C000090025

Social security and related matters
French-English glossary

First edition

Council of Europe Publishing

French edition:

Sécurité sociale et questions connexes – Glossaire anglais-français

ISBN 92-871-3131-7

Cover: Graphic Design Workshop of the Council of Europe

Council of Europe Publishing
F-67075 Strasbourg Cedex

ISBN 92-871-4014-6
© Council of Europe, August 1999
Printed in Germany

Preface

This glossary contains vocabulary used in the social security field. There are several reasons why we felt it necessary to deal with such a vast subject: the lack of recent relevant terminological material, the highly technical nature of some of the terms and concepts used and the internationalisation trend under way in this sphere, as indeed in others, with all the linguistic implications this has.

The difficulty of the exercise lay primarily in the choice of topics to be covered, for social security encompasses almost everything: employment, education, medicine, law, management, taxation, etc. We therefore analysed a large number of documents, official texts, comparative tables of social benefits in Europe, Canada and Australia, expert reports and dictionaries of all kinds relating either directly or indirectly to the social security field, not forgetting the two basic texts that are referred to almost routinely, viz. the European Social Charter and the International Standard Classification of Occupations (ISCO), the latter of which has been incorporated into the glossary. The material consulted thus processed represents about 15,000 entries.

We opted for as practical a layout as possible, so as to enable users of the glossary to find at a glance the equivalent of this or that term in the other language. We hope that the result of our efforts will come up to their expectations.

Terminology Office

ABAISSEMENT
lowering; reduction

abaissement de l'âge de la retraite
lowering of the retirement age

ABAISSER
abaisser la cotisation
to lower the contribution

ABANDON
discontinuation; cessation, termination;
waiver; abandonment; neglect; desertion

**abandon de l'activité (professionnelle /
salariée**
cessation of the employment / of the gainful
activity

abandon affectif
(moral) neglect

abandon de / du domicile conjugal
desertion (of the matrimonial home)

abandon d'enfant
abandonment of a child

abandon de famille
wilful neglect to maintain, non-support of
one's family

abandon d'une fonction
discontinuance of a function

abandon de foyer
desertion and failure to maintain

abandon matériel
physical neglect

abandon moral
(moral) neglect

abandon moral d'enfant
child neglect

abandon de poste
abandonment of post / of position; desertion
of one's post

abandon scolaire
drop-out, dropping out

abandon de la scolarité
(early) school-leaving

abandon volontaire d'un emploi
voluntary leaving of employment

clause d'abandon
waiver clause

déclaration d'abandon d'enfant
declaration of abandonment of a child

taux d'abandon (scolaire)
drop-out rate

ABANDONNER
abandonné
neglected; deserted

abandonner son épouse
to desert one's wife

abandonner ses études
to leave school; to drop out

abandonner sa famille
to desert one's family

abandonner son poste
to abandon one's post

abandonner un stage
to withdraw from a training course

abandonner le travail
to leave work

**allocation pour épouses abandonnées
(Irel.)**
deserted wife's allowance

enfant abandonné
neglected / abandoned child

épouse abandonnée
deserted wife

mère abandonnée
deserted mother

**prestation de femme abandonnée
(Irel.)**
deserted wife's benefit

ABATTEMENT
tax write-off / relief; allowance; deductible; reduction

abattement pour charges de famille
family allowance

abattement fiscal
tax allowance / reduction

abattement fiscal à la base
tax deduction at source

abattement fiscal sur le revenu professionnel de l'épouse
wife's earned income allowance

abattement fiscal sur le revenu du travail
earned income allowance

abattement d'impôts
tax allowance / reduction

abattement individuel
personal allowance

abattement légal / prévu par la loi
statutory deduction

abattement pour mouvements de personnel
adjustment for turnover of staff, turnover deduction

abattement personnel
personal allowance

ABOLIR
to abolish

ABONDANCE
affluence

société d'abondance
affluent society

ABONDEMENT
abondement de l'employeur
employer's complementary contribution to an employee savings scheme

ABORDABLE
logement à loyer abordable
affordable dwelling

ABRI
abri (sans)
homeless

personne sans abri
homeless person

personne seule et sans abri
single homeless

ABROGATION
abolishment, invalidation, revocation, repeal, termination

ABROGATOIRE
disposition abrogatoire
repealing provision

ABROGER
to abolish, to repeal, to rescind, to revoke

ABSENCE
absence, lack

absence autorisée
authorised absence, absence with leave

absence non autorisée
unauthorised absence, absence without leave

absence de consultation
failure to consult

absence pour convenance personnelle
compassionate leave

absence non expliquée
unexplained absence

absence illégale
absence without leave

absence injustifiée
unexcused / unexcusable absence

absence irrégulière
absence without leave, unauthorised absence

absence justifiée
excused / excusable absence

absence non justifiée
unexcused / unexcusable absence

absence pour maladie
sick leave

absence motivée
explained / excusable absence

absence pour raison(s) familiale(s) / de famille
compassionate leave

absence non réglementaire
absence without leave

absence régulière
absence with leave

absence rémunérée
paid leave

absence au travail
absence from work

autorisation d'absence
authorised absence, leave of absence

période d'absence du travail
time absent from work

rémunération inchangée en cas d'absence
pay not affected by absence

ABSENT (adj.)
absent

ABSENT (n.)
absentee

ABSENTÉISME
absenteeism

relevé concernant l'absentéisme
record of absenteeism

taux d'absentéisme
absenteeism rate, rate of absenteeism

ABSOLU
absolute, total

incapacité absolue
absolute disablement

invalidité absolue
total disability

invalidité absolue et définitive
total permanent disability

jour de carence absolu
absolute waiting day

misère absolue
absolute distress

niveau absolu de l'emploi
employment in absolute terms

ABSORBER
to absorb

absorber la main-d'oeuvre
to provide employment for labour force

ABSORPTION
capacité d'absorption du marché du travail
labour market absorption capacity

taux d'absorption des nouveaux venus sur le marché du travail
rate of absorption of labour market entrants

ABSTRACTION
abstraction (faire)
to disregard

ABUS
abus d'autorité
abuse of position / of authority

abus de confiance
breach of trust; misappropriation

abus de pouvoir
abuse of position / of authority

abus de prestations
(social security) benefit fraud

ABUSIF
undue

assiduités abusives
sexual harassment

clause abusive
unfair clause

licenciement abusif
unwarranted / unfair / wrongful dismissal,
wrongful discharge (USA)

licenciement non abusif
fair dismissal

licenciement abusif sans cause réelle et sérieuse
dismissal without just cause

licenciement abusif du fait de l'invocation tardive des motifs
waiver of breach of contract

prescription abusive
overprescription

protection contre le(s) licenciement(s) abusif(s)
unfair dismissal protection, protection against unfair dismissal

rupture abusive du contrat de travail
wrongful / unfair dismissal, wrongful discharge (USA)

ABUSIVEMENT
unreasonably, wrongfully

ACCÉDER
accéder à l'assurance
to enter insurance

accéder à une demande
to allow a claim

accéder à un nouveau poste
to take on a new job

accéder à un poste important
to rise to an important position

ACCÉLÉRATEUR
taux de chômage non accélérateur de l'inflation
non accelerating inflation rate of unemployment (NAIRU)

taux de chômage non accélérateur des salaires
non accelerating wage rate of unemployment (NAWRU)

ACCÉLÉRATION
principe d'accélération
acceleration principle

seuil d'accélération de l'emploi
employment threshold

ACCÉLÉRER
accélérer la cadence de travail
to speed up the production rate

augmentation de traitement accélérée
accelerated salary increment

cours de formation accélérée
intensive / crash (training) course

formation professionnelle accélérée
accelerated / intensive vocational training

programme accéléré
accelerated / crash programme

programme d'apprentissage accéléré
accelerated programme of apprenticeship

promotion accélérée
accelerated promotion

stage de formation accélérée
rapid training course

ACCEPTABLE
niveau acceptable d'exposition
acceptable level of exposure

niveau de vie minimum acceptable
minimum acceptable standard of living

ACCEPTATION
approval; acceptance

acceptation de l'emploi
acceptance of employment

acceptation d'une offre d'emploi
approval of a job offer

instrument d'acceptation
instrument of acceptance

ACCEPTER
accepter un emploi
to take / to accept a job, to take employment

accepter les fonctions
to assume office / duties

salaire minimum accepté
acceptance / reserve / reservation wage

ACCÈS
access, entrance, entry

accès à l'emploi
access to employment / to work / to the labour force; job access; opportunities of employment

accès au marché de l'emploi
access to the labour market

accès à un programme
access to / entry into a scheme

centre de formation à libre accès
open access training centre

condition d'accès
entry standard / requirement, requirement / condition for access / of admission / for entrance / for entry, entrance requirement

liberté d'accès (into a profession)
freedom of entry

libre accès
free / open access

limiter l'accès à
to restrict / to limit access

possibilité d'accès à l'emploi
accessibility to employment

professions et emplois d'accès réglementé
restricted occupations

programme d'accès à l'égalité
affirmative action programme

règles régissant l'accès
entrance rules

restreindre l'accès à
to restrict / to limit access

restriction d'accès
restriction on access / on entry, entrance / entry limitation / restriction, limitation on entrance / entry, restricted entrance / entry, admission restriction

ACCESSIBLE
accessible; available

ACCESSION
accession à la propriété
home ownership

ACCESSOIRE (adj.)
secondary; ancillary; subsidiary

activité accessoire
ancillary activity

avantage accessoire
supplementary / fringe / marginal benefit; perquisite, perk

dépenses accessoires
miscellaneous expenses

droit accessoire
ancillary right; (pl.) additional rights

frais accessoires
supplementary / extra cost / expenses

indemnité accessoire
subsidiary / supplementary allowance

occupation accessoire
extra work

prestation accessoire
collateral benefit

recettes accessoires
miscellaneous income

revenu accessoire
incidental / additional income; (pl.) subsidiary income

ACCESSOIRE (n.)
accessoires de salaire
fringe benefits

ACCIDENT
accident; injury; casualty

accident de la circulation
road / traffic accident

accident domestique
domestic accident

accident invalidant
disabling accident

accident de mines
mining accident

accident mortel
fatal accident / injury

accident non professionnel
non-occupational / non-industrial accident

accident de la route
traffic accident

accident lié au service
service-incurred injury

accident de / du trajet
injury / accident while travelling (to or from
work), accident between home and work,
commuting accident; accident in transit

accident de / du travail
accident at work, labour / work / industrial
accident, occupational accident / injury,
industrial / work / employment injury

accident survenu sur le chemin du travail
accident (or injury) while travelling (to or
from work); accident (or injury) in transit

**allocation d'incapacité par suite d'un
accident du travail (UK)**
industrial injury disability benefit

assurance-accidents
accident insurance

**assurance accidents corporels du secteur
public (Ger.)**
public accident insurance

assurance accidents individuelle
personal accident insurance

**assurance (contre les) accidents du
travail (et les maladies
professionnelles)**
industrial injury / injuries insurance,
insurance against accident at work;
employers' liability insurance; compensation scheme; accident insurance

**assurance décès-invalidité en cas
d'accident**
accidental death and dismemberment
(AD+D)

**caisse de compensation pour les acci-
dents du travail et les maladies
profes-sionnelles**
(occ.) workmen's compensation board

congé d'accident de travail
injury-on-duty leave

cotisation accident de travail (Fr.)
industrial injury contribution

**décès dû à un accident du travail ou à
une maladie professionnelle**
death from employment (injury)

déclaration d'accident
accident declaration / report(ing)

déclaration d'accident du travail
declaration / notification of an accident
at work

**demande d'indemnisation pour
accident du travail**
accident claim, workmen's
compensation claim

feuille d'accident du travail
work injury form

**indemnisation pour un / des
accident(s)**
accident compensation

**indemnisation des accidents du
travail**
worker's compensation (for industrial
injury)

indemnité (en cas) d'accident (Hung.)
compensation for injuries / for accident;
accident allowance

indemnité d'accident / pour accident de travail
workmen's compensation (award / benefit); employment / industrial injury benefit; injury benefit (UK, Irel., Malta)

indemnité d'invalidité pour accident du travail (ou maladie professionnelle)
industrial disablement payment / gratuity

indemnités maladie / accident du travail pour travailleurs indépendants
occupational sick pay for self-employed workers

invalidité totale consécutive à un accident du travail
total disability due to work injury

loi sur les accidents du travail
workmen's compensation law

nature de l'accident
nature of injury

organisme d'assurance contre les accidents
accident insurance institution

pension d'invalidité suite à un accident du travail (Hung.)
accident disability pension

pension payée en raison d'un accident civil
pension paid as a result of civil accident

pension de réversion à la suite d'un accident du travail
industrial death benefit

police d'assurance-accidents
accident policy

prédisposition aux accidents
accident proneness

prestation (en cas) d'accident du travail (et de maladies professionnelles)
accident benefit, benefit in respect of accidents at work, employment / industrial injury benefit, injury benefit (UK, Malta, Irel.)

prestations d'assurance-accident à recevoir
casualty insurance claim receivable

prestation de décès à la suite / résultant d'un accident du travail
industrial death benefit

prestation d'invalidité causée par un accident du travail (ou une maladie professionnelle)
industrial disablement benefit

prévention des accidents
accident prevention

prévention des accidents du travail
(occ.) industrial safety

prévention des accidents du travail et des maladies professionnelles
industrial / occupational health and safety

régime d'assurance contre les accidents personnels
personal injuries scheme

régime d'indemnisation en cas d'accident ou de maladie
compensation scheme for industrial injuries

registre des accidents du travail
accident book

rente d'accident du travail
industrial injury pension, pension for accident at work

réparation pour un / des accident(s)
accident compensation

réparation d'un accident du travail
compensation for an accident at work

réparation des accidents du travail et des maladies professionnelles
workmen's compensation (for industrial injuries and professional diseases)

risque d'accident du travail
occupational hazard / risk

taux (de fréquence) des accidents
accident frequency rate

taux de gravité des accidents
accident severity rate

victime d'accident de la circulation
road accident victim

victime d'(un) accident du travail
industrial accident / injury victim, person
who sustains an accident at work

ACCIDENTÉ (n.)
injured person, casualty

accidenté du travail
industrial injury / accident victim, person
who sustains an accident at work

accidenté de la vie
adventiously handicapped

ACCIDENTEL
chômage accidentel
intermittent / occasional unemployment

décès accidentel
accidental death

lésion accidentelle
accident injury

ACCOMPAGNEMENT
support, supportive care

accompagnement social
social support

**mesure d'accompagnement des sup-
pressions d'emplois**
redundancy mitigation measure

plan d'accompagnement
individual support scheme

**plan d'accompagnement des chômeurs
(Belg.)**
support plan for the unemployed

**plan d'accompagnement pour les
sortants de l'école et des études (SAVE)
(Belg.)**
support plan for school and college leavers

ACCOMPLIR
accomplir les périodes
to complete the periods

accomplir des tâches
to perform duties

années accomplies
complete years

travail accompli
work performed

ACCOMPLISSEMENT
completion; performance; discharge
accomplissement d'une période
d'assurance
completion of a period of insurance

accomplissement de soi
self-realisation

ACCORD
agreement; convention; understanding

accord (à l') amiable
out-of-court / friendly settlement

accord annexe
side agreement

accord d'assistance médicale
health care agreement

accord d'association
association / partnership agreement

accord d'autorisation
licensing agreement

accord de base
basic agreement

accord bilatéral
bilateral / reciprocal agreement

accord de branche
branch / industrial / sectoral agreement

accord-cadre
framework / outline / master / umbrella /
blanket agreement

accord collectif d'établissement
working / staff / works agreement

accord collectif sur les salaires
collective pay agreement

accord collectif (de travail)
collective agreement

accord de complaisance
convenience / (occ.) sweetheart arrangement

accord de détachement
secondment agreement

accord durable
long-lasting agreement

accord sur les effectifs
manning agreement

accord d'entreprise
staff / company / company-level / company-wide / plant agreement; works / labour agreement

accord de financement
contribution / funding agreement

accord fiscal bilatéral
double taxation agreement

accord de formation
training agreement

accord global
global / blanket agreement; (occ.) package deal

accord d'intéressement
profit-sharing agreement

accord intérimaire
temporary agreement

accord interprofessionnel
inter-branch / multi-industry / inter-trade agreement

accord librement conclu
voluntary agreement

accord de longue date
long-standing agreement

accord de modulation
adjustable hours agreement

accord multilatéral
multilateral agreement

accord ouvert
open-ended agreement

accord de participation
profit-sharing agreement

accord préalable
prior agreement

accord de principe
agreement in principle

accords de productivité
productivity bargaining / deal

accord professionnel
labour agreement

accord provisoire
interim / tentative agreement

accord de réciprocité
reciprocal agreement

accord réciproque
mutual agreement

accord de recrutement
recruitment agreement

accord salarial
wage / pay settlement

accord sectoriel
sectoral agreement

accord de travail partagé
work sharing agreement

accord(-)type
model agreement

accord unilatéral
unilateral / one-sided agreement

accord verbal
verbal agreement

commun accord (d'un / de)
by mutual agreement

cessation de service par accord mutuel
agreed termination

clauses d'un accord
terms of an agreement

commun accord (d'un / de)
by mutual agreement

dénonciation d'un accord
denunciation of / (unilateral) termination of an agreement

dispositions d'un accord
terms of an agreement

expiration d'un accord
termination of an agreement

licenciement par accord mutuel
agreed termination

mémorandum d'accord
memorandum of understanding

personnel visé par un accord
staff covered by an agreement

protocole d'accord
memorandum of understanding, statement
of agreement

recueil des accords d'entreprise
compendium of company agreements

résiliation d'un accord
termination of an agreement

ACCORDER
to grant, to allocate, to award

accorder un congé
to grant leave

accorder un congé payé
to grant paid leave; to release an employee
with pay

accorder une dérogation
to grant a waiver

accorder une indemnité
to award / to grant compensation (for
damages)

accorder une pension
to grant a pension

accorder une prestation
to grant a benefit

ACCOUCHEMENT
confinement; delivery

accouchement à domicile
home confinement

**allocation d'accouchement (Greece,
Sweden)**
childbirth allowance

centre d'accouchement
lying-in clinic

certificat d'accouchement
certificate of confinement

clinique d'accouchement
maternity home / hospital

date de l'accouchement
(actual) date of confinement

date effective de l'accouchement
effective date of confinement

date présumée de l'accouchement
expected date of confinement

date réelle de l'accouchement
effective date of confinement

prestation d'accouchement
confinement benefit

prime d'accouchement
confinement grant; (occ.) maternity
benefit

**prime d'accouchement à domicile
(UK)**
home confinement grant

semaine d'accouchement
week of confinement

semaine présumée d'accouchement
expected week of confinement

ACCRÉDITATION
accréditation patronale
certification of employer

accréditation syndicale
union certification

**retrait / révocation d'accréditation
syndicale**
withdrawal of union certification, (occ.)
decertification

système d'accréditation
certification / qualification system

ACCROISSEMENT
increase, increment, rise

accroissement de l'emploi
increase in employment

accroissement par migration
balance of migration

accroissement de / du personnel
staff increase, expansion of staff

accroissement de la population
population growth / increase

accroissement de la population active
labour force growth / increase

accroissement de la productivité
productivity increase

taux d'accroissement du personnel
accession rate

ACCROÎTRE
somme de travail accrue
increased workload

ACCUEIL
accueil et mise au courant des nouveaux agents
induction of new staff

allocation de premier accueil (Italy)
arrival grant

capacité d'accueil
intake capacity

centre d'accueil
receiving home; remand home; reception centre

centre d'accueil pour (jeunes) enfants
child-minding facility

centre d'accueil de jour
day care centre

centre d'accueil thérapeutique
(occ.) drop-in centre

centre de premier accueil
emergency home shelter

enfant placé dans une famille d'accueil
foster child

famille d'accueil
foster family / parents / home

livret d'accueil
employee handbook

maison d'accueil
residential home (for old people)

pays d'accueil
receiving / host country

permanence d'accueil, d'information et d'orientation (PAIO) (Fr.)
reception, information and guidance office

structure d'accueil pour (les) enfants
child care facility

ACCUMULATION
accumulation flexible
flexible accumulation

pourcentage de l'accumulation
rate of accumulation

ACCUMULER
to accumulate, to accrue

accumulé
accumulated; accrued

accumuler un congé
to accrue a leave

avoirs accumulés
accumulated assets

droits accumulés
accrued rights

fonds accumulés
accumulated assets

intérêts accumulés
accrued interests

jours de congé annuel accumulés
accrued annual leave

report de jours de congé accumulés
transfer of accrued leave

revenu accumulé
accrued income

solde de jours de congé annuel accumulés
accrued annual leave balance

total des congés annuels accumulés
accrued annual leave balance

ACCUSÉ
accusé de réception
receipt

ACHAT
achat de formation
purchase of training, training purchase

achat de services
purchase of services

baisse du pouvoir d'achat
loss of purchasing power

hausse du pouvoir d'achat
increase in purchasing power

maintien du pouvoir d'achat
maintenance of purchasing power

pouvoir d'achat
buying / purchasing power

pouvoir d'achat des salaires
(occ.) real wage / earnings

ACHETEUR
chefs de ventes et acheteurs [CITP-1968 (4-2)]
sales supervisors and buyers [ISCO-1968 (4-2)]

ACHÈVEMENT
date d'achèvement
completion / termination date

ACHEVER
achever sa formation
to complete / to finish one's training

ACOMPTE
advance, instalment

acompte sur salaire
advance on salary

ACOUSTIQUE (adj.)
appareil acoustique
hearing aid

ACQUÉRIR
acquérir de l'expérience
to acquire / gain experience

acquis
acquired; accrued; vested

acquis (non)
unvested

avantages acquis
established / vested rights

clause de maintien des avantages acquis
(occ.) grandfather clause

conférer un droit acquis
to endow with an acquired right

conservation des droits acquis
maintenance of acquired rights

droit acquis
existing right, vested interests; (pl.)
established / vested / accruing / accrual /
accrued / acquired rights

expérience acquise
past experience, previous work
experience; work background / history

expérience acquise en cours d'emploi
practical (work) / hands-on / on-the job
experience

maintien des droits acquis
maintenance of acquired / vested rights

montant acquis de la pension
accrued pension income

porter atteinte aux droits acquis
to jeopardise acquired rights

prévaloir de droits acquis (se)
to claim benefit of acquired rights

respect des droits acquis
respect for acquired rights

revenu acquis
accrued income

transfert des droits acquis d'une caisse à une autre (pension)
transferability / portability of pension rights

violation des droits acquis
breach of acquired rights

ACQUIS (n.)
knowledge; right

acquis social
social standard; (pl.) social rights

ACQUISITION
acquisition différée
deferred vesting (pensions)

acquisition de compétences
skill development

acquisition conditionnelle
conditional vesting (of a pension)

acquisition de connaissances
learning

acquisition de droits
vesting of rights

acquisition d'un droit à (des) prestations
acquisition of a right to benefits

conservation des droits en cours d'acquisition
maintenance of rights in course of acquisition

droit en cours d'acquisition
right in course of acquisition

système d'acquisition de compétences
skill acquisition system

taux d'acquisition du droit à pension
(pension) accrual rate

ACQUITTEMENT
payment

ACQUITTER
acquitté
paid; settled

acquitté (non)
unpaid

acquitter les cotisations
to pay contributions

acquitter les frais de
to pay the cost of

acquitter de ses responsabilités (s')
to fulfill one's duties / responsibilities

cotisation acquittée
paid contribution

ACTE
act; certificate; medical treatment

acte de baptême
baptismal certificate

acte de candidature pour un emploi (faire)
to apply for a job

acte commis à l'occasion d'un conflit du travail
act done in furtherance of a trade dispute

acte commis en vue d'un conflit du travail
act done in contemplation of a trade dispute

acte constitutif
articles

acte de décès
death certificate

acte discriminatoire
discriminatory practice; discrimination

acte législatif
legislation; statute

acte médical
item of care / service; medical treatment

acte de naissance
birth certificate

acte hors nomenclature (Fr.)
medical treatment not covered by the social
security scheme

actes de petite chirurgie
minor surgery

actes de pratique médicale courante
standard medical service

acte professionnel (med.) (Fr.)
medical treatment

acte de sécurité sociale (Fr.)
social security action

acte de société
articles of / deed of partnership

acte de la vie quotidienne
daily task

assimilation d'un acte professionnel (Fr.)
assimilation of medical treatment

codification des actes médicaux
codification of items of care

coefficient d'(un) acte médical
reimbursement rate of a medical treatment,
item of care coefficient

méthode de rémunération à l'acte
fee-for-service / item of service method of
remuneration

nomenclature des actes médicaux
classification of items of care

paiement à l'acte
fee-for-service (system)

prendre acte de
to act; to register

rémunération à l'acte
fee-for-service

système de paiement à l'acte
fee-for-service system

ACTIF (adj.)
(economically) active; proactive; working

accroissement de la population active
labour force growth / increase

actif (non)
inactive, unoccupied

âge actif
working age

âge actif (d')
of working age

âge très actif (d')
prime (work / working) age

âge d'entrée dans la vie active
age at entry into employment

âge limite de la vie active
maximum active working age

associé actif
working partner

augmentation de la population active
labour force growth / increase

**base de données projectives sur la
population active**
labour force projections data base

**caractéristiques de la population
active**
labour force characteristics

**cercle (Fr.) / club (Belg.) de recherche
active d'emploi**
job club

**charge supportée par la population
active**
dependency ratio

comportement de la population active
labour force behaviour

débutant dans la vie active
labour force entrant

dépense active
active expenditure

durée moyenne de la vie active
mean duration of working life

durée de la vie active
(duration of) working life

école active
active school

effectif de la population active
size of economically active population

enquête (par sondage) sur la population active
labour force (sample) survey

entrée dans la vie active
access to the labour force, access to / entrance into / entry into working life

entrer dans la vie active
to enter the labour force / market, to enter employment / into economic life, to take up employment, to begin / to start work

espérance brute de vie active
gross expectation of working life

espérance nette de vie active
net expectation of working life

espérance de vie active
expectation of working life

famille active
working family

insertion dans la vie active
integration into working life

intégration active
affirmative / positive action

intégration à la population active
labour force absorption

mesure active
active measure

passage à la vie active
transition to working life

passage de la vie active à la retraite
transition from work to retirement

période active (en)
of working age

personne active
(pl.) economically active persons

population active
economically active / gainfully occupied / gainfully employed / working / active population, labour / work force, gainful workers; (occ.) manpower

population non active
non-active / unoccupied / economically inactive population

population active agricole
agricultural workers

population active non agricole
non-agricultural workers

population active civile
civilian labour force / working population

population active ayant un emploi
gainfully occupied population

population active féminine
female labour (force)

population active industrielle
industrial population

population active intérieure
domestic labour force

population active masculine
male labour force

population active occupée
employed labour force / population

population active potentielle
potential labour force

population active primaire
primary labour force

population active de réserve
reserve labour force

population active secondaire
secondary labour force

population active à temps complet / à temps plein
full-time labour force

population d'âge actif
population of working age, working (-)age labour force

population économiquement active
economically active / gainfully occupied /
working population

population habituellement active
usually active population

productivité de la population active
productivity of the labour force

projection de la population active
labour force projection

quitter la vie active
to withdraw from / to leave the labour force

réintégrer la population active
to re-enter the labour force

répartition de la population active
labour force distribution

retirer de la vie active (se)
to withdraw from working life, to retire
(from work)

retour à la vie active
reintegration into / return to / re-entry into
working life

retrait de la population active
departure from the labour force

retrait de la vie active
withdrawal from work / from working life /
from employment

société active
active society

statistiques de la population active
labour force statistics

taux d'activité de la population active
labour force participation rate

travailleur actif
active / employed worker

travailleur d'âge très actif
prime-age worker

vie active
working life

ACTIF (n.)
active person / worker, (occ.) labour

market participant; (pl.) labour force
participants, manpower, economically
active / gainfully occupied / working /
active population / persons, labour /
work force; accumulated assets (pension
fund); (occ.) wealth

actif net
net asset; equity

actif net successoral
net assets by inheritance

actif occupé
employed; (pl.) population in
employment, employed labour force /
population

actif primaire
primary worker; (pl.) primary labour
force

actif secondaire
secondary worker

formation des actifs occupés (Fr.)
training for employed people

nouvel actif
labour force entrant, (new) entrant to the
workforce / labour force

pourcentage d'actifs
employment rate

proportion d'actifs
labour (force) participation; activity rate
/ ratio

rapport inactifs/actifs
dependency / support ratio, rate of
dependency

ACTION
action; activity; policy; work

action collective
collective / trade union / job / industrial
action

action collective en justice
class action

action corrective
corrective / remedial / affirmative /
positive action

action pour la défense des intérêts
professionnels
(occ.) industrial action

action en faveur de l'emploi et de la
formation
employment and training measures

action médico-éducative
medical and educational work / activities /
processes

action médico-sanitaire
health care

action médico-sociale
medical (and) social work

action palliative
affirmative / positive action, affirmative
action programme

action positive
affirmative / positive action

action préqualifiante
pre-skills training course

action revendicative
job / industrial action

action sanitaire
health measures / activities / promotion

action sanitaire et sociale
health and welfare activities, health and
social promotion

action de santé publique
(public) health work

action sociale
social measures / work, social welfare /
development / action

action sociale curative
remedial social action

action-travail
employee's share

centre d'action médico-sociale précoce
early medical social work centre

centre communal d'action sociale
social work municipal centre

centre d'information et de
coordination de l'action sociale
social work information and co-
ordination centre

champ d'action
scope

champ d'action et effet du travail
scope and effect of work

domaine d'action
policy area

fonds d'action générale
global funds

groupe d'action formé de citoyens
citizens' action group, public interest
group

journée d'action
day of action

ligne d'action
policy

mesure d'action sociale
socially supportive measure

moyens d'action
policy instruments

personnel d'action sociale
social work personnel / staff

plan d'action
action plan, plan of action

praticien de l'action sociale
social (welfare) worker

programme d'action prioritaire (Fr.)
priority action programme

programme d'action sociale
social action programme

rayon d'action
scope

recherche orientée vers l'action
action research

ACTIONNAIRE
shareholder

ACTIONNARIAT
shareholders; shareholding

plan / programme d'actionnariat du personnel / des salariés
employee share / stock ownership plan

ACTIVE (n.)
(pl.) female participants

armée d'active
regular / standing army

ACTIVER
to activate

ACTIVITÉ
activity, occupation, work; participation; labour (force) participation

abandon de l'activité salariée
cessation of the employment / of the gainful activity

activité (en)
in active employment

activité accessoire
ancillary activity

activité agricole
agricultural / farm work

activité d'appoint
subsidiary activity

activité artisanale
crafts

activité classique
mainstream activity

activité commerciale
business activity

activité conventionnelle
mainstream activity

activité dangereuse
hazardous occupation / work

activité délocalisée
offshore industry

activités dérivées
spin-off activities

activité économique
economic / business activity; business

activités économiques de caractère non matériel
non-productive labour

activité effectivement exercée
actual / current job / occupation, actual job

activité envisagée
planned activity

activités d'équipe
group activities

activités d'éveil du jeune enfant
early childhood stimulation

activité exercée
job / occupation held

activité extra-scolaire
extra-curricular activity

activité fonctionnelle
functional activity

activité de formation
training activity

activité génératrice d'emplois
employment-generating activity

activités de groupe
group activities

activité habituelle
normal business

activité indépendante
self-employment

activité industrielle
industrial / business activity

activité d'intérêt collectif
community business activity

activités de loisirs
leisure activities

activité lucrative
business / economic activity, gainful
activity / occupation / employment

activités de matière grise
knowledge industries

activités ménagères
homemaking, domestic activities, home
duties

activité mobile
(occ.) outreach activity

activité normale
normal activity

activité paraprofessionnelle
non-professional activity

activité périscolaire
extra-curricular activity; (pl.) extension /
extramural studies / work

activités péri-universitaires
university extension, extension / extramural studies / work

activité de pointe
leading industry

activité prévue
planned activity

activité primaire
primary activity

activité productrice de recettes
income-producing / revenue-producing /
income-generating / revenue-generating
activity

activité professionnelle
occupation, gainful activity / occupation,
occupational / professional / vocational
work, employment

activité professionnelle du conjoint
working status of the spouse

**activité professionnelle véritablement
rémunératrice**
substantially gainful occupation

activité hors programme (ed.)
extra-curricular activity

activité récréative
leisure activity

activité rémunératrice
income-producing / revenue-producing /
income-generating / revenue-generating
activity

activité rémunérée
gainful activity / occupation /
employment; economic activity; (occ.)
market work

activité non rémunérée
unpaid occupation / work / employment;
(occ.) non-market work

activité saisonnière
seasonal operation / business

activité salariée
gainful activity / occupation, activity as
an employed person; economic activity;
employment

activité non salariée
self-employment; activity as a self-
employed person

activité secondaire
secondary / ancillary activity

activité sociale et culturelle
social event

activité spéciale
special occupation

activité à temps partiel
part-time / subsidiary activity, part-time
job

activité de / sur le terrain
field work

activité tertiaire
service industry; (pl.) service / tertiary
industries, service / social trades

activité traditionnelle
traditional / mainstream activity

âge de cessation d'activité
age at retirement / at withdrawal / at
separation from the labour force,
retirement age

âge d'entrée en activité
age at accession to the labour force / at entry into employment

âge minimal d'activité professionnelle
minimum active working age

âge moyen de cessation d'activité
mean age at separation from the labour force

âge moyen d'entrée en activité
mean age at accession to the labour force

agents en activité
serving staff, staff in post

année d'activité
working year; (pl.) year's services

baisse d'activité
loss of work

branche d'activité
industry, line of business

branche d'activité (par)
by industry

branche d'activité en difficulté / en perte de vitesse
ailing industry

calendrier des activités d'un projet
project management schedule

cessation d'activité / de l'activité
going out of business; leaving the / separation from the / withdrawal from the labour force; withdrawal from work / from employment; retirement

cessation d'activité d'une entreprise
closing down of a business, business closure

cesser toute activité professionnelle
to drop out of / to leave the labour force; to leave work

choix de l'activité professionnelle
choice of job, job choice

classe d'âges de forte activité
prime (work / working) age (group)

classification par activité / par branche d'activité économique
industrial classification

début d'activité
entrance / entry into the labour force

début d'une activité indépendante / non salariée
entry into self-employment

deuxième activité professionnelle
second job

domaine d'activités
occupational area / field

double activité (qui exerce une)
dual job holder

durée d'activité
period of work

entrée en activité
accession to the labour force, entry into employment

entrer en activité
to begin work

exercer une activité lucrative
to be gainfully occupied / employed

exercer une activité professionnelle
to engage in an occupation, to hold a job

exercer une activité rémunérée
to be gainfully occupied / employed

exercice de plusieurs activités
multiple jobholding

exercice d'une double activité
double / dual jobholding

fluctuation de l'activité économique
business fluctuation, fluctuation in business / economic activity

mesure d'incitation à l'exercice d'une activité professionnelle
(occ.) in-work benefit

nomenclature des activités
industrial classification

ordre d'interruption d'une activité (dangereuse)
prohibition notice

période d'activité
working life / age; term of office; period of employment

période d'activité non salariée
period of self-employment

personne ayant une activité lucrative
(pl.) economically active / gainfully occupied / working population, labour force

personne n'exerçant pas d'activité rémunérée
non-employed person

personne qui exerce une double activité
double jobholder / jobber

personne qui exerce plusieurs activités
multiple jobholder

personnel en activité
serving staff

placement par secteur d'activité
placement by industry

population ayant une activité lucrative
economically active / gainfully occupied / working population, labour force

population en âge d'activité
population of working age, working (-)age labour force

première entrée en activité
first accession to the labour force; entrance / entry into the labour force

probabilité de cessation d'activité
probability of separation from the labour force

probabilité d'entrée en activité
probability of accession to the labour force

ralentissement de l'activité économique
economic slack / downswing / down-turn

rapport d'activité
activity / progress report, report on the activities

relevé statistique d'activité
statistical activity report

rémunération en début d'activité
beginning / starting salary

répartition par branche d'activité et par profession
industrial and occupational composition

reprise d'activité
re-entry into the labour force / into working life, return to working life

rester en activité
to continue to work, to remain / to stay in employment; to stay in the job

revenu d'activité
income from work

salaire en début d'activité
starting wage

secteur d'activité
branch of the economy; (sector of) industry; line of business

situation d'activité (en)
in active service

situation au regard de l'activité
activity status

table d'activité
table of working life

tableau statistique d'activité
statistical table of activity

taux d'activité
participation rate

taux d'activité des femmes / féminine
female (labour force) / women's participation rate

taux d'activité global
aggregate / total participation rate

taux d'activité de la main-d'oeuvre
labour force participation rate

taux d'activité masculine
male participation rate

taux d'activité de la population active
labour force participation rate

taux de cessation d'activité
rate of separation from the labour force

taux d'entrée en activité
rate of accession to the labour force

travailleur appartenant aux classes d'âge de forte activité
prime-age worker

type d'activité
kind / type of activity, type of job / of work

volume des activités
(volume of) work(-)load, volume level of activities

zone d'activité
enterprise zone

ACTUAIRE
actuary

actuaire-conseil
consulting actuary

ACTUALISATION
updating; uprating

taux d'actualisation
updating rate

ACTUALISER
to update; to adjust

coût actualisé
discounted cost

ACTUARIEL
conseiller actuariel
consulting actuary

déficit actuariel
actuarial / experience deficit

déséquilibre actuariel
actuarial imbalance

équivalent en valeur actuarielle
equivalent actuarial value

évaluation actuarielle
actuarial evaluation

mathématiques actuarielles
actuarial mathematics

principes actuariels équitables (selon des)
on an actuarial fair basis

réduction selon des calculs actuariels
actuarial reduction

surplus actuariel
actuarial / experience surplus

valeur actuarielle
actuarial value

ACTUEL
current

durée actuelle du chômage
(duration of) current spell of unemployment

effectif(s) actuel(s)
present workforce

emploi actuel
current employment / job

employeur actuel
present employer

niveau des compétences actuelles
current skill level

situation professionnelle actuelle
current employment status

ADAPTABILITÉ
adaptability; versatility

ADAPTATION
adaptation; adjustment

adaptation de la main-d'oeuvre
labour adjustment

adaptation au marché du travail
labour market adjustment

adaptation au travail
work adjustment

aide à l'adaptation (des structures)
adjustment assistance

chômage d'adaptation technologique
frictional / transitional unemployment

coefficient d'adaptation
corrective coefficient

contrat d'adaptation (Fr.)
adjustment contract

contrat d'adaptation à l'emploi (Fr.)
employment contract for integration into
working life

**contrat d'adaptation professionnelle
(Belg.)**
vocational adaptation contract

**contrat d'adaptation professionnelle
pour personnes handicapées (Belg.)**
vocational adaptation contract for the
disabled

indemnisation d'adaptation
adjustment compensation

pension d'adaptation (Sweden)
readjustment pension

**prestations d'adaptation pour les tra-
vailleurs**
labour adjustment benefits

service d'adaptation à l'emploi
employment adjustment service

ADAPTER
to adapt; to adjust

adapté
adapted; suitable

adapté aux besoins
geared to needs

**entreprise de travail adapté (ETA)
(Belg.)**
adapted work company

ADDITION
addition des périodes
totalling of periods

ADDITIONNALITÉ
additionality, incrementality

ADDITIONNEL
additional; supplementary; incremental

article additionnel
aditional article / provision, rider

avantage additionnel
incremental benefit

clause additionnelle
additional clause, rider

crédits additionnels
supplementary budget

frais généraux additionnels
incremental overhead costs

pension additionnelle (UK)
additional pension

revenu additionnel
secondary income

ADÉQUAT
appropriate, adequate, suitable

main-d'oeuvre adéquate
suitable labour

ADÉQUATION
appropriateness, adequacy; matching

**adéquation de l'offre et de la
demande**
matching supply and demand

**adéquation de l'offre et de la
demande d'emploi**
job-worker / worker-job matching,
matching of jobseekers and vacancies,
job matching

ADHÉRENT (n.)
member; (pl.) members, membership

adhérent cotisant
contributing member

**adhérent à jour / en règle de ses coti-
sations**
member in good standing

adhérent mutualiste
member of a mutual benefit society

adhérent non cotisant
non-contributing member

adhérent d'un syndicat
(trade) union member

carte d'adhérent
membership card

ADHÉRER
to join; to support

adhérer à une convention
to accede to / to join a convention

adhérer à un syndicat
to join a / to gain to a union

ADHÉSION
accession; support; entrance; enrolment;
membership

adhésion à l'assurance
entrance into insurance

adhésion individuelle (à l'assurance)
individual insurance cover

adhésion mutualiste
membership of a mutual benefit society

adhésion ouverte (sickness ins.)
open enrolment

adhésion tardive à l'assurance
late entrance into insurance

bulletin d'adhésion
enrolment form

clause (optionnelle) d'adhésion
opting-in clause

conditions d'adhésion
membership requirements

cotisation d'adhésion
membership fee

instrument d'adhésion
instrument of accession

libre adhésion (sur la base / sur une base de)
on a voluntary basis

ADJOINT (adj.)
administrateur adjoint
associate officer

directeur adjoint
deputy manager

directeur général adjoint
deputy managing director

ADJOINT (n.)
assistant

ADMETTRE
admettre dans un hôpital
to admit to a hospital

ADMINISTRATEUR
administrator; executive director; officer

administrateur adjoint
associate officer

administrateur d'une caisse de retraite
trustee of a pension fund

administrateur-délégué
managing director

administrateur d'école
school administrator / executive

administrateur externe
non-executive director

administrateurs et fonctionnaires de rang supérieur
(occ.) professional and higher categories

administrateur sanitaire
health officer / administrator

administrateur de (la) santé publique
(public) health officer / administrator

administrateur de service(s) socia(l)-(ux)
social (welfare) administrator

administrateur social
social welfare administrator

jetons de présence des administrateurs
directors' fees

poste d'administrateur
administrative job, (occ.) professional post

ADMINISTRATIF
administrative; clerical

agents administratifs (administration publique) [CITP-1968 (3-1)]
government executive officials [IS-CO-1968 (3-1)]

arrangement administratif
administrative agreement

autorisation administrative de licenciement
administrative authorisation to dismiss

autorités administratives
(administrative / regulatory) authorities; adjudicating authorities

blocage administratif
administrative bottleneck

contrôle administratif
administrative check

direction administrative
management office

emploi administratif
clerical occupation / job, office occupation

employés de type administratif [CITP-1988 (4)]
clerks [ISCO-1988 (4)]

enquête administrative
administrative inquiry

entraide administrative
administrative assistance, mutual assistance / aid in administrative matters

erreur administrative
administrative error

erreur et négligence administratives
administrative error and oversight

extension administrative
administrative extension (collective agreement)

faute administrative
administrative error

formule de notification administrative de décharge
personnel payroll clearance action form

frais administratifs
administration expenses, administrative / service / management cost(s)

gestion administrative
(occ.) management office

notification administrative
(occ.) personnel action / form

notification administrative de décharge
personnel payroll clearance action

personnel administratif
clerical staff / employees; support staff

poste administratif
professional post, administrative job

professions intermédiaires de la gestion administrative [CITP-1988 (344)]
administrative associate professionals [ISCO-1988 (343)]

recours administratif
appeal to a higher administrative authority

suspension de mesures administratives
suspension of administrative action

travail administratif
administrative / clerical work

voie administrative
official channel(s)

ADMINISTRATION
(public) administration; civil service; Government services; management; authority, authorities; (occ.) adjudicating authorities

administration d'assurance
insurance authority

Administration des contributions (UK)
Inland Revenue

administration directe
(occ.) direct rule

administration de l'emploi
labour / manpower administration

administration des finances publiques
fiscal administration

administration hospitalière
hospital authority

administration locale
local government / authority

administration pénitentiaire
prison service / administration

administration du personnel
staff / human resource(s) mnagement;
personnel policy

administration des premiers soins
provision of first aid

administration publique
government department

administration sanitaire
health administration / authorities

administration sanitaire intermédiaire
intermediate health administration

administration de (la) santé publique
(public) health administration

administration du / des service(s)
socia(l)(ux)
social (welfare) dministration

administration des soins infirmiers
provision of nursing care

administration territoriale
local government

administration du travail
labour administration

attaché d'administration
junior civil servant

cadres supérieurs de l'administration
publique [CITP-1988 (112)]
senior government officials [ISCO-1988
(112)]

conseil d'administration
board of directors; governing body

dépense(s) / frais d'administration
administrative / service / management
cost(s) / expenses

haute administration
senior civil service

organisme de l'administration locale
local government agency

poste de l'administration
civil service position

règlement d'administration publique
administrative regulation

système d'administration des soins
health care (delivery) system

ADMINISTRER
to administer; to manage, to run

administrer un programme
to manage / to run a programme

ADMIS
admitted, accepted; eligible, entitled

admis au bénéfice de
entitled to

ADMISSIBILITÉ
admissibility; eligibility, entitlement;
[qualifying]

âge d'admissibilité
qualifying age

condition d'admissibilité
qualifying condition; eligibility requirement

critère d'admissibilité
eligibility / acceptance criterion,
qualifier, qualifying factor

facteur d'admissibilité
qualifier, qualifying factor

taux d'admissibilité
eligibility rate

ADMISSIBLE
admissible, acceptable; recevable;
allowable

admissible (être à nouveau)
to reestablish one's eligibility

salaire hebdomadaire maximal admissible
maximum allowable weekly wage

ADMISSION
admission; membership

admission à l'aide sociale
social assistance / welfare entitlement,
eligibility for / admission to social
assistance / welfare

admission à l'assurance volontaire
admission to voluntary insurance

admission continue
continuous intake

admission dans un hôpital
admission to a hospital, hospital admission

admission permanente
permanent admission

âge d'admission à (la) pension
pensionable / retirement / pension age

Commission d'admission à l'aide sociale (Fr.)
Commission deciding on the eligibility for
social welfare

condition d'admission
qualifying condition; entry standard /
requirement, requirement for entry / for
access, entrance / admission requirement,
condition of admission; eligibility

condition d'admission au bénéfice de
eligibility criteria / requirement

conditions d'admission au bénéfice de (remplir les)
to be eligible

conditions d'admission à l'aide sociale
qualifying conditions to welfare benefits

critère d'admission
admission standard / rule, criterion for
membership

date d'admission
date of admission

demande d'admission à l'aide sociale
welfare benefits request

épreuve d'admission
pre-employment test

examen d'admission
entry / qualifying examination

jour de l'admission
intake day

modalités / procédure d'admission
admission / entitlement procedure

procédure d'admission à l'aide sociale
social assistance entitlement procedure

règles / réglementation régissant l'admission
entrance / admission rules

remplir les conditions d'admission
to qualify for membership

restriction d'admission / à l'admission
restriction on access / on entry, entrance
/ entry limitation / restriction, limitation
on entrance / entry, restricted entrance /
entry, admission restriction

taux d'admission
admission rate; (occ.) transfer rate

ADMONESTATION
admonition

ADOLESCENT
teenager; juvenile

ADOPTÉ (n.)
fichier de contact pour les adoptés (UK)
contact register for adopted persons

ADOPTER
adopter une loi
to introduce / to pass legislation

enfant adopté
adopted / foster child

ADOPTIF
enfant adoptif
adopted / foster child

parents adoptifs
adoptive parents

ADOPTION
adoption

congé d'adoption
adoption leave

foyer d'adoption
foster house / home

oeuvre d'adoption
adoption society

parents d'adoption
adoptive parents

prime d'adoption (Belg.)
adoption grant

ADRESSER
to send; to address; to refer

ADULTE (n.)
adulte à charge
adult dependant, dependent adult

adulte handicapé
disabled adult

âge adulte
adult age

allocation aux adultes handicapés
allowance for handicapped (Fr.) / disabled
adults

complément pour l'adulte (UK)
adult credit

crédit pour l'adulte (UK)
adult credit

éducation des / pour adultes
adult education

formation des adultes
adult training

formation professionnelle des adultes
adult occupational training

handicapé adulte
disabled adult

manoeuvre ordinaire adulte masculin
ordinary adult male labourer

**orientation professionnelle des
adultes**
adult vocational counselling

passage à l'âge adulte
transition to adult life

ADVERSATIF
relations professionnelles adversatives
adversarial industrial relations

ADVERSITÉ
adversity; hardship

AÉRÉ
centre aéré
outdoor centre

AÉRIEN
techniciens des moyens de transport
maritime et aérien [CITP-1988 (314)]
ship and aircraft controllers and
technicians [ISCO-1988 (314)]

AERIUM
sanatorium

AFFAIRE
matter; business

affaires courantes
day to day business

centre d'affaires
business centre / place

chiffre d'affaires
turnover

conseiller pour les / aux affaires sociales
social adviser

impôt sur le chiffre d'affaires
turnover tax

inspecteur des affaires sanitaires et sociales
health and sanitary inspector

inspection générale des affaires sociales
social affairs general inspectorate

milieux d'affaires
business community / circles

monde des affaires
business community

ralentissement des affaires
business recession

secteur des affaires
business community

AFFECTATION
posting, assignment, appointment; placement; allocation

affectation de crédits
allocation / appropriation of funds; earmarking

affectation flottante
floating assignment

affectation de fonds
allocation / appropriation of funds

affectation intérimaire
acting assignment

affectation internationale
international assignment

affectation de logement
allocation of accommodation

affectation à une mission
mission assignment

affectation particulière
specific job assignment

affectation du personnel
staff allocation

affectation provisoire
secondment

affectation des ressources
resource allocation, allocation of resources

affectation par rotation
rotational assignment

affectation hors siège
field service / assignment

affectation spéciale
special assignment, reserved occupation

affectation temporaire
temporary assignment

classement des lieux d'affectation
classification of duty stations

compte d'affectation spéciale
earmarked account

durée de l'affectation
length of assignment

fonds d'affectation spéciale
trust fund, funds-in-trust

indemnité d'affectation
assignment allowance

lieu d'affectation
duty station, assignment

lieu d'affectation initial
first duty station / assignment

lieu d'affectation officiel
official duty station / assignment

lieu d'affectation hors siège
field duty station, non-headquarters duty station

principal lieu d'affectation
main duty station

recrutement et affectations
(occ.) staffing

AFFECTER
to allocate, to earmark; to assign;
to affect

affecté à un poste (être)
(to be)assigned to a position

affecter suffisamment de personnel (ne pas)
to understaff, to underman

crédits affectés
apportioned / earmarked funds, ear-marking

crédits non affectés
unapportioned funds

fonds affectés à
funds earmarked for

recettes affectées
earmarked receipts

reliquat non affecté
unallotted balance

ressources affectées
income specially earmarked

solde non affecté
unallotted balance

AFFECTIF
abandon affectif
(moral) neglect

enfant présentant des troubles affectifs
emotionally disturbed child

AFFECTION
ailment, affection, illness, disease,
sickness, disorder, trouble

affection aiguë
acute illness / sickness / disorder / disease

affection dentaire
tooth disease

affection évolutive
active disease

affection de longue durée
long-term sickness / disease

affection préexistante
previous illness

affection prolongée et coûteuse
prolonged and expensive illness

enfant privé d'affection
emotionally deprived child

AFFICHAGE
posting

affichage des emplois
job posting

affichage obligatoire
compulsory posting

tableau d'affichage des offres d'emploi
(occ.) job board

AFFILIATION
membership; participation, entrance,
entry; enrolment

affiliation à l'assurance
entrance into insurance, insurance
membership

affiliation à une caisse de retraite
pension scheme membership

affiliation obligatoire
compulsory membership

affiliation à un régime de sécurité sociale
insurance under a social security
scheme

affiliation à la sécurité sociale
social security membership

affiliation syndicale
(trade) union membership

atelier pratiquant l'affiliation syndicale obligatoire
closed / union shop

caisse d'affiliation
insurance fund

condition d'affiliation
entry standard / requirement, requirement
for entry / for access, entrance requirement;
eligibility

cumul d'affiliation
overlapping of insurance

date d'affiliation
date of entry (into insurance)

dernière date d'affiliation à l'assurance
date of last entry into insurance

durée d'affiliation
period of / number of years of insurance;
insurance period; period of membership;
contributory service / period, period / length
of contributory service

numéro d'affiliation
membership number

période d'affiliation
period of / number of years of insurance;
insurance period; period of membership;
contributory service / period, period / length
of contributory service

période d'affiliation conventionnelle
notional period of contributory service

période minimum d'affiliation
(occ.) qualifying period

plafond d'affiliation
membership ceiling

règles régissant l'affiliation
entrance rules

**restitution d'une période d'affiliation
antérieure**
restoration of prior contributory service

restriction d'affiliation
restriction on access / on entry, entrance /
entry limitation / restriction, limitation on
entrance / entry, restricted entrance / entry,
admission restriction

AFFILIÉ (n.)
member, participant; (occ.) union member

AFFILIER
affilié à une institution (être)
to be insured with an institution

s'affilier à
to join

s'affilier à l'assurance
to enter insurance

s'affilier à un syndicat
to join a / to gain to a union

syndicat non affilié
non-affiliated union

AFFIRMATION
stage d'affirmation de soi
assertiveness training

AFFLUX
influx, inflow

afflux de chômeurs
inflow of unemployed

AFFRÉTEUR
shipper

AFFRONTEMENT
confrontation, showdown

ÂGÉ (adj.)
old

aide sociale aux personnes âgées
social assistance for old people, (occ.)
provision for old age

**allocation pour l'aide aux personnes
âgées (Belg.)**
allowance to assist the elderly

assistance aux personnes âgées
provision for / relief of old people

chômeur âgé
old(er) unemployed

**foyer-logement pour personnes âgées
(Fr.)**
residential housing for old people

foyer pour personnes âgées
residential / geriatric home

home pour personnes âgées
residential / geriatric home

maintien à domicile des personnes âgées
home care for the elderly

pension pour personnes âgées (Malta)
age pension

personne âgée
senior citizen; (pl.) old(er) people; the aged, the elderly

personne âgée non autonome
elderly dependent person

personnes âgées à charge
aged dependants

personnes âgées dépendantes
dependent / (occ.) frail elderly

personnes âgées et les vieillards (les)
the aged and the elderly

plan d'aide aux salariés pour la prise en charge de leurs parents âgés
elder care scheme

rapport de dépendance économique des personnes âgées
old age dependency ratio

rapport de soutien économique des personnes âgées
old age support ratio

service de soins infirmiers à domicile pour personnes âgées
home care nursing for the elderly

soins aux personnes âgées
care of old people

taux de dépendance des personnes âgées
old age dependency ratio

travailleur âgé
old(er) / elderly worker

ÂGE
age

abaissement de l'âge de la retraite
lowering of the retirement age

âge (par / selon l')
age-specific, age-related

âge actif
working age

âge actif (d')
of working age

âge très actif (d')
prime (work / working) age

âge d'admissibilité
qualifying age

âge d'admission à (la) pension
pensionable / retirement / pension age

âge adulte
adult age

âge d'aptitude à l'emploi / au travail
employable age

âge de cessation d'activité
age at retirement / at withdrawal / at separation from the labour force, retirement age

âge de départ obligatoire à la retraite
automatic / compulsory / mandatory retirement age

âge de départ à la retraite
retirement age

âge du droit à pension
age of pension entitlement, pensionable age

âge d'entrée en activité / au travail / dans la vie active
age at accession to the labour force / at entry into employment

âge de fin de scolarité (obligatoire)
school-leaving age

âge légal de départ à la / en retraite
statutory retirement age

âge légal de fin de scolarité
statutory school-leaving age

âge légal de la majorité
statutory majority age

âge légal de la retraite
(legal) retirement age, prescribed
pensionable age

âge limite de la vie active
maximum active working age

âge minimal
minimum age

âge minimal d'activité professionnelle
minimum active working age

âge minimum
minimum age

âge minimum légal pour travailler
minimum legal working age

âge de la mise à la retraite
pensionable age

**âge modulable de la prise de / du départ
à la retraite**
flexible pensionable / retirement age

âge moyen de cessation d'activité
mean age at separation from the labour
force

âge moyen d'entrée en activité
mean age at accession to the labour force

âge normal de fin de scolarité
normal / regular school-leaving age

âge normal de la retraite
normal retirement age

âge obligatoire de la retraite
automatic / compulsory / mandatory
retirement age

âge d'ouverture des droits
age of eligibility

**âge d'ouverture des droits à / ouvrant
droit à pension**
age of pension entitlement, pensionable age

âge de pension
age of pension entitlement, pensionable age

âge de pension (ayant atteint l')
of pensionable age

âge préscolaire (d')
under school age

**âge fixé pour la prise de / pour le
départ à la retraite anticipée**
age for early retirement

âge de la retraite
age at retirement / at withdrawal; pensionable / retiring age

âge de la retraite anticipée
age for early retirement

âge de retraite facultative
optional retirement age

âge scolaire
(compulsory) school age

âge de scolarité obligatoire
(compulsory) school age

âge de sortie de l'école
school-leaving age

âge statutaire de la retraite
statutory age of retirement

âge de travailler (en)
of working age

allocation selon l'âge (UK)
age allowance

arriver à l'âge
to attain the age

atteint par la limite d'âge
(occ.) superannuated

classe d'âge(s)
age group

classe d'âges de forte activité
prime (work / working) age (group)

classement par âge(s)
age distribution

cohorte d'âge
age cohort

composition par âge(s)
age distribution / pattern /structure

condition d'âge
age condition / qualification; qualifying age

effectif(s) d'âge scolaire (obligatoire)
school age population

enfant d'âge préscolaire
pre-school child

enfant d'âge scolaire
school(-)child

enfant en bas âge / du premier âge
baby, infant

femme en âge de procréer
woman of child-bearing age

groupe d'âge(s)
age group

limite d'âge
age limit

limite d'âge supérieure
upper age limit

majoration en fonction de l' / pour âge
age addition

passage à l'âge adulte
transition to adult life

personnes du quatrième âge
old / frail elderly

personnes du troisième âge
old people; (occ.) young elderly

population d'âge actif / en âge d'activité
population of working age, working
(-)age labour force

pyramide des âges
age / population pyramid, age distribution /
pattern / structure

quatrième âge
frail / old elderly

répartition par âge(s)
age distribution / pattern / structure

répartition des effectifs par âge
breakdown of headcount by age

retraite par limite d'âge
retirement on account of age

retraite nationale par limite d'âge (UK)
national superannuation

structure par âge(s)
age distribution / pattern / structure

tranche d'âge
age bracket

travailleur d'âge très actif
prime-age worker

travailleur d'un certain âge
older worker

travailleur appartenant aux classes d'âge de forte activité
prime-age worker

troisième âge
old people / age, (occ.) young elderly;
the aged, (occ.) the elderly

troisième et le quatrième âge (le)
the aged and the elderly

AGENCE
agency; branch, branch office;
subsidiary

agence pour l'emploi
employment agency / exchange, labour
exchange, employment bureau (USA),
job centre

agence d'intérim
temporary work (agency), staff / temp
agency

agence locale pour la création d'entre-prises
local enterprise agency

agence matrimoniale
marriage bureau

agence de missions de personnel
personnel dispatching agency

Agence nationale pour l'emploi (ANPE)
National Employment Agency

agence de placement
employment / placement agency, (labour) employment office, employment exchange / bureau, labour exchange (service)

agence de placement privée
private employment agency

agence de placement publique
public employment agency

agence pour la promotion des PME
SME / small business promotion agency

agence de recrutement
recruitment / staff agency

agence de travail intérimaire / temporaire
temporary work (agency), temp agency, temporary employment agency, temporary help contractor / service (USA)

AGENCEMENT
organisation, ordering; arrangement, layout; scheme

AGENT
agent; officer, staff member, official; operative; practitioner; worker; (pl.) staff, employees

accueil et mise au courant des nouveaux agents
induction of new staff

agents d'accompagnement et assimilés [CITP-1988 (511)]
travel attendants and related workers [ISCO-1988 (511)]

agents en activité
serving staff, staff in post

agents administratifs (administration publique) [CITP-1968 (3-1)]
government executive officials [ISCO-1968 (3-1)]

agent d'aide sociale
(social) welfare officer

agent approbateur
authorising officer / agent

agents d'assurances, agents immobiliers, courtiers en valeurs, agents de vente de services aux entreprises et vendeurs aux enchères [ISCO-1968 (4-4)]
insurance, real estate, securities and business services salesmen and auctioneers [ISCO-1968 (4-4)]

agent de l'assurance nationale (UK)
(national) insurance officer

agent auxiliaire
auxiliary worker

agent bénévole
voluntary worker

agents du cadre
established staff

agents commerciaux et courtiers [ISCO-1988 (342)]
business services agents and trade brokers [ISCO-1988 (342)]

agents commerciaux techniciens et voyageurs de commerce [CITP-1968 (4-3)]
technical salesmen, commercial travellers and manufacturers' agents [ISCO-1968 (4-3)]

agent à compétence générale
general purpose worker

agent compétent
responsible officer

agent comptable
accountant

agent contractuel
staff member under public employee contract

agent de contrôle
checking officer

agent contrôle de la sécurité sociale
social security inspector

agent enquêteur
investigating agent

agent d'entretien
maintenance worker

agent de l'Etat
Government employee, public official

agent d'exécution
field worker; manual worker; practitioner; (pl.) executing staff

agent d'exécution à compétence générale
general field worker

agent du fisc
Inland Revenue officer (UK); (pl.) revenue authorities

agent de la fonction publique
public / civil servant, public official

agent de formation
training officer, trainer

agent formé
trained worker

agent hospitalier
hospital employee / worker; (occ.) orderly; (pl.) hospital personnel / employees / workers / staff

agent de liaison
liaison officer; contact person

agent local
field / local worker; (pl.) local staff

agent local d'assurance
local insurance officer

agent de maîtrise
foreman, supervisor; technician; (pl.) lower management; supervisory staff

agents de maîtrise et assimilés [CITP-1968 (7-0)]
production supervisors and general foremen [ISCO-1968 (7-0)]

agent maritime
shipping agent

agent d'orientation / responsable de l'orientation
guidance officer

agent d'orientation professionnelle
career guidance officer

agent chargé du placement
(job) placement / placing officer

agent de planification de la famille / familiale
family-planning worker

agent polyvalent
multipurpose / front-line worker

agent principal
senior officer

agents de production
productive labour

agent de programme
programme officer

agent de projet
project officer

agent de protection de l'enfance
child welfare officer

agent de protection sociale
(social) welfare officer / worker, social worker, social service officer

agent public
public servant

agent qualifié
skilled employee, trained worker

agent recruté localement
locally recruited staff member

agent responsable
officer-in-charge

agent sanitaire
health (care) worker; (pl.) health personnel / staff

agent sanitaire primaire
primary health worker

agent sanitaire visiteur
(pl.) domiciliary health staff

agent de la santé
health (care) worker

agent de (la) santé mentale
mental health worker

agent de santé polyvalent
multipurpose health worker

agent de santé primaire
primary health worker, primary-level
worker

agent de santé publique
public health worker

agents de service
servicing staff

**agent de service social / des services
sociaux**
(social) welfare officer / worker, social
worker, social service officer

agent spécifiquement habilité
officer specifically authorised

agent de supervision
supervisor

agent technique
middle-level / sub-professional technician,
technician worker; maintenance worker;
clerk of works

agent non titulaire de l'Etat
non-established State employee

agent univalent
single purpose / single(-)skill worker

poste d'agent auxiliaire
ancillary post

poste d'agent local
local level post

statut des agents
staff status; staff regulations

AGGLOMÉRATION
urban / built-up area, town; settlement;
population cluster

AGGRAVATION
aggravation; deterioration; worsening;
increase

aggravation de l'invalidité
worsening of disability, aggravation of
invalidity

AGGRAVÉ
invalidité aggravée
aggravated disability

AGISSANT
active

agissant pour le compte de
acting

AGRÉER
to approve; to authorise; to certify

**aide à la famille pour l'emploi d'une
assistante maternelle agréée (Fr.)**
family benefit for hiring an approved
day-care attendant

agréé
authorised, certified; approved;
registered, State-registered

caisse agréée
approved fund

dépasser le tarif conventionnel agréé
to charge more than the standard agreed
fee

établissement agréé
approved institution

médecin agréé
approved doctor

régime de retraite agréé
registered pension plan

syndicat agréé
recognised union

AGRÉMENT
licensing agreement; approval; accreditation; registration; entertainment; (pl.)
amenities

certificat d'agrément
certificate of registration (pensions)

droit d'agrément
registration fee (pensions)

procédure d'agrément de l'entreprise
accreditation procedure for firms

retrait d'agrément
revocation / withdrawal of registration,
withdrawal of accreditation; deregistration

AGRICOLE
agricultural

activité agricole
agricultural / farm work

allocation de vieillesse agricole (Fr.)
agricultural old age allowance

**brevet d'études professionnelles agricoles
(BEPA) (Fr.)**
certificate of agricultural vocational
education

brevet de technicien agricole (BTA) (Fr.)
agricutural technician's certificate

**brevet de technicien supérieur agricole
(BTSA) (Fr.)**
agricultural senior technician's certificate

caisse d'assurance mutuelle agricole (Fr.)
agricultural mutual insurance fund

calamité agricole (Fr.)
agricultural disaster

**certificat d'aptitude professionnelle
agricole (CAPA) (Fr.)**
certificate of agricultural competence

collectivité agricole
farming community

demande de main-d'oeuvre agricole
agricultural labour demand

**directeurs et chefs d'exploitation
agricoles [CITP-1968 (6.0)]**
farm managers and supervisors [ISCO-1968
(6-0)]

emploi agricole
agricultural / farm employment

emploi agricole saisonnier
seasonal agriculture work

exploitant agricole
farm operator, farmer

exploitants agricoles [CITP-1968 (6-1)]
farmers [ISCO-1968 (6-1)]

**formation professionnelle initiale
agricole (Fr.)**
initial agricultural vocational training

industrie agricole
farming industry

**lycée professionnel agricole (LPA)
(Fr.)**
agricultural vocational upper secondary
school

main-d'oeuvre agricole
farm labour, agricultural manpower;
working farm population

manoeuvre non agricole
non-farm labourer

marché du travail agricole
agricultural / farm labour market

mutualité sociale agricole (Fr.)
agricultural social insurance agency

non-salarié des professions agricoles
self-employed agricultural worker

ouvrier agricole
agricultural / farm labourer / worker,
land worker

pénurie de main-d'oeuvre agricole
farm labour shortage

placement dans un emploi agricole
agricultural job placement

population active agricole
agricultural workers

population active non agricole
non-agricultural workers

population agricole
agricultural / farm population,
population dependent on agriculture

population non agricole
non-farm population

profession agricole
agricultural profession

régime agricole
agricultural scheme

revenu agricole
farm income

revenu agricole net
net farm income

saisonnier agricole
seasonal agricultural labourer

salarié agricole
agricultural / farm labourer / worker

salarié agricole permanent
full-time agricultural labourer

secteur agricole
agricultural sector

travail agricole
agricultural work

travail agricole saisonnier
seasonal agriculture work

travailleur agricole
farm / agricultural worker; (pl.) agricultural
manpower / workers

travailleurs agricoles [CITP-1968 (6-2)]
agriculture and animal husbandry workers
[ISCO-1968 (6-2)]

AGRICULTEUR
agriculteurs, éleveurs, forestiers, pêcheurs et
chasseurs [CITP-1968 (6)]
agriculture, animal husbandry and forestry
workers, fishermen and hunters [ISCO-
1968 (6)]

agriculteur exploitant
farm operator, farmer

agriculteur indépendant
self-employed farmer

**agriculteurs et ouvriers de l'agriculture
et de la pêche de subsistance [CITP-1988
(62)]**
subsistence agricultural and fishery workers
[ISCO-1988 (62)]

**agriculteurs et ouvriers de l'agriculture
et de la pêche de subsistance [CITP-1988
(621)]**
subsistence agricultural and fishery workers
[ISCO-1988 (621)]

**agriculteurs et ouvriers qualifiés de
l'agriculture et de la pêche [CITP-
1988 (6)]**
skilled agricultural and fishery workers
[ISCO-1988 (6)]

**agriculteurs et ouvriers qualifiés de
l'agriculture et de la pêche destinées
aux marchés [CITP-1988 (61)]**
market-oriented skilled agricultural and
fishery workers [ISCO-1988 (61)]

**agriculteurs et ouvriers qualifiés des
cultures destinées aux marchés
[CITP-1988 (611)]**
market gardeners and crop growers
[ISCO-1988 (611)]

**agriculteurs et ouvriers qualifiés de
polyculture et d'élevage destinés aux
marchés [CITP-1988 (613)]**
market-oriented crop and animal
producers [ISCO-1988 (613)]

pension des agriculteurs (Finl.)
farmers' pension

AGRICULTURE
population vivant de l'agriculture
agricultural / farm population,
population dependent on agriculture

AGRO-ALIMENTAIRE
industrie agro-alimentaire
food and agriculture industry; agri-food
industry

AIDANT
care taker, carer, helper

conjoint aidant
helping spouse, spouse helping

AIDE
help, assistance, care, support, relief,
aid;
welfare; incentive; grant; assistant,
helper

admission à l'aide sociale
social assistance / welfare entitlement,
eligibility for / admission to social
assistance / welfare

agent d'aide sociale
(social) welfare officer

aide à l'adaptation / à l'ajustement (des structures)
adjustment assistance

aide alimentaire de base (Ger.)
basic subsistence aid

aide aux chômeurs
unemployment assistance

aide constante d'un tiers / d'une tierce personne
constant attendance

aide au déplacement et à la prospection
relocation and exploratory assistance

aide didactique
training aid / material

aide directe
direct assistance

aide domestique
ancillary help

aide à domicile
home help

aide à l'embauche
employment subsidy

aide à l'emploi
employment assistance; labour / employment subsidy

aide aux employeurs
assistance for employers

aide à l'enfance
child assistance / care, aid to children

aide aux étudiants
student assistance

aide extérieure
outside help; substitute care (for children)

aide familiale
domestic / family worker / helper, (visiting) home(-)maker, family / home aid, home / mother's / family help

aide familial(e) non rémunéré(e)
unpaid family worker

aide à la famille pour l'emploi d'une assistante maternelle agréée (Fr.)
family benefit for hiring an approved day-care attendant

aide aux familles avec enfants à charge
aid to families with dependant children (AFDC)

aide financière
financial support / assistance; financial incentive

aide financière à la maternité (Czech Rep.)
financial assistance in maternity

aide fiscale
tax incentive

aide sur fonds publics
public / government aid

aide forfaitaire
lump-sum / flat-rate / fixed rate aid

aide à la / de formation
training assistance / aid

aide hospitalière
hospital assistance

aide aux indigents
poor relief

aide indirecte
indirect assistance

aide au logement et au relogement
housing and rehousing help

aide maternelle
child care worker, child-minder, day-care attendant

aide médicale
medical assistance

aide médicale à domicile
home medical care, medical home relief (USA)

aide médicale d'urgence
emergency medical aid

aides de ménage et autres aides, net-toyeurs et blanchisseurs [CITP-1988 (913)]
domestic and related helpers, cleaners and launderers [ISCO-1988 (913)]

aide ménagère
family / domestic help, home helper, home help (worker)

aide ménagère à domicile
home-making assistance

aide aux migrants
aid for migrants

aide à la mobilité
mobility assistance

aide à la mobilité des étudiants
student mobility grant

aide à la mobilité géographique
geographical mobility incentive

aide à la mobilité professionnelle
occupational mobility incentive

aide mutuelle
mutual aid

aide en nature
aid in kind

aide à l'obtention d'un emploi
assistance towards taking up work / employment

aide permanente (Denmark)
continuing maintenance assistance

aide personnalisée au logement (APL)
housing subsidy

aide au premier emploi
first job allowance

aide au premier emploi des jeunes (Fr.)
allowance for young new workers

aide prénatale
aid to expectant mothers

aide à la prospection
exploratory assistance

aide publique
public / government aid

aide à la recherche d'un emploi
assistance towards taking up work / employment, work assistance (Ger., Austr.)

aide à la reconversion (des structures)
adjustment assistance

aide aux réfugiés
aid for refugees

aide du secteur public
public / Government aid

aide sociale
social assistance / welfare, public / welfare assistance; supplementary benefit (UK)

aide sociale à l'enfance
child welfare (authorities); child care

aide sociale à la famille
social assistance for the family (members), family welfare

aide sociale aux handicapés
social assistance for disabled people

aide sociale aux personnes âgées
social assistance for old people, (occ.) provision for old age

aide et soins à domicile
home help and care

aide technique
technical assistance / aid

aide aux vacances
holiday subsidy

aide de voyage
travel assistance

allocation pour aide constante (UK)
attendance allowance

allocation pour l'aide aux personnes âgées (Belg.)
allowance to assist the elderly

allocation d'aide publique (Fr.)
State help allowance

allocation d'aide sociale
(occ.) supplementary allowance

bénéficiaire d'aide sociale
welfare / social assistance recipient; [on welfare]

bureau d'aide sociale
social assistance / social welfare office, welfare office

centre d'aide par le travail
work-based support centre

centre public d'aide sociale (CPAS) (Belg.)
public centre for social welfare, public welfare centre

Code de la famille et de l'aide sociale
Family and Social Welfare Code

Commission d'admission à l'aide sociale (Fr.)
Commission deciding on the eligibility for social welfare

Commission centrale d'aide sociale
Social Welfare Central Commission

conditions d'admission à l'aide sociale
qualifying conditions to welfare benefits

contentieux de l'aide sociale
social welfare claims

demande d'admission à l'aide sociale
welfare benefits request

demander une aide sociale
to apply for welfare benefits / for relief

financement de l'aide sociale
social welfare funding

mesure d'aide à l'emploi
employment incentive / stimulus

mineur confié à l'aide sociale (Fr.)
minor in custody of a social welfare institution

organisme d'aide sociale
(social) welfare agency

pension de l'aide sociale (UK)
supplementary pension

plan d'aide aux salariés pour la prise en charge de leurs parents âgés
elder care scheme

prestation d'aide sociale
welfare payment; supplementary benefit (UK); (pl.) welfare benefits, social fund (UK)

prestations générales d'aide sociale
general welfare assistance

prêt d'aide au budget (UK)
budgeting loan

prévoyance et aide sociale
social relief and welfare

procédure d'admission à l'aide sociale
social assistance entitlement procedure

programme d'aide à la collectivité / d'aide communautaire
community assistance programme

programme d'aide sociale
social support programme

recevoir des allocations d'aide / une aide sociale
to be on welfare

recours en matière d'aide sociale
legal action against a decision relating to social welfare

recours sur succession en matière d'aide sociale (Fr.)
action to recover social benefits from succession

régime d'aide sociale
welfare plan

service d'aide familiale / à la famille
home service; (pl.) family counselling; home-maker services

service d'aide maternelle / aux mères
mother care service; child care service; (pl.) home-maker services; child care facilities

service d'aide médicale d'urgence (SAMU)
emergency medical relief service

service d'aide à la petite enfance
infant care service

service d'aide sociale
(social) welfare service; (occ.) public charity

service d'hygiène et d'aide sociale
health and social welfare service

société d'aide à l'enfance
child helping society

système d'aide
support system

taux de prestations d'aide sociale
rate of welfare benefits, (occ.) welfare rate

AIDE-INFIRMIÈRE
nursing aid

AIDER
to help, to assist, to relieve, to support

AIDE-SOIGNANT(E)
nursing aid / assistant / auxiliary, auxiliary nurse; health assistant

AIGU
affection aiguë
acute illness / sickness / disorder / disease

chômage aigu
acute unemployment

hôpital de soins aigus
acute care / active treatment / somatic hospital

maladie aiguë
acute illness / sickness / disorder / disease

AIGUILLAGE
referral (med.)

service d'aiguillage
referral centre

système d'aiguillage
referral system

AIGUILLER
to refer (med.)

AÎNÉ (n.)
eldest; senior citizen; (pl.) old people; the aged, the elderly

aîné des enfants
eldest child

AIRE
aire d'attraction
catchment area

aire d'habitation
housing area

aire d'influence
catchment area

AISÉ (adj.)
classes (les) (plus) aisées
better-off (the)

AJOURNEMENT
postponement, deferment; adjournment

ajournement de l'option entre les prestations
deferment of choice of benefit

ajournement de la prise de retraite
deferred retirement

AJOURNER
to postpone, to defer; to adjourn

ajourner une promotion
to suspend (implementation of) a promotion

ajourner la prise de / le départ à la retraite
to defer retirement

départ à la retraite ajourné
deferred retirement

AJOUTÉ
effet travailleur ajouté
added worker effect

service à valeur ajoutée
value added / enhanced service

travailleur ajouté
added worker

valeur ajoutée
added value

AJUSTEMENT
adjustment

aide à l'ajustement (des structures)
adjustment assistance

ajustement annuel
annual adjustment

ajustement au coût de la vie
cost-of-living adjustment, consumer price index increase

ajustement des effectifs
labour adjustment

ajustement de l'emploi
employment adjustment

ajustement forfaitaire
lump-sum adjustment

ajustement des pensions aux variations du coût de la vie
cost-of-living pension adjustment

ajustement des prestations
benefit adjustment

ajustement saisonnier
seasonal adjustment

ajustement structurel
structural adjustment

ajustement dans le temps
time-to-time adjustment

annualisation du système d'ajustement des pensions
annualisation of the pension adjustment system

barème des ajustements de poste
schedule of post adjustments

classe d'ajustement
post adjustment class

classe d'ajustement négatif
negative post adjustment class

classement aux fins des ajustements
post adjustment classification

coefficient d'ajustement au coût de la vie
cost-of-living differential factor

indice d' / des ajustement(s)
post adjustment index

indice d'ajustement des pensions
pension adjustment index

indice révisé d'ajustement des pensions
revised pension adjustment index

méthode d'ajustement intérimaire
interim adjustment methodology

méthode d'ajustement proportionnel sur un an
annualised method of prorated adjustment

multiplicateur d'ajustement
post adjustment multiplier

système d'ajustement des pensions
pension adjustment system

système d'ajustement des prestations
benefit adjustment system

système révisé d'ajustement des pensions
revised pension adjustment system

AJUSTER
to adjust

ajusté selon l'évolution des prix
adjusted for price changes

prestation de pension ajustée
adjusted pension benefit

prestation périodique ajustée
periodically adjusted benefit

AJUSTEUR-MONTEUR
ajusteurs-monteurs, installateurs de
machines et mécaniciens de précision
(électriciens exceptés) [CITP-1968 (8-4)]
machinery fitters, machine assemblers and
precision instrument makers (except
electrical) [ISCO-1968 (8-4)]

ALÉA
aléa moral
moral hazard

ALÉATOIRE
échantillon aléatoire
random sample

erreur aléatoire
random error

sélection aléatoire
random assignment

sondage aléatoire
random sampling

ALERTE
droit d'alerte et de retrait (Fr.)
right of worker to notify a potential risk to
his safety and to stop work

procédure d'alerte
warning procedure

ALIÉNATION
aliénation (mentale)
mental disablement, insanity

ALIÉNÉ (n.)
aliéné (mental)
mentally disabled, mentally disordered
person

asile / hospice / maison d'aliénés
mental home

ALIGNEMENT
alignement des salaires
(occ.) pay comparability

ALIMENT
food; (pl.) (occ.) maintenance, support

aliment pour nourrissons
infant / baby food

créancier d'aliments
person entitled to maintenance

débiteur d'aliments
person liable to pay maintenance

ALIMENTAIRE
aide alimentaire de base (Ger.)
basic subsistence aid

avance sur pension alimentaire
advance on alimony

bon de réduction sur les denrées alimentaires (UK)
food rebate coupon

créance alimentaire
maintenance; right to claim / receive
maintenance

créancier alimentaire
person entitled to maintenance

intoxication alimentaire
food poisoning

obligation alimentaire
(alimony) maintenance order /
obligation / payment, obligation to
maintain

pension alimentaire
maintenance; maintenance / subsistence
allowance / payment; separation
allowance; alimony (and support); child
support

prestations alimentaires
(alimony) maintenance payments

provision alimentaire
maintenance

ALIMENTATION
food

bon d'alimentation
food stamp / voucher

ALIMENTER
to feed; (occ.) to finance

ALITEMENT
confinement to bed

ALLAITANT
mère allaitante
nursing / lactating mother

ALLAITEMENT
allaitement (naturel / maternel / au sein)
breast-feeding

allocation d'allaitement
nursing allowance (UK), allowance for
nursing mother (Port.)

indemnité d'allaitement
nursing benefit / allowance

pause d'allaitement
nursing break

prestation d'allaitement
nursing benefit

prime d'allaitement
nursing allowance

salle d'allaitement
nursing room

ALLAITER
to breast-feed

ALLÉGEMENT
relief; reduction; rebate

allégement fiscal / d'impôts
tax mitigation / relief / rebate / reduction;
tax subsidy

ALLÉGER
to relieve

ALLIANCE
affinal relationship

par alliance
by marriage

ALLOCATAIRE (adj.)
unité allocataire
benefit unit

ALLOCATAIRE (n.)
beneficiary, recipient; eligible person

allocataire de l'assurance chômage
unemployment insurance recipient

allocataire en fin de droit(s)
insurance exhaustee

allocataire potentiel
potential beneficiary

allocataire d'une prestation
benefit recipient

ALLOCATION
(cash) allowance; benefit; grant; indemnity; money; stipend; subsidy; allocation

**allocation d'accouchement (Greece,
Sweden)**
childbirth allowance

allocation aux adultes handicapés
allowance for handicapped (Fr.) /
disabled adults

allocation selon l'âge (UK)
age allowance

allocation pour aide constante (UK)
attendance allowance

**allocation pour l'aide aux personnes
âgées (Belg.)**
allowance to assist the elderly

allocation d'aide publique (Fr.)
State help allowance

allocation d'aide sociale
(occ.) supplementary allowance

allocation d'allaitement
nursing allowance (UK), allowance for
nursing mother (Port.)

allocation anticipative
advance allocation

allocation d'assistance
social assistance grant, attendance allowance

allocation d'assistance externe (Denmark)
outside assistance allowance

allocation d'assistance à la formation professionnelle (Ger.)
vocational assistance allowance

allocation d'assistance personnelle (It.)
personal assistance allowance

allocation d'attente (Belg.)
waiting allowance

allocation aux aveugles (Austr.)
blind persons' allowance

allocation de base
basic allowance

allocation de base vieillesse (Fr.)
old age basic allowance

allocation pour charges de famille
dependant care allowance

allocation de chauffage et d'électricité (Irel.)
fuel and electricity allowance

allocation de chômage
unemployment allowance / benefit / compensation; dole

allocation de chômage de base
basic unemployment allowance

allocation de chômage partiel
short-time working allowance

allocation de chômage total
total unemployment allowance

allocation de chômage de transition (Belg.)
transitional unemployment allowance

allocation compensatoire / compensatrice
equalisation / compensatory allowance; payment in lieu

allocation complémentaire
supplementary / additional allowance, supplement

allocation complémentaire de chômage
supplementary unemployment allowance

allocation complémentaire de veuve
widow's supplementary allowance

allocation complémentaire vieillesse (Fr.)
supplementary old age allowance

allocation au conjoint (Can.)
spouse allowance

allocation au conjoint pour veufs et veuves (Can.)
widowed spouse's allowance

allocation conventionnelle de solidarité (Fr.)
contractual solidarity allowance

allocation (de) (-) décès
death allowance / grant; (personal) death benefit, funeral benefit

allocation pour déclassement professionnel
allowance for lowered standard of occupation

allocation de déménagement
moving / removal / relocation allowance

allocation (de) (-) dépendance
dependency allowance; helpless person's allowance (Austr.), helplessness allowance (Liech.)

allocation de deuil (Austr.)
bereavement payment

allocation différentielle
compensatory / differential / equalisation allowance

allocation d'éducation
education allowance

allocation d'éducation du Commonwealth (Austr.)
Commonwealth education allowance

allocation pour l'éducation des enfants (Ger.)
child raising allowance

allocation d'éducation spéciale
special education allowance, allowance for severely disabled children (Fr.)

allocation pour éloignement géographique (Austr.)
remote area allowance

allocation pour enfant
child allowance

allocation pour enfant(s) à charge
dependent child allowance, children's allowance, child benefit (UK)

allocation pour enfant handicapé
child disability allowance (Austr.), handicapped child / children's allowance (Malta)

allocation d'entretien
maintenance allowance, subsistence allowance / payment; (occ.) training allowance

allocation pour épouses abandonnées (Irel.)
deserted wife's allowance

allocation familiale
family benefit / allowance, children's allowance, child benefit allowance (UK)

allocation familiale complémentaire (Port.)
supplementary family allowance

allocations familiales payables à partir du deuxième enfant
children's allowances from the second child

allocation familiale progressive
progressive family allowance

allocation pour femmes de détenus (Irel.)
prisoners wife's allowance

allocation de fin de droits
allowance for end of entitlement; follow-up benefit

allocation de fin de service
severance allowance

allocation financière
financial provision

allocation forfaitaire
flat-rate benefit, lump-sum grant, flat allowance

allocation de formation
training allowance / benefit

allocation de formation reclassement (Fr.)
resettlement / re-deployment (Fr.) training allowance (Fr.)

allocation de foyer
household allowance

allocation pour frais d'études
education(al) grant

allocation pour frais de garde (Fr.)
child-minding allowance, allowance for baby-sitting expenses

allocation pour frais de logement (Neth.)
housing cost allowance

allocation pour frais d'obsèques
funeral grant

allocation funéraire
funeral grant

allocation de garde (Pol.)
minding allowance

allocation de garde à domicile des enfants (Finl.)
child home care allowance

allocation pour garde d'enfant
child care allowance

allocation de garde d'enfant à domicile
home child care allowance

allocation globale
block grant; total allocation

allocation de guerre pour les civils
civilian war allowance

allocation d'habillement
clothing allowance

allocation par habitant
per capita allocation

allocation pour handicap (Denmark)
handicap allowance

allocation hebdomadaire
weekly allowance, allowance per week

allocation hebdomadaire maximale payable
maximum weekly allowance payable

allocation d'hébergement
overnight accommodation allowance

allocation d'hospitalisation
hospitalisation / treatment allowance

allocation aux implaçables
unemployability allowance

allocation d'impossibilité d'emploi
unemployability allowance / supplement (UK)

allocation pour imprévus
contingencies allowance

allocation d'incapacité par suite d'un accident du travail (UK)
industrial injury disability benefit

allocation pour / d'incapacité grave
severe disablement allowance

allocation pour incapacité de travail (UK)
disablement benefit

allocation d'incommodité (Finl.)
inconvenience allowance

allocation d'insertion
integration allowance, starting benefit, unemployment benefit for young first-job seekers (Fr.), young first-job seekers' allowance (Fr.)

allocation d'intégration (Belg.)
integration allowance

allocation d'invalidité (UK)
invalidity allowance

allocation d'invalidité partielle (Neth.)
partial disability allowance

allocation d'isolé (Irel.)
living alone allowance

allocation au /pour jeune enfant (Fr.)
young child allowance, allowance for young child

allocation journalière
daily allowance

allocation journalière de chômage
daily unemployment benefit

allocation journalière de maternité (Icel.)
daily maternity leave grant

allocation légale
statutory award

allocation (de) (-)logement
housing benefit / allowance, rental / rent subsidy, rent / accommodation / shelter allowance (Can.), rent assitance (Australia)

allocation logement social (Fr.)
social housing allowance

allocation de loyer
rent allowance

allocation de main-d'oeuvre
manpower allowance

allocation de mariage
marriage grant

allocation de maternité
maternity benefit / pay; (pl.) maternity allowances

allocation de ménage (Switz.)
household allowance

allocation aux mères de famille
mother's benefit

allocation de mère au foyer
allowance for mothers at home / for the housewife, non-working mother's allowance (UK)

allocation de mère veuve (UK)
widowed mother's allowance

allocation de mi-temps
half-time allowance

allocation de mobilité (UK)
mobility allowance

allocation de naissance
birth / childbirth grant / allowance; (occ.)
maternity grant

**allocation pour naissance multiple
(Austr.)**
multiple birth grant

allocation de nourriture
food allowance

allocation ordinaire
regular allowance

allocation pour / d'orphelin
orphan's allowance, allowance for orphans;
guardians's allowance (UK)

allocation de / pour parent isolé
one-parent benefit (UK), single-parent /
lone parent's (Fr.) allowance

allocations parentales (Finl.)
parents' allowance

allocation parentale d'éducation
parental child care allowance

allocation de paternité (Finl.)
paternity allowance

allocation de / pour personne à charge
dependant care allowance, dependant's /
dependency allowance

**allocation pour personnes impotentes
(UK)**
mobility allowance

allocation de premier accueil (It.)
arrival grant

allocation prénatale
pre(-)natal allowance, allowance for
pregnant women

allocation principale
principal allowance

allocation pour prothèse dentaire (Ger.)
dental replacement allowance

allocation provisoire
provisional benefit

**allocation pour recherche d'(un)
emploi (Austr.)**
job search allowance

allocation de reclassement
re-adjustment benefit

allocation de rééducation
(re)training allowance

**allocation prévue par le régime ordi-
naire d'indemnisation**
(occ.) standard benefit

**allocation prévue par les régimes
spéciaux d'indemnisation**
(occ.) special benefit

allocation régulière
regular allowance

allocation de réinstallation
reestablishment / resettlement allowance

allocation-relais
bridging allowance

allocation de remplacement (Fr.)
replacement allowance

**allocation de remplacement de
revenus (Belg.)**
income replacement allowance

allocation de rentrée scolaire
back-to-school allowance, back-to-
school clothing and footwear allowance
(Irel.)

allocation de revenus réduits (UK)
reduced earnings allowance

allocation des ressources
resource allocation, allocation of
resources

allocation de salaire unique
single wage allowance

allocation de séjour hors du foyer
living-away from home allowance

allocation des services ménagers (Fr.)
home help allowance

**allocation pour situation difficile /
pénible**
hardship allowance

**allocation pour situation particulière-
ment difficile (UK)**
special hardship allowance

allocation sociale
social allowance

allocation sociale complémentaire (Irel.)
supplementary welfare allowance

allocation pour soignant (Irel.)
carer's allowance

allocation de / pour soins
nursing / care allowance

allocation pour soins constants
(constant) attendance allowance, attendance benefit (Norw.)

allocation de soins à domicile (Irel.)
domiciliary care allowance

allocation pour soins aux enfants (Finl.)
child care allowance

allocation pour soins hospitaliers (UK)
hospital treatment allowance

allocation pour soins en institution (UK)
residential allowance

allocation pour soins à (un) invalide (UK)
invalid care allowance

allocation de soins majorée (Finl.)
increased care allowance

allocation pour soins médicaux
(medical) treatment allowance

**allocation de soins pour pensionnés
(Finl.)**
pensioner's care allowance

allocation de soins spéciale (Finl.)
special care allowance

allocation de soins aux tuberculeux
tuberculosis allowance

allocation de solidarité
solidarity allowance

**allocation de solidarité de chômage total
(Fr.)**
total unemployment solidarity allowance

**allocation de solidarité spécifique
(Fr.)**
specific solidarity allowance

**allocation de soutien de famille /
familial**
family support allowance

allocation spéciale
special allowance

allocation spéciale de chômage (Fr.)
special unemployment allowance

**allocation spéciale pour les enfants de
femmes divorcées (UK)**
child's special allowance

allocation spéciale de naissance
special childbirth allowance

allocation spéciale de solidarité (Fr.)
special solidarity allowance

allocation spéciale vieillesse (Fr.)
old age special allowance

allocation de stagiaire
trainee allowance

allocation de subsistance
subsistence / living allowance

**allocation de subsistance pour
invalides (UK)**
disability living allowance

**allocation de subsistance pour visite
préliminaire**
preliminary examination living
allowance

allocation supplémentaire
supplementary / additional allowance,
added benefit

**allocation supplémentaire d'attente
(Fr.)**
interim supplementary allowance

**allocation supplémentaire famille
(Fr.)**
supplementary family allowance

**allocation supplémentaire vieillesse
(Fr.)**
supplementary old age allowance

allocation à taux uniforme
flat-rate allowance / benefit

allocation temporaire
transitional allowance

allocation par tête
per capita allocation

allocation pour traitement hospitalier (UK)
hospital treatment allowance

allocation de trajets quotidiens
commuting allowance

allocation de transfert (Neth.)
transfer allowance

allocation de travail pour invalides (UK)
disability working allowance

allocation pour travaux insalubres et dangereux (Gr.)
unhealthy and dangerous work allowance

allocation de tutelle
after care allowance; guardian's allowance (UK)

allocation de tuteur (Austr.)
guardian allowance

allocation pour usure (anormale) des vêtements
allowance for wear and tear (of clothing)

allocation de vacances (Neth.)
holiday allowance

allocation de veuvage
widow's / widowhood (UK) allowance, widowed person's allowance (Australia)

allocation de veuve
widow's allowance

allocation viagère aux rapatriés (Fr.)
annuity for repatriates

allocation de victime de guerre (UK)
war pensioner's death benefit

allocation de vie chère
cost-of-living allowance / compensation / adjustment

allocation (de) vieillesse
old age allowance; (occ.) age allowance

allocation de vieillesse agricole (Fr.)
agricultural old age allowance

allocation aux vieux travailleurs
allowance for elderly / old workers

allocation aux vieux travailleurs salariés
allowance for old employees

allocation de visite préliminaire
preliminary examination allowance

allocation de voyage
travel allowance

barème des allocations
allowance table

bénéficiaire d'une allocation
beneficiary of an allowance

caisse d'allocations familiales
family allowance fund

Comité des allocations pour soins constants (UK)
Attendance Allowance Board

demande d'allocation
claim for a benefit / an allowance

droit aux allocations
eligibility for benefits / allowances

livret d'allocations (familiales)
allowance order book

logement ouvrant droit au versement d'une allocation
subsidised housing

percevoir une allocation
to be in receipt of a benefit

percevoir des allocations de chômage
to collect unemployment compensation, to live on / to draw unemployment benefit

recevoir des allocations d'aide / une aide sociale
to be on welfare

refuser une demande d'allocation
to reject a claim for benefit; (occ.) to disallow benefit

régime d'allocations familiales
family allowances scheme

régime d'allocations (de) logement
rental subsidy scheme

régime d'allocations (de) logement révisé
revised rental subsidy scheme

régime d'allocations et de retenues au titre du loyer
rental subsidy/deduction scheme

système de paiement / de versement des allocations
allowance payment system

taux des allocations
allowance rate / level, rate / level of allowances

taux des allocations de formation
rate / level of training allowances

titulaire d'une allocation
beneficiary of an allowance

toucher des allocations de chômage
to live on / to draw unemployment benefit

versement des allocations
payment of allowances

ALLONGER
allonger la durée du travail
to increase hours of work

ALLOUER
to grant, to allocate, to award

allouer une indemnité
to award / to grant compensation (for damages)

allouer une pension
to grant a pension

allouer une prestation
to allow a benefit

système du temps alloué
time-allowed system (piece work)

travail à la pièce obéissant au système du temps alloué
time piecework

ALPHABÉTISATION
literacy (education), basic literacy training

alphabétisation fonctionnelle
functional literacy

campagne d'alphabétisation
literacy campaign

ALTÉRATION
alteration; impairment

ALTÉRÉ
altéré (non)
unimpaired

ALTERNANCE
contrat en alternance
sandwich-type contract

contrat d'insertion en alternance (Fr.)
employment contract facilitating integration into working life, sandwich-type integration contract

études en alternance
day-release studies

formation en alternance
alternance / sandwich training / course, cooperative education; day-release studies (1-2 days/-week); block-release training (long period of absence)

programme d'alternance travail-études
work-study programme

stage de formation en alternance (Fr.)
sandwich integration course

ALTERNANT
équipe alternante
rotating shift

migrant alternant
commuter

migration alternante
journey to work; (pl.) commuting

poste alternant
rotating shift

système de travail par équipes alternant jour et nuit
alternating shift system

travailleur alternant
rotating worker

ALTERNATIF
coût alternatif
alternative cost

ALTERNÉ
enseignement alterné
work/study programme

système des classes alternées
double-shift system; dual sessions

AMBULANT
profession ambulante
itinerant trade

AMBULATOIRE
centre médico-pédagogique de cure ambulatoire (Fr.)
out-patient child care centre

malade (en traitement) ambulatoire
(hospital) out-patient

moyen de traitement ambulatoire
out-patient facility

régime ambulatoire (en)
on an out-patient basis

service de soins ambulatoires
ambulatory service

soins ambulatoires
ambulatory / out-patient care

soins en régime hospitalier ou ambulatoire
in-patient or out-patient care

traitement ambulatoire
out-patient / ambulatory treatment

AMÉLIORATION
improvement; development; upswing, upturn, upgrading

amélioration des compétences
skill improvement / development

amélioration de la couverture des risques
improvement in coverage

amélioration des qualifications
skill development, up-skilling

amélioration de la sécurité et de l'hygiène du travail
improvement in safety and health conditions at work

prêt à l'amélioration de l'habitat / du logement
loan for housing improvement

AMÉLIORER
to improve; to develop; to upgrade

AMÉNAGEMENT
adjustment; planning

aménagement du poste de travail
job adaptation / redesign

aménagement souple du temps de travail
variable / flexible working time

aménagement de statut
status adjustment

aménagement de structure
structural adjustment

aménagement du temps de travail
new patterns / redistribution of working time; flexible working hours / time

aménagement urbain
urban planning

convention d'aménagement et de réduction du temps de travail (ARTT) (Fr.)
agreement to reform and reduce working hours

coûts d'aménagement
fit-up cost

flexibilité dans l'aménagement du temps de travail
flexibility of working time arrangements

AMENDE (n.)
fine; penalty

AMENDEMENT
amendment

AMIABLE
accord (à l') amiable
out-of-court / friendly settlement

licenciement amiable
agreed termination

règlement (à l') amiable
out-of-court / friendly settlement

séparation à l'amiable
negotiated termination

AMONT
industrie / secteur en amont
(occ.) supplying sector

AMORÇAGE
capitaux d'amorçage
seed money

AMPLEUR
scale, size, scope

AMPLITUDE
amplitude de la journée de travail
work day span

AN
year

an (par)
per annum

ANALOGUE
emploi / travail analogue
equivalent occupation

ANALPHABÈTE
illiterate

ANALPHABÉTISME
illiteracy

analphabétisme fonctionnel
functional illiteracy

ANALYSE
analyse des besoins
needs analysis

analyse comparative
comparative analysis

analyse des compétences
skills analysis

analyse coûts-avantages
cost-benefit analysis

analyse coût-efficacité
cost-effectiveness analysis

analyse coûts-rendement
benefit-cost analysis

analyse des emplois
job analysis

analyse factorielle
factor analysis

analyse selon le / par groupe d'emplois
job group analysis

analyse du marché du travail
labour market analysis

analyse des professions
occupational analysis; (occ.)
occupational distribution / composition / pattern

analyse des professions et métiers
occupational and trade analysis

analyse de rendement
benefit-cost analysis

analyse sectorielle
sector analysis

analyse des tâches
task / job analysis, work study

analyse du travail
work study

laboratoire d'analyses médicales
medical analysis laboratory

ANALYTIQUE
évaluation analytique des tâches / du travail
analytical job evaluation

programme / système d'évaluation analytique des tâches / du travail
analytical job evaluation scheme

ANARCHIQUE
uncontrolled

ANATOMIQUE
consolidation anatomique
anatomical consolidation

ANCIEN (adj.)
ancien combattant
veteran, ex-serviceman

ancien déporté
war prisoner

ancien employeur
former employer

ancien militaire
ex-serviceman

association d' / des anciens élèves
former students' association

pension d'invalidité des anciens combattants
veterans' disability pension

ANCIEN (n.)
senior citizen; (pl.) old people; the aged, the elderly

ANCIENNETÉ
seniority; years of service; duration / length / period of employment / of service; time serving

ancienneté dans la classe
seniority in / within grade

ancienneté dans l'emploi
(job) tenure

ancienneté d'entreprise / à l'échelle de l'entreprise
corporate seniority

ancienneté requise
time-in-service requirement

ancienneté requise dans la classe
time-in-grade requirement

congé d'ancienneté
long-service / furlough leave

congé spécial d'ancienneté
special long-service leave

courbe d'ancienneté
(occ.) tenure profile

échelon d'ancienneté
longevity increment / step, long-service step

indemnité d'ancienneté
seniority allowance

médaille d'ancienneté
long-service award, seniority / service / long-service medal

minimum d'ancienneté exigible dans une classe
minimum time-in-grade requirement

pension d'ancienneté
company long-service pension, service pension, seniority pension (It.)

prestation d'ancienneté
long-service benefit

prime d'ancienneté
longevity / seniority pay / bonus

promotion à l'ancienneté
advancement / promotion by seniority

rappel d'ancienneté
grant of additional seniority / of (additional) years of service

reprise d'ancienneté
credit for previous service, restoration of earlier / of prior service

salarié ayant une longue / beaucoup d'ancienneté
long-serving employee, senior employee (USA)

transfert des droits d'ancienneté
transfer of seniority rights

travailleur ayant une longue / beaucoup d'ancienneté
long-serving worker, senior worker (USA)

ANIMATEUR
leader; (extension) worker

animateur bénévole
voluntary leader

animateur de groupe
group leader

animateur de groupes de jeunes
youth leader

animateur socio-culturel
community worker

animateur socio-pédagogique
social welfare organiser

formation d'animateurs
trainer training

ANIMATION
animation socio-culturelle
social and cultural activities; (occ.) community development

ANNÉE
year

années accomplies
complete years

année d'activité
working year; (pl.) year's services

année budgétaire
budget year

année civile
calendar year

année complète
full(-)year

année de cotisation
contribution year

années décomptées
credited service (old-age pension)

année ouvrant droit à
year of entitlement

année d'émission
year of issue

année d'études
year of study; grade

année fiscale
(income) tax year, taxable year

année d'imposition
assessment year, year of assessment, (income) tax year, taxable year

année partielle (en)
part(-)year

année pleine (en)
full(-)year

année de prestations
benefit year

année de qualification
qualifying year

année de référence
base / reckonable / relevant year

année de revenu
earning year

année révolue
complete year

année sabbatique
sabbatical year / (occ.) leave

année scolaire
school / academic year

années de service
seniority

année de travail
work(-)year, person-year, staff-year

année universitaire
academic year

compter trois années de résidence
to have complete three years' residence

cumul (de l') année
year to date

prime de fin d'année
Christmas / end-of-year bonus

régime salaire meilleures années
average best earnings plan

régularisation en fin d'année
year-end regularisation

reporter des congés d'une année à l'autre
to carry over outstanding holidays from one
year to the next

travail en année complète
full-year work

travail en année partielle
part-year work

travail en année pleine
full-year work

travailleur en année complète
full-year worker

travailleur en année partielle
part-year worker

travailleur en année pleine
full-year worker

unité travail-année
man-year unit, year work unit

ANNÉE-HOMME
année-homme
man-year

ANNÉE-PERSONNE
man-year, person-year, staff-year, work
(-)year

année-personne d'emploi
work-year of employment

année-personne de travail
work-year of employment

incidence sur les années-personnes
person-year impact

mouvement des années-personnes
person-year shift

ANNEXE (adj.)
accord annexe
side agreement

avantages annexes
fringe benefits

droit annexe
ancillary right

frais annexes
additional expenses

matériel annexe
ancillary equipment

ANNEXE (n.)
appendix, schedule; rider

annexe d'un contrat
schedule of a contract

annexe d'une loi
schedule of a law

ANNIVERSAIRE
date anniversaire d'entrée en fonction
anniversary date of hire

ANNONCE
annonce d'offre d'emploi
job advertisement

ANNUALISATION
annualisation; computation on an annual
basis

annualisation des horaires
annualised hours

annualisation du système d'ajustement des pensions
annualisation of the pension adjustment system

ANNUEL
annual, yearly

ajustement annuel
annual adjustment

avance sur congé annuel
advance annual leave

concours annuel
annual (competitive) examination

congé annuel
annual leave, (annual) vacation; (pl.) annual holiday

congé annuel payé, congé payé annuel
annual paid leave; paid vacation

cumul annuel
year to date

déclaration annuelle de données sociales (Fr.)
annual declaration of salaries

durée annuelle de travail
annual working time

durée annuelle effective du travail
annual hours worked

examen annuel
annual review

gains annuels
annual earnings

indemnité annuelle de départ
annuity for withdrawal from work

jours de congé annuel accumulés
accrued annual leave

montant annuel minimal
minimum annual rate

montant annuel normal
standard annual rate

montant annuel de la prestation de retraite
annual pension benefit (amount)

moyenne annuelle
annual / yearly average

rapport annuel
annual report

recueil annuel
annual series

régularisation annuelle des cotisations
annual regularisation of contributions

relevé de congé annuel
annual leave record

rémunération annuelle
annual remuneration

revenu annuel
yearly / annual income

révision annuelle
annual review

salaire annuel moyen de base
basic average annual wage

solde de jours de congé annuel accumulés
accrued annual leave balance

taux annuel
annual rate, annualised percentage rate

total des congés annuels accumulés
accrued annual leave balance

traitement annuel
annual salary

traitement annuel courant
current annual salary

ANNUELLEMENT
annually, yearly

ANNUITÉ
annuity, instalment, annual instalment / benefit; (occ.) pension unit; year's contribution; year of service

annuité différée
deferred annuity

annuité garantie (pour une période donnée)
annuity certain

annuité gratuite
free annuity

annuité réduite
reduced annual (periodic) benefit

ANNULATION
repeal, recision, annulment, termination

annulation de cotisation d'assurance (-)vieillesse (Fr.)
annulment of old age contribution

annulation du licenciement
rescission of termination

ANNULER
to repeal, to rescind, to revoke

annuler un décret
to revoke a decree

annuler un mot d'ordre de grève
to call off a strike

ANOMALIE
abnormality, abnormal condition

ANORMAL (adj.)
abnormal; unusual; undue

ANORMAL (n.)
mental(ly) deficient

ANORMALITÉ
abnormality

ANTAGONIQUE
relations professionnelles antagoniques
adversarial industrial relations

ANTÉCÉDENT
(pl.) record, case history / histories

antécédents d'emploi
employment record, work experience

antécédents médicaux
medical history

antécédents professionnels
employment / track record, occupational / employment / job / career / work history, past experience, (previous) work experience; work background

ANTENNE
unit; outposting

antenne locale d'un syndicat
(occ.) local union

antenne mobile
outreach unit; mobile field unit

antenne de reclassement
redeployment unit

ANTÉRIEUR
carrière antérieure
job history

emploi antérieur
previous employment

expérience professionnelle antérieure
past / previous (work) experience; work background; employment history

poste antérieur
previous position

prestation liée aux gains / revenus antérieurs
(previous) pay-related / earnings-related (insurance) benefit

restitution d'une période d'affiliation antérieure
restoration of prior contributory service

service antérieur
prior service

validation d'une période de service antérieure
validation of previous service

valider les services antérieurs
to have previous services credited

ANTÉRIORITÉ
clause d'antériorité
(occ.) grandfather clause

ANTICANCÉREUX
centre anticancéreux
cancer hospital / research centre

ANTICIPATIF
allocation anticipative
advance allocation

ANTICIPATION
anticipation (par)
in advance

anticipation de la pension
anticipation of the pension

anticipation de la prise de retraite
early retirement

paiement / versement par anticipation
advance payment

ANTICIPATIVEMENT
in advance

ANTICIPÉ
âge de / fixé pour la prise de / pour le départ
à la retraite anticipée
age for early retirement

appel anticipé
advance call (for contributions)

cessation anticipée de fonction
early termination of service

départ à la retraite anticipé
early retirement

indemnisation de départ anticipé
compensation for loss of office

liquidation anticipée
early vesting

mise à la retraite anticipée
advanced retirement

paiement anticipé
advance payment

pension anticipée
early / anticipated pension

pension individuelle anticipée (Finl.)
individual early pension

pension de retraite anticipée
early retirement allowance / benefit

prendre une retraite anticipée
to retire early

prestation anticipée de vieillesse
anticipatory old-age benefit

retraite anticipée
early retirement, pre-retirement

rupture anticipée
anticipatory breach

versement anticipé
advance payment

ANTICIPER
anticiper le départ à la retraite
to retire early

ANTICONJONCTUREL
counter-cyclical

ANTICUMUL
preventing the holding of more than one
office concurrently

ANTICYCLIQUE
counter-cyclical, anti-cyclic

ANTIDATÉ
backdated

ANTI-DISCRIMINATION
anti-discrimination à l'embauche
(occ.) affirmative action

ANTI-DISCRIMINATOIRE
mesures anti-discriminatoires à
l'embauche
(occ.) affirmative action programme

ANTI-ÉCONOMIQUE
uneconomic(al)

ANTI-HYGIÉNIQUE
unhygienic; insanitary

ANTI-INCENDIE
consignes anti-incendie
fire precautions / instructions

ANTI-INFLATIONNISTE
politique anti-inflationniste
anti-inflationary policy

ANTISOCIAL
comportement antisocial
anti-social behaviour

ANTI-SYNDICAL
discrimination anti-syndicale
anti-union discrimination

APATRIDE
stateless person

APERÇU
outline

APÉRIODIQUE
aperiodic

APLANIR
to level out

APPAREIL
appliance; machinery

appareil acoustique / auditif
hearing aid

appareil hospitalier
hospital system

appareil judiciaire
judicial machinery

appareil orthopédique
orthopaedic appliance

appareil de prothèse
prosthetic appliance

APPAREILLAGE
appliances

appareillage dentaire
dental plates

centre d'appareillage
appliance centre

commission d'appareillage
appliance commission

grand appareillage
major appliances / aids

petit appareillage
minor aids / appliances

APPARENT
chômage apparent
measured / open / overt / registered / visible unemployment

APPARENTÉ
catégorie apparentée
related category

emploi / métier apparenté
allied / related occupation / job

travailleur apparenté à l'employeur
employee / worker related to the employer

APPARIEMENT
matching

appariement informatique des offres et des demandes d'emploi
computerised matching of jobs and job seekers

APPARITION
start, beginning; onset (med.)

APPARTEMENT
appartment, flat

appartement loué à la municipalité
council flat

appartement thérapeutique
half-way house

APPARTENANCE
membership

appartenance religieuse
religious affiliation

appartenance syndicale / à un syndicat
(trade) union membership, membership of a trade union

appartenance à un syndicat
membership of a trade union

APPEL
appeal; call; use

appel (sans)
without appeal

appel de (faire)
to appeal

appel anticipé
advance call (for contributions)

appel à des concours extérieurs
use of outside expertise

appel de cotisations
call for / calling up of contributions

appel de cotisation complémentaire
supplementary call for contribution

appel d'une décision (faire)
to appeal against a decision

appel à de la main-d'oeuvre supplémentaire (faire)
(occ.) to take on extra hands

cour d'appel
Court of Appeal; (occ.) appeals tribunal (UK)

délai d'appel
time-limit for an appeal

droit d'appel / de former appel
right of / to appeal

interjeter appel
to appeal

juridiction d'appel
appeal body

lettre d'appel
letter of appeal

taux d'appel (Fr.)
coefficient used to calculate the effective rate of contributions

travail sur appel
work on call

APPELÉ (n.)
conscript, national serviceman (UK)

APPELER
appeler à la grève
to call a strike

APPELLATION
appellation d'emploi
occupational / job title

appellation d'emploi générique
generic job title

APPLICABLE
applicable; relevant

catégorie applicable
relevant class

directement applicable
immediately applicable; enforceable, self-executory

législation applicable
relevant legislation

taux applicable
appropriate rate

taux hebdomadaire applicable
appropriate weekly rate

APPLICATION
application, administration;
enforcement;
implementation

application automatique (d')
self-enforcing

application générale (d')
universally applicable

application d'un prorata
pro-rating

application sélective
differentiated application

arrêté d'application
implementing decree

champ d'application
field of application, scope; coverage

champ d'application matériel (ratione materiae)
material scope; substantive scope

champ d'application personnel (ratione personae)
personal scope

conditions d'application du contrat
terms and conditions of the agreement

date d'application
effective date

décret d'application
implementing decree

école d'application
practice school

entrée en application
entry into effect; (occ.) introduction

mettre en application
to implement

mise en application
implementation; enforcement; entry into effect

modalités d'application du contrat
terms and conditions of the agreement

règlement d'application
implementing regulation

APPLIQUER
to apply; to implement

appliquer (faire)
to enforce, to bring into force

recherche économique appliquée
applied economic research

APPOINT
activité d'appoint
subsidiary activity

matériel d'appoint
ancillary equipment

personnel d'appoint
contingent workers

programme d'appoint
(occ.) add-on programme

revenu d'appoint
secondary / complementary income

revenu d'appoint temporaire
temporary income support

salaire d'appoint
complementary / secondary income

travail d'appoint
subsidiary job

versement d'appoint
top-up / deficiency payment

APPOINTÉ (adj.)
salaried

APPOINTEMENTS
emoluments, pay, salary; allowance

APPORT
influx, inflow, input; contribution; increment

apport de l'Etat
contribution of the State

apports locaux
local input / content

apport de main-d'oeuvre
additional labour, labour input

APPORTEUR
apporteur de revenu
earner, breadwinner

deuxième apporteur de revenu
second (family) earner / breadwinner,
secondary family worker, secondary (wage)
earner

principal apporteur de revenus
main / principal (wage) earner, primary
earner

APPRÉCIATION
assessment, evaluation; rating; upgrading

appréciation globale
(occ.) general rating

appréciation du rendement
performance appraisal

échelle d'appréciation fondée sur des études de comportement type par fonction
behaviourally anchored rating scale (BARS)

rapport d'appréciation d'un travailleur
evaluation report of an employee

(système de) rapport d'appréciation du comportement professionnel
performance evaluation report (system)

APPRENTI
apprentice (trainee); apprenticeship
trainee; trainee

apprenti autonome
self-employed apprentice

apprenti sous contrat
indentured apprentice

apprenti stagiaire
trainee apprentice

centre de formation des apprentis (CFA) (Fr.)
tuition centre for working apprentices,
apprentice training centre

formation des apprentis
apprenticeship training, training of
apprentices

stagiaire non apprenti
non-apprentice trainee

APPRENTISSAGE
apprenticeship (training); (on-site /
on-the-job) training / learning

apprentissage de l'autonomie fonctionnelle
(occ.) life skills training

apprentissage à distance
distance learning

apprentissage par la pratique
learning by doing

atelier d'apprentissage
apprentice workshop

centre d'apprentissage
apprentice school

certificat d'apprentissage
certificate of apprenticeship

conseiller en apprentissage
apprenticeship counsellor

contrat d'apprentissage
apprenticeship contract; articles of
apprenticeship; indenture

contrat d'apprentissage «ordinaire» (Belg.)
"ordinary" apprenticeship contract

contrat d'apprentissage spécial (Belg.)
special apprenticeship contract

courbe d'apprentissage
learning curve

cours préparatoire à l'apprentissage
pre-apprenticeship course

crédit d'impôt relatif à l'apprentissage (Fr.)
tax credit for apprenticeship

difficulté d'apprentissage
learning disability

économie d'apprentissage
learning economy

exonération de la taxe d'apprentissage (Fr.)
exemption from apprenticeship tax

expérience d'apprentissage
learning experience

formation en apprentissage
apprenticeship training

matériel d'enseignement et d'apprentissage
teaching / learning material

métier d'apprentissage
apprenticeship / apprenticeable trade

période d'apprentissage
apprenticeship / learning period, period of apprenticeship

place en apprentissage
apprenticeship place

plan de formation en apprentissage
apprenticeship training plan

processus d'apprentissage
learning process

programme d'apprentissage
apprenticeship programme

programme d'apprentissage accéléré
accelerated programme of apprenticeship

programme de formation préalable à l'apprentissage
pre-apprenticeship training programme

schéma prévisionnel de l'apprentissage
appenticeship plan for the future

taxe d'apprentissage
apprenticeship tax; training levy (Fr.)

théorie de l'apprentissage
learning theory

APPROBATEUR
agent approbateur
authorising officer / agent

APPROBATION
approval; endorsement

approbation d'une offre d'emploi
approval of a job offer

approbation préalable
prior approval

approbation de principe
approval in principle

document d'approbation
record of approval

APPROCHE
approche prévisionnelle de l'emploi
manpower forecast approach

recrutement par approche directe
executive search

service d'approche
outreach service

APPROFONDISSEMENT
additional tuition (ed.)

APPROPRIÉ
adequate, relevant, suitable, due

emploi approprié
suitable employment

travailleur approprié
suitable worker

APPROUVÉ
congé de maladie approuvé
certified sick leave

effectifs approuvés
authorised establishment

APPROVISIONNEMENT
supply

APPUI
support

personnel d'appui
support staff

APPUYER
to support, to second

APTE
able, qualified

apte à l'(exercice d'un) emploi
fit for work / employement; employable

apte à reprendre le travail
(physically) fit to resume work

apte au travail
capable of work, able to work; able-bodied;
employable

chômeur apte au travail
able-bodied unemployed

entièrement apte à l'emploi
fully employable

personne handicapée apte au travail
employable person with disability / ies

**travailleur apte à occuper un emploi /
apte au travail**
employable worker

APTITUDE
ability, competence, competency, skill,
qualification

âge d'aptitude à l'emploi / au travail
employable age

aptitude à l'emploi
suitability for the job, fitness for work; job
readiness; employability

aptitude exigée
skill / job requirement

aptitude fonctionnelle
functional ability

aptitude manuelle
manual / manipulative skill

aptitudes nécessaires à la vie courante
living skills

aptitude personnelle
personal ability

aptitude physique
physical fitness

aptitude professionnelle
job / work / vocational skill,
occupational aptitude

aptitude psychomotrice
(occ.) manipulative skill

aptitude à reprendre le travail
(physical) fitness to return to / resume
work

aptitude au travail
occupational fitness; working ability,
ability to work; job readiness;
employability

aptitude à vivre en société
social skill(s)

brevet d'aptitude
certificate of competency

certificat d'aptitude professionnelle
certificate of competence, qualification /
occupational / trade proficiency / craft
certificate

**certificat d'aptitude professionnelle
agricole (CAPA) (Fr.)**
certificate of agricultural competence

**certificat médical d'aptitude profes-
sionnelle**
occupational medical certificate

degré d'aptitude
skill level

épreuve d'aptitude
skill test

niveau d'aptitude
skill level; functional level

profil d'aptitudes professionnelles
occupational aptitude pattern

test d'aptitude
aptitude test

test d'aptitude à l'emploi
employment aptitude test

test d'aptitude(s) générale(s)
general aptitude test

APUREMENT
(final) settlement; audit

ARBITRAGE
arbitration

arbitrage ayant force obligatoire (Malta)
binding arbitration

clause d'arbitrage
arbitration clause

commission d'arbitrage
board of arbitration / of arbitrators,
arbitration board / tribunal / commission;
(occ.) grievance committee

conseil d'arbitrage
adjudication tribunal

convention d'arbitrage
arbitration agreement

procédure de conciliation et d'arbitrage
conciliation and arbitration procedure

**Service de consultation, de conciliation et
d'arbitrage (UK)**
Advisory, Conciliation and Arbitration
Service (ACAS)

système paritaire d'arbitrage
joint arbitration machinery

taux de salaire fixé par arbitrage
award (wage) rate

tribunal d'arbitrage obligatoire
compulsory arbitration tribunal

ARBITRAIRE
congédiement arbitraire
arbitrary discharge

licenciement arbitraire
unfair / wrongful dismissal, wrongful
discharge (USA)

ARBITRAL
décision / sentence arbitrale
arbitration award

ARBITRE
arbitrator; (occ.) mediator

ARBITRER
arbitrer un litige
to mediate a dispute

ARCHITECTES
architectes, ingénieurs et assimilés
[CITP-1988 (214)]
architects, engineers and related professionals [ISCO-1988 (214)]

**architectes, ingénieurs et techniciens
assimilés [CITP-1968 (0-2/3)]**
architects, engineers and related technicians [ISCO-1968 (0-2/3)]

ARCHIVE
archives hospitalières
hospital records

ARCHIVISTE
archivistes, bibliothécaires, documentalistes et assimilés [CITP-1988 (-243)]
archivists, librarians and related information professionals [ISCO-1988 (243)]

ARGUER
to argue; to make representations

ARITHMÉTIQUE (adj.)
moyenne arithmétique
arithmetic mean / average

ARITHMÉTIQUE (n.)
programme d'initiation à l'arithmétique
numeracy programme

ARMATEUR
shipowner, ship operator

armateur transporteur
shipowner carrier

ARMÉ (adj.)
forces armées [CITP-1988 (0, 01, 011]
armed forces [ISCO-1988 (0, 01, 011)]

ARMÉE
armée d'active
regular / standing army

ARRANGEMENT
arrangement, agreement, understanding;
settlement; scheme

arrangement administratif
administrative agreement

**arrangement contractuel juridiquement
obligatoire**
legally binding contractual arrangement

ARRÉRAGES
arrears

arrérages au décès (Fr.)
death arrears

arrérages de pension échus
pension arrears due

arrérages des pensions de retraite (Fr.)
old age pension arrears

paiement des arrérages
payment of arrears

ARRÊT
interruption, stoppage; decision

arrêt de maladie / arrêt-maladie
sick leave, absence from work owing to
illness

arrêt de maladie (en)
absent from work owing to illness

arrêt de rémunération
interruption of earnings

arrêt de / du travail
absence from work; stoppage / suspension /
cessation of work, work stoppage, cessation
from work, walkout; disruption of
employment

arrêt de travail (en)
absent from work

arrêt de travail collectif
collective work stoppage

arrêt de travail pour maladie
sick leave, absence from work owing to
illness

arrêt de travail pour maladie (en)
absent from work owing to illness

arrêt de travail pour raison médicale
(occ.) medical suspension

avis d'arrêt de travail
notice of cessation of work / of having
ceased work; sick leave notice

certificat d'arrêt de travail
sick leave certificate

jour d'arrêt pour maladie
day off for illness

**nombre de jours d'arrêt pour
maladie**
number of days lost to illness

ARRÊTÉ (n.)
decree, ordinance; regulations

arrêté d'application
implementing decree

arrêté d'expulsion
deportation / expulsion order

arrêté préfectoral (Fr.)
prefectural order

arrêté royal (Belg.)
Royal decree

ARRIÉRATION
retardation

arriération mentale
mental retardation

ARRIÉRÉ (adj.)
cotisations arriérées
contribution arrears, outstanding contributions

ARRIÉRÉ (n.)
arrear, back payment, (pl.) arrearage;
subnormal person

arriéré de cotisation
contribution in arrears

arriéré mental
mentally retarded / defective, developmentally handicapped

arriéré profond
profoundly / severely mentally retarded

arriéré de salaire
arrear of wages, back wage / salary / pay, wage arrear

paiement des arriérés
payment of arrears

ARRIVANT
nouvel arrivant
(new) entrant

ARRIVÉE
date d'arrivée
date of arrival

ARRIVER
arriver à l'âge
to attain the age

arriver à terme
to expire

ARRONDISSEMENT
district

ARSENAL
arsenal juridique
panoply of legal instruments

ART
art; skill

arts ménagers
home management / economics; domestic arts

arts et métiers
applied / industrial arts and crafts

homme de l'art
professional

métier d'art
handicraft; (pl.) arts and crafts, (occ.) manual crafts

ARTICLE
clause; entry; section, subsection; item

article additionnel
additional article / provision, rider

article du budget
budget item

ARTIFICIEL
membre artificiel
artificial limb

ARTISAN
craftsman; (pl.) craft sector

artisans et ouvriers de l'alimentation et assimilés [CITP-1988 (741)]
food processing and related trades workers [ISCO-1988 (741)]

artisans et ouvriers de l'imprimerie et assimilés [CITP-1988 (734)]
printing and related trades workers [ISCO-1988 (734)]

artisans et ouvriers de la mécanique de précision, des métiers d'art de l'imprimerie et assimilés [CITP-1988 (73)]
precision, handicraft, printing and related trades workers [ISCO-1988 (73)]

artisans et ouvriers des métiers de l'extraction et du bâtiment [CITP-1988 (71)]
extraction and building trade workers [ISCO-1988 (71)]

artisans et ouvriers des métiers de la métallurgie, de la construction mécanique et assimilés [CITP-1988 (72)]
metal, machinery and related trades workers [ISCO-1988 (72)]

artisans et ouvriers des métiers du textile et de l'habillement et assimilés [CITP-1988 (743)]
textile, garment and related trades workers [ISCO-1988 (743)]

artisans et ouvriers du traitement du bois, ébénistes et assimilés [CITP-1988 (742)]
wood treaters, cabinet-makers and related trades workers [ISCO-1988 (742)]

artisans et ouvriers du travail du cuir, des peaux et de la chaussure [CITP-1988 (744)]
pelt, leather and shoemaking trades workers [ISCO-1988 (744)]

artisan rural (Fr.)
rural self-employed

autres artisans et ouvriers des métiers de type artisanal [CITP-1988 (74)]
other craft and related trades workers [ISCO-1988 (74)]

ARTISANAL
activité artisanale
crafts

autres artisans et ouvriers des métiers de type artisanal [CITP-1988 (74)]
other craft and related trades workers [ISCO-1988 (74)]

corporation artisanale
trade guild

établissement artisanal
handicraft establishment

industrie artisanale
cottage industry; (pl.) cottage industries / crafts

métier artisanal
handicraft; (pl.) arts and crafts, (occ.) manual crafts

non-salarié des professions artisanales
self-employed handicraft worker

profession artisanale
manual trade

zone artisanale
(occ.) development estate

ARTISANAT
handicraft, craft industry / sector / trades, (manual) crafts

artisanat de création
(occ.) arts and crafts

formation à l'artisanat
craft training

travail d'artisanat
handicraft

ARTISTE
artiste auteur (Fr.)
author artist

artiste professionnel / du spectacle
entertainer

ASCENDANCE
ascendance nationale
national extraction

ASCENDANT (adj.)
conjoncture / mouvement / tendance ascendant(e)
rising / upward trend

phase ascendante
upturn, upswing

ASCENDANT (n.)
ascendant

ASCENSION
ascension sociale
upward mobility

ASILE
home; poor house; hospital; shelter; establishment; asylum

asile d'aliénés
mental home

asile de nuit
night shelter

asile de vieillards, d'infirmes et de nécessiteux
home for the aged, infirm and needy

demandeur d'asile
asylum seeker

ASOCIAL
anti-social

comportement asocial
anti-social behaviour

ASPIRATION
aspiration professionnelle
career aspiration / expectation

aspirations salariales
wage aspirations / expectations

ASSAINISSEMENT
sanitation; rehabilitation

inspecteur de la santé et de l'assainissement
health and sanitary inspector

ASSEDIC (Fr.)
State unemployment fund

ASSEMBLAGE
conducteurs d'installations et de machines et ouvriers de l'assemblage ([CITP-1988 (8)]
plant and machine operators and assemblers [ISCO-1988 (8)]

conducteurs de machines et ouvriers de l'assemblage [CITP-1988 (82)]
machine operators and assemblers [ISCO-1988 (82)]

ouvriers de l'assemblage [CITP-1988 (828)]
assemblers [ISCO-1988 (828)]

ASSERVIR
enfant asservi
child bonded labourer, child slave

ASSERVISSEMENT
asservissement des enfants
child bondage / slavery

ASSIDU
travailleur assidu
steady worker

ASSIDUITÉ
class attendance; (pl.) harassment

assiduités abusives
sexual harassment

certificat d'assiduité
certificate of attendance

prime d'assiduité
attendance bonus

ASSIETTE
funding base; tax base; (basis of) assessment

assiette d'assujettissement (hand.); assiette de(s) cotisations
funding base for / assessment of contributions, contribution base

assiette des cotisations sociales
basis of social insurance contribution

assiette fiscale / de l'impôt
tax(able) base, basis of taxation

assiette mensuelle des cotisations
monthly assessment of contributions

assiette des prélèvements
contribution base

établissement de l'assiette fiscale
tax assessment

fixer l'assiette des cotisations
to assess contributions

limite inférieure pour l'assiette des cotisations de la catégorie n
lower earnings limit of class n contributions

limite supérieure pour l'assiette des cotisations de la catégorie n
upper earnings limit of class n contributions

ASSIGNER
to allocate, to assign

somme assignée
allocation

tâche assignée
assignment

ASSIMILATION
assimilation d'un acte professionnel (Fr.)
assimilation of medical treatment

ASSIMILÉ (adj.)
related; treated as such

période assimilée
period treated as such

personnel des professions scientifiques, techniques, libérales et assimilées [CITP-1968 (0/1)]
professional, technical and related workers [ISCO-1968 (0/1)]

professions scientifiques, techniques, libérales et assimilées
(occ.) professionals

régime spécial des fonctionnaires ou du personnel assimilé
special scheme for civil servants and persons treated as such

sculpteurs, peintres, photographes et artistes créateurs assimilés [CITP-1968 (1-6)]
sculptors, painters, photographers and related creative artists [ISCO-1968 (1-6)]

spécialistes des sciences physico-chimiques et techniciens assimilés [CITP-1968 (0-1)]
physical scientists and related technicians [ISCO-1968 (0-1)]

statisticiens, mathématiciens, analystes de systèmes et techniciens assimilés [CITP-1968 (0-8)]
statisticians, mathematicians, systems analysts and related technicians [ISCO-1968 (0-8)]

tailleurs, couturiers, couseurs, tapissiers et ouvriers assimilés [CITP-1968 (7-9)]
tailors, dressmakers, sewers, upholsterers and related workers [ISCO-1968 (7-9)]

travailleur assimilé
related worker

verriers, potiers et travailleurs assimilés [CITP-1968 (8-9)]
glass formers, potters and related workers [ISCO-1968 (8-9)]

ASSIMILÉ (n.)
treated as such

agents d'accompagnement et assimilés [CITP-1988 (511)]
travel attendants and related workers [ISCO-1988 (511)]

agents de maîtrise et assimilés [CITP-1968 (7-0)]
production supervisors and general foremen [ISCO-1968 (7-0)]

architectes, ingénieurs et assimilés [CITP-1988 (214)]
architects, engineers and related professionals [ISCO-1988 (214)]

architectes, ingénieurs et techniciens assimilés [CITP-1968 (0-2/3)]
architects, engineers and related technicians [ISCO-1968 (0-2/3)]

archivistes, bibliothécaires, documentalistes et assimilés [CITP-1988 (2-43)]
archivists, librarians and related information professionals [ISCO-1988 (243)]

artisans et ouvriers de l'alimentation et assimilés [CITP-1988 (741)]
food processing and related trades workers [ISCO-1988 (741)]

artisans et ouvriers de l'imprimerie et assimilés [CITP-1988 (734)]
printing and related trades workers [ISCO-1988 (734)]

artisans et ouvriers de la mécanique de précision, des métiers d'art de l'imprimerie et assimilés [CITP-1988 (73)]
precision, handicraft, printing and related trades workers [ISCO-1988 (73)]

artisans et ouvriers des métiers de la métallurgie, de la construction mécanique et assimilés [CITP-1988 (72)]
metal, machinery and related trades workers [ISCO-1988 (72)]

artisans et ouvriers des métiers du textile et de l'habillement et assimilés [CITP-1988 (743)]
textile, garment and related trades workers [ISCO-1988 (743)]

artisans et ouvriers du traitement du bois, ébénistes et assimilés [CITP-1988 (742)]
wood treaters, cabinet-makers and related trades workers [ISCO-1988 (742)]

assimilé cadre
employee with managerial status

astrologues, diseurs de bonne aventure et assimilés [CITP-1988 (515)]
astrologers, fortune-tellers and related workers [ISCO-1988 (515)]

athlètes, sportifs et assimilés [CITP-1968 (1-8)]
athletes, sportsmen and related workers [ISCO-1968 (1-8)]

auteurs, journalistes et écrivains assimilés [CITP-1968 (1-5)]
authors, journalists and related writers [ISCO-1968 (1-5)]

biologistes, agronomes et techniciens assimilés [CITP-1968 (0-5)]
life scientists and related technicians [ISCO-1968 (0-5)]

caissiers, guichetiers et assimilés [CITP-1988 (421)]
cashiers, tellers and related clerks [ISCO-1988 (421)]

chefs de groupe d'employés de maison et travailleurs assimilés [CITP-1968 (5-2)]
housekeeping and related service supervisors [ISCO-1968 (5-2)]

coiffeurs, spécialistes des soins de beauté et travailleurs assimilés [CITP-1968 (5-7)]
hairdressers, barbers, beauticians and related workers [ISCO-1968 (5-7)]

commis vendeurs, employés de commerce et travailleurs assimilés [CITP-1968 (4-5)]
salesmen, shop assistants and related workers [ISCO-1968 (4-5)]

compositeurs typographes et travailleurs assimilés [CITP-1968 (9-2)]
printers and related workers [ISCO-1968 (9-2)]

conducteurs d'installations et de matériels fixes et assimilés [CITP-1988 (81)]
stationary plant and related operators [ISCO-1988 (81)]

conducteurs d'installations de production d'énergie et assimilés [CITP-1988 (816)]
power-production and related plant operators [ISCO-1988 (816)]

conducteurs d'installations de verrerie et de céramique et assimilés [CITP-1988 (813)]
glass, ceramics and related plant-operators [ISCO-1988 (813)]

conducteurs de locomotives et assimilés [CITP-1988 (831)]
locomotive engine drivers and related workers [ISCO-1988 (831)]

ébénistes, menuisiers et travailleurs assimilés [CITP-1968 (8-1)]
cabinet makers and related woodworkers [ISCO-1968 (8-1)]

éboueurs et manoeuvres assimilés [CITP-1988 (916)]
garbage collectors and related labourers [ISCO-1988 (916)]

électriciens, électroniciens et travailleurs assimilés [CITP-1968 (8-5)]
electrical fitters and related electrical and electronics workers [ISCO-1968 (8-5)]

éleveurs et ouvriers qualifiés de l'élevage destiné aux marchés et assimilés [CITP-1988 (612)]
market-oriented animal producers and related workers [ISCO-1988 (612)]

employés de bibliothèque, de service du courrier et assimilés [CITP-1988 (414)]
library, mail and related clerks [ISCO-1988 (414)]

employés de comptabilité, caissiers et travailleurs assimilés [CITP-1968 (3-3)]
bookkeepers, cashiers and related workers [ISCO-1968 (3-3)]

employés de réception, caissiers, guichetiers et assimilés [CITP-1988 (42)]
customer service clerks [ISCO-1988 (42)]

fonctionnaires et assimilés
Government employees

forgerons, outilleurs et assimilés [CITP-1988 (722)]
blacksmiths, tool-makers and related trades workers [ISCO-1988 (722)]

gardiens d'immeubles, nettoyeurs et travailleurs assimilés [CITP-1968 (5-5)]
building caretakers, charworkers, cleaners and related workers [ISCO-1968 (5-5)]

manoeuvres de l'agriculture, de la pêche et assimilés [CITP-1988 (92) / (921)]
agricultural, fishery and related labourers [ISCO-1988 (92) / (921)]

matelots de pont et assimilés [CITP-1988 (834)]
ships' deck crews and related workers [ISCO-1988 (834)]

mathématiciens, statisticiens et assimilés [CITP-1988 (212)]
mathematicians, statisticians and related professionals [ISCO-1988 (212)]

médecins et assimilés (à l'exception des cadres infirmiers) [CITP-1988 (222)]
health professionals (except nursing) [ISCO-1988 (222)]

médecins, dentistes, vétérinaires et travailleurs assimilés [CITP-1968 (0-6/7)]
medical, dental, veterinary and related workers [ISCO-1968 (0-6/7)]

membres du clergé et assimilés [CITP-1968 (1-4)]
workers in religion [ISCO-1968 (1-4)]

messagers, porteurs, gardiens, portiers et assimilés [CITP-1988 (915)]
messengers, porters, doorkeepers and related workers [ISCO-1988 (915)]

mineurs, carriers, foreurs de puits et travailleurs assimilés [CITP-1968 (7-1)]
miners, quarrymen, well drillers and related workers [ISCO-1968 (7-1)]

mouleurs de fonderie, soudeurs, tôliers-chaudronniers, monteurs de charpentes métalliques et assimilés [CITP-1988 (721)]
metal moulders, welders, sheet-metal workers, structural-metal preparers, and related trades workers [ISCO-1988 (721)]

musiciens, acteurs, danseurs et artistes assimilés [CITP-1968 (1-7)]
composers and performing artists [ISCO-1968 (1-7)]

ouvriers du bâtiment (finitions) et assimilés [CITP-1988 (713)]
building finishers and related trades workers [ISCO-1988 (713)]

ouvriers du bâtiment (gros oeuvre) et assimilés [CITP-1988 (712)]
building frame and related trades workers [ISCO-1988 (712)]

ouvriers peintres, ravaleurs de façades et assimilés [CITP-1988 (714)]
painters, building structure cleaners and related trades workers [ISCO-1988 (714)]

pêcheurs, chasseurs et travailleurs assimilés [CITP-1968 (6-4)]
fishermen, hunters and related workers [ISCO-1968 (6-4)]

personnel administratif et travailleurs assimilés [CITP-1968 (3)]
clerical and related workers [ISCO-1968 (3)]

personnel du service d'immeuble, laveurs de vitres et assimilés [CITP-1988 (914)]
building caretakers, window and related cleaners [ISCO-1988 (914)]

physiciens, chimistes et assimilés [CITP-1988 (211)]
physicists, chemists and related professionals [ISCO-1988 (211)]

potiers, souffleurs de verre et assimilés [CITP-1988 (732)]
potters, glass-makers and related trades workers [ISCO-1988 (732)]

professions du forestage et assimilées [CITP-1988 (614)]
forestry and related workers [ISCO-1988 (614)]

professions intermédiaires de l'administration publique des douanes et des impôts, et assimilés [CITP-1988 (3-44)]
customs, tax and related government associate professionals [CITP-1988 (344)]

vendeurs ambulants et assimilés [CITP-1988 (911)]
street vendors and related workers [ISCO-1988 (911)]

ASSISTANAT
dependency; dependence on welfare

ASSISTANCE
assistance, help, care, aid; relief; attendance

accord d'assistance médicale
health care agreement

allocation d'assistance
social assistance grant, attendance allowance

allocation d'assistance externe (Denm.)
outside assistance allowance

allocation d'assistance à la formation professionnelle (Ger.)
vocational assistance allowance

allocation d'assistance personnelle (It.)
personal assistance allowance

assistance aux aveugles
assistance for the blind

assistance-chômage
unemployment assistance

assistance complémentaire
supplementary assistance

assistance constante d'un tiers / d'une tierce personne
constant attendance

assistance curative
remedial assistance

assistance dentaire
dental health services

assistance éducative
educational support

assistance éducative en milieu ouvert
open educational support

assistance à l'enfance
child welfare

assistance financière
financial assistance

assistance médicale
medical aid

assistance médicale à domicile
medical home relief (USA)

assistance aux mères et aux enfants
mother and child care

assistance autre que pécuniaire
non-cash assistance

assistance pénitentiaire
prison welfare

assistance permanente (Denm.)
continuing maintenance assistance

assistance aux personnes âgées
provision for / relief of old people

assistance publique
national assistance, public care / assistance, State care (institution), poor relief

assistance sociale
social assistance / welfare, welfare assistance

assistance sociale et médicale
social and medical assistance

assistance temporaire
temporary assistance

assistance d'une tierce personne
(occ.) invalid care allowance (UK)

bureau d'assistance sociale
social assistance / (social) welfare office

enfant sous assistance
child in the care of public authorities

organisme d'assistance
assistance body; charity

organisme d'assistance sociale
social assistance agency / body

prestation marginale d'assistance en espèces (Denm.)
marginal cash assistance benefit

prêter son assistance
to assist

prime d'assistance
assistance grant

régime d'assistance
assistance scheme

régime d'assistance publique (Can.)
assistance plan

service d'assistance
assistance board / department / service

ASSISTANT(E) (n.)
assistant, helper

aide à la famille pour l'emploi d'une assistante maternelle agréée (Fr.)
family benefit for hiring an approved day-care attendant

assistant(e) de direction
executive / personal assistant

assistante d'hygiène scolaire
school nurse

assistant-infirmier / assistante-infirmière
nursing assistant

assistants laïcs des cultes [CITP-1988 (348)]
religious associate professionals [ISCO-1988 (348)]

assistante maternelle
child care worker, child-minder, day-care attendant; (occ.) foster mother (Fr.)

assistant médical
medical assistant

assistant médico-social
medico-social worker; almoner

assistant sanitaire
health assistant

assistant social
welfare assistant / worker, social worker

assistante sociale de garderie
child-minder

assistant social d'hôpital / des hôpitaux
(occ.) almoner

assistant social du personnel
personnel social worker

pharmacien assistant
assistant pharmacist

prestation spéciale assistante maternelle (Fr.)
special benefit for day-care attendant

ASSISTÉ (n.)
person receiving / in receipt of public assistance / in receipt of relief, public welfare recipient; on relief, dependent

assisté social
welfare recipient; [on welfare]

statut d'assisté social
(occ.) welfare status

ASSISTER
to assist, to support; to attend

assisté (être)
to live off the State

emploi assisté
supported employment

enfant assisté
dependent child, child in the care of public authorities, foundling, child in care

placement assisté
assisted placement

région assistée (UK)
assisted area

ASSOCIATIF
secteur associatif
voluntary / third sector; community organisations

vie associative
associative / associational life; voluntary activities

ASSOCIATION
association, organisation, group; partnership

accord d'association
association / partnership agreement

association d' / des anciens élèves
former students' association

association à but non lucratif
non-profit-making organisation

association caritative
charity, charitable association / agency

association de citoyens
citizens' group

association communautaire
community group

association d'employeurs
employer's association / federation / organisation, association / organisation of employers

association d'entraide
self-help group, friendly society

association féminine
women's association / club

association locale
community group

association de médecins
medical association

association mutualiste
friendly society

association ouvrière
workman's / workmen's association

association patronale
employer's association / organisation, association / organisation of employers, trade association

association du personnel
staff association

association de praticiens libéraux
individual practices association (IPA)

association professionnelle
industrial board / association, professional / trade association, trade guild, professional organisation / body

association reconnue d'utilité publique
association recognised to be of public interest, charitable association; charity

association de salariés / de travailleurs
workers' organisation

caisse d'association (Switz.)
professional association fund

droit d'association
freedom of organisation; right to organise

loi régissant les associations à but non lucratif
law governing non-profit-making organisations

ASSOCIÉ (n.)
associé actif
working partner

associé d'exploitation
associate farmer

ASSORTIMENT
range; collection; (occ.) kit

ASSOUPLIR
to make more flexible; to liberalise

horaire de travail assoupli
flexible work schedule, flexible hours

ASSOUPLISSEMENT
liberalisation; easing

ASSUJETTI
liable

assujetti à l'assurance
liable to insurance

assujetti à l'assurance obligatoire
subject to compulsory insurance,
compulsorily covered

assujetti à une condition de ressources
subject to means test

assujetti à un contrôle des gains
earnings-tested

assujetti à l'impôt
subject to tax(ation), taxable

assujetti à l'impôt sur le revenu
subject to income tax(ation)

assujetti au versement d'une / de cotisation(s)
liable for contribution / to pay (a)
contribution(s)

emploi assujetti à l'assurance
insurable employment

ASSUJETTISSEMENT
compulsory insurability; qualifying
condition; liability for contribution

assujettissement à l'assurance obligatoire
liability to compulsory insurance

assujettissement à l'impôt
tax liability

assujettissement obligatoire
compulsory coverage

plafond d'assujettissement
liability ceiling

ASSURABLE
emploi assurable
insurable employment

plafond assurable
insurability ceiling

rémunération hebdomadaire assurable
weekly insurable earnings

ASSURANCE
insurance; (occ.) indemnity

accéder à l'assurance
to enter insurance

accomplissement d'une période d'assurance
completion of a period of insurance

adhésion à l'assurance
entrance into insurance

adhésion individuelle à l'assurance
individual insurance cover

adhésion tardive à l'assurance
late entrance into insurance

administration d'assurance
insurance authority

admission à l'assurance volontaire
admission to voluntary insurance

affiliation à l'assurance
entrance into insurance, insurance
membership

affilier à l'assurance (s')
to enter insurance

agent de l'assurance nationale (UK)
(national) insurance officer

agent local d'assurance
local insurance officer

allocataire de l'assurance chômage
unemployment insurance recipient

annulation de cotisation d'assurance-vieillesse (Fr.)
annulment of old age contribution

assujetti à l'assurance
liable to insurance

assujetti à l'assurance obligatoire
subject to compulsory insurance,
compulsorily covered

**assujettissement à l'assurance obliga-
toire**
liability to compulsory insurance

assurance-accidents
accident insurance

**assurance accidents corporels du secteur
public (Ger.)**
public accident insurance

assurance accidents individuelle
personal accident insurance

**assurance (contre les) accidents du
travail (et les maladies professionnelles)**
industrial injury / injuries insurance,
insurance against accident at work;
employers' liability insurance; compensation scheme; accident insurance

assurance automobile
car insurance

assurance(-)chômage
unemployment insurance / compensation

assurance-chômage obligatoire
compulsory unemployment insurance

assurance complémentaire
supplementary insurance, complementary
scheme

assurance à contribution / contributive
contributory insurance

**assurance à cotisation(s) / financée par
cotisations**
contributory insurance / scheme

assurance(-)décès
death insurance, insurance in respect of
death

**assurance décès-invalidité en cas
d'accident**
accidental death and dismemberment
(AD+D)

assurance-déplacement professionnel
travel accident insurance

assurance-dommages
damage / indemnity / loss insurance

assurance en cours d'emploi
in-service insurance

**assurance basée sur une entente
d'exonération mutuelle**
no fault insurance

**assurance extra-légale en matière
d'hospitalisation (Belg.)**
extra-legal hospitalisation insurance

assurance facultative
optional insurance

assurance facultative continuée
optional continued insurance

assurance générale
general insurance

**assurance générale risques graves
(Neth.)**
general insurance against serious risks

assurance contre la grève
strike insurance

**assurance gros frais médicaux / gros
risques**
major medical insurance

assurance de groupe
group insurance

assurance-groupe sur la vie
group life insurance

assurance-hospitalisation
hospital benefits insurance

assurance ininterrompue
continued insurance

assurance(-)invalidité
disability / disablement / invalidity
insurance, insurance in respect of
invalidity

assurance-invalidité permanente
long-term disability insurance

assurance légale
statutory insurance

assurance-maintien du salaire en cas d'arrêt de travail
salary continuation insurance

assurance(-)maladie
health / medical / sickness insurance,
medical benefits insurance

assurance-maladies graves
catastrophic health insurance

assurance (contre les) maladies professionnelles
insurance against occupational disease

assurance du mari
husband's insurance

assurance(-)maternité
maternity insurance

assurance mixte
(occ.) endowment insurance

assurance multirisques
comprehensive insurance

assurance mutualiste / mutuelle
mutual insurance

assurance nationale (UK)
national insurance

assurance obligatoire
compulsory insurance

assurance des ouvriers / ouvrière
workers' insurance

assurance-pension
pension insurance

assurance personnelle
personal insurance

assurance petits risques
minor medical insurance

assurance à prime
premium insurance

assurance privée
commercial insurance

assurance propre
own insurance

assurance-rente
pension insurance

assurance en responsabilité civile
third party insurance, liability insurance

assurance-responsabilité de l'employeur
employer's liability insurance

assurance(-)salaire
wage loss insurance

assurance-santé et perte de gains
health and loss of earnings insurance

assurance sociale
social insurance

assurance-soins dentaires
dental insurance, dental health scheme

assurance-soins de santé
health care insurance

assurance de survivant
survivor's assurance / insurance

assurance aux tiers
third party insurance

assurance tous risques
comprehensive insurance

assurance contre la tuberculose (It.)
tuberculosis insurance

assurance veuvage
widow's insurance

assurance-vie
life insurance, life assurance (UK)

assurance-vie à capital différé
endowment insurance

assurance-vie à capital récupérable
pure endowment insurance

assurance-vie privée
(occ.) non-occupational coverage

assurance(-)vieillesse
old-age insurance, insurance in respect
for old-age

assurance(-)vieillesse des employés
pensions insurance of salaried employees

assurance(-)vieillesse des ouvriers
manual workers' pension insurance,
pension insurance of manual workers

assurance(-)vieillesse et survivants
old age and survivors' insurance

assurance volontaire
voluntary / optional insurance

**assuré au titre d'une assurance faculta-
tive continuée**
insured on an optional continued basis

**assuré au titre d'une assurance obliga-
toire**
compulsorily insured

attestation d'assurance
certificate of insurance

attestation des périodes d'assurance
certification of periods of insurance,
certified statement specifying the periods of
insurance

bénéficiaire de l'assurance chômage
unemployment insurance recipient

bureau local d'assurance
local insurance office

caisse d'assurance
insurance fund

caisse d'assurance chômage
unemployment (insurance) fund

caisse d'assurance maladie
health (insurance) fund; sickness fund

caisse d'assurance mutuelle agricole (Fr.)
agricultural mutual insurance fund

caisse d'assurance nationale (UK)
national insurance fund

caisse d'assurances sociales
social insurance fund

caisse d'assurance(-)vieillesse
old age pension fund

**caisse primaire d'assurance maladie
(CPAM) (Fr.)**
local health fund

**caisse régionale d'assurance maladie
(CRAM) (Fr.)**
regional health fund

**carrière d'assurance: voir
reconstiuter la carrière d'assurance**

carte d'assurance (sociale)
(social) insurance card

**commissaire à l'assurance nationale
(UK)**
national insurance commissioner

compagnie d'assurance
insurance company

compagnie d'assurances mutuelles
mutual insurance company

contrat d'assurance collective
collective insurance contract

cotisation d'assurance
insurance contribution

cotisation à l'assurance-maladie
health / sickness insurance contribution

**cotisation à l'assurance nationale
(UK)**
national insurance contribution

**dernière date d'affiliation à
l'assurance**
date of last entry into insurance

**durée d'assurance ouvrant droit à
prestations**
qualifying insurance / qualification
period

durée d'assurance(-)vieillesse
period of old age insurance

emploi assujetti à l'assurance
insurable employment

entrée dans l' / en assurance
entrance into insurance

**fichier central des cotisations d'assu-
rance (UK)**
central record of insurance contributions

fonds assurance(-)formation (Fr.)
training insurance fund

fonds d'assurance(-)vieillesse
old age security fund

fonds public d'assurance
State insurance fund

immatriculation à l'assurance sociale
social insurance registration

indemnité d'assurance
insurance benefit

institut régional d'assurance
regional insurance office

institution d'assurance
insurance institute

institution d'assurance(-)chômage
unemployment insurance institution

institution d'assurance(-)maladie
sickness insurance institution

institution d'assurance(-)vieillesse
old-age insurance institution

interruption d'assurance
break in / interruption of / in insurance

manuel d'assurance-qualité (MQ)
quality assurance manual

numéro d'assurance nationale (UK)
national insurance number

numéro d'assurance sociale
social insurance number

organisme d'assurance
insurance institute

organisme d'assurance contre les accidents
accident insurance institution

pension versée sur la base de l'assurance du mari
pension by virtue of husband's contributions

pension versée sur la base de son assurance propre
pension by virtue of one's own contributions

pension relevant des assurances sociales
social insurance pension

pension proportionnelle (assurance mixte) (Irel.)
pro-rata (mixed insurance) pension

pension au titre de son propre régime d'assurance
pension on own insurance

période d'assurance
insurance period

période d'assurance obligatoire
period of compulsory insurance

période d'assurance requise pour l'ouverture du droit aux prestations
qualifying insurance / qualification period

police d'assurance
insurance policy

police d'assurance-accidents
accident policy

police d'assurance générale
(occ.) blanket (insurance) policy

police d'assurance mixte
endowment policy

police d'assurance-vie à capital différé
endowment policy

police d'assurance-vie à capital récupérable
pure endowment policy

prestations d'assurance-accident à recevoir
casualty insurance claim receivable

prestation de l'assurance chômage
unemployment (insurance) benefit

prestation de l'assurance maladie
sick(ness) benefit

prestation en nature de l'assurance maladie
health benefit in kind

prime d'assurance
insurance premium

principe d'assurance
insurance principle

production imputée de services d'assu-rance-dommages
imputed service charge for casualty insurance

production imputée de services d'assu-rance-vie
imputed service charge for life insurance

propre régime d'assurance (au titre de son)
on his own insurance

récapitulation des périodes d'assurance
summary of the periods of insurance

reconstituer la carrière d'assurance
to draw up someone's insurance history / record

régime d'assurance
insurance scheme

régime d'assurance contre les accidents personnels
personal injuries scheme

régime d'assurance-chômage
unemployment insurance (scheme)

régime d'assurance-maladie
health insurance scheme

régime d'assurance maladie ou mater-nité
sickness or maternity insurance scheme, scheme for sickness or maternity insurance

régime d'assurance obligatoire
compulsory insurance scheme

régime d'assurance salaire
wage loss insurance plan, wage loss replacement plan

régime d'assurance-traitement collectif
group salary insurance scheme

régime d'assurance(-)vieillesse
pension (insurance) scheme

régime d'assurance(-)vieillesse obliga-toire
compulsory pension insurance scheme

régime d'assurance(-)vieillesse propor-tionnelle au salaire
graduated pension scheme

régime d'assurance volontaire
voluntary insurance scheme

régime de retraite en assurance
insured pension plan

substitution d'assurance
substitution of insurance

superposition de périodes d'assurance
overlapping of periods of insurance

taux de pension de l'assurance (-)vieillesse
rate of the old age pension

timbre d'assurance (UK)
insurance stamp

totalisation des périodes d'assurance
adding (together) of periods of insurance, aggregation of / totalling of insurance pe-riods

ASSURÉ (n.)
insured person; insured; subscriber; claimant

assuré social
insured person; insured; (pl.) members of the National Insurance Scheme (UK)

carte d'assuré (social)
(social) insurance card

nouvel assuré
newly insured

ASSURER
assuré (non)
uninsured

assuré au titre d'une assurance facul-tative continuée
insured on an optional continued basis

**assuré contre une ou plusieurs éven-
tualités**
insured for one or more contingencies

**assuré à titre obligatoire / au titre d'une
assurance obligatoire**
compulsorily insured

assuré (à titre) volontaire
voluntarily insured

emploi assuré
secured / assured employment, secure job

ASSUREUR
insurer; underwriter; carrier

assureur subrogé
insurer substituting for ... / entering into the
rights of ... / involved

organisme assureur
insurance carrier, insuring body

ASTREINT
liable

**astreint à des strictes heures de bureau
(être)**
to be expected to keep strict office hours

ASTREINTE
constraint, obligation; daily penalty / fine

période d'astreinte
on-call time (USA)

prime d'astreinte
on-call / stand-by pay

ASTROLOGUE
astrologues, diseurs de bonne aventure et
assimilés [CITP-1988 (515)]
astrologers, fortune-tellers and related
workers [ISCO-1988 (515)]

ATELIER
workshop; task force / group; syndicate;
shop, shop floor (the); work

**atelier pratiquant l'affiliation
syndicale obligatoire / n'admettant
pas d'ouvriers non syndiqués**
closed / union shop

atelier d'apprentissage
apprentice workshop

atelier clandestin
sweat shop

**atelier d'entraînement à la recherche
d'emplois (Belg.)**
job-finding workshop

atelier flexible
flexible manufacturing system

atelier de formation
training workshop

atelier de gestion
management workshop

atelier de montage
assembly shop

**atelier d'objectif professionnel pour
demandeurs d'emploi (Belg.)**
vocational objectives workshop for
jobseekers

atelier ouvert
open workshop

atelier protégé
sheltered workshop

atelier syndical
closed / union shop

atelier non syndiqué
non-union / open shop

atelier thérapeutique
therapeutic workshop

chef d'atelier
workshop foreman / manager

délégué d'atelier
shop steward

école-atelier
production high school (Denm.),
workshop school (Sp.)

période en atelier
workshop period

règlement d'atelier
works regulations / rule-book

ATHLÈTE
athlètes, sportifs et assimilés [CITP-1968
(1-8)]
athletes, sportsmen and related workers
[ISCO-1968 (1-8)]

ATTACHÉ (n.)
attaché d'administration
junior civil servant

attaché de direction
executive / management assistant

ATTACHEMENT
attachment; support

attachement à l'emploi
job attachment

ATTAQUABLE
challengeable

ATTARDÉ (adj.)
enfant attardé
underdeveloped child

ATTARDÉ (n.)
attardé mental
mentally retarded / defective, developmentally handicapped

ATTEINT
atteint de
suffering from

atteint d'incapacité partielle
partially incapacitated

atteint d'invalidité partielle
partially disabled

atteint par la limite d'âge
(occ.) superannuated

ATTEINTE
impairment; violation

atteinte corporelle
personal injury

atteinte à la liberté du travail
violation of the freedom of labour

**indemnisation pour atteinte à
l'intégrité (Switz.)**
allowance for diminished faculty

porter atteinte à
to affect, to prejudice, to jeopardise

porter atteinte aux droits acquis
to jeopardise acquired rights

**porter atteinte au libre exercice de
l'industrie et du travail**
to impair / to restrict the freedom of
industry and labour

ATTENTE
expectation

allocation d'attente (Belg.)
waiting allowance

**allocation supplémentaire d'attente
(Fr.)**
interim supplementary allowance

attentes du personnel
staff aspirations

attente professionnelle
occupational expectation

chômage d'attente
search unemployment

compte d'attente
suspense account

**crédit d'attente pour le congé dans les
foyers**
credit for home leave travel

délai d'attente
qualifying period, waiting period / time;
(occ.) elimination period

emploi d'attente
bridge job

expiration d'un délai d'attente
completion of a waiting period

indemnité d'attente
tideover allowance

liste d'attente
stand-by / waiting list

période d'attente
waiting period

théorie des attentes
expectancy theory

ATTENTION
défaut d'attention
lack of care / of diligence

ATTESTATION
certificate, certification; evidence;
statutory declaration

attestation d'assurance
certificate of insurance

attestation de droit (aux prestations)
certificate of eligibility / of entitlement

attestation d'exactitude
certification of accuracy

attestation de médecin
doctor's certificate

attestation médicale
medical certificate

attestation des périodes d'assurance
certification of periods of insurance,
certified statement specifying the periods of
insurance

certificat d'attestation des frais
certificate of cost

ATTESTER
to certify

ATTITRÉ
regular, usual; accredited, registered,
appointed; certified

ATTITUDE
attitude d'insubordination
insubordinate attitude

ATTRACTION
aire d'attraction
catchment area

attraction du droit à prestations
(occ.) eligibility effect

zone d'attraction
catchment area

ATTRAIT
attraction; inducement, incentive; (pl.)
amenities

ATTRIBUABLE
attribuable au service
attributable to service

ATTRIBUER
to allocate, to grant, to assign; to
earmark

attribuer une prestation
to allow / to grant a benefit

**risques couverts et prestations
attribuées**
contingencies covered and benefits
granted

ATTRIBUTAIRE
recipient

ATTRIBUTION
allocation, assignment, provision,
granting, award; grant; (pl.) content of
job, responsibilities, competence,
competency, requirement, (terms of)
reference, function, work

attribution de crédits
award of credits

attribution d'indemnités de maladie
provision of sickness benefit(s)

attribution de places de formation
allocation of training places

attribution d'une prestation
provision / granting of a benefit

attribution des tâches
work assignment

classement (des postes) par attributions
duty classification (of posts)

condition d'attribution
qualifying condition; eligibility (requirement); condition of entitlement

conditions d'attribution des prestations
conditions governing eligibility for benefits

conflit d'attributions
(occ.) demarcation dispute

délégation d'attribution
delegation of authority

description des attributions
job / position description

éventail des attributions
range of duties

niveau des attributions
level of work

période d'attribution
period of payment

règle d'attribution
qualifying requirement

ATYPIQUE
forme d'emploi atypique
atypical form of employment

forme de travail atypique
non-standard form of working

travail atypique
atypical work

travailleur atypique
atypical worker

AUBAINE
revenu d'aubaine
windfall income

AUDIOLOGIE
hearing aid

AUDIOPHONE
hearing aid

AUDIOPROTHÈSE
hearing aid

AUDIOPROTHÉSISTE
hearing aid specialist

AUDIO-VISUEL
moyens audio-visuels
audio-visual material

AUDIT
audit social
social / personnel audit

AUDITEUR
auditeur libre
unregistered student

AUDITIF
appareil auditif
hearing aid

prothèse auditive
hearing aid

AUGMENTATION
increase, rise, uprating, increment

augmentation automatique
automatic / mandatory / statutory increase

augmentation barémique
(occ.) increment

augmentation des cotisations
raising of contributions

augmentation au titre du coût de la vie
cost-of-living increment / increase

augmentation échelonnée
incremental increase

augmentation d'impôts
tax increase

augmentation au mérite
merit increase

augmentation moyenne
average increase

augmentation en niveau des salaires
global percentage increase of salaries

augmentation périodique de traitement
salary increment, within-grade (salary) increment

augmentation de la population active
labour force growth / increase

augmentation préférentielle des salaires
premium wage increase

augmentation réglementaire
statutory increase

augmentation de la rémunération
salary increase

augmentation salariale
salary increase / award, salary / wage / pay rise / increase

augmentation salariale rétroactive
retroactive increase in wages

augmentation de / du / des salaire(s)
salary increase / award, salary / wage / pay rise / increase

augmentation du traitement
salary increase

augmentation de traitement accélérée
accelerated salary increment

augmentation uniforme
(occ.) across-the-board increase

courbe d'augmentation des salaires
salary progression curve

retenue d'une augmentation périodique de salaire
withholding of salary increment

AUGMENTER
to raise, to increase

augmenter les cotisations / le taux de la cotisation
to raise contributions

augmenter une prestation
to increase a benefit

AUSTERITÉ
austerity

plan / programme d'austérité
austerity programme

politique d'austérité
policy of restraint / of retrenchment

AUTARCIE
self-sufficiency

AUTARCIQUE
self-sufficient

AUTEUR
artiste auteur (Fr.)
author artist

auteur d'une demande
applicant

auteur d'une infraction
offender

auteurs, journalistes et écrivains assimilés [CITP-1968 (1-5)]
authors, journalists and related writers [ISCO-1968 (1-5)]

Etat auteur d'une réserve
reserving State (treaty)

AUTHENTIFIER
to certify

AUTHENTIQUE
certified; bona fide

offre d'emploi authentique
bona fide job offer

AUTO-ADMINISTRÉ
soins auto-administrés
self-care

AUTO-APPRENTISSAGE
self-instruction, self-education

AUTO-ASSISTANCE
self-help

groupement d'auto-assistance
self-help group

programme / projet d'auto-assistance
self-help project / scheme

AUTO-ASSISTÉ
logement auto-assisté
self-help housing / dwelling / construction

AUTO-ASSURANCE
self-insurance

AUTO-ASSURÉ
self-insured

AUTOCHTONE
travailleur autochtone
native / national / indigenous / aboriginal /
worker

AUTOCONSTRUCTION
self-help housing / construction

AUTO-ÉVALUATION
self-assessment; self-appraisal

questionnaire d'auto-évaluation
self-appraisal questionnaire

AUTODIAGNOSTIC
self-diagnosis

AUTODIDACTE (adj.)
self-taught

AUTODIDACTE (n.)
self-directed learner

AUTOFINANCÉ
plan autofinancé
self-funding scheme

AUTOFINANCEMENT
self-financing, self-funding

AUTOFORMATION
module d'autoformation
self-learning package

AUTOGESTION
autogestion par les travailleurs
workers' / personnel self-management

AUTO-INSCRIPTION
self-registration

AUTOMATIQUE
automatic; mandatory

application automatique (d')
self-enforcing

augmentation automatique
automatic / mandatory / statutory
increase

**plan d'épargne par prélèvement auto-
matique**
save-as-you-earn scheme

progression automatique des salaires
automatic wage progression

**réajustement automatique des
salaires**
automatic wage adjustment

AUTOMATISÉ
placement automatisé
computer-assisted placement

service de placement automatisé
computer-assisted placement service

AUTOMOBILE
assurance automobile
car insurance

AUTONOME
autonomous, self-operated, self-sufficient,
self-reliant, independent

apprenti autonome
self-employed apprentice

caisse autonome mutualiste (Fr.)
autonomous mutual aid fund

**établissement public (financièrement)
autonome**
governmental / Government-owned
corporation

organe autonome
autonomous / self-governing / self-
government body

personne âgée non autonome
elderly dependent person

recherche d'emploi autonome
independent job search

régime autonome
independent scheme

syndicat autonome
independent / non-affiliated (trade) union

travailleur autonome (Can.)
self-employed (person / worker)

AUTONOMIE
autonomy, self-sufficiency, self-reliance;
empowerment (ind.)

**apprentissage de l'autonomie fonc-
tionnelle**
(occ.) life skills training

autonomie fonctionnelle
(occ.) life skills

point d'autonomie (Belg.)
autonomy point

AUTONOMISATION
empowerment

AUTO-RENOUVELABLE
caisse / fonds auto-renouvelable
revolving fund

AUTORISATION
approval; authority; leave; permit;
license

accord d'autorisation
licensing agreement

autorisation d'absence
authorised absence, leave of absence

**autorisation administrative de
licenciement**
administrative authorisation to dismiss

autorisation d'avance
advance authorization

autorisation d'exercer
certification (med.)

autorisation d'exercer des fonctions
admission to the exercise of functions

autorisation d'exploitation
licensing

**autorisation de mise sur le marché
(Fr.)**
permit to market

autorisation préalable
prior approval

autorisation de séjour
residence permit

autorisation de travail
work / labour permit

AUTORISÉ
authorised; authoritative; eligible;
entitled

absence autorisée
authorised absence, absence with leave

absence non autorisée
unauthorised absence, absence without
leave

autorisé (non)
unauthorised

congé autorisé
authorised absence, approved leave, leave of absence

emploi non autorisé
unauthorised employment

légalement autorisé à travailler
legally entitled / eligible to work

travailleur non autorisé
illegal worker

voyage autorisé
official travel / journey

AUTORISER
to approve, to authorise; to entitle

AUTORITÉ
authority; power

abus d'autorité
abuse of position / of authority

autorité (avoir sous son)
to supervise

autorité (qui fait)
authoritative

autorités administratives
(administrative / regulatory) authorities; adjudicating authorities

autorité compétente
competent authority

autorités (responsables) de l'éducation / de l'enseignement
educational authorities

autorités financières
fiscal authorities

autorités fiscales
taxation authorities

autorité locale
local government

autorité locale de la santé (UK)
local health authority

autorités (responsables) du marché du travail
labour market institutions / authorities

autorités nationales
central government, national authorities

autorité parentale
parental authority; parental custody

autorité sanitaire
(pl.) health authorities
autorité sanitaire de circonscription (UK)
area health authority

autorité sanitaire de région
regional health authority

autorité territoriale
local government

autorité de tutelle
supervisory board

déchéance de l'autorité parentale
loss of parental authority

fonctionnaire d'autorité
official with a power to decide

tarif d'autorité (Fr.)
recommended medical fee, set rate

AUTOSUFFISANCE
self-sufficiency, self-reliance

AUTOSUFFISANT
self-sufficient

AUTRUI
responsabilité du fait d'autrui
vicarious liability

travailleur pour compte d'autrui
employee

AUXILIAIRE (adj.)
auxiliary; ancillary; subsidiary

agent auxiliaire
auxiliary worker

bureau auxiliaire
branch office, sub-office

comptabilité auxiliaire
subsidiary accounts

comptes auxiliaires
subsidiary accounts

emploi auxiliaire
casual employment

établissement de santé auxiliaire
peripheral health establishment

infirmière auxiliaire
nursing auxiliary

personnel auxiliaire
auxiliary / general duty personnel, servicing
/ ancillary staff; non-production workers

personnel infirmier auxiliaire
auxiliary nursing personnel

personnel des services auxiliaires
ancillary workers

poste d'agent auxiliaire
ancillary post

poste auxiliaire
servicing post

service auxiliaire
ancillary service

travailleur auxiliaire
auxiliary worker

AUXILIAIRE (n.)
assistant, aid, auxiliary; helper; support /
contingent worker, casual employee /
labourer / worker

auxiliaires de l'Etat
State auxiliary staff

auxiliaire familiale
domestic / family worker, (visiting) home
(-)maker, family / home aid / help / helper,
mother's help

auxiliaire familial(e) non rémunéré(e)
unpaid family worker

auxiliaire médical
medical aid / assistant / auxiliary

auxiliaire ménagère
family help

auxiliaire sanitaire
health assistant

auxiliaire social
social aid; unqualified social worker

auxiliaire de vie
home help

AVALISER
to approve; to back, to support; to
endorse, to guarantee

AVANCE (n.)
advance (payment); gap

autorisation d'avance
advance authorization

avance sur congé annuel
advance annual leave

avance sur pension alimentaire
advance on alimony

avance sur prestations
advance on benefits, advance payment
of benefits

avance récupérable
recoverable advance

avance sur salaire
salary advance

avance des salaires
wage gap

avance des salaires réels
real wage gap

demande d'avance de traitement
request for salary advance

recettes comptabilisées d'avance
deferred income

AVANCEMENT
step increase; career development;
up-ward mobility; advancement,
promotion

avancement dans la carrière
career progression, occupational advancement

avancement d'échelon
increment, within-grade (salary) increment

avancement professionnel
career progress / path / advancement,
professional advancement

concours d'avancement
competitive examination for promotion

inscrit au tableau d'avancement (être)
to be included in the promotion register

perspective d'avancement
promotion / advancement prospect, chance
for promotion

possibilité d'avancement
opportunity / chance for promotion / for advancement, potential for advancement,
promotability, promotional / career
opportunity, promotion / advancement
potential

recommander l'avancement
to recommend for promotion

tableau d'avancement
promotion roster / register, promotional
ladder

AVANTAGE
advantage; benefit; incentive

analyse coûts-avantages
cost-benefit analysis

avantage accessoire
supplementary / fringe / marginal benefit;
perquisite, perk

avantages acquis
established / vested rights

avantage additionnel
incremental benefit

avantages annexes
fringe benefits

avantages complémentaires
marginal benefits

**avantage complémentaire vieillesse
(Fr.)**
supplementary old age benefit

avantage contributif
contributory benefit

avantage non contributif
non-contributory benefit

avantage économique
economic benefit

avantage familial
(occ.) dependency benefit

avantage fiscal
tax benefit / incentive; (pl.) tax subsidies

avantage induit
induced benefit

avantages marginaux
fringe benefits

avantage en nature
benefit in kind; perk; fringe benefit

avantage négocié
negotiated benefit

avantage préférentiel
preferential benefit

avantage réglementaire
statutory benefit

avantage de salaire / salarial
wage premium

avantagessocial
fringe / marginal / social benefits; (pl.)
(occ.) staff amenities

avantage social contributif
contributory social benefit

avantage social non contributif
non-contributory social benefit

avantage social indirect
indirect (social) benefit

avantage supplémentaire
added benefit

avantage viager
annuity benefit

avantage (de) vieillesse
old age benefit / bonus

clause de maintien des avantages acquis
(occ.) grandfather clause

non-rétroactivité d'un avantage vieillesse
non-retroactivity of an old age benefit

responsable de la rémunération et des avantages sociaux (USA)
compensation and benefits manager

AVANTAGEUX
profitable

AVENANT (n.)
subsidiary / supplementary agreement;
additional provision / clause, rider

AVENIR
emploi sans avenir
dead-end job

nouveau secteur d'avenir
new growth industry

secteur d'avenir
growth sector

AVÉRÉ
risque avéré
proven risk

AVERTISSEMENT
warning, reprimand

avertissement écrit
written warning

avertissement oral
oral warning

avertissement verbal
verbal warning

grève d'avertissement
token (protest) / warning strike

AVEUGLE
blind

allocation aux aveugles (Austr.)
blind persons' allowance

assistance aux aveugles
assistance for the blind

aveugle de guerre
blind war victim, veteran blind / blinded

centre de rééducation pour aveugles
rehabilitation centre for the blind;
training centre for the blind

pension d'aveugle (Irel.)
blind pension

réadaptation des aveugles
rehabilitation of the blind

AVIS
notice; advice

avis d'arrêt de travail
notice of cessation of work / of having
ceased work; sick leave notice

avis de classement
classification notice

avis de concours
competition notice

avis d'inscription à une formation
notice of referral to training

avis d'interruption de la formation
training suspension notice

avis de licenciement
dismissal notice

avis de mutation
transfer notice

avis normalisé de vacance de poste
standardised notice of vacancy

avis de résiliation
notice of termination

avis de trop-payé
notice of overpayment

avis de vacance d'emploi
notice of a vacant post, notified vacancy,
vacancy announcement / notice

AVISER
to notify

aviser officiellement
to give formal notice

AVOIR (n.)
credit; (pl.) assets, holdings

avoirs accumulés
accumulated assets

avoir fiscal
tax credit

AVORTEMENT
abortion

AXÉ
axé sur ...
...-oriented

AYANT CAUSE
successor (in title)

AYANT DROIT (adj.)
eligible

AYANT DROIT (n.)
(eligible) beneficiary / person, person
entitled, (rightful) claimant; (occ.)
dependant

ayant droit à charge
eligible dependant

ayant droit mutualiste
beneficiary of a mutual fund

ayant droit à titre universel
residuary beneficiary

certificat d'ayant droit
certification of entitlement

pension d'ayant droit
dependant's pension

rente d'ayant droit
survivor's annuity

AZOÏQUE
composés azoïques
azo-compounds

BAGAGE
bagage scolaire
knowledge; schooling

BAIL
lease

louer à bail
to lease

BAISSE
decrease; decline; downward trend;
downswing, downturn

baisse d'activité
loss of work

baisse de l'emploi
decline in employment

baisse du pouvoir d'achat
loss of purchasing power

baisse de salaire
wage cut

réviser à la baisse
to review downwards

BAISSER
baisser la cotisation
to lower the contribution

BALANCE
balance commerciale
balance of trade, trade balance

balance migratoire
balance of migration, migration balance

balance des opérations courantes
current account

balance des paiements
balance of payments

balance des paiements courants
current account

déficit de la balance commerciale
balance of trade deficit

excédent de la balance commerciale
balance of trade surplus

BALNÉAIRE
cure balnéaire
spa (course of) treatment

BALNÉOTHERAPIE
balneotherapy

BALNÉOTHERAPIQUE
établissement balnéothérapique
spa

BANLIEUSARD
commuter

BANQUE
banque d'emplois
job bank

BAPTÊME
acte de baptême
baptismal certificate

BARÈME
scale (of rates), rate table, payment
schedule; level; range; schedule

barème des ajustements de poste
schedule of post adjustments

barème des allocations
allowance table

**barème des contributions du
personnel**
(occ.) staff assessment plan

**barème de conversion des points en
classes**
grade-point conversion scale

barème des cotisations
scale of contributions

barème courant de rémunération
ordinary scale of remuneration

barème des déductions
chart of deduction rates

barème fiscal
tax schedule

barème des / d'honoraires
scale of fees, fee schedule

barème d'imposition
tax rate / schedule

barème d'indemnisation
scale of compensation

barème des indemnités
allowance table

barème des indemnités de poste
schedule of post adjustments

barème d'invalidité
disablement / disability scale

barème local des salaires
local salary / wage scale

barème des prestations
schedule of benefits

barème des primes
schedule of premiums

barème des rémunérations considérées aux fins de la pension
scale of pensionable remuneration

barème des risques
scale of risks

barème des salaires
salary / wage scale

barème des traitements
salary / pay scales, salary rate, salaries range

barème des traitements de base
base salary scale

barème unique et uniforme de traite-ments de base
single uniform base salary scale

guide-barème
scale rate

tranche de barème fiscal
tax bracket

BARÉMIQUE
augmentation barémique
(occ.) increment

BARRIÈRE
barrière à l'entrée
barrier to entry, entry barrier

BAS (adj.)
bas âge
infancy

bas échelons (les)
lower ranks (the)

bas salaire
low wage

bas-salaires (les)
low-paid (the)

basse conjoncture
downward trend

emploi de bas niveau
low-level job

enfant en bas âge
baby, infant

pays à bas salaires
low-wage country

travailleur à bas salaire
low-wage earner

BAS (n.)
emploi / poste au bas de l'échelle
entry-level job

BASE
basis; the grass roots, rank and file (workers); shop floor (the), shop-floor workers

abattement fiscal à la base
tax deduction at source

accord de base
basic agreement

aide alimentaire de base (Ger.)
basic subsistence aid

allocation de base
basic allowance

allocation de base vieillesse (Fr.)
old age basic allowance

allocation de chômage de base
basic unemployment allowance

barème des traitements de base
base salary scale

barème unique et uniforme de traitements de base
single uniform base salary scale

base (de)
basic

base de calcul
assessment basis, basis for calculation

base de détermination
basis of assessment

base de données projectives sur la population active
labour force projections data base

base de l'évaluation
basis of assessment

base forfaitaire
fixed scale

base d'imposition
tax base

base mensuelle
monthly base

base mensuelle de calcul
monthly base for calculation

base syndicale (la)
shop floor (the), shop-floor workers

compétence de base
basic / generic / entry skill

connaissances de base
basic / (occ.) life skills

cotisation de base pour la catégorie n
primary class n contribution

données de base
baseline data / information

éducation / enseignement de base
basic education

enseignement médical de base
basic medical education

formation de base
basic / core education / training, foundation training

formation professionnelle de base
basic job training

formation aux techniques de base
basic skills training

gain journalier de base
basic daily earnings

indemnité de base
basic allowance

indicateur de base
basic indicator

industrie de base
basic / staple industry

majoration du taux de base
increase of the basic amount

montant de base
base / basic amount

pension de base
basic pension / benefit; basic retirement pension (UK)

pension de base de veuve (UK)
widow's basic pension

pension uniforme de base
basic flat-rate pension

prestation de base
basic benefit

principe de base
basic principle

qualification de base
basic / generic / entry skill; (pl.) key / core skills

régime de base
basic scheme

rémunération de base
basic remuneration

retraite de base
basic pension

salaire annuel moyen de base
basic average annual wage

salaire de base
base wage / pay / rate; (occ.) tariff wage

salaire de base pour le calcul de la retraite
pensionable earnings

salaire de base maximal imposable
maximum taxable wage rate

santé infantile de base
basic child health

services de base
basic services

service de santé de base
basic health service

soins de santé de base
basic health care

stage de formation de base
basic / low-level training course

tarif de base
basic rate

taux de base
basic rate / amount; basic wage; (occ.) straight-time rate

techniques de base
basic skill(s)

technologie de base
basic / core technology

traitement de base
basic salary

traitement de base net
net base salary

travailleurs de la base
rank and file workers

travailleurs des industries de base
(occ.) key workers

ville de base
base city

BASSIN
bassin d'emploi
labour / manpower / job catchment area, labour market / employment area; job pool

BATELLERIE
inland water navigation / transport

BÂTIMENT
building; building industry / trade; ship

artisans et ouvriers des métiers de l'extraction et du bâtiment [CITP-1988 (71)]
extraction and building trade workers [ISCO-1988 (71)]

bâtiment et travaux publics
building and civil industry

industrie du bâtiment
building industry / trade, construction industry

métiers du bâtiment
building trades

ouvrier du bâtiment
building worker

secteur du bâtiment
building / construction industry

travailleur du bâtiment
construction worker

BATTERIE
range

BÉNÉFICE
profit, gain; (pl.) earnings; receipt

bénéfice de (être admis au)
to qualify for, to be entitled to

bénéfice d'une pension (au)
in receipt of a pension

impôt sur les bénéfices
profit tax

impôt sur les bénéfices des sociétés
tax on corporate profits

participation aux bénéfices
profit-sharing

prétendre au bénéfice d'une / de pres-tation(s)
to claim benefit

régime de retraite à participation différée aux bénéfices
deferred profit-sharing pension plan

rémunération liée aux bénéfices
profit-related pay

BÉNÉFICIAIRE (adj.)
pays bénéficiaire
receiving country

population bénéficiaire
target population

unité bénéficiaire proratisée (Fr.)
pro-rata beneficiary unit

BÉNÉFICIAIRE (n.)
beneficiary, (income) recipient, payee; claimant; participant

bénéficiaire d'aide sociale
welfare / social assistance recipient; [on welfare]

bénéficiaire d'une allocation
beneficiary of an allowance

bénéficiaire de l'assurance chômage
unemployment insurance recipient

bénéficiaire sans contrepartie
free-rider

bénéficiaire en fin de droit
(unemployment) insurance exhaustee

bénéficiaire mutualiste
beneficiary of a mutual fund

bénéficiaire d'une pension
beneficiary of a pension

bénéficiaire d'une pension d'invalidité
invalidity pensioner

bénéficiaire d'une pension de vieillesse
old age pensioner

bénéficiaire potentiel
potential beneficiary

bénéficiaire d'une prestation
benefit recipient; (pl.) persons in receipt of benefits, recipients of benefits

bénéficiaire type
standard beneficiary

catégorie de bénéficiaires
class of beneficiaries

nombre de bénéficiaires
(occ.) coverage

BÉNÉFICIER
bénéficier de (faire)
to make available for

bénéficier d'une pension
to receive / to draw a pension

bénéficier d'une prestation
to receive a benefit

BÉNÉVOLAT
voluntary work

BÉNÉVOLE (adj.)
voluntary, unpaid, honorary

agent bénévole
voluntary worker

animateur bénévole
voluntary leader

bénévole (à titre)
on a voluntary basis

groupe bénévole
voluntary group

institution bénévole
voluntary agency

organisation / organisme bénévole
voluntary / volunteer agency / organisation

service bénévole
voluntary agency

travail bénévole
volunteer work

travailleur bénévole
voluntary / volunteer worker

BÉNÉVOLE (n.)
volunteer (worker)

BÉNÉVOLEMENT
on a voluntary basis

BESOIN
need, want; (pl.) wants and needs,
requirement; (means of) livelihood

adapté aux besoins
geared to needs

analyse des besoins
needs analysis

besoin (dans le)
in need

besoins éducatifs
educational need / requirement

besoins en effectifs
manpower needs

besoins de l'emploi / en matière d'emploi
employment requirements / needs

besoin essentiel
basic need; (pl.) basic needs / wants

besoins essentiels de l'être humain
basic human needs

besoins financiers / de financement
financial requirements

besoin fondamental
basic need

besoins en (matière de) formation
training needs / requirements

besoin global en personnel
overall staffing requirement

besoin individuel
individual need

besoins en main-d'oeuvre
work / worker / labour force
requirements, labour / manpower needs
/ requirements

besoins du marché du travail
labour market needs

besoin matériel
physical need; (occ.) bodily need / want

besoin(s) en personnel
manpower / labour / staff resource
requirement(s), personnel needs

besoins en personnel qualifié
skill needs / requirements

besoin reconnu / réel / ressenti
recognised / real / felt need

besoin sanitaire
health need

besoin social
social (welfare) need

besoin social non satisfait
unmet social need

besoins supplémentaires
additional needs / requirements /
demand

besoins de trésorerie
cash requirement / needs

**étude prévisionnelle des besoins de
main-d'oeuvre dans l'entreprise**
company manpower planning,
personnel planning at establishment
level

évaluation des besoins
needs assessment

évaluation des besoins essentiels
basic needs assessment

**incapable de subvenir à ses (propres)
besoins**
incapable of self-support

nouveaux besoins
additional needs / requirements /
demand

prévision des besoins
anticipation of needs

projection des besoins en main-d'oeuvre
projected manpower requirement

pyramide des besoins
needs hierarchy

société attentive aux besoins
caring society

stratégie des besoins essentiels
basic needs strategy

stratégie industrielle orientée vers la satisfaction des besoins essentiels
basic needs-oriented industrial strategy

subvenir aux besoins
to maintain, to support, to provide for

BI-ACTIF
ménage bi-actif
two-income family, dual income household

ménage bi-actif sans enfants
dual income with no kids (DINK)

BIAIS
bias (stat.)

BIBLIOGRAPHIQUE
étude / synthèse bibliographique
literature review / survey

BIEN (adv.)
bien payé
well-paid, high-paid, highly paid

bien portant
healthy

bien rémunéré
well-paid, high-paid, highly paid

BIEN (n.)
commodity; good; (pl.) assets

biens d'équipement
producer goods

biens immobiliers
real estate / property

biens médicaux
medical commodities

biens de production
producer goods

bien salarial
wage good

bien de santé
(pl.) health goods

industrie (productrice) de biens d'équipement
capital goods industry

BIEN-ÊTRE
well-being, welfare

bien-être économique
economic well-being

bien-être social
social welfare

espérance de vie corrigée en fonction du bien-être
quality-adjusted life-year (QUALY)

société de bien-être
welfare society

BIENFAISANCE
établissement de bienfaisance
charitable agency, charity

établissement de bienfaisance privé
private charitable agency / charity

institution de bienfaisance
charity, charitable association / agency / institution

oeuvre de bienfaisance
relief / charitable association, assistance fund, charitable agency / institution, charity

organisme de bienfaisance
charitable agency / institution, charity

organisme public de bienfaisance
public charity

BIEN-FONDÉ
adequacy; merit(s); justice

BIENVEILLANCE
congé de bienveillance
leave for compassionate reasons

BILAN
balance; record; assessment

bilan de compétence(s)
skills' / vocational assessment

bilan migratoire
balance of migration, migration balance

bilan professionnel
vocational assessment

bilan ressources-emploi
employment(-)resources balance sheet

bilan de santé
medical checkup, health check

bilan social
social audit / reporting

congé de bilan de compétence (Fr.)
vocational assessment leave

BILATÉRAL
accord bilatéral
bilateral / reciprocal agreement

accord fiscal bilatéral
double taxation agreement

convention bilatérale
bilateral convention

BIOLOGIE
biology

BIOLOGIQUE
famille biologique
biological family

BIOLOGISTE
biologist

biologistes, agronomes et techniciens assimilés [CITP-1968 (0-5)]
life scientists and related technicians
[ISCO-1968 (0-5)]

BIOMÉTRIE
biometrics

BIPARENTAL
two-parent

famille biparentale
two-parent family

BLÂME
reprimand; censure

blâme écrit
written censure

BLANC
veuve blanche
grass widow

BLANCHISSEUR
aides de ménage et autres aides,
nettoyeurs et blanchisseurs [CITP-1988
(913)]
domestic and related helpers, cleaners
and launderers [ISCO-1988 (913)]

blanchisseurs, dégraisseurs et presseurs [CITP-1968 (5-6)]
launderers, dry-cleaners and pressers
[ISCO-1968 (5-6)]

BLESSÉ (n.)
injured person, casualty

BLESSURE
injury

blessure de guerre
war injury

BLOCAGE
standstill, bottleneck; freeze

blocage administratif
administrative bottleneck

blocage des salaires
wage freeze

BLOQUER
to freeze; to withold; to peg

bloquer les salaires
to withhold wages

compte de garantie bloqué
escrow account

BON (n.)
bon d'alimentation
food stamp / voucher

bon d'emploi (Can.)
job voucher

bon de lait
milk voucher

bon de ravitaillement
food stamp / voucher

bon de réduction sur les denrées alimentaires (UK)
food rebate coupon

bon vacances
holiday voucher

BONI
profit; underexpenditure

BONIFICATION
bonus; subsidy

bonification pour enfant
child bonus

bonification d'intérêt
interest subsidisation / relief / reduction, interest relief grant

taux de bonification
bonus rate

BONIFIÉ
pension à fiscalité bonifiée
tax qualified pension

prêt bonifié
bonified loan

BONUS
bonus, premium

BORDEREAU
bordereau de cotisations
statement of contributions

bordereau de paiement
payment form

bordereau récapitulatif de cotisations
summary statement of contributions

BOIS
conducteurs de machines à bois [CITP-1988 (824)]
wood-products machine operators [ISCO-1988 (824)]

BOISSON
ouvriers de l'alimentation et des boissons [CITP-1968 (7-7)]
food and beverage processers [ISCO-1968 (7-7)]

BOTTIER-ORTHOPÉDISTE
orthopaedic shoemaker

bottiers, ouvriers de la chaussure et du cuir [CITP-1968 (8-0)]
shoemakers and leather goods makers [ISCO-1968 (8-0)]

BOUCHÉ (adj.)
carrière bouchée
blocked career path

emploi bouché
dead-end job

BOUCHE-TROU
emploi bouche-trou
stop-gap employment

BOUCHON
grève bouchon
bottleneck strike

BOULOT
petit boulot
odd job; (pl.) relief works

BOURSE
grant; fellowship; (stock) exchange

bourse de l'emploi / des emplois
labour / job exchange (service)

bourse d'études
bursary, scholarship, student / study grant

bourse de formation
training grant

bourse de formation professionnelle
vocational training grant

bourse du travail
job / labour exchange (service)

BOURSIER
fellow

BOUTIQUE
shop

boutique de l'emploi
job centre

boutique de gestion (Fr.)
small business promotion agency

BRANCHE
branch; class

accord de branche
branch / industrial / sectoral agreement

branche d'activité
industry, line of business

branche d'activité (par)
by industry

branche d'activité en difficulté / en perte de vitesse
ailing industry

branche de l'économie
economic sector

branche de l'industrie
industrial sector

branche professionnelle
occupation(al) sector, sector of industry

branche de (la) sécurité sociale
branch of social security

branche de services
service industry

convention (collective) de branche
industry-wide (collective) agreement

échelle d'une branche (à l')
industry-wide

répartition par branche d'activité et par profession
industrial and occupational composition

syndicat de branche
industrial union

BRAS
bras droit de
senior staffing...

grève les bras croisés
sit-down strike

BREF
brève échéance (à)
in the short-term, in the short-run

BREVET
certificate

brevet d'aptitude / de capacité
certificate of competency

brevet d'enseignement professionnel (BEP) (Fr.)
certificate of vocational education

brevet d'études professionnelles agricoles (BEPA) (Fr.)
certificate of agricultural vocational education

brevet de technicien agricole (BTA) (Fr.)
agricutural technician's certificate

brevet de technicien supérieur agricole (BTSA) (Fr.)
agricultural senior technician's certificate

BREVETÉ
patented; qualified; trained

marin breveté
able(-bodied) seaman

technicien breveté
professional technician

BRIGUER
to compete

briguer un poste
to compete for a post, to canvass for / to covet a job

BRISEUR
briseur de grève
strikebreaker, scab, blackleg

BROCHURE
leaflet

BRUT
espérance brute de vie active
gross expectation of working life

gains bruts
gross earnings

masse salariale brute
total gross earnings

montant brut
gross amount

produit intérieur brut (PIB)
Gross Domestic Product (GDP)

produit national brut (PNB)
Gross National Product (GNP)

recettes brutes
gross earnings

rémunération brute
gross pay / earnings / salary

rémunération brute à prendre en com-pte / en considération
gross reckonable earnings

revenu brut
gross income

revenu social brut
gross social (insurance) income

salaire brut
gross pay / wage / earnings

salaire brut moyen
average gross / gross average wage

salaire hebdomadaire brut
gross weekly pay, weekly earnings before deductions

salaire hebdomadaire brut normal
normal gross weekly earnings

traitement brut
gross salary

BUDGET
budget

article du budget
budget item

budget équilibré
balanced budget

budget d'équipement
investment / capital budget

budget d'exploitation
operational / operating budget

budget familial
family budget

budget de fonctionnement
operational / operating budget

budget de formation
training budget

budget global
global budget

budget d'investissement
investment / capital budget, below-the-line

budget du ménage
household budget

budget optimum
target budget

budget ordinaire
regular budget

budget de plein emploi
full(-)employment budget

budget de programme
programme budgeting

budget social
social budget

budget-temps
time budget

enquête sur les budgets-temps
time-use survey

inscription au budget
apportionment

inscrire au budget
to charge to the budget, to apportion

poste du budget
budget item / line

prêt d'aide au budget (UK)
budgeting loan

BUDGÉTAIRE
fiscal; [budget]

année budgétaire
budget year

collectif budgétaire
supplementary budget

compression budgétaire
budget cut

compte d'excédents budgétaires
surplus account

crédit budgétaire
budgetary provision, budget allocation

cycle budgétaire
budget cycle

déficit budgétaire
budget deficit

directive budgétaire
budget guideline

emploi budgétaire
established post

excédent budgétaire
budget surplus

excédent budgétaire de plein emploi
full-employment budget surplus

exercice budgétaire
budget year

limitation budgétaire (UK)
cash limit

objectif budgétaire
target budget

politique budgétaire
fiscal policy

poste budgétaire
budget item / line

provision budgétaire
budgetary provision

recettes budgétaires
fiscal revenue

restriction budgétaire
budgetary constraint

solde budgétaire en situation de plein emploi
full / high employment (budget) balance

BUDGÉTISATION
budgétisation intégrale
full budgeting

BULLETIN
schedule; form; certificate

bulletin d'adhésion / d'inscription
enrolment form

bulletin de paie
pay statement / slip, payroll

bulletin de paie détaillé
detailed / itemised pay statement

bulletin de salaire
payroll

vote à bulletin secret
secret ballot

BUREAU
office, bureau; branch

astreint à des strictes heures de bureau (être)
to be expected to keep strict office hours

autres employés de bureau [CITP-1988 (419)]
other office clerks [ISCO-1988 (419)]

bureau (de)
clerical

bureau d'aide / d'assistance sociale
social assistance / (social) welfare office

bureau auxiliaire
branch office, sub-office

bureau de conseils en personnel
personnel consultancy

bureau d'emploi
labour exchange (service)

bureaux de l'enfance (Scandinavia)
child welfare board system

bureau itinérant
itinerant office

bureau local
local office

bureau local d'assurance
local insurance office

bureau local de l'emploi
local employment office

bureau ouvert (Fr.)
mother and child care centre

bureau de paie
pay office

bureau de paiement des indemnités de chômage
unemployment benefit (paying) office

bureau paritaire de l'emploi
joint employment office

bureau du personnel
personnel office

bureau de placement
employment / placement agency, (labour) employment office, employment exchange / bureau, labour exchange (service)

bureau de placement payant
fee-charging employment agency

bureau privé de placement
private employment agency

bureau de protection de l'enfance
child welfare authority

bureau de recrutement
recruitment office

bureau régional
branch / regional office

bureau de renseignements
inquiry office

bureau de secteur
zone office

chefs de groupe d'employés de bureau [CITP-1968 (3-0)]
clerical supervisors [ISCO-1968 (3-0)]

emploi de bureau
clerical occupation / job, office occupation / work

employé de bureau
(office) clerk; office employee; clerical / of-fice worker, white-collar (worker); (pl.) clerical staff / employees

employés de bureau [CITP-1988 (41)]
office clerks [ISCO-1988 (41)]

fonctions d'employé de bureau
clerical duties

frais de bureau
(occ.) office allowance

heures de bureau
office hours

personnel de bureau
office staff, clerical personnel / staff /
employees, white-collar workers, white-
collars

services de bureau
clerical assistance

travail de bureau
clerical / office work; white-collar job /
occupation; office duty

BUT
but de carrière
occupational goal; vocational development
objective; career objective / goal

but lucratif (à)
profit-seeking, profit-making

but professionnel
occupational goal; vocational development
objective; career objective / goal

entreprise à but non lucratif
non-profit making firm

gestion sans but lucratif (Can.)
public administration

**loi régissant les associations à but non
lucratif**
law governing non-profit-making
organisations

BUTOIR
date butoir
deadline, cut-off date

CABINET
office; practice; surgery

cabinet de consultations
surgery, doctor's office, consulting room

cabinet dentaire
dental surgery

cabinet d'équipe (Fr.)
team surgery

cabinet de groupe (Fr.)
group surgery

cabinet médical
medical practice

cabinet de recrutement
(occ.) recruitment consultancy

consultation au cabinet
surgery consultation / visit

médecin de cabinet
doctor working in a town

CACHÉ
chômage caché
hidden / disguised / concealed unemployment

économie cachée
black / hidden / informal / moonlight / shadow / submerged / twilight / underground / grey / invisible economy

travail caché
disguised employment

CACHET
produit sous cachet (Fr.)
pharmaceutical product to be made up by the chemist

CADENCE
rate; (pl.) operating times

accélérer la cadence de travail
to speed up the production rate

cadence de production
production rate

étude des cadences
time and motion study

CADRE
framework; supervisory post / position; manager; officer, official; supervisor; (occ.) professional; establishment (staff); guideline; (pl.) professional / salaried / supervisory / senior / grade staff

accord-cadre
framework / outline / master / umbrella / blanket agreement

agents du cadre
established staff

assimilé cadre
employee with managerial status

autres cadres de direction [CITP-1988 (123)]
other department managers [ISCO-1988 (123)]

cadre confirmé
seasoned manager

cadre débutant
junior manager

cadre de direction
executive officer

cadres de direction, production et opérations [CITP-1988 (122)]
production and operations department managers [ISCO-1988 (122)]

cadre dirigeant
top / senior (level) / upper level manager, senior / top executive; director; (pl.) top management

cadre d'évaluation
evaluation framework

cadre exécutif
executive officer

cadre d'exploitation
operational framework

cadre familial
home; family environment

cadre fonctionnel
staff manager

cadre de fonctionnement
operational framework

cadre hiérarchique
line manager

cadres infirmiers et sages-femmes [CITP-1988 (223)]
nursing and midwifery professionals
[ISCO-1988 (223)]

cadre juridique / légal
legal framework

cadre moyen
middle manager; (pl.) middle (grade)
management, middle management staff,
middle-level manpower / personnel,
executive staff

cadre opérationnel
line manager

cadre organique
line manager

cadre de référence
terms of reference

cadre de service social
social work supervisor

cadre subalterne
junior official / executive; (pl.) executive
staff

cadre supérieur
top / senior (level) / upper level / executive
manager, senior / top / higher professional
executive, executive; technologist; (pl.)
(upper / senior / top) management, senior
directing staff, managerial / senior /
executive (supervisory) staff

cadres supérieurs de l'administration publique [CITP-1988 (112)]
senior government officials [ISCO-1988
(112)]

cadre syndical
union officer

cadre de travail
work setting / surroundings, working
environment

cadre unique de rémunération
single salary schedule

cadre de vie
home / human environment; setting of
life

collège de cadres
managerial body of electors

contrat-cadre
master contract

convention-cadre
umbrella convention, framework /
outline agreement

délai-cadre (Switz.)
standard period

formation de cadres
professional training

formation des cadres
management training

formation et gestion des carrières des cadres
management development

jeune cadre
junior manager

jeune cadre en formation
management trainee, trainee manager

loi-cadre
framework law

norme-cadre
master standard

organisme-cadre
umbrella organisation

perfectionnement des cadres
management development

politique-cadre
overall policy

profession de cadre supérieur
senior management occupation

programme de perfectionnement des cadres
(occ.) executive programme

rachat d'une entreprise par ses cadres avec effet de levier (RECEL)
leveraged management buy-out (LMBO)

régime de retraite des cadres
managers' pension scheme

statut-cadre
managerial status

CADUC
lapsed, discontinued, statute-barred, invalid

CADUCITÉ
lapse

CAHIER
cahier des charges
specifications

cahier des revendications syndicales
list of union demands

CAISSE
fund; agency

administrateur d'une caisse de retraite
trustee of a pension fund

affiliation à une caisse de retraite
pension scheme membership

caisse d'affiliation
insurance fund

caisse agréée
approved fund

caisse d'allocations familiales
family allowance fund

caisse d'association (Switz.)
professional association fund

caisse d'assurance
insurance fund

caisse d'assurance chômage
unemployment (insurance) fund

caisse d'assurance maladie
health (insurance) fund; sickness fund

caisse d'assurance mutuelle agricole (Fr.)
agricultural mutual insurance fund

caisse d'assurance nationale (UK)
national insurance fund

caisse d'assurances sociales
social insurance fund

caisse d'assurance(-)vieillesse
old age pension fund

caisse autonome mutualiste (Fr.)
autonomous mutual aid fund

caisse auto-renouvelable
revolving fund

caisse de chômage
unemployment (insurance) fund

caisse de compensation
compensation / equalisation / provident / fund

caisse de compensation pour les accidents du travail et les maladies professionnelles
(occ.) workmen's compensation board

caisse d'entreprise
fund operated by a firm, works provident fund

Caisse (fédérale) de garantie des pensions (USA)
Pension Benefit Guaranty Corporation

caisse de grève
strike fund

caisse (de) maladie
sick (benefit) fund, sickness (insurance) fund

caisse-maladie locale générale
general local sick fund

caisse mutuelle
mutual fund

caisse de pensions
pension fund

caisse de pension d'entreprise
enterprise pension fund

caisse de pensions financée suivant le principe de la capitalisation
funded pension fund

caisse de prévoyance (sociale)
provident / contingency / welfare fund, company life and disability insurance, social insurance fund

caisse primaire d'assurance maladie (CPAM) (Fr.)
local health fund

caisse régionale
regional fund

caisse régionale d'assurance maladie (CRAM) (Fr.)
regional health fund

caisse renouvelable
revolving fund

caisse de retraite
retirement fund / system, superannuation / pension fund

caisse de retraite complémentaire
complementary pension fund

caisse de secours
relief / contingency fund

caisse de sécurité sociale
social security fund

caisse de subsistance (Fr.)
subsistence fund

caisse supplétive (Switz.)
supplementary insurance fund

circonscription de caisse (de sécurité sociale)
(social security) fund district

contrat de gestion commune de caisses
pooled accounts funding contract

contrat de gestion distincte de caisse
segregated accounts funding contract

établissement de caisse (Fr.)
fund institution

fonds détenus par les caisses de pensions
pension fund accumulations

médecin de caisse
(social security) fund doctor (Fr.), sickness fund doctor (Ger.)

oeuvre de caisse (Fr.)
fund institution

production imputée de services de caisses de pension
imputed service charge for pension funds

transfert des droits acquis d'une caisse à une autre (pension)
transferability / portability of pension rights

CAISSIER
caissiers, guichetiers et assimilés [CITP-1988 (421)]
cashiers, tellers and related clerks [ISCO-1988 (421)]

CALAMITÉ
calamité agricole (Fr.)
agricultural disaster

calamité naturelle
natural disaster

CALCUL
calculation, computation

base de calcul
assessment basis, basis for calculation

base mensuelle de calcul
monthly base for calculation

calcul des cotisations
calculation / computation of contributions

calcul des coûts
costing

calcul du coût salarial
calculation of wage / salary cost(s), salary costing

calcul des coûts standard
standard costing

calcul des coûts unitaires
unit costing

calcul de l'expérience professionnelle
reckoning of professional experience

calcul fonctionnel des coûts
functional costing

calcul de la pension
calculation of the pension

calcul de la pension vieillesse
calculation of old age pension

calcul d'une prestation
calculation of a benefit

calcul-type
model calculation

coefficient de calcul des pensions vieillesse
factor applied to the calculation of old age pensions

formule de calcul de la pension
calculation of the pension

formule servant au calcul de...
computation formula

méthode de calcul
(method of) calculation; formula

méthode de calcul de la cotisation
calculation of the contribution; contribution formula

méthode de calcul de la pension
calculation of the pension; pension formula

méthode de calcul des prestations
calculation of the benefits; benefit formula

mode de calcul
method / mode of calculation

mode de calcul de la pension
calculation of the pension

nouveau calcul d'une prestation
recalculation of a benefit

réduction selon des calculs actuariels
actuarial reduction

salaire de base pour le calcul de la retraite
pensionable earnings

CALCULÉ
calculé sur la base de
calculated on the basis of

pension calculée sur la base de...
pension calculated on the basis of...

CALCULER
to calculate, to compute

calculer l'impôt sur le revenu
to assess income tax

calculer une pension / une prestation
to calculate a pension / a benefit

formule servant à calculer...
computation formula

CALENDAIRE
jour calendaire
calendar day

CALENDRIER
calendar; schedule; timetable

calendrier des activités d'un projet
project management schedule

calendrier des départs
separation schedule

calendrier de mise en oeuvre
implementation schedule

calendrier de négociation
bargaining schedule

calendrier de travail / des travaux
work schedule, scheduling of work

établissement de calendrier
scheduling

CAMARADE
colleague, co-worker

camarade de travail
fellow(-worker)

CAMP
camp de vacances
summer camp

CAMPAGNE
campagne d'alphabétisation / contre l'illettrisme
literacy campaign

campagne de recrutement
recruitment drive

CANCÉREUX (n.)
cancer patient

CANCÉRIGÈNE
carcinogen(ic)

CANDIDAT
canditate, (job) applicant; interviewee

candidat (se porter)
to apply for

candidat correspondant au profil recherché / requis
suitable candidate

candidat externe
external candidate

candidat malheureux
unsuccessful candidate

candidat n'ayant pas le profil recherché / requis
unsuitable candidate

candidat qualifié
suitable candidate

candidat non reçu
unsuccessful candidate

candidat retenu
successful candidate

candidat unique
sole candidate

fichier de candidats
roster of candidates

liste des candidats
list of candidates, nomination list

liste de candidats présélectionnés
shortlist of candidates

méthode de sélection de candidats en groupe
group selection method

présélection des candidats
shortlisting of candidates; screening of job applicants

CANDIDATURE
candidacy, (job) application

acte de candidature pour un emploi (faire)
to apply for a job

candidature non retenue
unsuccessful job application

candidature spéculative
speculative application

candidature spontanée
unsolicited candidacy / job application

date limite de réception des candidatures
application deadline

dossier de candidature
job application form, application blank (USA)

formulaire de candidature
application form

poser sa candidature à un emploi
to try / to apply for a job

présenter sa candidature à un poste
to submit one's candidacy for a post

retrait de candidature
withdrawal of candidacy

CAP
changement de cap
shift

CAPABLE
capable, competent, able, qualified

capable de travailler (pas)
incapable of working, not able / unable to work; (occ.) unemployable

CAPACITÉ
ability, power; skill, qualification, competence, competency; scope

brevet de capacité
certificate of competency

capacité d'absorption du marché du travail
labour market absorption capacity

capacité d'accueil
intake capacity

capacité de concurrence / concurrentielle
competitiveness

capacité contractuelle
bargaining power

capacité contributive
capacity to pay, taxable / tax-paying capacity

capacité fonctionnelle
functional capacity

capacité de gain
earning power / capacity

capacité d'hébergement
(occ.) bed capacity

capacité d'hospitalisation
bed capacity

capacité intellectuelle
mental capacity

capacité juridique
legal capacity; (occ.) ability

capacité de payer
ability to pay

capacité à pleine charge
full capacity

capacité de production
productive capacity

capacité (de production) excédentaire
excess (plant) capacity

capacité (de production) inutilisée
idle capacity

capacité professionnelle
work skill, professional ability

capacité professionnelle réduite
reduced occupational capacity

capacité résiduelle
residual capacity

capacité résiduelle de gain
residual capacity to earn

capacité de travail
capacity to / for work, ability to work, working capacity

capacité de travail réduite
reduced working capacity

capacité de travail rémunéré
wage-earning capacity

certificat de capacité
certificate of competence / competency, qualification / occupational / trade proficiency / craft certificate

chômage par insuffisance des capacités
classical unemployment

classification des capacités
taxonomy of skills

diminution de la capacité de gain
reduction / loss of earning capacity

diminution de la capacité de travail
reduction of working capacity

marge de capacité inutilisée
capacity slack

maximum de sa capacité (au)
to its full capacity

niveau de pleine capacité
full capacity level

perte de la capacité de gain / de travail
loss of earning capacity

pleine capacité
full capacity

récupération des capacités
recovery of capacities

sous-emploi des capacités
under-utilisation of capacity

taux de chômage en situation de plein emploi des capacités
full employment unemployment rate, equilibrium rate of unemployment, natural rate of unemployment

taux d'utilisation des capacités (de production)
rate of capacity utilisation

travailler à pleine capacité
to work at full capacity

CAPILLAIRE
prothèse capillaire
hair replacement

CAPILLARITÉ
capillarité sociale
inter-generational social mobility

CAPITAINE (marine marchande)
shipmaster

CAPITAL
capital; grant

assurance-vie à capital différé
endowment insurance

assurance-vie à capital récupérable
pure endowment insurance

capitaux d'amorçage
seed money

capitaux de couverture
insurance capital

capital(-)décès
(lump-sum) death benefit, death grant

capital de démarrage
seed capital

capital de départ
seed capital

capital humain
human capital / resources

capital initial
seed capital

capitaux de lancement
seed money

capital des services humanitaires
human overhead capital

capital des services sociaux
social overhead capital

capital temps-formation
right to a number of hours' training

capital versé en une seule fois
lump sum

conversion en capital
lump-sum commutation (of a part of the pension)

convertir une prestation en une somme en capital
to commute a benefit in a lump sum

participation au capital
equity stake

police d'assurance-vie à capital différé
endowment policy

police d'assurance-vie à capital récupérable
pure endowment policy

prestation en capital
lump-sum benefit / settlement

rachat en capital (d'une rente)
capital compensatory settlement

règlement en capital
lump-sum payment / settlement

somme en capital
capital sum; lump(-sum) payment

somme en capital résultant de / versée au titre de la conversion partielle de la pension
partial lump sum withdrawal benefit, partial lump sum commutation of pension benefit

subvention en capital
capital grant

valeur en capital
capital value

versement en capital
payment in capital, (payment of a) lump sum; capital compensation

CAPITALISATION
funding; capital (cover); accumulation

caisse de pensions financée suivant le principe de la capitalisation
funded pension fund

capitalisation individuelle
individual funding

capitalisation intégrale (par)
fully funded

facteur de capitalisation
accumulation factor

niveau de capitalisation d'un régime
level of funding of a scheme

pourcentage de capitalisation
funded ratio

pourcentage global de capitalisation
aggregate funded ratio

régime par / reposant sur la capitalisation
funded scheme

régime ne reposant pas sur la capitalisation
unfunded scheme

régime par / reposant sur la capitalisation intégrale
fully funded scheme

régime de retraite par capitalisation
funded pension plan / system

régime de retraite sans capitalisation
unfunded pension plan

régime de retraite par capitalisation intégrale
fully funded pension plan

régime de retraite par capitalisation partielle
partially funded-pension plan

régime de retraite personnel par capitalisation
personal pension scheme / plan

retraite par capitalisation
pre-funded pension plan / scheme

système par capitalisation
advance-funded plan

système de retraite par capitalisation
funded pension system

CAPITALISÉ
entièrement capitalisé
fully funded

système capitalisé
funded plan

CAPITATION
capitation; poll tax (UK)

paiement à la capitation
capitation payment

CARACTÉRIEL (adj.)
enfant caractériel
maladjusted / problem child

CARACTÉRIEL (n.)
maladjusted child

CARACTÉRISÉ
faute caractérisée
clear unquestionable misconduct

incompétence caractérisée
gross incompetence

CARACTÉRISTIQUE (adj.)
characteristic; typical

CARACTÉRISTIQUE (n.)
(pl.) requirement, specification, pattern, characteristics; particulars, details

caractéristiques de la population active
labour force characteristics

caractéristiques d'un / du poste (de travail)
particulars of a position, job specification / content

CARDIAQUE
simulateur cardiaque
pacemaker

CARENCE
deprivation; waiting time; inadequacy; handicap

délai de carence
benefit-waiting / benefit-free period, waiting period / time

jour de carence
waiting day

jour de carence absolu
absolute waiting day

CARITATIF
association / oeuvre caritative
charity, charitable association / agency

organisme caritatif
charity, charitable organisation

CARNET
carnet de grossesse
pregnancy record

carnet de maternité
maternity record

carnet médical
health record

carnet de santé
health booklet / passport / record

carnet de soins
health care booklet / record

CARRIÈRE
career, working life; work history; profession

avancement dans la carrière
career progression, occupational advancement

but de carrière
occupational goal; vocational development objective; career objective / goal

catégorie de carrière
career class

carrière (de)
professional

carrière (en cours de)
in service

carrière antérieure
job history

carrière d'assurance: voir reconstituer la carrière d'assurance

carrière bouchée
blocked career path

carrière civile
civilian career

carrière fictive
notional record of employment

carrière médicale
medical profession

carrière mixte
mixed career

carrière productive
productive career

choix de carrière
career decision / options, occupational / career / vocational choice

comité de carrières
careers committee

conseil en gestion de carrière
career counselling

débouché de carrière
career prospect

déroulement de carrière
career progress / path

durée de carrière
working life

échelons d'une carrière
(occ.) job ladder

enseignement axé sur les carrières
job-related education

entretien de carrière
career interview

étape de carrière
career ladder

étude du déroulement de carrière
career follow-up / career pattern study

étude d'évolution de la carrière
occupational follow-up study

évolution de carrière
career / occupational development

évolution de carrière en dents de scie
erratic career evolution

fonctionnaire de carrière
established civil servant

formation étalée sur toute la carrière
lifelong training

formation et gestion des carrières des cadres
management development

gestion de carrière
career development / management

grille de carrière
career lattice

indemnité de fin de carrière
end-of-service payment

information sur les carrières
occupational / vocational information

interruption de carrière
career break

marché des carrières
career market

militaire de carrière
professional / regular soldier

nomination de carrière
career appointment

objectif de carrière
occupational goal; vocational development objective; career objective / goal

organisation des carrières
(occ.) career development

parcours de carrière
career path

pension en cas de carrière mixte
mixed career pension

personnel de carrière
career staff

perspective de carrière
career opportunity, career / occupational outlook / prospect / development; promotional ladder

perspective d'évolution de carrière
career development prospect

plan de carrière
professional advancement, career development / advancement / planning, career (development) plan

planification de carrière
career planning

possibilité de carrière
opportunity for advancement, career opportunity

profil de carrière
career pattern / profile

progression dans la carrière
career progression / path

prospection des carrières
career exploration

reconstituer la carrière d'assurance
to draw up someone's insurance history / record

régime fin de carrière
final average earnings plan

régime salaire de carrière
career earnings pension plan

salaire en fin de carrière
final salary

schéma de carrière
career plan; (occ.) career structures

service de carrière
career system / service

service d'orientation sur les carrières (UK)
career service

sommet d'une carrière
peak of a career

taux de rétention des salariés à mi-carrière
(occ.) half-life survival rate

CARTE
carte d'adhérent
membership card

carte d'assurance (sociale) / d'assuré (social)
(social) insurance card

carte de cécité
blindness card

carte de cotisation
contribution card

carte d'immatriculation du salarié
employee registration card

carte médicale
health record

carte à mémoire
smart card

carte mutualiste
mutual insurance card

carte de pointage
attendance / time (clock) card

carte de présence
attendance card

carte de priorité
priority card

carte de résident
residence permit

carte des retenues (UK)
deduction card

carte de retraité
pension card

carte sanitaire
(occ.) list of health services

carte de séjour
residence permit

carte de séjour et de travail
work and residence permit, green card (USA)

carte syndicale
union card

carte de travail
work permit

horaire à la carte
flexible working hours / time, flexi-time

retraite à la carte
flexible retirement

CARTOGRAPHIE
cartographie des compétences
skills inventory

CARTON
carton de pointage
(time) clock card

confectionneurs d'articles en papier et en carton [CITP-1968 (9-1)]
paper and paperboard products makers [[ISCO-1968 (9-1)]]

CAS
case; event

cas concret
(occ.) case study

cas de détresse
hardship case

cas difficile / douloureux
hardship case

cas d'espèce
specific case

cas de force majeure
act of God

cas hospitaliers
hospital cases

cas résiduels
(occ.) hard core

cas social
person with social problems, needy /
hardship case, social misfit

durée moyenne des cas (de maladie)
average duration per case

étude de cas
case study

gestion par cas
case management

CASCADE
licenciements en cascade
spate of dismissals

CATASTROPHE
catastrophe naturelle
natural disaster

CATÉGORIE
category, class, group; grade

catégorie apparentée
related category

catégorie applicable
relevant class

catégorie de bénéficiaires
class of beneficiaries

catégorie de carrière
career class

catégorie de compétences
skill category

catégorie de cotisation
contribution class

catégorie d'emploi(s)
job category; service / job class

catégorie exemptée / d'exemption
excluded category

catégorie de personnes couvertes
group of persons covered; (pl.) range of
persons covered

**catégorie de personnes à faibles
revenus**
low-income (population) group

catégories de personnes protégées
population coverage

catégorie de population
segment / group of population

catégorie de prestations
category of benefits

catégorie de professions
type of occupations

catégorie des professions libérales
professional category

catégorie professionnelle
occupation(al) group / category, job
class; class of worker

catégorie de revenus
class of income

catégorie salariale
earnings category

catégorie sociale
social status / socio-economic group

**catégories sociales les plus
défavorisées**
lowest social classes

catégorie socio-professionnelle
social and economic category, social
status / socio-economic group; social
status

cotisation de base pour la catégorie n
primary class n contribution

**cotisation supplémentaire pour la
catégorie n**
secondary class n contribution

**répartition par catégorie
professionnelle**
industrial and occupational composition

CATÉGORIEL
sectional

revendication catégorielle
group claim; (pl.) sectional claims

CAUSE
cause (en)
concerned

cause juste
just cause

cause profonde
underlying cause

cause réelle et sérieuse
just cause; genuine and proper ground

cause réelle et sérieuse de licenciement
genuine and proper ground for dismissal

décès dû à quelque cause que ce soit
death from any cause

licenciement abusif sans cause réelle et sérieuse
dismissal without just cause

CAUTION / CAUTIONNEMENT
guarantee, guaranty, security

CÉCITÉ
carte de cécité
blindness card

pension de cécité (Malta)
blindness pension

CÉLIBAT
celibacy; bachelorhood; spinsterhood

survivant en état de célibat
single survivor

survivant en état de non-célibat
ever-married survivor

CÉLIBATAIRE
celibate, unmarried, never-married, single (person)

célibataire (non)
ever-married

mère célibataire
unmarried / single mother

parent non célibataire
non-single parent

père célibataire
unmarried father

travailleur célibataire
single worker

CELLULE
unit, cell

cellule familiale
family unit

cellule de reclassement
redeployment unit

CENTRAL (adj.)
comité central d'entreprise
central works committee

Commission centrale d'aide sociale
Social Welfare Central Commission

fichier central des cotisations d'assurance (UK)
central record of insurance contributions

hôpital central
(occ.) referral hospital

office central du logement
central authority for housing

pouvoir central
central government

siège central
head office

CENTRALE
centrale syndicale
central trade union organisation

CENTRE
centre

centre d'accouchement
lying-in clinic

centre d'accueil
receiving home; remand home; reception centre

centre d'accueil pour (jeunes) enfants
child-minding facility

centre d'accueil de jour
day care centre

centre d'accueil thérapeutique
(occ.) drop-in centre

centre d'action médico-sociale précoce
early medical social work centre

centre aéré
outdoor centre

centre d'affaires
business centre / place

centre d'aide par le travail
work-based support centre

centre anticancéreux
cancer hospital / research centre

centre d'appareillage
appliance centre

centre d'apprentissage
apprentice school

centre chirurgical de jour
day surgery centre

centre collectif de soins
community health centre

centre communal d'action sociale
social work municipal centre

centre communautaire
community (welfare) centre; (occ.) living community

centre de consultation
counselling centre; clinic

centre de consultation dentaire
dental clinic

centre de consultations psycho-médico-pédagogiques
child guidance clinic / centre

centre de convalescence, de cure ou de réadaptation (Fr.)
nursing, care or rehabilitation centre

centre de crise
crisis centre

centre de diagnostic
diagnosis centre

centre d'éducation motrice
education centre for people with motor impairment

centre d'éducation sensorielle
education centre for people with sensory disability

centre d'éducation surveillée
correctional school; (occ.) training school

centre d'emploi
job centre

centre d'entraide
self-help centre

centre d'évaluation
assessment centre

centre d'éveil
pre-school learning centre

centre d'examens de santé
medical examination centre

centre de formation
training centre / school

centre de formation des apprentis (CFA) (Fr.)
tuition centre for working apprentices, apprentice training centre

centre de formation de l'entreprise
company training centre

centre de formation en internat
residential training centre

centre de formation à libre accès
open access training centre

centre de formation professionnelle
vocational (training) centre

centre de guidance infantile
child guidance centre / clinic

centre pour handicapés
centre for disabled people

centre d'hébergement
reception / accommodation centre; hostel

centre d'hébergement nocturne
night hostel

centre hospitalier
hospital

centre hospitalier régional (CHR)
regional hospital

centre hospitalier universitaire (CHU)
university hospital

centre des impôts
local tax office

centre d'information et de coordination de l'action sociale
social work information and co-ordination centre

centre d'information et d'orientation (Fr.)
information and guidance centre

centre d'intégration (Sp.)
integration centre

centre interne de formation
company training centre

centre pour (les) jeunes
youth centre

centre de jour
day (care) centre; half-way house

centre de loisirs
vacation centre

centre de long séjour
nursing home

centre médical scolaire / de médecine scolaire
school health clinic / centre

centre de médecine sportive
sports medicine centre

centre médico-pédagogique
child guidance clinic / centre

centre médico-pédagogique de cure ambulatoire (Fr.)
out-patient child care centre

centre médico-scolaire
school health centre

centre médico-sportif
sports medicine centre

centre d'observation
observation centre

centre d'orientation
referral centre

centre de paiement
paying centre

centre de perfectionnement
(occ.) training school

centre de la petite enfance
early childhood reception centre

centre pilote
pilot centre

centre pilote de réadaptation
pilot rehabilitation centre

centre de placement familial
family placement centre

centre de post(-)cure
convalescent home, rest centre; after care centre

centre post-hospitalier général de réadaptation médicale
(occ.) medical rehabilitation centre

centre de premier accueil
emergency home shelter

centre de premier secours
emergency centre

centre de profit
profit centre

centre de protection maternelle et infantile
maternity child welfare centre

centre de proximité
community centre

centre psycho-médico-pédagogique
child guidance clinic / centre

centre public d'aide sociale (CPAS) (Belg.)
public centre for social welfare, public wlefare centre

centre de réadaptation
rehabilitation centre

centre de réadaptation physique
remedial exercise clinic

centre de rééducation
rehabilitation centre

centre de rééducation pour aveugles
rehabilitation centre for the blind; training centre for the blind

centre de référence
referral centre

centre sanitaire public
government / public health centre

centre de santé
health centre / unit

centre de santé intégré
integrated health centre

centre de santé publique
Government / public health centre

centre de services
service centre

centre social
welfare / social centre

centre social de quartier
neighbourhood (welfare / social) centre

centre socio-culturel
social / socio-cultural centre

centre de soins
(health / nursing) care centre

centre de soins primaires
primary care centre

centre témoin
pilot centre

CERCLE
cercle de qualité
quality circle, quality improvement group

cercle de recherche active d'emploi (Fr.)
job club

CERTIFICAT
certificate; certification

certificat d'accouchement
certificate of confinement

certificat d'agrément
certificate of registration (pensions)

certificat d'apprentissage
certificate of apprenticeship

certificat d'aptitude professionnelle
certificate of competence, qualification / occupational / trade proficiency / craft certificate

certificat d'aptitude professionnelle agricole (CAPA) (Fr.)
certificate of agricultural competence

certificat d'arrêt de travail
sick leave certificate

certificat d'assiduité
certificate of attendance

certificat d'attestation des frais
certificate of cost

certificat d'ayant droit
certification of entitlement

certificat de capacité
certificate of competence / competency, qualification / occupational / trade proficiency / craft certificate

certificat de conformité des moyens de sécurité incendie
fire certificate

certificat de consolidation
consolidation certificate

certificat d'embauche
certificate of employment

certificat d'enseignement secondaire inférieur (CESI)
lower secondary education certificate

certificat de fin d'études
(school-)leaving certificate

certificat de fin d'études secondaires
high-school leaving certificate

certificat de fin de scolarité
school-leaving certificate

certificat final
final certificate

certificat d'incapacité de travail
certificate of incapacity for work

certificat d'indigence
certificate of poverty

certificat initial
initial certificate

certificat de mariage
marriage certificate

certificat médical
health / medical / doctor's certificate

certificat médical d'aptitude professionnelle
occupational medical certificate

certificat prénuptial
prenuptial certificate

certificat professionnel
certificate of competence, qualification / occupational certificate

certificat de qualification
certificate of competence, qualification / occupational / trade proficiency / craft certificate

certificat de reconnaissance
recognition certificate

certificat de santé
health certificate; (occ.) medical clearance

certificat de scolarité
certificate of (school) attendance

certificat de service(s)
certificate of service

certificat de travail
certification / certificate of service, employment / work certificate

certificat de vie
life certificate

titres et certificats
(occ.) credentials

CERTIFICATION
authentication, certification

CERTIFIÉ
certified

certifié conforme par
authenticated by

instituteur / professeur certifié
certified teacher

CERTIFIER
to certify, to authenticate

CÉRUSE
white lead

CESSATION
âge de cessation d'activité
age at retirement / at withdrawal / at separation from the labour force, retirement age

âge moyen de cessation d'activité
mean age at separation from the labour force

cessation d'activité / de l'activité
going out of business; leaving the / separation from the / withdrawal from the labour force; withdrawal from work / from employment; retirement

cessation d'activité d'une entreprise
closing down of a business, business closure

cessation anticipée de fonction
early termination of service

cessation collective de travail
collective work stoppage

cessation d'un contrat de travail
termination of a contract of employment

cessation d'un droit à (des) prestations
cessation of entitlement to / of a right to benefits, exhaustion of entitlement to benefits

cessation d'emploi / de l'emploi
employment termination, termination (of employment), (job) separation; retirement

cessation de fonctions
(employment) termination, cessation / termination of employment, job separation; severance

cessation de fonctions par mise à la retraite
termination of appointment by retirement

cessation de la pension
cessation of the pension

cessation des prestations
exhaustion of benefits

cessation de la relation de travail
cessation / termination of employment

cessation de service
separation from service, termination, leaving

cessation des services
termination of services

cessation de service par accord mutuel
agreed termination

document de cessation de service
separation document

entretien de cessation d'emploi
exit interview

indemnité de cessation d'emploi / de cessation de fonctions / de cessation de service / lors de la cessation de service / versée à la cessation de service
separation / terminal / severance pay / payment / benefit, allowance for separation; (occ.) completion bonus

préavis de cessation d'emploi
end-of-employment notice

prestation de cessation de service
termination pay

probabilité de cessation d'activité
probability of separation from the labour force

réserve de cessation de l'emploi
(-sous)
subject to a retirement condition

somme due à la cessation de service
terminal entitlement

taux de cessation d'activité
rate of separation from the labour force

versement à la cessation de service
separation pay / payment

CESSER
cesser toute activité professionnelle
to drop out of / to leave the labour force; to leave work

cesser d'exercer un emploi
to separate from a job

cesser le travail
to stop work, to walk off the job; to leave work

CESSIBILITÉ
transferability

CESSION
transfer; assignment

cession d'entreprise
divestment

cession d'exploitation (agr.)
transfer of farm holding

cession de salaire
wage transfer

CHAÎNE
chaîne de fabrication
production line

chaîne de montage
assembly line

chaîne de production
production / assembly line

production à la chaîne
line production

travail à la chaîne
assembly-line work, flow process work,
production line work; flow / line
production,

travailler à la chaîne
to work on the production line

CHAMBRE
chambre de commerce (et d'industrie)
chamber of commerce

chambre commune (hosp.)
public ward

chambre des métiers
chamber of trades, guild chamber, trade(s)
association, trade guild

chambre particulière
private room

chambre privée (hosp.)
amenity bed

**chambre privée ou semi-privée (hosp.)
(Can.)**
preferred accommodation

chambres professionnelle
business chamber

chambre syndicale
employers' federation

obligation de garder la chambre
confinement to bed

supplément pour chambre privée
extra charge for private room

CHAMP
champ d'action
scope

champ d'action et effet du travail
scope and effect of work

champ d'application
field of application, scope; coverage

**champ d'application matériel (ratione
materiae)**
material scope; substantive scope

**champ d'application personnel
(ratione personae)**
personal scope

CHANCE
école de la deuxième chance
second-chance college

égalité des chances
equality of opportunities, equal opportunities

**égalité des chances sur le plan
éducatif**
equality of educational opportunity

égalité des chances dans l'emploi
equal employment opportunities

enseignement de la deuxième chance
second-chance education

inégalité des chances
opportunity gap

CHANGE
taux de change
exchange rate, rate of exchange

CHANGEMENT
change; shift

changement de cap
shift

changement de domicile
change of residence; removal, relocation

changement d'emploi
change of job, job change

changement d'orientation
change of track

changement de profession
change of occupation

changement de résidence
change of residence; removal, relocation

pièces attestant un changement de résidence
evidence of relocation

CHANTIER
site; works; work camp

chantier de construction
construction site

chef de chantier
site manager, (work)site foreman

ingénieur de chantier
site engineer

installations sur le chantier
on-site facilities

ouvrier sur chantier
building site labourer

CHARBONNAGE
régime complémentaire des travailleurs des charbonnages
colliery workers supplementary scheme

travailleur des charbonnages
colliery worker

CHARGE (n.)
office, charge; dependence; responsibi-lity; burden; expenditure, expense, cost

abattement pour charges de famille
family allowance

adulte à charge
adult dependant, dependent adult

aide aux familles avec enfants à charge
aid to families with dependant children (AFDC)

allocation pour charges de famille
dependant care allowance

allocation pour enfant(s) à charge
dependent child allowance, children's allowance, child benefit (UK)

allocation de / pour personne à charge
dependant care allowance, dependant's / dependency allowance

ayant droit à charge
eligible dependant

cahier des charges
specifications

capacité à pleine charge
full capacity

charge (à)
dependent

charge de (à la)
borne by; payable by

charge (avoir à sa)
to support

charge (ayant la) de
responsible for

charge de (être à la)
to be dependent on, to be in a dependent position, to be supported by, to be maintai-ned by

charge différée
deferred charge

charge élective
elective office

charges d'exploitation
running / operational / operating cost

charges familiales
family responsibilities

charges de famille
family expenses; family responsibilities

charge financière
financial cost / burden

charge fiscale
fiscal / tax burden

charge fixe
fixed cost; (pl.) overhead costs

charges de fonctionnement
running / operating cost(s) / expenditure

charges incombant à ...
costs to be borne by ...

charges indues
undue burden

charges patronales
employer's contributions

charge de la preuve
burden of proof, onus of the proof

charge publique
official duty

charge reportée
deferred charge

charge salariale
labour cost; (pl.) employee's contributions;
hired labour charges

charges salariales fixes
overhead labour costs

charges sociales
social burden / charges; payroll tax; social
security contributions; welfare costs

charge supportée par la population active
dependency ratio

charge de travail
(volume of) work()load

coefficient de charge
(old age) support ratio

compensation des charges
pooling of risks

conjoint à charge
dependent spouse

début de la prise en charge
commencement of benefit(s)

**déclaration de situation de famille et
demande d'indemnités pour charges de
famille**
family status report and request for payment
of dependency allowances

déduction pour charge de famille
dependants' allowance

dégrèvement pour charges de famille
dependency credit

délai de prise en charge
period of liability for compensation

déplacement de la charge du chômage
churning

durée de la prise en charge
duration of benefit, benefit duration

enfant à charge
dependent child

entièrement à la charge de quelqu'un
wholly dependent for support

exonération des charges
exemption from contributions

famille à charge
dependent relatives

frais à la charge de
costs to be borne by

garde de personnes à charge
dependant care

indemnité pour charge de famille
dependency / dependent allowance; (pl.)
family allowances; child benefit
allowances (UK)

indemnité pour personne à charge
dependent allowance

majoration pour charges de famille
dependency supplement

**majoration pour enfant à charge
(UK)**
child dependency addition

**majoration de la pension de retraite
pour conjoint à charge**
pension supplement / increase in respect
of a dependant spouse

majoration pour personne à charge
increase of benefits for a dependant,
supplement for dependant; family
supplement

**parent reconnu (légalement comme
parent) à charge**
dependent relative; (occ.) prescribed
relative

participation pour prise en charge exceptionnelle
contribution for exceptional expenses

pension de personnes indirectement à charge
secondary dependants' benefit

péréquation des charges familiales
equalisation of family burdens

période de prise en charge
period of coverage / of compensation, duration of benefit(s)

personnes âgées à charge
aged dependants

personne à charge
dependant

personne ayant des charges familiales
person with family responsibilities, breadwinner

personne directement à charge
primary dependent

personne non directement à charge
secondary dependent

plan d'aide aux salariés pour la prise en charge de leurs parents âgés
elder care scheme

prendre à sa charge
to assume responsibility for; to provide; to absorb

prendre à sa charge les frais de
to bear the cost of

prendre en charge
to cover, to compensate, to defray

prestation à la charge directe de l'employeur
employer-based benefit

prestation complémentaire pour charges locatives (Irel.)
rent supplement

prestation pour personne(s) à charge
benefit for dependents, dependent's benefit

prestation pour personne indirectement à charge
secondary dependent's benefit

prise en charge
compensation; acceptance of responsibility; reimbursement; defrayal, defrayment; liability; benefit(s)

prise en charge intégrale / totale
full payment; total subsidisation

répartition de la charge de travail
distribution of the workload

travailleur ayant charge de famille
worker with dependants / with family responsibilities

variation de la charge de travail
workload shift

CHARGÉ (adj.)
chargé de
responsible for

chargé de famille (être)
to be encumbered with family

personne chargée de famille
person with family responsabilities, breadwinner

CHARGÉ (n.)
chargé de cours
lecturer

chargé de famille
person with family responsibilities / with dependants

chargé de mission
special project manager

chargé de programme
programme manager

chargé de recrutement
recruitment officer

CHARGEMENT
facteur chargement
load factor

CHARITABLE
charitable

institution / oeuvre charitable
charity, charitable association / agency /
institution

CHARTE
charter; memorandum of association

CHASSEUR
agriculteurs, éleveurs, forestiers, pêcheurs et
chasseurs [CITP-1968 (6)]
agriculture, animal husbandry and forestry
workers, fishermen and hunters [ISCO-
1968 (6)]

CHAUFFAGE
allocation de chauffage et d'électricité
(Irel.)
fuel and electricity allowance

CHAUSSURE
artisans et ouvriers du travail du cuir, des
peaux et de la chaussure [CITP-1988 (744)]
pelt, leather and shoemaking trades workers
[ISCO-1988 (744)]

CHEF
head; chief; leader; officer-in-charge;
superintendent; supervisor

chef (de son propre)
in one's own right

chef d'atelier
workshop foreman / manager

chef de chantier
site manager, (work)site foreman

chef d'entreprise
manager; entrepreneur

chef d'équipe
head of shift, team leader; (occ.) charge
hand

chef d'établissement
manager; employer

chef de famille
family head, head of (the) family,
(family) breadwinner

chef de famille monoparentale
single household head

chef de groupe
supervisor; (occ.) adult leader

**chefs de groupe d'employés de
bureau [CITP-1968 (3-0)]**
clerical supervisors [ISCO-1968 (3-0)]

**chefs de groupe d'employés de
maison et travailleurs assimilés
[CITP-1968 (5-2)]**
housekeeping and related service
supervisors [ISCO-1968 (5-2)]

chef hiérarchique
official superior

chef de ménage
head of (the) household, householder

chef de projet
project manager

chef de quart
shift supervisor

chef de service (hosp.)
medical officer

chef des services médicaux
chief medical officer

**chefs de services de transports et de
communications [CITP-1968 (3-5)]**
transport and communications
supervisors [ISCO-1968 (3-5)]

**chefs traditionnels et chefs de village
[CITP-1988 (113)]**
traditional chiefs and heads of villages
[ISCO-1988 (113)]

**chefs de train et receveurs [CITP-
1968 (3-6)]**
transport conductors [ISCO-1968 (3-6)]

**chefs de ventes et acheteurs [CITP-
1968 (4-2)]**
sales supervisors and buyers [ISCO-
1968 (4-2)]

femme seule chef de famille
single woman family head

poste de chef de service
supervisor(y) post / position

qualité de chef d'entreprise
entrepreneur skill

CHÈQUE
chèque-éducation
education voucher

chèque-emploi
employment voucher

chèque-repas / chèque-restaurant
luncheon voucher

chèque de salaire
pay cheque

chèque vacances
holiday voucher

CHER
allocation / indemnité de vie chère
cost-of-living allowance / compensation / adjustment

main-d'oeuvre peu chère
cheap labour

prime de vie chère
cost-of-living allowance

CHERCHER
chercher un emploi / du travail
to look for employment / for a job, to seek employment / work

CHERCHEUR
researcher, research worker

CHERTÉ
indemnité de cherté de vie
cost-of-living allowance / compensation / adjustment

CHEVAUCHANT
système de travail par équipes chevau-chantes
coupled shift system

CHEVAUCHEMENT
overlapping

CHEVRONNÉ
experienced; proficient

travailleur chevronné
experienced worker

CHIFFRAGE
chiffrage des coûts / des dépenses
costing

CHIFFRÉ (adj.)
données chiffrées
facts and figures

CHIFFRE (n.)
figure, number; amount; level

chiffre d'affaires
turnover

chiffres du chômage
unemployment data

chiffres comparables
comparable figures

chiffres comparatifs
comparative figures

chiffres relatifs à l'emploi
employment figures

chiffre gonflé
inflated figure

chiffres trimestriels
quarterly figures

impôt sur le chiffre d'affaires
turnover tax

CHIFFRER
chiffrer à (se)
to amount to

CHIMIOTHÉRAPIQUE
traitement chimiothérapique
drug treatment

CHIMIQUE
conducteurs de fours et d'appareils
chimiques [CITP-1968 (7-4)]
chemical processers and related workers
[ISCO-1968 (7-4)]

conducteurs d'installations de traitement chimique [CITP-1988 (815)]
chemical-processing-plant operators [ISCO-1988 (815)]

conducteurs de machines pour la fabrication des produits chimiques [CITP-1988 (822)]
chemical-products machine operators
[ISCO-1988 (822)]

substance chimique dangereuse
hazardous chemical

CHIRURGICAL
centre chirurgical de jour
day surgery centre

CHIRURGIE
surgery

actes de petite chirurgie
minor surgery

chirurgie dentaire
dental surgery

chirurgie esthétique
plastic surgery

chirurgie non vitale
elective surgery

CHIRURGIEN
surgeon

chirurgien dentaire
dental surgeon

CHOIX
choice, option; kit

choix de l'activité professionnelle
choice of job, job choice

choix de carrière
career decision / options, occupational /
career / vocational choice

choix de la discipline / des matières
choice of subject (area) / of field of
study, subject choice

choix du médecin
choice of doctor

choix de profession / professionnels
career decision / options, occupational /
career / vocational choice

grille d'évaluation à choix forcé
forced choice rating (grid)

libre choix du médecin
free choice of doctor

questionnaire à choix multiples
multiple choice / ipsative test /
questionnaire

CHÔMAGE
unemployment; joblessness

allocataire de l'assurance chômage
unemployment insurance recipient

allocation de chômage
unemployment allowance / benefit /
compensation; dole

allocation de chômage de transition (Belg.)
transitional unemployment allowance

allocation complémentaire de chômage
supplementary unemployment
allowance

allocation journalière de chômage
daily unemployment benefit

allocation de solidarité de chômage total (Fr.)
total unemployment solidarity
allowance

allocation spéciale de chômage (Fr.)
special unemployment allowance

assistance-chômage
unemployment assistance

assurance-chômage
unemployment insurance /
compensation

assurance-chômage obligatoire
compulsory unemployment insurance

bénéficiaire de l'assurance chômage
unemployment insurance recipient

bureau de paiement des indemnités de chômage
unemployment benefit (paying) office

caisse d'assurance chômage
unemployment (insurance) fund

caisse de chômage
unemployment (insurance) fund

chiffres du chômage
unemployment data

chômage (au / en)
jobless, unemployed, without employment, out of work

chômage (être au)
to be unemployed / without employment; to be / to live on the dole

chômage accidentel
intermittent / occasional unemployment

chômage d'adaptation technologique
frictional / transitional unemployment

chômage aigu
acute unemployment

chômage apparent
measured / open / overt / registered / visible unemployment

chômage d'attente
search unemployment

chômage caché
hidden / disguised / concealed unemployment

chômage chronique
chronic / long-term unemployment

chômage classique
classical unemployment

chômage complet
full / total unemployment

chômage conjoncturel
cyclical unemployment

chômage croissant
rising unemployment

chômage cyclique
cyclical unemployment

chômage non cyclique
non-cyclical unemployment

chômage déclaré
measured / open / overt / registered / visible unemployment

chômage non déclaré
unrecorded / hidden / disguised / concealed unemployment

chômage découvert
recorded unemployment

chômage déguisé
hidden / disguised / concealed unemployment

chômage des (diplômés) universitaires
graduate unemployment, unemployment amongst graduates

chômage élevé
high unemployment

chômage endémique
long-term / chronic unemployment

chômage frictionnel
frictional / turnover / transitional / turn-around unemployment

chômage généralisé
general / large-scale / mass / massive unemployment

chômage global
aggregate unemployment

chômage grave
acute unemployment

chômage d'inadéquation
mismatch unemployment

chômage induit
induced unemployment

chômage par insuffisance des capacités
classical unemployment

chômage par insuffisance de la crois-sance
growth gap unemployment

chômage par insuffisance de la demande
demand-deficient unemployment

chômage par insuffisance d'équipements
capital shortage unemployment

chômage(-)intempéries
unemployment due to bad weather conditions

chômage intermittent
recurrent / frictional / casual unem-ployment

chômage invisible
hidden / disguised / unrecorded / concealed unemployment

chômage involontaire
involuntary unemployment

chômage irréductible
hard-core unemployment

chômage des jeunes
youth unemployment

chômage keynésien
demand-deficient / keynesian unem-ployment

chômage latent
unrecorded / hidden / disguised / concealed unemployment

chômage de longue durée
long duration / long-term / chronic unemployment

chômage de très longue durée
very long-term unemployment

chômage masqué
concealed unemployment

chômage massif
general / large-scale / mass unemployment

chômage mesuré
measured / open / overt / registered / visible unemployment

chômage partiel
short(-)time work(ing); partial unem-ployment; under-employment

chômage partiel (en)
under-employed

chômage partiel (être en)
to be under-employed, to work short-time, to be on short time

chômage permanent
persistent unemployment

chômage potentiel
threat of unemployment

chômage recensé
registered unemployment

chômage non recensé
unregistered / unrecorded unemployment

chômage record
peak unemployment

chômage récurrent
recurrent unemployment, multiple spells of unemployment

chômage résiduel
residual / hard-core / frictional / transitional unemployment

chômage saisonnier
seasonal unemployment

chômage sectoriel
sectoral unemployment

chômage sporadique
casual unemployment

chômage structurel
structural unemployment

chômage technique
(intermittent / temporary) lay(-)off

chômage technique (en)
(temporarily) laid-off, temporarily stopped, on furlough

chômage technologique
technological unemployment

chômage total
total unemployment

chômage total (au)
totally / wholly unemployed

chômage transféré
shift of unemployment, transferred unemployment

chômage transitionnel
transitional unemployment

chômage visible
measured / open / overt / visible unemployment

chômage volontaire
voluntary unemployment

courbe du chômage
unemployment pattern, pattern of unemployment

déplacement de la charge du chômage
churning

dilemme chômage-inflation
employment-inflation trade-off

données relatives au chômage
unemployment data

durée actuelle du chômage
(duration of) current spell of unemployment

durée de / du chômage
length / duration of unemployment

durée de l'indemnisation du chômage
duration of unemployment benefits

durée moyenne du chômage
average duration of unemployment

endiguer / enrayer le chômage
to stem / to reduce unemployment

entrées au chômage
flow into unemployment

fréquence du chômage
incidence of unemployment

incidence du chômage
incidence of unemployment

indemnisation du chômage
unemployment compensation

indemnisation pour chômage partiel
short-time working compensation

indemnité de chômage
unemployment allowance / benefit;
(occ.) dole

indemnité de chômage partiel
short-time working allowance

inscrire au chômage (s')
to register as unemployed; to go on the dole

inscrit au chômage (être)
to be on the unemployment register

institution d'assurance(-)chômage
unemployment insurance institution

interruption du / de chômage
break in unemployment

interruption de la durée / de la période de chômage
break in the period of unemployment

Lignes directrices du BIT pour la mesure du chômage
ILO Guidelines for measuring unemployment

lutter contre le chômage
to combat / to reduce unemployment

mettre au chômage
to make redundant

mettre en chômage technique, mettre temporairement au chômage
to lay off (temporarily)

niveau de chômage
unemployment level

noyau irréductible de chômage
hard-core unemployment

pension de préretraite-chômage (Finl.)
unemployment pension

percevoir des allocations / des indemnités de chômage
to collect unemployment compensation, to live on / to draw unemployment benefit

période de chômage
period / spell of unemployment

période de chômage complète
completed spell of unemployment

période de chômage en cours
spell of unemployment in progress

périodes de chômage répétées
multiple spells of unemployment

période complète de chômage
completed spell of unemployment

période d'indemnisation du chômage
period for which a claimant receives unemployment benefits

période isolée de chômage
single spell of unemployment

piège du chômage
unemployment trap

prestation de l'assurance chômage / (en cas) de chômage
unemployment (insurance) benefit

prestation pour chômage partiel
short-time working benefit

radié du chômage (être)
to be struck off the unemployment register

radier du chômage
to strike off the unemployment register

rapport chômage/population
unemployment/population ratio

réduire le chômage
to reduce unemployment

régime d'assurance-chômage
unemployment insurance (scheme)

régime d'indemnisation du chômage
unemployment compensation scheme

résorption du chômage
reduction of unemployment

secours chômage
unemployment relief

sortie du chômage
outflow from / flow out of unemployment

sorties du chômage pour reprise d'emploi
outflow to jobs from unemployment

statistiques du chômage
unemployment data / figures / statistics

taux de chômage
level of unemployment; unemployment / jobless rate

taux de chômage non accélérateur de l'inflation
non accelerating inflation rate of unemployment (NAIRU)

taux de chômage non accélérateur des salaires
non accelerating wage rate of unemployment (NAWRU)

taux de chômage familial
family unemployment rate

taux de chômage global
aggregate unemployment rate

taux de chômage naturel
full employment unemployment rate, equilibrium rate of unemployment, natural rate of unemployment, natural unemployment rate

taux de chômage normalisé / standardisé (TCS)
standardised unemployment rate (SUR)

taux de chômage en situation d'équilibre / de plein emploi (des capacités)
full employment unemployment rate, equilibrium / natural rate of unemployment

taux naturel de chômage
natural unemployment rate, natural rate of unemployment

taxe fédérale de chômage (USA)
employer's excise tax

tendance du chômage
unemployment pattern, pattern of unemployment

toucher des allocations / des indemnités de chômage
to live on / to draw unemployment benefit

travailleur en chômage technique
laid-off worker, (occ.) lay(-)off

vivre du chômage
to live on unemployment benefit

CHÔMÉ
heures chômées
not worked hours

jour chômé
non-working day; public / official holiday

CHÔMEUR
jobless, unemployed (person / worker); under-employed

afflux de chômeurs
inflow of unemployed

aide aux chômeurs
unemployment assistance

chômeur âgé
old(er) unemployed

chômeur apte au travail
able-bodied unemployed

chômeur chronique
chronically / long-term unemployed

chômeur complet
fully / wholly unemployed

chômeur conjoncturel
victim of cyclical unemployment

chômeur non déclaré
hidden unemployed

chômeur difficile à placer
hard-to-place unemployed

chômeur difficile à reclasser
(occ.) hard-core unemployed

chômeur en fin de droits
unemployment insurance / benefit exhaustee, unemployed person no longer entitled to receive unemployment benefit

chômeur indemnisé
unemployed (person) on benefit

chômeur inscrit
registered unemployed

chômeur latent
hidden unemployed

chômeur de longue date
chronically / long-term / long duration unemployed

chômeur de longue durée
chronically / long-term / long duration unemployed

chômeur partiel
under-employed, partially unemployed (worker), worker on short time, short-term worker

chômeur non qualifié
unemployed unskilled worker

chômeur récent
short-term / short-duration unemployed

chômeur à la recherche d'un emploi
job-seeking unemployed, unemployed job-seeker

chômeur secouru
unemployed on relief

chômeur volontaire
voluntary unemployed

flux de nouveaux chômeurs
flow into unemployment

formation des chômeurs (Fr.)
training for the unemployed

jeune chômeur
young unemployed

nombre de chômeurs
number of unemployed; unemployment (data / figures / statistics)

noyau irréductible de chômeurs
hard-core unemployment

plan d'accompagnement des chômeurs (Belg.)
support plan for the unemployed

stagiaire chômeur
unemployed trainee

CHRONIQUE
chômage chronique
chronic / long-term unemployment

chômeur chronique
chronically / long-term unemployed

hôpital pour malades chroniques
chronic disease hospital

malade chronique
chronic sick

maladie chronique
chronic disease / illness / sickness

pénurie chronique
persistent shortage

CHUTE
chute d'une hauteur
falling

CIBLAGE
targeting

CIBLÉ (adj.)
programme ciblé
target programme

CIBLE (n.)
groupe cible
target group; (occ.) priority group

population cible
target population

CINÉMA
opérateurs de stations d'émissions de radio et de télévision, opérateurs d'appareils de sonorisation et projectionnistes de cinéma [CITP-1968 (8-6)]
broadcasting station and sound equipment operators and cinema projectionists [ISCO-1968 (8-6)]

CIRCONSCRIPTION
district, area

autorité sanitaire de circonscription (UK)
area health authority

circonscription de caisse (de sécurité sociale)
(social security) fund district

circonscription hospitalière
hospital catchment area

circonscription sanitaire
health area

circonscription scolaire
school district

circonscription de service social
social service district

CIRCUIT
deuxième circuit de formation (Belg.)
"second chance" training facilities

CIRCULATION
accident de la circulation
road / traffic accident

liberté de circulation des travailleurs
freedom of movement for workers

libre circulation
free movement

libre circulation de la main-d'oeuvre / des travailleurs
free movement of workers

mise en circulation
(occ.) introduction

victime d'accident de la circulation
road accident victim

CIREUR
cireurs de chaussures et autres travailleurs
des petits métiers des rues [CITP-1988
(912)]
shoe cleaning and other street services
elementary occupations [ISCO-1988 (912)]

CITADIN
(pl.) urban dwellers

CITÉ
cité dortoir
dormitory town

CITOYEN
citizen; (pl.) members of the public

association de citoyens
citizens' group

groupe d'action formé de citoyens
citizens' action group, public interest group

groupe de citoyens
citizens' group

CITOYENNETÉ
citizenship

CIVIL (adj.)
année civile
calendar year

assurance en responsabilité civile
third party insurance, liability insurance

carrière civile
civilian career

emploi civil
civilian occupation

état civil
civil status

invalide civil
civilian disabled

jour civil
calendar day

journée civile
calendar day

libertés civiles
civil liberties

marché du travail civil
civilian labour market

mois civil
calendar month

**pension payée en raison d'un accident
civil**
pension paid as a result of civil accident

population active civile
civilian labour force / working
population

profession civile
civilian occupation

statistiques de l'état civil
vital statistics

victime civile de la guerre
civilian war victim

CIVIQUE
éducation / instruction civique
citizenship / civic education

organisation civique
civic organisation

CIVISME
public spirit, public-spiritedness

CLANDESTIN (adj.)
atelier clandestin
sweat shop

immigration clandestine
unauthorised / illegal immigration

immigré clandestin
illegal migrant / alien (USA)

main-d'oeuvre clandestine
unauthorised / undocumented labour

travail clandestin
black / hidden / moonlight / shadow /
submerged / twilight / underground / grey
economy; clandestine work, moonlighting

travailleur clandestin
illegal / clandestine / undeclared /
unauthorised / undocumented worker

CLANDESTIN (n.)
illegal migrant / alien (USA)

CLASSE
category, class; grade; level; bracket,
group

ancienneté dans la classe
seniority in / within grade

ancienneté requise dans la classe
time-in-grade requirement

**barème de conversion des points en
classes**
grade-point conversion scale

classe d'âge(s)
age group

classe d'âges de forte activité
prime (work / working) age (group)

classes (les) (plus) aisées
better-off (the)

classe d'ajustement
post adjustment class

classe d'ajustement négatif
negative post adjustment class

classe creuse
small age group

classe de début
(junior) entry / entrance level

classe laborieuse / ouvrière
working class

classes moyennes (Belg.)
small enterprises and traders

classe de perfectionnement
advanced / refresher / proficiency course

classe possédante
proprietary class

classe de salaire
wage class

classe sociale
social class

**fourchette de points pour les
différentes classes**
point range for classes

heures de classe
school hours

lutte des classes
class struggle

marin / matelot de deuxième classe
able(-bodied) seaman

**minimum d'ancienneté exigible dans
une classe**
minimum time-in-grade requirement

personnel hors classes
ungraded staff

poste hors classe
unclassified post

prime d'entrée dans les classes (Fr.)
allowance on entering the classes

**progression des traitements à
l'intérieur d'une même classe**
intra-grade salary progression

structure par classe
grade-level structure

structure des classes
grading structure

structure à n classes
n-grade level structure, n-level grading
structure

syndicat de classe (Spain)
non-corporatist union

système des classes alternées
double-shift system; dual sessions

**travailleur appartenant aux classes
d'âge de forte activité**
prime-age worker

CLASSEMENT
classification, ranking, grading (of a post-); codification

avis de classement
classification notice

classement par âge(s)
age distribution

classement aux fins des ajustements
post adjustment classification

classement des emplois
job classification

classement hiérarchique des emplois
labour ranking

classement des postes
job classification; codification of posts

classement (des postes) par attributions
duty classification of posts

classement (des postes) fondé sur le rang
rank classification of posts

classement des lieux d'affectation
classification of duty stations

demande de classement médical
medical clearance request

méthode du classement hiérarchique des emplois
job ranking method

norme de classement
standard of classification; grading standard

système de classement
system of classification, classification system; (occ.) grading system

système de classement des emplois par points
point-factor system of job classification

CLASSER
to classify; to rank; to dismiss

classer un poste
to classify a position

classer les traitements par ordre
to rank salary rates

CLASSIFICATION
classification; grading, ranking

classification par activité / par branche d'activité économique
industrial classification

classification des capacités
taxonomy of skills

classification des emplois
job classification / grading

Classification internationale des mala-dies (CIM)
International Classification of Diseases (ICD)

classification des maladies
classification of diseases

classification des postes
job classification

classification professionnelle
occupational classification

classification des tâches
classification of tasks; job grading

grille de classification (Fr.)
job category

système de classification des professions
occupational classification system

CLASSIQUE
classical; standard; academic

activité classique
mainstream activity

chômage classique
classical unemployment

enseignement de type classique
academic / formal education

CLAUSE
stipulation, clause, provision; (pl.) terms

clause d'abandon
waiver clause

clause abusive
unfair clause

clauses d'un accord
terms of an agreement

clause additionnelle
additional clause, rider

clause (optionnelle) d'adhésion
opting-in clause

clause d'antériorité
(occ.) grandfather clause

clause d'arbitrage
arbitration clause

clauses et conditions
terms

clause de dénonciation
termination clause

clause dérogatoire
escape / saving / dispensatory clause

clause (optionnelle) de désengagement
opting-out clause

clause de double indemnisation
double indemnity (clause)

clause d'embauche préférentielle
closed-shop clause

clause d'exclusion
exclusion clause

clauses de fond
substantive articles

clause de garantie (d'un accord)
guarantee clause; warranty

clause générale
standard clause

clause d'indexation
escalation / escalator clause, indexing /
indexation clause, pegging clause

clause d'intéressement
profit-sharing / incentive clause

clauses d'interprétation
understandings

clause de maintien des avantages acquis
(occ.) grandfather clause

clause de non-concurrence
non-competition clause, (occ.)
restrictive covenant

clause de paix sociale
no-strike / peace clause

clause de pénalité
penalty clause

clause de portée générale
(occ.) omnibus clause

clause de protection syndicale
closed-shop / union security clause

clauses de réduction, de suspension ou de suppression de prestations
provisions for reduction, suspension or
withdrawal of benefits

clause de renégociation
reopening clause

clause de résidence
residence clause

clause de résiliation
termination clause

clause restrictive
restrictive clause, proviso

clause de réversion
survivorship provision

clause de risque de grève
strikes clause

clause de rupture
termination clause

clause de sauvegarde
safety / escape / saving / hardship clause

clause de sécurité syndicale
closed-shop / union security clause

clause (optionnelle) de sortie
opting-out clause

clause-type
standard clause

dérogation aux clauses d'un contrat
deviation from the terms of a contract

résilier une clause
to annul a clause

CLAVIER
secrétaires et opérateurs sur claviers (411)]
secretaries and keyboard-operating clerks
[ISCO-1988 (411)]

CLÉ
clé de conversion
conversion key

contrat clés en mains
turn key job

emploi clé
key post / job / position

employeur clé
key employer

lettre clé
key letter

personnel clé
key staff / personnel

poste clé
key post / job / position

secteur clé
key sector

CLERGÉ
clergy

membres du clergé [CITP-1988 (246)]
religious professionals [ISCO-1988 (246)]

CLIENT
client, customer; user

organisme client
client body

**système de la rémunération d'après le
nombre de clients (med.)**
capitation-fee system

CLIENTÈLE
customers; users; practice

**clientèle de malades pris en charge
par le service public**
(occ.) public practice

clientèle privée (des médecins)
private practice

**employés de réception et
d'information de la clientèle [CITP-
1988) (422)]**
client information clerks [ISCO-1988
(422)]

CLIMAT
climat économique
business / economic climate

climat de travail
working atmosphere / environment,
work climate

CLIMATIQUE
station climatique
health resort

CLINIQUE (adj.)
soins cliniques
clinical care

CLINIQUE (n.)
clinic; nursing home

clinique d'accouchement
maternity home / hospital

clinique ouverte
open clinic

clinique privée
private clinic

directeur de clinique
nursing home administrator

CLOISONNEMENT
compartmentalisation

CLUB
club d'emploi
job club

club d'entreprise
staff club

club de femmes / féminin
women's club

club de jeunes
youth club

club de mères
mothers' club

club de recherche active d'emploi (Belg.)
job club

CODAGE
système de codage des postes
post coding system

CODE
code; coding scheme; statute book

code de bonne conduite
code of fair / good practice(s)

code de déontologie / déontologique
code of behaviour / of professional etiquette / of professional conduct

code d'éthique (professionnelle)
code of ethics / of behaviour

Code de la famille et de l'aide sociale
Family and Social Welfare Code

Code fiscal (UK)
Tax Code
code des impôts
tax law

Code de la mutualité
Code of mutual benefit societies

Code rural (Fr.)
rural Code

Code de la santé publique
Public Health Code

Code de la sécurité sociale
Social Security Code

Code du travail
Labour Code, labour laws

code d'usages / de l'usage
code of practice

CODÉCISION
co-determination

CODEX
Codex pharmacopoeia
Codex

CODIFICATION
codification

codification des actes médicaux
codification of items of care

codification des constats de décès
coding of death certificates

codification des fonctions
Common Directory of job Titles

COEFFICIENT
coefficient, ratio

coefficient d'(un) acte médical
reimbursement rate of a medical treatment, item of care coefficient

coefficient d'adaptation
corrective coefficient

coefficient d'ajustement au coût de la vie
cost-of-living differential factor

coefficient de calcul des pensions vieillesse
factor applied to the calculation of old age pensions

coefficient de charge
(old age) support ratio

coefficient de financement
funding ratio

coefficient d'invalidité
degree of disablement / invalidity

coefficient de longévité
vitality ratio

coefficient de minoration
reduction factor

coefficient de pondération
weight

coefficient de pondération constant
fixed weight

coefficient de recrutement différé
delayed recruitment factor

coefficient de réduction
reduction factor

coefficient de remplacement du revenu
income replacement ratio

coefficient de revalorisation
revalorisation coefficient

corrigé par un coefficient déflateur
deflated

CO(-)ENTREPRISE
joint venture

COERCITIF
mesure coercitive
enforcement measure

COFACTEUR
contributory factor

COGESTION
co-determination

COGNITIF
cognitive

compétence cognitive
cognitive skill

COHABITANT(E)
cohabitant, companion

COHABITATION
cohabitation; joint occupation

COHABITER
to cohabit

COHÉSION
cohésion sociale
social cohesion

COHORTE
cohorte d'âge
age cohort

COIFFEUR
coiffeurs, spécialistes des soins de
beauté et travailleurs assimilés [CITP-
1968 (5-7)]
hairdressers, barbers, beauticians and
related workers [ISCO-1968 (5-7)]

COIN
coin fiscal
tax wedge

CO-INVESTISSEMENT
co-investissement du salarié
employee's co-participation

COL
col blanc
white-collar (worker)

col bleu
blue-collar (worker)

COLLABORATEUR
contributor; collaborator; (pl.) staff

collaborateur indépendant
freelance (worker)

conjoint collaborateur
assisting spouse

**travailler comme collaborateur indé-
pendant**
to work freelance

COLLABORATION
collaboration, co-operation,
contribution;
partnership; team()work

convention de collaboration (Fr.)
collaboration agreement

COLLATÉRAL (adj.)
relations collatérales
(occ.) staff relations

COLLATÉRAL (n.)
(pl.) collaterals

COLLECTE
collection; collation

collecte de données
data collection

collecte de fonds
fund raising

COLLECTER
to collect; to raise

COLLECTIF (adj.)
community(-based); blanket

accord collectif d'établissement
working / staff / works agreement

accord collectif sur les salaires
collective pay agreement

accord collectif (de travail)
collective agreement

action collective
collective / trade union / job / industrial
action

action collective en justice
class action

activité d'intérêt collectif
community business activity

arrêt de travail collectif
collective work stoppage

centre collectif de soins
community health centre

cessation collective de travail
collective work stoppage

conflit collectif
labour dispute

contrat d'assurance collective
collective insurance contract

contrat collectif de retraite
group annuity policy

contrat collectif (de travail)
collective agreement

convention collective
collective (bargaining) / labour /
industrial agreement, labour(-
management) contract; union contract

**convention collective de branche /
sectorielle**
industry-wide collective agreement

convention collective du travail
collective labour agreement

crèche collective
collective day-care centre

équipements collectifs
(social / collective) infrastructure,
(public) utilities, community facilities

cycle de négociations collectives
collective bargaining round

domicile collectif
congregate housing

droit de / à la négociation collective
right to bargain collectively

entreprise d'intérêt collectif
community business venture

équipements collectifs
(social / collective) infrastructure,
(public) utilities, community facilities

habitat collectif
congregate housing

habitation collective
communal housing

hébergement collectif
communal living unit

intérêt collectif (d')
community(-based)

licenciement collectif
collective / mass dismissal, mass lay-off;
(mass) redundancy; blanket dismissal (in
case of offence committed by unindentified
worker)

**licenciement collectif pour motifs
économiques**
collective redundancy

logement collectif
congregate / shared housing

manifestation collective
mass manifestation

ménage collectif
collective / non-family household

négociation(s) collective(s)
collective bargaining / negotiations

organisme d'intérêt collectif
community(-based) organisation / agency

phase de négociations collectives
collective bargaining round

**politique en matière de négociation
collective**
collective bargaining policy

population des ménages collectifs (stat.)
institutional population

projet d'intérêt collectif
community project

propriété collective
collective ownership

régime d'assurance-traitement collectif
group salary insurance scheme

série de négociations collectives
collective bargaining round

service collectif
community service; (pl.) community
facilities

service d'intérêt collectif
community service

société en nom collectif
commercial partnership

tarification collective
collective rates

travail d'utilité collective (TUC)
community service / work; community
work scheme, workfare

COLLECTIF (n.)
collectif budgétaire
supplementary budget

collectif de défense des intérêts
citizens' action group, public interest
group

COLLECTIVITÉ
community; corporate body;
corporation; institutional / non-family
household

animateur de collectivité
community leader

collectivité agricole
farming community

collectivité locale
local government / authority

collectivité publique
public corporation

collectivité territoriale
local government

intérêt supérieur de la collectivité
ultimate interest of the community

médecine des collectivités
community medicine

participation de la collectivité
community involvement

programme d'aide à la collectivité
community assistance programme

**programme d'emploi des collectivités
locales**
community employment programme

**projet des / entrepris par les
collectivités locales**
community project

protection de la collectivité
community welfare

santé de la / des collectivité(s)
community health

service auprès de / fourni à la collectivité
community service / work; (pl.) (occ.)
community, social and personal services

service axé sur la collectivité et la famille
community and family-based service

service infirmier des collectivités
community health nursing service

**service sanitaire destiné à la collectivité /
service de santé des collectivités**
community health service

services sociaux de la collectivité
community welfare services

**services sociaux et services connexes
fournis à la collectivité**
social and related community services

COLLÈGE
college; panel; secondary school, middle
school

collège de cadres
managerial body of electors

collège électoral
body of electors

collège d'employés
non-managerial body of electors

collège de médecins
panel of doctors

collège privé (UK)
public school

COLLÈGUE
colleague, co-worker, fellow(-worker)

COLONIE
settlement

colonie pour enfants débiles (Belg.)
centre for underdeveloped children

colonie de squatters
squatter settlement

colonie de vacances
summer / holiday camp

COLONISATION
settlement

COMBATTANT
ancien combattant
veteran, ex-serviceman

pension d'invalidité des anciens combattants
veterans' disability pension

COMBINÉ
système combiné
dual / combined system

COMBLÉ (adj.)
taux de vacances comblées
vacancy fill rate

vacance comblée
vacancy filled

vacance non comblée
unfilled vacancy

COMBLER
vacance à combler
outstanding vacancy

COMITÉ
committee; board

**Comité des allocations pour soins
constants (UK)**
Attendance Allowance Board

comité de carrières
careers committee

comité central d'entreprise
central works committee

comité consultatif
advisory board / committee

comité directeur
steering committee

comité de direction
management / steering committee

Comité d'égalité (Austr.)
Equality Committee

comité d'entreprise
shop council; joint management - labour board, labour-management (joint) committee (Fr.), works council (Ger.), works committee

comité d'établissement
works committee / council (Ger.)

comité d'étude / d'examen
review board

comité d'hygiène, de sécurité et des conditions de travail (Fr.)
health and safety at work committee

comité d'hygiène et de sécurité
health and safety / safety and health committee

comité médical paritaire
joint medical committee

comité mixte
joint committee

comité mixte patronal - syndical
joint union - management committee

comité d'organisation
organising / (occ.) steering committee

comité d'orientation
steering committee

comité paritaire
joint committee

comité patronal - syndical
labour-management (joint) committee

comité de quartier
neighbourhood committee

comité régional de formation professionnelle (Fr.)
regional vocational training committee

comité des rentes
pensions committee

comité de révision
review board

Comité de supervision des pensions complémentaires (UK)
Reserve Pension Board

comité de surveillance
inspection / monitoring / supervising committee

comité technique paritaire
joint technical committee

Comité de travailleurs pour l'améliora-tion des conditions de travail (USA)
Employee Action Committee

comité de voisinage
neighbourhood committee

prestation sociale des comités d'entre-prise
social benefit paid by works committees

COMMANDE
travail à la commande
jobbing work; outwork

COMMERCE
agents commerciaux techniciens et voyageurs de commerce [CITP-1968 (4-3)]
technical salesmen, commercial travellers and manufacturers' agents [ISCO-1968 (4-3)]

chambre de commerce (et d'industrie)
chamber of commerce
commerce de détail
retail trade

école (supérieure) de commerce
business school

marin de commerce
merchant seaman

représentant de commerce
commercial traveller

secteur du commerce
trade industry

voyageur de commerce
commercial traveller

COMMERCIAL
activité commerciale
business activity

balance commerciale
balance of trade, trade balance

déficit de la balance commerciale
balance of trade deficit

déficit commercial
trade deficit

déséquilibre commercial
trade imbalance

droit commercial
business law

études commerciales
business studies

excédent de la balance commerciale
balance of trade surplus

excédent commercial
trade surplus

opération commerciale
(occ.) business venture

place commerciale
business place

pratiques commerciales
business practices

pratiques commerciales courantes
customary business practices

profession commerciale
commercial profession

professions industrielles et commerciales
industry and trade

revenus industriels et commerciaux
income from business

COMMIS (n.)
clerk

commis principal
principal / senior clerk

commis aux services aux usagers
help-desk clerk

commis vendeurs, employés de commerce et travailleurs assimilés [CITP-1968 (4-5)]
salesmen, shop assistants and related workers [ISCO-1968 (4-5)]

commis voyageur
commercial traveller

poste de commis
clerical post

premier commis
senior clerk

COMMISSAIRE
commissaire à l'assurance nationale (UK)
national insurance commissioner

commissaire du gouvernement
Government commissioner

COMMISSION
commission, committee, board; charge

Commission d'admission à l'aide sociale (Fr.)
Commission deciding on the eligibility for social welfare

commission d'appareillage
appliance commission

commission d'arbitrage
board of arbitration / of arbitrators, arbitration board / tribunal / commission; (occ.) grievance committee

Commission centrale d'aide sociale
Social Welfare Central Commission

commission de conciliation (Fr.)
conciliation board

commission consultative
advisory committee

commission de contrôle
supervisory board

Commission de l'équipement sanitaire
Health Facilities Commission

Commission d'évaluation des incapacités (Spain)
Incapacity Assessment Board

commission forfaitaire
lump-sum payment

Commission d'indemnisation (Austr.)
Compensation Board

Commission interparlementaire (UK)
Joint Committee

commission médicale
medical board

commission médicale périphérique
(occ.) district medical board

commission médico-psycho-pédagogique
child guidance commission

commission mixte
joint committee

commission paritaire
joint commission / committee

Commission des prestations complémentaires (UK)
Supplementary Benefits Commission

commission de recours
appeals board

commission de réforme
discharge board

commission salariale (paritaire)
wages council

commission scolaire
school board

Commission de séjour (Fr.)
Residence Committee

Commission spéciale (UK)
Select Committee

Commission des taux (UK)
Rating Board

rémunéré à la commission
employed on a commission basis

COMMODITÉ
convenience; (pl.) amenities, utilities

COMMONWEALTH
allocation d'éducation du
Commonwealth (Austr.)
Commonwealth education allowance

COMMUN
common; mutual

chambre commune (hosp.)
public ward

commun accord (d'un / de)
by mutual agreement

contrat de gestion commune de caisses
pooled accounts funding contract

mise en commun des revenus
income pooling

programmation commune
joint programming

régime commun
common system

régime commun des traitements
common salary scheme

système commun
common system

tronc commun
common core, core courses

COMMUNAL
centre communal d'action sociale
social work municipal centre

prestation pour taxe communale (UK)
community charge benefit

COMMUNAUTAIRE
community(-based)

association communautaire
community group

centre communautaire
community (welfare) centre; (occ.) living community

développement communautaire
community development

établissement d'enseignement post-secondaire communautaire (USA)
community college

médecine communautaire
community medicine

organisation / organisme communau-taire
community organisation

programme d'aide communautaire
community assistance programme

soins communautaires
community (health) care

COMMUNAUTÉ
community

communauté de vie
conjugal life

service social de communauté
community social work, social work with communities

travail au profit de la communauté
community service / work

COMMUNE
municipality

COMMUNICATION
chefs de services de transports et de communications [CITP-1968 (3-5)]
transport and communications supervisors [ISCO-1968 (3-5)]

communication obligatoire des emplois / offres d'emploi / postes vacants / vacances d'emploi
compulsory notification of vacancies

COMMUNIQUÉ (n.)
communiqué; press release; notice; statement

COMPAGNIE
compagnie d'assurance
insurance company

compagnie d'assurances mutuelles
mutual insurance company

compagnie maritime
shipping (line)

COMPAGNON
tradesman; craftsman; journeyman

compagnon de travail
fellow(-worker)

COMPAGNONNAGE
examen de compagnonnage
craftsman's / qualified / skilled workman's test

COMPARABILITÉ
comparability

COMPARABLE
chiffres / données comparables
comparable figures

postes de niveaux comparables
positions of the same level

COMPARAISON
comparaison intervilles
place to place comparison

comparaison portant sur la rémunération totale
total compensation comparison

comparaison temporelle / dans le temps
time-to-time comparison

point de comparaison
(occ.) comparator

COMPARATIF
comparative; standardised

analyse comparative
comparative analysis

chiffres /données comparati(fs)(ves)
comparative figures

tableau comparatif
comparative table

COMPENSATEUR
allocation / indemnité compensatrice
compensatory / equalisation allowance;
payment in lieu

indemnité compensatrice de congés payés
compensation in lieu of paid holidays,
holidays paid in lieu

indemnité compensatrice de préavis
compensation in lieu of notice, pay /
payment in lieu of notice

pension compensatrice
compensatory pension

repos compensateur
time off in lieu

COMPENSATION
compensation, set-off; equalisation;
replacement

caisse de compensation
compensation / equalisation / provident /
fund

caisse de compensation pour les accidents du travail et les maladies professionnelles
(occ.) workmen's compensation board

compensation des charges
pooling of risks

compensation monétaire
monetary compensation

compensation de / pour la perte de revenu(s)
compensation for loss of income,
income replacement / compensation

congé de compensation
compensatory leave / holiday

fonds de compensation
provident / compensation / equalisation
fund

indemnité de compensation (Pol.)
compensatory benefit

paiements de compensation
equalisation payments

taux de compensation
replacement ratio / rate

taux de compensation de la perte de revenu
income replacement ratio

taxe de compensation
compensatory charge; equalisation levy
(Neth.)

COMPENSATOIRE
allocation compensatoire
equalisation / compensatory allowance;
payment in lieu

complément compensatoire
equalisation supplement

congé compensatoire
compensatory leave / holiday

enseignement compensatoire
compensatory education

hausse salariale compensatoire
compensatory wage increase

indemnité compensatoire
hardship / compensatory / equalisation
allowance; payment in lieu

jour de congé compensatoire
day off in lieu

prélèvement compensatoire
compensatory levy

COMPENSER
to compensate, to make up; to indemnify

COMPÉTENCE
ability, skill, qualification, competence, competency; terms of reference; scope; function

acquisition de compétences
skill development

agent à compétence générale
general purpose worker

agent d'exécution à compétence générale
general field worker

amélioration des compétences
skill improvement / development

analyse des compétences
skills analysis

bilan de compétence(s)
skills' / vocational assessment

cartographie des compétences
skills inventory

catégorie de compétences
skill category

compétence pour (avoir)
to be competent for

compétence de base
basic / generic / entry skill

compétence cognitive
cognitive skill

compétences essentielles
key / core skills

compétence fonctionnelle
functional authority

compétences en gestion
management skills

compétences en mécanique
mechanical skills

compétence dans un / les métier(s)
trade(s) skill / ability

compétence obligatoire
compulsory jurisdiction

compétence particulière
specialised skill

compétences polyvalentes
(occ.) transferable skills

compétence professionnelle
vocational / occupational skill, employment / occupational / professional qualification

compétences recherchées
skill in demand

compétence requise
skill requirement; (pl.) necessary skills

compétence technique de haut niveau
high(er)-level technical skill

conflit de compétences
demarcation dispute

congé de bilan de compétence (Fr.)
vocational assessment leave

connaissances et compétences
skills and knowledge

degré de compétence
skill level

délégation de compétence
delegation of authority

domaine de compétence
field of expertise, specialised field, competency area

évaluation des compétences
assessment of skills, competency assessment

inventaire des compétences
skills inventory

manque de compétence
lack of skill

manque de compétences professionnelles
lack of occupational skills

niveau de compétence
competence / skill level, level of skill

niveau des compétences actuelles
current skill level

niveau de compétence professionnelle
occupational proficiency level

niveau élevé de compétence
high(er)-level skill

perfectionnement des compétences
skill improvement

profil des compétences
skill profile

revenu salarial proportionnel à ses compétences
salary commensurate with one's abilities

système d'acquisition de compétences
skill acquisition system

test de compétence
skill / proficiency test

transférabilité des compétences
skill transferability

travailleur à compétence unique
single-skilled employee

vivier de compétences
pool of talent

COMPÉTENT
capable, competent, able; skilled, qualified; trained; responsible for; relevant, concerned

agent compétent
responsible officer

autorité compétente
competent authority

Etat compétent
competent State

fonctionnaire compétent
appropriate official, authorised officer

institution compétente
appropriate / competent institution

ouvrier compétent
qualified worker

personne compétente
relevant person

travailleur compétent
skilled / suitable / qualified worker; skilled craftsman

COMPÉTITIF
Competitive

COMPÉTITION
competition

COMPÉTITIVITÉ
capacity to compete, competitiveness

COMPLAISANCE
accord de complaisance
convenience / (occ.) sweetheart arrangement

COMPLÉMENT
supplement; increment; supplementary benefit

complément pour l'adulte (UK)
adult credit

complément compensatoire
equalisation supplement

complément de dépendance (Finl.)
helplessness supplement

complément différentiel
equalisation supplement

complément pour l'enfant (UK)
child credit

complément extraordinaire de salaire (It.)
extraordinary wage supplement

complément (au / de revenu) familial
family supplement, family income supplement (UK); family credit (UK)

complément logement
housing supplement

complément ordinaire de salaire (It.)
ordinary wage supplement

complément de pension
pension supplement, topping-up pension

complément de pension générale (Swed.)
general pension supplement

complément de rémunération
earnings supplement

complément de revenu
income supplement, supplementary income, income support allowance

complément de salaire
pay / wage supplement

complément de salaire lié à la situation du marché de l'emploi (Swed.)
market pay supplement

complément salarial
remuneration supplement, top-up

complément social
(occ.) marginal benefit

COMPLÉMENTAIRE
additional, supplementary, complementary; incremental

allocation complémentaire
supplementary / additional allowance, supplement

allocation familiale complémentaire (Port.)
supplementary family allowance

allocation sociale complémentaire (Irel.)
supplementary welfare allowance

appel de cotisation complémentaire
supplementary call for contribution

assistance complémentaire
supplementary assistance

assurance complémentaire
supplementary insurance, complementary scheme

avantages complémentaires
marginal benefits

avantage complémentaire vieillesse (Fr.)
supplementary old age benefit

caisse de retraite complémentaire
complementary pension fund

Comité de supervision des pensions complémentaires (UK)
Reserve Pension Board

Commission des prestations complémentaires (UK)
Supplementary Benefits Commission

cotisation sociale complémentaire
supplementary welfare contribution

disposition complémentaire
additional provision

éducation complémentaire
further education

établissement d'éducation complémentaire
college of further education

formation complémentaire
further education, further (education and) training, post-initial / supplementary training; upgrading

formation complémentaire à l'obtention du diplôme de base
postbasic training

heures complémentaires
additional hours

opter pour la non-affiliation / le non-assujettissement au régime général de retraite complémentaire
to contract out

pension complémentaire (UK)
supplementary pension

pension complémentaire du régime général (UK)
reserve pension

prestation complémentaire
supplementary benefit

prestation complémentaire pour charges locatives (Irel.)
rent supplement
prestation complémentaire pour intérêts

hypothécaires (Irel.)
mortgage interest supplement

régime complémentaire
complementary scheme

régime complémentaire de retraite
company / occupational pension plan /
scheme

**régime complémentaire des travailleurs
des charbonnages / des houillères**
colliery workers supplementary scheme

**régime contributif de pensions com-
plémentaires du régime général (UK)**
contributory reserve pension scheme

**régime légal complémentaire profes-
sionnel**
occupation statutory complementary
scheme

régime de retraite complémentaire
complementary pension scheme

**régime de retraite complémentaire géré
par l'Etat**
State earnings-related pension scheme

régime de retraite complémentaire privé
private / contracted-out occupational
pension scheme

**régime de retraite complémentaire privé
en gestion directe**
self-administered pension scheme

**régime de retraite professionnelle
complémentaire (UK)**
occupational pension scheme

**rente complémentaire pour épouse
(Switz.)**
wife's supplementary pension

retraite complémentaire
company / occupational pension;
complementary pension

retraite professionnelle complémentaire
company / occupational pension

revenu complémentaire
secondary / complementary income

COMPLÉMENTARITÉ
additionality; complementarity

critère de complémentarité
additionality (criterion)

COMPLET
complete, total

année complète
full(-)year

chômage complet
full / total unemployment

chômeur complet
fully / wholly unemployed

complet (être au)
to be at full strength (staff)

**école dispensant un enseignement à
temps complet**
full-time school

emploi à temps complet
full-time job / employment

employé à temps complet
full-time employee

formation à temps complet
full-time training

garde complète d'enfants
full-time care for children

horaire complet (à)
full time

misère complète
absolute distress

orphelin complet
full orphan, orphan whose parents are
dead, orphan having lost both parents

pension complète
full pension, full retirement benefit

pension d'orphelin complet (Austr.)
double orphan pension

pension de retraite complète
standard retirement benefit, full pension

**période de chômage complète,
période complète de chômage**
completed spell of unemployment

personnel (employé) à temps complet
full-time staff

population active à temps complet
full-time labour force

retraite complète
full pension, full retirement benefit

soins complets
comprehensive care

stagiaire à temps complet
full-time trainee

statut de travailleur à temps complet
full-time status

temps complet (à)
full-time

travail en année complète
full-year work

travail à temps complet
full-time work / employment / job

travailleur en année complète
full-year worker

COMPLÉTER
to make up

compléter le salaire
to make up wage(s)

COMPLEXE (adj.)
ménage complexe
joint family, complex / composite
household

COMPLEXE (n.)
complexe de loisirs
recreational / holiday centre

complexe résidentiel
housing project / estate

complexe scientifique
science park

COMPORTEMENT
behaviour; pattern

bon comportement professionnel
good performance

**bon comportement professionnel
établi**
demonstrated good performance

comportement antisocial / asocial
anti-social behaviour

comportement dans l'emploi
employment behaviour

comportement injurieux
insulting behaviour

comportement de la main-d'oeuvre
labour force behaviour

comportement du marché du travail
labour market performance

comportement en termes de mobilité
mobility behaviour

comportement perturbateur
disruptive behaviour

comportement de la population active
labour force behaviour

comportement professionnel
employment behaviour; performance on
the job, job performance

**grille des comportements attendus
par type de fonction**
behaviour expectation scale

norme de comportement
standard of behaviour

**(système de) rapport d'appréciation
du comportement professionnel**
performance evaluation report (system)

variable de comportement
behaviour variable

COMPORTEMENTAL
behavioural

qualité comportementale
behavioural skill

COMPOSÉ (adj.)
intérêts composés
compound interest

COMPOSÉ (n.)
composés azoïques
azo-compounds

composés nitrés
nitro-compounds

COMPOSITE
famille composite
composite / joint family

COMPOSITEUR
compositeurs typographes et travailleurs
assimilés [CITP-1968 (9-2)]
printers and related workers [ISCO-1968 (9-2)]

COMPOSITION
composition; membership; pattern

composition par âge(s)
age distribution / pattern /structure

composition des effectifs
work force composition

composition du ménage
household structure

composition professionnelle
occupational distribution / composition /
pattern

COMPRESSION
compression budgétaire
budget cut

compression d'effectifs / de personnel
staff / manpower / work force reduction,
reduction in personnel / of staff, displacement; labour shake-out / shedding;
employment cut-back

compression des postes
job squeeze

compression des salaires
wage compression

politique de compression des dépenses
policy of retrenchment

**travailleur licencié pour compression
de personnel**
redundant worker

COMPROMETTRE
to endanger, to jeopardise, to prejudice

COMPROMIS
compromise; arrangement

compromis global
package deal

négociation de compromis
concession bargaining

COMPTABILISÉ
dépenses comptabilisées
recorded expenditure

recettes comptabilisées d'avance
deferred income

COMPTABILITÉ
comptabilité auxiliaire
subsidiary accounts

comptabilité nationale
national accounts

comptabilité publique
fiscal / public accounting

comptabilité sociale
social accounts / accounting

COMPTABLE (adj.)
agent comptable
accountant

exercice comptable
accounting year / period

COMPTABLE (n.)
comptables [CITP-1968 (1-1)]
accountants [ISCO-1968 (1-1)]

expert-comptable
chartered accountant

COMPTAGE
double comptage
double count / counting

méthode de comptage
counting method

COMPTE
account

compte d'affectation spéciale
earmarked account

compte d'attente
suspense account

comptes auxiliaires
subsidiary accounts

**compte économique de la formation
professionnelle (Fr.)**
vocational training economic account

compte d'excédents budgétaires
surplus account

compte de garantie bloqué
escrow account

comptes du ménage
household budget

comptes de la nation
national accounts / accounting

compte des opérations courantes
current account

compte d'ordre
suspense account

compte des paiements courants
current account

compte salaire
payroll account

compte satellite de la protection sociale
satellite account for social welfare

comptes sociaux de la nation
national social accounts

compte de tutelle
guardianship account

installer à son compte (s')
to set up on one's own

obligation de rendre compte
obligation to report; accountability

tenir compte (ne pas)
to disregard

personne travaillant à son compte
worker on own account; freelance
(worker)

personnel travaillant à son compte
freelance personnel

reçu pour solde de tout compte (Fr.)
receipt of final pay

**revenu à prendre en compte / en con-
sidération**
reckonable earnings

salaire pour solde de tout compte
terminated employee's final pay

travailleur pour compte d'autrui
employee

travailleur établi à son compte
self-employed (person / worker)

COMPTER
compter trois années de résidence
to have complete three years' residence

CONCENTRATION
industrie à forte concentration de main-
d'oeuvre
labour-intensive industry

CONCERTATION
consultation; dialogue

CONCERTÉ
concerted; consensual

planification concertée
joint planning

CONCILIATEUR
arbitrator, conciliation officer, conciliator

CONCILIATION
conciliation

commission de conciliation (Fr.)
conciliation board

conciliation individuelle
individual conciliation

conciliation entre partenaires sociaux
collective conciliation

conciliation sociale
collective conciliation

conseil de conciliation
conciliation board

procédure de conciliation
conciliation arrangement / procedure

procédure de conciliation et d'arbitrage
conciliation and arbitration procedure

procédure paritaire de conciliation
joint conciliation procedure

procès-verbal de conciliation
minutes of conciliation

Service de consultation, de conciliation et d'arbitrage (UK)
Advisory, Conciliation and Arbitration Service (ACAS)

tentative de conciliation
arbitration / conciliation attempt

CONCLU
accord librement conclu
voluntary agreement

CONCLUSION
conclusion; finding; termination

CONCOURIR
to contribute, to support; to compete

CONCOURS
assistance, support, aid, contribution;
competition, examination; overlapping

appel à des concours extérieurs
use of outside expertise

avis de concours
competition notice

concours annuel
annual (competitive) examination

concours d'avancement
competitive examination for promotion

concours de droits
overlapping of rights

concours d'entrée
(competitive) entrance examination

concours externe
open competition

concours public
open competition

mutation sans concours
transfer without competition

présenter à un concours (se)
to sit for a (competitive) examination

sélection sur / par / par voie de concours
competitive method of selection

CONCRET
cas concret
(occ.) case study

expérience concrète du travail
practical (work) / hands-on / on-the job experience

CONCUBIN(E)
cohabitant, companion

CONCUBINAGE
unmarried cohabitation

concubinage (en)
cohabiting

CONCURRENCE
competition

capacité de concurrence
competitiveness

concurrence de (à)
within the limits of

concurrence loyale
fair competition

emploi soumis à la concurrence
competitive employment

libre concurrence
freedom of competition

CONCURRENTIEL
competitive

capacité concurrentielle
competitiveness

emploi concurrentiel
open employment

salaire concurrentiel
competitive wage

CONDAMNÉ
malade condamné
terminally ill

CONDISCIPLE
fellow student

CONDITION
condition; qualification; position; proviso;
restriction; (pl.) terms, standard

assujetti à une condition de ressources
subject to means test

clauses et conditions
terms

**Comité d'hygiène, de sécurité et des
conditions de travail (Fr.)**
Health and Safety at Work Committee

**Comité de travailleurs pour l'améliora-
tion des conditions de travail (USA)**
Employee Action Committee

condition d'accès
entry standard / requirement,
requirement / condition for access / of
admission / for en-trance / for entry,
entrance requirement

conditions d'adhésion
membership requirements

condition d'admissibilité
qualifying condition; eligibility requirement

condition d'admission
qualifying condition; entry standard /
requirement, requirement for entry / for
access, entrance / admission
requirement, condition of admission;
eligibility

condition d'admission au bénéfice de
eligibility criteria / requirement

**conditions d'admission au bénéfice de
(remplir les)**
to be eligible

**conditions d'admission à l'aide
sociale**
qualifying conditions to welfare benefits

condition d'affiliation
entry standard / requirement,
requirement for entry / for access,
entrance requirement; eligibility

condition d'âge
age condition / qualification; qualifying
age

conditions d'application du contrat
terms and conditions of the agreement

condition d'attribution
qualifying condition; eligibility (requirement); condition of entitlement

**conditions d'attribution des
prestations**
conditions governing eligibility for
benefits

condition de cotisation
contribution condition

condition discriminatoire
discriminatory requirement

condition de durée de service
service requirement / eligibility

conditions d'embauche
terms and conditions / particulars of
employment; conditions of service / of
employment / of work

condition d'emploi
(pl.) terms of appointment; conditions of
service / of employment

condition d'emploi statutaire
statutory condition of service

conditions d'entrée
conditions for access / of admission / for
entrance / for entry, entrance requirements

conditions les plus favorables
best prevailing conditions

condition féminine
status of women

condition de fond
substantive restriction

condition de forme
formal restriction

condition d'inscription
admission requirement

condition légale de travail
legal employment requirement

condition minimale d'ouverture des droits
minimum qualifying condition

condition d'octroi
qualifying condition; (pl.) eligibility,
conditions of entitlement

conditions d'octroi des prestations
conditions governing eligibility for benefits

condition d'ouverture des droits
qualifying condition; condition of
entitlement; eligibility

conditions de paiement
terms of payment

condition préalable
pre-condition

conditions prévues (dans les)
on the conditions provided for

conditions de recevabilité
(occ.) eligibility

conditions de règlement
terms of settlement

condition réglementaire
statutory condition

condition requise
requirement, required / relevant
condition; qualification; (pl.) (occ.)
eligibility

conditions requises (qui ne remplit pas les)
unqualified

conditions requises (remplissant les / réunissant les / répondant aux)
eligible; qualified; suitable

conditions requises pour être promu (remplir les)
to be eligible for promotion

condition de résidence
residence requirement

condition de ressources
means test

condition de ressources (sans)
without means test

condition de ressources (sous)
on a means-test basis; means-tested

conditions salariales
wage conditions; details of salaries

condition sociale
social status; position

condition de stage
qualifying period

condition de stage (sans)
without qualifying period

conditions de travail
work(ing) / employment conditions,
conditions of work; work environment;
work practices

condition de / requise pour le versement des prestations
qualifying condition for benefits

conditions de vie
conditions of living, living conditions; (occ.) welfare

conditions de voyage
travel conditions / arrangements; standard of travel accommodation

enquête sur les conditions d'emploi les plus favorables
survey of best prevailing conditions of service

imposer aucune condition de stage (n')
to impose no qualifying period

mauvaises conditions de travail
poor working conditions

prestation ouverte sans condition
unconditional / (occ.) vested benefit

prestation liée à / soumise à / subordonnée à une / versée sous condition de ressources
means-tested / income-tested benefit

remplir une condition
to satisfy a condition; (pl.) to comply with / to fulfil the conditions

remplir les conditions (ne pas)
(occ.) to be ineligible

remplir les conditions d'admission
to qualify for membership

remplir les conditions d'ouverture des droits aux prestations
to be eligible for / to qualify for benefit, to satisfy the conditions for acquisition of the rights to benefits

remplir les conditions nécessaires / requises / voulues (pour bénéficier / avoir droit)
to qualify for; to fulfil requirements; to be eligible

remplir à nouveau les conditions requises pour
to requalify for

remplissant les conditions requises / voulues
qualified for; suitable; eligible

réunir les conditions
to fulfil the conditions

réunir les conditions (ne pas)
(occ.) to be ineligible

satisfaire à une condition
to satisfy a condition

satisfaire aux conditions requises pour être promu
to satisfy the standards required for promotion

soumis à (une) condition de ressources
subject to a means test, means-tested

subordonné à une condition de ressources
subject to a means test, means-tested

subordonné à une condition de stage
subject to a qualifying period

substitution de condition
substitution of condition

versé sous conditions de ressources
means-tested

versé sous condition de revenu
income-tested

CONDITIONNÉ
conditionné par
dependent on, conditioned by, affected by

CONDITIONNEL
conditional; qualified; provisional

acquisition conditionnelle
conditional vesting (of a pension)

inscription conditionnelle à un stage
conditional referral to a course

nomination conditionnelle
conditional appointment

CONDUCTEUR
operator

autres conducteurs de machines et ouvriers de l'assemblage [CITP-1988 (829)]
other machine operators and assemblers [ISCO-1988 (829)]

conducteurs de chaînes de montage automatiques et de robots industriels [CITP-1988 (817)]
automated-assembly-line and industrial-robot operators [ISCO-1988 (817)]

conducteurs d'engins de manutention et de terrassement, dockers et manu-tentionnaires [CITP-1968 (9-7)]
material-handling and related equipment operators, dockers and freight handlers [ISCO-1968 (9-7)]

conducteurs d'engins de transport [CITP-1968 (9-8)]
transport equipment operators [ISCO-1968 (9-8)]

conducteurs de fours et d'appareils chimiques [CITP-1968 (7-4)]
chemical processers and related workers [ISCO-1968 (7-4)]

conducteurs d'installations d'exploita-tion minière et d'extraction des miné-raux [CITP-1988 (811)]
mining and mineral-processing-plant operators [ISCO-1988 (811)]

conducteurs d'installations et de ma-chines et ouvriers de l'assemblage ([CITP-1988 (8)]
plant and machine operators and as-semblers [ISCO-1988 (8)]

conducteurs d'installations et de matériels fixes et assimilés [CITP-1988 (81)]
stationary plant and related operators [ISCO-1988 (81)]

conducteurs d'installations de produc-tion d'énergie et assimilés [CITP-1988 (816)]
power-production and related plant operators [ISCO-1988 (816)]

conducteurs d'installations de traite-ment chimique [CITP-1988 (815)]
chemical-processing-plant operators [ISCO-1988 (815)]

conducteurs d'installations pour le travail du bois et de la fabrication du papier [CITP-1988 (814)]
wood-processing-and papermaking-plant operators [ISCO-1988 (814)]

conducteurs d'installations de transfor-mation des métaux [CITP-1988 (812)]
metal-processing-plant operators [ISCO-1988 (812)]

conducteurs d'installations de verrerie et de céramique et assimilés [CITP-1988 (813)]
glass, ceramics and related plant-operators [ISCO-1988 (813)]

conducteur international
international transport worker

conducteurs de locomotives et assimilés [CITP-1988 (831)]
locomotive engine drivers and related workers [ISCO-1988 (831)]

conducteur de machine
machine operator

conducteurs de machines à bois [CITP-1988 (824)]
wood-products machine operators [ISCO-1988 (824)]

conducteurs de machines pour la fabrication de denrées alimentaires et de produits connexes [CITP-1988 (828)]
food and related products machine operators [ISCO-1988 (828)]

conducteurs de machines pour la fabrication de produits en caoutchouc et en matières plastiques [CITP-1988 (823)]
rubber- and plastic-products machine operators [ISCO-1988 (823)]

conducteurs de machines pour la fabrication des produits chimiques [CITP-1988 (822)]
chemical-products machine operators [ISCO-1988 (822)]

conducteurs de machines pour la fabrication de produits textiles et d'articles en fourrure et en cuir [ISCO-1988 (826)]
textile-, fur- and leather-products machine operators [ISCO-1988 (826)]

conducteurs de machines d'imprimerie, de machines à relier et de machines de papeterie [CITP-1988 (825)]
printing-, binding-and paper-products machine operators [ISCO-1988 (825)]

conducteurs de machines et d'installations fixes [CITP-1968 (9-6)]
stationary engine and related equipment operators [ISCO-1968 (9-6)]

conducteurs de machines et ouvriers de l'assemblage [CITP-1988 (82)]
machine operators and assemblers [ISCO-1988 (82)]

conducteurs de machines à travailler les métaux et les produits minéraux [CITP-1988 (821)]
metal-and mineral-products machine operators [ISCO-1988 (821)]

conducteurs de matériels mobiles agricoles et d'autres engins mobiles [CITP-1988 (833)]
agricultural and other mobile plant operators [ISCO-1988 (833)]

conducteur de travaux
site foreman

conducteurs de véhicules et d'engins lourds de levage et de manoeuvre [CITP-1988 (83)]
drivers and mobile plant operators [ISCO-1988 (83)]

conducteurs de véhicules à moteur [CITP-1988 (832)]
motor vehicle drivers [ISCO-1988 (832)]

CONDUITE
conduct; behaviour; practice

code de bonne conduite
code of fair / good practice(s)

conduite du traitement (med.)
(occ.) case management

ligne de conduite
guideline; course of action; policy

normes de conduite
standard of conduct

CONFECTIONNEUR
confectionneurs d'articles en papier et en carton [CITP-1968 (9-1)]
paper and paperboard products makers [[ISCO-1968 (9-1)]

CONFÉRENCIER
lecturer

CONFÉRER
conférer un droit acquis
to endow with an acquired right

CONFESSIONNEL
école confessionnelle
confessional school

CONFIANCE
confidence; trust

abus de confiance
breach of trust; misappropriation

confiance en soi
self-reliance

mesure visant à développer la confiance en soi
self-confidence-building measure

CONFIGURATION
layout; confirguration; shape; pattern

CONFINÉ
confiné chez soi
housebound

CONFIRMÉ
experienced, full fledged

cadre confirmé
seasoned manager

expérience confirmée
proven experience

travailleur confirmé
experienced worker

CONFIRMER
confirmer dans un poste / une fonction
to confirm in a job

CONFLICTUEL
objectifs conflictuels
conflict of objectives / of goals, goal
conflict

CONFLIT
conflict, dispute; confrontation

acte commis à l'occasion d'un conflit du travail
act done in furtherance of a trade dispute

acte commis en vue d'un conflit du travail
act done in contemplation of a trade dispute

conflit d'attributions
(occ.) demarcation dispute

conflit collectif
labour dispute

conflit de compétences
demarcation dispute

conflit de / des générations
generation gap
conflit individuel
individual dispute

conflit d'intérêts
conflict of interest

conflit professionnel
labour / industrial / trade dispute

conflit non réglé
unresolved dispute

conflit salarial
pay / wage dispute

conflit social
labour / industrial dispute; (pl.) labour / industrial unrest

conflit de / du travail
labour / industrial conflict / dispute, trade dispute

procédure de règlement d'un conflit social
(industrial) dispute procedure

règlement d'un conflit
dispute settlement / resolution, settlement of a dispute

CONFORME
certifié conforme par
authenticated by

conforme aux normes établies / fixées (être)
to fulfil requirements

travail non conforme
below-standard work

CONFORMER (se)
to abide by, to comply

CONFORMITÉ
conformity, compliance

certificat de conformité des moyens de sécurité incendie
fire certificate

CONFORT
éléments de confort
amenities

médicament de confort
comfort / ease drug

soins d'hygiène et de confort
basic nursing care

CONFRÈRE
(male) colleague; fellow member

CONFRÉRIE
guild

CONFRONTATION
confrontation; matching

confrontation des hommes et des postes
man-job matching

CONGÉ
holiday; leave; time off; absence; release;
notice

accorder un congé
to grant leave

accorder un congé payé
to grant paid leave; to release an employee
with pay

accumuler un congé
to accrue a leave

avance sur congé annuel
advance annual leave

congé d'accident de travail
injury-on-duty leave

congé d'adoption
adoption leave

congé d'ancienneté
long-service / furlough leave

congé annuel
annual leave, (annual) vacation; (pl.) annual
holiday

congé annuel payé, congé payé annuel
annual paid leave; paid vacation

congé autorisé
authorised absence, approved leave, leave
of absence

congé de bienveillance
leave for compassionate reasons

congé de bilan de compétence (Fr.)
vocational assessment leave

congé de compensation / compensatoire
compensatory leave / holiday

congé pour convenance(s) personnelle(s)
leave of absence for personal reasons;
casual / compassionate leave

congé de conversion
retraining leave

congé de déplacement
travel leave

congé de détente
(rest and) recuperation leave

congé-éducation / d'éducation (Ger.)
education(al) leave, child raising leave

congé-éducation payé
paid education(al leave)

congé enseignement (Fr.)
leave for teaching purposes

congé d'études
education(al) / study leave

congé pour événements familiaux (Fr.)
special family leave

congé examen (Fr.)
examination leave

congé pour exercice de fonctions publiques
time off (work) for public duties

congé (de)(-) formation
leave for training purposes, training /
study leave

congé de formation à l'Etat (Belg.)
State training leave

congé de formation jeunes travailleurs (Fr.)
young workers training leave

congé dans les foyers
home leave

congés fractionnés
split holidays

congé individuel de formation (Fr.)
individual / personal training leave

congé individuel de formation pour les salariés (Fr.)
individual training leave for employees

congé légal
statutory holiday

congé local
local holiday

congé de maladie
sick leave

congé de maladie approuvé
certified sick leave

congé de maladie à mi-temps
half-time sick leave

congé de maternité
maternity / pregnancy leave

congé mobile
floating holiday

congé de naissance
maternity / birth leave

congé pour obsèques
funeral leave

congé parental
parental leave

congé parental d'éducation (Fr.)
parental childcare leave

congé parental rémunéré
paid parental leave

congé de paternité
paternity leave

congé payé
paid leave, leave / time off with pay; (pl.)
holiday with pay, paid holiday, vacation pay
(USA)

congé non payé
absence / leave without pay

congé de perfectionnement
career / skill development leave, leave for
development purposes

congé postnatal
post(-)natal leave

congé prénatal
pre(-)natal leave

congé prolongé
extended leave

congé pour raisons de famille / familiales / personnelles / spéciales
leave of absence for personal / special
reasons; (occ.) compassionate leave

congé de réadaptation
rehabilitation leave

congé rémunéré
leave / time off with pay; (pl.) paid
holiday

congé de représentation (Fr.)
representation leave (in order to carry
out elected duties)

congé sabbatique
sabbatical leave

congé sans salaire
leave without pay

congés scolaires
school holidays / vacation

congé pour soins aux enfants (Swed.)
child care leave

congé sans solde
unpaid leave, leave without pay;
absence without pay

congé spécial
special leave

congé spécial d'ancienneté
special long-service leave

congé spécial à demi-traitement
special leave with half pay

congé spécial à plein traitement
special leave with full pay

congé spécial sans traitement
special leave without pay

congé spécial à traitement partiel
special leave with partial pay

congé (d'études) à temps partiel
part-time day release

congé sans traitement
leave without pay

crédit d'attente pour le congé dans les foyers
credit for home leave travel

décompte des jours de congé
leave record keeping

défalquer les congés d'un fonctionnaire
to undercredit a staff member for leave

délai-congé (Fr.)
notice of dismissal

délai de congé
term of notice

demande de congé
application for leave

demi-journée de congé
half day's leave

droit aux congés
vacation / holiday / leave entitlement

épuiser ses jours de congés payés
to use up one's holiday entitlement

état de congés
leave report

fractionnement des congés
split holidays; holiday splitting

indemnité compensatrice de congés payés
compensation in lieu of paid holidays,
holidays paid in lieu

indemnité de congé de maternité sans solde (Austr.)
unpaid maternity leave allowance

indemnité de congés payés
compensation for holiday leave

jours de congé annuel accumulés
accrued annual leave

jour de congé compensatoire
day off in lieu

jours de congé-études
day release education

lieu de congé dans les foyers
place of home leave

notification (de la date) du congé de maternité
notice of maternity absence

période de congé
holiday period

provisions pour congés payés
reserve for holiday leave

recevoir congé
to receive notice to quit

registre des congés
leave record

relevé de congé annuel
annual leave record

reliquat de congés
residual leave

report de jours de congé accumulés
transfer of accrued leave

reporter des congés d'une année à l'autre
to carry over outstanding holidays from
one year to the next

retour tardif de congés
late return from holidays

salaire dû pendant les congés
holiday / leave pay

solde de jours de congé annuel accumulés / total des congés annuels accumulés
accrued annual leave balance

CONGÉDIEMENT
discharge, dismissal

congédiement arbitraire
arbitrary discharge

lettre de congédiement
letter of discharge

CONGÉDIER
to dismiss

CONJOINT (adj.)
entreprise conjointe
joint venture

examen médical conjoint
joint medical examination

mineur sous protection conjointe (Fr.)
legally and socially protected minor

opération conjointe
joint venture

placement conjoint
associate placement

projet conjoint
joint project

CONJOINT (n.)
spouse; married person; (pl.) parties to a
marriage

activité professionnelle du conjoint
working status of the spouse

allocation au conjoint (Can.)
spouse allowance

**allocation au conjoint pour veufs et
veuves (Can.)**
widowed spouse's allowance

conjoint aidant
helping spouse, spouse helping

conjoint à charge
dependent spouse

conjoint collaborateur
assisting spouse

conjoint survivant
surviving spouse

majoration pour conjoint
increase / supplement in respect of spouse

**majoration de la pension de retraite pour
conjoint à charge**
pension supplement / increase in respect of
a dependent spouse

rente de conjoint
spouse life pension

CONJONCTURE
business situation / climate, economic
conditions; business conditions / cycle;
condition; (cyclical) trend

conjoncture ascendante
rising trend

conjoncture immobilière
housing trends

conjoncture du marché du travail
labour market conditions

**détérioration / fléchissement de la
conjoncture**
downturn of the economy

enquête de conjoncture
business (climate) survey

retournement de la conjoncture
cyclical upturn

**sensible aux variations de la
conjoncture**
(occ.) cyclically sensitive

CONJONCTUREL
conjunctural; cyclical; (econ.) short-
term

chômage conjoncturel
cyclical unemployment

chômeur conjoncturel
victim of cyclical unemployment

cycle conjoncturel
economic cycle

évolution conjoncturelle
economic development/ trend; business
/ cyclical trend

fluctuation conjoncturelle
business fluctuation, fluctuation in
business / economic activity

indicateur conjoncturel
business indicator

perspectives conjoncturelles
business outlook / prospect

politique conjoncturelle
business cycle policy

tendance conjoncturelle
business / cyclical trend

théorie conjoncturelle
business cycle theory

CONJUGAL
matrimonial

abandon de / du domicile conjugal
desertion (of the matrimonial home)

conseil d'orientation conjugale
marriage guidance council

conseiller conjugal
marriage counsellor

consultations conjugales
marriage counselling / guidance

domicile conjugal
marital domicile, matrimonial home

famille conjugale / du type noyau conjugal
conjugal family

service de consultations conjugales
marriage counselling / guidance

vie conjugale
married life

CONNAISSANCE
acquisition de connaissances
learning

bonnes connaissances pratiques
good working knowledge

connaissances de base
basic / (occ.) life skills

connaissances et compétences
skills and knowledge

connaissances élémentaires
basic / (occ.) life skills

connaissance pratique d'une langue
working knowledge of a language

connaissances techniques
(occ.) expertise, know-how

connaissances théoriques et pratiques
knowledge and skills

culture de la connaissance
culture of learning

intensité de connaissances
knowledge intensity

prime de connaissances linguistiques
language allowance / bonus

test de connaissances
knowledge test, test of knowledge

validation des connaissances
skill recognition, recognition of skills

CONNEXE
conducteurs de machines pour la fabrication de denrées alimentaires et de produits connexes [CITP-1988 (828)]
food and related products machine operators [ISCO-1988 (828)]

emploi / métier connexe
allied / related occupation / job

CONSACRÉ
usage consacré
established practice

CONSCIENCE
conscience ouvrière
working class consciousness

CONSCIENCIEUX
travail consciencieux
competent work

CONSCRIPTION
conscription

CONSCRIT
draftee, conscript, national serviceman (UK)

CONSÉCUTIF
orientation consécutive au placement
post-employment / post-placement counselling

CONSEIL
board, council; counsellor; (pl.) assistance, advice, counselling, guidance

actuaire-conseil
consulting actuary

bureau de conseils en personnel
personnel consultancy

conseil d'administration
board of directors; governing body

conseil d'arbitrage
adjudication tribunal

conseil de conciliation
conciliation board

conseil consultatif
advisory board / council

conseil de direction
governing body; management board

conseil de discipline
disciplinary board

conseil de gestion
management board

conseil en gestion de carrière
career counselling

conseil municipal
town council

conseil des oeuvres sociales
(occ.) community council

conseil d'orientation conjugale / matri-moniale
marriage guidance council

conseil ouvrier (Pol.)
workers' council

Conseil des pensions professionnelles (UK)
Occupational Pensions Board

conseil du personnel
staff council

Conseil privé du Roi (Norw.)
King in Council

conseil des prud'hommes (Fr.)
industrial court / tribunal (UK), labour court

conseil en matière de réadaptation
(pl.) rehabilitation counselling

conseil régional
county / district council

conseil régional des hôpitaux (UK)
hospital regional board

conseil des salaires (UK)
wage council

conseil scolaire
school board

conseil de surveillance
supervisory board

conseil syndical local
local labour council

conseil du travail (au niveau local)
local labour council

conseil de tutelle
supervisory board

expert-conseil
consultant

expert-conseil en gestion
managerial consultant

expert-conseil pour la jeunesse
youth consultant

expert-conseil sectoriel
industrial consultant

médecin-conseil
medical consultant / adviser,
supervising medical consultant

pharmacien-conseil
pharmaceutical adviser

praticien-conseil
health adviser

service de conseils
counselling service

service de conseils en matière d'emploi
employment advisory service

services de conseils familiaux
counselling for families, family
counselling

CONSEILLER (n.)
counsellor, adviser; mentor (trainees)

conseiller actuariel
consulting actuary

conseiller pour les / aux affaires sociales
social adviser

conseiller en apprentissage
apprenticeship counsellor

conseiller conjugal
marriage counsellor

conseiller en égalité (Norw.)
equality consultant

conseiller à l'emploi, conseiller emploi (Belg.)
employment / vocational adviser

conseiller de formation (Neth.)
training counsellor

conseiller des jeunes
youth advisor

conseiller juridique
legal advisor

conseiller matrimonial
marriage (guidance) counsellor

conseiller médical
medical adviser

conseiller municipal
town councillor

conseiller d'orientation
career(s) adviser / officer, guidance counsellor; school counsellor

conseiller en / d'orientation professionnelle
vocational (guidance) counsellor, career officer

conseiller principal
senior adviser

conseiller professionnel
careers adviser

conseiller prud'hommes
labour court member

conseiller en réadaptation / en rééducation
rehabilitation counsellor

conseiller sectoriel
industrial consultant

conseiller de service social
social welfare adviser

conseiller social
employment / staff / work counsellor; social adviser

conseiller spécialisé
specialist counsellor

conseiller technique
technical advisor

conseiller du travail
employment / work counsellor; industrial social / welfare worker; staff counsellor

conseillère-visiteuse
home visitor

formation des conseillers
counsellor training

CONSENSUEL
consensual

union consensuelle
companionate marriage, consensual union

CONSENTI
librement consenti
voluntary

CONSENTIR
to agree, to consent; to grant; to authorise

consentir un prêt
to grant a loan

CONSÉQUENCE
conséquence dommageable / préjudiciable
harmful effect

CONSERVATEUR
soins conservateurs
conservative treatment

CONSERVATION
maintenance, preservation

conservation des droits
preservation / maintenance of rights

conservation des droits acquis
maintenance of acquired rights

conservation des droits en cours d'acquisition / de formation
maintenance of rights in course of acquisition

conservation des droits à pension
preservation of rights to pension

conservation des prestations
preservation of benefits

délai de conservation
time for conservation

Système international de conservation des droits en matière de sécurité sociale
International System for the Maintenance of Rights in Social Security

taux de conservation des effectifs / des travailleurs / du personnel
retention rate, rate of retention

CONSERVATOIRE
protective; provisional

mesure conservatoire
protective measure

mise à pied conservatoire
suspension pending confirmation of dismissal / pending investigation; temporary lay-off

CONSERVER
to retain, to maintain, to keep

conserver un emploi
to retain employment, to stay on a job

CONSIDÉRATION
expérience à prendre en considération
reckonable experience

CONSIDÉRÉ
période considérée
period under review / under consideration / under observation, report period

CONSIGNE (n.)
order; directive; (pl.) regulations

consignes anti-incendie
fire precautions / instructions

consigne de la direction
managerial directive

consigne permanente
standing order

consigne de sécurité
safety regulation; (pl.) safety instructions / code

CONSIGNER
to record, to register

CONSOEUR
female colleague

CONSOLIDATION
consolidation; (occ.) permanent condition
(temporary incapacity becoming permanent incapacity)

certificat de consolidation
consolidation certificate

consolidation anatomique
anatomical consolidation

consolidation légale
legal consolidation

fonds de consolidation
stabilisation fund

CONSOLIDÉ
emploi consolidé (Fr.)
consolidated job

contrat d'emploi consolidé (CEC) (Fr.)
consolidated employment contract

CONSOMMATEUR
consumer; user

consommateur de soins de santé / de soins médicaux
medical consumer

CONSOMMATION
consumption

consommation médicale
consumption of medical care

consommation médicale finale
final consumption of medical care

consommation des ménages
household consumption

consommation de soins de santé / de soins médicaux
consumption of medical care

étude de consommation
consumer research / study

indice des prix à la consommation
consumer / retail price index

prix à la consommation
consumer price

salaire de la consommation réelle
real consumption wage

société de consommation
consumer society

CONSTANT
aide constante d'un tiers / d'une tierce personne
constant attendance

allocation pour aide constante (UK)
attendance allowance

allocation pour soins constants
(constant) attendance allowance, attendance benefit (Norw.)

assistance constante d'un tiers / d'une tierce personne
constant attendance

coefficient de pondération constant
fixed weight

Comité des allocations pour soins constants (UK)
Attendance Allowance Board

coût constant
fixed cost

exprimé en prix constants
deflated

francs constants (en)
in real value

prestation pour soins constants (Norw.)
attendance benefit

soins constants
constant attendance

surveillance constante
constant attendance

CONSTAT
codification des constats de décès
coding of death certificates

CONSTATATION
finding

CONSTITUÉ
corps constitué
corporate body; (pl.) constituent bodies

CONSTITUER
constituer une rente
to purchase an annuity

CONSTITUTIF
acte constitutif
articles

CONSTITUTION
devoir de fidélité à la Constitution (Ger.)
duty of loyalty to the Constitution

CONSTRUCTEUR
manufacturer

CONSTRUCTION
chantier de construction
construction site

construction de logements
housing construction

constructions navales
shipbuilding

construction subventionnée
social housing

**programme de construction d'habita-
tions / de logements**
housing programme

**programme de construction d'habita-
tions / de logements à bon marché / de
logements sociaux**
low-cost housing programme

secteur de la construction
building / construction industry

CONSULTANT
counsellor, consultant; (hospital) out-
patient, patient

infirmière consultante
nurse consultant

médecin consultant
(medical) consultant

psychiatre consultant
consultant psychiatrist

CONSULTATIF
advisory

comité / commission consultatif(ive)
advisory board / committee

conseil consultatif
advisory board / council

consultatif (à titre)
in an advisory capacity

instance consultative
consultative / advisory body

organe / organisme consultatif
consultative / advisory body

rôle consultatif
advisory capacity

service consultatif
consultative service; (pl.) provision of
advice

CONSULTATION
consultation; counselling; inspection;
surgery; (pl.) clinic

absence de consultation
failure to consult

cabinet de consultations
surgery, doctor's office, consulting
room

centre de consultation
counselling centre; clinic

centre de consultation dentaire
dental clinic

**centre de consultations psycho-
médico-pédagogiques**
child guidance clinic / centre

consultation au cabinet
surgery consultation / visit

consultations conjugales
marriage counselling / guidance

**consultations dentaires pour enfants
(Austr.)**
school dental clinic

consultation à domicile
domiciliary consultation

consultations pour enfants
child care / children's clinic

consultations externes
out-patient services / department / clinic
/ facilities

consultations familiales
counselling for families, family counselling

consultation d'hygiène mentale infantile
child mental health clinic

consultations infantiles
child care / children's clinic

consultations matrimoniales
marriage counselling / guidance

consultation de nourrissons
baby / infant clinic, infant welfare centre

consultations odontologiques
dental clinic

consultation d'orientation profession-nelle
vocational counselling

consultation paritaire
joint consultation

consultation permanente
ongoing consultation

consultations postnatales
post-natal clinic

consultation préalable
prior consultation

consultation de pré-évaluation
pre-assessment consultation

consultations prénatales
pre(-)natal clinic

consultations prénuptiales
pre(-)marital counselling

consultation de protection infantile
consulting centre for child health

consultations psycho(-médico)-péda-gogiques
child guidance clinic / centre

consultation pour la réadaptation
rehabilitation counselling

dispensaire de consultations prénatales
pre(-)natal clinic

engager des consultations
to enter into consultation

mécanisme de consultation
consultative mechanism

service de consultation
counselling service

Service de consultation, de conciliation et d'arbitrage (UK)
Advisory, Conciliation and Arbitration Service (ACAS)

service de consultations conjugales
marriage counselling / guidance

service de consultation dentaire
dental clinic

service de consultations pour enfants
child care / children's clinic

service de consultations externes
out-patient services / clinic / department; (pl.) out-patient facilities

service de consultations infantiles
child care / children's clinic

service de consultations matrimoniales
marriage counselling / guidance

service de consultations odontologiques
dental clinic

service de consultations postnatales
post-natal clinic

service de consultations prénatales
pre(-)natal clinic

service de consultations psycho-médico-pédagogiques
child guidance clinic / centre

soins médicaux en consultation externe
out-patient treatment

CONTACT
fichier de contact pour les adoptés (UK)
contact register for adopted persons

médecin de premier contact
physician of first contact

point de contact
contact person

verres de contact
contact lenses

CONTAGIEUX
maladie contagieuse
contagious disease

CONTENTIEUX (adj.)
procédure contentieuse
litigation procedure

susceptible de recours contentieux
challengeable

CONTENTIEUX (n.)
matters in dispute, litigation, claims;
adjudication; legal department

contentieux de l'aide sociale
social welfare claims

contentieux médical
medical claims

contentieux de la sécurité sociale
social security claims

contentieux technique
technical claims

service du contentieux
claims / legal department

CONTESTABLE
marché contestable
contestable market

CONTESTATION
claim, dispute, complaint

contestation sur
complaint as to

matière à contestation
case to answer

CONTESTER
contester une décision
to appeal against a decision

CONTEXTE
contexte économique
economic climate

CONTINGENT
quota; case-load

contingent d'immigration
immigration quota

CONTINU
admission continue
continuous intake

éducation continue
permanent / continuing /further
education

emploi continu
continuing / continuous / steady /
ongoing job / employment

engagements continus
continuous appointments

évaluation continue
continuous assessment

expectative d'emploi continu
expectancy of continued employment

formation continue
continuing / further education, in-
service (educational) training,
continuous learning, continuing /
continued training, further (education
and) training

formation continue dans l'entreprise
in-company continuing training

formation médicale continue
continuing medical education

formation professionnelle continue
ongoing vocational training

horaire continu
working hours without break

**industries appliquant des procédés de
fabrication en continu**
flow process industries

journée continue
non-stop working day; workday without lunch break

nomination de caractère continu
continuing appointment

système continu (3 x 8)
continuous work system

travail continu
non-stop work;

travail en continu
shift work(ing)

travail continu en équipe
continuous shiftwork

CONTINUÉ
assurance facultative continuée
optional continued insurance

assuré au titre d'une assurance facultative continuée
insured on an optional continued basis

CONTINUEL
soins continuels
regular care

CONTINUITÉ
continuité de l'emploi
continuity of employment

continuité du service
continuity of service

rapport de continuité
continuation rate

rupture dans la continuité du service
break in service

soins d'entretien et de continuité de la vie
daily care to compensate dependence

CONTRACEPTIF
contraceptive

CONTRACEPTION
contraception

CONTRACTION
phase de contraction
downswing, downturn

CONTRACTANT
pays contractant
contracting / (occ.) agreement country

CONTRACTÉ
obligation contractée
incurred obligation

CONTRACTUEL (adj.)
agent contractuel
staff member under public employee contract

arrangement contractuel juridiquement obligatoire
legally binding contractual arrangement

capacité contractuelle
bargaining power

droits contractuels
contractual rights

éléments contractuels
contractual elements

engagement contractuel
contractual commitment

fonctionnaire contractuel
temporary / non-established civil servant

force contractuelle
contractual force; bargaining power

hausse contractuelle de salaires
pay / wage settlement

liberté contractuelle
freedom of contract

main-d'oeuvre contractuelle
contract labour

obligation contractuelle
contractual obligation

salaire contractuel
contractual / negotiated wage

service contractuel
external contract

statut contractuel
contractual status

travailleur contractuel
contract labourer

CONTRACTUEL (n.)
contract employee / worker

CONTRAIGNANT
binding

contraignant (non)
non-binding

CONTRAINT
temps contraint
tied time

CONTRAINTE
requirement; constraint; coercion; hardship;
stress

contrainte (sous)
under duress

contrainte de recouvrement
enforced payment

contrainte sociale
inescapable social fact

**main-d'oeuvre assujettie à contrainte
d'employeur**
tied labour

procédure de contrainte
coercive measures / action

CONTRAIRE (adj.)
dispositions contraires (sauf)
unless otherwise provided

indication contraire (sauf)
unless otherwise stated / specified

CONTRAT
contract; indenture; policy (ins.); articles

annexe d'un contrat
schedule of a contract

apprenti sous contrat
indentured apprentice

cessation d'un contrat de travail
termination of a contract of employment

conditions d'application du contrat
terms and conditions of the agreement

contrat d'adaptation (à l'emploi) (Fr.)
employment contract for integration into
working life

**contrat d'adaptation professionnelle
(Belg.)**
vocational adaptation contract

**contrat d'adaptation professionnelle
pour personnes handicapées (Belg.)**
vocational adaptation contract for the
disabled

contrat en alternance
sandwich-type contract

contrat d'apprentissage
apprenticeship contract; articles of
apprenticeship; indenture

**contrat d'apprentissage «ordinaire»
(Belg.)**
"ordinary" apprenticeship contract

**contrat d'apprentissage spécial
(Belg.)**
special apprenticeship contract

contrat d'assurance collective
collective insurance contract

contrat-cadre
master contract

contrat clés en mains
turn key job

contrat collectif de retraite
group annuity policy

contrat collectif (de travail)
collective agreement

contrat de courte durée
short-term contract

contrat (de travail) à / de durée déter-minée
fixed-term / fixed-duration (employment / work) contract, fixed-term appointment

contrat à durée déterminée à terme imprécis (Fr.)
unspecified fixed-term contract

contrat à durée déterminée à terme précis (Fr.)
specified fixed-term contract

contrat à durée déterminée à terme non spécifié (Fr.)
unspecified (but fixed) term contract

contrat (de travail) à durée indéterminée
indefinite / open-ended (employment / work) contract, indefinite appointment

contrat d'emploi consolidé (CEC) (Fr.)
consolidated employment contract

contrat emploi-formation (Fr.)
employment training contract

contrat d'emploi de réadaptation (Irel.)
remedial work

contrat emploi-solidarité (CES) (Fr.)
solidarity employment contract, employment contract to facilitate reintegration of disadvantaged persons

contrat d'engagement des marins
ship's articles

contrat d'engagement de service
employment contract

contrat d'entreprise
services contract

contrat de formation
training contract / relationship; (occ.) training place

contrat de formation en entreprise
training-in-industry contract

contrat de formation professionnelle
vocational training contract

contrat de garantie
underwriting contract

contrat de gestion commune de caisses
pooled accounts funding contract

contrat de gestion de dépôts
deposit administration contract

contrat de gestion distincte
segregated funds contract

contrat de gestion distincte de caisse
segregated accounts funding contract

contrat individuel de retraite
individual annuity policy

contrat individuel de travail
(occ.) indenture contract

contrat initiative emploi
employment initiative contract

contrat d'insertion (Fr.)
integration contract

contrat d'insertion en alternance (Fr.)
employment contract facilitating integration into working life, sandwich-type integration contract

contrat de licence
licence agreement

contrat à long terme / de longue durée
long-term contract

contrat de louage de services
(institutional) service contract; (occ.) employment contract

contrat de louage de services individuels
individual service contract

contrat médical
medical contract

contrat de mise à disposition (Fr.)
contract making temporary staff available

contrat de mission (Fr.)
assignment contract

contrat d'orientation (Fr.)
guidance / employment orientation contract

contrat pédagogique
educational agreement

contrat permanent
permanent contract

contrat de progrès (Fr.)
contract for progress

contrat public
public contract

contrat de qualification
qualification / skills contract

contrat de réinsertion
return to work contract

contrat de retour à l'emploi (Fr.)
back-to-work contract

contrat de service
contract of service, service contract

contrat social
social contract

contrat de société
articles of / deed of partnership

contrat de solidarité
solidarity contract

contrat de sous-traitance
subcontracting; (occ.) contract for services

contrat spécial d'engagement / de service
special service agreement

contrat (de travail) subventionné
(Spain)
grant-assisted (employment) contract

contrat tarifaire
wage contract

contrat de travail
contract of employment / of labour / of
service, work contract / agreement, labour /
employment / service contract

contrat de travail intermittent
intermittent work contract

contrat de travail précaire
insecure employment contract

contrat de travail saisonnier
seasonal employment / work contract

contrat de travail temporaire
temporary work contract

contrat de travail à temps partiel
part-time employment contract

**contrat passé avec un travailleur
indé-pendant**
freelance contract

contrat-type de travail
standard service contract

contrat en vigueur
current contract

**date effective de la rupture du contrat
de travail**
effective date of termination

date de fin de contrat
termination date

dénoncer un contrat
to denounce a contract

dérogation aux clauses d'un contrat
deviation from the terms of a contract

durée d'un contrat
duration of a contract

exécuter un contrat
to administer a contract

**fonctionnaire à contrat de durée
déterminée**
fixed-term official

indemnité de fin de contrat
end-of-contract payment

main-d'oeuvre sous contrat
contract / indentured labour

manquement au contrat de travail
breach of contract of employment

médecin sous contrat
contract doctor

mettre fin à un contrat
to terminate a contract

modalités d'application du contrat
terms and conditions of the agreement

modification d'un contrat
variation of a contract

partie à un contrat
party to a contract

passer contrat avec
to contract with

prendre sous contrat
to sign up

prévoir au contrat
to set forth in a contract

prolongation de contrat
extension of contract

prolonger un contrat
to extend a contract

reconduction d'un contrat
renewal of a contract

régime de travail sous contrat
contract labour system

renouvellement d'un contrat
renewal of a contract

résiliation d'un contrat
termination of a contract

résilier / rompre un contrat
to terminate a contract

rupture abusive du contrat de travail
wrongful / unfair dismissal, wrongful discharge (USA)

rupture de contrat
breach of contract

rupture du contrat de travail
breach of contract of employment

rupture d'un contrat de travail
termination of a contract of employment

signataire d'un contrat
party to a contract

suspension d'un contrat de travail
suspension of an employment contract

système du travail sous contrat
contract labour system

terme d'un contrat
expiry date / end of contract; (pl.)
wording / terms and conditions of a contract

termes d'un contrat de travail
terms and conditions of employment

travail sous contrat
contract work; indentured labour

travailleur sous contrat
contract employee / worker

travailleurs engagés sur contrat
contract labour

venue à expiration du contrat
expiry of contract

CONTRE-INCITATION
disincentive effect

contre-incitation au travail
work disincentive

CONTRE-INDIQUÉ
unadvisable, unsuitable

CONTREMAÎTRE
foreman, headman; (occ.) charge hand

CONTREPARTIE
compensation; (occ.) consideration

bénéficiaire sans contrepartie
free-rider

contrepartie de (en)
in return for

CONTRE-PROPOSITION
counter-offer

CONTREVENANT
offender

CONTRE-VISITE
check visit / inspection, second inspection

CONTRIBUABLE
taxpayer

CONTRIBUER
to contribute

CONTRIBUTIF
contributory

assurance contributive
contributory insurance

avantage contributif
contributory benefit

avantage non contributif
non-contributory benefit

avantage social contributif
contributory social benefit

avantage social non contributif
non-contributory social benefit

capacité contributive
capacity to pay, taxable / tax-paying
capacity

contributif (non)
non-contributory; payable without regard to
contribution

faculté contributive
capacity to pay, taxable / tax-paying
capacity

pension contributive partielle (Irel.)
partial contributory pension

**pension non contributive de veuvage
(Irel.)**
widows non-contributory pension

pension d'invalidité non contributive
non-contributory invalidity pension

prestation contributive
contributory benefit

prestation non contributive
non-contributory benefit

régime contributif
contributory scheme

régime non contributif
non-contributory scheme

**régime contributif de pensions com-
plémentaires du régime général (UK)**
contributory reserve pension scheme

régime de retraite non contributif
non-contributory pension plan / scheme

régime de retraite contributif (mixte)
contributory pension scheme / plan

CONTRIBUTION
contribution; input; tax; charge (med.)

**Administration des contributions
(UK)**
Inland Revenue

assurance à contribution
contributory insurance

**barème des contributions du
personnel**
(occ.) staff assessment plan

contribution de l'Etat
contribution of the State

contribution indirecte
indirect tax

contribution du personnel
(occ.) staff assessment

contribution progressive
progressive contribution

**contribution au titre de la sécurité
sociale**
social security charge

**contribution sociale généralisée
(CSG) (Fr.)**
general social contribution

contribution de solidarité
solidarity contribution

fonctionnaire des contributions
tax official

CONTRÔLE
inspection; test(ing); check(ing); review; supervision, monitoring

agent de contrôle
checking officer

agent contrôle de la sécurité sociale
social security inspector

assujetti à un contrôle des gains
earnings-tested

commission de contrôle
supervisory board

contrôle administratif
administrative check

contrôle d'effectifs
attendance check

contrôle de l'emploi
employment control

contrôle financier
financial control

contrôle aux frontières
border control

contrôle de gestion
management control

contrôle de gestion interne
audit

contrôle médical
physical inspection, medical examination

contrôle des médicaments
drug control

contrôle sur place
on-site monitoring

contrôle (du niveau) des ressources
means testing

contrôle sanitaire
health control / checks, sanitary inspection

contrôle de la situation de fortune
means testing

contrôle surprise
random inspection

contrôle des tâches
job control

contrôle sur le tas / sur le vif
on-the-spot check

cycle de contrôle
control cycle

formation au contrôle
training in supervision

mécanisme de contrôle
supervisory procedure; monitoring mechanism

organe de contrôle
enforcement body

poste de contrôle du travail
supervisory work station

visite de contrôle
monitoring / follow-up visit; medical inspection at home

CONTRÔLEUR
supervisor; inspector; auditor; (occ.) team
leader

contrôleur de sécurité
safety inspector

médecin contrôleur
examining doctor

CONVALESCENCE
convalescence

centre de convalescence, de cure ou de réadaptation (Fr.)
nursing, care or rehabilitation centre

maison de convalescence
convalescent home, half-way house

CONVENABLE
emploi convenable
suitable employment

CONVENANCE
absence pour convenance personnelle
compassionate leave

congé pour convenance(s) personnelle(s)
leave of absence for personal reasons;
casual / compassionate leave

convenance personnelle (pour raison de)
for personal reasons

CONVENIR
rémunération à convenir
negotiable salary

CONVENTION
agreement; convention; covenant

adhérer à une convention
to accede to / to join a convention

convention d'aménagement et de réduction du temps de travail (ARTT) (Fr.)
agreement to reform and reduce working hours

convention d'arbitrage
arbitration agreement

convention bilatérale
bilateral convention

convention (collective) de branche
industry-wide (collective) agreement

convention-cadre
umbrella convention, framework / outline agreement

convention de collaboration (Fr.)
collaboration agreement

convention collective
collective (bargaining) / labour / industrial agreement, labour(-management) contract; union contract

convention collective du travail
collective labour agreement

convention de conversion
retraining agreement

convention emploi-formation (Belg.)
job-training agreement

convention d'entreprise
staff / company / works agreement

convention d'exclusivité syndicale
closed shop agreement

convention de formation professionnelle
vocational training agreement

convention de gestion financière (pensions)
funding instrument

convention locale mutualiste
local mutualistic convention / agreement

convention médicale
medical agreement

convention multilatérale
multilateral convention

convention multilatérale de sécurité sociale
multilateral social security convention

convention nationale
national convention / agreement

convention de placement (Fr.)
placement agreement

convention de recrutement
recruitment agreement

convention salariale
wage settlement

convention (collective) sectorielle
industry-wide (collective) agreement

convention de sécurité sociale
convention on social security, social security convention

convention de stage (Fr.)
training agreement

convention tarifaire
agreement on fees

convention trilatérale
trilateral convention

passer une convention
to contract with, to make a convention

tarif de convention
standard (agreed) fee

CONVENTIONNÉ
(National Health); government-regulated;
subsidised; low-interest

conventionné (non) (UK)
in private practice

établissement conventionné
national health institution

médecin conventionné
health service doctor, national health doctor,
panel doctor

médecin non conventionné
non-approved doctor

prêt conventionné
low-interest / subsidised loan

stage conventionné
agreement-regulated training course

CONVENTIONNEL
activité conventionnelle
mainstream activity

**allocation conventionnelle de solidarité
(Fr.)**
contractual solidarity allowance

dépasser le tarif conventionnel agréé
to charge more than the standard agreed fee

disposition conventionnelle
provision of an industrial agreement; (pl.)
(occ.) treaty provisions

droits conventionnels
contractual rights

obligation conventionnelle
treaty obligation

période d'affiliation conventionnelle
notional period of contributory service

tarif conventionnel
standard (agreed) fee

tarif médical conventionnel
standard medical fee

CONVENTIONNEMENT
national health contract

système du conventionnement
licensing regulations (health care
institutions)

CONVENU
agreed

**durée convenue du travail hebdoma-
daire**
standard working week, standard
weekly hours

salaire convenu
agreed / standard wage

taux salarial convenu
agreed wage rate

CONVERSION
(job) conversion; retraining;
redeployment; commutation

**barème de conversion des points en
classes**
grade-point conversion scale

clé de conversion
conversion key

congé de conversion
retraining leave

convention de conversion
retraining agreement

conversion en capital
lump-sum commutation (of a part of the
pension)

conversion partielle des pensions
partial commutation of retirement
benefits

conversion des postes
job conversion

conversion d'une rente
commutation of annuity

grille de conversion
conversion table

somme en capital résultant de / versée au titre de la conversion partielle de la pension
partial lump sum withdrawal benefit, partial lump sum commutation of pension benefit

table de conversion
conversion table

CONVERTIR
to commute; to change into

convertir une prestation en une somme en capital
to commute a benefit in a lump sum

CONVOQUER
convoquer à un entretien
to call for an interview

COOPÉRATIVE
coopérative de logement
housing co-operative

coopérative ouvrière
workers' cooperative

COORDINATION
co-ordination; co-ordinating committee (unions)

centre d'information et de coordination de l'action sociale
social work information and co-ordination centre

organisme de coordination
coordinating agency

COORDONNATEUR
coordonnateur de réadaptation
rehabilitation co-ordinator

COORDONNÉ
réseau de soins coordonnés
health maintenance organisation (HMO)

COPARTICIPATION
entreprise en coparticipation
joint venture

CORPORATIF
intérêt corporatif
professional interest

CORPORATION
guild

corporation artisanale
trade guild

CORPORATISTE
syndicat corporatiste
corporatist union

CORPOREL
assurance accidents corporels du secteur public (Ger.)
public accident insurance

atteinte corporelle
personal injury

dommages corporels
physical injury

lésion corporelle
bodily injury / harm, personal injury

préjudice corporel
personal injury

CORPS
body

corps constitué
corporate body; (pl.) constituent bodies

corps diplomatique
foreign service

corps enseignant
teaching staff / personnel

corps médical
medical profession

corps de métier
trade guild

corps professoral
teaching profession

corps social
social entity

syndicat de corps de métier
occupational / craft / (occ.) horizontal union

CORRECTEUR (adj.)
verres correcteurs
corrective lenses

CORRECTEUR (n.)
scorer (tests)

CORRECTIF
remedial

action corrective
corrective / remedial / affirmative / positive action

enseignement correctif
remedial tuition / teaching / education

mesure corrective
corrective / remedial measure

CORRECTION
correction des variations saisonnières
seasonal adjustment

multiplicateur corrigé par le facteur de correction de la rémunération
multiplier corrected by the remuneration correction factor

CORRÉLATION
interrelationship

CORRESPONDANCE
cours par correspondance
correspondence course

enseignement par correspondance
distance education

entreprise de vente par correspondance
mail-order business

mise en correspondance des offres et des demandes d'emploi
job matching

CORRESPONDANT (adj.)
corresponding; relevant

correspondant à
(occ.) suitable for

CORRESPONDANT (n.)
correspondent, contact person

correspondant d'entreprise
in-house correspondent

correspondant local
local correspondent

correspondant mutualiste (Fr.)
correspondent for a mutual benefit society

CORRIGÉ
corrigé par un coefficient déflateur
deflated

corrigé selon l'évolution des prix
adjusted for price changes

corrigé des variations du nombre d'heures supplémentaires
adjusted for overtime

corrigé des variations saisonnières
seasonally adjusted

multiplicateur corrigé par le facteur de correction de la rémunération
multiplier corrected by the remuneration correction factor

CORRIGER
to correct, to adjust

CORROBORER
to corroborate, to support

COTATION
cotation des emplois
job rating

cotation du travail
job evaluation

matrice de cotation par points
point-factor matrix

système de cotation des emplois
point-factor method of job evaluation

COTE
rating

COTISANT
subscriber; contributor

adhérent cotisant
contributing member

adhérent non cotisant
non-contributing member

membres cotisants
contributing members

COTISATION
contribution; charge; fee

abaisser la cotisation
to lower the contribution

acquitter les cotisations
to pay contributions

adhérent à jour / en règle de ses cotisations
member in good standing

année de cotisation
contribution year

annulation de cotisation d'assurance-vieillesse (Fr.)
annulment of old age contribution

appel de cotisations
call for / calling up of contributions

appel de cotisation complémentaire
supplementary call for contribution

arriéré de cotisation
contribution in arrears

assiette de(s) cotisations
funding base for / assessment of contributions, contribution base

assiette des cotisations sociales
basis of social insurance contribution

assiette mensuelle des cotisations
monthly assessment of contributions

assujetti au versement d'une / de cotisation(s)
liable for contribution / to pay (a) contribution(s)

assurance à cotisation(s) / financée par cotisations
contributory insurance / scheme

augmentation des cotisations
raising of contributions

augmenter les cotisations / le taux de la cotisation
to raise contributions

baisser la cotisation
to lower the contribution

barème des cotisations
scale of contributions

bordereau de cotisations
statement of contributions

bordereau récapitulatif de cotisations
summary statement of contributions

calcul des cotisations
calculation / computation of contributions

carte de cotisation
contribution card

catégorie de cotisation
contribution class

condition de cotisation
contribution condition

cotisation accident de travail (Fr.)
industrial injury contribution

cotisation acquittée
paid contribution

cotisation d'adhésion
membership fee

cotisations arriérées
contribution arrears, outstanding contributions

cotisation d'assurance
insurance contribution

cotisation à l'assurance-maladie
health / sickness insurance contribution

cotisation à l'assurance nationale (UK)
national insurance contribution

cotisation de base pour la catégorie n
primary class n contribution

cotisation créditée
credited contribution

cotisation différentielle
differential contribution

cotisation (de l') employeur
employer's contribution

cotisation d'équilibre
special payment (pensions)

cotisation (à taux) forfaitaire
flat-rate contribution

cotisation hebdomadaire
weekly contribution

cotisations impayées
outstanding contributions

cotisation indue
undue contribution

cotisation mensuelle
monthly contribution

cotisation minimale / minimum
minimum contribution

cotisation moyenne
average contribution

cotisation mutualiste
mutual insurance contribution

cotisation nominale
nominal contribution

cotisation normale
regular contribution

cotisation ouvrière
worker's contribution

cotisation patronale
employer's contribution

cotisation patronale de sécurité sociale
employers' social security contribution

cotisation payée
paid contribution

cotisation payée à l'étranger
contribution paid abroad

cotisation perçue sur le salaire (USA)
wages tax

cotisations à percevoir
contributions still due

cotisation proportionnelle au salaire
earnings-related contribution

cotisation salariale
worker's / employee's contribution

cotisation salariale de sécurité sociale
employees' social security contribution

cotisation de / à la / au titre de la sécurité sociale
social security contribution / charge / tax (USA)

cotisation sociale
welfare / social / insurance contribution

cotisation sociale complémentaire
supplementary welfare contribution

cotisations sociales du régime général de sécurité sociale
insurance contributions for the general social security scheme

cotisation sociale des travailleurs indépendants
self-employment insurance contribution

cotisation supplémentaire pour la catégorie n
secondary class n contribution

cotisation syndicale
union fee / subscription; (pl.) (trade) union dues

cotisation des travailleurs
workers' contribution

cotisation (à taux) uniforme
flat-rate contribution

cotisations versées
paid contributions, contribution record

cotisation volontaire
voluntary contribution

créditer les cotisations
to credit contributions

déduction de la cotisation
deduction of contribution

déduire la cotisation du salaire
to deduct contributions from wages

défaut de cotisation
contribution deficiency

échelonner les cotisations
to graduate contributions

établissement des cotisations
determination / assessment of contributions

exigibilité des cotisations
payability of contributions

exonération de cotisations
waiver of / exemption from / cancellation of
contributions

**exonérations et réductions des cotisa-
tions**
exemptions from and reductions of
contributions

**fichier central des cotisations d'assu-
rance (UK)**
central record of insurance contributions

**fixer les cotisations / l'assiette des
cotisations**
to assess contributions

graduer les cotisations
to graduate contributions

**limite inférieure pour l'assiette des
cotisations de la catégorie n**
lower earnings limit of class n contributions

**limite supérieure pour l'assiette des
cotisations de la catégorie n**
upper earnings limit of class n contributions

liste nominative des cotisations
list / statement of contributions per
person

majoration de cotisation
increase of contribution

méthode de calcul de la cotisation
calculation of the contribution;
contribution formula

niveau de / des cotisation(s)
contribution level, level of contributions

non-paiement des cotisations
non-payment of contributions

paiement des cotisations
payment of contributions, contribution
payment

paiement des cotisations syndicales
payment of union fees

payer les cotisations
to pay contributions

pension constituée par cotisations
contributory pension

**pension de vieillesse constituée par
cotisations**
contributory old age pension

perception des cotisations
collection of contributions, contribution
collection

percevoir des cotisations
to collect contributions

période de cotisation
contribution period, period of
contribution

plafond de cotisation
contribution ceiling

plafonnement des cotisations
upper limit on contributions

plan à cotisations définies
defined contribution plan

plan de retraite à cotisations fixes
fixed contribution retirement plan

rachat de cotisations
purchase of contributions

recettes tirées / provenant des cotisations
contribution revenue

recouvrement de(s) cotisations
recovery / collection of contributions,
contribution collection

recouvrer des cotisations
to collect contributions

régime à cotisations définies
defined contribution scheme

régularisation annuelle des cotisations
annual regularisation of contributions

relevé des cotisations (versées)
contribution record

relèvement des cotisations
raising of contributions

remboursement de cotisations
contribution refund, reimbursement of
contributions

remise de cotisation(s)
reduction / cancellation of (a) contribu-
tion(s)

remise gracieuse de cotisations
discretionary reduction of contributions

rentrées de cotisations
contribution revenue

retenir la cotisation sur le salaire
to deduct contributions from pay / wages

rétention des cotisations ouvrières
retention of workers' contributions

retenue de la cotisation
deduction of contribution

salaire donnant lieu / soumis à cotisation
earnings subject to contribution, contributory wage

semaine de cotisation
contribution week

soumis à cotisation
liable for / subject to contribution

stage de cotisation
qualifying period of contribution

supplément à la cotisation
supplement to contribution

**système de précompte des cotisations
/ de retenue de la cotisation sur le
salaire (UK)**
direct debit system

taux de (la) cotisation
contribution rate, amount / rate of
contribution; (pl.) level of contributions

timbre de cotisation (UK)
contribution stamp

verser les / des cotisations
to pay contributions, to contribute

COTISÉ
période cotisée
period for which contributions have
been paid

COTISER
to pay contributions, to contribute

cotiser à un syndicat
to contribute to a union

obligation de cotiser
liability for contribution

COUCHE
fausse couche
miscarriage

repos des femmes en couches (Fr.)
leave for women after childbirth

COUPLAGE
linkage

couplage des données / des dossiers
record linkage

COUPLE
(married) couple

couple dissocié
broken / dissolved marriage

couple marié
married couple

couple marié avec enfants
married couple with children, married couple family

rente pour couple (Switz.)
married couple's pension

COUR
cour d'appel
Court of Appeal; (occ.) appeals tribunal (UK)

Cour du travail
Labour Court of Appeal

COURANT (adj.)
current; standard

actes de pratique médicale courante
standard medical service

affaires courantes
day to day business

aptitudes nécessaires à la vie courante
living skills

balance des opérations courantes / des paiements courants
current account

barème courant de rémunération
ordinary scale of remuneration

compte des opérations courantes / des paiements courants
current account

dépenses courantes
running costs

fichiers courants de maladie
routine records of sickness

indice courant des retraites (Ger.)
current pension value

période d'emploi courante
current period of employment

pratiques commerciales courantes
customary business practices

pratique courante
standard / usual practice

rémunération courante
going salary

soins courants
routine care

solde des opérations courantes / des paiements courants
current account

taux courant
standard / going / prevailing rate

taux de rémunération / de salaire courant
prevailing rate of pay

traitement annuel courant
current annual salary

travail courant
normal workload; routine work

COURANT (n.)
trend; flow

courant migratoire
flow of migration

COURBE
courbe d'ancienneté
(occ.) tenure profile

courbe d'apprentissage
learning curve

courbe d'augmentation des salaires
salary progression curve

courbe du chômage
unemployment pattern, pattern of unemployment

courbe de la demande de main-d'oeuvre
demand curve for labour

courbe d'expérience
experience curve

courbe d'offre de main-d'oeuvre
supply curve of labour, labour supply schedule

courbe d'Okun
Okun curve

courbe de Phillips
Phillips curve

courbe de Phillips élargie
augmented Phillips curve

courbe des salaires
wage curve / trend

méthode de la double courbe des rémunérations
dual pay-line approach

COURONNE
fonctionnaire de la Couronne (UK)
Crown servant

COURS
course, tuition; rate; trend

chargé de cours
lecturer

cours (en)
current; active

cours par correspondance
correspondence course

cours pour débutants
beginners' course

cours d'emploi (en)
in-service, on-the-job

cours en externat
non-residential course

cours facultatif
optional / elective subject

cours de formation accélérée
intensive / crash (training) course

cours de formation pratique
practical training course

cours de formation préparatoire à l'emploi
pre-trades training course

cours d'initiation / d'intégration professionnelle
induction training / course, beginners' course

cours de langue
language course / training

cours de mise à niveau
remedial / refresher course

cours particuliers
private tuition

cours de perfectionnement
advanced / refresher / proficiency course

cours préparatoire à l'apprentissage
pre-apprenticeship course

cours préparatoire aux métiers
basic trades training

cours de rattrapage
remedial classes / course / training / teaching / education

cours de recyclage
refresher course

cours du soir
evening school / classes, night course / school / classes

cours théoriques
classroom / theoretical training

cours de vulgarisation
extension course, extramural studies

école / établissement dispensant des cours du soir
evening / night school

heures de cours
school hours

période de chômage en cours
spell of unemployment in progress

période en cours
current period, spell in progress

présence aux cours
class attendance

prêt en cours
outstanding loan

programme en cours d'emploi
on-the-job programme

COURSE
course entre les salaires
wage-wage spiral

COURT (adj.)
contrat de courte durée
short-term contract

courte durée
short-term

court de personnel (être à)
to be understaffed / undermanned / short-
handed / short-staffed / short of staff

court terme
short-term

court terme (à)
in the short-run

cycle court de formation
short training cycle

emploi de courte durée
short-term / temporary work / employment /
job

engagement de courte durée
short-term appointment

formation à court terme
short-term training

hôpital de court séjour
(occ.) somatic hospital

immigrant de courte durée
short-term immigrant

**personnel à court terme / engagé pour
une période de courte durée**
short-term staff

politique à court terme
short-term policy

**prestation de courte durée / à court
terme**
short-term benefit

COURTAGE
brokerage; job brokerage / broking

COURTIER
agents commerciaux et courtiers [ISCO-
1988 (342)]
business services agents and trade
brokers [ISCO-1988 (342)]

COURU
intérêts courus
accrued interests

COÛT
cost, charge

ajustement au coût de la vie
cost-of-living adjustment, consumer
price index increase

**ajustement des pensions aux
variations du coût de la vie**
cost-of-living pension adjustment

analyse coûts-avantages
cost-benefit analysis

analyse coût-efficacité
cost-effectiveness analysis

analyse coûts-rendement
benefit-cost analysis

**augmentation au titre du coût de la
vie**
cost-of-living increment / increase

calcul des coûts
costing

calcul du coût salarial
calculation of wage / salary cost(s),
salary costing

calcul des coûts standard
standard costing

calcul des coûts unitaires
unit costing

calcul fonctionnel des coûts
functional costing

chiffrage des coûts
costing

coefficient d'ajustement au coût de la vie
cost-of-living differential factor

coût actualisé
discounted cost

coût alternatif
alternative cost

coûts d'aménagement
fit-up cost

coût constant
fixed cost

coût direct
direct cost

coût-efficacité
cost-effectiveness

coût d'embauche
hiring cost

coût(s) d'embauche et de licenciement
hiring and firing cost(s), on and off costs
(Austr.)

coût estimatif
estimated cost

coût d'exploitation
running / operational / operating cost

coût extraordinaire
non-recurring cost

coût fixe
fixed cost

coût(s) de fonctionnement
running / operating cost(s) / expenditure

coûts de formation
training costs / charges

coût de gestion
administrative cost(s)

coût indirect
indirect cost

coût de licenciement
severance cost

coût de (la) main-d'oeuvre
labour cost / price

coût de main-d'oeuvre non salarial
non-wage labour cost

coût de main-d'oeuvre unitaire
unit labour cost

coût marginal
marginal cost

coût marginal du travail
marginal cost of labour

coût d'opportunité
opportunity cost

coût de production
production cost

coût de recrutement
hiring cost

coût de remplacement
replacement cost

coût des salaires nominaux
money-wage cost

coût salarial
wage / labour cost; (pl.) payroll / salary
costs, wage bill

coût non salarial
non-salary / non-wage cost

coûts salariaux directs
direct labour costs

coûts salariaux indirects
indirect labour costs

coûts non salariaux ordinaires
recurring non-salary costs

coût social du travail
social (opportunity) cost of labour

coût standard
standard cost

coût de substitution
replacement / opportunity cost

coûts de transaction
transaction costs (job seeking and hiring
of staff)

coût du travail
labour cost

coût unitaire
unit cost

coût unitaire de main-d'oeuvre
unit labour cost

coût d'usage
user cost

coût variable
variable cost

coût variable de la main-d'oeuvre
variable labour cost

coût de la vie
cost of living

différentiel de coût de la vie
cost-of-living differential factor

échelle mobile (des salaires) établie sur le coût de la vie
cost-of-living sliding scale

établissement du coût salarial
calculation of wage / salary cost(s), salary costing

facteur de coût
cost factor

incidence sur les coûts (sans)
cost-neutral

indexation sur le / au titre du coût de la vie
cost-of-living adjustment, adjustment to cost of living

indice du coût de l'emploi
employment cost index

indice du coût de la vie
cost-of-living index

maintenir les salaires au niveau du coût de la vie
to keep wages abreast of the cost of living

maîtrise des coûts
cost containment

participation au coût
cost-sharing

participation au coût de l'ordonnance
prescription fee / charge

rapport coût-rendement
cost-efficiency

recouvrement des coûts
cost recovery

salaire-coût
labour cost

COÛTANT
prix coûtant
cost price

COÛTEUX
affection prolongée et coûteuse / maladie longue et coûteuse
prolonged and expensive illness

COUVERT (adj.)
catégorie de personnes couvertes
group of persons covered; (pl.) range of persons covered

éventualité couverte
contingency covered

risques couverts et prestations attribuées
contingencies covered and benefits granted

type de risques couverts
type of coverage

COUVERTURE
coverage

amélioration de la couverture des risques
improvement in coverage

capitaux de couverture
insurance capital

couverture globale
blanket coverage

couverture maladie
health coverage / insurance

couverture maladie universelle (Fr.)
universal health coverage

couverture médicale
health coverage

couverture qualitative
qualitative coverage

couverture quantitative
quantitative coverage

couverture des risques de maladie
health insurance cover

couverture du risque vieillesse
old age coverage

couverture sanitaire (de la population)
health care coverage

couverture santé
health coverage

couverture de sécurité sociale
social security coverage

couverture sociale
social coverage; insurance coverage (USA)

couverture vieillesse
old age coverage

taux de couverture
coverage (ratio)

COUVRIR
to cover; to make good

éventualité à couvrir
contingency to be covered

CRÉANCE
(financial) claim

créance alimentaire
maintenance; right to claim / receive
maintenance

créance fiscale
tax claim

créance salariale
pay claim

garantie de créances de salaires
wage claim guarantee

CRÉANCIER (adj.)
institution créancière
creditor institution

organisme créancier
creditor body

CRÉANCIER (n.)
créancier alimentaire / d'aliments
person entitled to maintenance

CRÉATEUR
créateur d'entreprise
new entrepreneur

initiative créatrice d'emplois
employment-creation measure

mesure créatrice d'emplois
employment-creation / job-creation
measure

CRÉATION
agence locale pour la création
d'entreprises
local enterprise agency

artisanat de création
(occ.) arts and crafts

création directe d'emplois
direct job creation

création d'emplois
employment / job generation / development / creation, provision of employment

**création d'emplois par effet d'entraî-
nement / par effet multiplicateur**
employment spin-off

création de postes
job creation

**crédits / fonds affectés à la création
d'emplois**
job creation funds

**initiative locale de création d'emploi
(ILE)**
local employment initiative, local
initiative in promoting employment

possibilités de création d'emplois
employment-generating potential

**programme de création d'emplois /
favorisant la création d'emplois**
job-creation / work-creation / employment-creation programme / scheme, scheme aimed at creating employment / jobs

CRÈCHE
nursery, child care / day care centre;
early childhood care

crèche collective
collective day-care centre

crèche familiale
family day care

crèche parentale (Fr.)
family child care

services de crèche et de garderie
child care facilities

CRÉDIRENTIER
grantee for / of an annuity; annuitant

CRÉDIT
credit; provision; (pl.) supplies

affectation de crédits
allocation of / appropriation of funds;
earmarking

attribution de crédits
award of credits

crédits additionnels
supplementary budget

crédit pour l'adulte (UK)
adult credit

crédits affectés
apportioned / earmarked funds, earmarking

crédits non affectés
unapportioned funds

**crédit d'attente pour le congé dans les
foyers**
credit for home leave travel

crédit budgétaire
budgetary provision, budget allocation

**crédits affectés à la création
d'emplois**
job creation funds

crédit pour l'enfant (UK)
child credit

crédit aux entreprises
business credit

crédit d'études
school credit

crédit familial (UK)
family credit

crédits affectés à la formation
training funds

**crédit formation individualisé (CFI)
(Fr.)**
individualised training credit / loan
scheme

crédit formation jeunes (Fr.)
young people training tax credit

crédit d'heures
day release

crédit hypothécaire / immobilier
mortgage

crédit d'impôt
tax credit

**crédit d'impôt relatif à
l'apprentissage (Fr.)**
tax credit for apprenticeship

**crédit d'impôt (aux entreprises) en
faveur de l'emploi / pour la création
d'emplois / à l'emploi (Can.)**
employment tax credit (Can.); tax credit
for providing employment

crédit d'impôt pour enfant (Can.)
child tax credit (Can.)

crédit d'impôt-formation (Fr.)
training levy / tax credit

**crédit d'impôt au titre des revenus du
travail (USA)**
earned income tax credit

crédits ouverts
appropriations

crédit universitaire
university credit

dépassement de crédits
over-expenditure

ligne de crédit
appropriation line

porter au crédit de
to credit

programme de crédit-formation
training grants scheme

réaffectation de crédits
re-allocation of funds

transfert des crédits
credits transfer

CRÉDITÉ
cotisation créditée
credited contribution

CRÉDITER
credit (to)

créditer les cotisations
to credit contributions

CRÉER
créer des débouchés
to develop employment possibilities

créer des emplois
to create / to generate jobs / employment

CREUX (adj.)
classe creuse
small age group

heures creuses
off-peak / slack period

CRIANT
injustice criante
gross injustice

CRISE
crisis, slump; shortage; predicament

centre de crise
crisis centre

crise économique
economic crisis

crise de l'emploi
employment slump

crise du logement
housing shortage

négociation de crise
crisis bargaining

CRITÈRE
criterion; test; standard; (pl.)
requirement

critère d'admissibilité
eligibility / acceptance criterion,
qualifier, qualifying factor

critère d'admission
admission standard / rule, criterion for
membership

critère de complémentarité
additionality (criterion)

critère d'entrée
admission standard / rule

critère de financement
funding criterion

critère d'inscription
admission standard / rule

critère pédagogique
academic standard

**critère de recherche effective
d'emploi**
(occ.) work test

critère de ressources
means test

critère de revenu
income test

critère de sélection
criterion for selection, selection criterion

prestation liée à / soumise à / subordonnée à un critère de ressources
means-tested / income-tested benefit

subordonné au critère des ressources
subject to a means test, means-tested

CRITIQUE (adj.)
seuil critique
trigger level

zone critique
depressed area

CROISÉ
financement croisé
cross-subsidisation

CROISIÈRE
rythme de croisière d'un régime
mature status of scheme / plan

CROISSANCE
chômage par insuffisance de la croissance
growth gap unemployment

croissance économique
economic growth

croissance économique soutenue
sustained economic growth

croissance de l'emploi
employment growth

croissance équilibrée / harmonieuse
balanced growth

croissance du marché de l'emploi
labour market growth

croissance zéro
zero growth

intensité d'emploi de la croissance
employment / job content of growth

moteur de la croissance
engine of growth, growth engine

nouveau secteur de croissance
new growth industry

objectif de croissance
growth target

période de croissance
period of growth

perspective de croissance
growth perspective / prospect

phase de croissance
period of growth

pôle de croissance de l'emploi
employment growth area

politique de croissance
growth policy

potentiel de croissance
growth potential

salaire minimum interprofessionnel de croissance (SMIC) (Fr.)
guaranteed / statutory minimum wage

secteur de croissance
growth sector

secteur industriel à forte croissance
high-growth industrial sector

taux de croissance
growth rate

taux de croissance de l'emploi
employment growth rate

taux de croissance des professions
occupational growth rate

CROISSANT
chômage croissant
rising unemployment

CUIR
bottiers, ouvriers de la chaussure et du cuir [CITP-1968 (8-0)]
shoemakers and leather goods makers [ISCO-1968 (8-0)]

conducteurs de machines pour la fabrication de produits textiles et d'articles en fourrure et en cuir [ISCO-1988 (826)]
textile-, fur- and leather-products machine operators [ISCO-1988 (826)]

CUISINIER
cuisiniers, serveurs, barmen et travailleurs
assimilés [CITP-1968 (5-3)]
cooks, waiters, bartenders and related
workers [ISCO-1968 (5-3)]

CUJUS
cujus (de)
decendent; deceased person

CULTE
assistants laïcs des cultes [CITP-1988
(348)]
religious associate professionals [IS-CO-
1988 (348)]

ministre du culte
priest

CULTIVATEUR
petit cultivateur
smallholder

CULTURE
bonne culture générale
good general knowledge

culture de la connaissance
culture of learning

culture d'entreprise
corporate culture

culture générale
general culture / knowledge

enseignement de culture générale
academic education

CULTUREL
activité sociale et culturelle
social event

foyer récréatif et culturel
(occ.) community centre

CUMUL
overlapping; double dipping; accumulation, aggregation

cumul d'affiliation
overlapping of insurance

cumul (de l') année / annuel
year to date

cumul des déductions
overlapping of deductions

cumul de droits
overlapping entitlement

cumul de droits à (des) prestations
overlapping entitlement to benefits

cumul d'emplois
double-jobbing, dual / multiple job-holding, moonlighting

cumul de pensions
multiple receipt of pensions

cumul de / des prestations
overlapping (of) / plurality of / simultaneous payment of benefits, concurrent /
duplicate benefits

**cumul d'une prestation avec d'autres
prestations de sécurité sociale**
overlapping of one benefit with other
social security benefits

CUMULER
to cumulate, to accumulate

cumuler deux emplois
to hold two jobs, (occ.) to moonlight

cumuler des fonctions
to combine functions, to hold several
positions

CURATELLE
guardianship

CURATEUR
guardian

CURATIF
remedial

action sociale curative
remedial social action

assistance curative
remedial assistance

médecine curative
remedial medicine

service curatif
remedial service

soins curatifs
curative care

CURE
cure; course of treatment

centre de convalescence, de cure ou de réadaptation (Fr.)
nursing, care or rehabilitation centre

centre médico-pédagogique de cure ambulatoire (Fr.)
out-patient child care centre

cure balnéaire
spa (course of) treatment

cure marine
thalassatherapy

cure thermale
spa (course of) treatment, hydrotherapy

établissement de cure
spa establishment

foyer de cure (et de réadaptation)
half-way house

station de cure
health resort

CURIETHÉRAPIE
radium therapy

CURRICULUM VITAE
curriculum vitae, personal / career / work profile / record / history, bio data (USA), resume (USA)

CURSUS
curriculum

CYCLE
cycle budgétaire
budget cycle

cycle conjoncturel
economic cycle

cycle de contrôle
control cycle

cycle court de formation
short training cycle

cycle économique
business / economic cycle

cycle de formation
training course

cycle long de formation
long training cycle

cycle de négociations
bargaining round

cycle de négociations collectives
collective bargaining round

cycle de paie
pay cycle

cycle de travail
job / work cycle

deuxième cycle de l'enseignement secondaire
upper secondary (education)

enseignement secondaire du premier cycle
high school education

études de troisième cycle universitaire
postgraduate studies

étudiant du premier cycle
undergraduate student

étudiant du troisième cycle
(post)graduate student

examen d'entrée dans le second cycle universitaire (USA)
graduate record examination

premier cycle de l'enseignement secondaire
lower secondary

CYCLIQUE
cyclical

chômage cyclique
cyclical unemployment

chômage non cyclique
non-cyclical unemployment

emploi cyclique
cyclical job

DANGER
danger, hazard, insecurity

danger (hors de / sans)
safe

mettre en danger
to endanger, to jeopardise

mineur en danger
minor at risk

non-assistance à personne en danger
failure to render assistance to a person in danger

DANGEREUX
hazardous, unsafe

activité dangereuse
hazardous occupation / work

allocation pour travaux insalubres et dangereux (Gr.)
unhealthy and dangerous work allowance

emploi dangereux / occupation dangereuse
hazardous occupation / work

prime de zone dangereuse
danger zone bonus

substance chimique dangereuse
hazardous chemical

tâche dangereuse / travail dangereux
hazardous occupation / work

DATE
accord de longue date
long-standing agreement

chômeur de longue date
chronically / long-term / long duration unemployed

date de l'accouchement
(actual) date of confinement

date d'achèvement
completion / termination date

date d'admission
date of admission

date d'affiliation
date of entry (into insurance)

date anniversaire d'entrée en fonctions
anniversary date of hire

date d'application
effective date

date d'arrivée
date of arrival

date butoir
deadline, cut-off date

date de début de l'emploi
start date of the job

date de départ
date of departure

date d'échéance
due / target date

date d'échéance des prestations
date on which the benefits fall due

date effective de l'accouchement
effective date of confinement

date effective de la rupture du contrat de travail
effective date of termination

date d'effet
operative / effective date

date d'effet de la retraite
effective date of retirement

date d'embauche
hire date, date of hire

date d'entrée
date of entry, entry / starting date; date of hire

date d'entrée en fonctions
(date of) entry / entrance on duty

date d'entrée en vigueur
commencement / effective date

date d'expiration
termination / expiry date

date de fin de contrat
termination date

date limite
closing / cutoff date, deadline

date limite pour le dépôt de la demande
application deadline

date limite d'inscription
application deadline

date limite de réception des candidatures
application deadline

date de péremption
expiry date

date présumée de l'accouchement
expected date of confinement

date réelle de l'accouchement
effective date of confinement

date de référence
reference date

date de sortie
date of discharge; date of leaving (hosp.)

date de sortie d'un employé
departure date of an employee

dernière date d'affiliation à l'assurance
date of last entry into insurance

notification (de la date) du congé de maternité
notice of maternity absence

DÉBAUCHAGE
enticement (to quit employment); raiding; poaching; lay(-)off

DÉBAUCHER
to entice away, to entice (to quit employment), to hire away, to poach

DÉBILE
colonie pour enfants débiles (Belg.)
centre for underdeveloped children

débile mental
mentally retarded / disabled / deficient, mental deficient, developmentally handicapped

débile (mental) léger
mildly mentally retarded

débile (mental) profond
profoundly / severely mentally retarded

DÉBILITÉ
débilité mentale
mental retardation / deficiency

DÉBIRENTIER
grantor of an annuity

DÉBITEUR (adj.)
institution débitrice de prestations
institution responsible for payment / for provision of benefits

organisme débiteur
debtor / paying body, paying office

DÉBITEUR (n.)
débiteur d'aliments
person liable to pay maintenance

débiteur de prestations
liable for benefits

débiteur de sommes
liable to pay sums

DÉBLOCAGE
déblocage de fonds
release of funds

DÉBOUCHÉ
outlet, (job / employment) opening, opportunity for employment, work / job opportunity, job / employment prospect / outlook; (pl.) employment opportunities

créer des débouchés
to develop employment possibilities

débouché de carrière
career prospect

DÉBOURS
disbursement

DÉBRAYAGE
walkout, (work) stoppage

débrayage dans l'industrie
industrial stoppage

DÉBRAYER
to walk out

DÉBUT
beginning, commencement, starting; onset

classe de début
(junior) entry / entrance level

date de début de l'emploi
start date of the job

début d'activité
entrance / entry into the labour force

début d'une activité indépendante / non salariée
entry into self-employment

début de la prise en charge
commencement of benefit(s)

effectifs en début de mois
headcount on the first of the month

emploi de début
entrance level / entry(-)level job

rémunération en début d'activité
beginning / starting salary

salaire en début d'activité
starting wage

DÉBUTANT
beginner; junior (entrant)

cadre débutant
junior manager

cours pour débutants
beginners' course

débutant dans la vie active
labour force entrant

emploi de débutant
entrance level / entry(-)level job

formation des débutants
entry-level training

stage pour débutants
beginners' course

DÉBUTER
débuter dans un emploi
to start a job

débuter dans le métier
to start out in the profession

DÉCAISSEMENT
disbursement

DÉCALAGE
time lag

DÉCALÉ
horaire décalé
staggered hours

horaire décalé fixe
staggered working hours

DÉCALEMENT
décalement des horaires de travail
staggered working hours

DÉCEDÉ
deceased

mari décédé
late husband

DÉCENCE
seuil de décence
decency threshold

DÉCÈS
death

acte de décès
death certificate

allocation (de) (-) décès
death allowance / grant; (personal) death benefit, funeral benefit

arrérages au décès (Fr.)
death arrears

assurance décès
death insurance, insurance in respect of death

assurance décès-invalidité en cas d'accident
accidental death and dismemberment (AD+D)

capital(-)décès
(lump-sum) death benefit, death grant

codification des constats de décès
coding of death certificates

décès dû à un accident du travail ou à une maladie professionnelle
death from employment (injury)

décès accidentel
accidental death

décès dû à quelque cause que ce soit
death from any cause

décès prématuré
early death

indemnité pour décès
death, dependency and indemnity compensation

prestation (en cas) de décès
death benefit

prestation de décès à la suite / résultant d'un accident du travail
industrial death benefit

prestation pour décès professionnel
industrial death benefit

rente après décès
survivor's pension

DÉCHARGE
discharge

(formule de) notification administrative de décharge
personnel payroll clearance action (form)

DÉCHEANCE
deprivation; termination; lapse; loss
déchéance de l'autorité parentale
loss of parental authority

déchéance d'un droit
loss of right, forfeiture of a right; disqualification

déchéance des droits à pension
loss of pension rights

déchéance du droit aux prestations
disqualification for benefit

déchéance des fonctions
loss of office

déchéance professionnelle
professional disability

DÉCHOIR
to disqualify from receiving a benefit

DÉCHU
déchu du droit à prestation
disentitled

DÉCIDEUR
policy-maker

DÉCILE
decile

décile inférieur
lower decile

décile supérieur
upper decile

dernier décile
last decile

premier décile
first decile

DÉCISION
decision; commitment; order; adjudication

appel d'une décision (faire)
to appeal against a decision

contester une décision
to appeal against a decision

décision arbitrale
arbitration award

décision écrite formelle
formal / authoritative written determination
/ decision

décision d'expulsion
deportation / expulsion order

décision quant au fond
adjudication on the merits

décision gracieuse
ex gratia decision

décision faisant jurisprudence
test case

décision prise en haut lieu
high-level decision

décision de principe
policy decision

instance / organe de décision
decision-making body

participation à la prise de décisions
co-determination

pouvoir de décision
decision-making power

recourir contre une décision
to appeal against a decision

DÉCISIONNEL
organe décisionnel
decision-making body

DÉCLARANT
respondant; reporting

DÉCLARATIF
formule d'habilitation déclarative
declaratory authorisation arrangement

jugement déclaratif de faillite
adjudication order

DÉCLARATION
declaration, statement; beginning;
reporting, notification

déclaration d'abandon d'enfant
declaration of abandonment of a child

déclaration d'accident
accident declaration / report(ing)

déclaration d'accident du travail
declaration / notification of an accident
at work

**déclaration annuelle de données
sociales (Fr.)**
annual declaration of salaries

déclaration de faillite
adjudication of bankruptcy

déclaration frauduleuse
fraudulent declaration

déclaration de grossesse
notification of pregnancy

déclaration d'impôts
tax return

déclaration de l'impôt sur le revenu
income tax return / form

déclaration d'indigence
certificate of poverty

déclaration judiciaire
court declaration

déclaration de maladie
notification of sickness / of illness

déclaration de naissance
registration of birth

**déclaration préalable à l'embauche
(Fr.)**
prior registration of employee

déclaration de principe
policy statement

déclaration de revenus
statement of income

déclaration de revenus modifiée
modified statement of income, amended tax
return

**déclaration de situation de famille et
demande d'indemnités pour charges de
famille**
family status report and request for payment
of dependency allowances

erreur de déclaration
respondent error

fausse déclaration
false statement / declaration, misre-
presentation

maladie à déclaration obligatoire
notifiable / reportable disease; scheduled
disease

DÉCLARÉ
chômage déclaré
measured / open / overt / registered / visible
unemployment

chômage non déclaré
unrecorded / hidden / disguised / concealed
unemployment

chômeur non déclaré
hidden unemployed

emploi non déclaré
undeclared employment

gains déclarés
declared earnings

gains non déclarés
unreported earnings

travail non déclaré
undeclared / disguised / concealed /
unrecorded employment; unrecorded work

travailleur déclaré
regular employee

travailleur non déclaré
illegal / clandestine / undeclared /
unauthorised / undocumented worker

DÉCLARER
déclarer une vacance de poste
to declare a post vacant

DÉCLASSEMENT
de-grading, downgrading;
declassification; demotion

**allocation pour déclassement profes-
sionnel**
allowance for lowered standard of
occupation

déclassement d'un poste
downgrading of post

DÉCLASSER
to downgrade

DÉCLASSIFICATION
declassification; downgrading

DÉCLENCHEMENT
facteur de déclenchement
triggering factor

indice de déclenchement
trigger index

seuil de déclenchement
trigger level

DÉCLENCHER
déclencher une grève
to trigger a strike

DÉCLIN
secteur en déclin
declining industry

DÉCLOISONNEMENT
destreaming (ed.);

decompartmentisation
(ind.); deregulation (fin.)

DÉCOMPOSITION
disaggregation, disaggregating,
break-down

DÉCOMPTÉ
années décomptées
credited service (old-age pension)

DÉCOMPTE (n.)
count; breakdown

décompte direct
(occ.) direct settlement

décompte entre institutions
adjustment of accounts between institutions

décompte des jours de congé
leave record keeping

DÉCONDITIONNEMENT
untraining of staff

DÉCONVENTIONNEMENT
deregistration

DÉCONVENTIONNER
to deregister

DÉCOURAGÉ
effet travailleur découragé
discouraged worker effect

hypothèse travailleur découragé
discouraged worker hypothesis

main-d'oeuvre découragée
discouraged workforce

travailleur découragé
discouraged worker

DÉCOUVERT
chômage découvert
recorded unemployment

DÉCRET
decree; ordinance; order; statutory
instrument; regulations

annuler un décret
to revoke a decree

décret d'application
implementing decree

décret-loi
statutory order; Order-in-Council (UK)

décret de nomination
instrument of appointment

DÉCROCHAGE
décrochage scolaire
drop-out

DÉCROCHER
to find, to secure, to obtain; to drop out
(ed.)

décrocher un emploi
to obtain / to secure employment

DÉDIT
dédit-formation
forfeit for training

DÉDOMMAGEMENT
set-off, compensation; indemnification

droit à dédommagement
right to (receive) compensation

perte de soutien et dédommagement
death dependency and indemnity
compensation

DÉDOMMAGER
to compensate, to indemnify

DÉDOUBLEMENT
dédoublement de poste
job splitting

DÉDUCTIBLE
deductible, allowable

**déductible des impôts / du revenu
imposable**
tax(-)deductible

dépenses / frais déductibles
allowable expenses

DÉDUCTION
deduction; allowance; relief; tax write-off; negative post adjustment

barème des déductions
chart of deduction rates

cumul des déductions
overlapping of deductions

déduction pour charge de famille
dependants' allowance

déduction de la cotisation
deduction of contribution

déduction pour enfant (UK)
child relief

déduction familiale
dependants' allowance

déduction fiscale
tax allowance / deduction

déduction fiscale pour enfant (à charge)
child (tax) allowance

déduction d'impôt pour enfant (UK)
child relief

déduction (d'impôt) pour vieillesse (UK)
age relief

venir en déduction de
to be offset by

DÉDUIRE
to deduct (from)

déduire la cotisation du salaire
to deduct contributions from wages

DE FACTO
mariage de facto
common law marriage

DÉFAIRE
se défaire du personnel
to shed staff

DÉFALQUER
to write off, to credit against, to under-credit; to deduct

défalquer les congés d'un fonctionnaire
to undercredit a staff member for leave

DÉFAUT
lack; limitation; handicap

défaut d'attention
lack of care / of diligence

défaut de cotisation
contribution deficiency

défaut de mobilité de la main-d'oeuvre
manpower rigidity

zéro défaut
zero defect

DÉFAVORABLE
préjugé défavorable contre qqn
bias against somebody

DÉFAVORISÉ (adj.)
under(-)privileged, disadvantaged; deprived

catégories sociales les plus défavorisées
lowest social classes

famille socialement défavorisée
socially deprived family

groupe défavorisé
disadvantaged group

mesures en faveur de groupes défavorisés
(occ.) affirmative / positive action

personne défavorisée
disadvantaged person

socialement défavorisé
socially deprived

travailleur défavorisé
disadvantaged worker

zone défavorisée
depressed area

DÉFENDRE
to support

défendre les intérêts professionnels
to protect occupational interests

DÉFENSE
action pour la défense des intérêts
professionnels
(occ.) industrial action

collectif de défense des intérêts
citizens' action group, public interest group

défense sociale
social defence

DÉFICIENCE
disability; impairment; abnormality;
handicap; limitation; retardation;
(occ.) difficulty

déficience mentale
mental retardation / deficiency / disability

DÉFICIENT (adj.)
enfant déficient
defective / deficient child

mentalement déficient
mentally deficient

physiquement déficient
physically deficient

DÉFICIENT (n.)
disabled, handicapped; retarded

déficient (mental) léger
mildly mentally retarded

déficient mental
mentally retarded / disabled, mental(ly)
deficient, developmentally handicapped

déficient (mental) moyen
trainable mentally retarded

déficient (mental) profond
profoundly / severely mentally retarded

déficient semi-éducable
trainable mentally retarded

DÉFICIT
deficit; loss; shortage

déficit actuariel
actuarial / experience deficit

déficit de la balance commerciale
balance of trade deficit

déficit budgétaire
budget deficit

déficit commercial
trade deficit

déficit d'emplois
job gap

déficit de main-d'oeuvre qualifiée
(occ.) skill gap

déficit de qualifications
skill gap

déficit de la sécurité sociale
deficit in social security

DÉFINITIF
incapacité (de travail) définitive
permanent incapacity / disablement

invalidité absolue et définitive
total permanent disability

nomination définitive
permanent / career appointment

pension définitive
life / permanent pension

plan à cotisations définies
defined contribution plan

plan à prestations définies
defined benefit scheme

régime à cotisations définies
defined contribution scheme

régime à prestations définies
defined benefit plan

DÉFINITION
définition d'emploi
post / job description

définition des emplois
job classification

définition des fonctions / de poste
job description

définition du poste de travail
job specification

définition des tâches
job design / description, task definition;
work structuring

DÉFLATEUR
corrigé par un coefficient déflateur
deflated

DÉFORMATION
déformation professionnelle
job conditioning

DÉFUNT
decedent; deceased person

DÉGAGEMENT
dégagement d'emplois
job release

DÉGAGER
dégager des obligations professionnelles
to release from work

DÉGRADATION
deterioration; worsening; loss

DÉGRAISSAGE
shake-out, slimming down; shedding
labour; streamlining manpower

DÉGRAISSER
to streamline

dégraisser des effectifs
to reduce staff

DEGRÉ
degree; level

degré d'aptitude / de compétence
skill level

degré d'incapacité (de travail)
degree of incapacity / of disablement

degré d'instruction
educational status / level / achievement /
attainment

degré d'invalidité
degree of disablement / invalidity

degré d'occupation d'un logement
degree of crowding of a dwelling

degré de parenté
degree of relationship

degré de qualification
skill level

degré de satisfaction au travail
degree of job satisfaction

degré de scolarité
educational level

enseignement du premier degré
primary education

enseignement du second degré
secondary education

enseignement du troisième degré
tertiary education

DÉGRESSIF
degressive

impôt dégressif
degressive tax

DÉGRESSIVITÉ
dégressivité de l'impôt
regressive tax

DÉGRÈVEMENT
allowance; credit; relief; reduction,
rebate

dégrèvement pour charges de famille
dependency credit

dégrèvement fiscal / d'impôts
tax rebate / relief / reduction

dégrèvement légal / prévu par la loi
statutory deduction

dégrèvement de loyer
rent rebate

dégrèvement personnel
personal (tax) relief

DÉGROUPAGE
unbundling

DÉGUISÉ
chômage déguisé
hidden / disguised / concealed unemployment

emploi salarié déguisé
disguised wage employment

impôt déguisé
hidden tax

travail déguisé
disguised employment

DÉJEUNER
pause-déjeuner
meal interval

DÉLAI
term, time(-)limit, time frame (USA)

délai (dans le même)
within the same period

délai d'appel
time-limit for an appeal

délai d'attente
qualifying period, waiting period / time;
(occ.) elimination period

délai-cadre (Switz.)
standard period

délai de carence
benefit-waiting / benefit-free period,
waiting period / time

délai-congé (Fr.)
notice of dismissal

délai de congé
term of notice

délai de conservation
time for conservation

délai déterminé (dans un)
within a specified time

délai à exécution
extension for payment

délai d'exécution
lead(-)time

délai d'exposition au risque
risk exposure time

délai de forclusion
time-limit

délai de franchise (ins.)
waiting period

délai imparti
prescribed time-limit

délai impératif
strict time-limit

délai minimum légal de préavis
statutory notice

délai de paiement
term of payment

délai de préavis
period of notice, notice period

délai de prescription
period / term of limitation

délai prescrit
required / prescribed time(-limit)

délais prescrits (dans les)
in the required / prescribed time

délai de prise en charge
period of liability for compensation

délai de réalisation
lead time

délai de recours
time-limit for an appeal

délai réglementaire
prescribed time

délai de rigueur
strict time-limit

délai de route
travel(ling) time

dernier délai
final deadline

expiration d'un délai d'attente
completion of a waiting period

prorogation de délai
extension of deadline

proroger le délai prescrit
to extend the time-limit

terme d'un délai de préavis
end of a notice period

voies et délais de recours
legal remedies and periods allowed for
appeals

DÉLAISSÉ
neglected

enfant délaissé
abandoned / neglected / deprived child

DÉLAISSER
délaisser son épouse
to desert one's wife

délaisser sa famille
to desert one's family

DÉLÉGATION
delegation; assignment; devolution

**délégation d'attribution / de compétence /
de pouvoirs**
delegation of authority

délégation de solde
order to pay somebody's salary to
dependants

DÉLÉGUÉ
representative, delegate

administrateur-délégué
managing director

délégué d'atelier
shop steward

délégué électoral
electoral delegate

délégué patronal
management / employer's
representative, representative of
employer

délégué du personnel
staff representative; chief steward

délégué à la sécurité
safety representative

délégué de site (Fr.)
workplace staff representative

délégué syndical
(labour / trade) union representative /
delegate; (shop / union) steward

délégué des travailleurs
labour / union representative, union
steward

délégué à la tutelle
guardianship officer

DÉLESTAGE
délestage de main-d'oeuvre
labour shake-out / shedding /
displacement; dishoarding; lay(-)off

DÉLIBERÉ
insubordination délibérée
wilful disobedience

DÉLIT
délit d'entrave
obstruction offence

DÉLIVRANCE
grant, supply, issue, issuance; delivery;
relief

DÉLIVRER
to issue; to make available for

DÉLOCALISATION
relocation; offshore work

DÉLOCALISÉ
activité délocalisée
offshore industry

industrie délocalisée
footlose / offshore industry

DEMANDE
request, claim; application; demand

accéder à une demande
to allow a claim

adéquation de l'offre et de la demande
matching supply and demand

adéquation de l'offre et de la demande d'emploi
job-worker / worker-job matching,
matching of jobseekers and vacancies, job
matching

appariement informatique des offres et des demandes d'emploi
computerised matching of jobs and job
seekers

auteur d'une demande
applicant

chômage par insuffisance de la demande
demand-deficient unemployment

courbe de la demande de main-d'oeuvre
demand curve for labour

date limite pour le dépôt de la demande
application deadline

demande (à la)
on call

demande d'admission à l'aide sociale
welfare benefits request

demande d'allocation
claim for a benefit / an allowance

demande d'avance de traitement
request for salary advance

demande de classement médical
medical clearance request

demande de congé
application for leave

demande de dotation en personnel
staffing action request

demande d'emploi
application for a job, employment / job
application; situation wanted

demande excédentaire de main-d'oeuvre
excess demand for labour

demande frauduleuse
fraudulent claim

demande globale
aggregate / total demand

demande d'indemnisation
claim for compensation

demande d'indemnisation pour accident du travail
accident claim, workmen's
compensation claim

demande de main-d'oeuvre
demand for labour, labour / manpower /
worker demand

demande de main-d'oeuvre agricole
agricultural labour demand

demande sur le marché du travail
labour market demand

demande de mutation
request for transfer, transfer request

demande de pension
application / claim for (a) pension,
pension claim

demande préalable à l'emploi
pre-employment inquiry

demande de prestation
benefit claim, claim / application for benefit

demande de reclassement
request for reclassification

demande reconventionnelle
counter-claim

demande de remboursement
refund request / claim

demande saisonnière
seasonal demand

demande de services
service request

demande sociale d'éducation
social demand for education

demande tardive
late claim

demande de travail
demand for labour, labour demand

demande de travailleurs
worker / manpower demand

droit à une demande (faire)
to allow a claim

élasticité de la demande de main-d'oeuvre
elasticity of labour demand

élasticité de la demande par rapport au revenu
income elasticity of demand

évaluation des demandes
application assessment

formulaire de demande
claim / application form

formulaire de demande d'emploi
job application form

formulaire / formule de demande de remboursement
request for settlement form

inadéquation entre offres et demandes d'emploi
job mismatch

inadéquation de l'offre et de la demande de travail
(occ.) labour market mismatch

instruction d'une demande de prestations
investigation of a claim for benefits

instruire une demande
to consider an application, to investigate a claim

introduction d'une demande de presta-tions
submission of a claim for benefits

introduire une demande
to register / to make / to submit a claim

introduire une demande de prestations
to apply for / to lodge a claim for / to make an application for benefits

liquidation d'une demande de prestation
settlement of benefit claim, establishment of entitlement to benefit

mise en correspondance des offres et des demandes d'emploi
job matching

offre et la demande (l')
supply and demand

présenter une demande
to apply, to submit a claim

présenter une demande d'emploi
to apply for a job

profession à forte demande
high demand occupation

réception d'une demande
receipt of an application

refuser une demande d'allocation / de prestation
to reject a claim for benefit; (occ.) to disallow benefit

renchérissement de la demande
additional demand

Service des demandes (UK)
Claims Section

DEMANDER
demander une aide sociale
to apply for welfare benefits / for relief

demander à être indemnisé
to claim compensation

demander une / des prestation(s)
to claim benefit(s)

DEMANDEUR
applicant, claimant; customer

atelier d'objectif professionnel pour
demandeurs d'emploi (Belg.)
vocational objectives workshop for
jobseekers

demandeur d'asile
asylum seeker

demandeur d'emploi
applicant for work, person seeking work,
work-seeker, job applicant / seeker /
searcher / hunter; seeking, looking for work

demandeur d'emploi inscrit (comme tel)
registered job-seeker

demandeur d'un premier emploi
first(-time) job seeker, new entrant on the
labour market

demandeur d'une pension / d'une rente
pension claimant

DÉMARGINALISATION
(occ.) mainstreaming

DÉMARGINALISER
(occ.) to mainstream

DÉMARRAGE
capital de démarrage
seed capital

DÉMÉNAGEMENT
removal; relocation

allocation de déménagement
moving / removal / relocation allowance

frais de déménagement
moving / relocation / removal expenses /
costs

indemnité / prime de déménagement
moving / removal / relocation allowance

DÉMENCE
insanity

DÉMETTRE
démettre de ses fonctions (se)
to resign from one's post

DEMI-JOURNÉE
demi-journée de congé
half day's leave

DEMI-SALAIRE
half-pay, half-wage

DÉMISSION
resignation; quit(ting)

démission sans préavis
resignation without prior notice

donner sa démission
to submit one's resignation; to quit

préavis de démission écrit
written notice of resignation

DÉMISSIONNER
to resign, to quit

démissionner de ses fonctions
to resign from one's post

DÉMOBILISATEUR
effet démobilisateur
disincentive effect

DÉMOGRAPHIE
demography; population

démographie sociale
social demography

DÉMOGRAPHIQUE
perspective / prévision démographique
population forecast

projection démographique
population projection

statistiques démographiques
population statistics

DÉMONSTRATEUR
modèles, vendeurs et démonstrateurs
[CITP-1988 (52)]
models, salespersons and demonstrators
[ISCO-1988 (52)]

DÉMOTIVER
to demotivate, to remove incentive from

DÉMUNI (adj.)
deprived

DÉMUNI (n.)
the have-nots, the deprived

assurance-maladie pour les plus démunis (USA)
medicare

nantis et les démunis (les)
haves and the have-nots (the)

DÉMUNIR
to deprive

DENIER (n.)
deniers de l'Etat / publics
public money / monies / funds

deniers pupillaires
ward property

DÉNOMINATION
dénomination professionnelle
professional description

DÉNONCER
dénoncer un contrat
to denounce a contract

DÉNONCIATION
denunciation, termination

clause de dénonciation
termination clause

dénonciation d'un accord
denunciation of / (unilateral)
termination of an agreement

DENRÉE
bon de réduction sur les denrées alimentaires (UK)
food rebate coupon

DENTAIRE
affection dentaire
tooth disease

allocation pour prothèse dentaire (Ger.)
dental replacement allowance

appareillage dentaire
dental plates

assistance dentaire
dental health services

assurance-soins dentaires
dental insurance, dental health scheme

cabinet dentaire
dental surgery

centre de consultation dentaire
dental clinic

chirurgie dentaire
dental surgery

chirurgien dentaire
dental surgeon

consultations dentaires pour enfants (Austr.)
school dental clinic

formule dentaire
dental formula; dentition

hygiène dentaire
dental health

médecine dentaire
dentistry

prothésiste dentaire
dental technician

service de consultation dentaire
dental clinic

service de santé dentaire
dental health service

soins dentaires
dental treatment / care

soins dentaires d'entretien
conservative dental care

DENTISTERIE
dentistry

DÉNUEMENT
deprivation, destitution; want; distress

dénuement (dans le)
poverty-stricken

DÉONTOLOGIE
(professional) code of ethics, (professional) ethics

code de déontologie
code of behaviour / of professional etiquette / of professional conduct

DÉONTOLOGIQUE
code déontologique
code of behaviour / of professional etiquette / of professional conduct

DÉPART
departure; termination (of employment); separation

âge de départ obligatoire à la retraite
automatic / compulsolry / mandatory retirement age

âge de départ à la retraite
retirement age

âge légal de départ à la / en retraite
statutory retirement age

calendrier des départs
separation schedule

capital de départ
seed capital

date de départ
date of departure

départ forcé à la retraite
involuntary retirement

départs naturels
natural wastage of labour

départ à la / en retraite
retirement (from labour force); (pl.)
(occ.) staff attrition

départ à la retraite ajourné
deferred retirement

départ à la retraite anticipé
early retirement

départ à la retraite retardé
deferred retirement

départ volontaire
voluntary separation, quit(ting)

départ volontaire à la préretraite
early retirement on a voluntary basis

départ volontaire à la retraite
voluntary retirement

diminution des effectifs par le jeu naturel des départs
natural wastage of labour

entretien de départ
exit interview

indemnisation de départ anticipé
compensation for loss of office

indemnisation viagère de départ
annuity for withdrawal from work

indemnité annuelle de départ
annuity for withdrawal from work

indemnité de départ
severance pay / payment

jeu naturel des départs (par le)
by natural attrition

pourcentage des départs (naturels)
wastage rate

prime de départ
severance pay / payment; (occ.) golden handshake

prime de départ volontaire
voluntary leaving premium

programme de départs volontaires
voluntary severance / redundancy scheme

rémunération de départ
beginning / starting salary

retarder le départ à la retraite
to defer retirement

salaire de départ
starting wage

taux des départs
separation rate

versement de départ au titre de la liquidation des droits
withdrawal settlement

DÉPARTEMENT
department, division; unit

département externe (hosp.)
out-patient department

département hospitalier
hospital unit

département ministériel
Government department

département du personnel / des ressources humaines
personnel department

DÉPASSEMENT
dépassement de (en)
over and above

dépassement de crédits
over-expenditure

dépassement d'heures
surplus of hours worked

dépassement d'honoraires / de tarif
overbilling, extra-billing

droit permanent à dépassement (Fr.)
permanent right to overbilling

DÉPASSER
dépasser le tarif conventionnel agréé
to charge more than the standard agreed fee

DÉPENDANCE
dependence; dependency; helplessness; dependence on welfare

allocation (de) (-) dépendance
dependency allowance; helpless person's allowance (Austr.), helplessness allowance (Liech.)

complément de dépendance (Finl.)
helplessness supplement

dépendance médicamenteuse
drug dependence

état de dépendance
helplessness

rapport de dépendance économique
rate of dependency, dependency ratio

rapport de dépendance économique des personnes âgées
old age dependency ratio

substance engendrant une dépendance
dependence-producing drug

taux de dépendance (économique)
dependency ratio

taux de dépendance des personnes âgées
old age dependency ratio

DÉPENDANT
dependant

dépendant (non)
self-supporting

personnes âgées dépendantes
dependent / (occ.) frail elderly

travailleur dépendant
dependent worker

DÉPENSE
expenditure, expense; cost

chiffrage des dépenses
costing

dépenses accessoires
miscellaneous expenses

dépense active
active expenditure

dépense(s) d'administration
administrative / service / management
cost(s) / expenses

dépenses comptabilisées
recorded expenditure

dépenses courantes
running costs

dépenses déductibles
allowable expenses

dépenses exceptionnelles
below-the-line expenditure

dépenses d'exploitation
running / operational / operating cost

dépenses extraordinaires
below-the-line / non-recurrent expenditure

dépenses de fonctionnement
running / operating cost(s) / expenditure

dépense d'infrastructure sociale
social overhead cost

dépenses locales
local costs

dépenses ordinaires
recurrent expenditure

dépenses au titre des prestations
benefit expenditure

dépenses publiques
Government / public spending / expenditure

**dépenses raisonnablement et légitime-
ment engagées**
just and reasonable expenses

dépenses renouvelables
recurrent expenditure

dépenses non renouvelables
non-recurrent / non-recurring / one-time
expenditure

dépenses de santé
health expenditure

dépenses de sécurité sociale
social security expenditure

dépenses sociales
social expenditure

engagements de dépenses
financial obligations

engagement prévisionnel de dépenses
commitment

engager des dépenses
to incur expenses

justification des dépenses effectives
production of proof of actual
expenditure

maîtrise des dépenses
expenditure control

maîtrise des dépenses de santé
health expenditure control

**politique de compression des
dépenses**
policy of retrenchment

poste de dépenses
item of expenditure

**procédure de remboursement des
dépenses**
expense claim procedure

répartition des dépenses
(occ.) cost-sharing

restriction des dépenses
expenditure restraint

DÉPERDITION
déperdition d'effectifs
(labour) wastage, attrition; (ed.) drop-
out

déperdition (d'effectifs) scolaire(s)
educational wastage

déperdition naturelle
natural wastage of labour

taux de déperdition d'effectifs (ed.)
drop-out rate

DÉPISTAGE
screening (process), detection (med.);
identification

DÉPISTER
to screen

DÉPLACÉ
travailleur déplacé
displaced worker

DÉPLACEMENT
displacement; removal; relocation; shift;
travel

aide au déplacement et à la prospection
relocation and exploratory assistance

assurance-déplacement professionnel
travel accident insurance

congé de déplacement
travel leave

déplacement de la charge du chômage
churning

**déplacement domicile-travail / entre
domicile et lieu de travail**
travel / journey to work; commuting

déplacement de la main-d'oeuvre
manpower movement, movement of / flow
of workers

déplacement par mesure disciplinaire
disciplinary transfer

déplacement de service
official travel / journey

déplacement temporaire
temporary relocation

déplacement des travailleurs
manpower movement, movement of /
flow of workers

effet de déplacement
(job) displacement effect

frais de déplacement
transportation / travel expenses / costs

indemnité de déplacement
travel(ling) / mileage allowance,
mileage fee

indemnité spéciale de déplacement
special travel allowance

zone de déplacement domicile-travail
journey(-)to(-)work / travel(-)to(-)work
area

DÉPLAFONNEMENT
removal of ceiling

DÉPLAFONNER
to uncap

DÉPLIANT
leaflet

DÉPLOIEMENT
déploiement du personnel
deployment of staff

DÉPORTÉ (n.)
ancien déporté
war prisoner

DÉPOSER
déposer un préavis de grève
to give notice of strike action

DÉPOSITION
evidence

DÉPÔT
registration; deposit

contrat de gestion de dépôts
deposit administration contract

date limite pour le dépôt de la demande
application deadline

fonds en dépôt
funds-in-trust

DÉPRÉCIATION
dépréciation des qualifications
deskilling

DÉPRÉCIÉ
emploi déprécié
stigmatised job

DÉPUTATION
delegation

DÉQUALIFICATION
déqualification des tâches
deskilling

DÉRAPAGE
dérapage des salaires
earnings / wage drift

DÉRÉGLEMENTATION
deregulation

DÉRÉGLEMENTER
to deregulate

DÉRIVÉ (adj.)
activités dérivées
spin-off activities

droit social dérivé
subordinate social right

DÉRIVE (n.)
dérive des (niveaux de) salaire(s)
earnings / wage drift

DERNIER
dernière date d'affiliation à l'assurance
date of last entry into insurance

dernier décile
last decile

dernier délai
final deadline

dernier ressort (en)
without appeal; in the last instance

dernier salaire
final salary

DÉROGATION
derogation, dispensation; exception;
wai-ver; departure (from), deviation
(-from)

accorder une dérogation
to grant a waiver

dérogation aux clauses d'un contrat
deviation from the terms of a contract

DÉROGATOIRE
dispensatory

clause dérogatoire
escape / saving / dispensatory clause

régime dérogatoire (Fr.)
exceptional arrangement

DÉROGER
to waive

DÉROULEMENT
déroulement de carrière
career progress / path

étude du déroulement de carrière
career follow-up / career pattern study

DÉSACCORD
point de désaccord
area of contention

procès-verbal de désaccord
minutes of failure to agree

DÉSAISONNALISATION
seasonal adjustment, deseasonalisation

DÉSAVANTAGÉ (adj.)
disadvantaged

**mesures en faveur de groupes désa-
vantagés**
(occ.) affirmative / positive action

DÉSAVANTAGE (n.)
disadvantage; handicap

DÉSAVOUER
to disown

DESCENDANT (adj.)
phase descendante
downswing, downturn

DESCENDANT (n.)
descendant

DESCRIPTIF
descriptif de poste
job specification

DESCRIPTION
description des attributions / d'emploi / de
fonction / de poste / des tâches
job / position description

description sommaire de poste
summary job description

DÉSÉCONOMIE
déséconomie d'échelle
diseconomy of scale

DÉSENDETTEMENT
désendettement des ménages
reduction of household tax burden

DÉSENGAGEMENT
withdrawal

clause (optionnelle) de désengagement
opting-out clause

DÉSENGAGER (se)
to opt out

DÉSÉQUILIBRE
disequilibrium; imbalance;
maladjustment; mismatch

déséquilibre actuariel
actuarial imbalance

déséquilibre commercial
trade imbalance

**déséquilibre du marché de l'emploi /
du travail**
labour market imbalance, imbalance /
disequilibrium on the labour market

déséquilibre dans les professions
occupational imbalance

déséquilibre racial
racial imbalance

DÉSHERITÉ
under(-)privileged; deprived; castaway

enfance déshéritée
deprived children

zone déshéritée
depressed area

DÉSIGNATION
nomination, appointment; assignment

désignation de fonction
job title

désignation professionnelle
professional description

droit de désignation
right of nomination

DÉSIGNÉ
profession désignée
designated occupation

représentant désigné
official representative, (occ.) prescribed
person

travailleur nommément désigné
specific named worker

DÉSIGNER
to appoint

DÉSINSERTION
désinsertion sociale
(occ.) dropping out

DÉSINTÉRESSER
désintéresser de (se)
to disregard

DÉSISTEMENT
withdrawal

DÉSISTER (se)
to withdraw; to opt out

DÉSORGANISATION
désorganisation du marché du travail
labour market / manpower dislocation,
dislocation of the labour market

DESTINATAIRE (adj.)
pays destinataire
receiving country

DESTINATAIRE (n.)
recipient

DESTINATION
destination

DESTITUÉ
destitué de ses fonctions (être)
to be relieved of one's duties

DESTITUER
to dismiss

destituer de ses fonctions
to relieve of one's duties

DESTITUTION
dismissal

DÉSUET
profession désuète
obsolete occupation

DÉSYNDICALISER
to decline in trade union

DÉTACHÉ
détaché à (être)
to be seconded to

détaché par une entreprise
posted by an undertaking

personne détachée
secondee

personnel détaché
seconded staff

travailleur détaché
seconded worker

DÉTACHEMENT
deputation, detailment, detail, (out)
posting, secondment

accord de détachement
secondment agreement

détachement à l'étranger
secondment abroad

détachement de personnel
secondment of staff, staff secondment

détachement d'un travailleur salarié
posting of an employed person

période de détachement
period / term of posting

DÉTACHER
to second; to make available for; to
provide

DÉTAIL
commerce de détail
retail trade

directeurs (commerces de gros et de détail) [CITP-1968 (4-0)]
managers (wholesale and retail trade) [ISCO-1968 (4-0)]

prix de détail
retail price

propriétaires-gérants de commerces de gros et de détail [CITP-1968 (4-1)]
working proprietors (wholesale and retail trade) [ISCO-1968 (4-1)]

DÉTAILLÉ
bulletin / feuille / fiche de paie détaillé(e)
detailed / itemised pay statement

DÉTARTRAGE
scaling

DÉTECTIVE
inspecteurs de police judiciaire et détectives [CITP-1988 (345)]
police inspectors and detectives [ISCO-1988 (345)]

DÉTENTE
congé de détente
(rest and) recuperation leave

DÉTENTEUR
holder

DÉTENU (n.)
allocation pour femmes de détenus (Irel.)
prisoners wife's allowance

DÉTÉRIORATION
détérioration de la conjoncture
downturn of the economy

détérioration de l'emploi
(occ.) employment slump

usure et détérioration
wear and tear

DÉTERMINATION
determination; identification; assessment

base de détermination
basis of assessment

détermination du taux d'invalidité
determination of impairment / of invalidity

système de détermination du salaire minimum
minimum wage system

DÉTERMINÉ
specific; specified; prescribed

contrat (de travail) à / de durée déterminée
fixed-term / fixed-duration (employment / work) contract, fixed-term appointment

contrat à durée déterminée à terme imprécis (Fr.)
unspecified fixed-term contract

contrat à durée déterminée à terme précis (Fr.)
specified fixed-term contract

contrat à durée déterminée à terme non spécifié (Fr.)
unspecified (but fixed) term contract

délai déterminé (dans un)
within a specified time

emploi d'une durée déterminée
term employment

fonctionnaire à contrat de durée déterminée
fixed-term official

nomination pour une période déterminée / de durée déterminée
specified period / term appointment, fixed-term appointment

personnel engagé pour une durée déterminée
fixed-term staff

poste de durée déterminée
position on a fixed-term basis

profil professionnel déterminé
specific vocational profile

DÉTERMINER
to determine; to assess

déterminer le montant de l'impôt sur le revenu
to assess income tax

déterminer le montant des prestations
to assess benefits

rémunération à déterminer
negotiable salary

DÉTRESSE
hardship; plight

cas de détresse
hardship case

DETTE
debt; financial obligation; liability

rééchelonner une dette
to reschedule a debt

DEUIL
bereavement

allocation de deuil (Austr.)
bereavement payment

DEUXIÈME
allocations familiales payables à partir du deuxième enfant
children's allowances from the second child

deuxième activité professionnelle
second job

deuxième apporteur de revenu
second (family) earner / breadwinner, secondary family worker, secondary (wage) earner

deuxième circuit de formation (Belg.)
"second chance" training facilities

deuxième cycle de l'enseignement secondaire
upper secondary (education)

deuxième emploi
second job

deuxième notateur
second supervisor

école de la deuxième chance
second-chance college

enseignement de la deuxième chance
second-chance education

immigré de la deuxième génération
second-generation immigrant

marin / matelot de deuxième classe
able(-bodied) seaman

DÉVALORISATION
downgrading

dévalorisation du travail manuel
downgrading of manual labour

DÉVALORISER
to downgrade; to underrate

DÉVELOPPEMENT
développement communautaire
community development

développement économique équilibré
balanced economic development

développement de l'éducation
educational expansion

développement de l'emploi
employment development; job stimulation

développement local
community development

développement professionnel
staff development

développement des ressources humaines
human resources / manpower development

développement rural
rural development

développement social
social development

engagement de développement (EDDF) (Fr.)
development agreement

indicateur du développement humain
human development index

société de développement de l'emploi local
(occ.) community employment corporation

DEVOIR (n.)
duty

devoir de fidélité à la Constitution (Ger.)
duty of loyalty to the Constitution

devoir professionnel
official duty

devoir de secours
duty of assistance

manquement aux / violation des devoirs de fonction
breach of professional / official duty

DÉVOLUTION
vesting (USA)

DEXTÉRITÉ
dexterity; skill (in handling)

DIAGNOSTIC
diagnosis; assessment, evaluation

centre de diagnostic
diagnosis centre

diagnostic social
social diagnosis

DIAGRAMME
diagramme de flux / fonctionnel
flow chart

DIALOGUE
dialogue social
concertation, social dialogue

DIDACTIQUE
aide didactique
training aid / material

matériel didactique
training / teaching material / aid, instructional material

DIÉTÉTICIEN
dietetician / dietetitian

DIÉTÉTIQUE (n.)
dietetics

DIFFÉRÉ (adj.)
acquisition différée
deferred vesting (pensions)

annuité différée
deferred annuity

assurance-vie à capital différé
endowment insurance

charge différée
deferred charge

coefficient de recrutement différé
delayed recruitment factor

pension à jouissance différée
deferred pension

pension réduite de retraite différée
reduced deferred pension

police d'assurance-vie à capital différé
endowment policy

régime de retraite à participation différée aux bénéfices
deferred profit-sharing pension plan

rente différée
deferred annuity / pension

retraite différée
deferred pension / retirement benefit

revenu différé
deferred income

salaire différé
deferred wage

DIFFÉRÉ (n.)
deferment

différé d'indemnisation (Fr.)
waiting period

paiement en différé
deferred payment

DIFFÉRENCE
différence de rémunération
salary gap / disparity / differential, pay
differential

différences de revenus
income differential; earnings gap

différence de salaires / salariale
wage / earnings gap / differential, difference
in wages

DIFFÉRENCIÉ
salaires différenciés
differential wages

DIFFÉREND
dispute

différend du travail
industrial dispute

règlement d'un différend
dispute settlement / resolution, settlement of
a dispute

DIFFÉRENTIEL (adj.)
allocation différentielle
compensatory / differential / equalisation
allowance

complément différentiel
equalisation supplement

cotisation différentielle
differential contribution

indemnité différentielle
compensatory / equalisation allowance;
hardship allowance

régime différentiel
different treatment

taux différentiel (de traitement)
salary differential

DIFFÉRENTIEL (n.)
différentiel de coût de la vie
cost-of-living differential factor

DIFFÉRER
to defer

DIFFICILE
allocation pour situation difficile
hardship allowance

**allocation pour situation particulière-
ment difficile (UK)**
special hardship allowance

cas difficile
hardship case

enfant difficile
problem child

poste difficile
hardship post

poste difficile à pouvoir
hard-to-fill vacancy

situation difficile
hardship, predicament

DIFFICULTÉ
difficulty

difficulté d'apprentissage
learning disability

difficulté locomotrice
locomotor difficulty

élève en difficulté scolaire
under-achiever, low performer /
achiever

famille en difficulté
(occ.) problem family

**indemnité pour difficultés (exception-
nelles) d'existence**
hardship pay

industrie en difficulté
ailing industry

prime de difficulté de vie
hardship allowance

DIFFUSER
diffuser des offres d'emploi
to circulate job vacancies

DIFFUSION
circulation; distribution

DILEMME
dilemme chômage-inflation
employment-inflation trade-off

DILIGENCE
diligence raisonnable
due diligence

DILUTION
dilution de la main-d'oeuvre
dilution of labour

DIMANCHE
travail le dimanche
Sunday work

DIMENSION
dimension, size

dimension de la famille
family size

dimension du ménage
household size

dimension sociale
social dimension

DIMINUÉ
disabled, handicapped

diminué (non)
unimpaired

diminué physique
physically disabled / handicapped

diminué social
socially handicapped

enfant diminué
handicapped child

intellectuellement / mentalement diminué
mentally disabled

physiquement diminué
physically disabled / handicapped

DIMINUTION
reduction, decrease; loss; handicap

diminution de la capacité de gain
reduction / loss of earning capacity

diminution de la capacité de travail
reduction of working capacity

diminution des effectifs par le jeu naturel des départs
natural wastage of labour

diminution fonctionnelle
impairment of function, functional handicap / impairment

diminution de l'intégrité physique
(occ.) loss of faculty

taux de diminution des effectifs
attrition rate

DIPLÔMANT
stage diplômant
qualifying training period / working experience

DIPLOMATIQUE
corps / service diplomatique
foreign service

DIPLÔME (n.)
certificate; degree

diplôme reconnu
recognised diploma

diplôme universitaire
university diploma / degree

formation complémentaire à l'obtention du diplôme de base
postbasic training

titulaire d'un diplôme
diploma holder, holder of a diploma

titulaire d'un diplôme (être)
to hold a diploma

titulaire d'un diplôme universitaire
degree holder, holder of a degree

DIPLÔMÉ (adj.)
diploma holder; qualified; trained

diplômé (non)
unqualified

diplômé d'Etat
certified, State-registered

étudiant non diplômé
undergraduate

infirmière diplômée
trained / registered nurse

programme de formation pour jeunes diplômés
graduate training scheme

DIPLÔMÉ (n.)
chômage des diplômés universitaires
graduate unemployment, unemployment amongst graduates

diplômé de l'enseignement supérieur
college graduate, tertiary-education graduate

diplômé de niveau post-secondaire
post-secondary graduate

diplômé universitaire
graduate, degree holder, university graduate

niveau d'entrée des diplômés
graduate entry (in a company)

nouveau diplômé
recent graduate

recrutement de diplômés universitaires
graduate recruitment

DIRECT
administration directe
(occ.) direct rule

aide directe
direct assistance

coût direct
direct cost

coûts salariaux directs
direct labour costs

création directe d'emplois
direct job creation

décompte direct
(occ.) direct settlement

emploi direct
direct employment

entente directe
direct agreement

financement direct
direct funding

frais de formation directs
direct training costs

impôt direct
direct tax; (pl.) direct taxation

placement direct
direct placement

prestation à la charge directe de l'employeur
employer-based benefit

prestation sociale directe de l'employeur
unfunded employment welfare benefit

recrutement par approche directe
executive search

régime de retraite complémentaire privé en gestion directe
self-administered pension scheme

soins directs
direct care

subvention directe à l'emploi
direct employment subsidy

subvention salariale directe
direct wage subsidy

supérieur hiérarchique direct
immediate superior / supervisor

versement direct
direct payment

DIRECTEMENT
directement applicable
immediately applicable; enforceable, self-executory

frais directement liés à la formation
direct training costs

personne directement à charge
primary dependent

personne non directement à charge
secondary dependent

DIRECTEUR (adj.)
ligne directrice
guideline

Lignes directrices du BIT pour la mesure du chômage
ILO Guidelines for measuring unemployment

organe directeur
governing body; steering group; policy-making body

principe directeur
basic principle; (pl.) policy considerations / guidelines, guidelines, policy

schéma directeur
master plan

DIRECTEUR (n.)
manager; superintendent; warden

comité directeur
steering committee

directeurs [CITP-1968 (121)]
directors and chief executives [ISCO-1988 (121)]

directeur adjoint
deputy manager

directeurs et cadres administratifs supérieurs [CITP-1968 (2)]
administrative and managerial workers [ISCO-1968 (2)]

directeurs et cadres dirigeants (2-1)]
managers [ISCO-1968 (2-1)]

directeurs et chefs d'exploitation agricoles [CITP-1968 (6.0)]
farm managers and supervisors [ISCO-1968 (6-0)]

directeur de clinique
nursing home administrator

directeurs (commerces de gros et de détail) [CITP-1968 (4-0)]
managers (wholesale and retail trade) [ISCO-1968 (4-0)]

directeur exécutif
executive director

directeur général
executive / managing director, chief executive (officer) (CEO)

directeur général adjoint
deputy managing director

directeurs d'hôtels, de cafés ou de restaurants [CITP-1968 (5-0)]
managers (catering and lodging services) [ISCO-1968 (5-0)]

directeur du personnel
labour / work director, personnel manager

directeur de programme
programme manager

directeur de projet
project manager
directeur des ressources humaines
labour / work director, personnel manager

Directeur de la santé publique (UK)
State health officer

directeurs de société [CITP-1988 (12)]
corporate managers [ISCO-1988 (12)]

DIRECTIF
document directif
policy paper

entretien directif
guided / directed interview

DIRECTION
management; executive / managerial /
grade staff; managers; administration;
(head) office; leadership; trend

assistant(e) de direction
executive / personal assistant

attaché de direction
executive / management assistant

cadre de direction
executive officer

comité de direction
management / steering committee

conseil de direction
governing body; management board

consigne de la direction
managerial directive

direction administrative
management office

direction générale
top management

niveau de direction
executive level

personnel de direction
management; senior (directing / supervisory) staff, managerial staff

personnel d'encadrement et de direction
supervisory and management staff

poste de direction
executive position / job, managerial post

poste d'encadrement et de direction
supervisory and management position

poste de haute direction
upper level management position

représentant de la direction
management / employer's
representative, representative of
employer

secrétaire de direction
executive secretary, personal assistant

DIRECTIVE
guideline

directive budgétaire
budget guideline

DIRECTOIRE
executive board

DIRIGÉ
entretien dirigé
guided / directed interview

DIRIGEANT (n.)
(top) executive, manager; leader;
official;
policy-maker; (pl.) (senior / top)
management

cadre dirigeant
top / senior (level) / upper level
manager, senior / top executive;
director; (pl.) top management

directeurs et cadres dirigeants (2-1)]
managers [ISCO-1968 (2-1)]

**dirigeants et cadres supérieurs
d'organisations spécialisées [CITP-
1988 (114)]**
senior officials of special-interest
organisations [ISCO-1988 (114)]

**dirigeants et gérants [CITP-1988 (13,
131)]**
general managers [ISCO-1988 (13,
131)]

dirigeant syndical
(trade) union official / leader

DISCIPLINAIRE
déplacement par mesure disciplinaire
disciplinary transfer

droit disciplinaire
disciplinary law

intenter une procédure disciplinaire
to institute disciplinary proceedings

mesure disciplinaire
disciplinary measure / action

mise à pied disciplinaire
disciplinary lay-off, suspension without pay

mutation disciplinaire
disciplinary transfer

procédure disciplinaire
disciplinary procedure / proceedings

sanction disciplinaire
disciplinary sanction

DISCIPLINE
discipline, subject, branch / field of study;
subject area; subject group

choix de la discipline
choice of subject (area) / of field of study,
subject choice

conseil de discipline
disciplinary board

DISCONTINU
horaire discontinu
split working hours

journée discontinue
split workday

production en discontinu
batch production

DISCRÉTIONNAIRE
discretionary

pouvoir discrétionnaire
discretionary power

relever du pouvoir discrétionnaire de
to be within the discretion of

revenu discrétionnaire
discretionary income

DISCRIMINATION
discrimination

anti-discrimination à l'embauche
(occ.) affirmative action

discrimination antisyndicale
anti-union discrimination

discrimination à l'embauche
restrictive (hiring) practice(s)

discrimination dans l'emploi
discrimination in employment, employment discrimination

discrimination intentionnelle
intent discrimination

discrimination positive
positive discrimination

discrimination professionnelle
occupational segregation

discrimination pure et simple
outright discrimination

discrimination raciale
racial discrimination

discrimination à rebours
reverse discrimination

discrimination sexuelle
sexual discrimination

**discrimination structurelle /
systémati-que**
structural / systemic / systematic
discrimination

motif illicite de discrimination
prohibited ground of discrimination

DISCRIMINATOIRE
discriminatory

acte discriminatoire
discriminatory practice; discrimination

condition discriminatoire
discriminatory requirement

discriminatoire (non)
non-discriminatory

emploi non discriminatoire
non-discriminatory employment

exigence discriminatoire
discriminatory requirement

offre d'emploi discriminatoire
discriminatory job offer

pratique discriminatoire
discriminatory practice

régime discriminatoire
discriminatory / different treatment

système d'emploi non discriminatoire
neutral employment system

DISPARITÉ
disparity; differential

disparité de revenus
income differential; earnings gap

disparité de salaires
wage disparity

disparité de traitement
disparity of treatment

indice des disparités socio-économiques
socio-economic disparity index

DISPARITION
disparition d'emploi
job loss

disparition d'entreprises
death of companies

taux de disparition (des entreprises)
mortality rate (of companies)

DISPENSAIRE
public health outlet, (health) clinic

dispensaire de consultations prénatales
pre(-)natal clinic

dispensaire rattaché à une école
school clinic

dispensaire de médecine sociale
social medicine centre

dispensaire d'obstétrique
midwifery clinic

dispensaire prénatal
ante-natal / pre(-)natal clinic

DISPENSATEUR
dispensateur de soins
care giver / provider

dispensateur de soins médicaux
medical care provider

DISPENSÉ (adj.)
dispensé de légalisation
exempt from authentication

DISPENSE (n.)
dispensation; exemption; waiver;
remission

dispense générale
blanket exemption

dispense de préavis
release from working out one's notice

dispense de remboursement
waiver of reimbursement

liste de dispenses
waiver list

DISPENSER
to provide

dispenser des prestations
to provide services

DISPERSION
indicateur de dispersion des salaires
(occ.) comparatio

DISPONIBILITÉ
availability; (pl.) supply

disponibilité (en)
available for service

disponibilité de / en main-d'oeuvre
availability of manpower, manpower /
labour supply, supply of labour, worker(s)
availability

disponibilité pour le travail
availability for work

disponibilité de travailleurs
worker availability

**données sur la disponibilité (des tra-
vailleurs)**
(workers) availability data

durée de disponibilité du travailleur
length of time worker available

fonctionnaire en disponibilité
civil servant temporarily retired

mettre en disponibilité
to grant leave of absence, to place on
inactive status

mise en disponibilité
leave of absence; inactive status

DISPONIBLE
available

disponible pour un emploi
available for work

emploi disponible
available job

main-d'oeuvre disponible
availability of manpower, manpower /
labour supply, supply of labour, worker(s)
availability

poste disponible
available post

réserve de main-d'oeuvre disponible
(occ.) stand-by workforce

ressources humaines disponibles
human resources supply

revenu disponible
spendable / disposable income

revenu disponible des particuliers
disposable personal income

revenu personnel disponible
private disposable income, disposable
personal income

solde disponible
unexpended / unencumbered balance

travailleur disponible
available worker; (pl.) manpower
supply, supply of labour

DISPOSITIF
provision; machinery; scheme;
operative
provisions / part

dispositifs de formation
training facilities

DISPOSITION
rule; clause; arrangement; provision;
regulation(s), terms; willingness

contrat de mise à disposition (Fr.)
contract making temporary staff
available

disposition de (à la)
available

disposition abrogatoire
repealing provision

dispositions d'un accord
terms of an agreement

disposition complémentaire
additional provision

dispositions contraires (sauf)
unless otherwise provided

disposition conventionnelle
provision of an industrial agreement;
(pl.) (occ.) treaty provisions

dispositions diverses
miscellaneous provisions

dispositions d'espèce (sauf)
unless otherwise provided

disposition générale
general provision; (pl.) (occ.) blanket
clause

disposition prise à titre individuel
private arrangement

disposition légale / législative
statutory provision; (pl.) legislative
provisions, law

dispositions législatives et réglementaires
laws and regulations

disposition prise à titre personnel / privé
private arrangement

disposition réglementaire
regulatory rule; (pl.) regulation(s)

disposition spéciale
special provision

disposition statutaire
statutory provision, provision in the articles

disposition temporaire
transitional provision

disposition au travail
willingness to work; attitude to work

mettre à la disposition de
to make available for

personne mise à disposition
secondee

réserve des dispositions de (sous)
except as provided in, subject to the
provisions of

DISQUALIFIÉ
disentitled

DISSIMULÉ
sous-emploi dissimulé
concealed under-employment

travail dissimulé
disguised employment / work, concealed /
unrecorded employment

DISSOCIÉ
couple dissocié
broken / dissolved marriage

foyer dissocié
broken home

ménage dissocié
broken / dissolved household

DISSOLUTION
termination

DISSUASION
dissuasion; disincentive

effet de dissuasion
disincentive effect

DISTANCE
apprentissage à distance
distance learning

enseignement à distance
distance learning / education / teaching

travail à distance
remote control work; telecommuting,
telework(ing)

DISTINCT
contrat de gestion distincte
segregated funds contract

contrat de gestion distincte de caisse
segregated accounts funding contract

DISTRIBUABLE
réserve distribuable
revenue reserve

DISTRIBUTIF
négociation distributive
distributive / zero(-)sum bargaining

DISTRIBUTION
delivery

distribution des prestations
delivery of services

distribution du revenu
income distribution

distribution des soins médicaux
medical care delivery

- 245 -

distribution des soins de santé
health care delivery

distribution des tâches / du travail
work allocation / distribution, workload
breakdown

système national de distribution de soins
national system of health care

DISTRICT
agent sanitaire de district
district sanitarian

médecin de district
district physician

DIVERS
dispositions diverses
miscellaneous provisions

frais divers
miscellaneous expenses

DIVERSIFICATION
diversification des tâches
(occ.) job enlargement

DIVISION
division; department; branch

division internationale du travail
international division of work / of labour

**division du personnel / des ressources
humaines**
personnel department

division du travail
division of labour / of work

DIVORCÉ(E)
divorced (person)

**allocation spéciale pour les enfants de
femmes divorcées (UK)**
child's special allowance

personne divorcée
divorced (person)

veuf ou divorcé
ever-married

DOCKER
dock labourer

DOCTEUR
docteur en médecine
doctor of medicine

DOCTORAT
doctorate; postgraduate

études de doctorat
postgraduate studies

DOCUMENT
document; paper; record; evidence

document d'approbation
record of approval

document de cessation de service
separation document

document directif / d'orientation
policy paper

document récapitulatif
summary / round-up document

DOCUMENTAIRE
étude / synthèse documentaire
literature review / survey

DOCUMENTATION
documentation; evidence

DOLÉANCE
claim, grievance

DOMAINE
area, field

domaine d'action
policy area

domaine d'activités
occupational area / field

domaine de compétence
field of expertise, specialised field,
competency area

domaine du spectacle
entertainment industry; show business

emploi lié au domaine d'étude
school-related position

DOMESTICITÉ
household servants

DOMESTIQUE (adj.)
domestic

accident domestique
domestic accident

aide domestique
ancillary help

économie domestique
home economics; family budgeting;
homecraft

puériculture et économie domestique
home and mother craft

service domestique
domestic service

travail domestique
domestic / household work

travailleur domestique
domestic / household worker

DOMESTIQUE (n.)
(personal / domestic) servant; private
household worker

DOMICILE
domicile; home; (law) place of abode

abandon de / du domicile conjugal
desertion (of the matrimonial home)

accouchement à domicile
home confinement

aide à domicile
home help

aide médicale à domicile
home medical care, medical home relief
(USA)

aide ménagère à domicile
home-making assistance

aide et soins à domicile
home help and care

**allocation de garde à domicile des
enfants (Finl.)**
child home care allowance

**allocation de garde d'enfant à
domicile**
home child care allowance

allocation de soins à domicile (Irel.)
domiciliary care allowance

assistance médicale à domicile (USA)
medical home relief

changement de domicile
change of residence; removal, relocation

consultation à domicile
domiciliary consultation

**déplacement domicile-travail / entre
domicile et lieu de travail**
travel / journey to work; commuting

domicile collectif
congregate housing

domicile conjugal
marital domicile, matrimonial home

domicile familial
matrimonial / parental home

domicile fixe (sans)
homeless; of no fixed abode / address

domicile légal
legal domicile, place of abode

domicile d'origine
domicile of origin

domicile de secours (Fr.)
place of residence for welfare purposes

élire domicile
to make one's abode

garde à domicile
home care (children)

garde-malade à domicile
home nursing / care

hospitalisation à domicile
home (medical) care

industrie à domicile
home(-based) industry, home craft; cottage industry

infirmière à domicile
(occ.) community nurse

maintien à domicile des personnes âgées
home care for the elderly

navette entre son domicile et son lieu de travail (faire la)
to commute to and from work

personne sans domicile
person of / with no fixed abode, vagrant

prime d'accouchement à domicile (UK)
home confinement grant

repas à domicile
home meals

service de repas à domicile
(occ.) meals on wheels

service de soins à domicile
home care service

service de soins infirmiers à domicile pour personnes âgées
home care nursing for the elderly

soins à domicile
domiciliary / in-house care, home nursing, home (medical) care

soins infirmiers à domicile
home nursing, visiting nurse services

soins médicaux à domicile
home medical care, medical home relief (USA)

subvention pour le maintien à domicile (UK)
community care grant

trajet domicile-travail
work journey

travail à domicile
home business / work, (occ.) home-bound employment

travailleur à domicile
cottage / home worker, outworker

visite à domicile (med.)
doctor's home visit, domiciliary consultation / visiting, home call / visit

zone de déplacement domicile-travail
journey(-)to(-)work / travel(-)to (-)work area

DOMICILIÉ
population domiciliée
resident population

DOMINICAL
repos dominical
Sunday rest

travail dominical
Sunday work

visite dominicale
Sunday call

DOMMAGE
prejudice; loss

assurance-dommages
damage / indemnity / loss insurance

dommages corporels
physical injury

dommage immatériel
intangible loss

dommage matériel
pecuniairy / material damage

production imputée de services d'assurance-dommages
imputed service charge for casualty insurance

réparation des dommages de guerre
war damage compensation

responsabilité à raison de dommages
responsibility for injuries

DOMMAGEABLE
harmful; injurious

conséquence dommageable
harmful effect

DONNÉE
(pl.) data; figure(s); input; statistics

base de données projectives sur la population active
labour force projections data base

collecte de données
data collection

déclaration annuelle de données sociales (Fr.)
annual declaration of salaries

données de base
baseline data / information

données chiffrées
facts and figures

données relatives au chômage
unemployment data

données comparables
comparable figures

données comparatives
comparative figures

données sur la disponibilité (des travailleurs)
(workers) availability data

données relatives à l'emploi
employment figures / data

données de flux
flow data

données longitudinales
historical data

données relatives aux ménages
household data

données prévisionnelles sur les professions
occupational outlook information

données rétrospectives
retrospective / back data

données (statistiques) provenant d'un recensement
census material

données de stocks
stock data

interconnexion des données
record linkage

rassemblement de données
data collection

rassembler / réunir des données
to collect data

DONNER
donner sa démission
to submit one's resignation; to quit

donner droit
to entitle

donner effet
to implement

donner lieu à
to be liable to

donner mandat / pouvoir de
to authorise

donner un préavis
to give notice

donner suite
to follow up; to implement

DORTOIR
hostel

ville dortoir
dormitory town

DOSSIER
record, file; case history; papers; application; claim / benefit unit (UK); fact sheet

dossier de candidature
job application form, application blank (USA)

dossier hospitalier / d'hospitalisation
hospital record

dossier individuel
personal record / file

dossier individuel d'un salarié
employee file

dossier d'inscription
enrolment form, registration file

dossier médical
medical record; (pl.) health records; (occ.)
case histories

dossier militaire
service record
dossier de mutation
transfer record

dossier personnel
personal record / file

dossier du personnel
personnel file / record

dossier scolaire
school record

frais de dossier
administrative cost(s)

interconnexion des dossiers
record linkage

tenue de dossiers
record keeping

DOTATION
endowment; budget allocation

demande de dotation en personnel
staffing action request

dotation en effectifs
staffing, provision of staff, manning

dotation familiale
family endowment

dotation globale de fonctionnement
global operating budget

dotation globale hospitalière
global hospital budget

dotation en personnel
staffing, provision of staff, manning

dotation d'un poste
staffing of a position

dotation des postes par voie de recrutement externe
external staffing

gel de la dotation en personnel
staff freeze

DOTER
to provide

DOUBLE
clause de double indemnisation
double indemnity (clause)

double activité (qui exerce une)
dual job holder

double comptage
double count / counting

double emploi
overlapping

double indemnisation
double indemnity

double salaire sans enfants
double income no kids (DINK)

double taxation
double imposition

emplois en double pilotage
job shadowing

exercice d'une double activité
double / dual jobholding

méthode de la double courbe des rémunérations
dual pay-line approach

orphelin double
full orphan, orphan whose parents are
dead, orphan having lost both parents

personne qui exerce une double activité
double jobholder / jobber

système de la double filière (pensions)
two-track pension adjustment system

DOULOUREUX
cas douloureux
hardship case

DOUZIÈME
douzième provisoire
credit vote

DROIT
law; right; claim; fee; charge, duty

acquisition d'un droit à (des) prestations
acquisition of a right to benefits

acquisition de droits
vesting of rights

âge du droit à pension
pensionable age

âge d'ouverture des droits
age of eligibility

âge d'ouverture des droits à / ouvrant droit à pension
age of pension entitlement, pensionable age

allocataire en fin de droit(s)
insurance exhaustee

allocation de fin de droits
allowance for end of entitlement; follow-up benefit

année ouvrant droit à
year of entitlement

attestation de droit (aux prestations)
certificate of eligibility / of entitlement

attraction du droit à prestations
(occ.) eligibility effect

bénéficiaire en fin de droit
(unemployment) insurance exhaustee

cessation d'un droit à (des) prestations
cessation of entitlement to / of a right to benefits, exhaustion of entitlement to benefits

chômeur en fin de droits
unemployment insurance / benefit exhaustee, unemployed person no longer entitled to receive unemployment benefit

concours de droits
overlapping of rights

condition minimale d'ouverture des droits
minimum qualifying condition

condition d'ouverture des droits
qualifying condition; condition of entitlement; eligibility

conférer un droit acquis
to endow with an acquired right

conservation des droits
preservation / maintenance of rights

conservation des droits acquis
maintenance of acquired rights

conservation des droits en cours d'acquisition / de formation
maintenance of rights in course of acquisition

conservation des droits à pension
preservation of rights to pension

cumul de droits
overlapping entitlement

cumul de droits à (des) prestations
overlapping entitlement to benefits

déchéance d'un droit
loss of right, forfeiture of a right; disqualification

déchéance des droits à pension
loss of pension rights

déchéance du droit aux prestations
disqualification for benefit

déchu du droit à prestation
disentitled

donner droit
to entitle

droit (à)
entitlement

droit à (avoir)
to be eligible, to qualify for, to be entitled to

droit (ne pas avoir)
to be ineligible

droit (ayant) à
entitled

droit de (en)
entitled to

droit (qui a)
entitling
droit (qui de)
person entitled to a right

droit accessoire
ancillary right; (pl.) additional rights

droits accumulés
accrued rights

droit acquis
existing right, vested interests; (pl.)
established / vested / accruing / accrual /
accrued / acquired rights

droit en cours d'acquisition
right in course of acquisition

droit d'agrément
registration fee (pensions)

droit d'alerte et de retrait (Fr.)
right of worker to notify a potential risk to
his safety and to stop work

droit aux allocations
eligibility for benefits / allowances

droit annexe
ancillary right

droit d'appel
right of / to appeal

droit d'association
freedom of organisation; right to organise

droit commercial
business law

droit aux congés
vacation / holiday / leave entitlement

droits contractuels
contractual rights

droits conventionnels
contractual rights

droit à dédommagement
right to (receive) compensation

droit à une demande (faire)
to allow a claim

droit de désignation
right of nomination

droit disciplinaire
disciplinary law

droit écrit
statute law

droit à l'éducation
right to education

droits d'embauche
recruitment fee

**droits au regard de / dans l'emploi /
en matière d'emploi**
job / employment rights

droits de l'enfant
children's rights

droit d'enregistrement
registration fee

droit d'entrée
admission fee

droit d'établissement
right of establishment

droit exclusif
exclusive / proprietary / sole right

droit exclusif de placement des travailleurs
exclusive right to place workers in jobs,
placing monopoly

droit d'exercer
right to practice

droit d'expression des salariés
employees' right of expression

droit de former appel
right of / to appeal

droit de garde des parents
parental custody

droit de grève
right to strike

droit à indemnisation
right to (receive) compensation

droit à (une) indemnité
claim / allowance entitlement, entitlement / benefit claim

droit à l'information
information right

droit d'inscription
enrolment / registration fee

droit à l'instruction
right to education

droit de licenciement
right to dismiss

droits liquidés
claim settled

droit maintenu d'office
automatically maintained right, right automatically maintained

droit de la mutualité
law governing mutual benefit societies

droit de / à la négociation collective
right to bargain collectively

droits et obligations
rights and obligations

droit des obligations
law of obligations, contract law

droit d'option
right of option

droit d'organisation
freedom of organisation, right to organise

droit à pension
pension right, right to pension; (pl.) pension entitlement

droit à pension (faire valoir un)
to claim a pension

droit(s) à pension transférable(s)
portable pension right(s)

droit permanent à dépassement (Fr.)
permanent right to overbilling

droit de préemption des travailleurs
workers' right of pre-emption

droit à prestation (faire valoir un)
to claim benefit

droit à (des) prestations
right to / eligibility for / entitlement to benefit(s), benefit entitlement / claim

droit aux prestations (avoir)
to be eligible for / to qualify for benefit

droit de prétendre à (être en)
to be eligible

droit à une prime (avoir)
to be eligible for a grant

droit à une prime de rapatriement
entitlement to repatriation grant

droit à une promotion
right to promotion

droit de recours
right of / to appeal

droit de réexamen
right of review

droit de regard
right to examine

droit à réparation
(enforceable) right to (receive) compensation

droit de représentation syndicale
(occ.) representational right

droit de retrait (Fr.)
right to stop work

droit à la retraite (ayant)
eligible for retirement

droits à la retraite (faire valoir ses)
to claim retirement benefit

droit de réunion
right of assembly

droits des salariés
employee / employees' rights

droits de scolarité
tuition / school fees

droit à la sécurité sociale
right to social security

droit social
social / welfare law / legislation; (pl.) social rights

droit social dérivé
subordinate social right

droits de succession
death / estate duties

droit syndical
right of association / of union organisation / to organise; trade union law; (pl.) trade union rights

droit de se syndiquer
right to organise

droits et taxes
dues and taxes

droit au travail
right of / to work

droit du travail
labour law / legislation

durée du droit à prestations
duration of benefit entitlement

emploi ouvrant droit à pension
(recognised) pensionable employment

emploi n'ouvrant pas droit à pension
employment not recognised pensionable employment

enfant ouvrant droit aux prestations
eligible child

épuiser le droit aux prestations
to exhaust right / entitlement to benefit(s)

fin de droits
end of entitlement

fin de droits (être en)
reach the end of one's entitlement (to)

fins de droits (les)
exhaustees

fin des droits à (des) prestations
cessation / exhaustion of entitlement to / of a right to benefits

garder un droit sur son poste
to retain a lien on one's post

incessibilité des droits
non-transferability of rights

liquider des droits à prestations
to pay benefits

logement ouvrant droit au versement d'une allocation
subsidised housing

maintien des droits
maintenance / preservation of rights

maintien des droits acquis
maintenance of acquired / vested rights

maintien d'un droit à (des) prestations
retention of a right to benefits

mise en oeuvre des droits économiques et sociaux
realisation of economic and social rights

montant ouvrant droit à pension
pensionable amount

ouverture des droits
entitlement

ouverture d'un droit à (des) prestations
acquisition of a right to benefits

ouvrir un droit
to entitle; to grant / to confer a right

passible de droits
(occ.) taxable

perdre le droit à une / aux prestation(s)
to be disqualified for benefit, to disqualify from receiving benefit

période d'assurance requise pour l'ouverture du droit aux prestations
qualifying insurance / qualification period

période ouvrant droit
period of eligibility

période de service ouvrant droit à ...
period of qualifying service

personne ayant droit aux prestations
person eligible for benefits

personne en fin de droits
exhaustee

perte d'un droit
loss of (a) right

perte de droits à pension
loss of pension entitlements

perte du droit aux prestations
loss of entitlement

plein droit (de)
as of right

porter atteinte aux droits acquis
to jeopardise acquired rights

possibilité de transférer des droits
portability of rights

prescription d'un droit
limitation of a right

prestation servie de droit
benefit paid as of right

prestation servie par l'Etat
State benefit

prévaloir de droits acquis (se)
to claim benefit of acquired rights

priver du droit de faire qqch
to estop from doing something

recouvrement des droits
recovery of rights

recouvrement d'un droit à (des) prestations
recovery of a right to benefits

recouvrer le droit à (des) prestations
to requalify for / to recover the right to benefits

règle de droit
law

remplir les conditions d'ouverture des droits aux prestations
to be eligible for / to qualify for benefit, to satisfy the conditions for acquisition of the rights to benefits

renoncer à des droits
to waive / to relinquish rights

respect des droits acquis
respect for acquired rights

retrait du droit aux prestations
disqualification for benefit

revenu ouvrant droit à pension
pensionable income

salaire ouvrant droit à pension
pensionable wage

service ouvrant droit à pension
pensionable service

société de droit public
public corporation

solde des droits
balance of entitlements

survivant ayant droit
eligible survivor

Système international de conservation des droits en matière de sécurité sociale
International System for the Maintenance of Rights in Social Security

taux d'acquisition du droit à pension
(pension) accrual rate

titulaire d'un droit
person entitled to a right

traitement ouvrant droit à pension
pensionable salary

transfert des droits acquis d'une caisse à une autre (pension)
transferability / portability of pension rights

transfert des droits d'ancienneté
transfer of seniority rights

valoir ses droits à pension (faire)
to claim pension rights; to qualify for a pension

versement de départ au titre de la liquidation des droits
withdrawal settlement

violation des droits acquis
breach of acquired rights

DÛ
due, in arrears, payable

prestation due
benefit due

salaire dû
outstanding pay

DUAL
société duale
dual society

système dual (ed.)
dual system

DÛMENT
properly

dûment motivé
properly substantiated

DUMPING
dumping social
social dumping

DURABILITÉ
sustainability

DURABLE
accord durable
long-lasting agreement

DURÉE
duration, period; term

affection de longue durée
long-term sickness / disease

allonger la durée du travail
to increase hours of work

chômage de longue durée
long duration / long-term / chronic unemployment

chômage de très longue durée
very long-term unemployment

chômeur de longue durée
chronically / long-term / long duration unemployed

condition de durée de service
service requirement / eligibility

contrat (de travail) à / de durée déterminée
fixed-term / fixed-duration (employment / work) contract, fixed-term appointment

contrat à durée déterminée à terme imprécis (Fr.)
unspecified fixed-term contract

contrat à durée déterminée à terme précis (Fr.)
specified fixed-term contract

contrat à durée déterminée à terme non spécifié (Fr.)
unspecified (but fixed) term contract

contrat (de travail) à durée indéterminée
indefinite / open-ended (employment / work) contract, indefinite appointment

contrat de longue durée
long-term contract

courte durée
short-term

durée d'activité
period of work

durée actuelle du chômage
(duration of) current spell of unemployment

durée de l'affectation
length of assignment

durée d'affiliation
period of / number of years of insurance;
insurance period; period of membership;
contributory service / period, period / length
of contributory service

durée annuelle de travail
annual working time

durée annuelle effective du travail
annual hours worked

**durée d'assurance ouvrant droit à
prestations**
qualifying insurance / qualification period

durée d'assurance(-)vieillesse
period of old age insurance

durée de carrière
working life

durée de / du chômage
length / duration of unemployment

**durée convenue du travail hebdoma-
daire**
standard working week, standard weekly
hours

durée d'un contrat
duration of a contract

durée de disponibilité du travailleur
length of time worker available

durée du droit à prestations
duration of benefit entitlement

durée d'emploi
term / length of employment

durée de l'engagement
tenure of appointment

durée des études
duration / length of study

durée des fonctions
length / period / term of office; tenure

durée de la formation
duration of training

durée hebdomadaire du travail
hours worked weekly, weekly hours of
work, work(ing) week

**durée hebdomadaire du travail
prévue par la loi**
statutory working week

durée de l'hospitalisation
duration of hospitalisation

durée d'immatriculation (Lux.)
period of membership

durée de l'indemnisation du chômage
duration of unemployment benefits

durée légale du travail
statutory working hours

durée légale maximale du travail
statutory maximum working hours

durée d'un mandat
term / tenure of office

durée maximale / maximum
maximum duration

**durée maximale du travail prévue
par la loi**
statutory maximum working hours

durée minimale de service (benefits)
minimum period of payment

durée moyenne des cas (de maladie)
average duration per case

durée moyenne du chômage
average duration of unemployment

**durée moyenne de la vie active /
professionnelle**
mean duration of working life

durée normale du travail
standard working hours

**durée normale du travail
hebdomadaire**
standard working week, standard
weekly hours

durée d'occupation d'un emploi
job tenure

durée d'octroi des prestations
period for which benefit is allowed

durée de la période de stage
period of probationary service

durée de préavis
length of notice

durée de la prestation / de la prise en charge
duration of benefit, benefit duration

durée d'un programme
term of a programme

durée de résidence
period of residence

durée de séjour
duration / length of stay

durée de service
duration / length of service / of employment; period of payment (benefits)

durée de service des prestations
period for which benefit is allowed

durée du travail
hours of work, working time / hours

durée de travail réduite
short time

durée de vacance (de poste / d'emploi)
duration of vacancy, vacancy duration

durée de validité
period of validity

durée de la vie active / de la vie professionnelle
(duration of) working life

emploi de courte durée
short-term / temporary work / employment / job

emploi d'une durée déterminée
term employment

emploi de / à durée indéterminée
permanent job / employment, indefinite employment

emploi de longue durée
long-term employment

engagement de courte durée
short-term appointment

engagement pour une durée indéfinie
indefinite appointment

engagement à titre temporaire pour une durée indéfinie
temporary indefinite appointment

fonctionnaire à contrat de durée déterminée
fixed-term official

hôpital pour séjours de longue durée
long-term hospital

immigrant de courte durée
short-term immigrant

immigrant de longue durée
long-term immigrant

interruption de la durée de chômage
break in the period of unemployment

limitation de la durée du travail
restrictions on working hours

maladie de longue durée
long-term sickness / disease

nomination de durée déterminée
fixed-term appointmennt

nomination pour une durée indéfinie / de durée indéterminée
appointment of indefinite duration / without limit of time

occuper un emploi de longue durée
to work on a long-term basis

personnel engagé pour une durée déterminée
fixed-term staff

personnel engagé pour une période de courte durée
short-term staff

placement de longue durée dans une institution
long-term institutional care

poste de durée déterminée
position on a fixed-term basis

prestation de courte durée
short-term benefit

prestation sans limitation de durée
open-ended benefit

prestation de longue durée
long-term benefit

réduction de la durée du travail
reduction of / cut in working hours

réduction de la durée hebdomadaire du travail
reduction of the working week

réduction de la durée quotidienne du travail
reduction of daily hours

soins de longue durée
long-term care

temps réduit indemnisé longue durée (Fr.)
short-time work on benefit for a long period

DURETÉ
harshness

DYNAMIQUE (adj.)
politique dynamique de l'emploi
active employment policy

DYNAMIQUE (n.)
dynamics; trend

dynamique du marché du travail
labour market dynamics

ÉBÉNISTE
ébénistes, menuisiers et travailleurs
assimilés [CITP-1968 (8-1)]
cabinet makers and related woodworkers
[ISCO-1968 (8-1)]

ÉBOUEURS
éboueurs et manoeuvres assimilés [CITP-
1988 (916)]
garbage collectors and related labourers
[ISCO-1988 (916)]

ÉCART
range; disparity, difference, differential;
gap; lapse

écart interéchelons
inter-step differential

**écart introduit (à la marge) par la
fiscalité**
(marginal) tax wedge

écart de rémunération
salary gap / disparity / differential, pay
differential

écart entre les revenus
income differential; earnings gap

écart de salaires
wage / earnings gap / differential, difference
in wages

**écart des salaires par rapport à la
productivité**
real wage gap

écart salarial
wage / earnings gap / differential, difference
in wages

écart technologique
technological gap

ECCLÉSIASTIQUE (n.)
clergyman

ÉCHANGE
économie fondée sur l'échange
barter economy

termes de l'échange
terms of trade

ÉCHANTILLON
sample

échantillon aléatoire
random sample

échantillon de ménages
household sample, sample of
households

échantillon représentatif
representative / adequate sample

**enquête auprès d'un / sur échantillon
(restreint)**
sample survey

taille de l'échantillon
sample size

ÉCHANTILLONNAGE
erreur d'échantillonnage
sampling error

ÉCHÉANCE
due date; expiry; term

brève échéance (à)
in the short-term, in the short-run

date d'échéance
due / target date

date d'échéance des prestations
date on which the benefits fall due

longue échéance (à)
in the long run

période séparant deux échéances
period separating two dates for payment

ÉCHÉANCIER
schedule

ÉCHEC
failure; breakdown

échec scolaire
school failure; under-achievement

taux d'échec
failure rate

ÉCHELLE
scale; size; range

déséconomie d'échelle
diseconomy of scale

échelle d'appréciation fondée sur des études de comportement type par fonction
behaviourally anchored rating scale (BARS)

échelle d'une branche (à l')
industry-wide

échelle des emplois
job hierarchy

échelle mobile (des salaires)
sliding (wage) scale; incremental scale

échelle mobile (des salaires) établie sur le coût de la vie
cost-of-living sliding scale

échelle de notation du rendement
performance rating scale

échelle de rémunération
salary / pay / wage scale / range, range / scale of wages

échelle de(s) salaires / salariale
wage / pay / salary scale / range, range / scale of wages, wage bracket

échelle d'un secteur (à l')
industry-wide

échelle des taux
schedule of rates

échelle de traitement / des traitements
wage / pay / salary scale / range, range / scale of wages, wage bracket

économies d'échelle
economies of scale

emploi au bas de l'échelle
entry-level job

évaluation des emplois selon une échelle de points
point-factor method of job evaluation

perte d'échelle
diseconomy of scale

poste au bas de l'échelle
entry-level job

ÉCHELON
scale; (incremental) step; level

avancement d'échelon
increment, within-grade (salary) increment

échelon d'ancienneté
longevity increment / step, long-service step

échelons d'une carrière
(occ.) job ladder

échelon hiérarchique
hierarchical grade; level of authority

échelon inférieur
junior grade

échelon de mérite
meritorious increment

échelon de rémunération
pay grade; salary section

échelon supérieur
top grade

emploi aux échelons les plus élevés
high-level employment

emploi de premier échelon
entry-level job

ÉCHELONNÉ
graduated

augmentation échelonnée
incremental increase

horaire échelonné
staggered hours

système de primes échelonnées
scaled premium system

versement échelonné
instalment

ÉCHELONNEMENT
staging, scheduling

échelonnement des horaires de travail
scheduling of work

ÉCHELONNER
to graduate, to phase

échelonner les cotisations
to graduate contributions

échelonner les vacances
to stagger holidays

ÉCHO
(occ.) feedback

ÉCHU
arrérages de pension échus
pension arrears due

intérêts échus
outstanding interest

ÉCLAIR
grève éclair
lightning strike

ÉCOLE
administrateur d'école
school administrator / executive

âge de sortie de l'école
school-leaving age

dispensaire rattaché à une école
school clinic

école active
active school

école d'application
practice school

école-atelier
production high school (Denm.),
workshop school (Sp.)

école de commerce
business school

école confessionnelle
confessional school

école dispensant des cours du soir
evening / night school

école de la deuxième chance
second-chance college

école élémentaire
elementary / grade / primary school

école d'enseignement familial et ménager
home-making school

école (dispensant un enseignement) à temps complet
full-time school

école de gestion
business school

école libre
private school

école maternelle
infant / nursery school, kindergarten

école de médecine
medical college

école de métiers (Switz.)
vocational training college

école normale
college of education, teacher training
college / school

école parallèle
alternative school

école phare
magnet school

école polyvalente
comprehensive school

école post-secondaire
post-secondary school

école préparatoire
preparatory school

école primaire
elementary / grade school; grammar
school

école privée
private school

école professionnelle
training / trade / vocational school

école publique
government / public school

école secondaire
secondary school

école de secrétariat
secretarial college

école de service social
social work school

école du soir
evening / night school

école supérieure de commerce / de gestion
business school

effectifs sortis des écoles
school output

foyer-école
school home

hôpital-école
teaching hospital

jeune quittant prématurément l'école
early school leaver

jeune sortant de l'école / (déjà) sorti de l'école
school-leaver

plan d'accompagnement pour les sortants de l'école et des études (SAVE) (Belg.)
support plan for school and college leavers

professeur d'école normale
teacher of a college of education; (occ.) teacher(-)educator

ÉCOLIER
school(-)child

ÉCOLOGIQUE
éducation écologique
environmental education

ÉCONOMIE
economy; (pl.) savings

branche de l'économie
economic sector

économie d'apprentissage
learning economy

économie cachée
black / hidden / informal / moonlight / shadow / submerged / twilight / underground / grey / invisible economy

économie domestique
home economics; family budgeting; homecraft

économie fondée sur l'échange
barter economy

économies d'échelle
economies of scale

économie de l'éducation
economics of education

économies d'envergure
economies of scope

économie d'évasion
escapist economy

économies de gamme
economies of scope

économie immergée
black / hidden / informal / moonlight / shadow / submerged / twilight / underground / grey / invisible economy

économies de main-d'oeuvre
labour savings

économie de marché
market economy

économie de marché sociale
social market economy

économie ménagère
home economics

économie parallèle
parallel / black / hidden / informal / moonlight / shadow / submerged / twilight / underground / grey / invisible economy

économies de personnel
staff savings

économie de réseau
network economy

économie de salaires
wage economy

économie du savoir
knowledge(-based) economy

économie souterraine
black / hidden / informal / moonlight /
shadow / submerged / twilight /
underground / grey / invisible economy

économie du travail
labour market theory, labour economics

économie fondée sur le troc
barter economy

évolution de l'économie / économique
economic development / trend

générateur d'économies de main-
d'oeuvre
labour saving

mesure d'économie
economy measure

politique d'économies
policy of savings / of retrenchment

puériculture et économie domestique
home and mother craft

secteur de l'économie
economic sector, branche of the economy

secteur de l'économie sociale
(occ.) third sector

secteur formel de l'économie
formal economy sector

secteur informel / non organisé / parallèle
de l'économie
informal economy sector

secteur structuré de l'économie
formal economy sector

secteur non structuré de l'économie
informal economy sector

ÉCONOMIQUE
activité économique
economic / business activity; business

activités économiques de caractère
non matériel
non-productive labour

avantage économique
economic benefit

bien-être économique
economic well-being

classification par activité / par
branche d'activité économique
industrial classification

climat / contexte économique
business / economic climate

compte économique de la formation
professionnelle (Fr.)
vocational training economic account

crise économique
economic crisis

croissance économique
economic growth

croissance économique soutenue
sustained economic growth

cycle économique
business / economic cycle

développement économique équilibré
balanced economic development

évolution économique
economic development / trend

fluctuation de l'activité économique
business fluctuation, fluctuation in
business / economic activity

fonds d'indemnisation des
licenciements économiques
redundancy fund

indemnité de licenciement pour cause
/ raison économique
redundancy benefit / payment

indice de malaise économique
(economic) discomfort index

infrastructure économique et sociale
economic and social infrastructure /
facilities / overhead

licencié pour raisons économiques (être)
to be made redundant

licenciement collectif pour motifs économiques
collective redundancy

licenciement (pour motif) économique
dismissal for economic reasons, redundancy

logement économique
low-cost accomodation / housing unit

mise en oeuvre des droits économiques et sociaux
realisation of economic and social rights

perspectives économiques
economic outlook / prospects

politique économique
economic policy

principal soutien économique
primary / principal (wage) earner

ralentissement de l'activité économique
economic slack / downswing / down-turn

rapport de dépendance économique
rate of dependency, dependency ratio

rapport de dépendance économique des personnes âgées
old age dependency ratio

rapport de soutien économique
support ratio

rapport de soutien économique des personnes âgées
old age support ratio

récession économique
economic crisis

recherche économique appliquée
applied economic research

réfugié économique
economic refugee

relance / reprise économique
economic upswing / recovery

secteur économique
economic sector, branch of the economy

situation économique
economic / business situation

taux de dépendance économique
dependency ratio

tendance économique
economic trend

théorie économique
economic theory

travailleur licencié pour raisons économiques
redundant worker

ÉCONOMIQUEMENT
économiquement faible
person in need of financial assistance;
(occ.) underprivileged; low-income
people; (pl.) lower / lowest income
group

personne économiquement faible
person in need of financial assistance

population économiquement active
economically active / gainfully occupied
/ working population

population économiquement inactive
economically inactive / unoccupied
population

ÉCONOMISTE
économistes [CITP-1968 (0-9)]
economists [ISCO-1968 (0-9)]

ÉCOULÉ
période écoulée
completed period

ÉCOURTER
écourter un stage
to reduce a probationary period

ÉCRIT
avertissement écrit
written warning

blâme écrit
written censure

décision écrite formelle
formal / authoritative written determination
/ decision

droit écrit
statute law

instruction écrite
written submmission

préavis de démission écrit
written notice of resignation

preuves écrites
documentary evidence

ÉCRITURE
mécanismes de la lecture et de l'écriture
(occ.) literacy skills

ÉCRIVAIN
écrivains et artistes créateurs et exécutants
[CITP-1988 (245)]
writers and creative or performing artists
[ISCO-1988 (245)]

ÉDICTER
to issue

édicter des règlements
to issue / to make regulations

ÉDUCATEUR
educator; teacher; social worker

éducateur de rue
(community) supervision officer, street
educator

éducateur sanitaire
health educator

éducateur spécialiste du service social
social work educator

éducateur spécialisé
teacher of children with learning difficulties

moniteur éducateur
teaching instructor

ÉDUCATIF
assistance éducative
educational support

assistance éducative en milieu ouvert
open educational support

besoins éducatifs
educational need / requirement

**égalité des chances sur le plan
éducatif**
equality of educational opportunity

objectif éducatif
educational goal

système éducatif
education(al) system

ÉDUCATION
education

allocation d'éducation
education allowance

**allocation d'éducation du Common-
wealth (Austr.)**
Commonwealth education allowance

**allocation pour l'éducation des
enfants (Ger.)**
child raising allowance

allocation d'éducation spéciale
special education allowance, allowance
for severely disabled children (Fr.)

allocation parentale d'éducation
parental child care allowance

**autorités (responsables) de
l'éducation**
educational authorities

centre d'éducation motrice
education centre for people with motor
impairment

centre d'éducation sensorielle
education centre for people with sensory
disability

centre d'éducation surveillée
correctional school; (occ.) training
school

chèque-éducation
education voucher

congé-éducation / d'éducation (Ger.)
education(al) leave, child raising leave

congé-éducation payé
paid education(al) leave

congé parental d'éducation (Fr.)
parental childcare leave

demande sociale d'éducation
social demand for education

développement de l'éducation
educational expansion

droit à l'éducation
right to education

économie de l'éducation
economics of education

éducation des / pour adultes
adult education

éducation de base
basic education

éducation civique
citizenship / civic education

éducation complémentaire
further education

éducation continue
permanent / continuing / further education

éducation écologique
environmental education

éducation extrascolaire
out-of-school / informal education

éducation familiale
family education

éducation formelle
formal education

éducation ouvrière
workers' education

éducation permanente
continuing / lifelong / adult / further
education, lifelong training / learning

éducation à plein temps
full-time education

éducation préscolaire
early(-)childhood / pre(-)primary / pre-
school education

éducation professionnelle
vocational education

éducation récurrente
recurrent education

éducation sanitaire / pour / à la santé
health education

éducation spéciale
special education

**établissement d'éducation complé-
mentaire / d'éducation permanente /
d'éducation post-scolaire**
college of further education

établissement d'éducation spéciale
special school

indemnité d'éducation
education allowance

offre d'éducation
education provision

planification en matière d'éducation
educational planning

politique en matière d'éducation
educational policy

service d'éducation surveillée
correctional service

spécialiste en éducation sanitaire
health educator

zone d'éducation prioritaire (ZEP)
zone of educational priority (ZEP)

EFFECTIF (adj.)
effective; positive; actual; active

**critère de recherche effective
d'emploi**
(occ.) work test

date effective de l'accouchement
effective date of confinement

date effective de la rupture du contrat de travail
effective date of termination

durée annuelle effective du travail
annual hours worked

gains effectifs
actual earnings

justification des dépenses effectives
production of proof of actual expenditure

montant effectif d'une prestation
actual amount of a benefit

rémunération effective
actual earnings

rémunération effective nette mensuelle
monthly take-home pay

rémunération horaire effective
actual hourly earnings

revenus effectifs
actual earnings

salaire effectif
active / actual wage / earnings

taux effectif d'imposition sur le revenu
real income tax rate

taux marginaux d'imposition effectifs
marginal effective tax rates (METR)

traitement effectif
take-home salary

EFFECTIF (n.)
size; total number; strength; (pl.) staff, establishment, headcount, manning, manpower, work force, number of workers employed; membership; (school) enrolment

accord sur les effectifs
manning agreement

ajustement des effectifs
labour adjustment

besoins en effectifs
manpower needs

composition des effectifs
work force composition

compression d'effectifs
staff / manpower / work force reduction, reduction in personnel / of staff, displace-ment; labour shake-out / shedding; employment cut-back

contrôle d'effectifs
attendance check

dégraisser des effectifs
to reduce staff

déperdition d'effectifs
(labour) wastage, attrition; (ed.) drop-out

déperdition d'effectifs scolaires
educational wastage

diminution des effectifs par le jeu naturel des départs
natural wastage of labour

dotation en effectifs
staffing, provision of staff, manning

effectif(s) actuel(s)
present workforce

effectif(s) d'âge scolaire (obligatoire)
school age population

effectifs approuvés
authorised establishment

effectifs en début de mois
headcount on the first of the month

effectifs par enseignant
pupil/teacher ratio

effectif(s) de l'enseignement primaire
primary-school enrolment

effectifs excédentaires
labour redundancy

effectifs en fin de mois
month-end headcount

effectifs inscrits
employees under contract

effectifs de main-d'oeuvre
economically active / gainfully occupied / working population, labour force

effectif minimal
(occ.) skeleton staff

effectifs nécessaires
work / labour force requirements, labour /
manpower needs, labour requirements

effectif normal
normal workforce

effectifs nucléaires
core workforce / workers

effectifs occupés
employed population

effectifs périphériques
peripheral workers

effectif(s) permanent(s)
regular establishment, core workforce /
workers, permanent workers / work-force /
staff; established posts

effectifs du personnel
staffing

effectif de la population active
size of economically active population

effectifs présents
staff at work

effectif réduit
(occ.) skeleton staff

effectif non représentatif
non-representative workforce

effectifs salariés
salaried / payroll employees

effectifs scolaires / scolarisés
school population / enrolment

effectifs sortis des écoles
school output

effectifs en surnombre
labour redundancy, displaced / redundant
labour, workers made redundant, surplus
staff; overmanning

effectifs syndicaux
union membership

effectifs de terrain
field forces

employés faisant partie de l'effectif
staff on strength

enquête sur les effectifs
manpower survey

érosion des effectifs
personnel / staff attrition

étude des effectifs
manning / manpower survey

importance des effectifs
manning / staffing level

maintien de l'effectif / des effectifs
staff retention

modulation des effectifs
(occ.) flexible staffing

mouvement des effectifs
turnover of labour, labour turnover; staff
movement

niveau des effectifs
manning / staffing level

plan des effectifs
staffing plan

planification des effectifs
manpower / work force planning

porter à l'effectif
to take on strength

rajeunir les effectifs
to recruit younger employees

rayé de l'effectif
struck off strength

réaménagement des effectifs
labour force / manpower / work force
adjustment

redéploiement des effectifs
redeployment of labour, labour
adjustment

réduction des / d'effectifs
staff / manpower / work force reduction,
reduction in personnel / of staff, staff
cut; employment cut-back; post
reduction, reduction in staffing levels;
downsizing

réduire les effectifs
to reduce / to downsize / to shed staff

renforcement de l'effectif
staff increase

renouvellement des effectifs
labour turnover

répartition des effectifs par âge
breakdown of headcount by age

rétention d'effectifs
labour hoarding

rotation / roulement des effectifs
turnover (of staff), (staff) turnover

seuil d'effectifs
staff level

surcharger en effectif
to overstaff

tableau d' / des effectifs
staffing / manning table

taux de conservation des effectifs
retention rate, rate of retention

taux de déperdition d'effectifs (ed.)
drop-out rate

taux de diminution des effectifs
attrition rate

taux de rétention des effectifs
retention rate

taux de rotation des effectifs
staff turnover rate

usure naturelle des effectifs
natural wastage of labour

EFFECTIVEMENT
heure effectivement ouvrée / travaillée
hour actually worked

rémunération effectivement perçue
(occ.) take-home pay

EFFECTUÉ
heure de travail effectuée
worked hour; (pl.) hours (actually) worked

EFFECTUER
effectuer son préavis
to work out one's notice

effectuer un stage
to complete a training period

EFFET
champ d'action et effet du travail
scope and effect of work

date d'effet
operative / effective date

date d'effet de la retraite
effective date of retirement

donner effet
to implement

effet démobilisateur
disincentive effect

effet de déplacement
(job) displacement effect

effet de dissuasion
disincentive effect

effet sur l'emploi
employment effect

effet d'entraînement
linkage effect; spillover

effets induits
externalities

effet d'inertie
deadweight effect

effet majorateur
mark-up effect

effet de masse (wages)
percentage increase of the total wage
bill

effet multiplicateur / de multiplication
multiplier (effect); spin-off

effet nocif
harmful effect

effet redistributif
distributive effect

effet de report
carry-over effect

effet rétroactif (avec)
retroactively; backdated

effet de revenu
income effect (of a wage increase)

effet de substitution
displacement / substitution effect

effet du travail
impact of work

effet travailleur ajouté
added worker effect

effet travailleur découragé
discouraged worker effect

mesure à effet rétroactif
retroactive measure

prendre effet
to take effect

prise d'effet
entry into effect

EFFICACE
efficient, effective

EFFICACITÉ
effectiveness; adequacy

analyse coût-efficacité
cost-effectiveness analysis

coût-efficacité
cost-effectiveness

efficacité du marché du travail
labour market efficiency

EFFICIENCE
efficiency

efficience technique
technical efficiency

efficience-X
X-efficiency

salaire d'efficience
efficiency wage

EFFONDREMENT
effondrement de la natalité
baby bust

ÉGAL
principe à travail égal, salaire égal
equal pay for equal work principle

salaire égal
equal pay

travail égal
equal work

ÉGALISER
to level out

égaliser les revenus
to level out earnings

ÉGALITÉ
Comité d'égalité (Austr.)
Equality Committee

conseiller en égalité (Norw.)
equality consultant

égalité des chances
equality of opportunities, equal opportunities

égalité des chances sur le plan éducatif
equality of educational opportunity

égalité des chances dans l'emploi
equal employment opportunities

égalité professionnelle (femmes-hommes)
equal opportunities for women and men at work

égalité de / des rémunération(s)
equal pay, pay equity

égalité des salaires
equal pay, wage parity

égalité de situation
equality of condition

égalité de traitement
equal treatment, equality of treatment

principe de l'égalité de traitement
principle of equal treatment

programme d'accès à l'égalité
affirmative action programme

ÉLARGI
courbe de Phillips élargie
augmented Phillips curve

famille élargie
extended family

ÉLASTICITÉ
elasticity

élasticité de la demande de main-d'oeuvre
elasticity of labour demand

élasticité de la demande par rapport au revenu
income elasticity of demand

élasticité de l'offre de main-d'oeuvre
elasticity of labour supply

élasticité de l'offre de travail par rapport aux salaires
wage elasticity of labour supply

ÉLECTIF
charge / poste électif(ve)
elective office

ÉLECTORAL
collège électoral
body of electors

délégué électoral
electoral delegate

ÉLECTRICIEN
électriciens, électroniciens et travailleurs assimilés [CITP-1968 (8-5)]
electrical fitters and related electrical and electronics workers [ISCO-1968 (8-5)]

ÉLECTRICITÉ
allocation de chauffage et d'électricité (Irel.)
fuel and electricity allowance

ÉLECTRONIQUE (adj.)
mécaniciens et ajusteurs d'appareils électriques et électroniques [CITP-1988 (724)]
electrical and electronic equipment mechanics and fitters [ISCO-1988 (724)]

techniciens d'appareils optiques et électroniques [CITP-1988 (313)]
optical and electronic equipment operators [ISCO-1988 (313)]

télétravailleur électronique
computer-linked home worker

ÉLÉMENT
element, unit, component; (occ.) factor

éléments de confort
amenities

éléments contractuels
contractual elements
élément fixe des salaires
fixed wage element

élément de passif
liability

éléments de prestations
benefit components

éléments de preuve
evidence

élément soumis à retenue pour pension
pensionable element

élément non salarial de rémunération
non-wage award

ÉLÉMENTAIRE
connaissances élémentaires
basic / (occ.) life skills

école élémentaire
elementary / grade / primary school

enseignement élémentaire
primary education

formation aux techniques élémentaires
basic skills training

instruction élémentaire
basic / primary education; (occ.) literacy
and numeracy

ÉLEVÉ (adj.)
chômage élevé
high unemployment

emploi aux échelons les plus élevés
high-level employment

fonctionnaire de rang élevé
senior officer

niveau élevé de compétence
high(er)-level skill

poste élevé
high-ranking position

salaire élevé (à)
high-paid, highly paid

taux élevé
high rate

ÉLÈVE (n.)
pupil; student

association d' / des anciens élèves
former students' association

**élève en difficulté scolaire / ayant des
résultats scolaires médiocres**
under-achiever, low performer / achiever

élève lent
slow learner

élève-maître
teacher trainee

nombre d'élèves inscrits
(school) enrolment

travailleur-élève (Malta)
pupil worker

ÉLEVEUR
éleveurs et ouvriers qualifiés de
l'élevage destiné aux marchés et
assimilés [CITP-1988 (612)]
market-oriented animal producers and
related workers [ISCO-1988 (612)]

ÉLIGIBILITÉ
eligibility

ÉLIGIBLE
eligible

ÉLIMINATION
emplois résorbés par élimination
naturelle
jobs eliminated by attrition

ÉLIRE
élire domicile
to make one's abode

ÉLITE
exode de l'élite professionnelle
migration of highly trained personnel

ÉLOIGNEMENT
allocation pour éloignement
géographique (Austr.)
remote area allowance

éloignement du travail
distance from work

indemnité d'éloignement
foreign service (residence) allowance

prime d'éloignement
isolated post allowance

ÉLUSION
élusion des prestations sociales
evasion of social costs

EMBAUCHE
engagement, hiring; accession; manning

aide à l'embauche
employment subsidy

anti-discrimination à l'embauche
(occ.) affirmative action

certificat d'embauche
certificate of employment

clause d'embauche préférentielle
closed-shop clause

conditions d'embauche
terms and conditions / particulars of
employment; conditions of service / of
employment / of work

coût d'embauche
hiring cost

coût(s) d'embauche et de licenciement
hiring and firing cost(s), on and off costs
(Austr.)

date d'embauche
hire date, date of hire

déclaration préalable à l'embauche (Fr.)
prior registration of employee

discrimination à l'embauche
restrictive (hiring) practice(s)

droits d'embauche
recruitment fee

embauche sur poste(s) existant(s)
job replacement

embauche sur poste(s) existant(s) (par)
by replacement

embauche préférentielle
preferential hiring

gel de l'embauche
freeze in hiring

**législation interdisant le monopole
syndical d'embauche (USA)**
right-to-work laws

lettre d'embauche
letter of appointment

**mesures anti-discriminatoires à l'em-
bauche**
(occ.) affirmative action programme

**monopole syndical d'embauche /
d'emploi**
closed-union shop / system

niveau de salaire à l'embauche
accession rate of pay

**pratiques (suivies en matière) d'em-
bauche**
hiring practices

pré-contrôle d'embauche (USA)
employment verification

préférence à l'embauche
preferential hiring

promesse d'embauche
promise of employment

questionnaire d'embauche
employment questionnaire

salaire d'embauche
starting wage; recruitment ratio / rate,
hiring rate

subvention à l'embauche
recruitment subsidy

taux d'embauche du personnel
accession rate

visite médicale d'embauche
pre-employment medical examination

EMBAUCHER
to hire, to recruit, to engage, to take on;
to employ

embaucher (se faire)
to sign on

embaucher du personnel
to hire staff

EMBAUCHEUR
labour contractor

ÉMIGRATION
emigration

émigration interne
out-migration

pays d'émigration
country of emigration, emigration / sending country

ÉMIGRÉ (adj.)
envoi de fonds des travailleurs émigrés
workers' remittance

ÉMIGRÉ (n.)
migrant worker

ÉMISSION
année d'émission
year of issue

ÉMOLUMENT
(pl.) emoluments; salary

traitements et autres émoluments
salaries and emoluments

EMPIRIQUE
règle empirique
rule-of-thumb

EMPIRIQUEMENT
empirically; by rule of thumb

EMPLACEMENT
site; position

EMPLOI
employment, job, occupation, position, work, office; job opportunity; place; (pl.) (occ.) employment opportunities

abandon volontaire d'un emploi
voluntary leaving of employment

acceptation de l'emploi
acceptance of employment

acceptation d'une offre d'emploi
approval of a job offer

accepter un emploi
to take / to accept a job, to take employment

accès à l'emploi
access to employment / to work / to the labour force; job access; opportunities of employment

accès au marché de l'emploi
access to the labour market

accroissement de l'emploi
increase in employment

action en faveur de l'emploi et de la formation
employment and training measures

adéquation de l'offre et de la demande d'emploi
job-worker / worker-job matching, matching of jobseekers and vacancies, job matching

administration de l'emploi
labour / manpower administration

affichage des emplois
job posting

âge d'aptitude à l'emploi
employable age

agence pour l'emploi
employment agency / exchange, labour exchange, employment bureau (USA), job centre

Agence nationale pour l'emploi (ANPE)
National Employment Agency

aide à l'emploi
employment assistance; labour / employment subsidy

aide à la famille pour l'emploi d'une assistante maternelle agréée (Fr.)
family benefit for hiring an approved day-care attendant

aide à l'obtention d'un emploi
assistance towards taking up work / employment

aide au premier emploi
first job allowance

aide au premier emploi des jeunes (Fr.)
allowance for young new workers

aide à la recherche d'un emploi
assistance towards taking up work /
employment, work assistance (Ger., Austr.)

ajustement de l'emploi
employment adjustment

allocation d'impossibilité d'emploi
unemployability allowance / supplement
(UK)

**allocation pour recherche d'(un) emploi
(Austr.)**
job search allowance

analyse des emplois
job analysis

analyse selon le / par groupe d'emplois
job group analysis

ancienneté dans l'emploi
(job) tenure

année-personne d'emploi
work-year of employment

annonce d'offre d'emploi
job advertisement

antécédents d'emploi
employment record, work experience

**appariement informatique des offres et
des demandes d'emploi**
computerised matching of jobs and job
seekers

appellation d'emploi
occupational / job title

appellation d'emploi générique
generic job title

approbation d'une offre d'emploi
approval of a job offer

approche prévisionnelle de l'emploi
manpower forecast approach

apte à l'(exercice d'un) emploi
fit for work / employement; employable

aptitude à l'emploi
suitability for the job, fitness for work; job
readiness; employability

assurance en cours d'emploi
in-service insurance

**atelier d'entraînement à la recherche
d'emplois (Belg.)**
job-finding workshop

**atelier d'objectif professionnel pour
demandeurs d'emploi (Belg.)**
vocational objectives workshop for
jobseekers

attachement à l'emploi
job attachment

autre emploi
alternative / alternate employment,
replacement job

avis de vacance d'emploi
notice of a vacant post, notified
vacancy, vacancy announcement /
notice

baisse de l'emploi
decline in employment

banque d'emplois
job bank

bassin d'emploi
labour / manpower / job catchment area,
labour market / employment area; job
pool

**besoins de l'emploi / en matière
d'emploi**
employment requirements / needs

bilan ressources-emploi
employment(-)resources balance sheet

bon d'emploi (Can.)
job voucher

bourse de l'emploi / des emplois
labour / job exchange (service)

boutique de l'emploi
job centre

budget de plein emploi
full(-)employment budget

bureau d'emploi
labour exchange (service)

bureau local de l'emploi
local employment office

bureau paritaire de l'emploi
joint employment office

catégorie d'emploi(s)
job category; service / job class

centre d'emploi
job centre

cercle de recherche active d'emploi (Fr.)
job club

cessation d'emploi / de l'emploi
employment termination, termination (of employment), (job) separation; retirement

cesser d'exercer un emploi
to separate from a job

changement d'emploi
change of job, job change

chèque-emploi
employment voucher

chercher un emploi
to look for employment / for a job, to seek employment / work

chiffres relatifs à l'emploi
employment figures

chômeur à la recherche d'un emploi
job-seeking unemployed, unemployed job-seeker

classement des emplois
job classification

classement hiérarchique des emplois
labour ranking

classification des emplois
job classification / grading

club d'emploi / de recherche active d'emploi
job club

communication obligatoire des emplois / offres d'emploi / vacances d'emploi
compulsory notification of vacancies

complément de salaire lié à la situation du marché de l'emploi (Swed.)
market pay supplement

comportement dans l'emploi
employment behaviour

condition d'emploi
(pl.) terms of appointment; conditions of service / of employment

condition d'emploi statutaire
statutory condition of service

conseiller à l'emploi, conseiller emploi (Belg.)
employment / vocational adviser

conserver un emploi
to retain employment, to stay on a job

continuité de l'emploi
continuity of employment

contrat d'adaptation (Fr.)
adjustment contract

contrat d'adaptation à l'emploi (Fr.)
employment contract for integration into working life

contrat d'emploi consolidé (CEC) (Fr.)
consolidated employment contract

contrat emploi-formation (Fr.)
employment training contract

contrat d'emploi de réadaptation (Irel.)
remedial work

contrat emploi-solidarité (CES) (Fr.)
solidarity employment contract, employment contract to facilitate reintegration of disadvantaged persons

contrat initiative emploi
employment initiative contract

contrat de retour à l'emploi (Fr.)
back-to-work contract

contrôle de l'emploi
employment control

convention emploi-formation (Belg.)
job-training agreement

cotation des emplois
job rating

cours d'emploi (en)
in-service, on-the-job

cours de formation préparatoire à l'emploi
pre-trades training course

création directe d'emplois
direct job creation

création d'emplois
employment / job generation / development / creation, provision of employment

création d'emplois par effet d'entraînement / par effet multiplicateur
employment spin-off

crédits affectés à la création d'emplois
job creation funds

crédit d'impôt (aux entreprises) en faveur de l'emploi / pour la création d'emplois / à l'emploi (Can.)
employment tax credit (CND); tax credit for providing employment

créer des emplois
to create / to generate jobs / employment

crise de l'emploi
employment slump

critère de recherche effective d'emploi
(occ.) work test

croissance de l'emploi
employment growth

croissance du marché de l'emploi
labour market growth

cumul d'emplois
double-jobbing, dual / multiple job-holding, moonlighting

cumuler deux emplois
to hold two jobs, (occ.) to moonlight

date de début de l'emploi
start date of the job

débuter dans un emploi
to start a job

décrocher un emploi
to obtain / to secure employment

déficit d'emplois
job gap

définition d'emploi
post / job description

définition des emplois
job classification

dégagement d'emplois
job release

demande d'emploi
application for a job, employment / job application; situation wanted

demande préalable à l'emploi
pre-employment inquiry

demandeur d'emploi
applicant for work, person seeking work, work-seeker, job applicant / seeker / searcher / hunter; seeking, looking for work

demandeur d'emploi inscrit (comme tel)
registered job-seeker

demandeur d'un premier emploi
first(-time) job seeker, new entrant on the labour market

description d'emploi
job / position description

déséquilibre du marché de l'emploi
labour market imbalance, imbalance / disequilibrium on the labour market

détérioration de l'emploi
(occ.) employment slump

deuxième emploi
second job

développement de l'emploi
employment development; job stimulation

diffuser des offres d'emploi
to circulate job vacancies

discrimination dans l'emploi
discrimination in employment, employment discrimination

disparition d'emploi
job loss

disponible pour un emploi
available for work

données relatives à l'emploi
employment figures / data

double emploi
overlapping

droits au regard de / dans l'emploi / en matière d'emploi
job / employment rights

durée d'emploi
term / length of employment

durée d'occupation d'un emploi
job tenure

échelle des emplois
job hierarchy

effet sur l'emploi
employment effect

égalité des chances dans l'emploi
equal employment opportunities

emploi (ayant un)
employed

emploi (sans)
without employment, out of work

emploi actuel
current employment / job

emploi administratif
clerical occupation / job, office occupation

emploi agricole
agricultural / farm employment

emploi agricole saisonnier
seasonal agriculture work

emploi analogue
equivalent occupation

emploi antérieur
previous employment

emploi apparenté
allied / related occupation / job

emploi approprié
suitable employment

emploi assisté
supported employment

emploi assujetti à l'assurance / assurable
insurable employment

emploi assuré
secured / assured employment, secure job

emploi d'attente
bridge job

emploi non autorisé
unauthorised employment

emploi auxiliaire
casual employment

emploi sans avenir
dead-end job

emploi au bas de l'échelle
entry-level job

emploi de bas niveau
low-level job

emploi bouché
dead-end job

emploi bouche-trou
stop-gap employment

emploi budgétaire
established post

emploi de bureau
clerical occupation / job, office occupation / work

emploi civil
civilian occupation

emploi clé
key post / job / position

emploi soumis à la concurrence
competitive employment

emploi concurrentiel
open employment

emploi connexe
allied / related occupation / job

emploi consolidé (Fr.)
consolidated job

emploi continu
continuing / continuous / steady / ongoing
job / employment

emploi convenable
suitable employment

emploi de courte durée
short-term / temporary work / employment /
job

emploi cyclique
cyclical job

emploi dangereux
hazardous occupation / work

emploi de début / de débutant
entrance level / entry(-)level job

emploi non déclaré
undeclared employment

emploi déprécié
stigmatised job

emploi direct
direct employment

emploi non discriminatoire
non-discriminatory employment

emploi disponible
available job

emploi lié au domaine d'étude
school-related position

emplois en double pilotage
job shadowing

emploi ouvrant droit à pension
(recognised) pensionable employment

emploi n'ouvrant pas droit à pension
employment not recognised pensionable
employment

emploi d'une durée déterminée
term employment

emploi de / à durée indéterminée
permanent job / employment, indefinite
employment

emploi aux échelons les plus élevés
high-level employment

emploi effectivement occupé
current / actual job / occupation

emploi d'enfants
child employment

emploi envisagé
intended occupation

emploi d'été
summer employment / job

emploi d'été des / pour étudiants
student summer employment / job

emploi pour étudiant
student job

emploi dans la fonction publique
public service employment

emploi garanti
secured / assured employment, secure
job

emploi habituel
usual occupation

emploi indirect
indirect employment

emploi induit
induced job

emploi industriel
industrial employment

emploi insalubre
unhealthy occupation

emploi d'insertion
(occ.) make-work job

emploi intérimaire
interim job / employment

emploi intermittent
casual / odd job

emploi sans issue
dead-end job

emploi des jeunes
youth employment

emploi de longue durée
long-term employment

emploi lucratif
paid / gainful employment

emplois majoritairement féminins
female-dominated occupations

emplois majoritairement masculins
male-dominated occupations

emploi mal payé / mal rémunéré
low-wage job

emploi de manoeuvre
(occ.) labouring occupation

emploi non marchand
non-market job

emploi sur le marché primaire
mainstream job

emploi menacé
threatened job

emploi en milieu ordinaire / en milieu non protégé
open employment

emploi des mineurs
juvenile labour

emploi à mi-temps
half-time employment / work

emploi de morte-saison
off-season employment

emploi normal
regular employment

emploi non normalisé
non-standard job

emploi occasionnel
casual / odd job / employment

emploi occasionnel vacant
casual vacancy

emploi occupé
job / occupation held

emploi d'ouvrier spécialisé
semi-skilled occupation

emplois parallèles
dual jobholding

emploi périphérique
peripheral job

emploi permanent
permanent / regular job / employment / post; (pl.) establishment

emploi permanent à temps partiel
permanent part-time employment

emploi sur poste partagé
shared job

emploi à pourvoir
(unfilled) (job) vacancy

emploi pourvu
vacancy filled

emploi précaire
insecure / unstable job

emploi de premier échelon
entry-level job

emploi prescrit
prescribed employment

emploi prioritaire
preferential employment

emploi privilégié
preferred employment

emploi productif
productive employment, production job

emploi protégé
protected job; sheltered employment

emploi provisoire
interim job / employment

emploi de proximité
neighbourhood job

emploi public
public job / employment; (occ.) public office

emploi public temporaire
temporary public job

emploi qualifié
qualified / skilled job

emploi quantifiable
quantifiable employment

emploi redéfini
redesigned job

emploi régulier
regular employment

emploi régulier vacant
regular vacancy

emploi de remplacement
alternative / alternate employment,
replacement job

emploi peu rémunérateur
low-wage job

emploi rémunéré
paid /gainful employment

emploi repère
benchmark job

emploi réservé
(pre-)arranged employment; (pl.) job
reservation

emplois résorbés par élimination naturelle
jobs eliminated by attrition

emploi rétribué
paid / gainful employment

emploi saisonnier
employment of a seasonal nature, seasonal
job / employment / work

emploi saisonnier pour étudiants
(occ.) vacation job / work

emploi salarié
wage / dependent employment, employment as an employee, payroll job /
employment

emploi non salarié
non-wage employment, self-employment

emploi salarié déguisé
disguised wage employment

emploi de secrétariat
clerical occupation / job, office
occupation

emploi dans le secteur parapublic
semi-public / (occ.) non-government
employment

emploi dans le / du secteur privé
private (sector) employment

emploi dans le secteur public
public (sector) employment

emploi dans le secteur des / dans les services
service / tertiary employment

emploi semi-protégé
semi-sheltered employment

emploi de service
service job

emplois simultanés
dual jobholding

emploi stable
steady job, stable / secure employment

emploi de substitution
alternative / alternate employment,
replacement job

emploi subventionné
subsidised employment

emploi temporaire
interim / temporary job / employment

emploi à temps complet
full-time job / employment

emploi à temps partiel
part-time job / employment

emploi à temps plein
full-time job / employment

emploi tertiaire
service / tertiary employment

emploi dans le tiers secteur
third sector employment

emploi non traditionnel
non-traditional job

emploi unilingue
monolingual job

emploi de niveau universitaire
graduate-level job; (pl.) jobs for (university) graduates

emploi vacant
vacant position / post; (job) vacancy

emploi viable
(occ.) self-sustaining employment

emploi à vie
lifetime job / employment

emploi quasiment à vie
near lifetime job

enquête sur les conditions d'emploi les plus favorables
survey of best prevailing conditions of service

entièrement apte à l'emploi
fully employable

entretien de cessation / de fin d'emploi
exit interview

équilibre de l'emploi
adjustment of labour demand and supply

équilibre du marché de l'emploi
labour market equilibrium, balance of / equilibrium on the labour market

équité dans l'emploi
fair employment, employment equity

évaluation des emplois
job evaluation

évaluation des emplois selon une échelle de points
point-factor method of job evaluation

éventail d'emplois
range of jobs

évolution de l'emploi
employment trend

excédent budgétaire de plein emploi
full-employment budget surplus

exercer un emploi
to work, to hold a job, to be employed

exercer un emploi lucratif / rémunéré / rétribué
to be gainfully occupied / employed

expansion de l'emploi
employment development

expectative d'emploi continu
expectancy of continued employment

expérience acquise en cours d'emploi
practical (work) / hands-on / on-the job experience

famille d'emplois
job cluster / family

fléchissement de l'emploi
decline in employment

fluctuations de l'emploi
fluctuations in employment

fluctuations du niveau d'emploi
fluctuations in the level of employment

fluctuations saisonnières de l'emploi
seasonal employment variations

foire à l'emploi
job convention / fair / salon

fonctionnement du marché de l'emploi
functioning / operation of the labour market, labour market operation(s)

fonds affectés à la création d'emplois
job creation funds

fonds pour l'emploi
employment fund

formation avant l'emploi
pre-service / pre-employment training

formation en cours d'emploi
on-site / on-the-job training / learning, in-service (educational) training

formation hors emploi
off-the-job training

formation liée à l'emploi
job-related training

formation préalable à l'emploi
pre-service / pre-employment training

formation spécifique à un emploi
job-related training

forme d'emploi atypique / hors normes
atypical form of employment

formes d'emploi souples
flexible employment

formulaire de demande d'emploi
job application form

gains provenant / tirés d'un emploi
employment earnings, earnings from employment

garantie d'emploi / de l'emploi
security of employment; job assurance / guarantee

garantie de maintien dans l'emploi
job security

garder un emploi
to stay on a job, to retain employment

générateur d'emploi(s)
job(-)creating

gestion prévisionnelle de l'emploi (GPE)
(enterprise) manpower planning

gestion prévisionnelle de l'emploi dans l'entreprise
company manpower planning, personnel planning at establishment level

hausse de l'emploi
increase in / expansion of employment

inadéquation entre offres et demandes d'emploi
job mismatch

inapte à l'emploi
unfit for employment; unemployable

inaptitude à l'emploi
unfitness for employment; unemployability

incidence sur l'emploi
employment effect / impact

indemnité de cessation / de fin d'emploi
separation / terminal / severance pay / payment / benefit, allowance for separation; (occ.) completion bonus

indemnité de / pour perte d'emploi
indemnity for loss of job; redundancy payment, severance pay(ment)

indice du coût de l'emploi
employment cost index

initiative créatrice d'emplois
employment-creation measure

initiative en faveur de l'emploi et de la formation
employment and training measure

initiative locale de création d'emplois (ILE)
local employment initiative, local initiative in promoting employment

inscription en vue d'un / pour un emploi
employment registration, registration for work / for employment

intensité d'emploi
employment intensity

intensité d'emploi de la croissance
employment / job content of growth

interruption d'emploi
interruption of employment

législation en matière d'emploi / régis-sant l'emploi
employment legislation

lien formel avec l'emploi
formal job attachment

lieu d'emploi
place of business

maintenir les emplois
to preserve / to maintain (existing) jobs

maintenir le niveau d'emploi
to maintain employment level

maintien de l'emploi
job maintenance

maintien dans l'emploi
job retention / security

marché de l'emploi
labour / employment / job market

marché national de l'emploi
domestic / national labour market

marché primaire de l'emploi
mainstream / primary labour market

marché secondaire de l'emploi
secondary labour market

maximisation de l'emploi
maximisation of employment opportunities

menace pour l'emploi
employment threat

mesure d'accompagnement des suppressions d'emplois
redundancy mitigation measure

mesure d'aide à l'emploi
employment incentive / stimulus

mesure créatrice d'emplois / favorisant l'emploi / génératrice d'emplois
employment-creation / job-creation measure

mesures en faveur de l'emploi et de la formation
employment and training measures

mesure d'encouragement / d'incitation à l'emploi
employment incentive / stimulus; (occ.) in-work benefit

mesure préventive d'emploi
preventive employment measure

mesure sélective d'emploi
selective employment measure

mesure de stimulation de l'emploi
employment incentive, employment development measure

méthode du classement hiérarchique des emplois
job ranking method

méthode d'emploi neutre
neutral employment system

méthode de recherche d'emploi
job-finding / job-search skills / technique, job-hunting method

mise en correspondance des offres et des demandes d'emploi
job matching

monopole syndical d'embauche / d'emploi
closed-union shop / system

niveau absolu de l'emploi
employment in absolute terms

niveau d'emploi / de l'emploi
employment level, level of employment

niveau normal d'emploi
normal employment level

niveau de qualification / de technicité des emplois
skill content of jobs

norme d'emploi
employment standard

norme équitable en matière d'emploi
fair labour standard

notification obligatoire des emplois / des offres d'emploi / des vacances d'emploi
compulsory notification of vacancies

objectif de plein emploi
full employment target / objective

obstacle à l'emploi
barrier to employment, job barrier

obstacle lié à l'emploi
job-related barrier

occuper un emploi
to hold a job

occuper un emploi de longue durée
to work on a long-term basis

office de l'emploi
(labour) employment office, employment agency / bureau (USA)

offre d'emploi
job offer / advertisement / order; job opening / opportunity; job / appointment / situation vacant; (job) vacancy; (pl.) employment opportunities; availability of jobs

offre d'emploi authentique
bona fide job offer

offre d'emploi difficile à satisfaire
hard-to-fill vacancy

offre d'emploi discriminatoire
discriminatory job offer

offre d'emploi satisfaite
vacancy filled, filled vacancy

offre d'emploi non satisfaite
outstanding job / unfilled vacancy, unfilled
demand for worker

ouvrier sans emploi
jobless worker

ouvrir des emplois à
to provide employment for labour force

pacte pour l'emploi (Fr.)
employment scheme

partage d'emploi
job splitting / twinning / sharing

pension liée à l'emploi (Finl.)
employment pension

pénurie d'emplois
job scarcity / shortage, lack / scarcity /
shortage of jobs / of work

perdre son emploi
to lose one's job

performances sur le plan de l'emploi
labour market performance

période d'emploi
employment period, period of employment

période d'emploi courante
current period of employment

période d'emploi interrompue
split employment period

période d'emploi prévue
expected period of employment, period of
expected employment

période d'emploi proposée
proposed period of employment

**personne occupant un / exerçant un /
pourvue d'un emploi (rémunéré)**
employed, employee; (pl.) economically
active / gainfully occupied / working
population, labour force

**personnes en quête de leur premier
emploi [CITP-1968 (X-1)]**
new workers seeking employment
[ISCO-1968 (X-1)]

**personne à la recherche d'un emploi /
en quête d'emploi**
job hunter / seeker / searcher

perspective d'emploi
job / employment opening, opportunity
for employment, work opportunity, job
prospect / outlook, placing / placement
prospect; (pl.) employment outlook

Perspectives de l'emploi (OCDE)
Employment Outlook (OECD)

perte d'emploi / d'un emploi
loss of job, job loss

placement dans un emploi agricole
agricultural job placement

**placement dans un emploi
occasionnel**
casual job placement

placement dans un emploi régulier
regular job placement

plan personnel de recherche d'emploi
personal job-search plan

plein emploi
full employment

pôle de croissance de l'emploi
employment growth area

politique dynamique de l'emploi
active employment policy

politique de l'emploi
employment / manpower / labour
market policy

**politique d'emploi et de main-
d'oeuvre**
employment and manpower policy

politique de plein emploi
full employment policy, policy of full employment

politique de stimulation de l'emploi
employment development policy

population active ayant un emploi
gainfully occupied population

population occupant des emplois rémunérés
economically active / gainfully occupied / working population, labour force

porteur d'emploi
job creating

poser sa candidature à un emploi
to try / to apply for a job

possibilité d'accès à l'emploi
accessibility to employment

possibilités de création d'emplois
employment-generating potential

possibilité d'emploi
job / employment opening, opportunity for employment, work / job opportunity, job prospect / outlook, placing / placement prospect; (pl.) employment opportunities; availability of jobs

postuler un emploi
to apply for a job

pourvoir un emploi
to fill a post / a job / a vacancy, to staff a position

pourvu d'un emploi
in employment

pratique d'emploi impartiale / objective
neutral / objective employment practice

pratique d'emploi progressive
progressive employment practice

pratique loyale en matière d'emploi
fair employment practice

pratique restrictive en matière d'emploi
restrictive labour practice

préavis de cessation d'emploi
end-of-employment notice

précarité de l'emploi
job insecurity, lack of job security

prendre un emploi
to take / to accept a job, to enter into / to take employment

préparation à l'emploi
job preparation

présenter une demande d'emploi
to apply for a job

préserver des emplois
to safeguard / to preserve / to maintain (existing) jobs

prestation hors emploi
non-work benefit

prestation liée à l'exercice d'un emploi
in-work benefit

prévision en matière d'emploi
manpower forecast

primo-demandeur d'emploi
first(-time) job seeker, new entrant on the labour market

priorité d'emploi / de l'emploi
preferential access to employment, prior right of employment

prise d'emploi
appointment, assumption of duty / of office

professions et emplois d'accès réglementé
restricted occupations

profil d'emploi
employment profile

profil de l'emploi / des emplois
job / occupational characteristic

programme en cours d'emploi
on-the-job programme

programme de création d'emplois / favorisant la création d'emplois
job-creation / work-creation / employment-creation programme / scheme, scheme aimed at creating employment / jobs

programme pour / en faveur de l'emploi
employment scheme

programme d'emploi des collectivités locales
community employment programme

programme d'emploi et de formation
employment and training scheme

programme d'emploi d'intérêt local
community employment programme

programme de préparation à l'emploi
(occ.) bridging programme

progression de l'emploi
increase in / expansion of employment

prolongation d'emploi
extension of employment

promotion de l'emploi
employment promotion, promotion of employment / of job creation

proposition d'emploi
offer of employment

protection de l'emploi
job / employment protection

quête d'emploi (en)
looking for / seeking work

quête d'emploi (être en)
to seek employment / work

quitter un emploi volontairement
to voluntarily leave employment

rapport emploi/population
employment/population ratio

recherche d'emploi
job seeking / search / hunting

recherche d'un emploi (à la)
looking for / seeking work

recherche d'un emploi (être à la)
to seek employment / work

recherche d'emploi autonome
independent job search

recherche d'emploi individuelle
private job search

redéfinir un emploi
to redesign a job

réduction d'emplois
employment cut-back

refus d'emploi
denial of employment

refuser une offre d'emploi
to refuse a job offer

région d'emploi
region for work

registre des offres / des vacances d'emploi
register of vacancies

régression de l'emploi
decline in employment

réinsertion sur le marché de l'emploi
reintegration into the labour market

répartition des emplois
distribution of jobs

reprendre un emploi
to resume work, to re-enter employment, to return to employment / to work

réserve de cessation de l'emploi (-sous)
subject to a retirement condition

resserrement du marché de l'emploi
tightening of the job market

restructuration de l'emploi
employment adjustment

restructuration des emplois
job redefinition / restructuring

résultats sur le plan de l'emploi
labour market / employment performance

retrait d'emploi
removal from office

rétrécissement du marché de l'emploi
tightening of the job market

revenus provenant / tirés d'un emploi
employment earnings / income, earnings
from employment

**rotation des / d'emplois / d'un emploi à
l'autre**
job rotation

rouages du marché de l'emploi
functioning / operation of the labour market

sauver des emplois
to save / to safeguard / to preserve / to
maintain (existing) jobs

secteur du marché de l'emploi
labour market sector, segment of labour
market

sécurité de l'emploi / d'emploi
employment / job security, security of
employment, employment protection; job
guarantee

service d'adaptation à l'emploi
employment adjustment service

service de conseils en matière d'emploi
employment advisory service

service de l'emploi
labour / manpower administration / service,
employment agency / service; placing /
placement service; job service

service public de l'emploi
public employment service

seuil d'accélération de l'emploi
employment threshold

situation de l'emploi
employment / manpower / job situation

**situation relative à / au regard de
l'emploi**
employment / work situation / status

situation du marché de l'emploi
manpower / job situation, labour market
situation / conditions

**société de développement de l'emploi
local**
(occ.) community employment
corporation

**solde budgétaire en situation de plein
emploi**
full / high employment (budget) balance

solliciter un emploi
to apply for a job

**sorties du chômage pour reprise
d'emploi**
outflow to jobs from unemployment

sortie du marché de l'emploi
withdrawal from employment / from the
labour force

soutenir l'emploi
to sustain employment

spécialiste en emploi
employment specialist

stabilité d'emploi
job stability, security of tenure; job
tenure

stage d'emploi
qualifying period of employment

**stage d'insertion et de formation à
l'emploi (Fr.)**
employment integration and training
course

statistiques de l'emploi
labour market / manpower statistics;
employment figures

statistiques et prévisions d'emploi
employment statistics and estimates

stimulation de l'emploi
job stimulation; employment
development

stimuler l'emploi
to stimulate employment

stratégie d'emploi
employment strategy

structure de l'emploi
employment structure / pattern, patterns of employment

subvention directe à l'emploi
direct employment subsidy

subventionner un emploi
to subsidise a job

supplément pour impossibilité de se procurer un emploi (UK)
unemployability supplement

suppression d'emploi
job cut / loss; (pl.) job dislocation / displacement, labour displacement, redundancy

supprimer des emplois
to displace workers / labour

système de classement des emplois par points
point-factor system of job classification

système de cotation des emplois
point-factor method of job evaluation

système d'emploi neutre / non discri-minatoire
neutral employment system

système informatisé de traitement des offres d'emploi
automated job order system

tableau d'affichage des offres d'emploi
(occ.) job board

tableau des emplois
table of posts, establishment table

tableau nominatif des emplois
nominative table of posts

taux de chômage en situation de plein emploi (des capacités)
full employment unemployment rate, equilibrium / natural rate of unemployment

taux de croissance de l'emploi
employment growth rate

taux d'emploi
employment rate

taux de non-emploi
non-employment rate

taux naturel d'emploi
natural employment rate, natural rate of employment

taux de rotation des emplois
job turnover rate

taux de vacances d'emploi
vacancy rate

technique(s) de recherche d'emploi
job(-)search / job-finding skill(s) / technique; job-hunting method

tendance (du marché) de l'emploi / du travail
labour market trend

tenue de l'emploi
labour market / employment performance

test d'aptitude à l'emploi
employment aptitude test

titulaire d'un emploi
job holder

titulaire de deux emplois
second job holder

travailleur apte à occuper un emploi
employable worker

travailleur ayant un emploi
employed worker

travailleur sans emploi
unemployed (worker), jobless worker

travailleur occupant un emploi
employee in employment

travailleur occupant plus d'un emploi
multiple jobholder

travailleur sans emploi régulier
casual labourer / worker, occasional worker

travailleur dont l'emploi a été supprimé
displaced / redundant worker

travailleurs du marché primaire de l'emploi
primary labour force, mainstream workers

travailleur victime de suppressions d'emploi(s)
redundant / displaced worker

trouver un emploi
to find / to obtain / to secure employment

type d'emploi
kind of job

vacance d'emploi
(job) vacancy

vacance d'emploi notifiée
vacancy notified

volume (global) de l'emploi
(overall) level of employment

EMPLOYABILITÉ
employability; job readiness

entretien d'évaluation de l'employabilité
employability assessment interview

EMPLOYÉ (adj.)
employé de façon intermittente
periodically / occasionally / casually / marginally employed

personne employée (par)
per employee

EMPLOYÉ (n.)
employee; salary earner, salaried worker / employee; non-manual worker; white-collar (worker); officer, official; servant; (pl.) staff, employees, clerical and office workers, non-industrial / salaried staff

assurance(-)vieillesse des employés
pensions insurance of salaried employees

autres employés de bureau [CITP-1988 (419)]
other office clerks [ISCO-1988 (419)]

collège d'employés
non-managerial body of electors

date de sortie d'un employé
departure date of an employee

employés de type administratif [CITP-1988 (4)]
clerks [ISCO-1988 (4)]

employés d'approvisionnement, d'ordonnancement et des transports [CITP-1988 (413)]
material-recording and transport clerks [ISCO-1988 (413)]

employés de bibliothèque, de service du courrier et assimilés [CITP-1988 (414)]
library, mail and related clerks [ISCO-1988 (414)]

employé de bureau
(office) clerk; office employee; clerical / of-fice worker, white-collar (worker); (pl.) clerical staff / employees

employés de bureau [CITP-1988 (41)]
office clerks [ISCO-1988 (41)]

employés de comptabilité, caissiers et travailleurs assimilés [CITP-1968 (3-3)]
bookkeepers, cashiers and related workers [ISCO-1968 (3-3)]

employés faisant partie de l'effectif
staff on strength

employé de l'Etat
public servant

employé de maison
domestic employee / servant; (pl.) service personnel, domestic servants

employés de maison et travailleurs assimilés non classés ailleurs [CITP-1968 (5-4)]
maids and related housekeeping service workers not elsewhere classified [ISCO-1968 (5-4)]

employé des mines
mine employee

employé occasionnel
casual employee; (pl.) short-term staff

employé permanent
permanent employee

employé permanent à temps partiel
permanent part-time employee

employé permanent à temps plein
permanent full-time employee

employé à plein temps
full-time employee

employé non qualifié
unskilled employee

**employés non qualifiés des services et de
la vente [CITP-1988 (91)]**
sales and services elementary occupations
[ISCO-1988 (91)]

**employés de réception, caissiers, gui-
chetiers et assimilés [CITP-1988 (42)]**
customer service clerks [ISCO-1988 (42)]

**employés de réception et d'information
de la clientèle [CITP-1988) (422)]**
client information clerks [ISCO-1988 (422)]

employé saisonnier
seasonal employee

employé salarié
wage earner

employé du secteur parapublic
semi-public employee

employé du secteur public
public employee

employé du secteur des services
service worker

employé du secteur de la vente
sales worker

employé de service
employee on duty

**employés des services comptables et
financiers [CITP-1988 (412)]**
numerical clerks [ISCO-1988 (412)]

employé d'un service public
public servant

employés subalternes
junior staff

employé temporaire
temporary employee

employé à temps complet
full-time employee

employé à temps partiel
part-time employee

employé titularisé
employee with tenure

employé d'usine
factory employee

fonctions d'employé de bureau
clerical duties

licencier un employé
to terminate an employee

ouvriers et employés
industrial and non-industrial staff,
manual workers and salaried employees,
wage and salary workers

ouvriers et employés des mines
mineworkers and mine employees

part employé
employee's contribution

permutation des employés
staff interchange

**programme d'initiation des nouveaux
employés**
orientation programme for new
employees

proportion ouvriers - employés
(occ.) labour mix

rapport sur la situation des employés
status report on employees

régime applicable aux employés
scheme applicable to clerical workers

relations employeur-employé
staff relations

EMPLOYER
to employ, to hire

EMPLOYEUR
employer; (pl.) (occ.) management

abondement de l'employeur
employer's complementary contribution to an employee savings scheme

aide aux employeurs
assistance for employers

ancien employeur
former employer

association d'employeurs
employer's association / federation / organisation, association / organisation of employers

assurance-responsabilité de l'employeur
employer's liability insurance

cotisation (de l') employeur
employer's contribution

employeur actuel
present employer

employeur clé
key employer

employeur éventuel
prospective / potential employer

employeur local
local / (occ.) outside employer

employeur potentiel
potential employer

employeur du secteur privé
private sector employer

employeur unique
sole employer

formation coordonnée par l'employeur
employer-based training

futur employeur
prospective employer

licenciement du fait de l'employeur
(occ.) compulsory redundancy

main-d'oeuvre assujettie à contrainte d'employeur
tied labour

mise en rapport avec l'employeur
introduction to employer

mutation chez un même employeur
interplant transfer

organisation d'employeurs
organisation of employers

organisme employeur
employing agency

part (de l') employeur
employer's contribution

prestation à la charge directe de l'employeur
employer-based benefit

prestation sociale directe de l'employeur
unfunded employment welfare benefit

recommandation à un employeur
introduction to employer

régime relatif aux obligations de l'employeur
scheme concerning the employer's liability

régime fondé sur la responsabilité de l'employeur
employer's liability scheme

régime de retraite proposé / mis en place par l'employeur
employer-sponsored pension plan

relations employeur-employé
staff relations

relations employeurs-travailleurs
labour-management / industrial relations

représentant de l'employeur
management / employer's representative, representative of employer

représentant auprès des employeurs
employment representative

responsabilité de l'employeur
employer's liability

second employeur
secondary employer

services aux employeurs
employer services, services to employers

syndicat d'employeurs
employer's association / federation /
organisation

travailleur apparenté à l'employeur
employee / worker related to the employer

travailleurs et employeurs
(occ.) labour and management

EMPOISONNEMENT
poisoning

ENCADRÉ
formation encadrée
supervised training

ENCADREMENT
management; mentorship, mentoring;
guidance; control

encadrement des salaires
wage control

encadrement supérieur
top / executive management

fonction d'encadrement
supervisory duty / function

personnel d'encadrement
senior directing / supervisory staff, grade /
managerial staff

personnel d'encadrement et de direction
supervisory and management staff

poste d'encadrement et de direction
supervisory and management position

taux d'encadrement (ed.)
teacher/pupil ratio

ENCHÈRE
agents d'assurances, agents
immobiliers, courtiers en valeurs, agents
de vente de services aux entreprises et
vendeurs aux enchères [ISCO-1968 (4-
4)]
insurance, real estate, securities and
business services salesmen and
auctioneers [ISCO-1968 (4-4)]

ENCOURAGEMENT
inducement; incentive

mesure d'encouragement à l'emploi
employment incentive / stimulus; (occ.)
in-work benefit

prime d'encouragement
incentive award / bonus

programme d'encouragement
incentive programme

système de primes d'encouragement
bonus incentive scheme

ENDÉMIQUE
chômage endémique
long-term / chronic unemployment

ENDIGUER
endiguer le chômage
to stem / to reduce unemployment

ENFANCE
childhood

agent de protection de l'enfance
child welfare officer

aide à l'enfance
child assistance / care, aid to children

aide sociale à l'enfance
child welfare (authorities); child care

assistance à l'enfance
child welfare

bureaux de l'enfance (Scand.)
child welfare board system

bureau de protection de l'enfance
child welfare authority

centre de la petite enfance
early childhood reception centre

enfance déshéritée
deprived children

enfance inadaptée
maladjusted children

établissement de protection sanitaire et sociale de l'enfance
health and social care institution for children

inspecteur de l'enfance (Fr.)
child care inspector

petite enfance
early childhood, very young age

première enfance
infancy
protection de l'enfance
child care / welfare

protection de la famille et de l'enfance
family and child welfare

protection médico-sociale de l'enfance
medical and social child welfare

protection sociale et juridique de l'enfance
social and legal child welfare

secours à l'enfance
aid to children

service d'aide à la petite enfance
infant care service

services intégrés en faveur de l'enfance
integrated services for children

service de protection de la famille et de l'enfance
family and child welfare service

société d'aide à l'enfance
child helping society

ENFANT
child

abandon d'enfant
abandonment of a child

abandon moral d'enfant
child neglect

activités d'éveil du jeune enfant
early childhood stimulation

aide aux familles avec enfants à charge
aid to families with dependant children (AFDC)

aîné des enfants
eldest child

allocation pour l'éducation des enfants (Ger.)
child raising allowance

allocation pour enfant
child allowance

allocations familiales payables à partir du deuxième enfant
children's allowances from the second child

allocation de garde à domicile des enfants (Finl.)
child home care allowance

allocation pour garde d'enfant
child care allowance

allocation de garde d'enfant à domicile
home child care allowance

allocation au /pour jeune enfant (Fr.)
young child allowance, allowance for young child

allocation pour soins aux enfants (Finl.)
child care allowance

allocation spéciale pour les enfants de femmes divorcées (UK)
child's special allowance

asservissement des enfants
child bondage / slavery

assistance aux mères et aux enfants
mother and child care

bonification pour enfant
child bonus

centre d'accueil pour (jeunes) enfants
child-minding facility

colonie pour enfants débiles (Belg.)
centre for underdeveloped children

complément pour l'enfant (UK)
child credit

congé pour soins aux enfants (Swed.)
child care leave

consultations dentaires pour enfants (Austr.)
school dental clinic

consultations pour enfants
child care / children's clinic

couple marié avec enfants
married couple with children, married couple family

crédit pour l'enfant (UK)
child credit

crédit d'impôt pour enfant (Can.)
child tax credit

déclaration d'abandon d'enfant
declaration of abandonment of a child

déduction pour enfant (UK)
child relief

déduction fiscale pour enfant (à charge)
child (tax) allowance

déduction d'impôt pour enfant (UK)
child relief

double salaire sans enfants
double income no kids (DINK)

droits de l'enfant
children's rights

emploi d'enfants
child employment

enfant abandonné
neglected / abandoned child

enfant adopté / adoptif
adopted / foster child

enfant d'âge préscolaire
pre-school child

enfant d'âge scolaire
school(-)child

enfant asservi
child bonded labourer, child slave

enfant sous assistance
child in the care of public authorities

enfant assisté
dependent child, child in the care of public authorities, foundling, child in care

enfant attardé
underdeveloped child

enfant en bas âge
baby, infant

enfant caractériel
maladjusted / problem child

enfant à charge
dependent child

enfant déficient
defective / deficient child

enfant délaissé
abandoned / neglected / deprived child

enfant difficile
problem child

enfant diminué
handicapped child

enfant ouvrant droit aux prestations
eligible child

enfant issu de famille ouvrière
child of working-class family

enfant sans foyer
homeless child

enfant sous la garde de
child in the care of

enfant sous la garde de parents nourriciers
foster child

enfant handicapé
disabled / handicapped child

enfant illégitime
illegitimate child, child born out of wedlock

enfant inadapté
maladjusted child

enfant inadapté physique
physically handicapped child

enfant invalide
incapacitated child

enfant livré à lui-même
neglected child

enfant mentalement inadapté
mentally handicapped child

enfant mineur
under-age child

enfant mort-né
stillborn child

enfant naturel
illegitimate child, child born out of wedlock

enfant né hors mariage
child born out of wedlock

enfant nécessiteux
deprived child

enfant (placé en) en nourrice
foster child

enfant perturbé
emotionally disturbed child

enfant placé dans une famille d'accueil / en foyer
foster child

enfant placé en internat
child boarded out

enfant du premier âge
baby, infant

enfant privé d'affection
emotionally deprived child

enfant protégé
protected child

enfant recueilli
foster child

enfant retardé
(mentally) retarded child

enfant des rues
street child

enfant scolarisé
school child

enfant non scolarisé
out-of-school child

enfant secouru
child on relief

enfant surveillé
supervised child

enfant temporairement recueilli
temporarily fostered child

enfant présentant des troubles affectifs
emotionally disturbed child

enfant vagabond
vagrant child

établissement pour enfants
children's home

exploitation pornographique des enfants
child pornography

exposition d'enfant
child exposure

famille sans enfants
childless family

famille à enfant unique
one-child family

foyer pour enfants
children's home

garde complète d'enfants
full-time care for children

garde d'un / des enfants
child-minding, child care, custodial care, custody of a child

garderie d'enfants
child care centre, day-care centre, day-care
of children

gardienne d'enfants
day-care attendant

jardin d'enfants
kindergarten, nursery school

jeune enfant
young child

majoration pour enfant
child supplement / increase

majoration pour enfant à charge (UK)
child dependency addition

majoration de pension pour enfants
increase in pensions / pension increase /
pension supplement in respect of children

maltraitance des enfants
child abuse

mauvais traitements à enfant
child abuse

médiateur pour enfants (Norw.)
commissioner for children

ménage bi-actif sans enfants
dual income with no kids (DINK)

mère élevant seule son / ses enfant(s)
single mother

pension d'enfant
child's benefit

pension pour enfant (Icel.)
child pension

placement des enfants
fostering / placement of children

placement des enfants en établissement
institutional care of children

placement libre d'enfant
voluntary placement of a child

pornographie impliquant des enfants
child pornography

pourvoir à l'entretien d'un enfant
to provide for a child

prestation pour enfant (UK)
child benefit

prostitution d'enfants
child prostitution

**régime de prestations pour enfants
(UK)**
child benefit scheme

santé de l'enfant
child health

service de consultations pour enfants
child care / children's clinic

service de garderie d'enfants
day nursery; (pl.) day-care facilities for
children

servitude des enfants
child bondage / slavery

sévices à enfant
child abuse

soins aux enfants
child care

soins aux mères et aux enfants
mother and child care

structure d'accueil pour (les) enfants
child care facility

supplément pour enfant
child's supplement

supplément de pension pour enfants
pension supplement / supplement to
pensions in respect of children

trafic / traite d'enfants
child trafficking

travail des enfants
child employment / labour

ENFANTIN
main-d'oeuvre enfantine
child labour
population enfantine
child population

prostitution enfantine
child prostitution

ENGAGÉ
dépenses raisonnablement et légitimement
engagées
just and reasonable expenses

engagé à l'essai
on probation; probationer

solde non engagé
unobligated balance

ENGAGEMENT
undertaking; commitment; liability;
appointment; hiring; covenant

contrat d'engagement des marins
ship's articles

contrat d'engagement de service
employment contract

contrat spécial d'engagement
special service agreement

durée de l'engagement
tenure of appointment

engagements continus
continuous appointments

engagement contractuel
contractual commitment

engagement de courte durée
short-term appointment

engagements de dépenses
financial obligations

engagement pour une durée indéfinie
indefinite appointment

engagement à l'essai
hiring with probationary period

**engagement de développement (EDDF)
(Fr.)**
development agreement

engagement financier
financial commitment

engagement sur l'honneur
solemn and binding agreement

engagement pour une période de stage
probationary appointment

engagement à titre permanent
permanent appointment

**engagement prévisionnel (de
dépenses)**
commitment

engagement à titre régulier
regular appointment

engagement au titre des retraites
pension liability

engagement à titre temporaire
temporary appointment

**engagement à titre temporaire pour
une durée indéfinie**
temporary indefinite appointment

**expectative juridique du
renouvellement d'un engagement**
legal expectation of renewal of contract

mettre fin à l'engagement de qqn
to terminate the appointment of
somebody

offre d'engagement
offer of appointment

prolongation d'un engagement
extension of appointment

prolonger un engagement
to extend an appointment

ENGAGER
to engage, to take on, to hire, to recruit;
to retain; to undertake; (occ.) to contract
in

engager des consultations
to enter into consultation

engager des dépenses
to incur expenses

ENGIN
véhicules et engins
vehicles and equipment

ENGRENAGE
engrenage de la pauvreté
poverty trap

ENQUÊTE
inquiry; survey; test

enquête administrative
administrative inquiry

enquête sur les budgets-temps
time-use survey

enquête sur les conditions d'emploi les plus favorables
survey of best prevailing conditions of service

enquête de conjoncture
business (climate) survey

enquête auprès d'un / sur échantillon (restreint)
sample survey

enquête sur les effectifs
manpower survey

enquête sur les forces de travail
labour force survey

enquête intervilles
place to place survey

enquête sur le logement
housing survey

enquête auprès des / sur les ménages, enquête-ménages
household survey

enquête par panel
panel survey

enquête sur la population active
labour force survey

enquête sur les salaires
salary survey

enquête sanitaire
health survey

enquête sur la / de santé
health survey

enquête de satisfaction du personnel
staff satisfaction survey

enquête sociale
social inquiry

enquête par sondage
sample survey

enquête par sondage sur la population active
labour force sample survey

enquête de suivi
follow-up survey

enquête sur le terrain
field survey

période couverte par l'enquête
inquiry / survey period

rapport d'enquête sociale
social (inquiry) report

suspension pendant enquête
suspension pending investigation

ENQUÊTEUR
agent enquêteur
investigating agent

ENRAYER
enrayer le chômage
to stem / to reduce unemployment

ENREGISTREMENT
registration; entry; recording

droit d'enregistrement
registration fee

enregistrement des maladies
registration of diseases

ENREGISTRER
to register

enregistrer (se faire)
to register, to enter

ENRICHISSANT
travail enrichissant
rewarding work

ENRICHISSEMENT
enrichissement des tâches / du travail
job enrichment

ENSEIGNANT (adj.)
corps enseignant
teaching staff / personnel

formation du personnel enseignant
teacher training

personnel enseignant
teaching staff / personnel

personnel enseignant du service social
social work educators

ENSEIGNANT (n.)
teacher

effectifs par enseignant
pupil/teacher ratio

enseignants spécialisés dans l'éducation des handicapés [CITP-1988)]
special education teaching professionals [ISCO-1988 (234)]

formateur des enseignants
teacher(-)educator

formation des enseignants en cours de service
INSET (in-service training)

ENSEIGNÉ (adj)
matières enseignées
content of teaching

ENSEIGNEMENT
teaching; education; learning

autorités (responsables) de l'enseignement
educational authorities

brevet d'enseignement professionnel (BEP) (Fr.)
certificate of vocational education

certificat d'enseignement secondaire inférieur (CESI)
lower secondary education certificate

congé enseignement (Fr.)
leave for teaching purposes

deuxième cycle de l'enseignement secondaire
upper secondary (education)

diplômé de l'enseignement supérieur
college graduate, tertiary-education graduate

école d'enseignement familial et ménager
home-making school

école dispensant un enseignement à temps complet
full-time school

effectif(s) de l'enseignement primaire
primary-school enrolment

enseignement alterné
work/study programme

enseignement assisté par ordinateur (EAO)
computer-assisted learning (CAL)

enseignement de base
basic education

enseignement axé sur les carrières
job-related education

enseignement de la deuxième chance
second-chance education

enseignement de type classique
academic / formal education

enseignement compensatoire
compensatory education

enseignement correctif
remedial tuition / teaching / education

enseignement par correspondance
distance education

enseignement de culture générale
academic education

enseignement à distance
distance learning / education / teaching

enseignement élémentaire
primary education

enseignement dispensé par des établissements spécialisés
(occ.) institutionalised education

enseignement extra-scolaire
out-of-school / informal education

enseignement général (l')
general school system, general education (system)

enseignement à horaire réduit
part-time education

enseignement infirmier
nursing education

enseignement initial
initial education

enseignement libre
private education

enseignement médical de base
basic medical education

enseignement ménager
home economics

enseignement ordinaire
formal education, mainstream education / schooling

enseignement parallèle
informal education

enseignement post-obligatoire
post-compulsory education

enseignement post-secondaire
post-secondary / further education

enseignement post-universitaire
postgraduate training

enseignement pratique
(occ.) field teaching

enseignement du premier degré
primary education

enseignement préprimaire
pre-school / pre-primary education

enseignement pré(-)professionnel
pre(-)vocational education

enseignement préscolaire
early(-)childhood / pre(-)primary / pre-school education

enseignement primaire
primary education

enseignement privé
private education

enseignement professionnel
vocational education

enseignement régulier
formal education

enseignement scolaire
formal education

enseignement non scolaire
non-formal education

enseignement du second degré / secondaire
secondary education

enseignement secondaire du premier cycle
high school education

enseignement de soutien
remedial teaching / education

enseignement structuré
organised education

enseignement supérieur
college / higher education

enseignement technique
technical education

enseignement technique et formation professionnelle
vocational and technical education and training (VOTEC)

enseignement à temps partiel
part-time instruction / education

enseignement tertiaire
tertiary education

enseignement non traditionnel
non-formal education

enseignement du troisième degré
tertiary education

enseignement universitaire pratique
graduate training

établissement d'enseignement
educational institution / establishment

établissement d'enseignement général
(occ.) mainstream school

établissement d'enseignement mixte
co-educational institution

établissement d'enseignement post-secondaire
post-secondary educational institution

établissement d'enseignement post-secondaire communautaire (USA)
community college

établissement d'enseignement secondaire
secondary school, high school (USA)

établissement d'enseignement spécial
special school

établissement d'enseignement supérieur
establishment / institution of higher education, (higher education) college

étudiant de l'enseignement supérieur
student in higher education; (occ.) scholar

étudiant des quatre premières années de l'enseignement supérieur
undergraduate

indicateur de l'enseignement
educational indicator

matériel d'enseignement
teacher equipment

matériel d'enseignement et d'apprentissage
teaching / learning material

personnel de l'enseignement
educational personnel

premier cycle de l'enseignement secondaire
lower secondary

professions intermédiaires de l'enseignement [CITP-1988 (33)]
teaching associate professionals [ISCO-1988 (33)]

programme d'enseignement
curriculum

réforme de l'enseignement
educational reform

spécialistes de l'enseignement [CITP-1988 (23)]
teaching professionals [ISCO-1988 (23)]

spécialiste de l'enseignement du service social
social work educator

système d'enseignement post-secondaire
post-secondary system

ENSEMBLE (adv.)
vivant ensemble séparément
living apart together

ENSEMBLE (n.)
ensemble immobilier
housing project / estate

ensemble pédagogique
training package (multimedia)

ensemble de la population
general population

grand ensemble
housing project / estate

ENTENTE
agreement; understanding

assurance basée sur une entente d'exonération mutuelle
no fault insurance

entente directe
direct agreement

entente préalable
prior agreement, pre-agreement

mémorandum d'entente
memorandum of understanding

protocole d'entente
memorandum of understanding, statement
of agreement

ENTIER
membre à part entière
full member

pension / retraite entière
full pension, full retirement benefit

ENTIÈREMENT
entièrement apte à l'emploi
fully employable

entièrement capitalisé
fully funded

entièrement à la charge de quelqu'un
wholly dependent for support

ENTRAIDE
(co-operative / mutual) self-help

association d'entraide
self-help group, friendly society

centre d'entraide
self-help centre

entraide administrative
administrative assistance, mutual assistance
/ aid in administrative matters

entraide mutualiste
mutualistic help

fonds d'entraide
(occ.) welfare fund

groupe d'entraide
(mutual) self-help group

permanence d'entraide sociale (UK)
Citizens' Advice Bureau

projet d'entraide
self-help project / scheme

ENTRAÎNEMENT
training; practice

**atelier d'entraînement à la recherche
d'emplois (Belg.)**
job-finding workshop

**création d'emplois par effet d'entraî-
nement**
employment spin-off

effet d'entraînement
linkage effect; spillover

ENTRANT
entrant

ENTRAVE
obstruction; interference; obstacle

délit d'entrave
obstruction offence

entrave à la liberté du travail
interference with freedom of
employment

entrave au travail
work hindrance

ENTRÉE
access, admission, entrance, entry;
influx, inflow

**âge d'entrée en activité / au travail /
dans la vie active**
age at accession to the labour force / at
entry into employment

âge moyen d'entrée en activité
mean age at accession to the labour
force

barrière à l'entrée
barrier to entry, entry barrier

concours d'entrée
(competitive) entrance examination

conditions d'entrée
conditions for access / of admission / for
entrance / for entry, entrance
requirements

date anniversaire d'entrée en fonction
anniversary date of hire

date d'entrée
date of entry, entry / starting date; date of hire

date d'entrée en fonctions
(date of) entry / entrance on duty

date d'entrée en vigueur
commencement / effective date

droit d'entrée
admission fee

entrée en activité
accession to the labour force, entry into employment

entrée en application
entry into effect; (occ.) introduction

entrée dans l' / en assurance
entrance into insurance

entrées au chômage
flow into unemployment

entrée en fonctions
entry on / assumption of duty, assumption of office

entrées de fonds
income

entrée en jouissance
commencement date (of a pension)

entrée au travail
entry into employment

entrée dans la vie active
access to the labour force, access to / entrance into / entry into working life

entrée en vigueur
entry into effect

examen d'entrée
entrance / entry examination

examen d'entrée dans le second cycle universitaire (USA)
graduate record examination

grade d'entrée
entry grade

modalités d'entrée
admission procedure

niveau d'entrée
entry level

niveau d'entrée des diplômés dans une entreprise
graduate entry

niveau d'entrée en fonction
entrance level

pointage à l'entrée
clocking-on

première entrée en activité
first accession to the labour force; entrance / entry into the labour force

prime d'entrée dans les classes (Fr.)
allowance on entering the classes

probabilité d'entrée en activité
probability of accession to the labour force

procédure d'entrée
admission procedure

règles / réglementation régissant l'entrée
admission / entrance rules

restriction à l'entrée
admission restriction, restriction / limitation on entry, entry limitation, restricted entry

table d'entrée en invalidité
disability table

taux d'entrée en activité
rate of accession to the labour force

visa d'entrée
entry permit

ENTREPRENARIAL, ENTREPRENEURIAL
entrepreneurial

ENTREPRENARIAT
entrepreneurship

ENTREPRENEUR
contractor; undertaker; entrepreneur; employer; operator

entrepreneur indépendant
self-employed entrepreneur, independent
contractor

entrepreneur individuel
sole trader; self-employed (person / worker)

entrepreneur principal
principal contractor

talent d'entrepreneur
entrepreneurial skill

ENTREPRISE
(business) enterprise, firm, plant,
undertaking, venture, company; installation;
workplace: (occ.) work

accord d'entreprise
staff / company / company-level / company-
wide / plant agreement; works / labour
agreement

**agence locale pour la création d'entre-
prises**
local enterprise agency

**ancienneté d'entreprise / à l'échelle de
l'entreprise**
corporate seniority

caisse d'entreprise
fund operated by a firm, works provident
fund

caisse de pension d'entreprise
enterprise pension fund

centre de formation de l'entreprise
company training centre

cessation d'activité d'une entreprise
closing down of a business, business closure

cession d'entreprise
divestment

chef d'entreprise
manager; entrepreneur

club d'entreprise
staff club

comité central d'entreprise
central works committee

comité d'entreprise
shop council; joint management - labour
board, labour-management (joint)
committee (Fr.), works council (Ger.),
works committee

contrat d'entreprise
services contract

contrat de formation en entreprise
training-in-industry contract

convention d'entreprise
staff / company / works agreement

correspondant d'entreprise
in-house correspondent

créateur d'entreprise
new entrepreneur

crédit aux entreprises
business credit

culture d'entreprise
corporate culture

détaché par une entreprise
posted by an undertaking

disparition d'entreprises
death of companies

entreprise (en)
in-house

entreprise à but non lucratif
non-profit making firm

entreprise conjointe
joint venture

entreprise en coparticipation
joint venture

entreprise d'Etat
State-owned / State-controlled
enterprise

entreprise familiale
family firm / establishment / enterprise /
business / concern

**entreprise de formation par le travail
(EFT) (Belg.)**
training-through-work venture

entreprise horizontale
horizontal corporation

entreprise individuelle
non-corporate / one-man business, (sole) proprietorship; (occ.) self-employment

entreprise industrielle
industrial undertaking

entreprise d'intérêt collectif
community business venture

entreprise intermédiaire
non-profit making firm

entreprise migratrice
runaway shop (in order to avoid trade union activism)

entreprise mixte
joint venture

entreprise nodale
network firm

entreprise à participation mixte
joint venture

entreprise personnelle
(sole) proprietorship

entreprise privée
private enterprise

entreprise publique
public undertaking / utility / corporation

entreprise-réseau
network firm

entreprise du secteur public
public undertaking / utility / corporation

entreprise de service
service enterprise

entreprise de service public
public utility

entreprise constituée en société
corporate business / enterprise, incorporated business / enterprise

entreprise transnationale
transnational company

entreprise de travail adapté (ETA) (Belg.)
adapted work company

entreprise de vente par correspondance
mail-order business

esprit d'entreprise
entrepreneurship, entrepreneurial spirit

étude prévisionnelle des besoins de main-d'oeuvre dans l'entreprise
company manpower planning, personnel planning at establishment level

expansion des entreprises
business development

fermeture d'(une) entreprise
closing down of a business, business / plant closure, closure of an establishment

fonds de pension d'entreprise
corporate / enterprise pension fund

formation continue dans l'entreprise
in-company continuing training

formation assurée par les entreprises
enterprise-based training

formation en / dans l'entreprise
in-firm / on-site / in-house / in-plant / industry / industrial training, training-in-industry, entreprise-based training

formation à l'extérieur de l'entreprise
off-the-job training

formation professionnelle auprès d'une entreprise
vocational training with a company

frais d'entreprise
company charges

gestion des entreprises
business administration / management

gestion prévisionnelle de l'emploi dans l'entreprise
company manpower planning, personnel planning at establishment level

grande entreprise
large-scale enterprise

groupement d'entreprises locales
local enterprise trust

hôtel pour entreprise
enterprise house / workshop; industry hotel

implantation d'entreprises
industrial settlement

infirmière d'entreprise
occupational health nurse

institut d'entreprise
corporate college

logement d'entreprise
accommodation supplied by the employing
business

médecin en / d'entreprise
industrial doctor; company medical officer,
company / works doctor

**membres de l'exécutif et des corps
législatifs, cadres supérieurs de l'administration publique, dirigeants et
cadres supérieurs d'entreprise [CITP-
1988 (1)]**
legislators, senior officials and managers
[ISCO-1988 (1)]

négociation au niveau de l'entreprise
plant bargaining

**participation des travailleurs à la gestion
des entreprises**
workers' participation in management

pépinière d'entreprises
business / enterprise incubator

personnel extérieur à l'entreprise
out-house staff

petite entreprise
small business

petites et moyennes entreprises (PME)
small and medium-sized enterprises (SME)

plan d'épargne d'entreprise (Fr.)
company / employee savings scheme

**planification de la main-d'oeuvre / du
personnel / des ressources humaines
dans l'entreprise / des entreprises**
company manpower planning,
personnel planning at establishment
level

portage d'entreprise
(occ.) piggy-backing

**prestation sociale des comités d'entre-
prise**
social benefit paid by works committees

prévisions des entreprises
business expectations

procédure d'agrément de l'entreprise
accreditation procedure for firms

projet d'entreprise
business plan; mission statement

qualité de chef d'entreprise
entrepreneur skill

rachat d'une entreprise
buy-out

**rachat d'une entreprise par ses cadres
avec effet de levier (RECEL)**
leveraged management buy-out
(LMBO)

**rachat d'une entreprise par ses
salariés (RES)**
leveraged management buy-out
(LMBO)

**recensement effectué auprès des
entre-prises**
establishment census

recueil des accords d'entreprise
compendium of company agreements

**régime d'entreprise
enterprise-based / employer-based /
occupational scheme**

régime de pension d'entreprise
occupational pension scheme

règlement d'entreprise
works / staff regulations, works rule-
book

rentabilité des entreprises
business profitability

responsable d'entreprise
(occ.) workers' representative, shop steward

secteur des entreprises
corporate sector

services aux entreprises
business services

service social d'entreprise
industrial social work

spécialistes des fonctions administratives et commerciales des entreprises [CITP-1988 (241)]
business professionals [ISCO-1988 (241)]

sport d'entreprise
sports activities for workers

stage en entreprise
(occ.) internship

stage de fin de formation en entreprise (Belg.)
enterprise-based end of training course

syndicat d'entreprise
works / in-house union

taux de disparition des entreprises
mortality rate of companies

transparence dans l'entreprise
accessibility of information within a company

travail social d'entreprise
industrial social work

travailleur social d'entreprise
industrial social / welfare worker

zone d'entreprises
enterprise zone

ENTRER
to join

entrer en activité
to begin work

entrer dans ses fonctions / en fonction
to take / to assume office, to begin employment, to take up one's duties, to commence work, to assume duties

entrer au service de ... en qualité de
to be recruited by ... as

entrer dans la vie active
to enter the labour force / market, to enter employment / into economic life, to take up employment, to begin / to start work

entrer en vigueur
to come into force

ENTRETENIR
to support

ENTRETIEN
maintenance; support, subsistence; up-keep; (job) interview

agent d'entretien
maintenance worker

allocation d'entretien
maintenance allowance, subsistence allowance / payment; (occ.) training allo-wance

convoquer à un entretien
to call for an interview

entretien de carrière
career interview

entretien de cessation d'emploi / de départ
exit interview

entretien directif / dirigé
guided / directed interview

entretien d'évaluation
appraisal / assessment interview

entretien d'évaluation de l'employabilité
employability assessment interview

entretien de fin d'emploi
exit interview

entretien ménager
household operation

entretien préalable à la formation
pre-training interview

entretien préalable au licenciement
preliminary discussion before dismissal

entretien de présentation
referral interview

entretien structuré
directed interview

passer un entretien pour un poste
to interview for a job

pourvoir à l'entretien d'un enfant
to provide for a child

présenter à un entretien (se)
to report for an interview

refus d'entretien
failure to maintain; non-support

soins dentaires d'entretien
conservative dental care

soins d'entretien et de continuité de la vie
daily care to compensate dependence

technique d'entretien
interviewing skill

thérapeutique d'entretien
maintenance therapy

ENTREVUE
interview

entrevue de présélection
screening interview

ENVELOPPE
enveloppe globale
global budget

enveloppe de paie / de salaire
pay / wage packet

ENVERGURE
économies d'envergure
economies of scope

ENVIRONNEMENT
hygiène de l'environnement
environmental health

salubrité du milieu
environmental health

ENVISAGÉ
activité envisagée
planned activity

emploi / profession envisagé(e)
intended occupation

ENVOI
envois de fonds
cash remittances

envoi de fonds des travailleurs émigrés / immigrés
workers' remittance

ENVOYER
to send; to refer

envoyer en (stage de) formation
to refer for training

ÉPANOUISSEMENT
épanouissement de l'individu
self-development

épanouissement personnel
self-fulfilment

ÉPARGNE
savings

fonds d'épargne
savings fund

plan d'épargne
savings scheme / plan

plan d'épargne d'entreprise (Fr.)
company / employee savings scheme

plan d'épargne logement
home (loan) saving plan (Fr.), private
home ownership plan (USA)

plan d'épargne par prélèvement auto-matique
save-as-you-earn scheme

plan d'épargne retraite (Fr.)
savings-related retirement scheme

société d'épargne et de financement immobilier
(occ.) building society

ÉPIDEMIOLOGIE
epidemiology

ÉPOUSE
spouse; wife

abandonner son épouse
to desert one's wife

abattement fiscal sur le revenu profes-sionnel de l'épouse
wife's earned income allowance

allocation pour épouses abandonnées (Irel.)
deserted wife's allowance

délaisser son épouse
to desert one's wife

épouse abandonnée
deserted wife

épouse sans profession
housewife

rente complémentaire pour épouse (Switz.)
wife's supplementary pension

supplément pour épouse (Swed.)
wife's supplement

ÉPOUX
spouse; husband; (pl.) married couple; parties to a marriage

ÉPREUVE
test; plight

épreuve d'admission
pre-employment test

épreuve d'aptitude
skill test

épreuve de force
showdown

mettre à l'épreuve
to test

ÉPUISEMENT
exhaustion

ÉPUISER
épuiser le droit aux prestations
to exhaust right / entitlement to benefit(s)

épuiser ses jours de congés payés
to use up one's holiday entitlement

ÉQUATION
équation de type Phillips
Phillips type equation

ÉQUILIBRÉ (adj.)
budget équilibré
balanced budget

croissance équilibrée
balanced growth

développement économique équilibré
balanced economic development

ÉQUILIBRE (n.)
equilibrium, balance; (occ.) well-being

atteindre l'équilibre
to break even

cotisation d'équilibre (pensions)
special payment

équilibre de l'emploi
adjustment of labour demand and supply

équilibre du marché de l'emploi / du travail
labour market equilibrium, balance of / equilibrium on the labour market

équilibre racial
racial balance

taux de chômage en situation d'équilibre
full employment unemployment rate,
equilibrium / natural rate of unemployment

ÉQUIPE
team; shift

activités d'équipe
group activities

cabinet d'équipe (Fr.)
team surgery

chef d'équipe
head of shift, team leader; (occ.) charge
hand

équipe alternante
rotating shift

équipe fixe
regular shift

équipe de jour
day shift

équipe du matin
morning shift

équipe de nuit
night / twilight shift

équipe de réadaptation
rehabilitation team

équipe de remplacement
relief shift

équipe de rotation rapide
rapid rotation shift work

équipe sanitaire / soignante
health team

équipe du soir
backs / evening shift

équipes successives
successive shifts

équipe tournante
rotating / swing shift

équipe de travail
work shift

équipe volante
floating staff

médecine d'équipe
team / group medicine

première équipe
prime shift

**système de travail par équipes
alternant jour et nuit**
alternating shift system

**système de travail par équipes
chevau-chantes**
coupled shift system

travail continu en équipe
continuous shiftwork

travail d'équipe
team work

travail en / par équipe
shift work(ing)

travail par équipes fixes
fixed shift system

ÉQUIPEMENT
facilities

biens d'équipement
producer goods

budget d'équipement
investment / capital budget

**chômage par insuffisance
d'équipements**
capital shortage unemployment

**Commission de l'équipement
sanitaire**
Health Facilities Commission

équipements collectifs
(social / collective) infrastructure,
(public) utilities, community facilities

équipements de loisirs
recreation(al) facilities

équipements de quartier
neighbourhood facilities

équipements récréatifs
recreational facilities

équipement sanitaire
health equipment / (pl.) facilities

équipement sanitaire et médical
health and medical equipment / facilities

équipement de sécurité
safety equipment

équipement de service social
social welfare (material) facility

équipement social
social resources / development / facilities /
services, community / welfare facilities

équipement socio-éducatif
socio-educational facility

équipement thérapeutique
treatment facility

**industrie (productrice) de biens d'é-
quipement**
capital goods industry

plan d'équipement social
social development plan

prime d'équipement (Fr.)
equipment allowance

programme d'équipement
capital programme

ÉQUITABLE
indemnité équitable
fair compensation

norme équitable en matière d'emploi
fair labour standard

norme du travail équitable
fair labour standard

principes actuariels équitables (selon des)
on an actuarial fair basis

répartition géographique équitable
equitable geographical distribution

traitement juste et équitable
fair and equitable treatment

ÉQUITÉ
equity; reasonableness

équité dans l'emploi
fair employment, employment equity

ÉQUIVALENT (adj.)
période équivalente
equivalent period

salaire équivalent
equivalent earnings

ÉQUIVALENT (n.)
équivalent de main-d'oeuvre à temps
plein
full-time man equivalent

équivalent plein temps
full-time equivalent (FTE)

équivalent en valeur actuarielle
equivalent actuarial value

ÉREINTANT
stressful

ERGONOMIE
ergonomics; (occ.) human (factors)
engineering (USA)

ERGOTHÉRAPEUTE
occupational therapist

ERGOTHÉRAPIE
vocational / work / working / occupational therapy, vocational rehabilitation

ÉROSION
érosion des effectifs
personnel / staff attrition

ERREUR
erreur administrative
administrative error

erreur aléatoire
random error

erreur de déclaration
respondent error

erreur d'échantillonnage
sampling error

erreur et négligence administratives
administrative error and oversight

erreur de rétrospection
recall error

erreur-type
standard error

ESCOMPTER
fondé à escompter une promotion (être)
to have a justified expectation to be
promoted

ESCROQUERIE
fraud

escroquerie à la sécurité sociale
(social security) benefit fraud

ESPÈCE
cas d'espèce
specific case

dispositions d'espèce (sauf)
unless otherwise provided
espèces (en)
in cash

indemnité en espèces
compensation in cash

indemnité de maladie versée en espèces
cash sickness benefit

plafond du montant en espèces
cash limit

prestation en espèces
cash benefit, benefit / payment in cash

prestations autres qu'en espèces
non-cash benefits

**prestation marginale d'assistance en
espèces (Denm.)**
marginal cash assistance benefit

prestation de maternité en espèces
maternity cash benefit

prestation périodique en espèces
periodical cash benefit

**prestation supplémentaire en espèces
en cas d'invalidité**
supplementary disability income benefit

récompense en espèces
money / cash award

remboursement en espèces
cash refund

rémunération en espèces
salary paid in cash

salaire en espèces
(occ.) money wage

secours en espèces
relief in cash

subvention en espèces
cash grant

versement en espèces
payment in cash

ESPÉRANCE
expectation

espérance brute de vie active
gross expectation of working life

espérance mathématique
actuarial expectation

espérance nette de vie active
net expectation of working life

espérance de vie
life expectancy

espérance de vie active
expectation of working life

espérance de vie en bonne santé
health expectation, healthy life
expectancy

espérance de vie corrigée en fonction du bien-être
quality-adjusted life-year (QUALY)

espérance de vie à la naissance
life expectancy at birth

ESPRIT
esprit d'entreprise
entrepreneurship, entrepreneurial spirit

esprit d'initiative
initiative, entrepreneurial spirit, ressourcefulness

esprit de / du service social
social work approach

faible d'esprit
mental(ly) deficient, mentally defective

ESSAI
test, trial

engagé à l'essai
on probation; probationer

engagement à l'essai
hiring with probationary period

essai (à l')
on probation; on a trial basis

essai (à titre d')
on a trial basis

période d'essai
period of probation, probation (period), conditional employment / trial / probationary period

prendre à l'essai
to take on probation

travailleur à l'essai
probationary employee / worker

ESSAIMAGE
hiving off

ESSAIMER
to hive off

ESSENTIEL (adj.)
besoin essentiel
basic need; (pl.) basic needs / wants

besoins essentiels de l'être humain
basic human needs

compétences essentielles
key / core skills

évaluation des besoins essentiels
basic needs assessment

gestes essentiels de la vie quotidienne
basic activities of daily life

médicament essentiel
essential medicine / drug

services essentiels
basic facilities

stratégie des besoins essentiels
basic needs strategy

stratégie industrielle orientée vers la satisfaction des besoins essentiels
basic needs-oriented industrial strategy

ESSOR
upturn, upswing

ESTHÉTIQUE (adj.)
chirurgie esthétique
plastic surgery

ESTIMATIF (adj.)
coût estimatif
estimated cost

ESTIMATION
estimate, rating

estimation grossière
(occ.) guestimate

estimation de référence
benchmark estimate

ESTIMÉ (adj.)
gains estimés
(occ.) hypothetical earnings

pension estimée
(occ.) hypothetical pension

ESTROPIÉ
disabled

ESTUDIANTIN
population estudiantine
number of students, student numbers

ÉTABLI
norme établie
set standard

travailleur établi à son compte
self-employed (person / worker)

usage établi
established practice

ÉTABLISSEMENT
establishment; place of business; office;
settlement; (occ.) facility; work

accord collectif d'établissement
working / staff / works agreement

chef d'établissement
manager; employer

comité d'établissement
works committee / council (Ger.)

droit d'établissement
right of establishment

**enseignement dispensé par des établis-
sements spécialisés**
(occ.) institutionalised education

établissement agréé
approved institution

établissement artisanal
handicraft establishment

établissement de l'assiette fiscale
tax assessment
établissement balnéothérapique
spa

établissement de bienfaisance
charitable agency, charity

établissement de bienfaisance privé
private charitable agency / charity

établissement de caisse (Fr.)
fund institution

établissement de calendrier
scheduling

établissement conventionné
national health institution

établissement des cotisations
determination / assessment of
contributions

**établissement dispensant des cours du
soir**
evening / night school

établissement du coût salarial
calculation of wage / salary cost(s),
salary costing

établissement de cure
spa establishment

**établissement d'éducation
complémen-taire / d'éducation
permanente / d'é-ducation post-
scolaire**
college of further education

établissement d'éducation spéciale
special school

établissement pour enfants
children's home

établissement d'enseignement
educational institution / establishment

établissement d'enseignement général
(occ.) mainstream school

établissement d'enseignement mixte
co-educational institution

**établissement d'enseignement post-
secondaire**
post-secondary educational institution

**établissement d'enseignement post-
secondaire communautaire (USA)**
community college

établissement d'enseignement secon-daire
secondary school, high school (USA)

établissement d'enseignement spécial
special school

établissement d'enseignement supérieur
establishment / institution of higher education, (higher education) college

établissement de formation
training institution

établissement de formation des maîtres
college of education

établissement hospitalier
hospital; (occ.) residential institution; (pl.) hospital facilities

établissement d'hospitalisation
in-patient establishment

établissement de jour (med.)
day-care patient facility

établissement post-secondaire
post-secondary educational institution

établissement privé
private institution

établissement d'un profil professionnel
vocational assessment

établissement de protection sanitaire et sociale de l'enfance
health and social care institution for children

établissement public
Government-owned establishment / corporation, public institution, govern-mental corporation; statutory body

établissement public (financièrement) autonome
governmental / Government-owned corporation

établissement de la quote-part
assessment of contributions

établissement des rôles d'imposition
tax assessment

établissement sanitaire
health facility

établissement de santé auxiliaire
peripheral health establishment

établissement scolaire
educational institution

établissement secondaire technique
technical college

établissement de séjour
residential facility

établissement de soins
health facility

établissement spécialisé
specialised institution

établissement stable
permanent establishment

établissement non syndiqué
non-union establishment

établissement pour tuberculeux
tuberculosis clinic

établissement d'utilité publique
charitable corporation; charity

formation en établissement
institutional training

formation spécialisée en établissement
institutional skill training

frais d'établissement
start-up cost

frais de premier établissement
initial outlay

liberté d'établissement
freedom of establishment

personnel d'établissement
residential staff

placement des enfants en établissement
institutional care of children

placement en établissement
institutional care

placer dans un établissement
to institutionalise (in a social or medical structure)

programme de formation en établissement scolaire
in-school training programme

soins en établissement
institutional / residential care

soins dans des établissements de jour
day care

soins en établissement privé
private care

système d'établissement des rapports périodiques
periodic reporting system

traitement en établissement
institutional / residential care

travailleur social en établissement pénitentiaire
prison welfare officer

ÉTALEMENT
étalement du risque
spreading the risk

étalement des vacances
staggered holidays

ÉTALON
standard

modèle médical étalon
standardised medical experience

ÉTAPE
étape de carrière
career ladder

formation par étapes
phased / (occ.) analytical training

retraite par étapes
phased retirement

ÉTAT
condition, status; statement, position; State; (pl.) returns

agent de l'Etat
Government employee, public official

agent non titulaire de l'Etat
non-established State employee

apport de l'Etat
contribution of the State

auxiliaires de l'Etat
State auxiliary staff

congé de formation à l'Etat (Belg.)
State training leave

contribution de l'Etat
contribution of the State

deniers de l'Etat
public money / monies / funds

diplômé d'Etat
certified, State-registered

employé de l'Etat
public servant

entreprise d'Etat
State-owned / State-controlled enterprise

Etat auteur d'une réserve
reserving State (treaty)

état civil
civil status

Etat compétent
competent State

état de congés
leave report

état de dépendance
helplessness

état des gains
statement of income

état handicapant
handicapping condition

état d'indigence
state of need

état du marché du travail
labour market conditions

états de paie
payroll

état de présence
attendance record

Etat protecteur / providence
welfare State

état récapitulatif
summary / consolidated statement

état sanitaire / de santé
health / physical condition, state of health,
health status

état de santé d'une population
health profile of a population

état de service
service record, record / length of service

état nécessitant des soins médicaux
condition requiring medical care

fonctionnaire de l'Etat (UK)
Crown servant

indicateur de l'état de santé
health status indicator

inscrit sur les états de paie
in pay status

**logements financés / subventionnés par
l'Etat**
public housing

maintien en état
maintenance

médecin de l'Etat (Malta)
Government practitioner

organisme d'Etat
government(al) body / agency

participation de l'Etat
State's contribution / share

pension de l'Etat liée aux revenus (UK)
State earnings-related pension

prestation servie par l'Etat
State benefit

propriété de l'Etat
State ownership

pupille de l'Etat
child in care

quatrième état
working class

questionnaire d'état de santé
medical questionnaire

**régime de retraite complémentaire
géré par l'Etat**
State earnings-related pension scheme

remise en état
rehabilitation

ressortissant d'un Etat membre
national of a Member State

retraite versée par l'Etat
State pension

salarié de l'Etat
Government employee

statistiques de l'état civil
vital statistics

subvention de l'Etat
State / Government subsidy

**travailleur handicapé reconnu par
l'Etat**
registered disabled person

ÉTAT-MAJOR
staff (mil.); administrative staff; top /
senior management

personnel d'état-major
staff personnel (mil.)

ÉTATIQUE
State-owned

ÉTATISÉ
médecine étatisée
State medicine

ÉTÉ
emploi d'été
summer employment / job

emploi d'été des / pour étudiants
student summer employment / job

horaire d'été
summer time

stage d'été
summer course

université d'été
summer school

vacances d'été
summer holidays

ÉTENDU
famille étendue
extended / joint family

prestation étendue
extended benefit

ÉTENDUE
size, range, scope

étendue de la / des garantie(s)
degree of coverage, extent / range of cover

ÉTHIQUE
code d'éthique (professionnelle)
code of ethics / of behaviour

éthique professionnelle
professional code of ethics

ÉTRANGER
alien, foreigner

cotisation payée à l'étranger
contribution paid abroad

détachement à l'étranger
secondment abroad

étranger (à l')
abroad

étranger de passage
alien visitor, non-resident / visiting alien

étranger résident
resident alien

étranger en situation irrégulière
illegal alien

fonctionnaire en poste à l'étranger
expatriate civil servant

implantations à l'étranger / étrangères
(occ.) establishment trade

main-d'oeuvre étrangère
foreign / off-shore labour

paiement à l'étranger
payment abroad

paiement des prestations à un titulaire à l'étranger
payment of benefits abroad

pension payée (à un titulaire) à l'étran-ger
pension paid abroad

recrutement à l'étranger / de travailleurs étrangers
foreign recruiting, foreign worker recruitment; off-shore recruitment

résidence à l'étranger
residence abroad

résident étranger
alien resident

séjour à l'étranger
stay abroad

service des prestations à un titulaire à l'étranger
payment of benefits abroad

soins à l'étranger
health care abroad

travailleur étranger
foreign worker

ÉTUDE
study; survey, review; research; engineering; (pl.) education, schooling

abandonner ses études
to leave school; to drop out

allocation pour frais d'études
education(al) grant

année d'études
year of study; grade

bourse d'études
bursary, scholarship, student / study grant

brevet d'études professionnelles agricoles (BEPA) (Fr.)
certificate of agricultural vocational education

certificat de fin d'études
(school-)leaving certificate

certificat de fin d'études secondaires
high-school leaving certificate

comité d'étude
review board

congé d'études
education(al) / study leave

congé d'études à temps partiel
part-time day release

crédit d'études
school credit

durée des études
duration / length of study

emploi lié au domaine d'étude
school-related position

études (faire des)
to study; to attend school

études en alternance
day-release studies

étude bibliographique
literature review / survey

étude des cadences
time and motion study

étude de cas
case study

études commerciales
business studies

étude de consommation
consumer research / study

étude du déroulement de carrière
career follow-up / career pattern study

études de doctorat
postgraduate studies

étude documentaire
literature review / survey

étude des effectifs
manning / manpower survey

étude d'évolution de la carrière
occupational follow-up study

étude de l'historique professionnel
career follow-up / career pattern study

études de médecine
undergraduate medical studies

étude par panel
panel design / study

études à plein temps
full-time education

étude de(s) poste(s) de travail
job analysis

étude prévisionnelle des besoins de main-d'oeuvre dans l'entreprise
company manpower planning, personnel planning at establishment level

étude spécifique
case study

étude des tâches
work study

étude des traitements
review of salary scales

études de troisième cycle universitaire
postgraduate studies

études universitaires supérieures
postgraduate studies

groupe d'étude
task force / group; (occ.) syndicate

hautes études universitaires
postgraduate studies

indemnité pour frais d'études
education(al) grant

institut de hautes études
graduate school

jeune ayant abandonné ses études
early leaver, drop-out

jeune ayant terminé ses études
school-leaver

jours de congé-études
day release education

journées d'étude
(occ.) workshop

mesure d'incitation à l'étude des langues
language incentive

moyens d'étude et de formation
study and training facilities

niveau d'études
educational level, level of study / of
education / of schooling, academic /
educational achievement / attainment

période couverte par l'étude
inquiry / survey period

plan d'accompagnement pour les sortants de l'école et des études (SAVE) (Belg.)
support plan for school and college leavers

plan d'études
curriculum

poursuite des / d'études
continuation of studies

poursuivre l'étude de
to keep under review

programme d'alternance travail-études
work-study programme

situation au regard des études
school attendance status

stage de travail et d'étude
(occ.) work study

suivre des études
to attend school

voyage d'étude de travailleurs
study tour for workers

ÉTUDIANT
student

aide aux étudiants
student assistance

aide à la mobilité des étudiants
student mobility grant

emploi d'été des / pour étudiants
student summer employment / job

emploi pour étudiant
student job

emploi saisonnier pour étudiants
(occ.) vacation job / work

étudiant non diplômé
undergraduate

étudiant de l'enseignement supérieur
student in higher education; (occ.) scholar

étudiant des quatre premières années de l'enseignement supérieur
undergraduate

étudiant en pédagogie
teacher trainee

étudiant du premier cycle
undergraduate student

étudiant salarié
student employee, working student

étudiant de service social
social work student

étudiant du troisième cycle
(post)graduate student

main-d'oeuvre étudiante
student labour

notation par les étudiants (USA)
course student rate

personnel étudiant
student staff

placement d'étudiants
student placement

prêt étudiant
student loan

**subvention de mobilité des étudiants /
destinée aux étudiants**
student mobility grant

ÉVALUATION
evaluation, assessment; appraisal; estimate, rating

base de l'évaluation
basis of assessment

cadre d'évaluation
evaluation framework

centre d'évaluation
assessment centre

**Commission d'évaluation des incapacités
(Spain)**
Incapacity Assessment Board

entretien d'évaluation
appraisal / assessment interview

entretien d'évaluation de l'employabilité
employability assessment interview

évaluation actuarielle
actuarial evaluation

**évaluation analytique des tâches / du
travail**
analytical job evaluation

évaluation des besoins
needs assessment

évaluation des besoins essentiels
basic needs assessment

évaluation des compétences
assessment of skills, competency
assessment

évaluation continue
continuous assessment

évaluation des demandes
application assessment

évaluation des emplois
job evaluation

**évaluation des emplois selon une échelle
de points**
point-factor method of job evaluation

évaluation formative
formative assessment

évaluation globale
overall assessment

évaluation de l'impôt
tax assessment

évaluation inverse
inverted appraisal

évaluation du personnel au mérite
merit rating / rate

évaluation d'un poste
audit of a job / post

évaluation des postes de travail
job evaluation

évaluation professionnelle
vocational assessment

évaluation du rendement
performance appraisal / rating

évaluation sommative
summative assessment

évaluation des tâches
job evaluation

évaluation du travail
work assessment

fiche d'évaluation
assessment sheet

grille d'évaluation
appraisal / evaluation grid

grille d'évaluation à choix forcé
forced choice rating (grid)

méthode d'évaluation du rendement
performance evaluation system

**programme d'évaluation analytique
des tâches / du travail**
analytical job evaluation scheme

rapport d'évaluation d'un travailleur
evaluation report of an employee

structure d'évaluation
evaluation framework

système d'évaluation
evaluation system

système d'évaluation analytique des tâches / du travail
analytical job evaluation scheme

système d'évaluation du rendement
performance evaluation system

ÉVASION
économie d'évasion
escapist economy

évasion fiscale
tax evasion / avoidance

possibilité d'évasion fiscale
tax loophole

ÉVEIL
activités d'éveil du jeune enfant
early childhood stimulation

centre d'éveil
pre-school learning centre

ÉVÉNEMENT
congé pour événements familiaux (Fr.)
special family leave

ÉVENTAIL
éventail des attributions
range of duties

éventail d'emplois
range of jobs

éventail de prix
price range

éventail de qualifications
range of skills, skill mix

éventail des salaires
range of wages; (occ.) wage differential

éventail des traitements
salaries range

ÉVENTUALITÉ
contingency, risk; event

assuré contre une ou plusieurs éventualités
insured for one or more contingencies

éventualité couverte
contingency covered

éventualité à couvrir
contingency to be covered

éventualité d'ordre physique
physical contingency

ÉVENTUEL
employeur éventuel
prospective / potential employer

salarié éventuel
prospective employee

ÉVOLUTIF
affection / maladie évolutive
active / progressive disease

maladie non évolutive
inactive disease

ÉVOLUTION
development; trend

ajusté / corrigé selon l'évolution des prix
adjusted for price changes

étude d'évolution de la carrière
occupational follow-up study

évolution de carrière
career / occupational development

évolution de carrière en dents de scie
erratic career evolution

évolution conjoncturelle
economic development/ trend; business / cyclical trend

évolution de l'économie / économique
economic development / trend

évolution de l'emploi
employment trend

évolution du marché du travail
labour market development

évolution des mentalités
change of attitudes

évolution de l'offre sur le marché du travail
changes in labour supply

évolution prévisionnelle de la main-d'oeuvre
occupational forecast

évolution professionnelle
occupational development

évolution des techniques / technologique
technological change

modulé selon l'évolution des prix
adjusted for price changes

perspective d'évolution de carrière
career development prospect

suivre l'évolution de
to keep under review

EXACTITUDE
attestation d'exactitude
certification of accuracy

EXAMEN
examination; review; test; inspection
centre d'examens de santé
medical examination centre

comité d'examen
review board

congé examen (Fr.)
examination leave

examen d'admission
entry / qualifying examination

examen annuel
annual review

examen de compagnonnage
craftsman's / qualified / skilled workman's test

examen d'entrée
entrance / entry examination

examen d'entrée dans le second cycle universitaire (USA)
graduate record examination

examen final
final examination

examen de maîtrise
(occ.) master craftsman's examination

examen médical
health check, physical inspection, medical examination

examen médical conjoint
joint medical examination

examen médical de routine
routine medical test

examen d'orientation professionnelle
vocational testing

examen partiel
intermediate examination

examen professionnel
trade examination

examen radiographique
x-ray examination

examen de santé
health examination

passer / présenter un examen
to take an examination

résultats obtenus à l'examen / aux examens
examination performance

réussir un examen
to pass an examination

EXAMINATEUR
tester

EXCÉDANT
in excess of

EXCÉDENT
surplus

compte d'excédents budgétaires
surplus account

excédent de la balance commerciale
balance of trade surplus

excédent budgétaire
budget surplus

excédent budgétaire de plein emploi
full-employment budget surplus

excédent commercial
trade surplus

excédent de main-d'oeuvre
surplus labour / manpower, labour /
manpower surplus, manpower redundancy,
redundancy of manpower

excédent de personnel
redundancy

excédent de rémunération
salary surplus

excédent de travailleurs
over-supply of workers, worker surplus

indicateur-repère d'excédent de main-d'oeuvre
benchmark (labour / manpower) surplus
indicator

profession en excédent de main-d'oeuvre
surplus occupation

région à excédent de main-d'oeuvre
labour surplus area

EXCÉDENTAIRE
surplus, supernumerary

capacité (de production) excédentaire
excess (plant) capacity

demande excédentaire de main-d'oeuvre
excess demand for labour

effectifs excédentaires
labour redundancy

main-d'oeuvre excédentaire
labour / manpower surplus / redundancy,
surplus manpower, redundancy of manpower, displaced / redundant labour, workers
made redundant

**offre excédentaire de main-d'oeuvre,
offre de main-d'oeuvre excédentaire**
excess supply / oversupply of labour

personnel excédentaire
labour redundancy, displaced /
redundant labour, workers made
redundant

**recouvrement des versements excé-
dentaires**
over-payment recovery

remboursement excédentaire
over-reimbursement

**taux de la main-d'oeuvre
excédentaire des jeunes**
youth labour surplus rate

travailleur excédentaire
redundant worker; surplus employee

versement excédentaire
over-payment

EXCÉDER
excéder ses pouvoirs
to act beyond one's authority

EXCEPTION
exception; departure (from)

traitement d'exception
special treatment

EXCEPTIONNEL
dépenses exceptionnelles
below-the-line expenditure

octroi exceptionnel
exceptional / extra-statutory award

paiement exceptionnel
(occ.) one-off payment

**participation pour prise en charge
exceptionnelle**
contribution for exceptional expenses

prélèvement fiscal exceptionnel
exceptional tax levy

prestation exceptionnelle
exceptional / special benefit

prime exceptionnelle
exceptional / special bonus

secours exceptionnel
exceptional relief

versement exceptionnel
(occ.) one-off payment

EXCÈS
recours pour excès de pouvoir
application to set aside a decision on
grounds of exceeding or misusing one's
authority

EXCESSIF
undue

paiement excessif
overpayment

EXCESSIVEMENT
unduly

EXCLU
exclu de la sécurité sociale
not protected by social security

**prestation exclue de la rémunération
considérée aux fins de la pension**
non-pensionable benefit

EXCLURE
to exclude; to disregard; to expel

exclure d'un syndicat
to expel from a union

EXCLUSIF
droit exclusif
exclusive / proprietary / sole right

**droit exclusif de placement des tra-
vailleurs**
exclusive right to place workers in jobs,
placing monopoly

EXCLUSION
exclusion, expulsion

clause d'exclusion
exclusion clause

exclusion d'un syndicat
expulsion from a union

convention d'exclusivité syndicale
closed shop agreement

EX-CONJOINT
former spouse

EXÉCUTANT
operator; practitioner; (pl.) operational
staff / personnel

**écrivains et artistes créateurs et exé-
cutants [CITP-1988 (245)]**
writers and creative or performing
artists [ISCO-1988 (245)]

poste d'exécutant
working level post

EXÉCUTER
to execute; to enforce, to implement; to
administer

exécuter un contrat
to administer a contract

exécuter son préavis
to work out one's notice

exécuter un programme
to administer a programme

EXÉCUTIF
cadre exécutif
executive officer

directeur exécutif
executive director

EXÉCUTION
execution; performance; workmanship;
enforcement; implementation; discharge

agent d'exécution
field worker; manual worker;
practitioner; (pl.) executing staff

agent d'exécution à compétence géné-rale
general field worker

délai à exécution
extension for payment

délai d'exécution
lead(-)time

exécution sans faute
(occ.) zero defect

exécution d'un programme
programme delivery

mesure d'exécution
enforcement measure

ordre d'exécution
mandatory injunction

personnel d'exécution
basic staff, operative workers, unskilled
staff for executory work

sursis à exécution
stay of execution

voies d'exécution
means of enforcement

EXÉCUTOIRE
enforceable

force exécutoire (ayant)
enforceable, binding

EXEMPT
exempt d'impôts
tax-free

exempt de service
excused from duty

EXEMPTÉ
catégorie exemptée
excluded category

travailleur exempté
excluded employee

EXEMPTION
exemption; waiver; remission; release

catégorie d'exemption
excluded category

exemption générale
blanket exemption

exemption du ticket modérateur
exemption from patient's contribution

EXERCÉ
activité effectivement exercée
actual / current job / occupation, actual
job

activité exercée
job / occupation held

EXERCER
to perform; to engage in; (med.) to be in
practice

autorisation d'exercer (méd.)
certification

autorisation d'exercer des fonctions
admission to the exercise of functions

droit d'exercer
right to practice

**exercer une activité lucrative / un
emploi lucratif**
to be gainfully occupied / employed

exercer une activité professionnelle
to engage in an occupation, to hold a job

**exercer une activité rémunérée / un
emploi rémunéré**
to be gainfully occupied / employed

exercer un emploi
to work, to hold a job, to be employed

exercer un emploi rétribué
to be gainfully occupied / employed

exercer des fonctions
to perform duties

exercer légalement
to be registered in / to practice

frapper d'une interdiction d'exercer
to suspend from practice

habilité à exercer
qualified to practice

médecin habilité à exercer (Can.)
licensed physician

EXERCICE
exercise; practice; year, period; discharge;
financial / fiscal / accounting period /
year

apte à l'exercice d'un emploi
fit for work / employement; employable

**congé pour exercice de fonctions
publiques**
time off (work) for public duties

exercice (en)
in service, serving

exercice de plusieurs activités
multiple jobholding

exercice budgétaire
budget year

exercice comptable
accounting year / period

exercice d'une double activité
double / dual jobholding

exercice fiscal
tax(able) year

exercice de ses fonctions (dans l')
in the course of one's duties / of
employment, in the line of duty

exercice de fonctions officielles
performance of official duties

exercice de groupe prépayé
prepaid group practice (PGP)

exercice d'imposition
assessment year, year of assessment

exercice libéral (d')
in private practice

exercice libéral de la médecine
free medical practice, free practice of
medicine

exercice de la profession infirmière
nursing practice

**imputable à l'exercice de fonctions
officielles**
attributable to the performance of
official duties

**porter atteinte au libre exercice de
l'industrie et du travail**
to impair / to restrict the freedom of
industry and labour

**prestation liée à l'exercice d'un
emploi**
in-work benefit

EX GRATIA
paiement ex gratia
ex gratia payment

EXIGÉ
aptitude exigée
skill / job requirement

salaire exigé
wage required

EXIGENCE
requirement

exigence discriminatoire
discriminatory requirement

exigence explicite
specific requirement

exigences en matière de formation
training requirements

exigence du poste
job requirement

exigence précise
specific requirement

exigence professionnelle
skill requirement; (pl.) occupational
requirements

EXIGIBILITÉ
exigibilité des cotisations
payability of contributions

EXIGIBLE
due, payable, exigible, chargeable

EXISTANT
embauche sur poste(s) existant(s)
job replacement

embauche sur poste(s) existant(s) (par)
by replacement

EXISTENCE
garantie des moyens d'existence
income security

garantir les moyens d'existence
to maintain income

**indemnité pour difficultés (exception-
nelles) d'existence**
hardship pay

**minimum de moyens d'existence
(MINIMEX) (Belg.)**
minimum income security, minimum
subsistence income

moyens d'existence
means of support / subsistence, subsistence
means, (means of) livelihood; income;
welfare

perte de moyens d'existence
loss of income support

EXODE
exode de l'élite professionnelle
migration of highly trained personnel

exode de personnel
outflow of personnel

exode rural
rural depopulation

EXONÉRATION
exemption; disregard, remission

assurance basée sur une entente
d'exonération mutuelle
no fault insurance

**exonération des charges / de(s) cotisa-
tions**
waiver of / exemption from / cancellation of
contributions

exonération fiscale / d'impôt
tax exemption

exonération du paiement des primes
waiver of premiums

**exonérations et réductions des cotisa-
tions**
exemptions from and reductions of
contributions

**exonération de la taxe
d'apprentissage (Fr.)**
exemption from apprenticeship tax

plafond d'exonération fiscale
tax exemption limit

**seuil d'exonération fiscale des
revenus**
lower earnings limit of tax exemption

EXONÉRÉ
exonéré d'impôt
exempt from tax / taxation, tax-free

revenus exonérés d'impôts
tax-free income

EXPANSION
expansion de l'emploi
employment development

expansion des entreprises
business development

industrie en expansion
growth / sunrise industry

potentiel d'expansion
growth potential

secteur en expansion
growth industry

EXPATRIATION
indemnité d'expatriation
expatriation allowance, overseas
premium / allowance

prestation liée à l'expatriation
expatriate benefit

prestation non liée à l'expatriation
non-expatriate benefit

prime d'expatriation
expatriation allowance / bonus, overseas premium / allowance

EXPATRIÉ
expatriate

EXPECTATIVE
expectative d'emploi continu
expectancy of continued employment

expectative juridique du renouvellement d'un engagement
legal expectation of renewal of contract

EXPÉRIENCE
acquérir de l'expérience
to acquire / gain experience

calcul de l'expérience professionnelle
reckoning of professional experience

courbe d'expérience
experience curve

expérience acquise
past experience, previous work experience; work background / history

expérience acquise en cours d'emploi
practical (work) / hands-on / on-the job experience

expérience d'apprentissage
learning experience

expérience concrète du travail
practical (work) / hands-on / on-the job experience

expérience confirmée
proven experience

expérience à prendre en considération
reckonable experience

expérience professionnelle
professional / job / work experience; work history

expérience professionnelle antérieure
past / previous (work) experience; work background; employment history

expérience suffisante (avoir / posséder une)
(occ.) to qualify for

expérience du terrain
field experience

expérience de travail
job / work experience

expérience en milieu de travail
practical (work) / hands-on / on-the job experience

manque d'expérience pratique
lack of practical experience /of work experience

EXPÉRIMENTAL
expérimental (à titre)
on an experimental basis, tentative

programme expérimental
pilot programme

projet expérimental
pilot project

EXPÉRIMENTÉ
experienced

main-d'oeuvre expérimentée
experienced workforce

travailleur expérimenté
experienced worker

EXPERT (adj.)
able; expert; proficient

EXPERT (n.)
expert; professional

compétence d'experts
expertise

expert-comptable
chartered accountant

expert-conseil
consultant

expert-conseil en gestion
managerial consultant

expert-conseil pour la jeunesse
youth consultant

expert-conseil sectoriel
industrial consultant

expert en matière de sécurité (Gr.)
safety technician

groupe d'experts
panel of experts

médecin-expert
medical expert

EXPERTISE
expertise médicale
expert medical report / opinion

expertise médico-légale
expert forensic report

expertise psychiatrique
expert psychiatric report

protocole d'expertise
(occ.) memorandum of appraisal

EXPIRATION
expiry; termination

date d'expiration
termination / expiry date

expiration d'un accord
termination of an agreement

expiration d'un délai d'attente
completion of a waiting period

venir à expiration
to lapse, to expire

venue à expiration du contrat
expiry of contract

EXPIRÉ
expired

expiré (non)
unexpired

EXPIRER
to expire

EXPLICITE
exigence explicite
specific requirement

EXPLIQUÉ
absence non expliquée
unexplained absence

EXPLOITANT
operator; land holder

agriculteur exploitant
farm operator, farmer

exploitant agricole
farm operator, farmer

exploitants agricoles [CITP-1968 (6-1)]
farmers [ISCO-1968 (6-1)]

exploitant principal
main farmer

petit exploitant
smallholder

propriétaire exploitant
self-employed farmer; farm-owner;
owner-operator, owner-manager;
working proprie-tor

EXPLOITATION
associé d'exploitation
associate farmer

autorisation d'exploitation
licensing

budget d'exploitation
operational / operating budget

cadre d'exploitation
operational framework

cession d'exploitation (agr.)
transfer of farm holding

charges / coût / dépenses d'exploitation
running / operational / operating cost

exploitation minière
mine

exploitation pornographique des enfants
child pornography

exploitation type (agr.)
standard farm

frais d'exploitation
running / operational / operating cost

horaire d'exploitation
opening hours

petite exploitation
smallholding

EXPLOITÉ
main-d'oeuvre exploitée
slave / sweated labour

EXPLOSION
explosion nataliste
baby boom

EXPOSÉ (adj.)
at risk; subject to

groupe particulièrement exposé
particular risk group

groupe très exposé
high-risk group

personne exposée
person at risk

EXPOSÉ (n.)
exposé succinct
summary statement

EXPOSER
exposer à des frais (s')
to incur costs

EXPOSITION
délai d'exposition au risque
risk exposure time

exposition d'enfant
child exposure

niveau acceptable d'exposition
acceptable level of exposure

EXPRESSION
droit d'expression des salariés
employees' right of expression

EXPRIMÉ
exprimé en prix constants
deflated

EXPULSION
deportation, expulsion

arrêté / décision / mesure / ordre d'expulsion
deportation / expulsion order

EXTENSION
extension; increase

extension administrative
administrative extension (collective agreement)

extension des prestations
increasing provision of benefits

EXTÉRIEUR
aide extérieure
outside help; substitute care (for children)

appel à des concours extérieurs
use of outside expertise

formation extérieure
off-the-job training

migration extérieure
external migration

organisme extérieur
external / outside agency

personnel extérieur à l'entreprise
out-house staff

placement extérieur (familial)
boarding out

recours à des ressources extérieures
out(-)sourcing

recrutement extérieur
external recruitment

recrutement à l'extérieur
outside recruitment

signe extérieur de richesse
external indication of wealth

travailleur extérieur
outside worker

travailleur extérieur à la production
non-production worker

EXTERNALISATION
externalisation des services
facilities management

EXTERNAT
cours en externat
non-residential course

EXTERNE (adj.)
administrateur externe
non-executive director

allocation d'assistance externe
(Denmark)
outside assistance allowance

candidat externe
external candidate

concours externe
open competition

consultations externes
out-patient services / department / clinic /
facilities

département externe (hosp.)
out-patient department

**dotation des postes par voie de recru-
tement externe**
external staffing

facteurs externes
externalities

formation externe
external training

malade externe
(hospital) out-patient

marché du travail externe
external labour market

migration externe
external migration

organisme externe
external / outside agency

reclassement externe
out(-)placement

recrutement externe
external recruitment

revenus externes
outside earnings

service de consultations externes
out-patient services / clinic /
department; (pl.) out-patient facilities

**soins médicaux en consultation
externe**
out-patient treatment

travailleur externe
outside worker

EXTERNE (n.)
day pupil; (med.) non-resident student at
a teaching hospital, extern

EXTINCTION
termination

EXTRA (n.)
occasional help / hand; peripheral
worker;
(pl.) casual labour

travailler comme extra
to work as an extra

EXTRACTIF
industries extractives
mining (industries / activities)

EXTRA-LÉGAL
assurance extra-légale en matière
d'hospitalisation (Belg.)
extra-legal hospitalisation insurance

prestation extra-légale
non-statutory benefit

EXTRAORDINAIRE
extraordinary; non-recurrent

complément extraordinaire de salaire (It.)
extraordinary wage supplement

coût extraordinaire
non-recurring cost

dépenses extraordinaires
below-the-line / non-recurrent expenditure

recettes extraordinaires
below-the-line income

EXTRASCOLAIRE
out-of-school; extra-curricular

activité extrascolaire
extra-curricular activity

éducation / enseignement extrascolaire
out-of-school / informal education

FABRICANT
manufacturer

FABRICATION
chaîne de fabrication
production line

industries appliquant des procédés de fabrication en continu
flow process industries

ouvrier de fabrication
production worker

système de fabrication flexible
flexible manufacturing system

FABRIQUE
factory; shop

FAÇADE (ass.)
fronting

FACILITÉ
facility; (pl.) amenities; accomodation;
incentive; facilities

FAÇON
workmanship

ouvrier à façon
jobbing workman

travail à façon
hire service contract; special order work;
jobbing work; outwork

FAÇONNIER
jobbing workman

FACTEUR
facteur d'admissibilité
qualifier

facteur de capitalisation
accumulation factor

facteur chargement
load factor

facteur de coût
cost factor

facteur de déclenchement
triggering factor

facteurs externes
externalities

facteur des gains
earnings factor

facteur des gains globaux
total earnings factor

facteurs et messagers [CITP-1968 (3-7)]
mail distribution clerks [ISCO-1968 (3-7)]

facteur mobilité
mobility factor

facteur de personnalité
personality factor

facteur de production
production factor; input

facteur saisonnier
seasonal factor

multiplicateur corrigé par le facteur de correction de la rémunération
multiplier corrected by the remuneration correction factor

procédé à facteur travail prédominant
labour-intensive technology

FACTORIEL
analyse factorielle
factor analysis

FACULTATIF
optional; voluntary

âge de retraite facultative
optional retirement age

assurance facultative
optional insurance

assurance facultative continuée
optional continued insurance

**assuré au titre d'une assurance facul-
tative continuée**
insured on an optional continued basis

cours / matière facultatif(ve)
optional / elective subject

prestation facultative
optional benefit

régime de retraite facultatif
optional pension plan

repos prénatal facultatif
optional pre(-)natal leave

retraite facultative
optional retirement

FACULTÉ
ability, power; entitlement; branch;
college

faculté de (avoir la)
to be entitled

faculté contributive
capacity to pay, taxable / tax-paying
capacity

faculté intellectuelle
mental capacity

faculté de médecine
medical college

faculté mentale
mental capacity

FAIBLE (adj.)
catégorie de personnes à faibles revenus
low-income (population) group

économiquement faible
person in need of financial assistance; (occ.)
underprivileged; low-income people; (pl.)
lower / lowest income group

groupe à faibles revenus
low-income (population) group

**logements pour les groupes sociaux à
faibles revenus**
low-income housing

ménage à faible revenu
low-income household

personne économiquement faible
person in need of financial assistance

prêt à faible taux d'intérêt
low-interest loan

seuil de faible revenu
low-income cut-off / threshold / limit

travailleur à faibles revenus
worker with low income

FAIBLE (n.)
faible d'esprit
mental(ly) deficient, mentally defective

FAIBLESSE
weakness; limitation; handicap

faiblesse structurelle d'un système
inbuilt weakness of a system

FAILLITE
business failure; bankruptcy

déclaration de faillite
adjudication of bankruptcy

jugement déclaratif de faillite
adjudication order

FAIT (n.)
fact; event

fait de guerre
act of war

personne recueillie de fait
de facto dependant

responsabilité du fait d'autrui
vicarious liability

FAMILIAL
absence pour raison(s) familiale(s)
compassionate leave

agent de planification familiale
family-planning worker

aide familiale
domestic / family worker / helper, (visiting) home(-)maker, family / home aid, home / mother's / family help

aide familial(e) non rémunéré(e)
unpaid family worker

allocation familiale
family benefit / allowance, children's allowance, child benefit allowance (UK)

allocation familiale complémentaire (Port.)
supplementary family allowance

allocations familiales payables à partir du deuxième enfant
children's allowances from the second child

allocation familiale progressive
progressive family allowance

allocation de soutien familial
family support allowance

auxiliaire familiale
domestic / family worker, (visiting) home(-)maker, family / home aid / help / helper, mother's help

auxiliaire familial(e) non rémunéré(e)
unpaid family worker

avantage familial
(occ.) dependency benefit

budget familial
family budget

cadre familial
home; family environment

caisse d'allocations familiales
family allowance fund

cellule familiale
family unit

centre de placement familial
family placement centre

charges familiales
family responsibilities

complément (au / de revenu) familial
family supplement, family income supplement (UK); family credit (UK)

congé pour événements familiaux (Fr.)
special family leave

congé pour raisons familiales
compssionate leave

consultations familiales
counselling for families, family counselling

crèche familiale
family day care

crédit familial (UK)
family credit

déduction familiale
dependants' allowance

domicile familial
matrimonial / parental home

dotation familiale
family endowment

école d'enseignement familial et ménager
home-making school

éducation familiale
family education

entreprise familiale
family firm / establishment / enterprise / business / concern

foyer de placement familial
foster house / home

guidance familiale
family guidance

halte-garderie familiale
family occasional care centre

industries familiales
cottage industries / crafts

livret d'allocations familiales
allowance order book

logement familial
family home

maison familiale de vacances
family holiday home

ménage non familial
non-family household

milieu familial
family environment

monitrice familiale
teaching homemaker

noyau familial
family nucleus

orientation familiale
family guidance

pension à titre familial
family pension

péréquation des charges familiales
equalisation of family burdens

personne ayant des charges familiales
person with family responsibilities,
breadwinner

placement extérieur familial
boarding out

placement familial
family placement; foster (home) care

placement familial de vacances
holiday family placement

planification familiale
family planning, planned parenthood; birth
control

planning familial
family planning, planned parenthood; birth
control

préparation à la vie familiale
family life education

prestation familiale
family benefit

prime familiale (Malta)
family bonus

programme de planification familiale
family-planning programme

quotient familial
dependants' allowance set against tax,
tax relief with respect to dependants

régime d'allocations familiales
family allowances scheme

regroupement familial
family reunion

**regroupement familial des
travailleurs migrants**
reuniting of migrant workers' families

relations familiales
family / (occ.) domestic relations

revenu familial
family / household income

revenu minimum familial
family minimum income

santé familiale
family health

service d'aide familiale
home service; (pl.) family counselling;
home-maker services

services de conseils familiaux
counselling for families, family
counselling

service de santé familiale
family health service

service de travailleuses familiales
home help service

situation familiale
marital / conjugal / dependency / family
/ parental status

soutien du revenu familial
family income support

structures familiales
(occ.) family patterns

supplément de revenu familial (UK)
family income supplement

système du quotient familial
system of (income) tax relief with
respect to dependants

taux de chômage familial
family unemployment rate

taux de prestations familiales
rate of family benefits

travail familial
family work; (occ.) cottage industry

travailleur familial non rémunéré
unpaid family worker

travailleuse familiale
home-maker, home / mother's help; family /
home aid, family help / helper / worker;
(pl.) home-maker services (Fr.)

tutelle aux prestations familiales (Fr.)
control on family benefits

voyage de visite familiale
family visit travel

FAMILLE
family; relatives; household

abandon de famille
wilful neglect to maintain, non-support of
one's family

abandonner sa famille
to desert one's family

abattement pour charges de famille
family allowance

absence pour raison(s) de famille
compassionate leave

agent de planification de la famille
family-planning worker

**aide à la famille pour l'emploi d'une
assistante maternelle agréée (Fr.)**
family benefit for hiring an approved day-
care attendant

aide aux familles avec enfants à charge
aid to families with dependant children
(AFDC)

aide sociale à la famille
social assistance for the family (members),
family welfare

allocation pour charges de famille
dependant care allowance

allocation aux mères de famille
mother's benefit

allocation de soutien de famille
family support allowance

**allocation supplémentaire famille
(Fr.)**
supplementary family allowance

chargé de famille (être)
to be encumbered with family

charges de famille
family expenses; family responsibilities

chargé de famille
person with family responsibilities /
with dependants

chef de famille
family head, head of (the) family,
(family) breadwinner

chef de famille monoparentale
single household head

Code de la famille et de l'aide sociale
Family and Social Welfare Code

congé pour raisons familiales
compssionate leave

**déclaration de situation de famille et
demande d'indemnités pour charges
de famille**
family status report and request for
payment of dependency allowances

déduction pour charge de famille
dependants' allowance

dégrèvement pour charges de famille
dependency credit

délaisser sa famille
to desert one's family

dimension de la famille
family size

enfant issu de famille ouvrière
child of working-class family

**enfant placé dans une famille
d'accueil**
foster child

famille d'accueil
foster family / parents / home

famille active
working family

famille biologique
biological family

famille biparentale
two-parent family

famille à charge
dependent relatives

famille composite
composite / joint family

famille conjugale
conjugal family

famille en difficulté
(occ.) problem family

famille élargie
extended family

famille d'emplois
job cluster / family

famille sans enfants
childless family

famille à enfant unique
one-child family

famille étendue
extended / joint family

famille monoparentale
lone-parent / one-parent / single-parent family

famille nombreuse
large family
famille peu nombreuse
small family

famille nourricière
foster family

famille du type noyau conjugal
conjugal family

famille nucléaire
nuclear family

famille d'origine
natural family

famille à parent unique
lone-parent / one-parent / single-parent family

famille proche
close relatives / relations

famille recomposée / reconstituée
reconstituted family, stepfamily

famille à deux revenus
two-income / two-earner family

famille à plusieurs revenus / à revenus multiples
multi-earner family

famille à revenu unique / à salaire unique
one-earner family

famille socialement défavorisée
socially deprived family

femme seule chef de famille
single woman family head

garde dans une famille hôte
family day care

indemnité pour charge de famille
dependency / dependent allowance; (pl.) family allowances; child benefit allowances (UK)

livret de famille (Fr.)
family record book

majoration pour charges de famille
dependency supplement

médecin de famille
family doctor

membre de la famille
member of the family; relative

membres salariés de la famille
earning members of the family

personne chargée de famille
person with family responsibilities, breadwinner

placement dans une famille
family placement; foster (home) care

plan famille (Fr.)
family scheme

préparation à la vie de famille
family life education

prestation aux familles
family / dependency benefit

prestation supplémentaire pour la famille
family supplement

programme en faveur de la famille
family scheme

protection de la famille
family welfare

protection de la famille et de l'enfance
family and child welfare

résidence de famille
family / matrimonial home

santé de la famille
family health

service d'aide à la famille
home service; (pl.) family counselling;
home-maker services

service axé sur la collectivité et la famille
community and family-based service

**service de protection de la famille et de
l'enfance**
family and child welfare service

service de santé de la famille
family health service

situation de famille
marital / conjugal / dependency / family /
parental status

soins dispensés par la famille
family care / support

soutien de famille
primary / principal (wage) earner; (family)
breadwinner; family support

taille de la famille
(average) family size

travailleur ayant charge de famille
worker with dependants / with family
responsibilities

FARDEAU
burden

FASCICULE
leaflet

FAUTE
error; misconduct; negligence

exécution sans faute
(occ.) zero defect

faute administrative
administrative error

faute caractérisée
clear unquestionable misconduct

faute grave
serious misconduct, gross misconduct /
negligence

faute inexcusable
gross negligence

faute intentionnelle
wilful misconduct

faute légère
slight misconduct

faute lourde
serious misconduct, gross misconduct /
negligence

faute patente
patent misconduct

faute professionnelle
professional misconduct, malpractice

faute de service
administrative / official error

licenciement pour faute
dismissal for misconduct

licenciement pour faute grave
disciplinary lay-off

renvoyer pour faute
to dismiss for misconduct

FAUTEUIL
fauteuil roulant
wheel-chair

FAUX
fausse couche
miscarriage

fausse déclaration
false statement / declaration, misrepre-
sentation

faux frais
incidental expenses

faux malade
malingerer

faux ménage
irregular household

FAVEUR
traitement de faveur
preferential treatment

FAVORABLE
conditions les plus favorables
best prevailing conditions

**enquête sur les conditions d'emploi les
plus favorables**
survey of best prevailing conditions of
service

parti pris favorable
favourably discriminatory treatment

préjugé favorable pour qqn
bias towards somebody

FAVORISER
to promote

FAVORITISME
patronage

FÉDÉRAL
taxe fédérale de chômage (USA)
employer's excise tax

FÉDÉRATION
fédération patronale
employers' federation, industrial
federation (USA)

FÉMININ
association féminine
women's association / club

club féminin
women's club

condition féminine
status of women

emplois majoritairement féminins
female-dominated occupations

**main-d'oeuvre / population active
féminine**
female labour (force)

taux d'activité féminine
female (labour force) / women's participation rate

FEMME
allocation pour femmes de détenus
(Irel.)
prisoners wife's allowance

club de femmes
women's club

femme en âge de procréer
woman of child-bearing age

femme au foyer
home-maker, housewife

femme mariée
married woman

femme mariée qui travaille
working wife

femme rentrante (Belg.)
woman re-entering the labour market

femme seule chef de famille
single woman family head

formation des femmes dans les métiers non traditionnels
non-traditional training for women

prestation de femme abandonnée (Irel.)
deserted wife's benefit

programme destiné aux / en faveur des / intéressant les femmes
women's programme

promotion de la / des femme(s)
advancement of women

renforcement du pouvoir des femmes
empowerment of women

repos des femmes en couches (Fr.)
leave for women after childbirth

service en faveur des / s'adressant aux femmes
women's service

taux d'activité des femmes
female (labour force) / women's participation rate

taux de représentativité des femmes
women's participation rate

FÉRIÉ
jour férié
public / official / statutory holiday; bank holiday

jour férié payé
paid public holiday

FERMAGE
rent(al)

FERME
offre ferme
firm offer

FERMETURE
fermeture d'(une) entreprise
closing down of a business, business / plant closure, closure of an establishment

FERMIER
tenant farmer

FÊTE
fête légale
bank holiday, public / official / statutory holiday

fête religieuse
religious holiday

fête du travail
Mayday, Labor Day (USA)

FEUILLE
form; sheet; schedule

feuille d'accident du travail
work injury form

feuille d'heures
time sheet

feuille d'impôt
tax form

feuille journalière de présence
daily attendance sheet

feuille de maladie
medical record; medical (expenses refund) claim form (Fr.)

feuille de ménage
household schedule

feuille de paie
paylist, paysheet, payroll, earnings record, pay statement / slip

feuille de paie détaillée
detailed / itemised pay statement

feuille de pointage
punctuality record

feuille des présences
attendance sheet / list, record of attendance

feuille de rémunération / de salaire
paylist, paysheet, payroll, earnings record, pay statement / slip

feuille de soins (Fr.)
medical (expenses refund) claim form

feuille de travail
worksheet

FICHE
sheet; (record) card

fiche d'évaluation
assessment sheet

fiche d'information
information sheet

fiche médicale
health record

fiche de paie
paylist, paysheet, payroll, earnings record,
pay statement / slip

fiche de paie détaillée
detailed / itemised pay statement

fiche de pointage
time card

fiche de position (Fr.)
benefit statement

fiche de poste à pourvoir
requisition form

fiche de présence
attendance sheet / list, record of attendance

fiche de renseignements
fact sheet

fiche de santé infantile
child health card

fiche signalétique
identification sheet

fiche de travail
worksheet

FICHIER
file; record; register; roster

**fichier central des cotisations d'assu-
rance (UK)**
central record of insurance contributions

fichier de candidats
roster of candidates

fichier de contact pour les adoptés (UK)
contact register for adopted persons

fichiers courants de maladie
routine records of sickness

fichier de fonctions
task data sheet

fichier de sécurité sociale
social security record

FICTIF
notional

carrière fictive
notional record of employment

gains fictifs
notional earnings

rémunération fictive
notional earnings

FIDÉLITÉ
devoir de fidélité à la Constitution
(Ger.)
duty of loyalty to the Constitution

FIDUCIE
trust

régime de retraite en fiducie
trusteed pension plan

FILET
filet de protection sociale
social security net

filet de sécurité
safety net

filet de sécurité sociale
social security net

FILIALE
branch, subsidiary

FILIÈRE
sector; path; (occ.) scheme

filière professionnelle
occupational career path

système de la double filière (pensions)
two-track pension adjustment system

FILLE
jeune fille au foyer
non-working girl

FIN
end; termination; exhaustion

âge de fin de scolarité (obligatoire)
school-leaving age

âge légal de fin de scolarité
statutory school-leaving age

âge normal de fin de scolarité
normal / regular school-leaving age

allocataire en fin de droit(s)
insurance exhaustee

allocation de fin de droits
allowance for end of entitlement; follow-up
benefit

allocation de fin de service
severance allowance

bénéficiaire en fin de droit
(unemployment) insurance exhaustee

certificat de fin d'études
(school-)leaving certificate

certificat de fin d'études secondaires
high-school leaving certificate

certificat de fin de scolarité
school-leaving certificate

chômeur en fin de droits
unemployment insurance / benefit
exhaustee, unemployed person no longer
entitled to receive unemployment benefit

date de fin de contrat
termination date

effectifs en fin de mois
month-end headcount

entretien de fin d'emploi
exit interview

fin de droits
end of entitlement

fin de droits (être en)
reach the end of one's entitlement (to)

fins de droits (les)
exhaustees

fin des droits à (des) prestations
cessation / exhaustion of entitlement to /
of a right to benefits

fin de non-recevoir
demurrer, objection; blunt refusal;
dismissal

indemnité de fin d'emploi
separation / terminal / severance pay /
payment / benefit

indemnité de fin de carrière
end-of-service payment

indemnité de fin de contrat
end-of-contract payment

indemnité de fin de mission
end-of-assignment payment

mettre fin à un contrat
to terminate a contract

mettre fin à l'engagement de qqn
to terminate the appointment of
somebody

personne en fin de droits
exhaustee

prendre fin
to expire

prime de fin d'année
Christmas / end-of-year bonus

régime fin de carrière
final average earnings plan

régularisation en fin d'année
year-end regularisation

salaire en fin de carrière
final salary

**stage de fin de formation en
entreprise (Belg.)**
enterprise-based end of training course

versement de fin de service
end-of-service payment

FINAL
certificat final
final certificate

consommation médicale finale
final consumption of medical care

examen final
final examination

rémunération moyenne finale
final average remuneration

FINANCE
administration des finances publiques
fiscal administration

finances publiques
public finance

FINANCEMENT
financing, funding; supply of finance;
source of funds; provision

accord de financement
contribution / funding agreement

besoins de financement
financial requirements

coefficient de financement
funding ratio

financement de l'aide sociale
social welfare funding

financement croisé
cross-subsidisation

financement direct
direct funding

financement par l'impôt
tax financing

financement intégral
full funding / financing

financement par répartition
current(-)income / pay-as-you-go financing

financement de la sécurité sociale
financing of social security

financement tripartite
tripartite / three-party financing

moyens de financement
financial facilities

niveau de financement
funding level

société d'épargne et de financement immobilier
(occ.) building society

source de financement
funding source

FINANCER
to fund, to finance; to support

FINANCIER
financial; fiscal

aide financière
financial support / assistance; financial
incentive

aide financière à la maternité (Cz.)
financial assistance in maternity

allocation financière
financial provision

assistance financière
financial assistance

autorités financières
fiscal authorities

besoins financiers
financial requirements

charge financière
financial cost / burden

contrôle financier
financial control

convention de gestion financière (pensions)
funding instrument

**employés des services comptables et
financiers [CITP-1988 (412)]**
numerical clerks [ISCO-1988 (412)]

engagement financier
financial commitment

frais financiers
interest charges

incitation financière
financial incentive

motivation non financière
(occ.) intrinsic reward

organisme financier
financial institution

péréquation financière
financial adjustment / equalisation

**position financière précaire, précarité
financière**
financial insecurity

recettes financières
fiscal revenue

ressources financières
financial resources

situation financière
fiscal position

situation financière précaire
financial insecurity

tiers financier
funding agency

FINANCIÈREMENT
établissement public financièrement
autonome
governmental / Government-owned
corporation

financièrement indépendant
(occ.) self-supporting

FISC
fiscal administration, revenue authorities,
Inland Revenue (UK), Internal Revenue
Service (USA)

agent du fisc
Inland Revenue officer (UK); (pl.)
revenue authorities

FISCAL
[tax]; fiscal

abattement fiscal
tax allowance / reduction

abattement fiscal à la base
tax deduction at source

**abattement fiscal sur le revenu
profes-sionnel de l'épouse**
wife's earned income allowance

**abattement fiscal sur le revenu du
travail**
earned income allowance

accord fiscal bilatéral
double taxation agreement

aide fiscale
tax incentive

allégement fiscal
tax mitigation / relief / rebate; tax
subsidy

année fiscale
(income) tax year, taxable year

assiette fiscale
tax(able) base; basis of taxation

autorités fiscales
taxation authorities

avantage fiscal
tax benefit / incentive; (pl.) tax subsidies

avoir fiscal
tax credit

barème fiscal
tax schedule

charge fiscale
fiscal / tax burden

Code fiscal (UK)
Tax Code

coin fiscal
tax wedge

créance fiscale
tax claim

déduction fiscale
tax allowance / deduction

déduction fiscale pour enfant (à charge)
child (tax) allowance

dégrèvement fiscal
tax rebate / relief / reduction

établissement de l'assiette fiscale
tax assessment

évasion fiscale
tax evasion / avoidance

exercice fiscal
tax(able) year

exonération fiscale
tax exemption

foyer fiscal
household as defined for tax purposes

incitation fiscale
tax incentive

lacune (de la législation) fiscale
tax loophole

optimisation fiscale
(occ.) tax avoidance

paradis fiscal
tax haven

part fiscale
tax unit

perception fiscale
revenue receipt

péréquation fiscale
tax equalisation

plafond d'exonération fiscale
tax exemption limit

politique fiscale
fiscal / tax policy

possibilité d'évasion fiscale
tax loophole

prélèvement fiscal
tax levy

prélèvement fiscal exceptionnel
exceptional tax levy

pression fiscale
tax burden / load

recettes fiscales
financial / tax / fiscal revenue

redressement fiscal
tax adjustment

réduction fiscale
tax reduction / cut

réforme fiscale
fiscal reform

régime fiscal
(system of) taxation

rentrée fiscale
tax receipt

semaine fiscale
income tax week

seuil d'exonération fiscale des revenus
lower earnings limit of tax exemption

tranche de barème fiscal
tax bracket

trêve fiscale
tax holiday

FISCALISATION
fiscalisation des ressources
funding by taxation of revenue

FISCALISTE
tax consultant

FISCALITÉ
(system of) taxation

écart introduit (à la marge) par la fiscalité
(marginal) tax wedge

pension à fiscalité bonifiée
tax qualified pension

poids de la fiscalité
fiscal / tax burden

réforme de la fiscalité
fiscal reform

FIXATION
determination; assessment

fixation de la quote-part
assessment of contributions

fixation des salaires
salary determination

FIXE (adj.)
fixed; flat; statutory; settled

charge fixe
fixed cost; (pl.) overhead costs

charges salariales fixes
overhead labour costs

**conducteurs de machines et d'installa-
tions fixes [CITP-1968 (9-6)]**
stationary engine and related equipment
operators [ISCO-1968 (9-6)]

coût fixe
fixed cost

domicile fixe (sans)
homeless; of no fixed abode / address

élément fixe des salaires
fixed wage element

équipe fixe
regular shift

frais fixe
fixed cost; (pl.) fixed expenditure / charges

horaire décalé fixe
staggered working hours

horaire fixe
fixed working hours

personne sans résidence fixe
person of / with no fixed abode, vagrant

plage fixe
hard core, core hours / time

plage horaire fixe
fixed time bracket

plan de retraite à cotisations fixes
fixed contribution retirement plan

plan de retraite à prestations fixes
fixed benefit retirement plan

régime à taux fixe
flat-rate scheme

rémunération fixe
basic / fixed salary

revenu fixe
fixed / regular income

salaire fixe
basic / fixed wage

somme fixe
fixed sum

taux fixe
flat / set rate

taux fixe (à)
at flat rate

traitement fixe
basic / fixed salary

travail par équipes fixes
fixed shift system

FIXER
to determine; to assess; to set; to provide
for

**fixer l'assiette des cotisations / les
cotisations / la quote-part**
to assess contributions

fixer sa résidence
to make one's abode

fixer les salaires
to set wages

FLAGRANT
injustice flagrante
gross injustice

FLÉCHISSEMENT
downward trend, downswing, downturn

fléchissement de la conjoncture
downturn of the economy

fléchissement de l'emploi
decline in employment

FLEXIBILITÉ
flexibilité dans l'aménagement du temps de travail
flexibility of working time arrangements

flexibilité fonctionnelle
functional / task flexibility

flexibilité de la main-d'oeuvre
labour force flexibility

flexibilité du marché du travail
labour market flexibility

flexibilité quantitative
numerical flexibility

flexibilité salariale
wage flexibility

horaires à flexibilité maximale
(occ.) maniflex

FLEXIBLE
accumulation flexible
flexible accumulation

atelier flexible
flexible manufacturing system

horaire de travail flexible
flexible working hours / time, flexible work schedule, flexitime

plage horaire flexible
flexible time bracket

spécialisation flexible
flexible specialisation

système de fabrication flexible
flexible manufacturing system

FLEXITOUR
flexitour

FLOTTANT
affectation flottante
floating assignment

FLUCTUATION
fluctuation de l'activité économique / fluctuation conjoncturelle
business fluctuation, fluctuation in business / economic activity

fluctuations de l'emploi
fluctuations in employment

fluctuations du niveau d'emploi
fluctuations in the level of employment

fluctuation saisonnière
seasonal fluctuation / variation

fluctuations saisonnières de l'emploi
seasonal employment variations

FLUX
flow; influx, inflow

diagramme de flux
flow chart

données de flux
flow data

flux de main-d'oeuvre
labour force flow

flux migratoire
flow of migration

flux de nouveaux chômeurs
flow into unemployment

production en flux tendus
just-in-time production

statistiques de flux
flow statistics

FOI
foi (qui fait)
authoritative

textes faisant également foi
texts equally authoritative

FOIRE
foire à l'emploi
job convention / fair / salon

FONCIER
impôt foncier
land / property tax

revenu foncier
land income

système foncier
land-tenure system

taxe foncière
property tax

FONCTION
charge, duty; responsibility; position;
(occ.) employment; (pl.) activity; office;
service; terms

abandon d'une fonction
discontinuance of a function

accepter les fonctions
to assume office / duties

agent de la fonction publique
public / civil servant, public official

autorisation d'exercer des fonctions
admission to the exercise of functions

cessation anticipée de fonction
early termination of service

cessation de fonctions
(employment) termination, cessation /
termination of employment, job separation;
severance

cessation de fonctions par mise à la retraite
termination of appointment by retirement

codification des fonctions
Common Directory of job Titles

confirmer dans une fonction
to confirm in a job

congé pour exercice de fonctions publiques
time off (work) for public duties

cumuler des fonctions
to combine functions, to hold several
positions

date anniversaire d'entrée en fonctions
anniversary date of hire

date d'entrée en fonctions
(date of) entry / entrance on duty

déchéance des fonctions
loss of office

définition des fonctions
job description

démettre (se) / démissionner de ses fonctions
to resign from one's post

description de fonction
job / position description

désignation de fonction
job title

destitué de ses fonctions (être)
to be relieved of one's duties

destituer de ses fonctions
to relieve of one's duties

durée des fonctions
length / period / term of office; tenure

emploi dans la fonction publique
public service employment

entrée en fonctions
entry on / assumption of duty,
assumption of office

entrer dans ses fonctions / en fonction
to take / to assume office, to begin
employment, to take up one's duties, to
commence work, to assume duties

exercer des fonctions
to perform duties

exercice de ses fonctions (dans l')
in the course of one's duties / of
employment, in the line of duty

exercice de fonctions officielles
performance of official duties

fichier de fonctions
task data sheet

fonction (en)
in service, in office, in charge

fonction de (faire)
to act as / for, to represent

fonction de (faisant)
acting

fonctions d'employé de bureau
clerical duties

fonction d'encadrement
supervisory duty / function

fonction mineure
minor duty

fonction motrice
motor function

fonction nourricière
material need function

fonction officielle
official function / duty; (pl.) public office

fonctions organiques
bodily processes

fonction parentale
parenthood

fonction de production
production function

fonction publique
public administration / service; civil service
(corps); official duty

fonction de risque
hazard function

fonction de surveillance
supervisory duty / function

fonction (d') utilité
utility function

fusionner des fonctions
to integrate functions

**grille des comportements attendus par
type de fonction**
behaviour expectation scale

immunité de fonctions
immunity by virtue of one's office

**imputable à l'exercice de fonctions
officielles**
attributable to the performance of
official duties

indemnité de cessation de fonctions
separation / terminal / severance pay /
payment / benefit, allowance for
separation; (occ.) completion bonus

indemnité de fonction
post / duty allowance, per diem duty;
official expenditure allowance

**indemnité de fonctions
supplémentaires**
extra-duty pay

investir qqn d'une fonction
to vest someone with a function

logement de fonction
official / service accommodation;
company flat

maintien en fonction
retention

manquement aux devoirs de fonction
breach of professional / official duty

membre de la fonction publique
civil servant

**mutation du personnel déjà en
fonctions**
reassignment of existing staff

niveau d'entrée en fonction
entrance level

occuper une fonction
to hold a position

personnel de fonction
professional staff

prendre ses fonctions
to take office, to report for / to duty

préposer à une fonction
to appoint to an office

prise de fonctions
appointment, assumption of duty / of office

reconduit dans ses fonctions
re-designated

redistribution des fonctions
reassignment of duties

relèvement de fonctions
removal from office

relever de ses fonctions
to dismiss, to relieve of one's duties, to discharge

remplir les fonctions de
to serve as

rémunération des fonctions
remuneration for duties

secret de fonctions
official secret

suppression d'une fonction
discontinuance of a function

suspendu de ses fonctions (être)
to be suspended from one's position

suspension de fonctions
suspension from office

taux de maintien en fonction
retention rate, rate of retention

violation des devoirs de fonction
breach of professional / official duty

voiture de fonction
company car

FONCTIONNAIRE
civil / public servant, public (service) employee, (public) officer / official; (pl.) (occ.) (career) staff

administrateurs et fonctionnaires de rang supérieur
(occ.) professional and higher categories

fonctionnaires et assimilés
Government employees

fonctionnaire d'autorité
official with a power to decide

fonctionnaire de carrière
established civil servant

fonctionnaire compétent
appropriate official, authorised officer

fonctionnaire contractuel
temporary / non-established civil servant

fonctionnaire à contrat de durée déterminée
fixed-term official

fonctionnaire des contributions
tax official
fonctionnaire de la Couronne (UK)
Crown servant

fonctionnaire en disponibilité
civil servant temporarily retired

fonctionnaire de l'Etat (UK)
Crown servant (UK)

fonctionnaire international
international civil servant

fonctionnaire municipal
local authority employee

fonctionnaire permanent
permanent civil servant

fonctionnaire en poste à l'étranger
expatriate civil servant

fonctionnaire de rang élevé
senior officer

fonctionnaires de rang supérieur
staff in the higher categories

fonctionnaire en instance de réaffecta-tion
civil servant awaiting reappointment (redundant)

fonctionnaire de réserve
relieving officer

fonctionnaire retraité
retired staff member

fonctionnaire de la santé publique
(public) health officer

fonctionnaire stagiaire
civil servant on probation

fonctionnaire titulaire / titularisé
established civil servant

fonctionnaire non titulaire / non titularisé
temporary / non-established civil servant

garantie des fonctionnaires
protection of public officials

haut fonctionnaire
high-ranking / senior official, senior officer / civil servant; (pl.) Government officials

médecin fonctionnaire
employed doctor

mutation de fonctionnaire
transfer of staff member

muter un fonctionnaire
to transfer a staff member

régime de retraite des fonctionnaires
public service pension scheme

régime spécial des fonctionnaires ou du personnel assimilé
special scheme for civil servants and persons treated as such

serment de fonctionnaire
official oath

FONCTIONNARIAT
civil service

FONCTIONNEL
functional; work-oriented; substantive

activité fonctionnelle
functional activity

alphabétisation fonctionnelle
functional literacy

analphabétisme fonctionnel
functional illiteracy

apprentissage de l'autonomie fonctionnelle
(occ.) life skills training

aptitude fonctionnelle
functional ability

autonomie fonctionnelle
(occ.) life skills

cadre fonctionnel
staff manager

calcul fonctionnel des coûts
functional costing

capacité fonctionnelle
functional capacity

compétence fonctionnelle
functional authority

diagramme fonctionnel
flow chart

diminution fonctionnelle
impairment of function, functional handicap / impairment

flexibilité fonctionnelle
functional / task flexibility

gêne fonctionnelle
functional handicap / impairment

impotence / incapacité fonctionnelle
functional impairment / disability

liaisons fonctionnelles
functional relationships

mobilité fonctionnelle
functional mobility

mutation fonctionnelle
functional transfer

personnel fonctionnel
(field) support staff

perte fonctionnelle
functional loss

poste fonctionnel
functional / staff position

réadaptation / rééducation fonctionnelle
functional rehabilitation

relations fonctionnelles
functional relations

titre fonctionnel
functional / post title

trouble fonctionnel
functional disturbance, disturbance of
function

FONCTIONNEMENT
budget de fonctionnement
operational / operating budget

cadre de fonctionnement
operational framework

**charges / coût(s) / dépenses de fonc-
tionnement**
running / operating cost(s) / expenditure

dotation globale de fonctionnement
global operating budget

**fonctionnement du marché de l'emploi /
du travail**
functioning / operation of the labour market,
labour market operation(s)

frais de fonctionnement
running / operational / operating cost

frais généraux de fonctionnement
general operating costs

subvention de fonctionnement
operating subsidy

FOND
merit(s)

clauses de fond
substantive articles

condition de fond
substantive restriction

décision quant au fond
adjudication on the merits

fond (de / sur le)
substantive

ouvrier du fond
underground worker

règle de fond
substantive rule

FONDAMENTAL
fundamental, substantive, basic;
under-lying

besoin fondamental
basic need

normes fondamentales du travail
basic / core labour standards

recherche fondamentale
basic research

technologie fondamentale
basic / core technology

textes législatifs fondamentaux
basic legislation

FONDATION
foundation; trust

FONDÉ
fondé (être)
to have good cause; to be entitled to

**fondé à escompter une promotion
(être)**
to have a justified expectation to be
promoted

**fondé à réclamer une indemnisation
pour perte de salaire (être)**
to be entitled to claim restitution of lost
salary / wage / earnings

FONDEMENT
ground

fondement (sans)
groundless

FONDER
fonder des syndicats
to form trade unions

FONDS
fund(s); assets

affectation de fonds
allocation / appropriation of funds

aide sur fonds publics
public / government aid

collecte de fonds
fund raising

déblocage de fonds
release of funds

entrées de fonds
income

envois de fonds
cash remittances

**envoi de fonds des travailleurs émigrés /
immigrés**
workers' remittance

fonds accumulés
accumulated assets

fonds d'action générale
global funds

fonds d'affectation spéciale
trust fund, funds-in-trust

fonds affectés à
funds earmarked for

fonds affectés à la création d'emplois
job creation funds

fonds assurance(-)formation (Fr.)
training insurance fund

fonds d'assurance(-)vieillesse
old age security fund

fonds auto-renouvelable
revolving fund

fonds détenus par les caisses de pensions
pension fund accumulations

fonds de compensation
provident / compensation / equalisation
fund

fonds de consolidation
stabilisation fund

fonds en dépôt
funds-in-trust

fonds pour l'emploi
employment fund

fonds d'entraide
(occ.) welfare fund

fonds d'épargne
savings fund

fonds destinés à la formation
training funds

fonds de grève
strike fund

**fonds d'indemnisation des
licenciements économiques / des
travailleurs licenciés (pour raisons
économiques)**
redundancy fund

fonds de pension
pension fund / foundation

fonds de pension d'entreprise
corporate / enterprise pension fund

fonds de péréquation
equalisation fund

fonds de prévoyance
provident / contingency fund

fonds de prévoyance sociale
welfare fund

fonds propres
equity base

fonds publics
public funds / money, Government
funds

fonds public d'assurance
State insurance fund

fonds recouvrés
recovery funds

fonds renouvelable
revolving fund

fonds de réserve
reserve fund

fonds de secours
relief / contingency fund

fonds social
social fund

fonds de solidarité
solidarity fund

fonds de solidarité vieillesse (Fr.)
old age solidarity fund

fonds syndical
union fund

provenance des fonds
source of funds

recueillir / réunir des fonds
to raise funds

transfert de fonds (migr.)
remittance

FORCÉ (adj.)
départ forcé à la retraite
involuntary retirement

grille d'évaluation à choix forcé
forced choice rating (grid)

inactivité forcée
enforced idleness

recouvrement forcé
enforced payment

travail forcé
forced labour

FORCE (n.)
force; power

cas de force majeure
act of God

enquête sur les forces de travail
labour force survey

épreuve de force
showdown

forces armées [CITP-1988 (0, 01, 011]
armed forces [ISCO-1988 (0, 01, 011)]

force contractuelle
contractual force; bargaining power

force exécutoire (ayant)
enforceable, binding

force de loi (ayant)
binding

force majeure
act of God, force majeure

forces du marché
market forces

force obligatoire (ayant)
binding

forces de l'ordre
police

**membres des forces de l'ordre
(Malta)**
members of a disciplined force

rapport de forces
power relationship; bargaining power

reconduite de force
forcible return

travailleur de force
heavy worker

FORCLOS
time-barred, out of time

FORCLUSION
délai de forclusion
time-limit

FORDIEN
Fordist

FORDISME
Fordism

FORESTIER
travailleurs forestiers [CITP-1968 (6-3)]
forestry workers [ISCO-1968 (6-3)]

FORFAIT
fixed / lump sum; lump-sum payment

forfait (à)
on a lump-sum basis

forfait hospitalier (Fr.)
patient's fixed contribution per day of
hospitalisation

forfait journalier hospitalier
patient's daily charge for hospitalisation

**forfait journalier de soins et d'héber-
gement**
patient's daily charge for care and
accommodation

forfait par personne
capitation

forfait thermal (Fr.)
fixed rate for spa course of treatment

remboursement sur la base de forfaits
refund on the basis of lump-sum payments

travail à forfait
contract work

FORFAITAIRE
lump; flat; notional

aide forfaitaire
lump-sum / flat-rate / fixed rate aid

ajustement forfaitaire
lump-sum adjustment

allocation forfaitaire
flat-rate benefit, lump-sum grant, flat
allowance

base forfaitaire
fixed scale

commission forfaitaire
lump-sum payment

cotisation (à taux) forfaitaire
flat-rate contribution

gain forfaitaire
standard earnings

imposition forfaitaire
presumptive taxation

indemnité forfaitaire
flat(-rate) / one-off / lump-sum allowance,
lump-sum / capital compensation / grant,
lump sum

indemnité forfaitaire pour veuve
widow's (lump sum)payment, widow's
grant

montant forfaitaire
flat-rate amount, lump sum

**montant minimal / minimum
forfaitaire**
(occ.) standard amount
paiement forfaitaire
lump-sum / one-off payment

pension forfaitaire
standard pension

prestation forfaitaire
flat-rate benefit, lump-sum grant

prix forfaitaire
overhead price

remboursement forfaitaire
lump-sum reimbursement / refund,
refund in a lump sum

**rémunération forfaitaire par
personne**
(occ.) capitation

réparation forfaitaire
lump-sum / standard compensation

retraite forfaitaire
flat-rate pension

somme forfaitaire
lump(-sum) / single payment, lump sum

subvention forfaitaire
lump-sum grant

tarif forfaitaire
flat rate

taux forfaitaire
flat / standard / fixed rate

taux forfaitaire (à)
at flat rate

versement forfaitaire (unique)
lump-sum / flat-rate payment

FORFAITAIREMENT
for a lump sum

FORFAITURE
breach of duty

FORGERON
forgerons, outilleurs et assimilés [CITP-1988 (722)]
blacksmiths, tool-makers and related trades workers [ISCO-1988 (722)]

FORMALITÉ
formality; procedure

FORMATEUR (adj.)
travail formateur
formative work

FORMATEUR (n.)
instructor; training officer, trainer

formateur des enseignants
teacher(-)educator

formation de formateurs
trainer training

FORMATIF
évaluation formative
formative assessment

FORMATION
training; learning; education; training system; unit

accord de formation
training agreement

achat de formation
purchase of training, training purchase

achever sa formation
to complete / to finish one's training

action en faveur de l'emploi et de la formation
employment and training measures

activité de formation
training activity

agent de formation
training officer, trainer

aide à la / de formation
training assistance / aid

allocation d'assistance à la formation professionnelle (Ger.)
vocational assistance allowance

allocation de formation
training allowance / benefit

allocation de formation reclassement (Fr.)
resettlement / re-deployment (Fr.) training allowance

atelier de formation
training workshop

attribution de places de formation
allocation of training places

avis d'inscription à une formation
notice of referral to training

avis d'interruption de la formation
training suspension notice

besoins en (matière de) formation
training needs / requirements

bourse de formation
training grant

bourse de formation professionnelle
vocational training grant

budget de formation
training budget

capital temps-formation
right to a number of hours' training

centre de formation
training centre / school

centre de formation des apprentis (CFA) (Fr.)
tuition centre for working apprentices, apprentice training centre

centre de formation de l'entreprise
company training centre

centre de formation en internat
residential training centre

centre de formation à libre accès
open access training centre

centre de formation professionnelle
vocational (training) centre

centre interne de formation
company training centre

comité régional de formation professionnelle (Fr.)
regional vocational training committee

compte économique de la formation professionnelle (Fr.)
vocational training economic account

congé (de)(-) formation
leave for training purposes, training / study leave

congé de formation à l'Etat (Belg.)
State training leave

congé de formation jeunes travailleurs (Fr.)
young workers training leave

congé individuel de formation (Fr.)
individual / personal training leave

congé individuel de formation pour les salariés (Fr.)
individual training leave for employees

conseiller de formation (Neth.)
training counsellor

conservation des droits en formation
maintenance of rights in course of acquisition

contrat emploi-formation (Fr.)
employment training contract

contrat de formation
training contract / relationship; (occ.) training place

contrat de formation en entreprise
training-in-industry contract

contrat de formation professionnelle
vocational training contract

convention emploi-formation (Belg.)
job-training agreement

convention de formation professionnelle
vocational training agreement

cours de formation accélérée
intensive / crash (training) course

cours de formation pratique
practical training course

cours de formation préparatoire à l'emploi
pre-trades training course

coûts de formation
training costs / charges

crédits affectés à la formation
training funds

crédit formation individualisé (CFI) (Fr.)
individualised training credit / loan scheme

crédit formation jeunes (Fr.)
young people training tax credit

crédit d'impôt-formation (Fr.)
training levy / tax credit

cycle court de formation
short training cycle

cycle de formation
training course

cycle long de formation
long training cycle

dédit-formation
forfeit for training

deuxième circuit de formation (Belg.)
"second chance" training facilities

dispositifs de formation
training facilities

durée de la formation
duration of training

enseignement technique et formation professionnelle
vocational and technical education and training (VOTEC)

entreprise de formation par le travail (EFT) (Belg.)
training-through-work venture

entretien préalable à la formation
pre-training interview

envoyer en (stage de) formation
to refer for training

établissement de formation
training institution

établissement de formation des maîtres
college of education

exigences en matière de formation
training requirements

fonds assurance(-)formation (Fr.)
training insurance fund

fonds destinés à la formation
training funds

formation (sans)
untrained

formation des actifs occupés (Fr.)
training for employed people

formation des adultes
adult training

formation en alternance
alternance / sandwich training / course,
cooperative education; day-release studies
(1-2 days/-week); block-release training
(long period of absence)

formation d'animateurs
trainer training

formation des apprentis
apprenticeship training, training of
apprentices

formation en apprentissage
apprenticeship training

formation à l'artisanat
craft training

formation de base
basic / core education / training, foundation
training

formation de cadres
professional training

formation des cadres
management training

formation étalée sur toute la carrière
lifelong training

formation des chômeurs (Fr.)
training for the unemployed

formation complémentaire
further education, further (education
and) training, post-initial /
supplementary training; upgrading

**formation complémentaire à
l'obtention du diplôme de base**
postbasic training

formation des conseillers
counsellor training

formation continue
continuing / further education, in-
service (educational) training,
continuous learning, continuing /
continued training, further (education
and) training

formation continue dans l'entreprise
in-company continuing training

formation au contrôle
training in supervision

formation à court terme
short-term training

formation des débutants
entry-level training

formation avant l'emploi
pre-service / pre-employment training

formation en cours d'emploi
on-site / on-the-job training / learning,
in-service (educational) training

formation hors emploi
off-the-job training

formation liée à l'emploi
job-related training

**formation coordonnée par
l'employeur**
employer-based training

formation encadrée
supervised training

formation des enseignants en cours de service
INSET (in-service training)

formation assurée par les entreprises
enterprise-based training

formation en / dans l'entreprise
in-firm / on-site / in-house / in-plant / industry / industrial training, training-in-industry, entreprise-based training

formation à l'extérieur de l'entreprise
off-the-job training

formation en établissement
institutional training

formation par étapes
phased / (occ.) analytical training

formation extérieure
off-the-job training

formation externe
external training

formation des femmes dans les métiers non traditionnels
non-traditional training for women

formation de formateurs
trainer training

formation générale
basic / foundation training / education

formation en gestion
management training

formation et gestion des carrières des cadres
management development

formation individuelle
individual / one-to-one training

formation initiale
basic education, initial training

formation d'instructeurs
trainer training

formation intensive
intensive training

formation interne
on-the-job training / learning, in-house / internal training

formation intra-entreprise
in-house training

formation itinérante
mobile training

formation de / des jeunes youth training

formation sur les lieux de travail
on-the-job training / learning

formation linguistique
language training

formation de la main-d'oeuvre
labour force / manpower training

formation médicale continue
continuing medical education

formation sur mesure
(occ.) learner-centred training

formation aux métiers
trades training

formation aux / dans les métiers spécialisés
skilled trades training

formation par mise en situation
vestibule training

formation par modules
modular training

formation nécessaire
required training

formation ouvrière
workers' education

formation parallèle
concurrent training

formation pédagogique
teacher training

formation périodique
recurrent training

formation permanente
continuing / continued / continuous / ongoing / further education, lifelong training / learning

formation du personnel
staff training, training of personnel

formation du personnel enseignant
teacher training

formation de personnel qualifié
(occ.) skill training

formation sur place
local training

formation polyvalente
broadly-based skill training, multi-skilling

formation hors poste
off-the-job training

formation post-secondaire
post-secondary training

formation poussée
intensive training

formation pratique
on-the-job training

formation pratique par simulation
simulated on-the-job training

formation préalable
pre-training

formation préalable à l'emploi
pre-service / pre-employment training

formation de première insertion (Fr.)
initial integration training

formation préparatoire
preparatory / vestibule training

formation préprofessionnelle
pre(-)vocational training

formation sans production
out-of-production training

formation professionnelle
vocational education; occupational / vocational / job / skill training; professional education / training; skills development

formation professionnelle accélérée
accelerated / intensive vocational training

formation professionnelle des adultes
adult occupational training

formation professionnelle de base
basic job training

formation professionnelle continue
ongoing vocational training

formation professionnelle auprès d'une entreprise
vocational training with a company

formation professionnelle générale
generic skill training, general vocational training / education

formation professionnelle initiale
initial vocational training

formation professionnelle initiale agricole (Fr.)
initial agricultural vocational training

formation professionnelle spécialisée
occupational skills training, specialised vocational training

formation qualifiante
skill formation

formation pour la réadaptation
rehabilitation education

formation de reconversion
retraining, conversion training

formation régulière
formal training

formation de réinsertion
(occ.) remedial training

formation des salaires
wage formation

formation sanitaire
hospital / health unit; health training

formation en santé publique
public health training

formation en milieu scolaire
in-school / (occ.) classroom training

formation à la sécurité
safety training

formation en cours de service
in-service (educational) training

formation au service social
social work education

formation spécialisée
specialised / specialisation / specialist
training

formation hautement spécialisée
high-skill training

formation peu spécialisée
lower-level skill training

formation spécialisée en établissement
institutional skill training

formation spécifique à un emploi
job-related training

formation des stagiaires
training of trainees

formation structurée
formal training

formation non structurée
informal training

formation supérieure
advanced / postbasic education

formation supérieure (de)
(occ.) professional

formation sur le tas
on-site / on-the job / in-service training /
learning

formation technique
technical training

**formation aux techniques de base /
élémentaires**
basic skills training

formation à temps complet
full-time training

formation à temps partiel
part-time training

formation à temps plein
full-time training

formation théorique
theoretical / off-the-job training

formation tournante
carousel training

formation en milieu de travail
on-the-job training / learning

frais directement liés à la formation
direct training costs

frais de formation
training costs / charges

frais de formation directs
direct training costs

homologation d'une formation
official approval for a training course

impôt-formation
training levy

**initiative en faveur de l'emploi et de
la formation**
employment and training measure

**inscrire en formation / à un stage de
formation**
to refer for training

institut de formation pédagogique
teacher training college / school

jeune cadre en formation
management trainee, trainee manager

marché de la formation
training market

matériel de formation
training material / aid

mécanisme de formation des prix
price mechanism

**mesures en faveur de l'emploi et de la
formation**
employment and training measures

méthode de formation
training method

module de formation
training package / module

moyens d'étude et de formation
study and training facilities

moyens de formation
training facilities

niveau de formation
education level

offre de formation
training provision / proposal, proposal for training

organisme de formation
training agency

passeport-formation
skills passport

période de formation
period of training, training period

place de / en formation
training place

place de formation vacante
training vacancy

plan de formation
training plan

plan de formation en apprentissage
apprenticeship training plan

plan de formation-insertion (Belg.)
employment-plus-training scheme

politique de formation
educational / training policy

possibilité de formation
training opportunity

poste de formation
training / trainee position

prélèvement destiné à financer la formation
training levy

prestation de formation
training benefit

programme de crédit-formation
training grants scheme

programme d'emploi et de formation
employment and training scheme

programme de formation
training programme / scheme

programme de formation en établisse-ment scolaire
in-school training programme

programme de formation individuelle
individual training programme

programme de formation pour jeunes diplômés
graduate training scheme

programme de formation préalable à l'apprentissage
pre-apprenticeship training programme

programme de formation universitaire
university-based training programme

projet de formation
training project / initiative

proposition de formation
proposal for training, training proposal

rendement de la formation
pay-offs to training

responsable de la formation
training officer

salaire de formation
training wage

séance de formation
training session

service de formation
training service

stage de fin de formation en entreprise (Belg.)
enterprise-based end of training course

stage de formation
training course

stage de formation accélérée
rapid training course

stage de formation en alternance (Fr.)
sandwich integration course

stage de formation de base
basic / low-level training course

stage de formation intensive
intensive / rapid training course

stage de formation professionnelle
occupational / skill / vocational course

stage de formation qualifiante
skill training course

stage de formation reconnu
approved training course

stage d'insertion et de formation à l'emploi (Fr.)
employment integration and training course

stagiaire en formation
active trainee

subside pour la formation
training grant / subsidy

système de formation
training system

taux des allocations de formation
rate / level of training allowances

technique de formation
training technique

terminer sa formation
to finish / to complete one's training

travailleur en formation
(occ.) trainee worker

FORMÉ (adj.)
agent formé
trained worker

personnel formé
trained workers

travailleur formé
trained worker

FORME (n.)
form; pattern

condition de forme
formal restriction

forme d'emploi atypique / hors normes
atypical form of employment

formes d'emploi souples
flexible employment

formes de travail
work patterns

forme de travail atypique
non-standard form of working

forme de travail souple
flexible work

FORMEL
décision écrite formelle
formal / authoritative written determination / decision

éducation formelle
formal education

lien formel avec l'emploi
formal job attachment

secteur formel de l'économie
formal economy sector

FORMER
droit de former appel
right of / to appeal

former le personnel
to train staff

former un piquet de grève
to picket

former un recours
to enter / to lodge an appeal, to appeal

former un travailleur
to train a worker

FORMULAIRE
form

formulaire de candidature
application form

formulaire de demande
claim / application form

formulaire de demande d'emploi
job application form

**formulaire de demande de rembourse-
ment**
request for settlement form

formulaire d'inscription
application form

FORMULE
formula; scheme; form

formule de calcul de la pension
calculation of the pension

**formule servant à calculer... / au calcul
de...**
computation formula

formule de demande de remboursement
request for settlement form

formule dentaire
dental formula; dentition

formule d'habilitation déclarative
declaratory authorisation arrangement

**formule de notification administrative de
décharge**
personnel payroll clearance action form

formule de pondération des prestations
weighted benefit formula

FORTUNE (n.)
contrôle de la situation de fortune
means testing

impôt sur la fortune
wealth / property tax

logement de fortune
emergency dwelling

FOURCHETTE
range, bracket

fourchette indicative
guideline range

**fourchette de points pour les
différentes classes**
point range for classes

fourchette de prix
price range

fourchette de salaires
wage range / band / bracket

fourchette des traitements
salary range / band / bracket

FOURNISSEUR
supplier; provider

fournisseur spécialisé
specialised supplier

FOURNITURE
supply; provision

FOYER
home; hostel; nursing home; social
centre;
focal point

abandon de foyer
desertion and failure to maintain

allocation de foyer
household allowance

allocation de mère au foyer
allowance for mothers at home / for the
housewife, non-working mother's
allowance (UK)

allocation de séjour hors du foyer
living-away from home allowance

congé dans les foyers
home leave

**crédit d'attente pour le congé dans les
foyers**
credit for home leave travel

enfant sans foyer
homeless child

enfant placé en foyer
foster child

femme au foyer
home-maker, housewife

foyer (sans)
homeless

foyer d'adoption
foster house / home

foyer de cure (et de réadaptation)
(occ.) half-way house

foyer dissocié
broken home

foyer-école
school home

foyer pour enfants
children's home

foyer fiscal
household as defined for tax purposes

foyer pour (les) jeunes
youth centre

foyer de jeunes travailleurs
young workers hostel

**foyer-logement pour personnes âgées
(Fr.)**
residential housing for old people

foyer nourricier
foster home

foyer ouvert
open-door house

foyer permanent d'habitation
normal / permanent home

foyer pour personnes âgées
residential / geriatric home

foyer de placement (familial)
foster house / home

foyer de post-cure (et de réadaptation)
(occ.) half-way house

foyer récréatif et culturel
(occ.) community centre

foyer-restaurant (Fr.)
home meals

foyer de semi-liberté
semi-custodial home

foyer social
(occ.) settlement (house)

foyer de transition
transit home

foyer de voisinage
neighbourhood house

jeune fille au foyer
non-working girl

lieu de congé dans les foyers
place of home leave

mère au foyer
non-working mother

FRACTION
fraction au prorata du temps / prorata
temporis
pro-rata fraction

versé en trois fractions
paid in three instalments

FRACTIONNÉ
congés fractionnés
split holidays

horaire fractionné
split hours

poste fractionné
split shift

FRACTIONNEMENT
fractionnement des congés
split holidays; holiday splitting

FRAIS (n.)
cost; charge; fee; disbursement;
expenditure; expense

acquitter les frais de
to pay the cost of

allocation pour frais d'études
education(al) grant

allocation pour frais de garde (Fr.)
child-minding allowance, allowance for
baby-sitting expenses

allocation pour frais de logement (Neth.)
housing cost allowance

allocation pour frais d'obsèques
funeral grant

assurance gros frais médicaux
major medical insurance

certificat d'attestation des frais
certificate of cost

exposer à des frais (s')
to incur costs

faux frais
incidental expenses

frais accessoires
supplementary / extra cost / expenses

frais administratifs / d'administration
administrative / service / management
cost(s) / expenses

frais annexes
additional expenses

frais de bureau
(occ.) office allowance

frais à la charge de
costs to be borne by

frais déductibles
allowable expenses

frais de déménagement
moving / relocation / removal expenses /
costs

frais de déplacement
transportation / travel expenses / costs

frais directement liés à la formation
direct training costs

frais divers
miscellaneous expenses

frais de dossier
administrative cost(s)

frais d'entreprise
company charges

frais d'établissement
start-up cost

frais d'exploitation
running / operational / operating cost

frais financiers
interest charges

frais fixe
fixed cost; (pl.) fixed expenditure /
charges

frais de fonctionnement
running / operational / operating cost

frais de formation
training costs / charges

frais de formation directs
direct training costs

frais funéraires
cost of funeral, funeral expenses

frais généraux
overall / overhead costs, overhead
(expenses)

frais généraux additionnels
incremental overhead costs

frais généraux de fonctionnement
general operating costs

frais de gestion
administration / administrative expenses
/ cost(s), service cost

frais d'hébergement
accommodation expenses

frais d'hospitalisation
hospital expenses

frais hôteliers (hosp.) (Switz.)
room and board expenses

frais de justice
legal costs

frais médicaux
medical expenses

frais d'obsèques
cost of funeral, funeral expenses

frais de premier établissement
initial outlay

frais professionnels
professional expenses

frais de recrutement
recruitment costs

frais réels
real cost, actual expenses, total expenses
incurred

frais de repas
meal expenses

frais de représentation
entertainment expenses / allowance,
expense account, office allowance

frais de scolarité
tuition / school fees

frais de séjour
subsistence expenses

frais de subsistance
living costs / expenses

frais supplémentaires
additional expenses; extras

frais de transport
travelling / travel / transportation expenses

frais de voyage
transportation / travel expenses / costs

frais de voyage et de séjour
travel and accommodation / travel and
subsistence expenses

indemnité pour frais d'études
education(al) grant

indemnité pour / de frais funéraires
funeral / death grant

indemnité de frais professionnels
professional expenditure allowance

indemnité de frais de service
official expenditure allowance

partage des frais
cost-sharing

participation aux frais
contribution towards / participation in
cost / expenses

participation aux frais médicaux
contribution towards medical expenses,
patient's contribution

participation du malade aux frais
cost-sharing

prendre à sa charge les frais de
to bear the cost of

prestation pour frais funéraires
funeral benefit

programme à frais partagés
shared-cost programme

**récupération des frais afférents au
paiement des prestations**
recovery of expenses incurred in the
payment of benefits

**remboursement partiel des frais sala-
riaux**
partial wage reimbursement

système de partage des frais
cost-sharing system

**système de participation du malade
aux frais**
cost-sharing system

système de recouvrement des frais
cost recovery system

FRANCHISAGE
franchising

FRANCHISE (n.)
franchise; excess; deductible

délai de franchise (ins.)
waiting period

FRANCHISÉ (n.)
franchisee

FRANCHISEUR
franchiser

FRANC (adj.)
jour franc
calendar / clear / full day

FRANC (n.)
francs constants (en)
in real value

FRAPPER
frapper d'une interdiction d'exercer
to suspend from practice

FRATRIE
sibling

majoration de fratrie (Finl.)
sibling increase

FRAUDULEUX
déclaration frauduleuse
fraudulent declaration

demande frauduleuse
fraudulent claim

FRÉQUENCE
incidence; periodicity

fréquence du chômage
incidence of unemployment

taux de fréquence des accidents
accident frequency rate

FRÉQUENTATION
attendance, enrolment, participation

fréquentation scolaire
school enrolment, school attendance (rate)

taux de fréquentation
participation rate

taux de fréquentation scolaire
school attendance (rate), attendance ratio

FRÉTEUR
ship operator, shipowner

FRICTIONNEL
chômage frictionnel
frictional / turnover / transitional / turn-
around unemployment

FRONTALIER (adj.)
travailleur frontalier
border / frontier worker; cross-border
worker (Belg.)

zone frontalière
frontier zone

FRONTALIER (n.)
border / frontier worker

FRONTIÈRE
contrôle aux frontières
border control

reconduite à la frontière
deportation

FRUSTRATION
frustration; deprivation

FUNÉRAILLES
funeral

FUNÉRAIRE
allocation funéraire
funeral grant

frais funéraires
cost of funeral, funeral expenses

indemnité pour / de frais funéraires
funeral / death grant

indemnité funéraire
funeral benefit

prestation pour frais funéraires
funeral benefit

FUSIONNER
fusionner des fonctions
to integrate functions

FUTUR
futur employeur
prospective employer

future main-d'oeuvre
oncoming labour force

future mère
expectant mother

GAGNÉ
revenu gagné
accrued income; (pl.) earned income

revenu non gagné
investment / unearned income

GAGNE-PAIN
(means of) livelihood

GAGNER
indemnité pour manque à gagner
compensation for loss of wages / earnings

manque à gagner
loss of profit / of wages / of (potential) earnings

GAIN
gain; earnings; wage, pay

assujetti à un contrôle des gains
earnings-tested

assurance-santé et perte de gains
health and loss of earnings insurance

capacité de gain
earning power / capacity

capacité résiduelle de gain
residual capacity to earn

diminution de la capacité de gain
reduction / loss of earning capacity

état des gains
statement of income

facteur des gains
earnings factor

facteur des gains globaux
total earnings factor

gains annuels
annual earnings

gains bruts
gross earnings

gains déclarés
declared earnings

gains non déclarés
unreported earnings

gains effectifs
actual earnings

gains provenant / tirés d'un emploi
employment earnings, earnings from employment

gains estimés
(occ.) hypothetical earnings

gains fictifs
notional earnings

gain forfaitaire
standard earnings

gains hebdomadaires
weekly earnings

gain horaire
hourly remuneration; (pl.) hourly earnings

gain après impôt
take-home pay

gain journalier de base
basic daily earnings

gain moyen
average earnings

gain net
take-home pay, (pl.) net earnings

gain de productivité
productivity gain

gains réels
actual earnings

gains salariaux
wage earnings

gains non signalés
unreported earnings

gain de survie
advantage accruing to the survivor

gains théoriques
notional earnings

incapacité de gain
earning incapacity

indemnisation de / pour la perte de gain
compensation for loss of earnings,
earnings replacement / compensation

limite inférieure des gains
lower earnings level / limit

limite supérieure des gains
upper earnings limit / level

niveau des gains
earnings level

niveau général des gains
general level of earnings

pension liée aux gains (antérieurs)
earnings-related pension

perspective de gains
earnings prospect

perte de la capacité de gain
loss of earning capacity

perte de gain
loss of earnings

perte du gain
cessation of earnings

plafond des gains
earnings limit / ceiling

prestation liée / dont le taux est lié aux gains (antérieurs)
(previous) pay-related / earnings-related
(insurance) benefit

proportionnel aux gains
earnings-related

relevé des gains
statement of income

suspension du gain
suspension of earnings

taux de remplacement des gains
earnings replacement ratio / rate

GAMME
range

économies de gamme
economies of scope

gamme de prix
price range

GARANT
système du tiers garant (Switz.)
third party guarantee system

GARANTI
annuité garantie (pour une période
donnée)
annuity certain

emploi garanti
secured / assured employment, secure job

régime non garanti (Can.)
uninsured plan

revenu minimum garanti
guaranteed minimum income

salaire garanti
warranted wage

salaire minimum garanti
guaranteed minimum wage, minimum
wage rate; (occ.) fall-back pay (when
linked to performance)

**salaire minimum interprofessionnel
garanti**
intertrade minimum wage

supplément de revenu garanti (Can.)
guaranteed income supplement, supplemental security income

taux garanti
guaranteed rate

GARANTIE
guarantee; indemnity; collateral (USA);
benefit; security

**Caisse (fédérale) de garantie des pen-
sions (USA)**
Pension Benefit Guaranty Corporation

clause de garantie (d'un accord)
guarantee clause; warranty

compte de garantie bloqué
escrow account

contrat de garantie
underwriting contract

étendue de la / des garantie(s)
degree of coverage, extent / range of cover

garantie de créances de salaires
wage claim guarantee

garantie d'emploi / de l'emploi
security of employment; job assurance / guarantee

garantie des fonctionnaires
protection of public officials

garantie de maintien dans l'emploi
job security

garantie maladie
sickness coverage

garantie des moyens d'existence
income security

garantie de ressources
income guarantee / maintenance, guaranteed minimum income, minimum income security; income support (allowance)

garantie des ressources après la re-traite
income maintenance after retirement

garantie de revenu
income maintenance / support

garantie de revenu minimal
minimum / basic income support

garantie des revenus après la retraite
income maintenance after retirement

garantie sociale
social guarantee

radié des garanties (être)
to be excluded form insurance coverage

rétribution garantie-traitement (Belg.)
guaranteed remuneration

GARANTIR
to underwrite; to indemnify; to guarantee

garantir les moyens d'existence
to maintain income

GARDE
care; custody

allocation pour frais de garde (Fr.)
child-minding allowance, allowance for baby-sitting expenses

allocation de garde (Pol.)
minding allowance

allocation de garde à domicile des enfants (Finl.)
child home care allowance

allocation pour garde d'enfant
child care allowance

allocation de garde d'enfant à domicile
home child care allowance

droit de garde des parents
parental custody

enfant sous la garde de
child in the care of

enfant sous la garde de parents nour-riciers
foster child

garde (sous la)
in the care

garde complète d'enfants
full-time care for children

garde à domicile
home care (children)

garde d'un / des enfants
child-minding, child care, custodial care, custody of a child

garde dans une famille hôte
family day care

garde de nuit
night nurse

garde de personnes à charge
dependant care

rétablissement de la garde
restoration of custody

GARDE-MALADE
nurse

garde-malade à domicile
home nursing / care

GARDER
to retain

garder un droit sur son poste
to retain a lien on one's post

garder un emploi
to stay on a job, to retain employment

GARDERIE
nursery; child-minding place; day care
(centre)

assistante sociale de garderie
child-minder

garderie d'enfants
child care centre, day-care centre, day-
care of children

garderie sur les lieux
on-site day care facility

garderie parascolaire
(occ.) school-based care

garderie sur place
on-site day care facility

services de crèche et de garderie
child care facilities

service de garderie (d'enfants)
day nursery; (pl.) day-care facilities for
children

GARDIEN
warden

gardien d'immeuble
caretaker

**gardiens d'immeubles, nettoyeurs et
travailleurs assimilés [CITP-1968 (5-5)]**
building caretakers, charworkers, cleaners
and related workers [ISCO-1968 (5-5)]

GARDIENNE
gardienne d'enfants
day-care attendant

GEL
freeze

gel de la dotation en personnel
staff freeze

gel de l'embauche
freeze in hiring

gel du recrutement
freeze in recruitment

gel des salaires
wage / pay freeze

GÊNE
constraint; handicap; hardship, distress;
impairment

gêne fonctionnelle
functional handicap / impairment

gêne professionnelle
vocational disablement

gêne pour le travail
work hindrance

GÉNÉRAL (adj.)
general; standard; blanket

agent à compétence générale
general purpose worker

**agent d'exécution à compétence géné-
rale**
general field worker

application générale (d')
universally applicable

assurance générale
general insurance

assurance générale risques graves (Neth.)
general insurance against serious risks

bonne culture générale
good general knowledge

caisse-maladie locale générale
general local sick fund

centre post-hospitalier général de réadaptation médicale
(occ.) medical rehabilitation centre

clause générale
standard clause

clause de portée générale
(occ.) omnibus clause

complément de pension générale (Swed.)
general pension supplement

cotisations sociales du régime général de sécurité sociale
insurance contributions for the general social security scheme

culture générale
general culture / knowledge

directeur général
executive / managing director, chief executive (officer) (CEO)

directeur général adjoint
deputy managing director

direction générale
top management

dispense générale
blanket exemption

disposition générale
general provision; (pl.) (occ.) blanket clause

enseignement de culture générale
academic education

enseignement général (l')
general school system, general education (system)

établissement d'enseignement général
(occ.) mainstream school

exemption générale
blanket exemption

fonds d'action générale
global funds

formation générale
basic / foundation training / education

formation professionnelle générale
generic skill training, general vocational training / education

frais généraux
overall / overhead costs, overhead (expenses)

frais généraux additionnels
incremental overhead costs

frais généraux de fonctionnement
general operating costs

grève générale
general strike

hôpital général
general hospital

indice de satisfaction générale
general satisfaction rating

inspection générale des affaires sociales
social affairs general inspectorate

intérêt général
public interest

invalidité générale
general invalidity

maladie générale
(occ.) systemic disease

médecine générale
general (medical) practice

niveau général des gains
general level of earnings

opter pour la non-affiliation / le non-assujettissement au régime général de retraite complémentaire
to contract out

orientation générale
(general) policy

pension complémentaire du régime général (UK)
reserve pension

plan général
outline

police d'assurance générale
(occ.) blanket (insurance) policy

prestations générales d'aide sociale
general welfare assistance

prestation du régime général
basic scheme benefit

recettes générales
general revenue

régime contributif de pensions complémentaires du régime général (UK)
contributory reserve pension scheme

régime général
general / basic scheme

régime général de (la) sécurité sociale
general social security scheme, standard social security health and retirement insurance (for private industry)

rendement général
overall performance

révision générale
general review

révision générale des traitements
major salary review

service de santé général
general health service

soins de médecine générale
general medical care, general practitioner care

syndicat général
general (workers') union

test d'aptitude(s) générale(s)
general aptitude test

travail d'intérêt général (TIG)
community service / work

trésorier payeur général
accountant-general, paymaster-general

GÉNÉRALISÉ
chômage généralisé
general / large-scale / mass / massive unemployment

contribution sociale généralisée (CSG) (Fr.)
general social contribution

grève généralisée
widespread strike

GÉNÉRALISTE (adj.)
médecin généraliste
general practitioner

GÉNÉRALISTE (n.)
general practitioner

GÉNÉRATEUR (adj.)
activité génératrice d'emplois
employment-generating activity

générateur d'économies de main-d'-oeuvre
labour(-)saving

générateur d'emploi(s)
job(-)creating

mesure génératrice d'emplois
employment-creation / job-creation measure

GÉNÉRATION
conflit de / des générations
generation gap

immigré de la deuxième génération
second-generation immigrant

remplacement / renouvellement des générations
generation replacement

GÉNÉRIQUE
appellation d'emploi générique
generic job title

GÉNÉSIQUE
santé / soins génésique(s)
reproductive health

GÉNÉTIQUE
génie génétique
genetic engineering

GÉNIE
engineering

génie génétique
genetic engineering

génie sanitaire
public health engineering

ingénieur du génie civil
civil engineer

GENS
gens de maison
domestic servants

gens de mer
seamen; sailors

gens du métier
tradespersons; profession

GÉOGRAPHIQUE
aide à la mobilité géographique
geographical mobility incentive

allocation pour éloignement géographique (Austr.)
remote area allowance

inadéquation géographique
regional mismatch

mobilité géographique
geographic / spatial mobility

répartition géographique équitable
equitable geographical distribution

répartition géographique du personnel
geographical distribution of staff

GÉRANT
manager; managing director

dirigeants et gérants [CITP-1988 (13, 131)]
general managers [ISCO-1988 (13, 131)]

GÉRER
gérer un programme
to manage / to run / to administer a programme

GESTE
gestes essentiels de la vie quotidienne
basic activities of daily life

geste de la vie quotidienne
daily task

GESTION
administration; management

atelier de gestion
management workshop

boutique de gestion (Fr.)
small business promotion agency

compétences en gestion
management skills

conseil de gestion
management board

conseil en gestion de carrière
career counselling

contrat de gestion commune de caisses
pooled accounts funding contract

contrat de gestion de dépôts
deposit administration contract

contrat de gestion distincte
segregated funds contract

contrat de gestion distincte de caisse
segregated accounts funding contract

contrôle de gestion
management control

contrôle de gestion interne
audit

convention de gestion financière (pensions)
funding instrument

coût de gestion
administrative cost(s)

école (supérieure) de gestion
business school

expert-conseil en gestion
managerial consultant

formation en gestion
management training

formation et gestion des carrières des cadres
management development

frais de gestion
administration / administrative expenses / cost(s), service cost

gestion administrative
(occ.) management office

gestion sans but lucratif (Can.)
public administration

gestion de carrière
career development / management

gestion par cas
case management

gestion des entreprises
business administration / management

gestion au plus juste
lean management

gestion participative
participative management, worker participation

gestion du personnel
human resources / personnel management; manpower / personnel practices

gestion prévisionnelle de l'emploi (GPE)
(enterprise) manpower planning

gestion prévisionnelle de l'emploi dans l'entreprise
company manpower planning, personnel planning at establishment level

gestion prévisionnelle du personnel
staff planning

gestion des rémunérations
salary administration

gestion des ressources humaines
human resources / personnel management

gestion des vacances de poste
vacancy management

participation des travailleurs à la gestion des entreprises
workers' participation in management

régime de retraite complémentaire privé en gestion directe
self-administered pension scheme

système de gestion de la qualité
quality management system

technique de gestion
management technique

GESTIONNAIRE (adj.)
tiers gestionnaire
funding agency

GESTIONNAIRE (n.)
administrator; manager

GLISSEMENT
shift

glissement de salaires
incidental wage increase, wage drift / shift

GLOBAL
aggregate; holistic; blanket; total; global

accord global
global / blanket agreement; (occ.) package deal

allocation globale
block grant; total allocation

appréciation globale
(occ.) general rating

besoin global en personnel
overall staffing requirement

budget global
global budget

chômage global
aggregate unemployment

compromis global
package deal

couverture globale
blanket coverage

demande globale
aggregate / total demand

dotation globale de fonctionnement
global operating budget

dotation globale hospitalière
global hospital budget

enveloppe globale
global budget

évaluation globale
overall assessment

facteur des gains globaux
total earnings factor

indemnité globale
lump-sum allowance

médecine globale
comprehensive medicine

offre globale
aggregate / total supply

politique globale
overall policy

pourcentage global de capitalisation
aggregate funded ratio

rémunération globale
comprehensive package; pay / remuneration package, compensation package (USA); emoluments

somme globale
lump(-sum) / single payment, lump sum

subvention globale
block grant

taux d'activité global
aggregate / total participation rate

taux de chômage global
aggregate unemployment rate

visa global
blanket visa

volume global de l'emploi
overall level of employment

GONFLÉ
chiffre gonflé
inflated figure

salaire gonflé
inflated salary

GOUVERNANCE
(corporate) governance

GOUVERNEMENT
commissaire du Gouvernement
Government commissioner

GOUVERNEMENTAL
organisation non gouvernementale semi-autonome
quasi-autonomous non-governmental organisation (quango)

service gouvernemental
Government department

GRABATAIRE
(permanently) bedridden

GRACIEUX
décision gracieuse
ex gratia decision

gracieux (à titre)
free of charge

indemnité accordée à / paiement à titre gracieux
ex gratia payment

procédure gracieuse
non-contentious proceedings / procedure

recours gracieux
application to reconsider a decision;
submission for an out-of-court settlement

remise gracieuse de cotisations
discretionary reduction of contributions

versement à titre gracieux
ex gratia payment

GRADE
grade, degree

grade d'entrée
entry grade

grade attribué à titre personnel
personal grade

grade professionnel
service grade

GRADUÉ
graduated

soins gradués
progressive patient care

GRADUEL
graduated

GRADUER
to graduate, to phase

graduer les cotisations
to graduate contributions

GRAND
grand appareillage
major appliances / aids

grande échelle (à)
large-scale

grand ensemble
housing project / estate

grande entreprise
large-scale enterprise

grand groupe
major group

grand groupe professionnel
broad occupational group

grand handicapé
substantially handicapped

grand infirme / grand invalide
severely handicapped / disabled, seriously disabled person; (pl.) badly
disabled (the)

grandes orientations
policy formulations, guidelines

grande pauvreté
(occ.) destitution

grande profession
core occupation

grande série
long production run

grandes vacances
summer holidays

GRANDEUR
ordre de grandeur
order of magnitude, range, estimate

ordre de grandeur de salaire
salary estimation / estimate

GRATIFIANT
travail gratifiant
rewarding work

GRATIFICATION
bonus, premium; gratuity

GRATUIT
free of charge

annuité gratuite
free annuity

- 384 -

validation gratuite
free validation

GRATUITÉ
gratuité des soins
free medical care

GRAVE
allocation pour / d'incapacité grave
severe disablement allowance

assurance générale risques graves (Neth.)
general insurance against serious risks

chômage grave
acute unemployment

faute grave
serious misconduct, gross misconduct / negligence

incapacité / infirmité / invalidité grave
major / severe disability

lésion grave
serious injury

licenciement pour faute grave
disciplinary lay-off

maladie grave
dangerous / major / serious / severe illness

personne souffrant d'une incapacité grave
seriously disabled person

GRAVEMENT
personne gravement handicapée
seriously disabled person

GRAVITÉ
severity

taux de gravité
severity rate

taux de gravité des accidents
accident severity rate

GRÉ
gré (de son plein)
voluntary

GRÈVE
strike; work stoppage; direct action

annuler un mot d'ordre de grève
to call off a strike

appeler à la grève
to call a strike

assurance contre la grève
strike insurance

briseur de grève
strikebreaker, scab, blackleg

caisse de grève
strike fund

clause de risque de grève
strikes clause

déclencher une grève
to trigger a strike

déposer un préavis de grève
to give notice of strike action

droit de grève
right to strike

fonds de grève
strike fund

former un piquet de grève
to picket

grève d'avertissement
token (protest) / warning strike

grève bouchon
bottleneck strike

grève les bras croisés
sit-down strike

grève éclair
lightning strike

grève générale
general strike

grève généralisée
widespread strike

grève illégale
unlawful strike

grève illicite
illegal strike

grève illimitée
indefinite strike

grève insurrectionnelle
revolutionary strike

grève largement suivie
widespread strike

grève légale
official / lawful strike

grève avec occupation des locaux
sit-in / stay-in strike; worker occupation

grève perlée
slow-down strike, go-slow (strike);
slowing down of work, work slow-down;
work-to-rule (strike)

grève ponctuelle
selective strike

grève sans préavis
wild(-)cat strike

grève de protestation
protest strike

grève de protestation contre des / les licenciements
redundancy strike

grève du règlement
work-to-rule (strike)

grève sauvage
outlaw / unofficial / wild(-)cat strike

grève sectorielle
industry-wide strike

grève sélective
whipsaw strike

grève de solidarité
secondary / sympathetic / sympathy strike, secondary industrial action

grève surprise
lightning / guerilla strike

grève symbolique
token (protest) strike

grève sur le tas
sit-down / sit-in / stay-in strike; worker occupation

grève tournante
rotating / staggered / selective / guerilla strike

grève par le travail
work-in

grève du zèle
work(ing)-to-rule (strike), go-slow (strike)

grève du zèle (faire la)
to work to rule

mettre en grève (se)
to take strike action

licenciement pour fait de grève
dismissal resulting from strike

mot d'ordre de grève
strike call

mouvement de grève
strike movement

piquet de grève
(strike) picket; (pl.) picketing

piquet de grève mobile
roving picket

piquet de grève volant
flying picket

préavis de grève
strike notice

scrutin / vote décidant de la tenue d'une grève
strike vote / ballot

GRÉVISTE
striker

salaire de gréviste
strike pay

GRIEF
grievance, claim

GRILLE
grille de carrière
career lattice

grille de classification (Fr.)
job category

grille des comportements attendus par type de fonction
behaviour expectation scale

grille de conversion
conversion table

grille d'évaluation
appraisal / evaluation grid

grille d'évaluation à choix forcé
forced choice rating (grid)

grille des salaires
salary scale

GROS
assurance gros frais / gros risques médicaux
major medical insurance

GROSSESSE
pregnancy

carnet de grossesse
pregnancy record

déclaration de grossesse
notification of pregnancy

grossesse pathologique
pathological pregnancy

interruption de grossesse
termination of pregnancy

interruption volontaire de grossesse (IVG)
voluntary termination of pregnancy

prestation de grossesse
pregnancy benefit

prime de grossesse (Icel.)
pregnancy subsidy

GROSSIER
estimation grossière
(occ.) guestimate

GROUPE
group; category; panel; unit; (occ.) bracket

activités de groupe
group activities

analyse selon le / par groupe d'emplois
job group analysis

animateur de groupe
group leader

animateur de groupes de jeunes
youth leader

assurance de groupe
group insurance

assurance-groupe sur la vie
group life insurance

cabinet de groupe (Fr.)
group surgery

chef de groupe
supervisor; (occ.) adult leader

exercice de groupe prépayé (PGP)
prepaid group practice (PGP)

grand groupe
major group

grand groupe professionnel
broad occupational group

groupe d'action formé de citoyens
citizens' action group, public interest group

groupe d'âge(s)
age group

groupe bénévole
voluntary group

groupe cible
target group; (occ.) priority group

groupe de citoyens
citizens' group

groupe défavorisé
disadvantaged group

groupe d'entraide
(mutual) self-help group

groupe d'étude
task force / group; (occ.) syndicate

groupe d'experts
panel of experts

groupe particulièrement exposé
particular risk group

groupe très exposé
high-risk group

groupe à faibles revenus
low-income (population) group

groupe d'habitants
population cluster

groupe d'habitations
housing project / estate

groupe à haut(s) risque(s)
high-risk group

groupe homogène de malades (GHM)
diagnosis related group

groupe d'intérêt
interest group

groupe local
community group

groupe minoritaire
minority group

groupe de population
segment of population

groupe de pression
pressure group, lobby

groupe prioritaire
priority / target group

groupe de professions
job family

groupe professionnel
occupational group / class; (occ.) industry,
branch of economic activity

groupe récréatif
play group

groupe de référence
comparison / control group

groupe sanitaire
health unit

groupe sanitaire rural
rural health unit

groupe social
social (status) group, socio-economic
group

groupe de solidarité
(mutual) self-help group

groupe témoin
comparison / control group

groupe de travail
task force / group; (occ.) syndicate

groupe de voisinage
neighbourhood group

**logements pour les groupes sociaux à
faibles revenus**
low-income housing

mécanisme de groupe
group process

médecine de groupe
group medicine, group (medical) practice

**mesures en faveur de groupes désa-
vantagés / défavorisés**
(occ.) affirmative / positive action

méthode de groupe
group process

**méthode de sélection de candidats en
groupe**
group selection method

pratique médicale de groupe
group (medical) practice

responsable de groupe
group leader

service social de groupe
social group work

travail de / en groupe
group work

travailleur social de groupe
group (social) worker

GROUPEMENT
groupement d'auto-assistance
self-help group

groupement d'entreprises locales
local enterprise trust

groupement inter-hospitalier
interhospital group

groupement médical prépayé (PGP)
prepaid group practice (PGP)

groupement mutualiste
mutual benefit society

groupement patronal
employer's association / federation /
organisation

GUÉRISON
recovery

GUÉRISSEUR
praticiens de la médecine traditionnelle et
guérisseurs [CITP-1988]
traditional medicine practitioners and faith
healers [ISCO-1988 (324)]

GUERRE
allocation de guerre pour les civils
civilian war allowance

allocation de victime de guerre (UK)
war pensioner's death benefit

aveugle de guerre
blind war victim, veteran blind / blinded

blessure de guerre
war injury

fait de guerre
act of war

invalide / mutilé de guerre
disabled veteran / ex-serviceman, war
invalid / disabled / cripple

orphelin de guerre
war orphan

pension de guerre
war pension

pension de veuve de guerre
war widow's pension

pension de victime de guerre (UK)
war pensioner's death benefit

prisonnier de guerre
war prisoner

réparation des dommages de guerre
war damage compensation

veuve de guerre
war widow

victime civile de la guerre
civilian war victim

victime de (la) guerre
war victim, war handicapped, victim of
war; (occ.) war pensioner

GUIDANCE
guidance

centre de guidance infantile
child guidance centre / clinic

guidance familiale
family guidance

guidance infantile
child guidance

GUIDE
guide-barème
scale rate

GYMNASE
gymnasium

HABILE
able; skilful

HABILETÉ
craftsmanship, skill

HABILITANT
enabling

technologie habilitante
enabling technology

HABILITATION
accreditation; empowerment

formule d'habilitation déclarative
declaratory authorisation arrangement

habilitation de responsables syndicaux
accreditation of union officials

loi d'habilitation
enabling act

HABILITÉ (adj.)
authorised; entitled to; competent; qualified; eligible

agent spécifiquement habilité
officer specifically authorised

habilité à exercer
qualified to practice

médecin habilité à exercer (Can.)
licensed physician

personne habilitée
authorised / approved person

HABILITÉ (n.)
habilité motrice
motor skill

HABILITER
to authorise, to entitle; to empower

HABILLEMENT
allocation / indemnité / prime d'habillement
clothing allowance; (occ.) allowance for wear and tear (of clothing)

HABITABILITÉ
logement ne répondant pas aux normes d'habitabilité minimale
sub(-)standard housing

HABITANT
allocation par habitant
per capita allocation

groupe d'habitants
population cluster

habitant (par)
per capita, per head

revenu par habitant
per capita income

HABITAT
housing; settlement

habitat collectif
congregate housing

habitat humain
human habitat

habitat protégé
sheltered housing

habitat spontané
squatter settlement

mode d'habitat
settlement pattern

prêt à l'amélioration de l'habitat
loan for housing improvement

HABITATION
housing, accommodation

aire d'habitation
housing area

foyer permanent d'habitation
normal / permanent home

groupe d'habitations
housing project / estate

habitations à bon marché
low-cost housing

habitation collective
communal housing

habitation à loyer modéré (HLM)
council flat / housing, rent controlled
premises; (pl.) low-cost housing

programme de construction d'habitations
housing programme

programme de construction d'habitations à bon marché
low-cost housing programme

programme subventionné (de construction) d'habitations
social housing scheme, subsidised
housing programme

taxe d'habitation (Fr.)
community charge

unité d'habitation
dwelling (unit), housing unit

HABITUDE
habit; practice

habitudes d'hygiène
health habits / practices

habitude de travail
work habit, working pattern; attitude to
work

HABITUEL
activité habituelle
normal business

emploi habituel
usual occupation

population de résidence habituelle
resident population

profession habituelle
usual occupation

résidence habituelle
normal / ordinary / regular residence

résident habituel
normal resident

tâche habituelle
routine task

HABITUELLEMENT
population habituellement active
usually active population

profession habituellement exercée par des hommes
(occ.) male-dominated occupation

HALTE-GARDERIE
occasional care centre

halte-garderie familiale
family occasional care centre

HANDICAP
handicap, abnormality, impairment, deficiency; difficulty

allocation pour handicap (Denm.)
handicap allowance

handicap mental
mental disability / disablement

handicap physique
physical handicap; bodily disablement

HANDICAPANT
état / maladie handicapant(e)
handicapping condition

HANDICAPÉ
handicapped / disabled (person); crippled;
(pl.) people with disabilities, the disabled

adulte handicapé
disabled adult

aide sociale aux handicapés
social assistance for disabled people

allocation aux adultes handicapés
allowance for handicapped (Fr.) / disabled
adults

allocation pour enfant handicapé
child disability allowance (Austr.),
handicapped child / children's allowance
(Malta)

centre pour handicapés
centre for disabled people

contrat d'adaptation professionnelle pour personnes handicapées (Belg.)
vocational adaptation contract for the disabled

enfant handicapé
disabled / handicapped child

enseignants spécialisés dans l'éducation des handicapés [CITP-1988]
special education teaching professionals [ISCO-1988 (234)]

grand handicapé
substantially handicapped

handicapé adulte
disabled adult

handicapé mental
mentally retarded / disabled / handicapped, developmentally handicapped; (pl.) people with mental disabilities

handicapé mineur
disabled child

handicapé physique
physically disabled / handicapped; (pl.) people with physical disabilities

handicapé social
socially handicapped; social misfit

main-d'oeuvre handicapée
disabled labour force

mineur handicapé
disabled child

personne gravement handicapée
seriously disabled person

personne handicapée
handicapped person

personne handicapée apte au travail
employable person with disability / ies

professions intermédiaires de l'éducation des handicapés [CITP-1988 (333)]
special education teaching associate professionals [ISCO-1988 (333)]

travailleur handicapé
disabled / handicapped worker

travailleur handicapé reconnu par l'Etat
registered disabled person

travailleur physiquement handicapé
physically disabled worker

voiture pour handicapé
(occ.) invalid carriage; trike

HARCÈLEMENT
harcèlement en raison de la race
racial harassment

harcèlement sexuel
sexual harassment

HARMONIEUX
croissance harmonieuse
balanced growth

HARMONISATION
harmonisation, harmonising

harmonisation interne (des salaires)
internal alignment (of wages)

HAUSSE
increase, rise

hausse contractuelle de salaires
pay / wage settlement

hausse de l'emploi
increase in / expansion of employment

hausse inflationniste de salaires
wage inflation

hausse du pouvoir d'achat
increase in purchasing power

hausse de la productivité
productivity increase

hausse du / des salaire(s) / salariale
wage / salary rise / increase, pay increase

hausse salariale compensatoire
compensatory wage increase

réviser à la hausse
to review upwards

révision en hausse
upward adjustment

révision à la hausse des traitements
upward adjustment of salaries

tendance à la hausse
upward trend

HAUT (adj.)
compétence technique de haut niveau
high(er)-level technical skill

groupe à haut(s) risque(s)
high-risk group

industrie de haute technologie
high(-)technology industry

haute administration
senior civil service

hautes études universitaires
postgraduate studies

haut fonctionnaire
high-ranking / senior official, senior
officer / civil servant; (pl.) Government
officials

haute personnalité
(high-ranking) official

haut placé
highly placed

haute qualification (de)
(occ.) professional

haut rang (de)
high-ranking

haut responsable
senior executive

institut de hautes études
graduate school

métier de haute spécialisation
highly skilled / higher-skill trade

poste de haute direction
upper level management position

**profession de haute qualification /
spécialisation**
highly skilled / higher-skill / qualified
occupation

responsable de haut rang
senior-ranked official

HAUT (n.)
haut de la hiérarchie des revenus
upper income bracket

HAUTEMENT
hautement qualifié / spécialisé
highly qualified / skilled; professional

main-d'oeuvre hautement qualifiée
highly qualified / skilled manpower

métier hautement spécialisé
highly skilled / higher-skill trade

ouvrier hautement qualifié
highly skilled worker

personne hautement spécialisée
(occ.) professional

profession hautement spécialisée
highly skilled / higher-skill / qualified
occupation

professionnel hautement qualifié
highly skilled professional employee

travail hautement spécialisé
highly skilled work

travail technique hautement spécialisé
high-skill technical work

travailleur hautement qualifié
highly skilled worker

HAUTEUR
chute d'une hauteur
falling

HEBDOMADAIRE
weekly

allocation hebdomadaire
weekly allowance, allowance per week

**allocation hebdomadaire maximale
payable**
maximum weekly allowance payable

cotisation hebdomadaire
weekly contribution

**durée convenue du travail hebdoma-
daire**
standard working week, standard weekly
hours

durée hebdomadaire du travail
hours worked weekly, weekly hours of
work, work(ing) week

**durée hebdomadaire du travail prévue
par la loi**
statutory working week

**durée normale du travail hebdoma-
daire**
standard working week, standard weekly
hours

gains hebdomadaires
weekly earnings

horaire hebdomadaire normal
standard weekly hours

indemnité hebdomadaire
allowance per week

jour de repos hebdomadaire
weekly rest day

paiement hebdomadaire
weekly payment

**réduction de la durée hebdomadaire du
travail**
reduction of the working week

rémunération hebdomadaire assurable
weekly insurable earnings

repos hebdomadaire
weekly rest

revenu hebdomadaire
weekly earnings

salaire hebdomadaire
weekly wage / pay, earnings / wage per
week

salaire hebdomadaire brut
gross weekly pay, weekly earnings before
deduction

salaire hebdomadaire brut normal
normal gross weekly earnings

**salaire hebdomadaire maximal admis-
sible**
maximum allowable weekly wage

salaire hebdomadaire moyen
average weekly earnings

soutien du revenu hebdomadaire
weekly income support

taux hebdomadaire
weekly rate

taux hebdomadaire applicable
appropriate weekly rate

taux de rémunération hebdomadaire
weekly wage / pay rate

HÉBERGEMENT
accommodation; housing

allocation d'hébergement
overnight accommodation allowance

capacité d'hébergement
(occ.) bed capacity

centre d'hébergement
reception / accommodation centre; hostel

centre d'hébergement nocturne
night hostel

**forfait journalier de soins et d'héber-
gement**
patient's daily charge for care and
accommodation

frais d'hébergement
accommodation expenses

hébergement collectif
communal living unit

indemnité d'hébergement
accommodation allowance

HERBORISTE
herbalist

HÉRITIER
heir; next of kin

HEURE
astreint à des strictes heures de bureau
(être)
to be expected to keep strict office hours

**corrigé des variations du nombre
d'heures supplémentaires**
adjusted for overtime

crédit d'heures
day release

dépassement d'heures
surplus of hours worked

feuille d'heures
time sheet

heures de bureau
office hours

heures chômées
not worked hours

heures de classe
school hours

heures complémentaires
additional hours

heures de cours
school hours

heures creuses
off-peak / slack period

heure effectivement ouvrée / travaillée
hour actually worked

heure-homme
manpower-hour, man-hour

heures de loisirs
leisure time

heure de main-d'oeuvre
man-hour, hour of operation

heures normales de travail
scheduled hours of work

heures d'ouverture
trading / opening hours

heure ouvrée
worked hour; (pl.) hours worked

heures ouvrées dans la journée
daily working hours

heure-personne
man-hour

heures de présence
hours spent at work

heure de prise de service
starting time

heures de récupération
hours off in lieu, hours (not worked) to be
made up later

heures de service
hours of duty; working time

heures supplémentaires
overtime (work / working)

heures supplémentaires (faire des)
to work overtime, to work after / extra
hours

heures de travail
hours of work, working hours

heure de travail effectuée
worked hour; (pl.) hours (actually)
worked

heure travaillée
worked hour; (pl.) hours / time worked

heure unitaire de main-d'oeuvre
unit hour of operation

heure-unité
unit hour

interdiction d'heures supplémentaires
overtime ban

paiement des heures supplémentaires
overtime compensation / pay

payé à l'heure (être)
to be paid on an hourly basis / by the
hour; to be assigned to hourly rates

prime d'heures supplémentaires
premium for extra duty, overtime pay

**rémunération des heures supplémen-
taires**
overtime compensation / pay

salaire au prorata des heures ouvrées
wage in proportion to time worked

taux d'heures supplémentaires
overtime rate

taux de rémunération des heures sup-
plémentaires
overtime rate of pay

travail à l'heure
time work

travailler aux heures normales
to work regular hours

travailler en dehors des heures norma-
les
to work unsocial hours

travailleur rémunéré à l'heure
hourly paid worker

HIÉRARCHIE
hierarchy; ranking; scale

haut de la hiérarchie des revenus
upper income bracket

hiérarchie des revenus / des salaires
salary scale; wage bracket; scale of
income / salaries

HIÉRARCHIQUE
hierarchical; superior

cadre hiérarchique
line manager

chef hiérarchique
official superior

classement hiérarchique des emplois
labour ranking

échelon hiérarchique
hierarchical grade; level of authority

méthode du classement hiérarchique
des emplois
job ranking method

niveau hiérarchique
layer of hierarchy

recours hiérarchique
application for disciplinary proceedings,
disciplinary complaint; appeal to superior
administrative authority

relation hiérarchique
managerial relationship

supérieur hiérarchique
(official / hierarchical) superior

supérieur hiérarchique direct
immediate superior / supervisor

voie hiérarchique
official channel(s); (occ.) chain of
command

HIÉRARCHIQUEMENT
by reference to a superior authority, by
seniority

HIPPOCRATE
serment d'Hippocrate
Hippocratic oath

HISTORIQUE (n.)
étude de l'historique professionnel
career follow-up / career pattern study

HIVER
horaire d'hiver
winter time

HOME
establishment; home

home pour personnes âgées
residential / geriatric home

HOMME
année-homme
man-year

heure-homme
manpower-hour, man-hour

jour-homme
man-day

homme de l'art
professional

homme marié
married man

homme de métier
tradesman; craftsman; journeyman

homme de métier qualifié
qualified journeyman

homme du sérail
insider

profession habituellement exercée par des hommes
(occ.) male-dominated occupation

HOMOGÈNE
groupe homogène de malades (GHM)
diagnosis related group

HOMOLOGATION
certification; authentication; approval; validation; accreditation

homologation d'une formation
official approval for a training course

responsable de l'homologation des syndicats (UK)
certification officer

HOMOLOGUE (adj.)
authorised; certified

HOMOLOGUER
to certify; to authenticate; to approve

HONNEUR
engagement sur l'honneur
solemn and binding agreement

prêt d'honneur
loan on trust

HONORAIRE
(pl.) (professional) fees; fee-for-service

barème des / d'honoraires
scale of fees, fee schedule

dépassement d'honoraires
overbilling, extra-billing

honoraires de médecin / médicaux
doctor's / medical fees

honoraire tarifé
scheduled fee

méthode de rémunération par honoraires
fee-for-service / item of service method of remuneration

paiement par honoraires (système de)
fee-for-service system

provision sur honoraires
retainer fee

secteur à honoraires libres (Fr.)
free-fee sector

HÔPITAL
hospital

admettre dans un hôpital
to admit to a hospital

admission dans un hôpital
admission to a hospital, hospital admission

assistant social d'hôpital / des hôpitaux
(occ.) almoner

conseil régional des hôpitaux (UK)
hospital regional board

hôpital central
(occ.) referral hospital

hôpital de court séjour
(occ.) somatic hospital

hôpital-école
teaching hospital

hôpital général
general hospital

hôpital de jour
day hospital; half-way house

hôpital local
local hospital

hôpital de long séjour
long-term hospital

hôpital pour malades chroniques
chronic disease hospital

hôpital de nuit
night hospital

hôpital ouvert
open-door hospital

hôpital privé
voluntary / private hospital

hôpital psychiatrique
mental home / hospital, psychiatric hospital

hôpital public
public hospital

hôpital régional
regional hospital

hôpital pour séjours de longue durée
long-term hospital

hôpital de soins aigus
acute care / active treatment / somatic hospital

hôpital spécialisé
specialised hospital

hôpital thermal
hydropathic hospital

hôpital universitaire
teaching / training hospital, hospital school

médecin d'hôpital / des hôpitaux
doctor in hospital, hospital medical officer, hospital doctor

pharmacien d'hôpital
hospital pharmacist

régime des hôpitaux
hospital regulations

salle d'hôpital
ward

service social à l'hôpital
hospital social work

soins médicaux en consultation externe
out-patient treatment

sortie de l'hôpital
release from hospital

visites du médecin traitant à l'hôpital
in-hospital doctor's care

HORAIRE (adj.)
gain horaire
hourly remuneration; (pl.) hourly earnings

personnel horaire
hourly paid personnel

plage horaire
time frame / bracket

plage horaire fixe
fixed time bracket

plage horaire flexible / mobile / variable
flexible time bracket

productivité horaire de la main-d'oeuvre
hourly productivity of labour

rémunération horaire
hourly earnings

rémunération horaire effective / réelle
actual hourly earnings

salaire horaire
hourly / time wage

tâche horaire
hour task

taux horaire
hourly / time rate

taux horaire minimal
minimum hourly rate

taux horaire de salaire, taux de salaire horaire
hourly wage rate

travailleur horaire
hourly paid worker

HORAIRE (n.)
hours; schedule

annualisation des horaires
annualised hours

décalement des horaires de travail
staggered working hours

échelonnement des horaires de travail
scheduling of work

enseignement à horaire réduit
part-time education

horaire à la carte
flexible working hours / time, flexitime

horaire complet (à)
full time

horaire continu
working hours without break

horaire décalé
staggered hours

horaire décalé fixe
staggered working hours

horaire discontinu
split working hours

horaire échelonné
staggered hours

horaire d'été
summer time

horaire d'exploitation
opening hours

horaire fixe
fixed working hours

horaires à flexibilité maximale
(occ.) maniflex

horaire fractionné
split hours

horaire hebdomadaire normal
standard weekly hours

horaire d'hiver
winter time

horaire libre
variable working hours

horaire mobile / modulés
flexible working hours / time, flexible
time / hours; flexitime

horaire réduit (à)
part-time; short(-)time

horaire souple
flexible working hours / time, flexible
time / hours; flexitime

horaire de travail
working time / hours; work(ing) schedule

horaire de travail assoupli / flexible
flexible work schedule, flexible hours

horaire de travail individualisé
personalised hours of work, personalised
working hours

horaire de travail normal
normal working hours

**horaire de travail personnel / person-
nalisé**
personalised working hours

horaire (de travail) souple / variable
flexible working hours / time, flexible
work schedule, flexitime

modulation des horaires
adjustable hours

salaire en horaire normal
straight-time pay; (occ.) regular wage

souplesse des horaires de travail
flexibility of working hours

tableau d'horaires
duty roster

travail à horaires réduits
short-time work / working; partial
unemployment

travailler en horaires réduits
to be on / to work short-time

HORIZONTAL
entreprise horizontale
horizontal corporation

relations horizontales
lateral relations

HOROKILOMÉTRIQUE
indemnité horokilométrique
mileage fee / allowance

HOSPICE
nursing home; establishment; poor house;
(occ.) hospital

hospice d'aliénés
mental home

HOSPITALIER (adj.)
hospital

administration hospitalière
hospital authority

agent hospitalier
hospital employee / worker; (occ.)
orderly; (pl.) hospital personnel /
employees / workers / staff

aide hospitalière
hospital assistance

**allocation pour soins hospitaliers / pour
traitement hospitalier (UK)**
hospital treatment allowance

appareil hospitalier
hospital system

archives hospitalières
hospital records

cas hospitaliers
hospital cases

centre hospitalier
hospital

centre hospitalier régional (CHR)
regional hospital

centre hospitalier universitaire (CHU)
university hospital

circonscription hospitalière
hospital catchment area

département hospitalier
hospital unit

dossiers hospitaliers
hospital records

dotation globale hospitalière
global hospital budget

établissement hospitalier
hospital; (occ.) residential institution; (pl.)
hospital facilities

forfait hospitalier (Fr.)
patient's fixed contribution per day of
hospitalisation

forfait journalier hospitalier
patient's daily charge for hospitalisation

médecin hospitalier
doctor in hospital, hospital medical
officer, hospital doctor

personnel hospitalier
hospital staff / personnel / employees /
workers

régime hospitalier
hospital system

relevé hospitalier
hospital record

réseau / secteur hospitalier
hospital network / system

service hospitalier
in-patient unit / service; (pl.) hospital
services

service public hospitalier
hospital public service

soins hospitaliers / en milieu hospitalier
hospital care / treatment; (occ.)
institutional care

soins non hospitaliers
(occ.) out-patient care

**soins en régime hospitalier ou ambu-
latoire**
in-patient or out-patient care

traitement (en milieu) hospitalier
hospital care / treatment; institutional care

HOSPITALIER (n.)
hospital medical officer

HOSPITALISATION
stay in hospital, admission to a hospital,
entry into hospital, hospitalisation; indoor
relief; institutional / hospital treatment;
(in-)hospital care

allocation d'hospitalisation
hospitalisation / treatment allowance

**assurance extra-légale en matière
d'hospitalisation (Belg.)**
extra-legal hospitalisation insurance

assurance-hospitalisation
hospital benefits insurance

capacité d'hospitalisation
bed capacity

dossier d'hospitalisation
hospital record

durée de l'hospitalisation
duration of hospitalisation

établissement d'hospitalisation
in-patient establishment

frais d'hospitalisation
hospital expenses

hospitalisation à domicile
home (medical) care

hospitalisation libre
informal hospitalisation, voluntary
admission

hospitalisation d'office
involuntary hospitalisation

journée d'hospitalisation
bed-day, hospital day

maladie donnant lieu à hospitalisation
hospitalised illness

service d'hospitalisation
in-patient department; (occ.) ward

temps d'hospitalisation
stay in hospital

traitement sans hospitalisation
out-patient treatment

HOSPITALISÉ
malade hospitalisé
(hospital) in-patient

malade non hospitalisé
ambulatory patient, (hospital) out-patient

personne hospitalisée
(hospital) in-patient

**services recevant des malades hospita-
lisés**
in-patient facilities / units

soins aux malades hospitalisés
(occ.) residential care

soins aux malades non hospitalisés
(occ.) non-residential care

HÔTE
garde dans une famille hôte
family day care

HÔTEL
hôtel pour entreprise
enterprise house / workshop; industry
hotel

hôtel maternel (Fr.)
mother and child accommodation centre

HÔTELIER (adj.)
frais hôteliers (hosp.) (Switz.)
room and board expenses

HÔTELLERIE
hotel business; catering; hotel management (ed.)

hôtellerie-restauration
catering

HOUILLER
industrie houillère
coal(-mining) industry

HOUILLÈRE
colliery

**régime complémentaire des travailleurs
des houillères**
colliery workers supplementary scheme

travailleur des houillères
colliery worker

HUMAIN
besoins essentiels de l'être humain
basic human needs

capital humain
human capital / resources

département des ressources humaines
personnel department

développement des ressources humaines
human resources / manpower development

directeur des ressources humaines
labour / work director, personnel manager
division des ressources humaines
personnel department

gestion des ressources humaines
human resources / personnel management

habitat humain
human habitat

indicateur du développement humain
human development index

mise en valeur des ressources humaines
labour / human resources / manpower / staff development

planification des ressources humaines
personnel / human resources planning

planification des ressources humaines dans l'entreprise
company manpower planning, personnel planning at establishment level

relations humaines
interpersonal relations

ressources humaines
manpower, human capital / resources

ressources humaines disponibles
human resources supply

sciences humaines
humanistic studies, humanities

service des ressources humaines
personnel department

spécialistes des sciences sociales et humaines [CITP-1988 (244)]
social science and related professionals [ISCO-1988 (244)]

valorisation des ressources humaines
human resources / manpower / staff development

HUMANITAIRE
capital des services humanitaires
human overhead capital

raisons humanitaires
humanitarian reasons; compassionate circumstances

HYGIÈNE
hygiene; personal care; health; sanitation

amélioration de la sécurité et de l'hygiène du travail
improvement in safety and health conditions at work

assistante d'hygiène scolaire
school nurse

Comité d'hygiène, de sécurité et des conditions de travail (Fr.)
Health and Safety at Work Committee

comité d'hygiène et de sécurité
health and safety / safety and health committee

consultation d'hygiène mentale infantile
child mental health clinic

habitudes d'hygiène
health habits / practices

hygiène dentaire
dental health

hygiène de l'environnement
environmental health

hygiène industrielle
industrial health (and safety), occupational health and safety, occupational hygiene

hygiène infantile
child health

hygiène du milieu
environmental health

hygiène de la nutrition
nutritional health

hygiène professionnelle
occupational health

hygiène publique
public health

hygiène et santé individuelles
personal health

hygiène scolaire
school health; health education

hygiène et sécurité
health and safety

hygiène et sécurité du travail
industrial / occupational health and safety

hygiène et sécurité sur le lieu de travail / au travail
health and safety at work

hygiène sociale
preventive medicine and social welfare

hygiène du travail
industrial / occupational health

niveau d'hygiène
sanitation level

règles d'hygiène
health practices

responsable de l'hygiène et de la sécurité
(health and) safety officer

sécurité et hygiène (du travail)
safety and health (at work)

service d'hygiène et d'aide sociale
health and social welfare service

service de visiteuses d'hygiène
health visiting service

soins d'hygiène et de confort
basic nursing care

visiteuse d'hygiène
health visitor

HYPOTHÉCAIRE
crédit hypothécaire
mortgage

prestation complémentaire pour inté-rêts hypothécaires (Irel.)
mortgage interest supplement

rente hypothécaire
reverse mortgage

HYPOTHÈQUE
mortgage

hypothèque légale
statutory charge

HYPOTHÈSE
hypothèse nulle
null hypothesis

hypothèse travailleur découragé
discouraged worker hypothesis

hypothèse travailleur supplémentaire
additional worker hypothesis

HYSTÉRÈSE
hysteresis

ILLÉGAL
absence illégale
absence without leave

grève illégale
unlawful strike

ILLÉGITIME
enfant illégitime
illegitimate child, child born out of
wedlock

union illégitime
illegitimate union

ILLETTRÉ
illiterate

ILLETTRISME
(functional) illiteracy

campagne contre l'illettrisme
literacy campaign

ILLICITE
grève illicite
illegal strike

immigration illicite
illegal immigration

motif illicite de discrimination
prohibited ground of discrimination

travail illicite
irregular employment, illegal work

ILLIMITÉ
grève illimitée
indefinite strike

IMMATÉRIEL
dommage immatériel
intangible loss

IMMATRICULATION
registration

carte d'immatriculation du salarié
employee registration card

durée d'immatriculation (Lux.)
period of membership

immatriculation à l'assurance sociale
social insurance registration

numéro d'immatriculation
identification / registration number;
insurance number

période d'immatriculation (Lux.)
period of membership

IMMATRICULÉ
infirmière immatriculée
registered nurse

IMMÉDIAT
indemnisation immédiate
immediate payment

licenciement / renvoi immédiat
dismissal without notice, immediate /
summary dismissal

IMMERGÉ
économie immergée
black / hidden / informal / moonlight /
shadow / submerged / twilight /
underground / grey / invisible economy

IMMEUBLE
building; block of flats, tenement house

gardien d'immeuble
caretaker

immeuble (à usage) locatif
rental house, tenement

IMMIGRANT
immigrant; incomer

immigrant de courte durée
short-term immigrant

immigrant de longue durée
long-term immigrant

IMMIGRATION
immigration

contingent d'immigration
immigration quota

immigration clandestine
unauthorised / illegal immigration

immigration illicite
illegal immigration

issu de l'immigration
from immigrant origin

pays d'immigration
immigration country

IMMIGRÉ
immigrant

envoi de fonds des travailleurs immi-grés
workers' remittance

immigré clandestin (USA)
illegal migrant / alien

immigré de la deuxième génération
second-generation immigrant

main-d'oeuvre immigrée
immigrant labour / workers

travailleur immigré
migrant / immigrant worker

travailleur immigré temporaire
temporary immigrant / migrant worker;
(occ.) guest worker

IMMOBILIER (adj.)
biens immobiliers
real estate / property

conjoncture immobilière
housing trends

crédit immobilier
mortgage

ensemble immobilier
housing project / estate

parc immobilier
housing stock

précompte immobilier (Belg.)
property tax deduction

propriété immobilière
real estate / property

société d'épargne et de financement immobilier
(occ.) building society

IMMOBILIER (n.)
real estate; property; property / real-estate
business

IMMUNITÉ
immunité de fonctions
immunity by virtue of one's office

levée de l'immunité
waiver of immunity

IMPARTI
délai imparti
prescribed time-limit

IMPARTIAL
pratique d'emploi impartiale
neutral / objective employment practice

IMPAYÉ
unpaid; (pl.) outstanding payments

cotisations impayées
outstanding contributions

prêt impayé
outstanding loan

IMPÉRATIF (adj.)
mandatory; binding

délai impératif
strict time-limit

règle impérative
mandatory rule

IMPÉRATIF (n.)
requirement; demand; necessity

IMPÉRITIE
incompetence, inefficiency

IMPLAÇABLE (n.)
allocation aux implaçables
unemployability allowance

IMPLANTATION
settlement; siting

implantation d'entreprises
industrial settlement

implantations à l'étranger / étrangères
(occ.) establishment trade

implantation syndicale
union density

IMPLICITE
licenciement implicite
(occ.) constructive discharge / dismissal

IMPONDÉRABLE (n.)
intangible factor

IMPORTANCE
importance des effectifs
manning / staffing level

importance numérique
strength

prestation en nature de grande importance
major / substantial benefit in kind

IMPOSABLE
liable to tax(ation), taxable; chargeable

déductible du revenu imposable
tax(-)deductible

imposable (non)
tax-free

personne imposable
taxpayer

revenu imposable
assessed / assessable / taxable income

revenu non imposable
tax-free income

salaire de base maximal imposable
maximum taxable wage rate

IMPOSÉ
imposé à la source
taxed at source

tarif imposé
set rate

IMPOSER
imposer aucune condition de stage (n')
to impose no qualifying period

imposer à la source
to tax at source

IMPOSITION
taxation; (tax) assessment; enforcement

année d'imposition
assessment year, year of assessment,
(income) tax year, taxable year

barème d'imposition
tax rate / schedule

base d'imposition
tax base

établissement des rôles d'imposition
tax assessment

exercice d'imposition
assessment year, year of assessment

imposition forfaitaire
presumptive taxation

mode d'imposition
taxation method

niveau d'imposition
level of taxation

plafond d'imposition
(tax) assessment ceiling

première tranche d'imposition
basic rate tax

rôle d'imposition
tax roll

seuil d'imposition
tax threshold

taux effectif d'imposition sur le revenu
real income tax rate

taux d'imposition marginal
marginal rate of tax, marginal tax rate

taux marginaux d'imposition effectifs
marginal effective tax rates (METR)

tranche d'imposition
tax bracket

tranche d'imposition inférieure
lower income bracket

tranche d'imposition supérieure
upper income bracket

tranche supérieure d'imposition
higher tax bracket

IMPOSSIBILITÉ
allocation d'impossibilité d'emploi,
supplément pour impossibilité de se
procurer un emploi
unemployability allowance / supplement
(UK)

IMPÔT
tax; levy; charge; taxation; duty

abattement d'impôts
tax allowance / reduction

allégement d'impôts
tax mitigation / relief / rebate / reduction;
tax subsidy

assiette de l'impôt
tax(able) base, basis of taxation

assujetti à l'impôt
subject to tax(ation), taxable

assujetti à l'impôt sur le revenu
subject to income tax(ation)

assujettissement à l'impôt
tax liability

augmentation d'impôts
tax increase

calculer l'impôt sur le revenu
to assess income tax

centre des impôts
local tax office

code des impôts
tax law

crédit d'impôt
tax credit

crédit d'impôt relatif à l'apprentissage (Fr.)
tax credit for apprenticeship

crédit d'impôt (aux entreprises) en faveur de l'emploi / pour la création d'emplois / à l'emploi
employment tax credit (Can.); tax credit
for providing employment

crédit d'impôt pour enfant (Can.)
child tax credit

crédit d'impôt-formation (Fr.)
training levy / tax credit

crédit d'impôt au titre des revenus du travail (USA)
earned income tax credit

déclaration d'impôts
tax return

déclaration de l'impôt sur le revenu
income tax return / form

déductible des impôts
tax(-)deductible

déduction d'impôt pour enfant (UK)
child relief

déduction d'impôt pour vieillesse (UK)
age relief

dégressivité de l'impôt
regressive tax

dégrèvement d'impôts
tax rebate / relief / reduction

déterminer le montant de l'impôt sur le revenu
to assess income tax

évaluation de l'impôt
tax assessment

exempt d'impôts
tax-free

exonération d'impôt
tax exemption

exonéré d'impôt
exempt from tax / taxation, tax-free

feuille d'impôt
tax form

financement par l'impôt
tax financing

gain après impôt
take-home pay

impôt sur les bénéfices
profit tax

impôt sur les bénéfices des sociétés
tax on corporate profits

impôt sur le chiffre d'affaires
turnover tax

impôt dégressif
degressive tax

impôt déguisé
hidden tax

impôt direct
direct tax; (pl.) direct taxation

impôt foncier
land / property tax

impôt-formation
training levy

impôt sur la fortune
wealth / property tax

impôt indirect
indirect tax; (pl.) indirect taxation

impôt local
community charge; rate (UK); poll tax (UK)

impôt sur la masse des salaires / salariale
payroll tax

impôt négatif
negative tax, tax credit system

impôt de progrès social
social development tax

impôt progressif
graded / graduated tax

impôt progressif sur le revenu
graduated / progressive income tax

impôt proportionnel
proportional tax

impôt réel
property tax

impôt sur le revenu
income tax

impôt sur les revenus des personnes physiques (Fr.)
personal income tax

impôt sur le revenu progressif / fondé sur la progressivité
graduated / progressive income tax

impôt sur les salaires
payroll tax

impôt de sécurité sociale des travailleurs indépendants
self-employment social security tax

impôt sur les sociétés
corporate tax

impôt de solidarité
solidarity tax

impôt prélevé / retenu à la source
tax deducted at source, pay-as-you-earn (PAYE) tax, withholding tax

impôt spécial
special tax

impôts et taxes
taxes and dues

impôt par tranches
graduated tax (rate)

impôt des travailleurs indépendants
self-employment tax

majoration d'impôts
tax increase

minoration d'impôts
tax reduction

net d'impôts
tax-free

passible de l'impôt
liable to tax

perception des impôts
tax(-)collection

produit de l'impôt
tax proceeds / receipt

progressivité de l'impôt sur le revenu
graduated / progressive income tax

rappel d'impôt(s)
back tax(es)

recouvrement des impôts
tax collection

réduction d'impôts
tax abatement / concession / cut /
reduction

rémunération après impôts
after-tax pay

revenus exonérés d'impôts
tax-free income

revenu de l'impôt
tax yield

salaire après impôt
take-home / after-tax pay

situation devant l'impôt
tax status

soumis à l'impôt
taxable

IMPOTENCE
impotence fonctionnelle
functional impairment / disability

IMPOTENT
disabled, invalid

**allocation pour personnes impotentes
(UK)**
mobility allowance

IMPRÉCIS
contrat à durée déterminée à terme
imprécis (Fr.)
unspecified fixed-term contract

IMPRÉVU (n.)
allocation pour imprévus
contingencies allowance

IMPRIMÉ (n.)
printed form; leaflet

IMPROMPTU
visite impromptue
(occ.) cold call

IMPROPRE
unsuitable; unfit

IMPUTABILITÉ
présomption d'imputabilité
presumption of responsibility / of liability

IMPUTABLE
chargeable

**imputable à l'exercice de fonctions
officielles**
attributable to the performance of official
duties

imputable au service
service-incurred

imputable au service (non)
non-service connected

IMPUTÉ
production imputée de services d'assurance-dommages
imputed service charge for casualty
insurance

**production imputée de services d'assu-
rance-vie**
imputed service charge for life insurance

production imputée de services de caisses de pension
imputed service charge for pension funds

INACTIF (adj.)
not in / out of the labour force; inactive; without employment

population (économiquement) inactive
non working / unoccupied population, persons not in the labour force, non-labour force, economically inactive population

INACTIF (n.)
non-labour force participant; (pl.) persons not in the labour force; non-labour force; non working population

poids des inactifs
dependency ratio

rapport inactifs/actifs
dependency / support ratio, rate of dependency

INACTIVITÉ
inactivité forcée
enforced idleness

taux d'inactivité
inactivity rate

INADAPTATION
maladjustment

INADAPTÉ (adj.)
maladjusted

enfance inadaptée
maladjusted children

enfant inadapté
maladjusted child

enfant inadapté physique
physically handicapped child

enfant mentalement inadapté
mentally handicapped child

INADAPTÉ (n.)
inadapté social
social misfit; socially maladjusted / inadequate

INADÉQUAT
inadequate

INADÉQUATION
mismatch; inadequacy

chômage d'inadéquation
mismatch unemployment

inadéquation géographique
regional mismatch

inadéquation entre offres et demandes d'emploi
job mismatch

inadéquation de l'offre et de la demande de travail
(occ.) labour market mismatch

inadéquation des qualifications
skill mismatch

INADMISSIBILITÉ
ineligibility; inadmissibility; disqualification

période d'inadmissibilité
period of disqualification

INAMOVIBILITÉ
irremovability; tenure; absolute security of office

INAPPROPRIÉ
unsuitable, inadequate

INAPTE
unfit; maladjusted

inapte à l'emploi
unfit for employment; unemployable

inapte au service
unfit for service

inapte au travail
incapable for / of work; unfit for work;
not able / unable to work

INAPTITUDE
inability, incapacity

inaptitude à l'emploi
unfitness for employment;
unemployability

inaptitude au travail
inability to work, incapacity for / to work,
unfitness for work

INCAPABLE
incapable, incompetent; (jur.) incapacitated

**incapable de subvenir à ses (propres)
besoins**
incapable of self-support

incapable de travailler
incapable of working, not able / unable to
work; (occ.) unemployable

INCAPACITÉ
incapacity; disability; handicap; disablement

**allocation d'incapacité par suite d'un
accident du travail (UK)**
industrial injury disability benefit

allocation pour / d'incapacité grave
severe disablement allowance

**allocation pour incapacité de travail
(UK)**
disablement benefit

atteint d'incapacité partielle
partially incapacitated

certificat d'incapacité de travail
certificate of incapacity for work

**Commission d'évaluation des incapa-
cités (Sp.)**
Incapacity Assessment Board

degré d'incapacité (de travail)
degree of incapacity / of disablement

incapacité absolue
absolute disablement

incapacité (de travail) définitive
permanent incapacity / disablement

incapacité fonctionnelle
functional impairment / disability

incapacité de gain
earning incapacity

incapacité grave
major / severe disability

incapacité initiale
initial incapacity

incapacité légère
minor disability

incapacité mentale
mental disability / disablement / infirmity
/ impairment / handicap

incapacités multiples
multiple / several disabilities

incapacité (de travail) partielle
partial disablement / incapacity

**incapacité (de travail) partielle perma-
nente**
permanent partial incapacity / disablement

incapacité (de travail) permanente
permanent incapacity /disablement

incapacité physique
physical disability / disablement /
incapacity

incapacité professionnelle
incapacity for work in one's profession;
occupational invalidity / disablement,
vocational disablement

incapacité prolongée
prolonged / long-term disability

incapacité résiduelle
residual disability

incapacité sensorielle
sensory disability

incapacité stabilisée
arrested incapacity

incapacité (de travail) temporaire
short-term / temporary disablement /
incapacity

incapacité (de travail) totale
total / absolute disablement, total
incapacity

incapacité de travail
disablement / incapacitation / disability
for work, industrial / occupational /
vocational disablement, working disability, working / vocational incapacity,
inability to work, incapacity for / to work,
unfitness for work

incapacité de travail primaire (Belg.)
primary incapacity for work

incapacité de travailler (dans l')
unfit for work, not able / unable to work

indemnité d'incapacité
disability payment / gratuity

indemnité pour incapacité permanente
permanent disability payment;
permanency award (USA)

jour d'incapacité
day of incapacity

**personne souffrant d'une incapacité
grave**
seriously disabled person

prestation d'incapacité (UK)
disablement benefit

rente d'incapacité
disablement / disability pension

rente d'incapacité permanente
permanent disability pension

taux d'incapacité
degree of incapacity / of disablement

travailleur atteint d'incapacité
disabled worker

INCHANGÉ
rémunération inchangée en cas d'absence
pay not affected by absence

INCENDIE
certificat de conformité des moyens de
sécurité incendie
fire certificate

INCESSIBILITÉ
incessibilité des droits
non-transferability of rights

incessibilité de pension de vieillesse
non-transferability of old age pension

INCIDENCE
incidence; effect, impact

incidence sur les années-personnes
person-year impact

incidence du chômage
incidence of unemployment

incidence sur les coûts (sans)
cost-neutral

incidence sur l'emploi
employment effect / impact

incidence sur les revenus
income effect

taux d'incidence
incidence rate

INCITANT (n.)
inducement

INCITATION
inducement; incentive

incitation financière
financial incentive

incitation fiscale
tax incentive

mesure d'incitation
incentive (measure)

mesure d'incitation à l'emploi
employment incentive / stimulus; (occ.)
in-work benefit

mesure d'incitation à l'étude des langues
language incentive

mesure d'incitation au travail / à l'exercice d'une activité professionnelle
(occ.) in-work benefit

prime d'incitation
incentive bonus

programme d'incitation
incentive programme

système d'incitation
incentive scheme

INCOMBANT
charges incombant à ...
costs to be borne by ...

INCOMMODITÉ
allocation d'incommodité (Finl.)
inconvenience allowance

INCOMPATIBILITÉ
incompatibilité professionnelle
professional disqualification

INCOMPÉTENCE
incapability; incompetence; inefficiency

incompétence caractérisée
gross incompetence

INCONDITIONNEL
obligation inconditionnelle
absolute liability

INCONDUITE
misconduct

INCORPORATION
induction

INCURABILITÉ
incurability, incurableness; (occ.) intractability

INCURABLE
incurable; untreatable

malade incurable
terminally ill

INCURIE
incompetence, inefficiency, negligence, malpractice

INDÉFINI
engagement pour une durée indéfinie
indefinite appointment

engagement à titre temporaire pour une durée indéfinie
temporary indefinite appointment

nomination pour une durée indéfinie
appointment of indefinite duration

INDÉLICATESSE
misconduct

INDEMNE
uninjured

INDEMNISATION
compensation; payment

allocation prévue par le régime ordinaire d'indemnisation
(occ.) standard benefit

allocation prévue par les régimes spéciaux d'indemnisation
(occ.) special benefit

barème d'indemnisation
scale of compensation

clause de double indemnisation
double indemnity (clause)

Commission d'indemnisation (Austr.)
Compensation Board

demande d'indemnisation
claim for compensation

**demande d'indemnisation pour acci-
dent du travail**
accident claim, workmen's compensation
claim

différé d'indemnisation (Fr.)
waiting period

double indemnisation
double indemnity

droit à indemnisation
right to (receive) compensation

durée de l'indemnisation du chômage
duration of unemployment benefits

**fondé à réclamer une indemnisation
pour perte de salaire (être)**
to be entitled to claim restitution of lost
salary / wage / earnings

**fonds d'indemnisation des licencie-
ments économiques / des travailleurs
licenciés (pour raisons économiques)**
redundancy fund

**indemnisation pour un / des ac-
cident(s)**
accident compensation

indemnisation des accidents du travail
worker's compensation (for industrial
injury)

indemnisation d'adaptation
adjustment compensation

**indemnisation pour atteinte à l'inté-
grité (Switz.)**
allowance for diminished faculty

indemnisation du chômage
unemployment compensation

indemnisation pour chômage partiel
short-time working compensation

indemnisation de départ anticipé
compensation for loss of office

indemnisation immédiate
immediate payment

indemnisation de / pour la perte de gain
compensation for loss of earnings,
earnings replacement / compensation

indemnisation viagère de départ
annuity for withdrawal from work

période d'indemnisation du chômage
period for which a claimant receives
unemployment benefits

régime d'indemnisation
compensation scheme; benefit plan

**régime d'indemnisation en cas d'acci-
dent ou de maladie**
compensation scheme for industrial
injuries

régime d'indemnisation du chômage
unemployment compensation scheme

supplément d'indemnisation
additional compensation

tarif d'indemnisation
rate of compensation

INDEMNISÉ
chômeur indemnisé
unemployed (person) on benefit

demander à être indemnisé
to claim compensation

maladie professionnelle indemnisée
occupational disease for which the benefit
has been awarded

**temps réduit indemnisé longue durée
(Fr.)**
short-time work on benefit for a long
period

INDEMNISER
to compensate, to grant compensation (for
damages)

INDEMNITÉ
allowance, benefit; grant; compensation;
indemnity; gratuity; money; extra pay

accorder / allouer une indemnité
to award / to grant compensation (for
damages)

attribution d'indemnités de maladie
provision of sickness benefit(s)

barème des indemnités
allowance table

barème des indemnités de poste
schedule of post adjustments

bureau de paiement des indemnités de chômage
unemployment benefit (paying) office

déclaration de situation de famille et demande d'indemnités pour charges de famille
family status report and request for payment of dependency allowances

droit à (une) indemnité
claim / allowance entitlement, entitlement / benefit claim

indemnité accessoire
subsidiary / supplementary allowance

indemnité (en cas) d'accident
compensation for injuries / for accident; accident allowance (Hung.)

indemnité d'accident / pour accident de travail
workmen's compensation (award / benefit); employment / industrial injury benefit; injury benefit (UK, Irel., Malta)

indemnité d'affectation
assignment allowance

indemnité d'allaitement
nursing benefit / allowance

indemnité d'ancienneté
seniority allowance

indemnité annuelle de départ
annuity for withdrawal from work

indemnité d'assurance
insurance benefit

indemnité d'attente
tideover allowance

indemnité de base
basic allowance

indemnité de cessation d'emploi / de cessation de fonctions / de cessation de service / lors de la cessation de service / versée à la cessaition de service
separation / terminal / severance pay / payment / benefit, allowance for separation; (occ.) completion bonus

indemnité pour charge de famille
dependency / dependent allowance; (pl.) family allowances; child benefit allowances (UK)

indemnité de cherté de vie
cost-of-living allowance / compensation / adjustment

indemnité de chômage
unemployment allowance / benefit; (occ.) dole

indemnité de chômage partiel
short-time working allowance

indemnité de compensation (Pol.)
compensatory benefit

indemnité compensatoire / compensatrice
compensatory / equalisation allowance; payment in lieu

indemnité compensatrice de congés payés
compensation in lieu of paid holidays, holidays paid in lieu

indemnité compensatrice de préavis
compensation in lieu of notice, pay / payment in lieu of notice

indemnité de congé de maternité sans solde (Austr.)
unpaid maternity leave allowance

indemnité de congés payés
compensation for holiday leave

indemnité pour décès
death, dependency and indemnity compensation

indemnité de déménagement
moving / removal / relocation allowance

indemnité de départ
severance pay / payment

indemnité de déplacement
travel(ling) / mileage allowance, mileage fee

indemnité différentielle
compensatory / equalisation allowance; hardship allowance

indemnité pour difficultés (exception-nelles) d'existence
hardship pay

indemnité d'éducation
education allowance

indemnité d'éloignement
foreign service (residence) allowance

indemnité équitable
fair compensation

indemnité en espèces
compensation in cash

indemnité d'expatriation
expatriation allowance, overseas pre-mium / allowance

indemnité de fin de carrière
end-of-service payment

indemnité de fin de contrat
end-of-contract payment

indemnité de fin d'emploi
separation / terminal / severance pay / payment / benefit, allowance for separation; (occ.) completion bonus

indemnité de fin de mission
end-of-assignment payment

indemnité de fonction
post / duty allowance, per diem duty; official expenditure allowance

indemnité de fonctions supplémentai-res
extra-duty pay

indemnité forfaitaire
flat(-rate) / one-off / lump-sum allo-wance, lump-sum / capital compensation / grant, lump sum

indemnité forfaitaire pour veuve
widow's (lump sum) payment, widow's grant

indemnité pour frais
expenditure allowance

indemnité pour frais d'études
education(al) grant

indemnité pour / de frais funéraires
funeral / death grant

indemnité de frais professionnels
professional expenditure allowance

indemnité de frais de service
official expenditure allowance

indemnité funéraire
funeral benefit

indemnité globale
lump-sum allowance

indemnité accordée à titre gracieux
ex gratia payment

indemnité d'habillement
clothing allowance; (occ.) allowance for wear and tear (of clothing)

indemnité hebdomadaire
allowance per week

indemnité d'hébergement
accommodation allowance

indemnité horokilométrique
mileage fee / allowance

indemnité d'incapacité
disability payment / gratuity

indemnité pour incapacité permanente
permanent disability payment, permanency award (USA)

indemnité d'installation
installation / settling-in grant

indemnité d'intégrité (Austr.)
integrity compensation

indemnité pour intempéries
bad weather allowance / payment

indemnité d'invalidité
disability payment / gratuity

indemnité d'invalidité pour accident du travail (ou maladie professionnelle)
industrial disablement payment / gratuity

indemnité pour invalidité permanente
permanent disability payment, permanency award (USA)

indemnité journalière
daily allowance, daily benefit

indemnité journalière de maladie
daily sickness benefit

indemnité journalière de repos
daily rest allowance

indemnité journalière de subsistance
daily subsistence / living allowance; per diem

indemnité journalière de subsistance au taux spécial
special rate of daily subsistence allowance

indemnité kilométrique
mileage fee / allowance

indemnités légales de maladie (UK)
statutory sick pay

indemnités légales de maternité (UK)
statutory maternity pay

indemnité de licenciement
dismissal indemnity / payment / compensation, termination indemnity, severance pay / payment

indemnité de licenciement pour cause / raison économique
redundancy benefit / payment

indemnité de logement
rent(al) allowance / subsidy, housing allowance / grant

indemnité de maladie
sickness allowance / benefit; sick pay

indemnités maladie / accident du travail pour travailleurs indépendants
occupational sick pay for self-employed workers

indemnité de maladie versée en espèces
cash sickness benefit

indemnité pour manque à gagner
compensation for loss of wages / earnings

indemnité de naissance
birth grant

indemnité de non-titulaire
service benefit

indemnité de nuit
night shift allowance

indemnité de panier
meal(s) allowance

indemnité partielle
partial compensation

indemnité pécuniaire
cash benefit

indemnités périodiques
regular benefits

indemnité pour personne à charge
dependent allowance

indemnité personnelle provisoire
personal transitional allowance

indemnité de / pour perte d'emploi
indemnity for loss of job; redundancy payment, severance pay(ment)

indemnité pour perte de salaire
compensation for loss of wage(s)

indemnité pharmaceutique (Austr.)
pharmaceutical allowance

indemnité de poste
assignment allowance; post adjustment (allowance)

indemnité de préavis
compensation in lieu of notice

indemnité prénatale
allowance for pregnant women

indemnités et prestations
allowances and benefits

indemnité pour privation de jouissance
compensation for loss of property

indemnité provisionnelle
provisional compensation

indemnité de rapatriement
repatriation allowance

indemnité de réadaptation
retraining (Hung.) / rehabilitation (Pol.)
allowance

indemnité sans reconnaissance de responsabilité
without prejudice payment

indemnité de redémarrage (Austr.)
new start allowance

indemnité de réinstallation
reestablishment / resettlement allowance

indemnité de renvoi
dismissal compensation

indemnité de réparation
rehabilitation allowance

indemnité de repas
meal(s) allowance

indemnité de représentation
entertainment / hospitality allowance

indemnité de résidence
residence allowance

indemnité de responsabilité
liability allowance

indemnité de salaire
wage replacement / compensation

indemnité se substituant au salaire
compensation in lieu of salary

indemnité de séjour
subsistence / living allowance

indemnité de séparation
separation allowance

indemnité de soins aux tuberculeux
tuberculosis allowance

indemnité spéciale de déplacement
special travel allowance

indemnité de subsistance
subsistence allowance / payment,
maintenance allowance; stipend

indemnité de traitement
wage / salary replacement

indemnité de transport
travel allowance

indemnité de vacances
vacation allowance

indemnité vestimentaire
clothing allowance

indemnité de veuve
widow's (lump sum) payment, widow's
grant

indemnité de vie chère
cost-of-living allowance / compensation /
adjustment

juste indemnité
fair / reasonable compensation

justes indemnités en cas de maladie, accident ou de décès
reasonable compensation in the event of
illness, accident or death

moyenne pondérée des indemnités de poste
weighted average of post adjustments

octroi d'une indemnité
award of compensation

percevoir des indemnités de chômage
to collect unemployment compensation, to
draw unemployment benefit, to live on
unemployment benefit

relèvement de l'indemnité de poste
increase of post adjustment

système des indemnités de poste
post adjustment system

système de paiement / de versement des indemnités
allowance payment system

taux des indemnités
allowance rate, rate of allowances

toucher des indemnités de chômage
to draw unemployment benefit, to live on
unemployment benefit

traitements et indemnités
salaries and allowances

versement d'indemnités
compensation payment, payment of
benefits / allowances

INDÉPENDANCE
independence; self-reliance

INDÉPENDANT (adj.)
activité indépendante
self-employment

agriculteur indépendant
self-employed farmer

collaborateur indépendant
freelance (worker)

**contrat passé avec un travailleur indé-
pendant**
freelance contract

**cotisation sociale des travailleurs
indépendants**
self-employment insurance contribution

début d'une activité indépendante
entry into self-employment

entrepreneur indépendant
self-employed entrepreneur, independent
contractor

financièrement indépendant
(occ.) self-supporting

**impôt de sécurité sociale des travail-
leurs indépendants**
self-employment social security tax

impôt des travailleurs indépendants
self-employment tax

**indemnités maladie / accident du
travail pour travailleurs indépendants**
occupational sick pay for self-employed
workers

**pension des travailleurs indépendants
(Finl.)**
self-employed persons' pension

professions indépendantes (les)
professions (the)

syndicat indépendant
independent / non-affiliated (trade) union

travail indépendant
self-employment

**travailler comme collaborateur indé-
pendant**
to work freelance

travailleur indépendant
self-employed (earner / worker / person);
freelance / independent / own-account
worker, worker on own account

travailleur indépendant permanent
permanent self-employed

INDÉPENDANT (n.)
independent, self-reliant; self-employed;
sole trader; (pl.) (n.) freelance personnel

travailler comme indépendant
to work freelance

INDÉTERMINÉ
contrat (de travail) à durée indéterminée
indefinite / open-ended (employment/
work), indefinite appointment

emploi de / à durée indéterminée
permanent job / employment, indefinite
employment

**nomination pour une période indéter-
minée**
indeterminate appointment

INDEXATION
indexing, indexation index-linking; adjustment based on an index figure

clause d'indexation
escalation / escalator clause, indexing /
indexation clause, pegging clause

indexation sur le / au titre du coût de la vie
cost-of-living adjustment, adjustment to cost of living

indexation des salaires / salariale
wage indexation

indexation des salaires sur l'inflation
indexing of wages to inflation

saut d'indexation
not applied index-adjustment

système d'indexation des salaires
pay indexation system

INDEXÉ
index-linked, index-tied, indexed

indexé sur l'inflation
geared to inflation

pension indexée
indexed / (occ.) dynamised / pegged pension

pension de retraite indexée
index-linked pension

rémunération / salaire indexé(e)
index-tied wage, indexed pay

salaires indexés sur l'inflation
wages geared to inflation

INDEXER
to index, to peg

INDICATEUR
indicator

indicateur de base
basic indicator

indicateur conjoncturel
business indicator

indicateur du développement humain
human development index

indicateur de dispersion des salaires
(occ.) compa-ratio

indicateur de l'enseignement
educational indicator

indicateur de l'état de santé
health status indicator

indicateur du niveau de vie
standard-of-living indicator

indicateur de performance
performance indicator

indicateur-repère d'excédent de main-d'oeuvre
benchmark (labour / manpower) surplus indicator

indicateur-repère de pénurie de main-d'oeuvre
benchmark (labour / manpower) shortage indicator

indicateur de résultat
performance indicator

indicateur social
social indicator; (pl.) (occ.) key personnel statistical data

indicateur socio-économique
socio-economic indicator

indicateur supplétif
proxy measure

indicateur synthétique
summary indicator / measure

INDICATIF
fourchette indicative
guideline range

INDICATION
indication contraire (sauf)
unless otherwise stated / specified

INDICE
index; rate, rating; evidence

indice d' / des ajustement(s)
post adjustment index

indice d'ajustement des pensions
pension adjustment index

indice courant des retraites (Ger.)
current pension value

indice du coût de l'emploi
employment cost index

indice du coût de la vie
cost-of-living index

indice de déclenchement
trigger index

indice des disparités socio-économiques
socio-economic disparity index

indice intervilles
place to place index

indice de malaise économique
(economic) discomfort index

indice pivot (Belg.)
reference index

indice des prix
price index

indice des prix à la consommation
consumer / retail price index

indice de référence
benchmark / reference index

indice révisé d'ajustement des pensions
revised pension adjustment index

indice des salaires
wage index

indice de satisfaction générale
general satisfaction rating

indice de seuil
threshold index

indice de stabilité du personnel
labour stability index

indice temporel
time-to-time index

point d'indice
index point

INDICIAIRE
valeurs indiciaires des traitements
(salary) scale relativities

INDIFFÉRENCE
seuil d'indifférence
range of indifference

INDIGENCE
poverty; destitution

certificat / déclaration d'indigence
certificate of poverty

état d'indigence
state of need

indigence (dans l')
in necessity

seuil de l'indigence
poverty line / threshold / level

totale indigence
absolute distress

INDIGENT
indigent, poor; destitute

aide aux indigents
poor relief

INDIQUÉ
suitable

INDIRECT
aide indirecte
indirect assistance

avantage social indirect
indirect (social) benefit

contribution indirecte
indirect tax

coût indirect
indirect cost

coûts salariaux indirects
indirect labour costs

emploi indirect
indirect employment

impôt indirect
indirect tax; (pl.) indirect taxation

main-d'oeuvre indirecte
non-production worker

salaire indirect
indirect wage / compensation

soins indirects
indirect care

système indirect de prestations médicales
indirect system / pattern of providing medical care

INDIRECTEMENT
pension de personnes indirectement à charge
secondary dependants' benefit

prestation pour personne indirectement à charge
secondary dependent's benefit

INDISPENSABLE
médicament indispensable
essential medicine / drug

personnel indispensable
key personnel

INDIVIDU
épanouissement de l'individu
self-development

soins aux individus
individual patient care

INDIVIDUALISÉ
crédit formation individualisé (CFI) (Fr.)
individualised training credit / loan scheme

horaire de travail individualisé
personalised hours of work, personalised working hours

INDIVIDUEL
individual, personal

abattement individuel
personal allowance

adhésion individuelle (à l'assurance)
individual insurance cover

assurance accidents individuelle
personal accident insurance

besoin individuel
individual need

capitalisation individuelle
individual funding

conciliation individuelle
individual conciliation

conflit individuel
individual dispute

congé individuel de formation (Fr.)
individual / personal training leave

congé individuel de formation pour les salariés (Fr.)
individual training leave for employees

contrat individuel de retraite
individual annuity policy

contrat individuel de travail
(occ.) indenture contract

contrat de louage de services individuels
individual service contract

disposition prise à titre individuel
private arrangement

dossier individuel
personal record / file

dossier individuel d'un salarié
employee file

entrepreneur individuel
sole trader; self-employed (person / worker)

entreprise individuelle
non-corporate / one-man business, (sole) proprietorship; (occ.) self-employment

formation individuelle
individual / one-to-one training

hygiène et santé individuelles
personal health

logement individuel
private / (occ.) single family dwelling

individuel (à titre)
on a personal basis

maison individuelle
private house

médiation individuelle
individual conciliation

moyens de protection individuelle
body / individual protection equipment

orientation individuelle
individual counselling

pension individuelle anticipée (Finl.)
individual early pension

prestation individuelle
personal benefit / allowance

programme de formation individuelle
individual training programme

recherche d'emploi individuelle
private job search

service préventif individuel
personal preventive service

service de santé individuel
personal health service

soins individuels
personal health care

traitement social individuel
individual social treatment

INDU
undue

charges indues
undue burden

cotisation indue
undue contribution

récupération de prestations indues
recovery of benefits which were not due

INDUIT
avantage induit
induced benefit

chômage induit
induced unemployment

effets induits
externalities

emploi induit
induced job

INDUSTRIALISATION
industrialisation

INDUSTRIE
industry; secondary sector; sector

branche de l'industrie
industrial sector

débrayage dans l'industrie
industrial stoppage

industrie agricole
farming industry

industrie agro-alimentaire
food and agriculture industry; agri-food
industry

industrie en amont
(occ.) supplying sector

industrie artisanale
cottage industry; (pl.) cottage industries /
crafts

industrie de base
basic / staple industry

industrie du bâtiment
building industry / trade, construction
industry

industrie de biens d'équipement
capital goods industry

industrie délocalisée
footlose / offshore industry

industrie en difficulté
ailing industry

industrie à domicile
home(-based) industry, home craft;
cottage industry

industrie en expansion
growth / sunrise industry

industries extractives
mining (industries / activities)

industries familiales
cottage industries / crafts

**industrie à forte concentration de main-
d'oeuvre / à forte intensité de travail**
labour-intensive industry

industrie de haute technologie
high(-)technology industry

industrie houillère
coal(-mining) industry

industrie légère
light industry

industrie lourde
heavy / basic industry

industrie de main-d'oeuvre
labour industry

industrie à main-d'oeuvre importante
labour-intensive industry

industries manufacturières
manufacturing industries

industrie mécanique
engineering industry

industrie minière
mining industry

industrie mobile
(occ.) footloose industry

industrie en perte de vitesse
sunset / ailing industry

industrie de pointe
high(-)technology industry

industrie primaire
primary industry

**industries appliquant des procédés de
fabrication en continu**
flow process industries

**industrie productrice de biens d'équi-
pement**
capital goods industry

industrie relocalisée
migrant industry

industrie de services
service / tertiary industry

industrie du spectacle
entertainment industry; show business

industrie de transformation
processing / manufacturing industry

petite industrie
small-scale industries

**porter atteinte au libre exercice de
l'industrie et du travail**
to impair / to restrict the freedom of
industry and labour

salaires dans l'industrie
industrial wages

secteur de l'industrie
sector of industry; industrial sector

service social dans l'industrie
industrial welfare service

subvention à l'industrie
industrial incentive

travail dans l'industrie
industrial work

travailleur de l'industrie
industrial worker; (pl.) industrial staff

travailleurs des industries de base
(occ.) key workers

travailleurs salariés de l'industrie
employed persons in industry

INDUSTRIEL (adj.)
industrial

activité industrielle
industrial / business activity

conducteurs de chaînes de montage automatiques et de robots industriels [CITP-1988 (817)]
automated-assembly-line and industrial-robot operators [ISCO-1988 (817)]

emploi industriel
industrial employment

entreprise industrielle
industrial undertaking

hygiène industrielle
industrial health (and safety), occupational health and safety, occupational hygiene

ingénierie industrielle
industrial engineering

masse des salaires industriels
industrial payroll

population active industrielle
industrial population

professions industrielles et commerciales
industry and trade

recensement industriel
industrial census

reconversion / redéploiement industriel(le)
industrial redeployment

revenus industriels et commerciaux
income from business

secteur industriel
sector of industry; industrial sector

secteur industriel à forte croissance
high-growth industrial sector

site industriel
industrial site

stage préparatoire aux techniques industrielles
basic industrial skill course

stratégie industrielle orientée vers la satisfaction des besoins essentiels
basic needs-oriented industrial strategy

zone industrielle
development / enterprise zone; industrial estate

INDUSTRIEL (n.)
industrialist; manufacturer

INEFFICACITÉ
inefficiency

INEFFICIENCE
inefficience technique
technical inefficiency

inefficience-X
X-inefficiency

INÉGAL
traitement inégal
unequal treatment

INÉGALITÉ
inégalité des chances
opportunity gap

inégalité de salaires
wage disparity

inégalité de traitement
unequal treatment, (occ.) discrimination

INÉLASTICITÉ
rigidity

INÉLIGIBILITÉ
ineligibility

INEMPLOI
taux d'inemploi
non-employment rate

INEMPLOYÉ
main-d'oeuvre inemployée
slack labour

INÉQUITABLE
traitement inéquitable
unfair treatment

INERTIE
effet d'inertie
deadweight effect

INEXCUSABLE
faute inexcusable
gross negligence

INEXÉCUTION
inexécution des obligations de service
failure to discharge the duties attaching to
a post

INEXPERIMENTÉ
inexperienced

INFANTILE
centre de guidance infantile
child guidance centre / clinic

**centre de protection maternelle et
infantile**
maternity child welfare centre

consultation d'hygiène mentale infantile
child mental health clinic

consultations infantiles
child care / children's clinic

consultation de protection infantile
consulting centre for child health

fiche de santé infantile
child health card

guidance infantile
child guidance

hygiène infantile
child health

pornographie infantile
child pornography

protection infantile
child care / welfare

protection maternelle et infantile
maternal and child welfare

santé infantile de base
basic child health

santé maternelle et infantile
maternal and child health

service de consultations infantiles
child care / children's clinic

service de protection infantile
child / infant welfare service

**service de protection maternelle et
infantile**
maternal and child health service

INFECTIEUX
maladie infectieuse
infectious disease

INFÉRIEUR
lower

**certificat d'enseignement secondaire
inférieur (CESI)**
lower secondary education certificate

décile inférieur
lower decile

échelon inférieur
junior grade

**limite inférieure pour l'assiette des
cotisations de la catégorie n**
lower earnings limit of class n contributions

limite inférieure des gains
lower earnings level / limit

tranche d'imposition inférieure
lower income bracket

tranche inférieure des salaires (la)
lower paid (the)

INFIRME
handicapped, disabled, invalid, physically
disabled / handicapped, infirm; (pl.)
people with (physical) disabilities, the
disabled

**asile de vieillards, d'infirmes et de
nécessiteux**
home for the aged, infirm and needy

grand infirme
severely handicapped / disabled, seriously disabled person; (pl.) badly disabled (the)

infirme mental
mental(ly) deficient, mentally disabled

INFIRMERIE
infirmary; first-aid centre

INFIRMIER (adj.)
administration des soins infirmiers
provision of nursing care

enseignement infirmier
nursing education

exercice de la profession infirmière
nursing practice

personnel infirmier
nursing staff / personnel

personnel infirmier auxiliaire
auxiliary nursing personnel

pratique infirmière
nursing practice

prestations infirmières
(occ.) nursing

prestation de soins infirmiers
provision of nursing care

profession infirmière
nursing profession

professions intermédiaires de la médecine moderne (à l'exception du personnel infirmier) [ISCO-1988 (322)]
modern health associate professionals (except nursing) [ISCO-1988 (322)]

service infirmier
nursing service

service infirmier des collectivités
community health nursing service

service infirmier de santé publique
public health nursing service

service public de soins infirmiers
public health nursing service, district nursing service (UK)

service de soins infirmiers à domicile pour personnes âgées
home care nursing for the elderly

soins infirmiers
nursing (care)

soins infirmiers à domicile
home nursing, visiting nurse services

soins infirmiers intensifs
intensive nursing care

soins infirmiers aux malades mentaux
mental health nursing

soins infirmiers néonatals
neo-natal nursing

soins infirmiers de pédiatrie / pédiatriques
paediatric nursing

travaux infirmiers
nursing work

INFIRMIER / INFIRMIÈRE
nurse

assistant-infirmier / assistante-infirmière
nursing assistant

infirmière auxiliaire
nursing auxiliary

infirmière consultante
nurse consultant

infirmière diplômée
trained / registered nurse

infirmière à domicile
(occ.) community nurse

infirmière d'entreprise
occupational health nurse

infirmière immatriculée
registered nurse

infirmière libérale
private / agency nurse

infirmière monitrice
teaching nurse; (occ.) sister tutor

infirmière de nuit
night nurse

infirmière qualifiée
trained nurse

infirmière de santé publique
public health nurse

infirmier scolaire
school nurse

infirmière du secteur psychiatrique
psychiatric nurse

infirmière visiteuse
domiciliary / home / district nurse, health visitor

INFIRMITÉ
disability, handicap, disablement, infirmity, impairment functional impairment

infirmité grave
major / severe disability

infirmité mentale
mental disability / disablement / infirmity / impairment / handicap

infirmités multiples
several disabilities

infirmité permanente
permanent disablement / disability / invalidity, long-term disability

infirmité physique
physical handicap / disability / disablement / impairment / infirmity

infirmité professionnelle
occupational / vocational disablement

INFLATION
inflation

dilemme chômage-inflation
employment-inflation trade-off

indexation des salaires sur l'inflation
indexing of wages to inflation

inflation rampante
creeping inflation

inflation par les / des salaires
wage(-push) inflation

salaires indexés sur l'inflation
wages geared to inflation

taux de chômage non accélérateur de l'inflation
non accelerating inflation rate of unemployment (NAIRU)

INFLATIONNISTE
hausse inflationniste de salaires
wage inflation

spirale inflationniste
inflationary spiral

INFLUENCE
aire / zone d'influence
catchment area

INFOGÉRANCE
facilities management

INFORMATION
centre d'information et de coordination de l'action sociale
social work information and co-ordination centre

centre d'information et d'orientation (Fr.)
information and guidance centre

droit à l'information
information right

fiche d'information
information sheet

information sur les carrières
occupational / vocational information

informations personnelles
personal information / data

information sur les professions
occupational / vocational information

information professionnelle
vocational orientation

information en retour
feedback

opérateurs sur machines à traiter l'information [CITP-1968 (3-4)]
computing machine operators [ISCO-1968 (3-4)]

permanence d'accueil, d'information et d'orientation (PAIO) (Fr.)
reception, information and guidance office

rassembler / réunir des informations
to collect information / data

système d'information sanitaire
health information system

INFORMATIQUE (adj.)
pupitreurs et autres opérateurs de matériels informatiques [CITP-1988 (312)]
computer associate professionals [IS-CO-1988 (312)]

INFORMATIQUE (n.)
spécialistes de l'informatique [CITP-1988 (213)]
computing professionals [ISCO-1988 (213)]

INFORMATISÉ
orientation professionnelle informatisée
computerised vocational guidance

système informatisé de traitement des offres d'emploi
automated job order system

système d'orientation professionnelle informatisé
computer-based career orientation system

INFORMEL
secteur informel de l'économie
informal economy sector

INFRACTION
offence; failure to comply; departure from

auteur d'une infraction
offender

INFRASTRUCTURE
facilities; infrastructure; basic equipment / services

dépense d'infrastructure sociale
social overhead cost

infrastructure économique et sociale
economic and social infrastructure / facilities / overhead

infrastructure sanitaire
health infrastructure, health care (delivery) system

infrastructure sanitaire et sociale
health and welfare infrastructure

infrastructure sociale
social overhead / facilities / infrastructure

services d'infrastructure
(occ.) basic services

INGÉNIERIE
engineering

ingénierie industrielle
industrial engineering

ingénierie sociale
social engineering

INGÉNIEUR
ingénieur de chantier
site engineer

ingénieur du génie civil
civil engineer

ingénieur des méthodes
industrial engineer

ingénieur de sécurité (Ger.)
safety engineer

sciences de l'ingénieur
engineering sciences

INGÉNIEUR-CONSEIL
consultant engineer

ingénieur-conseil en organisation
management consultant

INGÉRENCE
interference

INGRAT
tâche ingrate
invidious task

travail ingrat
unrewarding work

INHUMATION
lieu d'inhumation
place of burial

ININTERROMPU
assurance ininterrompue
continued insurance

temps de présence ininterrompue au travail
(occ.) continuous employment

INITIAL
certificat initial
initial certificate

capital initial
seed capital

enseignement initial
initial education

formation initiale
basic education, initial training

formation professionnelle initiale
initial vocational training

formation professionnelle initiale agricole (Fr.)
initial agricultural vocational training

incapacité initiale
initial incapacity

lieu d'affectation initial
first duty station / assignment

rémunération initiale
starting salary

salaire initial
starting wage

INITIATION
induction, orientation, vestibule training

cours d'initiation professionnelle
induction training / course, beginners' course

initiation au monde du travail
introductory training; (occ.) career(s) education

initiation à la profession
pre-vocational training; vocational preparation

initiation aux techniques professionnelles
work-skill training

initiation au travail
pre-employment orientation, (job) induction; job training

initiation à la vie professionnelle
introductory training to working life

programme d'initiation
induction programme

programme d'initiation à l'arithmétique
numeracy programme

programme d'initiation des nouveaux employés
orientation programme for new employees

stage d'initiation
beginners' / introductory / induction course

stage d'initiation au travail
pre-employment course

stage d'initiation à la vie professionnelle (SIVP)
work experience programme

INITIATIVE
initiative, measure; enterprise

contrat initiative emploi
employment initiative contract

esprit d'initiative
initiative, entrepreneurial spirit, ressourcefulness

initiative créatrice d'emplois
employment-creation measure

initiative en faveur de l'emploi et de la formation
employment and training measure

initiative locale de création d'emplois (ILE)
local employment initiative, local initiative in promoting employment

initiative privée
voluntary effort

projet fondé sur l'initiative personnelle
self-help project / scheme

INJONCTION
injunction

injonction interlocutoire / provisoire
interim / interlocutory injunction

INJURIEUX
comportement injurieux
insulting behaviour

INJUSTICE
inequity

injustice criante / flagrante
gross injustice

injustice sociale
social inequality

INJUSTIFIABLE
retard injustifiable
unjustifiable delay

INJUSTIFIÉ
unjustified; unwarranted; undue

absence injustifiée
unexcused / unexcusable absence

INNOCUITÉ
innocuousness; harmlessness; safety

INOBSERVANCE
failure to observe / to comply

INOCCUPÉ
not working

INOPPORTUN
unsuitable

INSALUBRE
insanitary, unhealthy

allocation pour travaux insalubres et dangereux (Gr.)
unhealthy and dangerous work allowance

emploi / métier insalubre
unhealthy occupation

travail insalubre
unhealthy work

INSALUBRITÉ
poor sanitation

prime d'insalubrité
allowance for unhealthy working conditions

INSATISFACTION
insatisfaction professionnelle / au travail
job dissatisfaction

mobilité d'insatisfaction
dissatisfaction mobility

INSCRIPTION
admission, entry; registration; enrolment; posting

avis d'inscription à une formation
notice of referral to training

bulletin d'inscription
enrolment form

condition d'inscription
admission requirement

date limite d'inscription
application deadline

dossier d'inscription
enrolment form, registration file

droit d'inscription
enrolment / registration fee

formulaire d'inscription
application form

inscription au budget
apportionment

inscription conditionnelle à un stage
conditional referral to a course

inscription en vue d'un / pour un emploi
employment registration, registration for work / for employment

inscription à un programme
entry into a scheme

inscription provisoire
provisional registration

inscription du travailleur
worker registration

jour de l'inscription
intake day

nombre d'inscriptions
(occ.) enrolment

réglementation régissant l'inscription
admission rules

stage à inscription préétablie
scheduled intake course

taux d'inscription
enrolment rate

INSCRIRE
to register; to refer; to enrol, to enter

inscrire (se faire)
to enter

inscrire au budget
to charge to the budget, to apportion

inscrire au chômage (s')
to register as unemployed; to go on the dole

inscrire en formation / à un stage de formation
to refer for training

INSCRIT
registered; participant

chômeur inscrit
registered unemployed

demandeur d'emploi inscrit (comme tel)
registered job-seeker

effectifs inscrits
employees under contract

inscrit au chômage (être)
to be on the unemployment register

inscrit sur les états de paie
in pay status

inscrit maritime
seaman registered for service in the navy

inscrit au tableau d'avancement (être)
to be included in the promotion register

médecin inscrit au registre
registered practitioner

nombre d'élèves inscrits
(school) enrolment

nouvel inscrit à un programme
entrant into a scheme

patient inscrit
registered patient

personnel inscrit
employees on the payroll

poste vacant inscrit
vacancy recorded

(système de la) rémunération par malade inscrit
capitation(-fee) system

INSÉCURITÉ
insecurity

INSERTION
integration; activation (Denm.)

allocation d'insertion
integration allowance, starting benefit, unemployment benefit for young first-job seekers (Fr.), young first-job seekers' allowance (Fr.)

contrat d'insertion (Fr.)
integration contract

contrat d'insertion en alternance (Fr.)
employment contract facilitating integration into working life, sandwich-type integration contract

emploi d'insertion
(occ.) make-work job

formation de première insertion (Fr.)
initial integration training

insertion professionnelle
vocational integration; integration into employment; job entry

insertion sociale
social integration

insertion dans la vie active
integration into working life

organisme d'insertion socio-professionnelle (OISP) (Belg.)
social and vocational integration organisation / agency

plan de formation-insertion (Belg.)
employment-plus-training scheme

revenu minimum d'insertion (RMI)
minimum social income, guaranteed minimum income

salaire minimum d'insertion (Sp.)
minimum integration wage

stage d'insertion
work-experience job

stage d'insertion et de formation à l'emploi (Fr.)
employment integration and training course

stage d'insertion à la vie profession-nelle
integration to working life course

INSOUMISSION
insubordination; failure to report for duty

INSPECTEUR
inspector, supervisor

inspecteur des affaires sanitaires et sociales
health and sanitary inspector

inspecteur de l'enfance (Fr.)
child care inspector

inspecteurs d'immeubles, de sécurité, d'hygiène et de qualité [CITP-1988 (315)]
safety and quality inspectors [ISCO-1988 (315)]

inspecteurs de police judiciaire et détectives [CITP-1988 (345)]
police inspectors and detectives [IS-CO-1988 (345)]

inspecteur de salubrité / sanitaire
sanitary inspector

inspecteur de la santé et de l'assainis-sement
health and sanitary inspector

inspecteur du travail
labour inspector

médecin-inspecteur
medical inspector

médecin-inspecteur du travail
occupational health inspector

INSPECTION
inspection; supervision; inspectorate

inspection générale des affaires sociales
social affairs general inspectorate

inspection du lieu de travail
inspection of work surroundings

inspection sur le lieu de travail
on-site inspection

inspection sanitaire
sanitary inspection

inspection de la santé
health inspectorate

inspection du travail
labour inspectorate, factory inspectorate / inspection; Occupational Safety and Health Administration (USA)

visite d'inspection
monitoring visit

INSTABILITE
instabilité de la main-d'oeuvre
labour instability

INSTALLATION
installation, facility; settlement; induction; (pl.) facilities

indemnité d'installation
installation / settling-in grant

installations sur le chantier
on-site facilities

prime d'installation
installation / settling-in grant

sous-utilisation de la main-d'oeuvre et des installations
under-utilisation of labour and capacity

INSTALLER
installer à son compte (s')
to set up on one's own

INSTANCE
body

instance consultative
consultative / advisory body

instance de décision
decision-making body

instance de recours
appeal body

INSTITUT
institut d'entreprise
corporate college

institut de formation pédagogique
teacher training college / school

institut de hautes études
graduate school

institut médico-professionnel
medical (and) occupational institute

institut pédagogique
teacher training college / school

institut régional d'assurance
regional insurance office

institut de technologie
institute of technology

INSTITUTEUR
(primary school) teacher

instituteur certifié
certified teacher

instituteurs de l'enseignement primaire et préprimaire [CITP-1988 (233)]
primary and pre-primary education teaching professionals [ISCO-1988 (233)]

instituteur spécialisé (Fr.)
special school teacher

INSTITUTION
institution; establishment; body; agency

affilié à une institution (être)
to be insured with an institution

allocation pour soins en institution (UK)
residential allowance

décompte entre institutions
adjustment of accounts between institutions

institution d'assurance
insurance institute

institution d'assurance(-)chômage
unemployment insurance institution

institution d'assurance(-)maladie
sickness insurance institution

institution d'assurance(-)vieillesse
old-age insurance institution

institution bénévole
voluntary agency

institution de bienfaisance / charitable
charity, charitable association / agency / institution

institution compétente
appropriate / competent institution

institution créancière
creditor institution

institution débitrice de prestations
institution responsible for payment / for provision of benefits

institution d'instruction
institution investigating the claim, investigating institution

institution du lieu de résidence
institution of the place of residence

institution du lieu de séjour
institution of the place of stay

institution mutualiste
mutual benefit society

institution de prévoyance
welfare institute

institution de retraite
pension institute

institution sanitaire
health agency

institution de sécurité sociale
social security agency / institution

institutions sociales
social / welfare agency / institution; (pl.) social services

institution sociale privée
private / voluntary welfare agency

organe d'une institution de sécurité sociale
organ of a social security institution

personnel d'institution
residential staff

placement en institution
placement in institution; institutional care

placement de longue durée dans une institution
long-term institutional care

remboursement entre institutions
reimbursement between institutions

soins / traitement en institution
institutional / residential care

INSTITUTIONNALISATION
institutionalisation

INSTITUTIONNALISER
to institutionalise

INSTRUCTEUR
instructor; trainer

formation d'instructeurs
trainer training

INSTRUCTION
instruction; education, schooling; provision; processing; (pl.) (occ.) terms of reference

degré d'instruction
educational status / level / achievement / attainment

droit à l'instruction
right to education

institution d'instruction
institution investigating the claim, investigating institution

instruction civique
citizenship / civic education

**instruction d'une demande de presta-
tions**
investigation of a claim for benefits

instruction écrite
written submmission

instruction élémentaire
basic / primary education; (occ.) literacy
and numeracy

instruction ministérielle
ministerial directive

**instruction relative au mode de
paiement**
payment instruction

instruction obligatoire
compulsory education

instruction en salle
bench / vestibule training

instruction à temps plein
full-time instruction

niveau d'instruction
educational level, level of study / of
education / of schooling, academic /
educational achievement / attainment

relèvement du niveau d'instruction
educational upgrading

INSTRUIRE
instruire une demande
to consider an application, to investigate a
claim

INSTRUMENT
instrument d'acceptation
instrument of acceptance

instrument d'adhésion
instrument of accession

**instrument d'orientation profession-
nelle**
vocational counselling tool

instrument de ratification
instrument of ratification

INSUBORDINATION
insubordination

attitude d'insubordination
insubordinate attitude

insubordination délibérée
wilful disobedience

INSUFFISAMMENT
logement insuffisamment occupé
under-occupied accommodation

INSUFFISANCE
shortage, lack; limitation; impairment;
handicap

chômage par insuffisance des capacités
classical unemployment

**chômage par insuffisance de la crois-
sance**
growth gap unemployment

**chômage par insuffisance de la de-
mande**
demand-deficient unemployment

**chômage par insuffisance d'équipe-
ments**
capital shortage unemployment

INSURRECTIONNEL
grève insurrectionnelle
revolutionary strike

INTÉGRAL
budgétisation intégrale
full budgeting

capitalisation intégrale (par)
fully funded

financement intégral
full funding / financing

paiement intégral
full payment

prise en charge intégrale
full payment; total subsidisation

régime par / reposant sur la capitalisation intégrale
fully funded scheme

régime de retraite par capitalisation intégrale
fully funded pension plan

réparation intégrale
full / global compensation

salaire intégral
full wage

INTÉGRATIF
négociation intégrative
positive-sum bargaining

INTÉGRATION
integration; absorption

allocation d'intégration (Belg.)
integration allowance

centre d'intégration (Sp.)
integration centre

cours d'intégration professionnelle
induction training / course, beginners' course

intégration active
affirmative / positive action

intégration au marché du travail
labour market integration / entry

intégration à la population active
labour force absorption

intégration professionnelle
vocational integration

période d'intégration
induction period

problème d'intégration au marché du travail
labour market entry difficulty

stage d'intégration professionnelle
induction course

INTÉGRÉ
integrated

centre de santé intégré
integrated health centre

non intégré
(occ.) non integrated

politique sociale intégrée
integrated social policy

services intégrés en faveur de l'enfance
integrated services for children

système intégré
integrated system / scheme / model

zone non intégrée
(occ.) marginal area

INTÉGRITÉ
diminution de l'intégrité physique
(occ.) loss of faculty

indemnisation pour atteinte à l'intégrité (Switz.)
allowance for diminished faculty

indemnité d'intégrité (Austr.)
integrity compensation

intégrité professionnelle
professional integrity

INTELLECTUEL
intellectual; cognitive; mental

capacité / faculté intellectuelle
mental capacity

travail intellectuel
intellectual / professional work

travailleur intellectuel
intellectual / professional worker; (occ.) salaried worker / employee

INTELLECTUELLEMENT
intellectuellement diminué
mentally disabled

INTEMPÉRIE
chômage(-)intempéries
unemployment due to bad weather conditions

indemnité pour / prime d'intempéries
bad weather allowance / payment

INTENDANT
paymaster; bailiff

intendants et personnel des services de restauration [CITP-1988 (512)]
housekeeping and restaurant services workers [ISCO-1988 (512)]

INTENSIF
formation intensive
intensive training

programme intensif
crash programme

soins infirmiers intensifs
intensive nursing care

soins intensifs
intensive care

stage de formation intensive
intensive / rapid training course

stage intensif
intensive / crash course

traitement intensif
intensive care

unité de soins intensifs
intensive care unit

INTENSITÉ
industrie à forte intensité de travail
labour-intensive industry

intensité de connaissances
knowledge intensity

intensité d'emploi
employment intensity

intensité d'emploi de la croissance
employment / job content of growth

intensité (relative) de main-d'oeuvre / de travail
labour intensity

intensité de qualification
skill intensity

INTENTER
intenter une procédure disciplinaire
to institute disciplinary proceedings

INTENTIONNNEL
discrimination intentionnelle
intent discrimination

faute intentionnelle
wilful misconduct

INTERACTIF
techniques interactives
interacting skills

INTERACTION
interrelationship

INTERBRANCHE
syndicat interbranches
multi-industry union

INTERCONNEXION
interconnexion des données / des dossiers
record linkage

INTERDÉPENDANCE
interdepence; interrelationship

INTERDÉPENDANT
interdependent; interrelated

INTERDICTION
frapper d'une interdiction d'exercer
to suspend from practice

interdiction d'heures supplémentaires
overtime ban

interdiction de recrutement
ban on recruitment, recruitment ban

INTERÉCHELON
écart interéchelons
inter-step differential

INTÉRESSEMENT
profit-sharing; incentive

- 439 -

accord d'intéressement
profit-sharing agreement

clause d'intéressement
profit-sharing / incentive clause

plan d'intéressement
profit-sharing scheme

prime d'intéressement
profit-sharing bonus; wage dividend

INTÉRÊT
interest; inducement; incentive

**action pour la défense des intérêts
professionnels**
(occ.) industrial action

activité d'intérêt collectif
community business activity

bonification d'intérêt
interest subsidisation / relief / reduction,
interest relief grant

collectif de défense des intérêts
citizens' action group, public interest
group

conflit d'intérêts
conflict of interest

défendre les intérêts professionnels
to protect occupational interests

entreprise d'intérêt collectif
community business venture

groupe d'intérêt
interest group

intérêt (sans)
interest-free

intérêts accumulés
accrued interests

intérêt collectif (d')
community(-based)

intérêts composés
compound interest

intérêt corporatif
professional interest

intérêts courus
accrued interests

intérêts échus
outstanding interest

intérêt général
public interest

intérêt professionnel
occupational interest

intérêt supérieur de la collectivité
ultimate interest of the community

**organisation / organisme d'intérêt local
/ d'intérêt collectif**
community(-based) organisation / agency

**prestation complémentaire pour inté-
rêts hypothécaires (Irel.)**
mortgage interest supplement

prêt à faible taux d'intérêt
low-interest loan

prêt sans intérêt
interest-free loan

programme d'emploi d'intérêt local
community employment programme

projet d'intérêt collectif
community project

service d'intérêt collectif
community service

travail d'intérêt général (TIG)
community service / work

travaux d'intérêt public
public works

INTER-ÉTATIQUE
interstate

INTERFÉRENCE
interference; interrelationship

INTERGOUVERNEMENTAL
intergovernmental

INTER-HOSPITALIER
groupement / syndicat inter-hospitalier
interhospital group

INTÉRIEUR
marché du travail intérieur
domestic labour market

migration intérieure
internal migration

population active intérieure
domestic labour force

produit intérieur brut
Gross Domestic Product (GDP)

règlement intérieur
works regulations / rule-book; rules of
procedure; standing orders

INTÉRIM
interim; temporary work (agency); (occ.)
temping

agence d'intérim
temporary work (agency), staff / temp
agency

intérim (par)
acting; interim

INTÉRIMAIRE (adj.)
interim; provisional; temporary; acting

accord intérimaire
temporary agreement

affectation intérimaire
acting assignment

agence de travail intérimaire
temporary work (agency), temp agency,
temporary employment agency,
temporary help contractor / service (USA)

emploi intérimaire
interim job / employment

main-d'oeuvre intérimaire
temporary labour

méthode d'ajustement intérimaire
interim adjustment methodology

nomination intérimaire
acting appointment

paiement intérimaire
interim payment

rapport intérimaire
progress report

travail intérimaire
temporary work; temping

travailleur intérimaire
temporary / casual worker

versement intérimaire
interim payment

INTÉRIMAIRE (n.)
temporary / occasional worker, casual
labourer; temp; (pl.) temporary staff

INTERINSTITUTION
mutation interinstitutions
inter-agency transfer

INTERJETER
interjeter appel
to appeal

INTERLOCUTEUR
interlocuteurs sociaux
social partners

INTERLOCUTOIRE
provisional

injonction interlocutoire
interim / interlocutory injunction

INTERMÉDIAIRE (adj.)
administration sanitaire intermédiaire
intermediate health administration

entreprise intermédiaire
non-profit making firm

personnel intermédiaire
middle-level personnel

professions intermédiaires [CITP-1988 (3)]
technical and associate professionals [ISCO-1988 (3)]

qualification intermédiaire
intermediate skill

revenu intermédiaire
middle income

service de santé intermédiaire
intermediate health service

soins intermédiaires (Can.)
intermediate care

INTERMÉDIAIRE (n.)
intermédiaire de placement
boarding-out intermediary

INTERMITTENCE
travail en intermittence
periodic work

INTERMITTENT
chômage intermittent
recurrent / frictional / casual unemployment

contrat de travail intermittent
intermittent work contract

emploi intermittent
casual / odd job

employé de façon intermittente
periodically / occasionally / casually / marginally employed

main-d'oeuvre intermittente
casual labour

poste temporaire intermittent
recurrent temporary post

travail intermittent
periodic work

travailleur intermittent
casual / occasional worker

INTERNAT
residential institution; residential / boarding school; internship

centre de formation en internat
residential training centre

enfant placé en internat
child boarded out

placement en internat
boarding out

INTERNATIONAL
international; interstate; cross-country, cross-national; overseas

affectation internationale
international assignment

Classification internationale des maladies (CIM)
International Classification of Diseases (ICD)

conducteur international
international transport worker

division internationale du travail
international division of work / of labour

fonctionnaire international
international civil servant

personnel recruté sur le plan international
internationally recruited staff

Système international de conservation des droits en matière de sécurité sociale
International System for the Maintenance of Rights in Social Security

travailleur salarié des transports internationaux
person employed in international transport

INTERNATIONALISATION
internationalisation; globalisation

INTERNE (adj.)
internal; in-house

centre interne de formation
company training centre

contrôle de gestion interne
audit

émigration interne
out-migration

formation interne
on-the-job training / learning, in-house /
internal training

harmonisation interne (des salaires)
internal alignment (of wages)

main-d'oeuvre interne
internal labour force

marché du travail interne
internal labour market

migration interne
internal migration

**programme pour la promotion interne
(Sp.)**
internal development programme

promotion interne
internal advancement, promotion from
within; (occ.) inbreeding

reclassement interne
in-placement

règlement interne
rules of association

INTERNE (n.)
house doctor; houseman (UK); intern
(USA)

INTERPARLEMENTAIRE
Commission interparlementaire (UK)
Joint Committee

INTERPERSONNEL
relations interpersonnelles
interpersonal relations

INTERPRÉTATION
interpretation, understanding

clauses d'interprétation
understandings

INTERPROFESSIONNEL
interprofessional; intertrade; inter-branch

accord interprofessionnel
inter-branch / multi-industry / inter-trade
agreement

mobilité interprofessionnelle
inter-occupation / intertrade mobility

négociations interprofessionnelles
multi-trade bargaining

**salaire minimum interprofessionnel
(Sp.)**
minimum interprofessional wage

**salaire minimum interprofessionnel de
croissance (SMIC) (Fr.)**
guaranteed / statutory minimum wage

**salaire minimum interprofessionnel
garanti**
intertrade minimum wage

syndicat interprofessionnel
general union, interprofessional union
(Cyp.)

INTERROMPRE
to interrupt, to suspend; to stop out (ed.)

INTERROMPU
période d'emploi interrompue
split employment period

INTERRUPTION
interruption, discontinuation; suspension;
stoppage; stopping out (ed.)

avis d'interruption de la formation
training suspension notice

interruption d'assurance
break in / interruption of / in insurance

interruption de carrière
career break

interruption du / de chômage
break in unemployment

interruption de la durée / de la période de chômage
break in the period of unemployment

interruption d'emploi
interruption of employment

interruption de grossesse
termination of pregnancy

interruption des services
break in service

interruption de travail
interruption of employment / of work

interruption du travail
cessation of / from work

interruption volontaire de grossesse (IVG)
voluntary termination of pregnancy

ordre d'interruption d'une activité (dangereuse)
prohibition notice

période d'interruption de travail
period of interruption of employment

INTERSECTORIEL
cross-sector(al)

INTERVALLE
lapse

intervalles réguliers (à)
periodically

INTERVENANT
intervenant sur le marché du travail
labour market partner

INTERVENTION
moyens d'intervention
policy instruments

politique d'intervention (directe) sur le marché du travail
active labour market policy

politique de non-intervention
laissez-faire policy

seuil d'intervention
trigger level

INTERVIEW
interview

INTERVILLE
comparaison intervilles
place to place comparison

enquête intervilles
place to place survey

indice intervilles
place to place index

INTITULÉ
title; heading

intitulé de poste
job title

INTOXICATION
poisoning

intoxication alimentaire
food poisoning

intoxication d'origine professionnelle
vocational poisoning

intoxication saturnine
lead poisoning

INTRA-ENTREPRISE
formation intra-entreprise
in-house training

INTRAPRENARIAT
intrapreneurship

INTRAPRENEUR
intrapreneur

INTRODUCTION
introduction d'une demande de prestations
submission of a claim for benefits

INTRODUIRE
introduire une demande
to register / to make / to submit a claim

introduire une demande de prestations
to apply for / to lodge a claim for / to
make an application for benefits

INUTILISÉ
capacité (de production) inutilisée
idle capacity

main-d'oeuvre inutilisée
slack labour

**marge / ressources de main-d'oeuvre
inutilisée(s)**
employment / labour market slack

INVALIDANT
accident invalidant
disabling accident

maladie invalidante
disabling disease / illness / incapacitating
illness, crippling disease

INVALIDE
disabled / handicapped (person);
incapacitated; infirm; invalid; (pl.) people
with disabilities, the disabled

**allocation pour soins à (un) invalide
(UK)**
invalid care allowance

**allocation de subsistance pour invali-
des (UK)**
disability living allowance

**allocation de travail pour invalides
(UK)**
disability working allowance

enfant invalide
incapacitated child

grand invalide
severely handicapped / disabled, seriously disabled person; (pl.) badly
disabled (the)

invalide civil
civilian disabled

invalide de guerre
disabled veteran / ex-serviceman, war
invalid / disabled / cripple

invalide de naissance
congenitally disabled

invalide profond
severely disabled

personne invalide
disabled / handicapped person

**préposé au reclassement (profession-
nel) des invalides (UK)**
disablement resettlement officer

réadaptation des invalides
disablement rehabilitation, rehabilitation
of the disabled

**réadaptation professionnelle des
invalides**
vocational rehabilitation of the disabled

rééducation des invalides
disablement rehabilitation, rehabilitation
of the disabled

travailleur invalide
disabled worker

INVALIDÉ
invalid

INVALIDITÉ
disability, disablement, impairment; infirmity; invalidity; handicap

aggravation de l'invalidité
worsening of disability, aggravation of
invalidity

allocation d'invalidité (UK)
invalidity allowance

allocation d'invalidité partielle (Neth.)
partial disability allowance

**assurance décès-invalidité en cas
d'accident**
accidental death and dismemberment
(AD+D)

- 445 -

assurance(-)invalidité
disability / disablement / invalidity insurance, insurance in respect of invalidity

assurance-invalidité permanente
long-term disability insurance

atteint d'invalidité partielle
partially disabled

barème d'invalidité
disablement / disability scale

bénéficiaire d'une pension d'invalidité
invalidity pensioner

coefficient / degré d'invalidité
degree of disablement / invalidity

détermination du taux d'invalidité
determination of impairment / of invalidity

indemnité d'invalidité
disability payment / gratuity

indemnité d'invalidité pour accident du travail (ou maladie professionnelle)
industrial disablement payment / gratuity

indemnité pour invalidité permanente
permanent disability payment, permanency award (USA)

invalidité absolue
total disability

invalidité absolue et définitive
total permanent disability

invalidité aggravée
aggravated disability

invalidité générale
general invalidity

invalidité grave
major / severe disability

invalidité partielle
partial disability

invalidité permanente
permanent disablement / disability / invalidity, long-term disability

invalidité professionnelle
occupational disability

invalidité temporaire
short-term / temporary disability / invalidity

invalidité totale
absolute disablement, total disability

invalidité totale consécutive à un accident du travail
total disability due to work injury

maladie entraînant l'invalidité
disabling disease / illness, incapacitating illness, crippling disease

pension d'invalidité
disability / invalidity pension

pension d'invalidité suite à un accident du travail (Hung.)
accident disability pension

pension d'invalidité des anciens combattants
veterans' disability pension

pension d'invalidité non contributive
non-contributory invalidity pension

pension d'invalidité de veuve
invalid widow's pension (Fr.)

pension militaire d'invalidité
military disablement pension

pension sociale d'invalidité (Port.)
social invalidity pension

pourcentage d'invalidité
degree of disability

prestation d'invalidité
disablement / disability / invalidity benefit

prestation d'invalidité causée par un accident du travail (ou une maladie professionnelle)
industrial disablement benefit

prestation d'invalidité permanente
industrial disablement benefit

prestation supplémentaire en espèces en cas d'invalidité
supplementary disability income benefit

rente d'invalidité
disability / invalidity / disablement
pension

risque d'invalidité
probability / risk of disability

table d'(entrée en) invalidité
disability table

taux d'invalidité
degree of invalidity / of disability,
disability / invalidity rate

INVENTAIRE
inventory; survey; evaluation; schedule

inventaire des compétences
skills inventory

service d'inventaires
(occ.) referral centre

INVERSE
évaluation inverse
inverted appraisal

INVESTI
masse salariale investie (dans...)
invested pay, investment wage

INVESTIR
investir qqn d'une fonction
to vest someone with a function

INVESTISSEMENT
budget d'investissement
investment / capital budget, below-the-
line

investissement sanitaire et social
health and social investment

**participation aux investissements
sanitaires**
contribution in health investments

subvention à l'investissement
(incremental) investment subsidy

INVISIBLE
chômage invisible
hidden / disguised / unrecorded /
concealed unemployment

sous-emploi invisible
invisible under-employment

travail invisible
disguised employment

INVOCABLE
enforceable

INVOLONTAIRE
chômage involontaire
involuntary unemployment

INVOQUÉ
pouvoir être invoqué devant les tribunaux
to be enforceable in a court of law

IRRÉDUCTIBLE
chômage irréductible, noyau irréductible
de chômage / de chômeurs
hard-core unemployment

IRRÉGULARITÉ
irregularity; flaw

IRRÉGULIER
absence irrégulière
absence without leave, unauthorised
absence

étranger en situation irrégulière
illegal alien

main-d'oeuvre en situation irrégulière
unauthorised / undocumented labour

travail irrégulier
irregular employment

travailleur en situation irrégulière
illegal / undeclared / unauthorised /
undocumented worker

ISOLAT
isolate

ISOLÉ
single (person / householder); (pl.) housebound (the)

allocation d'isolé (Irel.)
living alone allowance

allocation de / pour parent isolé
one-parent benefit (UK), single-parent /
lone parent's (Fr.) allowance

parent isolé
one(-)parent, lone(-)parent, single parent,
sole(-)parent

pension de parent isolé (Aust.)
sole parent pension

période isolée
single spell

période isolée de chômage
single spell of unemployment

personne isolée
single person / householder

ISOLEMENT
prime d'isolement
isolation pay

ISSU
issu de l'immigration
from immigrant origin

ISSUE
emploi sans issue
dead-end job

ITINÉRAIRE
itinéraire de reclassement
outplacement schedule

ITINÉRANT
bureau itinérant
itinerant office

formation itinérante
mobile training

travailleur itinérant
itinerant / transient worker

JARDIN
jardin d'enfants
kindergarten, nursery school

JETON
jetons de présence des administrateurs
directors' fees

JEU
game; range; kit

jeu naturel des départs (par le)
by natural attrition

jeu à somme nulle
zero-sum game

matériel de jeux
play equipment / material

matériel pour terrains de jeux
playground equipment

terrain de jeux
recreation ground, playground

JEUNE
young (people)

aide au premier emploi des jeunes (Fr.)
allowance for young new workers

allocation au /pour jeune enfant (Fr.)
young child allowance, allowance for
young child

animateur de groupes de jeunes
youth leader

centre pour (les) jeunes
youth centre

chômage des jeunes
youth unemployment

club de jeunes
youth club

**congé de formation jeunes travailleurs
(Fr.)**
young workers training leave

conseiller des jeunes
youth advisor

crédit formation jeunes (Fr.)
young people training tax credit

emploi des jeunes
youth employment

formation de / des jeunes
youth training

foyer pour (les) jeunes
youth centre

foyer de jeunes travailleurs
young workers hostel

jeune cadre
junior manager

jeune cadre en formation
management trainee, trainee manager

jeune chômeur
young unemployed

jeune quittant prématurément l'école
early school leaver

**jeune sortant de l'école / (déjà) sorti de
l'école**
school-leaver

jeune enfant
young child

jeune ayant abandonné ses études
early leaver, drop-out

jeune ayant terminé ses études
school-leaver

jeune fille au foyer
non-working girl

jeune ménage
young couple

jeunes non scolarisés
out-of-school young people / youth

**jeune ayant achevé sa scolarité / en fin
de scolarité / sorti du système scolaire**
school-leaver

jeune travailleur
young worker

organisation de jeunes
youth organisation

personnes encore jeunes
non aged, non elderly

prêt aux jeunes ménages
loan for young couples

programme de formation pour jeunes diplômés
graduate training scheme

programme axé sur / orienté vers les jeunes
youth-specific programme

taux de la main-d'oeuvre excédentaire des jeunes
youth labour surplus rate

JEUNESSE
expert-conseil pour la jeunesse
youth consultant

JOAILLIER
joailliers et orfèvres [CITP-1968 (8-8)]
jewellery and precious metal workers
[ISCO-1968 (8-8)]

JOUISSANCE
entrée en jouissance
commencement date (of a pension)

indemnité pour privation de jouissance
compensation for loss of property

pension à jouissance différée
deferred pension

sécurité de jouissance
security of tenure

JOUR
day

centre d'accueil de jour
day care centre

centre chirurgical de jour
day surgery centre

centre de jour
day (care) centre; half-way house

décompte des jours de congé
leave record keeping

épuiser ses jours de congés payés
to use up one's holiday entitlement

équipe de jour
day shift

établissement de jour (med.)
day-care patient facility

hôpital de jour
day hospital; half-way house

jour de l'admission
intake day

jour de l'An
New Year's Day

jour d'arrêt pour maladie
day off for illness

jour calendaire
calendar day

jour de carence
waiting day

jour de carence absolu
absolute waiting day

jour civil
calendar day

jour chômé
non-working day; public / official holiday

jours de congé annuel accumulés
accrued annual leave

jour de congé compensatoire
day off in lieu

jours de congé-études
day release education

jour férié
public / official / statutory holiday; bank holiday

jour férié payé
paid public holiday

jour franc
calendar / clear / full day

jour-homme
man-day

jour d'incapacité
day of incapacity

jour de l'inscription
intake day

jour ouvrable / ouvré
business / working / work day, week-day

jour non ouvrable / non ouvré
non-working day

jour de paie
pay(-)day

jour-personne
person-day

jour plein
full day

jour de récupération
day off in lieu, day (not worked) to be
made up later

jour de référence
reference day / date

jour de repos
rest day, day off, non-working day

jour de repos hebdomadaire
weekly rest day

jour restant à prendre
remaining day

jour supplémentaire
additional day

jour de travail
work day

malade en traitement de jour
day patient

nombre de jours d'arrêt pour maladie
number of days lost to illness

poste de jour
day shift

report de jours de congé accumulés
transfer of accrued leave

service de traitement de jour
day-care patient facility

soins dans des établissements de jour
day care

soins aux malades en traitement de jour
day patient care

solde de jours de congé annuel accu-mulés
accrued annual leave balance

veuve de jour
grass widow

vivre au jour le jour
living on a hand-to-mouth basis

JOURNALIER (adj.)
daily

allocation journalière
daily allowance

allocation journalière de chômage
daily unemployment benefit

allocation journalière de maternité (Icel.)
daily maternity leave grant

feuille journalière de présence
daily attendance sheet

forfait journalier hospitalier
patient's daily charge for hospitalisa-tion

forfait journalier de soins et d'héber-gement
patient's daily charge for care and
accommodation

gain journalier de base
basic daily earnings

indemnité journalière
daily allowance, daily benefit

indemnité journalière de maladie
daily sickness benefit

indemnité journalière de repos
daily rest allowance

indemnité journalière de subsistance
daily subsistence / living allowance; per
diem

indemnité journalière de subsistance au taux spécial
special rate of daily subsistence allowance

migration journalière
(pl.) commuting

prestation journalière
daily benefit

rayon de migration journalière
commuting distance

salaire journalier
daily wage

tarif / taux journalier
day / daily rate

trajet journalier
day haul; (pl.) commuting

JOURNALIER (n.)
daily worker; (day) labourer; farm hand

JOURNÉE
day

amplitude de la journée de travail
work day span

heures ouvrées dans la journée
daily working hours

journée d'action
day of action

journée civile
calendar day

journée continue
non-stop working day; workday wi-thout lunch break

journée discontinue
split workday

journées d'étude
(occ.) workshop

journée d'hospitalisation
bed-day, hospital day

journée de revendication
day of action

journée de travail
work()day, working day

journée de travail normale
normal working day

journée de travail normale à temps partiel
normal part-time working day

nombre moyen de journées de maladie
mean number of days of illness

ouvrier à la journée
day labourer

prix de journée (Fr.)
charge by the day, daily rate

travailleur payé à la journée
daily wage worker

JUDICIAIRE
appareil judiciaire
judicial machinery

déclaration judiciaire
court declaration

passible de poursuites judiciaires
subject to legal proceedings

JUGE
juge prud'hommes
labour court member

juge social
(occ.) social assessor

JUGEMENT
judgment, (legal) decision; decree; adjudication

jugement déclaratif de faillite
adjudication order

JURIDICTION
juridiction d'appel
appeal body

JURIDIQUE
arsenal juridique
panoply of legal instruments

cadre juridique
legal framework

capacité juridique
legal capacity; (occ.) ability

conseiller juridique
legal advisor

**expectative juridique du renouvelle-
ment d'un engagement**
legal expectation of renewal of con-tract

personnalité juridique
legal status

**protection sociale et juridique de
l'enfance**
social and legal child welfare

recours juridique
legal action

service juridique
legal department

JURIDIQUEMENT
arrangement contractuel juridiquement
obligatoire
legally binding contractual arrange-ment

JURISPRUDENCE
décision faisant jurisprudence
test case

JURISTE
juristes [CITP-1968 (1-2)]
jurists [ISCO-1968 (1-2)]

juristes [CITP-1988 (242)]
legal professionals [ISCO-1988 (242)]

JURY
jury de présélection
screening board

jury de sélection
selection board

JUSTE
cause juste
just cause

gestion au plus juste
lean management

juste indemnité
fair / reasonable compensation

**justes indemnités en cas de maladie,
accident ou de décès**
reasonable compensation in the event of
illness, accident or death

juste salaire
fair wage

production au plus juste
lean production

production juste à temps
just-in-time production

traitement juste et équitable
fair and equitable treatment

JUSTICE
justice; law; fairness

action collective en justice
class action

frais de justice
legal costs

justice sociale
social fairness

JUSTICIABLE (adj.)
subject to

JUSTICIABLE (n.)
person subject to trial; person under the
court's jurisdiction

JUSTIFICATIF (adj.)
pièce justificative
supporting document, voucher; proof;
(pl.) documentary evidence

**pièces justificatives requises attestant le
pays de résidence**
required proof of the country of resi-dence

JUSTIFICATION
justification; evidence; rationale

justification (sur)
upon presentation of proof

justification des dépenses effectives
production of proof of actual expendi-ture

JUSTIFIÉ
absence non justifiée
unexcused / unexcusable absence

refus justifié
(occ.) non-disqualifying refusal

JUVÉNO-INFANTILE
population juvéno-infantile
child population

KEYNÉSIEN
chômage keynésien
demand-deficient / keynesian unemployment

KILOMÉTRIQUE
indemnité kilométrique
mileage fee / allowance

KINÉSITHÉRAPEUTE
physical therapist, physiotherapist

KINÉSITHÉRAPIE
physical therapy, physiotherapy

LABORANTIN
laboratory assistant

LABORATOIRE
laboratoire d'analyses médicales
medical analysis laboratory

technicien de laboratoire
laboratory technician

LABORIEUX
classe laborieuse
working class

LACUNE
gap; deficiency; limitation; handicap

lacune (de la législation) fiscale
tax loophole

LAISSÉ (n.)
laissé pour compte (de la société)
cast-off from society; (pl.) under-class

LAIT
bon de lait
milk voucher

lait maternisé
infant formula

substitut du lait maternel
infant formula

LANCEMENT
introduction

capitaux de lancement
seed money

LANGUE
connaissance pratique d'une langue
working knowledge of a language

cours de langue
language course / training

mesure d'incitation à l'étude des langues
language incentive

prime de langue
language allowance / bonus

LATENT
chômage latent
unrecorded / hidden / disguised /
concealed unemployment

chômeur latent
hidden unemployed

travail latent
disguised employment

LATITUDE
scope

LAYETTE
baby clothes

LECTURE
mécanismes de la lecture et de l'écriture
(occ.) literacy skills

LÉGAL
lawful, legal, statutory

abattement légal
statutory deduction

âge légal de départ à la / en retraite
statutory retirement age

âge légal de fin de scolarité
statutory school-leaving age

âge légal de la majorité
statutory majority age

âge légal de la retraite
(legal) retirement age, prescribed
pensionable age

âge minimum légal pour travailler
minimum legal working age

allocation légale
statutory award

assurance légale
statutory insurance

cadre légal
legal framework

condition légale de travail
legal employment requirement

congé légal
statutory holiday

consolidation légale
legal consolidation

dégrèvement légal
statutory deduction

délai minimum légal de préavis
statutory notice

disposition légale
statutory provision; (pl.) legislative
provisions, law

domicile légal
legal domicile, place of abode

durée légale du travail
statutory working hours

durée légale maximale du travail
statutory maximum working hours

fête légale
bank holiday, public / official / statutory
holiday

grève légale
official / lawful strike

hypothèque légale
statutory charge

indemnités légales de maladie (UK)
statutory sick pay

indemnités légales de maternité (UK)
statutory maternity pay

médecine légale
forensic medicine

moyens légaux
legal means

prestation légale
statutory benefit

régime légal
statutory scheme

**régime légal complémentaire profes-
sionnel**
occupation statutory complementary
scheme

régime légal de retraite
statutory pension scheme

régime légal de sécurité sociale
statutory social security scheme

revenu minimum légal
statutory minimum income

salaire légal de maternité (UK)
statutory maternity pay

salaire minimum légal
statutory minimum wage

statut légal
legal status

taux légal
prescribed rate

LÉGALEMENT
exercer légalement
to be registered in / to practice

légalement autorisé à travailler
legally entitled / eligible to work

LÉGALISATION
certification, authentication

dispensé de légalisation
exempt from authentication

LÉGALISER
to authenticate

LÉGER
débile léger
mildly mentally retarded

déficient (mental) léger
mildly mentally retarded

faute légère
slight misconduct

incapacité légère
minor disability

industrie légère
light industry

lésion / traumatisme léger / légère
minor injury

travaux légers
light work

LÉGIFÉRER
to introduce / to pass legislation

LÉGISLATIF
legislative; legal

acte législatif
legislation; statute

disposition législative
legal provision; (pl.) legislative provisions, law

**dispositions législatives et réglemen-
taires**
laws and regulations

**membres de l'exécutif et des corps
législatifs [CITP-1988 (111)]**
legislators [ISCO-1988 (111)]

texte législatif
legal / statutory instrument; (pl.)
legislation

textes législatifs fondamentaux
basic legislation

textes législatifs et/ou réglementaires
statutory instruments / regulations

LÉGISLATION
legislation, (statute) law, laws

législation applicable
relevant legislation

**législation en matière d'emploi / régis-
sant l'emploi**
employment legislation

**législation interdisant le monopole
syndical d'embauche (USA)**
right-to-work laws

législation sociale
welfare / social legislation

législation du travail
labour law / legislation

LÉGITIME
lawful, legal

licenciement légitime
lawful dismissal

motif légitime (sans)
without just cause

union légitime
legitimate union, (occ.) marriage

LÉGITIMEMENT
dépenses raisonnablement et légitime-
ment engagées
just and reasonable expenses

LÉSION
injury; impairment

lésion accidentelle
accident injury

lésion corporelle
bodily injury / harm, personal injury

lésion grave
serious injury

lésion légère
minor injury

lésion professionnelle
employment injury

**maladies et lésions d'origine
professionnelle**
work-related / occupational diseases and
injuries

nature de la lésion
nature of injury

**prestation pour lésion ou maladie
(professionnelle) (UK)**
injury benefit (UK, Irel., Malta), industrial injury / employment injury
benefit

LETTRE
letter; notice

lettre d'appel
letter of appeal

lettre clé
key letter

lettre de congédiement
letter of discharge

lettre d'embauche
letter of appointment

lettre de licenciement
dismissal notice, letter of dismissal; notice of lay-off

lettre de promotion
letter of promotion

lettre de recommandation / de réfé-rence
letter of reference / of recommendation

notifier une lettre de promotion
to issue a letter of promotion

LEVÉE
(jur.) waiver

levée de l'immunité
waiver of immunity

LEVIER
rachat d'une entreprise par ses cadres avec effet de levier (RECEL)
leveraged management buy-out (LMBO)

LIAISON
agent de liaison
liaison officer; contact person

liaison avec (assurer la)
to liaise with

liaisons fonctionnelles
functional relationships

organisme de liaison
liaison body

LIBELLÉ
wording; version

LIBÉRAL
liberal; concessional

association de praticiens libéraux
individual practices association (IPA)

catégorie des professions libérales
professional category

exercice libéral (d')
in private practice

exercice libéral de la médecine
free medical practice, free practice of medicine

infirmière libérale
private / agency nurse

médecin libéral
private doctor

médecine libérale (la)
free practice of medicine

membre d'une profession libérale
professional (worker)

profession libérale
independent / learned / liberal profession, professional occupation / job; (pl.) professions

professions scientifiques, techniques, libérales et assimilées
(occ.) professionals

LIBÉRALISATION
liberalisation, deregulation

LIBÉRALISER
to liberalise, to deregulate

LIBÉRATION
(jur.) release

LIBÉRATOIRE
paiement / versement libératoire
payment in full discharge

LIBÉRÉ
poste libéré
vacated position

LIBÉRER
to release

libérer un poste
to vacate a position

libérer qqn de son travail
to release someone from work

LIBERTÉ
atteinte à la liberté du travail
violation of the freedom of labour

entrave à la liberté du travail
interference with freedom of employment

liberté d'accès (into a profession)
freedom of entry

liberté de circulation des travailleurs
freedom of movement for workers

libertés civiles
civil liberties

liberté contractuelle
freedom of contract

liberté d'établissement
freedom of establishment

liberté de licenciement (USA)
employment at will

liberté de prescription
freedom of prescription

liberté de réunion
freedom of assembly

liberté syndicale
right of association / of union organisation / to organise; freedom of association

LIBRE
auditeur libre
unregistered student

centre de formation à libre accès
open access training centre

école libre
private school

enseignement libre
private education

horaire libre
variable working hours

hospitalisation libre
informal hospitalisation, voluntary admission

libre accès
free / open access

libre adhésion (sur la base / sur une base de)
on a voluntary basis

libre choix du médecin
free choice of doctor

libre circulation
free movement

libre circulation de la main-d'oeuvre / des travailleurs
free movement of workers

libre concurrence
freedom of competition

libre service
self-service

médicament en vente libre
over-the-counter drug

placement libre d'enfant
voluntary placement of a child

porter atteinte au libre exercice de l'industrie et du travail
to impair / to restrict the freedom of industry and labour

secteur à honoraires libres (Fr.)
free-fee sector

temps libre(s)
leisure / spare time

union libre
free / non-marital union; cohabitation

union libre (en)
cohabiting

vivre en union libre
to cohabit

LIBREMENT
librement consenti
voluntary

LICENCE
licence; (bachelor's) degree

contrat de licence
licence agreement

octroi de licence
licensing

LICENCIÉ
fonds d'indemnisation des travailleurs
licenciés (pour raisons économiques)
(UK)
redundancy fund

**licencié pour raisons économiques
(être)**
to be made redundant

**travailleur licencié pour compression
de personnel / pour raisons économiques**
redundant worker

LICENCIEMENT
termination of (a contract of) employment, dismissal (from employment), lay-
off; severance; (pl.) labour shake-out /
shedding; redundancy; employment
dislocation

annulation du licenciement
rescission of termination

**autorisation administrative de
licenciement**
administrative authorisation to dismiss

avis de licenciement
dismissal notice

cause réelle et sérieuse de licenciement
genuine and proper ground for dismissal

coût(s) d'embauche et de licenciement
hiring and firing cost(s), on and off costs
(Austr.)

coût de licenciement
severance cost

droit de licenciement
right to dismiss

entretien préalable au licenciement
preliminary discussion before dismissal

**fonds d'indemnisation des licencie-
ments économiques**
redundancy fund

**grève de protestation contre des / les
licenciements**
redundancy strike

indemnité de licenciement
dismissal indemnity / payment / compensation, termination indemnity,
severance pay / payment

**indemnité de licenciement pour cause /
raison économique**
redundancy benefit / payment

lettre de licenciement
dismissal notice, letter of dismissal; notice
of lay-off

liberté de licenciement (USA)
employment at will

licenciement abusif
unwarranted / unfair / wrongful dismissal, wrongful discharge (USA)

licenciement non abusif
fair dismissal

**licenciement abusif sans cause réelle et
sérieuse**
dismissal without just cause

**licenciement abusif du fait de l'invo-
cation tardive des motifs**
waiver of breach of contract

**licenciement par accord mutuel /
amiable**
agreed termination

licenciement par appel au volontariat
voluntary redundancy

licenciement arbitraire
unfair / wrongful dismissal, wrongful discharge (USA)

licenciements en cascade
spate of dismissals

licenciement collectif
collective / mass dismissal, mass lay-off; (mass) redundancy; blanket dismissal (in case of offence committed by unindentified worker)

licenciement collectif pour motifs économiques
collective redundancy

licenciement (pour motif) économique
dismissal for economic reasons, redundancy

licenciement du fait de l'employeur
(occ.) compulsory redundancy

licenciement pour faute
dismissal for misconduct

licenciement pour faute grave
disciplinary lay-off

licenciement pour fait de grève
dismissal resulting from strike

licenciement immédiat
dismissal without notice, immediate / summary dismissal

licenciement implicite
(occ.) constructive discharge / dismissal

licenciement légitime
lawful dismissal

licenciement avec préavis
dismissal with notice

licenciement sans préavis
dismissal without notice

licenciement pour raisons objectives (Sp.)
dismissal on objective grounds

licenciement sur-le-champ
summary / immediate dismissal

motif de licenciement
ground / reason for dismissal

plan de licenciement
redundancy plan

préavis de licenciement
dismissal / termination notice, notice of dismissal / of termination

prime de licenciement
severance pay / payment

procédure de licenciement
dismissal procedure

protection contre le(s) licenciement(s) (abusif(s))
(unfair) dismissal protection, protection against (unfair) dismissal

rapport spécial relatif au licenciement
special report relating to termination

recevoir un préavis de licenciement
to be served with a notice of termination

LICENCIER
to dismiss; to terminate

licencier un employé
to terminate an employee

licencier temporairement
to lay off (temporarily)

LICITE
lawful, legal

LIEN
relationship

lien avec (assurer le)
to liaise with

lien formel avec l'emploi
formal job attachment

liens avec le marché du travail
labour market attachment

liens de parenté
kinship

LIER
(jur.) to be binding upon

LIEU
place; site

classement des lieux d'affectation
classification of duty stations

décision prise en haut lieu
high-level decision

déplacement entre domicile et lieu de travail
travel / journey to work; commuting

donner lieu à
to be liable to

formation sur les lieux de travail
on-the-job training / learning

garderie sur les lieux
on-site day care facility

inspection du lieu de travail
inspection of work surroundings

inspection sur le lieu de travail
on-site inspection

institution du lieu de résidence
institution of the place of residence

institution du lieu de séjour
institution of the place of stay

lieu d'affectation
duty station, assignment

lieu d'affectation initial
first duty station / assignment

lieu d'affectation officiel
official duty station / assignment

lieu d'affectation hors siège
field duty station, non-headquarters duty station

lieu de congé dans les foyers
place of home leave

lieu d'emploi
place of business

lieu d'inhumation
place of burial

lieu de recrutement
place of recruitment

lieu de résidence
place of residence

lieu de séjour
place of stay

lieu sûr
safe place

lieu de travail
job site, place of work / of employment, work site, work()place; (pl.) work premises

lieu(x) de travail (sur le / les)
on-the-job

lieu de vie
(occ.) sheltered home

navette entre son domicile et son lieu de travail (faire la)
to commute to and from work

occupation des lieux
occupation of premises

principal lieu d'affectation
main duty station

sécurité sur le lieu de travail
job / occupational safety, safety at work

LIGNE
ligne d'action
policy

ligne de conduite
guideline; course of action; policy

ligne de crédit
appropriation line

ligne directrice
guideline

Lignes directrices du BIT pour la mesure du chômage
ILO Guidelines for measuring unemployment

LIMITATION
limitation; limit

limitation budgétaire (UK)
cash limit

limitation de la durée du travail
restrictions on working hours

limitation des salaires
wage restraint

prestation sans limitation de durée
open-ended benefit

LIMITE (n.)
limit

âge limite de la vie active
maximum active working age

atteint par la limite d'âge
(occ.) superannuated

date limite
closing / cutoff date, deadline

limite d'âge
age limit

limite d'âge supérieure
upper age limit

limite inférieure pour l'assiette des cotisations de la catégorie n
lower earnings limit of class n contributions

limite inférieure des gains
lower earnings level / limit

limite minimale
minimum level

limite supérieure
maximum / upper limit; ceiling; high cutoff point

limite supérieure pour l'assiette des cotisations de la catégorie n
upper earnings limit of class n contributions

limite supérieure des gains
upper earnings limit / level

retraite par limite d'âge
retirement on account of age

retraite nationale par limite d'âge (UK)
national superannuation

LIMITER
to restrict, to limit; (occ.) to qualify

limiter l'accès à
to restrict / to limit access

LIMOGEAGE
dismissal

LIMOGER
to dismiss

LINGUISTIQUE
formation linguistique
language training

personnel des services linguistiques
language staff

prime (de connaissances) linguistique(s)
language allowance / bonus

LIQUIDATION
settlement; award

liquidation anticipée
early vesting

liquidation d'une demande de prestation
settlement of benefit claim, establishment of entitlement to benefit

liquidation d'une pension
award of pension; calculation / determination of a pension

liquidation d'une prestation
award of a benefit

liquidation de retraite
pension calculation

versement de départ au titre de la liquidation des droits
withdrawal settlement

LIQUIDÉ
droits liquidés
claim settled

LIQUIDER
to claim; to award; to pay

liquider des droits à prestations
to pay benefits

LISTE
list; panel; schedule; register

liste d'attente
stand-by / waiting list

liste des candidats
list of candidates, nomination list

liste de candidats présélectionnés
shortlist of candidates

liste de dispenses
waiver list

liste de maladies professionnelles
list of professional diseases

liste nominative des cotisations
list / statement of contributions per person

liste de paie
paylist, paysheet, earnings record

liste de rationnaires
relief roll

liste de roulement
rota

liste des syndiqués
union roll

LIT
nombre de lits
bed capacity

LITIGE
dispute; litigation

arbitrer un litige
to mediate a dispute

litige concernant des / relatif aux prestations
benefit dispute

procédure de litige
litigation procedure

règlement d'un litige
dispute settlement / resolution, settlement of a dispute

LIVRE
livre de paie
paybook, wage book, payroll ledger

LIVRET
book; handbook; order book (UK)

livret d'accueil
employee handbook

livret d'allocations (familiales)
allowance order book

livret de famille (Fr.)
family record book

livret de longue maladie
long-term sickness order book

livret de retraite
pension book

livret de travail (Gr.)
labour permit

LOCAL (adj.)
local; community(-based)

administration locale
local government / authority

agence locale pour la création d'entreprises
local enterprise agency

agent local
field / local worker; (pl.) local staff

agent local d'assurance
local insurance officer

antenne locale d'un syndicat
(occ.) local union

apports locaux
local input / content

association locale
community group

autorité locale
local government

autorité locale de la santé (UK)
local health authority

barème local des salaires
local salary / wage scale

bureau local
local office

bureau local d'assurance
local insurance office

bureau local de l'emploi
local employment office

caisse-maladie locale générale
general local sick fund

collectivité locale
local government / authority

congé local
local holiday

conseil syndical local
local labour council

convention locale mutualiste
local mutualistic convention / agreement

correspondant local
local correspondent

dépenses locales
local costs

développement local
community development

employeur local
local / (occ.) outside employer

groupe local
community group

groupement d'entreprises locales
local enterprise trust

hôpital local
local hospital

impôt local
community charge; rate (UK); poll tax
(UK)

**initiative locale de création d'emplois
(ILE)**
local employment initiative, local
initiative in promoting employment

main-d'oeuvre locale
local labour

marché du travail local
local labour market

mission locale (Fr.)
local agency

mobilité locale
local / residential mobility

organisation / organisme d'intérêt local
community(-based) organisation / agency

organisme de l'administration locale
local government agency

poste d'agent local
local level post

pouvoirs locaux
local authorities

**programme d'emploi des collectivités
locales / d'intérêt local**
community employment programme

**projet des / entrepris par les
collectivités locales**
community project

recrutement sur le plan local
local recruitment

recrutement dans les services locaux
local authority appointment

réduction des taxes locales (UK)
rate rebate

réseau local de soutien
neighbourhood support system

section locale d'un / des syndicat(s)
(trade) union local / branch

**service local de la santé, service de
santé local**
local health service

société de développement de l'emploi local
(occ.) community employment corporation

taux de rémunération local
local wage / pay rate

taxe locale (UK)
rate

unité sanitaire locale (It.)
local health unit

LOCAL (n.)
room; (pl.) premises; facilities

grève avec occupation des locaux
sit-in / stay-in strike; worker occupation

locaux (destinés à être) occupés par plus d'un ménage
multi-household living quarters

locaux professionnels
work / business premises

local syndical
union room

LOCALEMENT
agent recruté localement
locally recruited staff member

personnel recruté localement
locally recruited staff

LOCALISATION
localisation; siting

LOCATIF
immeuble (à usage) locatif
rental house, tenement

prestation complémentaire pour charges locatives (Irel.)
rent supplement

valeur locative
rental value

LOCATION
tenancy

LOCK-OUT
lock-out

travailleur soumis à un lock-out
locked-out worker

LOCOMOTEUR
difficulté locomotrice
locomotor difficulty

LOGEMENT
housing, home, dwelling (unit); rental; living quarter; shelter; accommodation

affectation de logement
allocation of accommodation

aide au logement et au relogement
housing and rehousing help

aide personnalisée au logement (APL)
housing subsidy

allocation pour frais de logement (Neth.)
housing cost allowance

allocation (de) (-)logement
housing benefit / allowance, rental / rent subsidy, rent / accommodation / shelter allowance (Can.), rent assitance (Australia)

allocation logement social (Fr.)
social housing allowance

complément logement
housing supplement

construction de logements
housing construction

coopérative de logement
housing co-operative

crise du logement
housing shortage

degré d'occupation d'un logement
degree of crowding of a dwelling

enquête sur le logement
housing survey

foyer-logement pour personnes âgées (Fr.)
residential housing for old people

indemnité de logement
rent(al) allowance / subsidy, housing allowance / grant

logement (sans)
homeless

1% logement (Fr.)
company contributions (1%) to a fund offering bonified loans for housing purposes

logement auto-assisté
self-help housing / dwelling / construction

logement collectif
congregate / shared housing

logement ouvrant droit au versement d'une allocation
subsidised housing

logement économique
low-cost accomodation / housing unit

logement d'entreprise
accommodation supplied by the employing business

logement familial
family home

logements financés / subventionnés par l'Etat / les pouvoirs publics
public housing

logement de fonction
official / service accommodation; company flat

logement de fortune
emergency dwelling

logements pour les groupes sociaux à faibles revenus
low-income housing

logement individuel
private / (occ.) single family dwelling

logement à loyer abordable
affordable dwelling

logements à bon marché
low-cost housing

logement meublé
furnished dwelling

logement ne répondant pas aux normes d'habitabilité minimale
sub(-)standard housing

logement insuffisamment occupé
under-occupied accommodation

logement ouvrier
tenement

logements de promotion publique (Sp.)
public promotion housing

logement occupé par son propriétaire
owner-occupied dwelling

logement protégé
sheltered housing

logement de mauvaise qualité / de qualité médiocre
sub(-)standard housing

logement social
social housing, low-cost dwelling / housing unit; (pl.) low-cost / council / subsidised / public housing

logement sous-peuplé
insufficiently occupied dwelling

logement stable (Icel.)
secure dwelling

logement subventionné
social housing

logement surpeuplé
overcrowded dwelling

logement urbain
urban housing

logement vacant
unoccupied dwelling

marché du logement
housing market

modernisation du logement
housing rehabilitation

occupation d'un logement en (toute) propriété
owner-occupancy

office central du logement
central authority for housing

personne sans logement
homeless person

plan d'épargne logement
home (loan) saving plan (Fr.), private home ownership plan (USA)

prêt à l'amélioration du logement
loan for housing improvement

prêt au logement
home loan

programme de construction de logements
housing programme

programme de construction de logements à bon marché / de logements sociaux
low-cost housing programme

programme de logements
housing programme

programme subventionné (de construction) de logements
social housing scheme, subsidised housing programme

projet de logements sociaux
low-income housing project

propriétaire de son logement (Austr.)
homeowner

recherche de logement
house hunting

régime d'allocations (de) logement
rental subsidy scheme

régime d'allocations (de) logement révisé
revised rental subsidy scheme

système d'obligations-logement (Icel.)
house-bond system

unité de logement
dwelling (unit), housing unit

LOGIS
logis (sans)
homeless

LOI
law, statute; legislation

abattement prévu par la loi
statutory deduction

adopter une loi
to introduce / to pass legislation

annexe d'une loi
schedule of a law

décret-loi
statutory order; Order-in-Council (UK)

dégrèvement prévu par la loi
statutory deduction

durée hebdomadaire du travail prévue par la loi
statutory working week

durée maximale du travail prévue par la loi
statutory maximum working hours

force de loi (ayant)
binding

loi de 1901 (Fr.)
law governing non-profit-making organisations

loi sur les accidents du travail
workmen's compensation law

loi régissant les associations à but non lucratif
law governing non-profit-making organisations

loi-cadre
framework law

loi d'habilitation
enabling act

loi organique
organic law

loi de redressement
economic recovery act

lois et règlements
laws and regulations

loi rétroactive
retroactive statute

loi sociale
(pl.) social legislation

loi de synthèse
consolidation act

loi tarifaire
collective (wage) agreements act

loi unifiée
consolidation act

prestation prévue par la loi
statutory benefit

prestation non prévue par la loi
non-statutory benefit

procédure régulière conforme à la loi
due process of law

recueil des lois
statute book

texte de loi
act, legal / statutory instrument; (pl.)
legislation

voter une loi
to introduce / to pass legislation

LOISIR
leisure (activities / time); entertainment

activités de loisirs
leisure activities

centre de loisirs
vacation centre

complexe de loisirs
recreational / holiday centre

équipements de loisirs
recreation(al) facilities

heures de loisirs
leisure time

LONG
accord de longue date
long-standing agreement

affection de longue durée
long-term sickness / disease

centre de long séjour
nursing home

chômage de longue durée
long duration / long-term / chronic
unemployment

chômage de très longue durée
very long-term unemployment

**chômeur de longue date / de longue
durée**
chronically / long-term / long duration
unemployed

contrat à long terme / de longue durée
long-term contract

cycle long de formation
long training cycle

emploi de longue durée
long-term employment

**hôpital de long séjour / pour séjours de
longue durée**
long-term hospital

immigrant de longue durée
long-term immigrant

livret de longue maladie
long-term sickness order book

longue échéance (à)
in the long run

longue haleine (de)
long-term

longue maladie
long-term sickness / disease

longue portée (à)
long-run, long-range

long terme
long-term, long-run, long-range

malade atteint de longue maladie
long-term patient

maladie longue et coûteuse
prolonged and expensive illness

maladie de longue durée
long-term sickness / disease

occuper un emploi de longue durée
to work on a long-term basis

placement de longue durée dans une institution
long-term institutional care

prestation de longue durée / à long terme
long-term benefit

soins de longue durée
long-term care

temps réduit indemnisé longue durée (Fr.)
short-time work on benefit for a long period

LONGÉVITÉ
coefficient de longévité
vitality ratio

LONGITUDINAL
données longitudinales
historical data

LOTI
mieux lotis (les)
the better-off, the well-to-do

LOUAGE
contrat de louage de services
(institutional) service contract; (occ.) employment contract

contrat de louage de services individuels
individual service contract

LOUER
louer (à bail)
to lease

LOURD
faute lourde
serious misconduct, gross misconduct / negligence

industrie lourde
heavy / basic industry

LOYAL
concurrence loyale
fair competition

pratique loyale en matière d'emploi
fair employment practice

LOYER
rent(al)

allocation de loyer
rent allowance

dégrèvement de loyer
rent rebate

habitation à loyer modéré (HLM)
council flat / housing, rent controlled premises; (pl.) low-cost housing

logement à loyer abordable
affordable dwelling

montant des loyers
rent quotations

quittance de loyer
rent receipt

réduction du loyer
rent rebate

régime d'allocations et de retenues au titre du loyer
rental subsidy/deduction scheme

retenue (opérée) au titre du loyer
rental deduction

système de modulation des loyers (Irel.)
differential rent scheme

LUCRATIF
profitable

activité lucrative
business / economic activity, gainful
activity / occupation / employment

association à but non lucratif
non-profit-making organisation

but lucratif (à)
profit-seeking, profit-making

emploi lucratif
paid / gainful employment

entreprise à but non lucratif
non-profit making firm

**exercer une activité lucrative / un
emploi lucratif**
to be gainfully occupied / employed

gestion sans but lucratif (Can.)
public administration

**loi régissant les associations à but non
lucratif**
law governing non-profit-making
organisations

occupation lucrative
remunerated employment

**personnes / population ayant une
activité lucrative**
economically active / gainfully occupied /
working population, labour force

LUNDI
lundi de Pâques
Easter Monday

LUNETTES
spectacles

monture de lunettes
spectacle frame

LUTTE
lutte des classes
class struggle

lutte contre les maladies
disease control

lutte contre les maladies transmissibles
communicable disease control

LUTTER
lutter contre le chômage
to combat / to reduce unemployment

LYCÉE
secondary school; grammar school (UK);
high school (USA)

lycée professionnel
vocational upper secondary school

**brevet d'études professionnelles
agricoles (BEPA) (Fr.)**
certificate of agricultural vocational
education

MACHINE
conducteur de machine
machine operator

mécaniciens et ajusteurs de machines [CITP-1988 (723)]
machinery mechanics and fitters [ISCO-1988 (723)]

opérateur sur machine
machine operator

MACHINISTE
machine operator

MAÇON
maçons, charpentiers et autres travailleurs de la construction [CITP-1968 (9-5)]
bricklayers, carpenters and other construction workers [ISCO-1968 (9-5)]

MACRO-ÉCONOMIE
macroeconomics

MACROPLANIFICATION
macroplanning

MAGASIN
vendeurs et démonstrateurs en magasin [CITP-1988 (522)]
shop salespersons and demonstrators [ISCO-1988 (522)]

MAGISTRAL
médicament magistral
magistral drug

MAIN-D'OEUVRE
manpower, work force, labour; economically active / gainfully occupied / working / active population, labour force

absorber la main-d'oeuvre
to provide employment for labour force

adaptation de la main-d'oeuvre
labour adjustment

allocation de main-d'oeuvre
manpower allowance

appel à de la main-d'oeuvre supplémentaire (faire)
(occ.) to take on extra hands

apport de main-d'oeuvre
additional labour, labour input

besoins en main-d'oeuvre
work / worker / labour force requirements, labour / manpower needs / requirements

comportement de la main-d'oeuvre
labour force behaviour

courbe de la demande de main-d'oeuvre
demand curve for labour

courbe d'offre de main-d'oeuvre
supply curve of labour, labour supply schedule

coût de (la) main-d'oeuvre
labour cost / price

coût de main-d'oeuvre non salarial
non-wage labour cost

coût de main-d'oeuvre unitaire / coût unitaire de main-d'oeuvre
unit labour cost

coût variable de la main-d'oeuvre
variable labour cost

défaut de mobilité de la main-d'oeuvre
manpower rigidity

déficit de main-d'oeuvre qualifiée
(occ.) skill gap

délestage de main-d'oeuvre
labour shake-out / shedding / displacement; dishoarding; lay(-)off

demande excédentaire de main-d'oeuvre
excess demand for labour

demande de main-d'oeuvre
demand for labour, labour / manpower / worker demand

demande de main-d'oeuvre agricole
agricultural labour demand

déplacement de la main-d'oeuvre
manpower movement, movement of /
flow of workers

dilution de la main-d'oeuvre
dilution of labour

disponibilité de / en main-d'oeuvre
availability of manpower, manpower /
labour supply, supply of labour, worker(s)
availability

économies de main-d'oeuvre
labour savings

effectifs de main-d'oeuvre
economically active / gainfully occupied /
working population, labour force

élasticité de la demande de main-d'oeuvre
elasticity of labour demand

élasticité de l'offre de main-d'oeuvre
elasticity of labour supply

équivalent de main-d'oeuvre à temps plein
full-time man equivalent

étude prévisionnelle des besoins de main-d'oeuvre dans l'entreprise
company manpower planning, personnel
planning at establishment level

évolution prévisionnelle de la main-d'oeuvre
occupational forecast

excédent de main-d'oeuvre
surplus labour / manpower, labour /
manpower surplus, manpower redundancy, redundancy of manpower

flexibilité de la main-d'oeuvre
labour force flexibility

flux de main-d'oeuvre
labour force flow

formation de la main-d'oeuvre
labour force / manpower training

future main-d'oeuvre
oncoming labour force

générateur d'économies de main-d'oeuvre
labour saving

heure de main-d'oeuvre
man-hour, hour of operation

heure unitaire de main-d'oeuvre
unit hour of operation

indicateur-repère d'excédent de main-d'oeuvre
benchmark (labour / manpower) surplus
indicator

indicateur-repère de pénurie de main-d'oeuvre
benchmark (labour / manpower) shortage
indicator

industrie à forte concentration de main-d'oeuvre
labour-intensive industry

industrie de main-d'oeuvre
labour industry

industrie à main-d'oeuvre importante
labour-intensive industry

instabilité de la main-d'oeuvre
labour instability

intensité (relative) de main-d'oeuvre
labour intensity

libre circulation de la main-d'oeuvre
free movement of workers

main-d'oeuvre adéquate
suitable labour

main-d'oeuvre agricole
farm labour, agricultural manpower;
working farm population

main-d'oeuvre peu chère
cheap labour

main-d'oeuvre clandestine
unauthorised / undocumented labour

main-d'oeuvre contractuelle
contract labour

main-d'oeuvre assujettie à contrainte d'employeur
tied labour

main-d'oeuvre sous contrat
contract / indentured labour

main-d'oeuvre découragée
discouraged workforce

main-d'oeuvre disponible
availability of manpower, manpower /
labour supply, supply of labour, worker(s)
availability

main-d'oeuvre enfantine
child labour

main-d'oeuvre étrangère
foreign / off-shore labour

main-d'oeuvre étudiante
student labour

main-d'oeuvre excédentaire
labour / manpower surplus / redundancy,
surplus manpower, redundancy of manpower, displaced / redundant labour,
workers made redundant

main-d'oeuvre expérimentée
experienced workforce

main-d'oeuvre exploitée
slave / sweated labour

main-d'oeuvre féminine
female labour (force)

main-d'oeuvre handicapée
disabled labour force

main-d'oeuvre hautement qualifiée
highly qualified / skilled manpower

main-d'oeuvre immigrée
immigrant labour / workers

main-d'oeuvre indirecte
non-production worker

main-d'oeuvre inemployée
slack labour

main-d'oeuvre intérimaire
temporary labour

main-d'oeuvre intermittente
casual labour

main-d'oeuvre interne
internal labour force

main-d'oeuvre inutilisée
slack labour

main-d'oeuvre locale
local labour

main-d'oeuvre bon marché
cheap labour

main-d'oeuvre nucléaire
core workforce / workers

main-d'oeuvre occasionnelle
casual labour

main-d'oeuvre périphérique
peripheral workers

main-d'oeuvre potentielle
manpower potential

main-d'oeuvre prestataire
statute labour

main-d'oeuvre à bas prix
cheap labour

main-d'oeuvre à la production
productive labour

main-d'oeuvre qualifiée
qualified / skilled manpower, skilled
labour

main-d'oeuvre non qualifiée
common / unskilled labour

main-d'oeuvre saisonnière
seasonal manpower / labour force

main-d'oeuvre salariée
dependent labour force / working
population, hired labour

main-d'oeuvre semi-qualifiée
semi-skilled labour

main-d'oeuvre en situation irrégulière
unauthorised / undocumented labour

main-d'oeuvre spécialisée
semi-skilled labour

main-d'oeuvre stable
stable workforce

main-d'oeuvre en surnombre
labour redundancy, displaced / redundant
labour, workers made redundant, surplus
staff; overmanning

main-d'oeuvre syndiquée
unionised labour

main-d'oeuvre temporaire
interim / temporary / casual labour

manque de main-d'oeuvre
lack / shortage / under-supply of workers,
labour / manpower / worker shortage

manque de main-d'oeuvre qualifiée
lack / shortage of skilled workers / labour
/ manpower

marché de la main-d'oeuvre
employment / labour market

marge de main-d'oeuvre inutilisée
employment / labour market slack

médecin de la main-d'oeuvre (Fr.)
labour medical adviser

**méthode fondée sur l'utilisation de la
main-d'oeuvre**
labour-intensive method

migration de main-d'oeuvre
manpower / labour migration, migration
of labour

mobilité de la main-d'oeuvre
labour / manpower / work force / worker
mobility

mouvement de la main-d'oeuvre
turnover of labour, labour turnover; staff
movement

offre excédentaire de main-d'oeuvre
excess supply of labour

offre de main-d'oeuvre
manpower / labour supply, supply of
labour; worker availability

offre de main-d'oeuvre excédentaire
oversupply of labour

offre potentielle de main-d'oeuvre
potential manpower supply

pays recruteur de main-d'oeuvre
labour(-)recruiting country

pénurie de main-d'oeuvre
labour deficit / shortage / scarcity,
shortage of labour / manpower, manpower
/ occupational / worker shortage, under-
supply of workers; labour / manpower
bottleneck

pénurie de main-d'oeuvre agricole
farm labour shortage

pénurie de main-d'oeuvre qualifiée
skilled labour / skill shortage, shortage /
lack of skilled labour

pénurie persistante de main-d'oeuvre
long-term / persistent manpower shortage

perfectionnement de la main-d'oeuvre
development of manpower, manpower
development

planification de la main-d'oeuvre
manpower / work force planning

**planification de la main-d'oeuvre des
entreprises**
company / corporate manpower planning

politique d'emploi et de main-d'oeuvre
employment and manpower policy

politique de rétention de main-d'oeuvre
labour hoarding policy

potentiel de main-d'oeuvre
labour force / manpower potential

prêt de main-d'oeuvre
labour detachment

prix de la main-d'oeuvre
labour price

prix d'offre de la main-d'oeuvre
supply price of labour

**productivité horaire de la main-
d'oeuvre**
hourly productivity of labour

productivité de la main-d'oeuvre
productivity of labour, labour productivity

**profession en excédent de main-
d'oeuvre**
surplus occupation

profession en pénurie de main-d'oeuvre
shortage occupation, occupation in short
supply

**programme en faveur de la main-
d'oeuvre**
manpower programme

**projection des besoins en main-
d'oeuvre**
projected manpower requirement

réaffectation de la main-d'oeuvre
redeployment of labour

recrutement de la main-d'oeuvre
manpower recruitment

recyclage de la main-d'oeuvre
retraining of manpower

redéploiement de la main-d'oeuvre
redeployment of labour

région à excédent de main-d'oeuvre
labour surplus area

rencensement de la main-d'oeuvre
manpower inventory

renouvellement de la main-d'oeuvre
labour / staff turnover

répartition de la main-d'oeuvre
allocation of labour

réserve de main-d'oeuvre
labour / manpower reserve

réserve de main-d'oeuvre disponible
(occ.) stand-by workforce

réservoir de main-d'oeuvre
labour pool, pool of workers / of labour

ressources de / en main-d'oeuvre
labour / manpower resources / supply

ressources de main-d'oeuvre inutilisées
labour market slack

rétention de main-d'oeuvre
labour hoarding; overmanning

**rotation / roulement de la main-
d'oeuvre**
turnover (of labour), (labour) turnover

service de la main-d'oeuvre
employment service; (pl.) labour services

source de main-d'oeuvre
manpower / supply source

sous-emploi de la main-d'oeuvre
under-utilisation of labour

sous-traitance de main-d'oeuvre
labour sub-contracting

sous-utilisation de la main-d'oeuvre
under-utilisation of labour

**sous-utilisation de la main-d'oeuvre et
des installations**
under-utilisation of labour and capacity

**système de prestation de services de
main-d'oeuvre**
manpower delivery system

taux d'activité de la main-d'oeuvre
labour force participation rate

**taux de la main-d'oeuvre excédentaire
des jeunes**
youth labour surplus rate

taux de rotation de la main-d'oeuvre
labour turnover rate

trafic de main-d'oeuvre
labour traffic / trafficking

utilisation de la main-d'oeuvre
utilisation of manpower

viscosité de la main-d'oeuvre
manpower rigidity

volant de main-d'oeuvre
labour / manpower reserve

zone de recrutement de main-d'oeuvre
labour recruiting area

MAINTENANCE
maintenance

MAINTENIR
to retain; to preserve; to maintain

maintenir les emplois
to preserve / to maintain (existing) jobs

maintenir le niveau d'emploi
to maintain employment level

maintenir les salaires au niveau du coût de la vie
to keep wages abreast of the cost of living

MAINTENU
droit maintenu d'office
automatically maintained right, right automatically maintained

MAINTIEN
assurance-maintien du salaire en cas d'arrêt de travail
salary continuation insurance

clause de maintien des avantages acquis
(occ.) grandfather clause

garantie de maintien dans l'emploi
job security

maintien à domicile des personnes âgées
home care for the elderly

maintien des droits
maintenance / preservation of rights

maintien des droits acquis
maintenance of acquired / vested rights

maintien d'un droit à (des) prestations
retention of a right to benefits

maintien de l'effectif / des effectifs
staff retention

maintien de l'emploi
job maintenance

maintien dans l'emploi
job retention / security

maintien en état
maintenance

maintien en fonction
retention

maintien du personnel
employee retention

maintien du pouvoir d'achat
maintenance of purchasing power

maintien du salaire
continued payment of wage, wage continuation

maintien du service des prestations
continued payment of benefits

subvention pour le maintien à domicile (UK)
community care grant

taux de maintien en fonction
retention rate, rate of retention

MAISON
house, home; (occ.) in-house

employé de maison
domestic employee / servant; (pl.) service personnel, domestic servants

employés de maison et travailleurs assimilés non classés ailleurs [CITP-1968 (5-4)]
maids and related housekeeping service workers not elsewhere classified [ISCO-1968 (5-4)]

gens de maison
domestic servants

maison d'accueil
residential home (for old people)

maison d'aliénés
mental home

maison de convalescence
convalescent home, half-way house

maison familiale de vacances
family holiday home

maison individuelle
private house

maison maternelle
maternal home

maison de quartier
neighbourhood centre

maison de refuge
assistance home

maison de repos
convalescent / rest / nursing home

maison de retraite
old people home, nursing home (USA);
custodial care

maison de santé
nursing home

maison de santé mentale
mental home

personnel de maison
domestic servants

syndicat maison
house / in-house / company union

MAÎTRE
master; teacher

établissement de formation des maîtres
college of education

MAÎTRISE
workmanship; (ed.) master's degree

agent de maîtrise
foreman, supervisor; technician; (pl.)
lower management; supervisory staff

examen de maîtrise
(occ.) master craftsman's examination

maîtrise des coûts
cost containment

maîtrise des dépenses
expenditure control

maîtrise des dépenses de santé
health expenditure control

maîtrise totale de la qualité (MTQ)
total quality control (TQC)

MAJEUR (adj.)
major; of age

(cas de) force majeure
act of God, force majeure

MAJORATEUR
effet majorateur
mark-up effect

MAJORATION
rise; increase, increment; additional charge, surcharge; supplement
majoration en fonction de l' / pour âge
age addition

majoration pour charges de famille
dependency supplement

majoration pour conjoint
increase / supplement in respect of spouse

majoration de cotisation
increase of contribution

majoration pour enfant
child supplement / increase

majoration pour enfant à charge (UK)
child dependency addition

majoration de fratrie (Finl.)
sibling increase

majoration d'impôts
tax increase

majoration de pension pour enfants
increase in pensions / pension increase /
pension supplement in respect of children

**majoration de la pension de retraite
pour conjoint à charge**
pension supplement / increase in respect
of a dependent spouse

majoration pour personne à charge
increase of benefits for a dependant,
supplement for dependant; family
supplement

majoration des prestations
benefit increase, increase of benefits

majoration de revalorisation
revalorisation increase

majoration du / des salaire(s) / salariale
salary / wage / pay rise / increase

majoration du taux de base
increase of the basic amount

majoration pour tierce personne
attendance allowance for third person,
constant attendance allowance (UK)

MAJORÉ
allocation de soins majorée (Finl.)
increased care allowance

taux majoré
increased / enhanced rate

taux majoré de moitié
(occ.) time and a half rate

MAJORER
to increase; to raise

majorer une prestation
to increase a benefit

MAJORITAIRE
participation majoritaire
majority shareholding

MAJORITAIREMENT
emplois majoritairement féminins
female-dominated occupations

emplois majoritairement masculins
male-dominated occupations

MAJORITÉ
âge légal de la majorité
statutory majority age

MAL
mal payé / rémunéré
low / badly / ill / poorly paid

emploi mal payé / mal rémunéré
low-wage job

MALADE (adj.)
ill; sick

porter malade (se faire)
to report sick

tomber malade
to be taken ill

MALADE (n.)
patient

**clientèle de malades pris en charge par
le service public**
(occ.) public practice

faux malade
malingerer

groupe homogène de malades (GHM)
diagnosis related group

hôpital pour malades chroniques
chronic disease hospital

malade ambulatoire
ambulatory patient, (hospital) out-patient

malade chronique
chronic sick

malade condamné
terminally ill

malade externe
ambulatory patient, (hospital) out-patient

malade hospitalisé
(hospital) in-patient

malade non hospitalisé
ambulatory patient, (hospital) out-patient

malade incurable
terminally ill

malade atteint de longue maladie
long-term patient

malade mental
mentally disordered person

malade mourant / en phase terminale
terminal patient

malade en traitement ambulatoire
(hospital) out-patient

malade en traitement de jour
day patient

participation du malade aux frais
cost-sharing, patient's contribution

rémunération par malade inscrit
capitation(-fee) system

**services recevant des malades hospita-
lisés**
in-patient facilities / units

soins infirmiers aux malades mentaux
mental health nursing

soins aux malades
patient care

soins aux malades hospitalisés
(occ.) residential care

soins aux malades non hospitalisés
(occ.) non-residential care

soins aux malades en traitement de jour
day patient care

système de participation du malade aux frais
cost-sharing system

système de la rémunération par malade inscrit
capitation-fee system

MALADIE
illness, disease; sickness; ill health

absence pour maladie
sick leave

arrêt de maladie / arrêt-maladie
sick leave, absence from work owing to illness

arrêt de maladie (en)
absent from work owing to illness

arrêt de travail pour maladie
sick leave, absence from work owing to illness

arrêt de travail pour maladie (en)
absent from work owing to illness

assurance (contre les) accidents du travail et les maladies professionnelles
industrial injury / injuries insurance, insurance against accident at work; employers' liability insurance; compensation scheme; accident insurance

assurance(-)maladie
health / medical / sickness insurance, medical benefits insurance

assurance-maladie pour les plus démunis (USA)
medicare

assurance (contre les) maladies professionnelles
insurance against occupational disease

attribution d'indemnités de maladie
provision of sickness benefit(s)

caisse d'assurance maladie
health (insurance) fund; sickness fund

caisse de compensation pour les accidents du travail et les maladies professionnelles
(occ.) workmen's compensation board

caisse (de) maladie
sick (benefit) fund, sickness (insurance) fund

caisse-maladie locale générale
general local sick fund

caisse primaire d'assurance maladie (CPAM) (Fr.)
local health fund

caisse régionale d'assurance maladie (CRAM) (Fr.)
regional health fund

Classification internationale des maladies (CIM)
International Classification of Diseases (ICD)

classification des maladies
classification of diseases

congé de maladie
sick leave

congé de maladie approuvé
certified sick leave

congé de maladie à mi-temps
half-time sick leave

cotisation à l'assurance-maladie
health / sickness insurance contribution

couverture maladie
health coverage / insurance

couverture maladie universelle (Fr.)
universal health coverage

couverture des risques de maladie
health insurance cover

décès dû à un accident du travail ou à une maladie professionnelle
death from employment (injury)

déclaration de maladie
notification of sickness / of illness

durée moyenne des cas de maladie
average duration per case

enregistrement des maladies
registration of diseases

feuille de maladie
medical record; medical (expenses refund) claim form (Fr.)

fichiers courants de maladie
routine records of sickness

garantie maladie
sickness coverage

indemnité journalière de maladie
daily sickness benefit

indemnités légales de maladie (UK)
statutory sick pay

indemnité de maladie
sickness allowance / benefit; sick pay

indemnités maladie / accident du travail pour travailleurs indépendants
occupational sick pay for self-employed workers

indemnité de maladie versée en espèces
cash sickness benefit

institution d'assurance(-)maladie
sickness insurance institution

jour d'arrêt pour maladie
day off for illness

liste de maladies professionnelles
list of professional diseases

livret de longue maladie
long-term sickness order book

longue maladie
long-term sickness / disease

lutte contre les maladies
disease control

lutte contre les maladies transmissibles
communicable disease control

malade atteint de longue maladie
long-term patient

maladie aiguë
acute illness / sickness / disorder / disease

maladie chronique
chronic disease / illness / sickness

maladie contagieuse
contagious disease

maladie à déclaration obligatoire
notifiable / reportable disease; scheduled disease

maladie évolutive
active / progressive disease

maladie non évolutive
inactive disease

maladie générale
(occ.) systemic disease

maladie grave
dangerous / major / serious / severe illness

maladie handicapante
handicapping condition

maladie donnant lieu à hospitalisation
hospitalised illness

maladie infectieuse
infectious disease

maladie invalidante / entraînant l'invalidité
disabling disease / illness, incapacitating illness, crippling disease

maladies et lésions d'origine professionnelle
work-related / occupational diseases and injuries

maladie longue et coûteuse
prolonged and expensive illness

maladie de longue durée
long-term sickness / disease

maladie mentale
mental infirmity / illness

maladie dans sa / en phase terminale
terminal illness

maladie prévalente
prevalent disease

maladie professionnelle
occupational illness, industrial / occupational / professional disease

maladie non professionnelle
non-occupational disease

maladie professionnelle indemnisée
occupational disease for which the benefit has been awarded

maladie professionnelle reconnue
prescribed industrial disease

maladie prolongée
prolonged illness

maladie reconnue
prescribed / scheduled disease

maladie la plus répandue
prevalent disease

maladie du système ostéo-articulaire et des muscles
musculo-skeletal disease

maladie transmissible
communicable disease

maladie du travail
industrial / occupational / professional disease

maladie de la vieillesse
geriatric disorder

nombre de jours d'arrêt pour maladie
number of days lost to illness

nombre moyen de journées de maladie
mean number of days of illness

période de maladie
period of sickness

prestation de l'assurance maladie
sick(ness) benefit

prestation pour lésion ou maladie (professionnelle) (UK)
injury benefit (UK, Irel., Malta), industrial injury / employment injury benefit

prestation (en cas) (de) maladie
sick(ness) / medical benefit

prestation de maladie-maternité
sickness-maternity benefit

prestation de maladie professionnelle
benefit in respect of occupational disease(s)

prestation en nature de l'assurance maladie
health benefit in kind

prestation en nature de maladie ou de maternité
sickness or maternity benefit in kind

prestation réglementaire de maladie (UK)
statutory sick pay

prévalence des maladies
prevalence of diseases

prévention des accidents du travail et des maladies professionnelles
industrial / occupational health and safety

prévention des maladies
prevention of diseases

régime d'assurance-maladie
health insurance scheme

régime d'assurance maladie ou maternité
sickness or maternity insurance scheme, scheme for sickness or maternity insurance

régime d'indemnisation en cas d'accident ou de maladie
compensation scheme for industrial injuries

rente de maladie professionnelle
pension for / in respect of an occupational disease

réparation des accidents du travail et des maladies professionnelles
workmen's compensation (for industrial injuries and professional diseases)

tableau des maladies professionnelles
table of occupational diseases

taux de maladies professionnelles
occupational illness rate

taux de mortalité par suite de maladie professionnelle
occupational fatality rate

victime d'une maladie professionnelle
person who contracts an occupational
disease

MALAISE
indice de malaise économique
(economic) discomfort index

malaise social
industrial / labour unrest

MALENTENDANT
travailleur malentendant
hearing-impaired worker

MALFAÇON
malpractice

MALFORMATION
malformation

MALHEUREUX
candidat malheureux
unsuccessful candidate

MALTRAITANCE
maltraitance des enfants
child abuse

MALTRAITÉ
neglected

MALVERSATION
malpractice; embezzlement

MALVOYANT (n.)
visually impaired person

MANDAT
authority; (term of) office; terms of reference, terms; responsibility; work

donner mandat de
to authorise

durée d'un mandat
term / tenure of office

mandat Colbert (Fr.)
Colbert money order

prorogation d'un mandat
renewal of tenure

renouvellement de mandat
re(-)appointment (on the expiry of the
term of office)

MANDATER
to appoint; to commission; to empower; to
give a mandate to

MANIFESTATION
demonstration; manifestation

manifestation collective
mass manifestation

MANIFLEX
maniflex

MANNEQUIN
mannequins et autres modèles [CITP-
1988 (521)]
fashion and other models [ISCO-1988
(521)]

MANOEUVRE
general workman, unskilled worker /
labourer, (occ.) manual worker

**conducteurs de véhicules et d'engins
lourds de levage et de manoeuvre
[CITP-1988 (83)]**
drivers and mobile plant operators [ISCO-
1988 (83)]

emploi de manoeuvre
(occ.) labouring occupation

manoeuvre non agricole
non-farm labourer

**manoeuvres de l'agriculture, de la
pêche et assimilés [CITP-1988 (92) /
(921)]**
agricultural, fishery and related labourers
[ISCO-1988 (92) / (921)]

manoeuvres non classés ailleurs [CITP-1968 (9-9)]
labourers not elsewhere classified [ISCO-1968 (9-9)]

manoeuvres des industries manufacturières [CITP-1988 (932)]
manufacturing labourers [ISCO-1988 (932)]

manoeuvres des mines, du bâtiment et des travaux publics [CITP-1988 (931)]
mining and construction labourers [ISCO-1988 (931)]

manoeuvres des mines, du bâtiment et des travaux publics, des industries manufacturières et des transports [CITP-1988 (93)]
labourers in mining, construction, manufacturing and transport [ISCO-1988 (93)]

manoeuvre ordinaire
ordinary labourer

manoeuvre ordinaire adulte masculin
ordinary adult male labourer

manoeuvres des transports et manutentionnaires [CITP-1988 (933)]
transport labourers and freight handlers [ISCO-1988 (933)]

manoeuvre(-)type
typical unskilled male worker, person deemed typical of unskilled labour

ouvriers et manoeuvres
production and related workers

profession de manoeuvre
labouring occupation

MANOEUVRE-BALAI
unskilled labourer

MANQUE
lack, shortage, scarcity; want

indemnité pour manque à gagner
compensation for loss of wages / earnings

manque de compétence
lack of skill

manque de compétences professionnelles
lack of occupational skills

manque d'expérience pratique
lack of practical experience / of work experience

manque à gagner
loss of profit / of wages / of (potential) earnings

manque de main-d'oeuvre
lack / shortage / under-supply of workers, labour / manpower / worker shortage

manque de main-d'oeuvre qualifiée
lack / shortage of skilled workers / labour / manpower

manque de motivation
lack of incentive / of motivation

manque de moyens
lack of means

manque de personnel
shortage of staff, staff shortage, understaffing, undermanning

manque de personnel qualifié
lack / shortage of skilled workers / labour / manpower

manque de ponctualité
unpunctuality

manque à produire
foregone output

manque de qualification
lack of skill

manque de travail
lack / shortage of work, work shortage

manque de travailleurs
lack / shortage / under-supply of workers, labour / manpower / worker shortage

MANQUEMENT
failure to observe; violation, breach; departure (from); default

manquement au contrat de travail
breach of contract of employment

manquement aux devoirs de fonction
breach of professional / official duty

MANQUER
manquer de personnel
to be understaffed / undermanned / short-handed / short-staffed, to be short of staff

MANUEL (adj.)
aptitude manuelle
manual / manipulative skill

dévalorisation du travail manuel
downgrading of manual labour

métier manuel
manual work / occupation, craft

régime applicable aux travailleurs manuel
scheme applicable to manual workers

revalorisation du travail manuel
upgrading of manual work

travail manuel
manual work / labour

travail non manuel
non-manual /white-collar job / work / occupation

travailleur manuel
blue-collar (worker); manual worker; (pl.) (occ.) industrial staff

travailleur non manuel
clerical / office / non-manual worker, white-collar (worker); (pl.) (occ.) clerical and office workers

travailleur manuel spécialisé
semi-skilled manual worker

MANUEL (n.)
manual

manuel d'assurance-qualité (MQ)
quality assurance manual

MANUFACTURIER
industries manufacturières
manufacturing industries

manoeuvres des industries manufacturières [CITP-1988 (932)]
manufacturing labourers [ISCO-1988 (932)]

MANUTENTION
manutentions portuaires
dock work

MANUTENTIONNAIRE
conducteurs d'engins de manutention et de terrassement, dockers et manutentionnaires [CITP-1968 (9-7)]
material-handling and related equipment operators, dockers and freight handlers [ISCO-1968 (9-7)]

manoeuvres des transports et manutentionnaires [CITP-1988 (933)]
transport labourers and freight handlers [ISCO-1988 (933)]

MARC
marc le franc (au)
proportionally, pro rata

MARCHAND (adj.)
emploi non marchand
non-market job

marin de la marine marchande
merchant seaman

travail marchand
market work

travail non marchand
non-market work

MARCHANDISE
good; commodity

MARCHE
marche à suivre
procedure

marche du travail
work flow

MARCHÉ
market; contract

accès au marché de l'emploi
access to the labour market

adaptation au marché du travail
labour market adjustment

agriculteurs et ouvriers qualifiés de l'agriculture et de la pêche destinées aux marchés [CITP-1988 (61)]
market-oriented skilled agricultural and fishery workers [ISCO-1988 (61)]

agriculteurs et ouvriers qualifiés des cultures destinées aux marchés [CITP-1988 (611)]
market gardeners and crop growers [ISCO-1988 (611)]

agriculteurs et ouvriers qualifiés de polyculture et d'élevage destinés aux marchés [CITP-1988 (613)]
market-oriented crop and animal producers [ISCO-1988 (613)]

analyse du marché du travail
labour market analysis

autorisation de mise sur le marché (Fr.)
permit to market, licensing authorisation

autorités (responsables) du marché du travail
labour market institutions / authorities

besoins du marché du travail
labour market needs

capacité d'absorption du marché du travail
labour market absorption capacity

complément de salaire lié à la situation du marché de l'emploi (Swed.)
market pay supplement

comportement du marché du travail
labour market performance

conjoncture du marché du travail
labour market conditions

croissance du marché de l'emploi
labour market growth

demande sur le marché du travail
labour market demand

déséquilibre du marché de l'emploi / du travail
labour market imbalance, imbalance / disequilibrium on the labour market

désorganisation du marché du travail
labour market / manpower dislocation, dislocation of the labour market

dynamique du marché du travail
labour market dynamics

économie de marché
market economy

économie de marché sociale
social market economy

efficacité du marché du travail
labour market efficiency

emploi sur le marché primaire
mainstream job

équilibre du marché de l'emploi / du travail
labour market equilibrium, balance of / equilibrium on the labour market

état du marché du travail
labour market conditions

évolution du marché du travail
labour market development

évolution de l'offre sur le marché du travail
changes in labour supply

flexibilité du marché du travail
labour market flexibility

fonctionnement du marché de l'emploi / du travail
functioning / operation of the labour market, labour market operation(s)

forces du marché
market forces

habitations à bon marché
low-cost housing

intégration au marché du travail
labour market integration / entry

intervenant sur le marché du travail
labour market partner

liens avec le marché du travail
labour market attachment

logements à bon marché
low-cost housing

main-d'oeuvre bon marché
cheap labour

marché des carrières
career market

marché contestable
contestable market

marché de l'emploi
labour / employment / job market

marché de la formation
training market

marché du logement
housing market

marché de la main-d'oeuvre
employment / labour market

marché matrimonial
marriage market

marché national de l'emploi / du travail
domestic / national labour market

marché ouvert
open market

marché primaire de l'emploi / du travail
mainstream / primary labour market

marché secondaire de l'emploi / du travail
secondary labour market

marché de la sécurité sociale
social security contract

marché du travail
employment / job / labour market

marché du travail agricole
agricultural / farm labour market

marché du travail civil
civilian labour market

marché du travail externe
external labour market

marché du travail intérieur
domestic labour market

marché du travail interne
internal labour market

marché du travail local
local labour market

marché du travail naturel
natural labour market

marché du travail normal
normal / open labour market

marché du travail officiel / organisé
official / organised / formal labour market

marché du travail restreint / serré / tendu
tight labour market

mécanismes du marché
market forces

mesures visant le marché du travail
labour market policy

mouvements sur le marché du travail
labour market flow

nouveau venu sur le marché du travail
labour force entrant, (new) entrant on the labour market

observation du marché du travail
labour market monitoring

participation au marché du travail
labour market / labour force attachment, attachment to the labour force

personnel des services et vendeurs de magasin et de marché [CITP-1988 (5)]
service workers and shop and market sales workers [ISCO-1988 (5)]

perturbation du marché du travail
labour market / manpower dislocation, dislocation of the labour market

politique d'intervention (directe) sur le marché du travail
active labour market policy

politique du marché du travail
labour market policy

pression(s) exercée(s) sur le marché du travail
labour market pressure

problème d'intégration au marché du travail
labour market entry difficulty

programme de construction d'habitations à bon marché
low-cost housing programme

programme du / intéressant le marché du travail
labour market programme / scheme

prospection du marché du travail
(occ.) job exploration

ralentissement du marché du travail
labour market slack

réajustement / réaménagement du marché du travail
adjustment of the labour market

réinsertion sur le marché de l'emploi / du travail
reintegration into the labour market

réintégrer le marché du travail
to re-enter the labour force

rendement du marché du travail
labour market performance

rentrée sur le marché du travail
re-entry into the labour force

rentrer sur le marché du travail
to re-enter the labour force

resserrement du marché du travail / de l'emploi
tightening of the job market

retirer du marché du travail (se)
to withdraw from the labour force

retour sur le marché du travail
re-entry (into the labour force)

rétrécissement du marché du travail / de l'emploi
tightening of the job market

revenir sur le marché du travail
to re-enter the labour force

rigidité du marché du travail
labour market rigidity

rouages du marché de l'emploi / du travail
functioning / operation of the labour market

salaire du marché
market salary

secteur du marché de l'emploi / du travail
labour market sector, segment of labour market

segmentation du marché du travail
labour market segmentation

situation du marché de l'emploi / du travail
manpower / job situation, labour market situation / conditions

sortie du marché de l'emploi / du travail
withdrawal from employment / from the labour force

stabilisation du marché du travail
labour market stabilisation

statistiques relatives au marché du travail
labour market statistics

structure du marché du travail
labour market structure

suivi du marché du travail
labour market monitoring

système du marché du travail
labour market system

taux d'absorption des nouveaux venus sur le marché du travail
rate of absorption of labour market entrants

taux du marché
market rate

tendance du marché de l'emploi / du travail
labour market trend

travailleurs du marché primaire de l'emploi
primary labour force, mainstream workers

travailleurs du marché secondaire
secondary labour force

vendeurs à l'étal et sur les marchés [CITP-1988 (523)]
stall and market salespersons [ISCO-1988 (523)]

MARGE
scope

écart introduit à la marge par la fiscalité
marginal tax wedge

marge de capacité inutilisée
capacity slack

marge de main-d'oeuvre inutilisée
employment / labour market slack

marge entre les rémunérations nettes
net remuneration margin

marge de résistance au travail
work(ing) tolerance

MARGINAL (adj.)
marginal; incremental

avantages marginaux
fringe benefits

coût marginal
marginal cost

coût marginal du travail
marginal cost of labour

prestation marginale
marginal / fringe benefit

prestation marginale d'assistance en espèces (Denm.)
marginal cash assistance benefit

produit marginal du travail
marginal product of labour

revenu marginal du travail
marginal revenue of labour

taux d'imposition marginal
marginal rate of tax, marginal tax rate

taux marginaux d'imposition effectifs
marginal effective tax rates (METR)

travailleur marginal
marginal worker

MARGINAL (n.)
social misfit; (occ.) drop-out

MARGINALISATION
marginalisation, marginality

MARGINALITÉ
fringe / marginal status

MARI
husband

assurance du mari
husband's insurance

mari décédé
late husband

pension versée sur la base de l'assurance du mari
pension by virtue of husband's contributions

MARIAGE
marriage; wedding

allocation de mariage
marriage grant

certificat de mariage
marriage certificate

enfant né hors mariage
child born out of wedlock

mariage de facto
common law marriage

prime de mariage
marriage grant / gratuity

MARIÉ
married (person); ever-married

couple marié
married couple

couple marié avec enfants
married couple with children, married couple family

femme mariée
married woman

femme mariée qui travaille
working wife

homme marié
married man

personne mariée
married person

MARIN (adj.)
cure marine
thalassatherapy

MARIN (n.)
seaman, seafarer; mariner

contrat d'engagement des marins
ship's articles

marin breveté
able(-bodied) seaman

marin de commerce
merchant seaman

marin de deuxième classe
able(-bodied) seaman

marin de la marine marchande
merchant seaman

marin pêcheur
fisherman, seafisherman

MARINE
marin de la marine marchande
merchant seaman

MARITAL
vie maritale
cohabitation

MARITALEMENT
vivre maritalement
to cohabit, to live as husband and wife

MARITIME
agent maritime
shipping agent

compagnie maritime
shipping (line)

inscrit maritime
seaman registered for service in the navy

transport maritime
shipping

MASCULIN
emplois majoritairement masculins
male-dominated occupations

manoeuvre ordinaire adulte masculin
ordinary adult male labourer

ouvrier masculin qualifié
skilled manual male employee

population active masculine
male labour force

profession à prédominance masculine
male-dominated occupation

taux d'activité masculine
male participation rate

MASQUÉ (adj.)
chômage masqué
concealed unemployment

travail masqué
disguised employment

MASSE
effet de masse (wages)
percentage increase of the total wage bill

impôt sur la masse des salaires / salariale
payroll tax

masse des salaires industriels
industrial payroll

masse salariale
wage / pay bill, total payroll / wage (bill);
payroll; total earnings

masse salariale brute
total gross earnings

masse salariale investie (dans...)
invested pay, investment wage

production de masse
large-scale / mass production

réduire la masse salariale
to cut the payroll

taxe sur la masse des salaires / sur la masse salariale
payroll tax

MASSEUR-KINÉSITHÉRAPEUTE
physiotherapist

MASSIF
large-scale

chômage massif
general / large-scale / mass unemployment

MATELOT
seaman

matelot de deuxième classe
able(-bodied) seaman

matelots de pont et assimilés [CITP-1988 (834)]
ships' deck crews and related workers [ISCO-1988 (834)]

MATÉRIEL (adj.)
material; physical

abandon matériel
physical neglect

activités économiques de caractère non matériel
non-productive labour

besoin matériel
physical need; (occ.) bodily need / want

champ d'application matériel (ratione materiae)
material scope; substantive scope

dommage matériel
pecuniairy / material damage

obstacle matériel
physical barrier

organisation matérielle
physical organisation

ressource matérielle
physical resource

MATÉRIEL (n.)
matériel annexe / d'appoint
ancillary equipment

matériel didactique
training / teaching material / aid,
instructional material

matériel d'enseignement
teacher equipment

matériel d'enseignement et d'apprentissage
teaching / learning material

matériel de formation
training material / aid

matériel de jeux
play equipment / material

matériel pédagogique
teacher equipment

matériel récréatif
play equipment / material

matériel roulant
rolling stock (railways)

matériel de sensibilisation
sensitivity material

matériel pour terrains de jeux
playground equipment

MATERNAGE
mothering

MATERNANT
personne maternante
mothering person

MATERNEL
aide à la famille pour l'emploi d'une
assistante maternelle agréée (Fr.)
family benefit for hiring an approved day-
care attendant

aide maternelle
child care worker, child-minder, day-care
attendant

assistante maternelle
child care worker, child-minder, day-care
attendant; (occ.) foster mother (Fr.)

**centre de protection maternelle et
infantile**
maternity child welfare centre

école maternelle
infant / nursery school, kindergarten

hôtel maternel (Fr.)
mother and child accommodation centre

maison maternelle
maternal home

**prestation spéciale assistante
maternelle (Fr.)**
special benefit for day-care attendant

protection maternelle
maternal welfare; maternity care

protection maternelle et infantile
maternal and child welfare

santé maternelle
maternal health

santé maternelle et infantile
maternal and child health

service d'aide maternelle
mother care service; child care service;
(pl.) home-maker services; child care
facilities

service de protection maternelle
maternity service

**service de protection maternelle et
infantile**
maternal and child health service

substitut du lait maternel
infant formula

MATERNISÉ
lait maternisé
infant formula

MATERNITÉ
maternity; motherhood; lying-in clinic

aide financière à la maternité (Cz.)
financial assistance in maternity

**allocation journalière de maternité
(Icel.)**
daily maternity leave grant

allocation de maternité
maternity benefit / pay; (pl.) maternity
allowances

assurance maternité
maternity insurance

carnet de maternité
maternity record

congé de maternité
maternity / pregnancy leave

**indemnité de congé de maternité sans
solde (Austr.)**
unpaid maternity leave allowance

indemnités légales de maternité (UK)
statutory maternity pay

**notification (de la date) du congé de
maternité**
notice of maternity absence

prestation de maladie-maternité
sickness-maternity benefit

prestation (en cas) de maternité
maternity benefit

prestation de maternité en espèces
maternity cash benefit

prestation médicale en cas de maternité
maternity medical benefit

**prestation en nature de maladie ou de
maternité**
sickness or maternity benefit in kind

**prestation réglementaire de maternité
(UK)**
statutory maternity pay

prime de maternité
maternity grant / payment (UK)

protection de la maternité
maternity protection / care

régime d'assurance maladie ou maternité
sickness or maternity insurance scheme, scheme for sickness or maternity insurance

repos de maternité
maternity leave

salaire légal de maternité (UK)
statutory maternity pay

service de maternité
maternity unit; (occ.) lying-in clinic

soins de maternité
maternity care

trousse de maternité
maternity pack

MATHÉMATICIEN
mathématiciens, statisticiens et assimilés [CITP-1988 (212)]
mathematicians, statisticians and related professionals [ISCO-1988 (212)]

MATHÉMATIQUE (adj.)
espérance mathématique
actuarial expectation

réserve mathématique
mathematical reserve

MATHÉMATIQUE (n.)
mathématiques actuarielles
actuarial mathematics

MATIÈRE
branch, discipline, field of study; subject (area / group)

activités de matière grise
knowledge industries

choix des matières
choice of subject (area) / of field of study, subject choice

matière à contestation
case to answer

matières enseignées
content of teaching

matière facultative / en option / optionnelle
optional / elective subject

MATIN
équipe du matin
morning shift

MATRICE
matrice de cotation par points
point-factor matrix

MATRICULE
registration (certificate)

numéro matricule
identification / registration number; insurance number

MATRIMONIAL
matrimonial

agence matrimoniale
marriage bureau

conseil d'orientation matrimoniale
marriage guidance council

conseiller matrimonial
marriage (guidance) counsellor

consultations matrimoniales
marriage counselling / guidance

état matrimonial
marital status / condition

marché matrimonial
marriage market

service de consultations matrimoniales
marriage counselling / guidance

situation matrimoniale
marital / civil / conjugal status, marital condition

MATURATION
maturation (social schemes)

MATURITÉ
maturity

venue à maturité
maturation

MAUVAIS
mauvaises conditions de travail
poor working conditions

mauvais résultats scolaires
(occ.) under-achievement

mauvais traitements
ill treatment, abuse

mauvais traitements à enfant
child abuse

MAXIMAL
maximum

allocation hebdomadaire maximale payable
maximum weekly allowance payable

durée légale maximale du travail
statutory maximum working hours

durée maximale
maximum duration

durée maximale du travail prévue par la loi
statutory maximum working hours

horaires à flexibilité maximale
(occ.) maniflex

montant maximal
maximum amount / rate

montant maximal théorique
highest theoretical amount

niveau maximal de rendement
maximum performance level

période maximale requise
maximum period required

prestation maximale supérieure
overall highest maximum benefit

remboursement maximal au titre des salaires
maximum wage reimbursement

salaire de base maximal imposable
maximum taxable wage rate

salaire hebdomadaire maximal admissible
maximum allowable weekly earnings / wage

taux de rémunération / de salaire maximal
maximum rate of pay

MAXIMISATION
maximisation de l'emploi
maximisation of employment opportunities

MAXIMUM
maximum; ceiling

durée maximum
maximum duration

maximum de sa capacité (au)
to its full capacity

montant maximum
maximum amount / rate

montant maximum théorique
highest theoretical amount

période maximum requise
maximum period required

prestation maximum supérieure
overall highest maximum benefit

MÉCANICIEN
mécaniciens et ajusteurs d'appareils électriques et électroniques [CITP-1988 (724)]
electrical and electronic equipment mechanics and fitters [ISCO-1988 (724)]

mécaniciens et ajusteurs de machines [CITP-1988 (723)]
machinery mechanics and fitters [ISCO-1988 (723)]

mécaniciens de précision sur métaux et matériaux similaires [CITP-1988 (731)]
precision workers in metal and related materials [ISCO-1988 (731)]

pilotes, officiers de pont et officiers mécaniciens (marine et aviation) [CITP-1968 (0-4)]
aircraft and ships' officers [ISCO-1968 (0-4)]

MÉCANIQUE
mechanics; engineering : mechanical

compétences en mécanique
mechanical skills

industrie mécanique
engineering industry

MÉCANISME
mechanism; procedure, system; scheme; (pl.) machinery

mécanisme de consultation
consultative mechanism

mécanisme de contrôle
supervisory procedure; monitoring mechanism

mécanisme de formation des prix
price mechanism

mécanisme de groupe
group process

mécanismes de la lecture et de l'écriture
(occ.) literacy skills

mécanismes du marché
market forces

MÉCONNAÎTRE
to disregard; to be in breach of

MÉCONTENTEMENT
discontent

mécontentement social
social discontent

MÉDAILLE
médaille d'ancienneté / du travail
long-service award, seniority / service / long-service medal

MÉDECIN
doctor, physician; medical practitioner / officer; (pl.) medical profession

association de médecins
medical association

attestation de médecin
doctor's certificate

choix du médecin
choice of doctor

collège de médecins
panel of doctors

honoraires de médecin
doctor's / medical fees

libre choix du médecin
free choice of doctor

médecin agréé
approved doctor

médecins et assimilés (à l'exception des cadres infirmiers) [CITP-1988 (222)]
health professionals (except nursing) [ISCO-1988 (222)]

médecin de cabinet
doctor working in a town

médecin de caisse
(social security) fund doctor (Fr.), sickness fund doctor (Ger.)

médecin-conseil
medical consultant / adviser, supervising medical consultant

médecin consultant
(medical) consultant

médecin sous contrat
contract doctor

médecin contrôleur
examining doctor

médecin conventionné
health service doctor, national health doctor, panel doctor

médecin non conventionné
non-approved doctor

médecins, dentistes, vétérinaires et travailleurs assimilés [CITP-1968 (0-6/7)]
medical, dental, veterinary and related workers [ISCO-1968 (0-6/7)]

médecin de district
district physician

médecin en / d'entreprise
industrial doctor; company medical officer, company / works doctor

médecin de l'Etat (Malta)
Government practitioner

médecin-expert
medical expert

médecin de famille
family doctor

médecin fonctionnaire
employed doctor

médecin généraliste
general practitioner

médecin habilité à exercer (Can.)
licensed physician

médecin d'hôpital / des hôpitaux / hospitalier
doctor in hospital, hospital medical officer, hospital doctor

médecin inscrit au registre
registered practitioner

médecin-inspecteur
medical inspector

médecin-inspecteur du travail
occupational health inspector

médecin libéral
private doctor

médecin de la main-d'oeuvre (Fr.)
labour medical adviser

médecin praticien
medical practitioner

médecin de premier contact
physician of first contact

médecin principal
senior medical officer

médecin référant (Fr.)
refering doctor

médecin de (la) santé publique
medical officer of health, public health physician / medical officer

médecin (de santé) scolaire
school health doctor / medical officer

médecin de santé publique
medical officer of health, public health physician / medical officer

médecin traitant
attending physician; family doctor; doctor in attendance

médecin du travail
occupational health doctor; works (Gr.) / industrial medical officer, industrial doctor

médecin vacataire
part-time doctor

médecin de ville
non-hospital doctor; doctor working in a town

Ordre des Médecins (Fr.)
medical association

profession de médecin
medical profession

titre médecin (Fr.)
coupon for medical consultation in a third party system

visites du médecin traitant à l'hôpital
in-hospital doctor's care

MÉDECINE
medicine; medical profession

centre de médecine scolaire
school health clinic / centre

centre de médecine sportive
sports medicine centre

dispensaire de médecine sociale
social medicine centre

docteur en médecine
doctor of medicine

école de médecine
medical college

études de médecine
undergraduate medical studies

exercice libéral de la médecine
free medical practice, free practice of
medicine

faculté de médecine
medical college

**médecine des collectivités / commu-
nautaire**
community medicine

médecine curative
remedial medicine

médecine dentaire
dentistry

médecine d'équipe
team / group medicine

médecine étatisée
State medicine

médecine générale
general (medical) practice

médecine globale
comprehensive medicine

médecine de groupe
group medicine, group (medical) practice

médecine légale
forensic medicine

médecine libérale (la)
free practice of medicine

médecine naturelle
naturopathy; natureopathy

médecine préhospitalière d'urgence
prehospital medicine

médecine préventive
preventive medicine

médecine au rabais
cheap medicine

médecine rééducative
rehabilitation medicine

médecine réparatrice
restorative services

médecine scolaire
school health

médecine sociale
social medicine

médecine du travail
industrial / occupational medicine / health

médecine d'urgence
emergency medicine

médecine de ville
general medicine as practised in towns

**service d'aide médicale d'urgence
(SAMU)**
emergency medical relief service

service de médecine du travail
occupational health service

soins de médecine générale
general medical care, general practitioner
care

MÉDIAN
salaire médian
median wage

MÉDIATEUR
arbitrator, conciliator, mediator; ombuds-
man

médiateur pour enfants (Norw.)
commissioner for children

MÉDIATION
conciliation, mediation

médiation individuelle
individual conciliation

MÉDICAL
medical

accord d'assistance médicale
health care agreement

acte médical
item of care / service; medical treatment

actes de pratique médicale courante
standard medical service

aide médicale
medical assistance

aide médicale à domicile
home medical care, medical home relief (USA)

aide médicale d'urgence
emergency medical aid

allocation pour soins médicaux
(medical) treatment allowance

antécédents médicaux
medical history

arrêt de travail pour raison médicale
(occ.) medical suspension

assistance médicale
medical aid

assistance médicale à domicile
medical home relief (USA)

assistance sociale et médicale
social and medical assistance

assistant médical
medical assistant

assurance gros frais médicaux
major medical insurance

attestation médicale
medical certificate

auxiliaire médical
medical aid / assistant / auxiliary

biens médicaux
medical commodities

cabinet médical
medical practice

carnet médical
health record

carrière médicale
medical profession

carte médicale
health record

centre médical scolaire
school health clinic / centre

centre post-hospitalier général de réadaptation médicale
(occ.) medical rehabilitation centre

certificat médical
health / medical / doctor's certificate

certificat médical d'aptitude professionnelle
occupational medical certificate

chef des services médicaux
chief medical officer

codification des actes médicaux
codification of items of care

coefficient d'(un) acte médical
reimbursement rate of a medical treatment, item of care coefficient

comité médical paritaire
joint medical committee

commission médicale
medical board

commission médicale périphérique
(occ.) district medical board

conseiller médical
medical adviser

consommateur de soins médicaux
medical consumer

consommation médicale
consumption of medical care

consommation médicale finale
final consumption of medical care

consommation de soins médicaux
consumption of medical care

contentieux médical
medical claims

contrat médical
medical contract

contrôle médical
physical inspection, medical examination

convention médicale
medical agreement

corps médical
medical profession

couverture médicale
health coverage

demande de classement médical
medical clearance request

dispensateur de soins médicaux
medical care provider

distribution des soins médicaux
medical care delivery

dossier médical
medical record; (pl.) health records; (occ.)
case histories

enseignement médical de base
basic medical education

équipement sanitaire et médical
health and medical equipment / facilities

état nécessitant des soins médicaux
condition requiring medical care

examen médical
health check, physical inspection, medical
examination

examen médical conjoint
joint medical examination

examen médical de routine
routine medical test

expertise médicale
expert medical report / opinion

fiche médicale
health record

formation médicale continue
continuing medical education

frais médicaux
medical expenses

groupement médical prépayé (PGP)
prepaid group practice (PGP)

honoraires médicaux
doctor's / medical fees

laboratoire d'analyses médicales
medical analysis laboratory

modèle médical étalon
standardised medical experience

monopole médical
medical monopoly

nomenclature des actes médicaux
classification of items of care

octroi des soins médicaux
provision of medical care

ordonnance médicale
medical prescription

participation aux frais médicaux
contribution towards medical expenses

personnel médical
medical personnel

personnel non médical
non-medical personnel

poste médical
health station / post

pratique médicale de groupe
group (medical) practice

prestataire de soins médicaux
medical care provider

prestation médicale
medical benefit; (pl.) medicare (Austr.)

prestation médicale en cas de maternité
maternity medical benefit

profession médicale
medical profession

questionnaire médical
medical questionnaire

rapport médical
medical record

réadaptation médicale
medical rehabilitation

rééducation médicale
medical rehabilitation

référence médicale opposable (Fr.)
valid medical norm

registre de suivi médical
health register

secret médical
medical secrecy

services médicaux
medical care services

soins médicaux
medical care / treatment / (occ.) attention,
course of treatment

soins médicaux en consultation externe
out-patient treatment

soins médicaux à domicile
home medical care, medical home relief
(USA)

soins médicaux primaires
primary medical care

soins médicaux secondaires
secondary medical care

soins médicaux tertiaires
tertiary medical care

substance médicale
medicine, drug

surconsommation médicale
excessive medical demand

surveillance médicale (ultérieure)
medical supervision / follow-up

surveillance médicale (sous)
under medical supervision

**système indirect de prestations
médicales**
indirect system / pattern of providing
medical care

tarif médical conventionnel
standard medical fee

traitement médical
medical treatment, course of treatment

urgence médicale
emergency health care

visite médicale
medical inspection / examination

visite médicale d'embauche
pre-employment medical examination

visite médicale de reprise
medical examination before returning to
work

visiteur médical
medical representative

MÉDICALISÉ
résidence médicalisée
(occ.) serviced flat

MÉDICAMENT
medicine, drug, medicinal product

contrôle des médicaments
drug control

médicament de confort
comfort / ease drug

médicament essentiel / indispensable
essential medicine / drug

médicament magistral
magistral drug

**médicament délivré / vendu sur or-
donnance**
prescription drug

médicament spécialisé
patent medicine

médicament en vente libre
over-the-counter drug

MÉDICAMENTEUX
dépendance médicamenteuse
drug dependence

MÉDICO-ÉDUCATIF
action médico-éducative
medical and educational work / activities /
processes

MÉDICO-HOSPITALIER
réseau médico-hospitalier
health care (delivery) system

MÉDICO-LÉGAL
expertise médico-légale
expert forensic report

MÉDICO-PÉDAGOGIQUE
centre médico-pédagogique
child guidance clinic / centre

centre médico-pédagogique de cure ambulatoire (Fr.)
out-patient child care centre

service médico-pédagogique
child guidance clinic / centre

MÉDICO-PROFESSIONNEL
institut médico-professionnel
medical (and) occupational institute

MÉDICO-PSYCHO-PÉDAGOGIQUE
commission médico-psycho-pédagogique
child guidance commission

MÉDICO-SANITAIRE
action médico-sanitaire
health care

personnel médico-sanitaire
health personnel / staff / officers

protection médico-sanitaire
health care

système national de protection médico-sanitaire
national system of health care, health care national system

système de protection médico-sanitaire
health care (delivery) system

MÉDICO-SCOLAIRE
centre médico-scolaire
school health centre

MÉDICO-SOCIAL
action médico-sociale
medical (and) social work

assistant médico-social
medico-social worker; almoner

centre d'action médico-sociale précoce
early medical social work centre

protection médico-sociale de l'enfance
medical and social child welfare

service médico-social
medical and social service / (occ.) work

travail médico-social
medical and social work; almoning (UK)

MÉDICO-SPORTIF
centre médico-sportif
sports medicine centre

MÉDIOCRE
élève ayant des résultats scolaires médiocres
under-achiever, low performer / achiever

MEMBRE
member; limb; (pl.) membership

membre artificiel
artificial limb

membres du clergé [CITP-1988 (246)]
religious professionals [ISCO-1988 (246)]

membres du clergé et assimilés [CITP-1968 (1-4)]
workers in religion [ISCO-1968 (1-4)]

membres des corps législatifs et cadres supérieurs de l'administration publique [CITP-1968 (2-0)]
legislative officials and governments administrators [ISCO-1968 (2-0)]

membres cotisants
contributing members

membres de l'exécutif et des corps législatifs [CITP-1988 (111)]
legislators [ISCO-1988 (111)]

membres de l'exécutif et des corps législatifs, et cadres supérieurs de l'administration publique [CITP-1988 (11)]
legislators and senior officials [ISCO-1988 (11)]

membres de l'exécutif et des corps législatifs, cadres supérieurs de l'administration publique, dirigeants et cadres supérieurs d'entreprise [CITP-1988 (1)]
legislators, senior officials and managers [ISCO-1988 (1)]

membre de la famille
member of the family; relative

membre de la fonction publique
civil servant

membres des forces de l'ordre (Malta)
members of a disciplined force

membre du ménage
member of the household

membre à part entière
full member

membre d'une profession libérale
professional (worker)

membres salariés de la famille
earning members of the family

membre des services sociaux
social (welfare) worker

membre d'un syndicat
(trade) union member; unionist

MÉMOIRE
carte à mémoire
smart card

MÉMORANDUM
mémorandum d'accord / d'entente
memorandum of understanding

MENACÉ (adj.)
emploi menacé
threatened job

MENACE (n.)
menace pour l'emploi
employment threat

menace de renvoi
threat of dismissal

MÉNAGE
married couple; household (unit)

allocation de ménage (Switz.)
household allowance

budget du ménage
household budget

chef de ménage
head of (the) household, householder

composition du ménage
household structure

comptes du ménage
household budget

consommation des ménages
household consumption

désendettement des ménages
reduction of household tax burden

dimension du ménage
household size

données relatives aux ménages
household data

échantillon de ménages
household sample, sample of households

enquête auprès des / sur les ménages, enquête-ménages
household survey

faux ménage
irregular household

feuille de ménage
household schedule

jeune ménage
young couple

locaux (destinés à être) occupés par plus d'un ménage
multi-household living quarters

membre du ménage
member of the household

ménage (de)
domestic

ménage bi-actif
two-income family, dual income household

ménage bi-actif sans enfants
dual income with no kids (DINK)

ménage collectif
collective / non-family household

ménage complexe
joint family, complex / composite
household

ménage dissocié
broken / dissolved household

ménage à faible revenu
low-income household

ménage non familial
non-family household

ménage monoactif
one-earner family

ménage monoparental
single-parent / sole-parent household

ménage multifamilial
multi-family / multiple(-)family household

ménage multiple
multi-person household

ménage ordinaire
family / private household

ménage d'une personne
one-person / single person household

ménage privé
private household

ménage à revenu / à salaire unique
one-earner family

ménage à salaires multiples
multiple earner household

ménage unifamilial
one-family household

population des ménages collectifs (stat.)
institutional population

prêt aux jeunes ménages
loan for young couples

revenu du ménage
household income

soins du ménage
household care

taille du ménage
household size

MÉNAGER (adj.)
activités ménagères
homemaking, domestic activities, home
duties

aide ménagère
family / domestic help, home helper,
home help (worker)

aide ménagère à domicile
home-making assistance

allocation des services ménagers (Fr.)
home help allowance

arts ménagers
home management / economics; domestic
arts

auxiliaire ménagère
family help

**école d'enseignement familial et
ménager**
home-making school

économie / enseignement ménager (ère)
home economics

entretien ménager
household operation

sciences ménagères
home economics

unité ménagère
household unit

MÉNAGÈRE
housewife, home-maker

panier de la ménagère
basket of goods, shopping basket

MENSUALISATION
monthly payment

MENSUALITÉ
monthly instalment

MENSUEL
assiette mensuelle des cotisations
monthly assessment of contributions

base mensuelle
monthly base

base mensuelle de calcul
monthly base for calculation

cotisation mensuelle
monthly contribution

montant mensuel
monthly amount

moyenne mensuelle
monthly average

ordre mensuel de paiement
monthly payment order

paiement mensuel
monthly payment

rémunération effective nette mensuelle
monthly take-home pay

rémunération mensuelle
monthly salary

salaire mensuel
monthly wage

taux de salaire mensuel
monthly wage rate

versement mensuel
monthly instalment / payment

MENSUELLEMENT
on a monthly basis

MENTAL
mental

agent de (la) santé mentale
mental health worker

aliénation mentale
mental disablement, insanity

aliéné mental
mentally disabled, mentally disordered
person

arriération mentale
mental retardation

arriéré / attardé mental
mentally retarded / defective, developmentally handicapped

**consultation d'hygiène mentale
infantile**
child mental health clinic

débile mental
mentally retarded / disabled / deficient,
mental deficient, developmentally
handicapped

débile mental léger
mildly mentally retarded

débile mental profond
profoundly / severely mentally retarded

débilité / déficience mentale
mental retardation / deficiency / disability

déficient mental
mentally retarded / disabled, mental(ly)
deficient, developmentally handicapped

déficient mental léger
mildly mentally retarded

déficient mental moyen
trainable mentally retarded

déficient mental profond
profoundly / severely mentally retarded

faculté mentale
mental capacity

handicap mental
mental disability / disablement

handicapé mental
mentally retarded / disabled / handicapped, developmentally handicapped;
(pl.) people with mental disabilities

incapacité mentale
mental disability / disablement / infirmity
/ impairment / handicap

infirme mental
mental(ly) deficient, mentally disabled

infirmité mentale
mental disability / disablement / infirmity
/ impairment / handicap

maison de santé mentale
mental home

malade mental
mentally disordered person

maladie mentale
mental infirmity / illness

retardé mental
mentally retarded, developmentally handicapped

santé mentale
mental / (occ.) emotional health

soins infirmiers aux malades mentaux
mental health nursing

trouble mental
mental disorder; (pl.) mental disability

MENTALEMENT
enfant mentalement inadapté
mentally handicapped child

mentalement déficient
mentally deficient

mentalement diminué
mentally disabled

MENTALITÉ
évolution / modification des mentalités
change of attitudes

MENTION
diplôme obtenu sans mention
pass degree

MENTORAT
mentorship, mentoring

MER
gens de mer
seamen; sailors

unité en mer (Denm.)
offshore unit

MÈRE
mother

allocation aux mères de famille
mother's benefit

allocation de mère au foyer
allowance for mothers at home / for the housewife, non-working mother's allowance (UK)

allocation de mère veuve (UK)
widowed mother's allowance

assistance aux mères et aux enfants
mother and child care

club de mères
mothers' club

future mère
expectant mother

mère abandonnée
deserted mother

mère allaitante
nursing / lactating mother

mère célibataire
unmarried / single mother

mère élevant seule son / ses enfant(s)
single mother

mère au foyer
non-working mother

mère nourricière
house / foster mother

orphelin de mère
orphan whose mother is dead

orphelin de père et de mère
full orphan, orphan whose parents are dead, orphan having lost both parents

orphelin de père ou de mère
orphan having lost one parent

service d'aide aux mères
mother care service; child care service; (pl.) home-maker services; child care facilities

soins aux mères et aux enfants
mother and child care

MÉRITE
augmentation au mérite
merit increase

échelon de mérite
meritorious increment

évaluation / notation au mérite
merit rating / rate

principe du mérite
merit principle

promotion au mérite
promotion according to merit

régime de rémunération au mérite
merit pay system

rémunération au mérite
merit pay

MESSAGER
facteurs et messagers [CITP-1968 (3-7)]
mail distribution clerks [ISCO-1968 (3-7)]

messagers, porteurs, gardiens, portiers et assimilés [CITP-1988 (915)]
messengers, porters, doorkeepers and related workers [ISCO-1988 (915)]

MESURÉ (adj.)
chômage mesuré
measured / open / overt / registered / visible unemployment

MESURE (n.)
measure, arrangement; provision; standard; (pl.) (occ.) facilities

déplacement par mesure disciplinaire
disciplinary transfer

formation sur mesure
(occ.) learner-centred training

Lignes directrices du BIT pour la mesure du chômage
ILO Guidelines for measuring unemployment

mesure (outre)
unduly

mesure d'accompagnement des suppressions d'emplois
redundancy mitigation measure

mesure d'action sociale
socially supportive measure

mesure active
active measure

mesure d'aide à l'emploi
employment incentive / stimulus

mesures anti-discriminatoires à l'embauche
(occ.) affirmative action programme

mesure coercitive
enforcement measure

mesure visant à développer la confiance en soi
self-confidence-building measure

mesure conservatoire
protective measure

mesure corrective
corrective / remedial measure

mesure disciplinaire
disciplinary measure / action

mesure d'économie
economy measure

mesure à effet rétroactif
retroactive measure

mesure créatrice d'emplois / favorisant l'emploi / génératrice d'emplois
employment-creation / job-creation measure

mesures en faveur de l'emploi et de la formation
employment and training measures

mesure d'encouragement à l'emploi
employment incentive / stimulus; (occ.) in-work benefit

mesure d'exécution
enforcement measure

mesure d'expulsion
deportation / expulsion order

**mesures en faveur de groupes désa-
vantagés / défavorisés**
(occ.) affirmative / positive action

mesure d'incitation
incentive (measure)

mesure d'incitation à l'emploi
in-work benefit; employment incentive /
stimulus

**mesure d'incitation à l'étude des
langues**
language incentive

**mesure d'incitation à l'exercice d'une
activité professionnelle / au travail**
(occ.) in-work benefit

mesure passive
passive measure

mesure de la performance
performance measure

mesure préventive
preventive measure

mesure préventive d'emploi
preventive employment measure

mesure de prophylaxie
preventive health measure

mesure quantitative du travail
work count

mesure de redressement
remedial action / measure

mesures de relance
reflationary measures / policy

mesure du rendement
performance measure

mesure de représailles
retaliatory measure

mesure de restriction
restraint measure

mesure de rétorsion
retaliatory measure

mesure de salubrité
health measure; (pl.) sanitation

mesure de sécurité
safety measure / precaution

mesure sélective
selective measure

mesure sélective d'emploi
selective employment measure

mesure de soutien
support measure

mesure de stimulation de l'emploi
employment incentive, employment
development measure

mesure du travail
work measurement

mesure d'urgence
emergency measure

norme de mesure du travail
work measurement standard

suspension de mesures administratives
suspension of administrative action

**système de mesure de la performance /
du rendement**
performance measure system

train de mesures
series of measures; (occ.) package deal

MÉTAL
conducteurs d'installations de transformation des métaux [CITP-1988 (812)]
metal-processing-plant operators [ISCO-
1988 (812)]

**ouvriers du façonnage et de l'usinage
des métaux [CITP-1968 (8-3)]**
blacksmiths, toolmakers and machine-tool
operators [ISCO-1968 (8-3)]

**ouvriers de la production et du
traitement des métaux [CITP-1968 (7-
2)]**
metal processers [ISCO-1968 (7-2)]

MÉTALLIQUE
plombiers soudeurs, tôliers-chaudronniers, monteurs de charpentes et de
structures métalliques [CITP-1968 (8-7)]
plumbers, welders, sheet metal and
structural metal preparers and erectors
[ISCO-1968 (8-7)]

MÉTALLURGIE
metallurgical industry; metal trades

MÉTAYER
sharecropper, tenant farmer

MÉTHODE
method, procedure; skill

ingénieur des méthodes
industrial engineer

méthode d'ajustement intérimaire
interim adjustment methodology

**méthode d'ajustement proportionnel
sur un an**
annualised method of prorated adjustment

méthode de calcul
(method of) calculation; formula

méthode de calcul de la cotisation
calculation of the contribution;
contribution formula

méthode de calcul de la pension
calculation of the pension; pension
formula

méthode de calcul des prestations
calculation of the benefit; benefit formula

**méthode du classement hiérarchique
des emplois**
job ranking method

méthode de comptage
counting method

**méthode de la double courbe des
rémunérations**
dual pay-line approach

méthode d'emploi neutre
neutral employment system

méthode d'évaluation du rendement
performance evaluation system

méthode de formation
training method

méthode de groupe
group process

méthode des points
point method

méthode de recherche d'emploi
job-finding / job-search skills / technique,
job-hunting method

**méthode de rémunération à l'acte / par
honoraires**
fee-for-service / item of service method of
remuneration

méthode de sélection
selection procedure

**méthode de sélection de candidats en
groupe**
group selection method

méthode de / du service social
social work method / process

méthode des timbres
stamp method

méthode de travail
work process; (pl.) work practices

**méthode fondée sur l'utilisation de la
main-d'oeuvre**
labour-intensive method

**procédés et méthodes de production
(PMP)**
process and production methods (PPM)

MÉTIER
occupation; job; profession

analyse des professions et métiers
occupational and trade analysis

arts et métiers
applied / industrial arts and crafts

chambre des métiers
chamber of trades, guild chamber, trade(s)
association, trade guild

compétence dans un / les métier(s)
trade(s) skill / ability

corps de métier
trade guild

cours préparatoire aux métiers
basic trades training

débuter dans le métier
to start out in the profession

école de métiers (Switz.)
vocational training college

formation des femmes dans les métiers non traditionnels
non-traditional training for women

formation aux métiers
trades training

formation aux / dans les métiers spécialisés
skilled trades training

gens du métier
tradespersons; profession

homme de métier
tradesman; craftsman; journeyman

homme de métier qualifié
qualified journeyman

métier (de)
professional

métier apparenté
related occupation / job

métier d'apprentissage
apprenticeship / apprenticeable trade

métier d'art / artisanal
handicraft; (pl.) arts and crafts, (occ.) manual crafts

métiers du bâtiment
building trades

métier connexe
allied occupation, related job

métier de haute spécialisation / hautement spécialisé
highly skilled / higher-skill trade

métier insalubre
unhealthy occupation

métier manuel
manual work / occupation, craft

métier pénible
arduous occupation

métier qualifié
skilled trade

métier secondaire
alternative / alternate / secondary employment

ouvrier de métier
craftsman

petits métiers de la rue
light street industries

profession ou métier
profession or trade

répertoire des métiers
trades register

syndicat (de corps) de métier
professional organisation / association; industrial association; occupational / craft / horizontal union

usages du métier
professional practices

METTRE
mettre en application
to implement

mettre au chômage
to make redundant

mettre en chômage technique
to lay off (temporarily)

mettre en danger
to endanger, to jeopardise

mettre en disponibilité
to grant leave of absence, to place on inactive status

mettre à la disposition de
to make available for

mettre à l'épreuve
to test

mettre fin à un contrat
to terminate a contract

mettre fin à l'engagement de qqn
to terminate the appointment of somebody

mettre à jour
to update

mettre en oeuvre
to implement

mettre opposition sur un traitement
to attach salary

mettre à pied
to dismiss, to lay off, to suspend (from duty)

mettre à la retraite
to pension off

mettre temporairement au chômage
to lay off (temporarily)

mettre en vigueur
to enforce, to bring into force

MEUBLÉ (adj.)
logement meublé
furnished dwelling

MICRO-ÉCONOMIE
microeconomics

MICROPLANIFICATION
microplanning

MIGRANT
migrant

aide aux migrants
aid for migrants

migrant alternant / quotidien
commuter

migrant de retour
returning migrant

regroupement familial des travailleurs migrants
reuniting of migrant workers' families

travailleur migrant
migrant labourer / worker; transient worker; (pl.) migrant labour

MIGRATEUR (adj.)
entreprise migratrice
runaway shop (in order to avoid trade union activism)

MIGRATION
accroissement par migration
balance of migration

migration alternante
journey to work; (pl.) commuting

migration extérieure / externe
external migration

migration intérieure / interne
internal migration

migration journalière
(pl.) commuting

migration de main-d'oeuvre
manpower / labour migration, migration of labour

migration pendulaire
journey to work; (pl.) commuting

migration quotidienne
(pl.) commuting

migration de retour
return migration

migration sociale
social mobility

migration de travail
labour migration

rayon de migration journalière
commuting distance

MIGRATOIRE
balance / bilan migratoire
balance of migration, migration balance

courant / flux migratoire
flow of migration

mouvement migratoire
migration / migratory movement

pression migratoire
migratory pressure

solde migratoire
balance of migration, migration balance

MILIEU
emploi en milieu ordinaire / en milieu non
protégé
open employment

hygiène du milieu
environmental health

milieux d'affaires
business community / circles

milieu familial
family environment

milieu ouvrier
working(-)class environment

milieu professionnel
occupational environment

milieu protégé
sheltered (working) environment

milieu social
social environment / background

milieu de travail
work(ing) environment

milieu de vie
human environment

salubrité du milieu
environmental health

soins en milieu hospitalier
hospital care / treatment; (occ.)
institutional care

MILITAIRE (adj.)
dossier militaire
service record

obligations militaires
(compulsory) military service

pension militaire d'invalidité
military disablement pension

service militaire
military service

service militaire obligatoire
compulsory military service

MILITAIRE (n.)
soldier; serviceman; (pl.) military personnel

ancien militaire
ex-serviceman

militaire de carrière
professional / regular soldier

MILITANT (n.)
active member

militant syndical
trade union worker, militant unionist

MILITANTISME
militantisme syndical
union militancy

MINE
accident de mines
mining accident

employé des mines
mine employee

ouvriers et employés des mines
mineworkers and mine employees

**travailleur des mines et des établisse-
ments assimilés**
worker in mines and similar undertakings

mine de charbon
colliery

ouvrier des mines
mineworker

MINÉRAL (adj.)
conducteurs de machines à travailler les
métaux et les produits minéraux [CITP-
1988 (821)]
metal-and mineral-products machine
operators [ISCO-1988 (821)]

MINÉRAL (n.)
conducteurs d'installations d'exploitation
minière et d'extraction des minéraux
[CITP-1988 (811)]
mining and mineral-processing-plant
operators [ISCO-1988 (811)]

MINEUR (adj.)
enfant mineur
under-age child

fonction mineure
minor duty

handicapé mineur
disabled child

MINEUR (n.)
miner, colliery worker; under age, minor

emploi des mineurs
juvenile labour

mineur confié à l'aide sociale (Fr.)
minor in custody of a social welfare
institution

**mineurs, carriers, boutefeux et tailleurs
de pierre [CITP-1988 (711)]**
miners, shotfirers, stone cutters and
carvers [ISCO-1988 (711)]

**mineurs, carriers, foreurs de puits et
travailleurs assimilés [CITP-1968 (7-1)]**
miners, quarrymen, well drillers and
related workers [ISCO-1968 (7-1)]

mineur en danger
minor at risk

mineur handicapé
disabled child

mineur sous protection conjointe (Fr.)
legally and socially protected minor

MINI-CRÈCHE
mini day-care centre

MINIER
exploitation minière
mine

industrie minière
mining industry

MINIÈRE
open-cast mine

MINIMAL
minimum

âge minimal
minimum age

âge minimal d'activité professionnelle
minimum active working age

**condition minimale d'ouverture des
droits**
minimum qualifying condition

cotisation minimale
minimum contribution

durée minimale de service (benefits)
minimum period of payment

effectif minimal
(occ.) skeleton staff

garantie de revenu minimal
minimum / basic income support

limite minimale
minimum level

**logement ne répondant pas aux normes
d'habitabilité minimale**
sub(-)standard housing

montant annuel minimal
minimum annual rate

montant minimal
minimum amount

montant minimal forfaitaire
(occ.) standard amount

niveau minimal
minimum level

norme minimale
minimum standard

pension minimale
minimum pension

personnel minimal
minimum / (occ.) skeleton staff

prestation minimale
minimum benefit

salaire minimal
minimum wage

salaire social minimal (Lux.)
minimum social salary

soins minimaux
minimum care

taux horaire minimal
minimum hourly rate

MINIMEX
minimum de moyens d'existence
(MINIMEX) (Belg.)
minimum income security, minimum
subsistence income

MINIMEXÉ (Belg.)
living on the minimum income security /
minimum subsistence income

MINIMUM
minimum; lower limit

âge minimum
minimum age

âge minimum légal pour travailler
minimum legal working age

cotisation minimum
minimum contribution

délai minimum légal de préavis
statutory notice

**minimum d'ancienneté exigible dans
une classe**
minimum time-in-grade requirement

**minimum de moyens d'existence
(MINIMEX) (Belg.)**
minimum income security, minimum
subsistence income

minimum des pensions vieillesse
old age pension minimum

minimum vieillesse
basic old-age pension, old age minimum
(Fr.)

minimum vital
subsistence level / minimum; living /
subsistence wage; (occ.) demogrant;
poverty line

montant minimum
minimum amount

montant minimum forfaitaire
(occ.) standard amount

niveau minimum
minimum level

niveau de vie minimum acceptable
minimum acceptable standard of living

norme minimum
minimum standard

normes minima de sécurité sociale
minimum standards for social security

pension minimum
minimum pension

pension de retraite minimum (Belg.)
minimum retirement pension

pension de survie minimum (Belg.)
minimum survivors' pension

période minimum d'affiliation
(occ.) qualifying period
wage

revenu minimum
minimum income, income support (UK)

revenu minimum familial
family minimum income

revenu minimum garanti
guaranteed minimum income

revenu minimum d'insertion (RMI)
minimum social income, guaranteed
minimum income

revenu minimum légal
statutory minimum income

salaire minimum
minimum wage

salaire minimum accepté
acceptance / reserve / reservation wage

salaire minimum garanti
guaranteed minimum wage, minimum
wage rate; (occ.) fall-back pay (when
linked to performance)

salaire minimum d'insertion (Sp.)
minimum integration wage

salaire minimum interprofessionnel (Sp.)
minimum interprofessional wage

salaire minimum interprofessionnel de croissance (SMIC) (Fr.)
guaranteed / statutory minimum wage

salaire minimum interprofessionnel garanti
intertrade minimum wage

salaire minimum légal
statutory minimum wage

salaire minimum vital
minimum living wage

service minimum
minimum (level of) service

système (de détermination) du salaire minimum
minimum wage system

taux de salaire minimum
minimum wage rate

MINISTÉRIEL
département ministériel
Government department

instruction ministérielle
ministerial directive

officiers publics et ministériels
public and ministerial officers

MINISTRE
ministre du culte
priest

MINORATION
coefficient de minoration
reduction factor

minoration d'impôts
tax reduction

MINORÉ
reduced; deflated

pension / retraite à taux minoré
reduced (rate) pension / retirement benefit

MINORITAIRE
groupe minoritaire
minority group

participation minoritaire
minority shareholding

MINORITÉ
minorité nationale
national minority

MISE
accueil et mise au courant des nouveaux agents
induction of new staff

autorisation de mise sur le marché (Fr.)
permit to market

calendrier de mise en oeuvre
implementation schedule

contrat de mise à disposition (Fr.)
contract making temporary staff available

cours de mise à niveau
remedial / refresher course

formation par mise en situation
vestibule training

mise en application
implementation; enforcement; entry into effect

mise en circulation
(occ.) introduction

mise en commun des revenus
income pooling

mise en correspondance des offres et des demandes d'emploi
job matching

mise au courant
(occ.) post-induction training

mise en demeure
(enforcement) notice

mise en disponibilité
leave of absence; inactive status

mise à l'écart des syndicats
labour exclusion

mise en garde
warning

mise à jour
update

mise en oeuvre
implementation; enforcement

mise en oeuvre des droits économiques et sociaux
realisation of economic and social rights

mise en pension
boarding out

mise à pied
lay(-)off; suspension (without pay)

mise à pied conservatoire
suspension pending confirmation of dismissal / pending investigation; temporary lay-off

mise à pied disciplinaire
disciplinary lay-off, suspension without pay

mise à pied temporaire
intermittent / temporary lay-off

mise en préretraite
compulsory early retirement

mise en rapport avec l'employeur
introduction to employer

mise à la retraite
retirement; superannuation

mise à la retraite anticipée
advanced retirement

mise à la retraite d'office
compulsory retirement

mise en valeur des ressources
resource development

mise en valeur des ressources humaines
labour / human resources / manpower / staff development

mise en vigueur
enforcement

procédure de mise à pied
lay-off procedure

MISÈRE
distress, destitution, poverty

misère absolue / complète
absolute distress

salaire de misère
subsistence wage

MISÉREUX
poverty-stricken

MISSION
mission, assignment (of duties), duty; responsibility; work

affectation à une mission
mission assignment

agence de missions de personnel
personnel dispatching agency

chargé de mission
special project manager

contrat de mission (Fr.)
assignment contract

indemnité de fin de mission
end-of-assignment payment

mission locale (Fr.)
local agency

mission principale d'un poste
main job duty

mission spéciale
special assignment

personnel de mission
dispatched workers

service de missions de personnel
personnel dispatching service

voyage en mission
travel on official business

MI-TAUX
half rate

MI-TEMPS
half-time

allocation de mi-temps
half-time allowance

congé de maladie à mi-temps
half-time sick leave

emploi / travail à mi-temps
half-time employment / work

travailler à mi-temps
to work half-time

travailleur à mi-temps
half-time worker; half-timer

MIXTE
joint, mixed

assurance mixte
(occ.) endowment insurance

carrière mixte
mixed career

comité mixte
joint committee

comité mixte patronal - syndical
joint union - management committee

commission mixte
joint committee

entreprise (à participation) mixte
joint venture

établissement d'enseignement mixte
co-educational institution

pension en cas de carrière mixte
mixed career pension

pension proportionnelle (assurance mixte) (Irel.)
pro-rata (mixed insurance) pension

projet mixte
joint project

régime de retraite contributif mixte
contributory pension scheme / plan

société mixte
joint venture

MOBILE (adj.)
activité mobile
(occ.) outreach activity

antenne mobile
outreach unit; mobile field unit

conducteurs de matériels mobiles agricoles et d'autres engins mobiles [CITP-1988 (833)]
agricultural and other mobile plant operators [ISCO-1988 (833)]

congé mobile
floating holiday

échelle mobile (des salaires)
sliding (wage) scale; incremental scale

échelle mobile (des salaires) établie sur le coût de la vie
cost-of-living sliding scale

horaire mobile
flexible working hours / time, flexible time / hours; flexitime

industrie mobile
(occ.) footloose industry

moyenne mobile
moving average

personnel mobile
mobile staff

piquet de grève mobile
roving picket

plage horaire mobile
flexible time bracket

plage mobile
flexible hours / band

service mobile d'urgence et de réanimation (SMUR)
mobile emergency and intensive care service

taux mobile
loose rate

MOBILIER (adj.)
valeur mobilière
security

MOBILISATION
mobilisation des ressources
(occ.) resource securing

MOBILITÉ
mobility; outreach

aide à la mobilité
mobility assistance

aide à la mobilité des étudiants
student mobility grant

aide à la mobilité géographique
geographical mobility incentive

aide à la mobilité professionnelle
occupational mobility incentive

allocation de mobilité (UK)
mobility allowance

comportement en termes de mobilité
mobility behaviour

défaut de mobilité de la main-d'oeuvre
manpower rigidity

facteur mobilité
mobility factor

mobilité fonctionnelle
functional mobility

mobilité géographique
geographic / spatial mobility

mobilité d'insatisfaction
dissatisfaction mobility

mobilité interprofessionnelle
inter-occupation / intertrade mobility

mobilité locale
local / residential mobility

mobilité de la main-d'oeuvre
labour / manpower / work force / worker
mobility

mobilité physique
geographic / spatial mobility

mobilité professionnelle
job / occupational / professional / inter-
occupation mobility; occupational change

mobilité régionale
regional mobility

mobilité résidentielle
residential mobility

mobilité sectorielle
inter-industry / sectoral mobility

mobilité sociale
social mobility

mobilité des travailleurs
labour / manpower / work force / worker
mobility

mobilité verticale
upward / vertical mobility

obstacle à la mobilité
mobility barrier

personne à mobilité réduite
people with mobility handicap(s)

prime de mobilité
mobility grant / allowance (UK)

subvention à la mobilité
mobility grant

**subvention de mobilité des étudiants /
destinée aux étudiants**
student mobility grant

MODALITÉ
mode; (pl.) arrangements, terms,
procedure, method

modalités d'admission
admission procedure

modalités d'application du contrat
terms and conditions of the agreement

modalités d'entrée
admission procedure

modalités de paiement / de règlement
method of payment

modalités de remboursement
repayment terms

modalités de travail
work patterns

modalités de versement
method of payment

MODE
mode; method; pattern

instruction relative au mode de paiement
payment instruction

mode de calcul
method / mode of calculation

mode de calcul de la pension
calculation of the pension

mode d'habitat
settlement pattern

mode d'imposition
taxation method

mode d'occupation
tenancy, tenure

mode de recrutement
recruitment process

mode de remboursement
method of reimbursement

mode de vie
lifestyle, life pattern, living arrangement

MODÈLE
model; pattern

mannequins et autres modèles [CITP-1988 (521)]
fashion and other models [ISCO-1988 (521)]

modèle médical étalon
standardised medical experience

modèle de répartition
allocative model

modèles, vendeurs et démonstrateurs [CITP-1988 (52)]
models, salespersons and demonstrators [ISCO-1988 (52)]

MODÉRATEUR
exemption du ticket modérateur
exemption from patient's contribution

ticket modérateur
cost of medical expenses, part not reimbursed to insured persons; patient's contribution; co-payment (lump sum), co-insurance (proportional)

MODÉRATION
modération salariale
pay restraint, wage moderation

MODÉRÉ
habitation à loyer modéré (HLM)
council flat / housing, rent controlled premises; (pl.) low-cost housing

MODERNISATION
modernisation, rehabilitation

modernisation du logement
housing rehabilitation

modernisation rurale
rural modernisation

MODERNISER
to modernise, to streamline, to upgrade

MODESTE
personne aux revenus modestes
person on low income / with small means

MODIFICATION
change, modification; amendment; shift; variation

modification d'un contrat
variation of a contract

modification des mentalités
change of attitudes

MODIFIÉ
déclaration de revenus modifiée
modified statement of income, amended tax return

MODULABLE
âge modulable de la prise de / du départ à
la retraite
flexible pensionable / retirement age

MODULATION
accord de modulation
adjustable hours agreement

modulation des effectifs
(occ.) flexible staffing

modulation des horaires
adjustable hours

modulation du temps de travail
flexible working hours / scheduling

système de modulation des loyers (Irel.)
differential rent scheme

MODULÉ (adj.)
flexible, graduated

horaires modulés
flexible working hours / time, flexible
time / hours; flexitime

modulé selon l'évolution des prix
adjusted for price changes

retraite modulée
flexible retirement

MODULE (n.)
module; package

formation par modules
modular training

module d'autoformation
self-learning package

module de formation
training package / module

MODULER
to adjust; to graduate

MOINS-PAYÉ
underpayment

MOIS
effectifs en début de mois
headcount on the first of the month

effectifs en fin de mois
month-end headcount

mois civil
calendar month

mois de référence
base month

mois de travail
(occ.) staff-month

treizième mois
extra month's salary

MOIS-HOMME
man-month

MOIS-PERSONNE
person-month; staff-month

MOMENT
moment de la réalisation du risque
time when risk / the contingency arises

MONDE
initiation au monde du travail
introductory training; (occ.) career(s)
education

monde des affaires
business community

monde du spectacle
entertainment industry

monde du travail
working life

MONÉTAIRE
compensation monétaire
monetary compensation

transfert monétaire
cash transfer

MONITEUR
instructor, trainer; community leader; (pl.)
training staff

infirmière monitrice
teaching nurse; (occ.) sister tutor

moniteur éducateur
teaching instructor

monitrice familiale
teaching homemaker

moniteur de service social
social work educator

moniteur socio-pédagogique
social welfare instructor

MONOACTIF
ménage monoactif
one-earner family

MONOGRAPHIE
case study, monograph

MONOPARENTAL
one(-)parent, lone(-)parent, sole(-)parent

chef de famille monoparentale
single household head

famille monoparentale
lone-parent / one-parent / single-parent
family

ménage monoparental
single-parent / sole-parent household

MONOPATRONAL
négociation monopatronale
single-employer bargaining

MONOPOLE
législation interdisant le monopole
syndical d'embauche
right-to-work laws (USA)

monopole médical
medical monopoly

monopole de placement des travailleurs
exclusive right to place workers in jobs,
placing monopoly

**monopole syndical d'embauche /
d'emploi**
closed-union shop / system

MONOTONE
travail monotone
monotonous / repetitive work

MONTAGE
chaîne de montage
assembly line

atelier de montage
assembly shop

MONTANT (n.)
amount, sum; rate; size, level; charge

**déterminer le montant de l'impôt sur le
revenu**
to assess income tax

déterminer le montant des prestations
to assess benefits

montant acquis de la pension
accrued pension income

montant annuel minimal
minimum annual rate

montant annuel normal
standard annual rate

**montant annuel de la prestation de
retraite**
annual pension benefit (amount)

montant de base
base / basic amount

montant brut
gross amount

montant ouvrant droit à pension
pensionable amount

montant effectif d'une prestation
actual amount of a benefit

montant forfaitaire
flat-rate amount, lump sum

montant des loyers
rent quotations

montant maximal / maximum
maximum amount / rate

montant maximal / maximum théorique
highest theoretical amount

montant mensuel
monthly amount

montant minimal / minimum
minimum amount

montant minimal / minimum forfaitaire
standard amount

montant moyen
average amount

montant net
net amount

montant de la pension
amount of the pension

montant de la prestation
amount of the / rate of benefit; (pl.) benefit level

montants recouvrés
recovery funds

montant des rémunérations
amounts earned

montant de la rémunération considérée aux fins de la pension
amount / level of pensionable remune-ration

montant théorique
theoretical amount

montant total
total amount

plafond du montant en espèces
cash limit

MONTÉE
increase, rise, growth

MONTER
monter à (se)
to amount to

MONTURE
monture de lunettes
spectacle frame

MORAL
abandon moral
(moral) neglect

abandon moral d'enfant
child neglect

aléa moral
moral hazard

organisme doté de la personnalité morale
corporate body

personnalité morale
legal personnality

personne morale
legal entity / person, corporate body

référence morale
character reference

risque moral
moral hazard

MORALE
morale professionnelle
professional ethics

MORBIDE
état morbide
morbid condition

MORBIDITÉ
morbidity; disease pattern

tableau de morbidité
disease pattern

MORT (n.)
death

MORTALITÉ
mortality

mortalité par profession / professionnelle
occupational mortality

probabilité / quotient de mortalité
probability of dying

taux de mortalité
mortality / death / fatality rate

taux de mortalité par suite de maladie professionnelle
occupational fatality rate

MORTEL
accident mortel
fatal accident / injury

MORTE-SAISON
off-season period

emploi de morte-saison
off-season employment

MORT-NÉ
enfant mort-né
stillborn child

MOT
annuler un mot d'ordre de grève
to call off a strike

mot d'ordre de grève
strike call

MOTEUR (adj.)
centre d'éducation motrice
education centre for people with motor impairment

fonction motrice
motor function

habilité motrice
motor skill

troubles moteurs
motor disability

MOTEUR (n.)
conducteurs de véhicules à moteur [CITP-1988 (832)]
motor vehicle drivers [ISCO-1988 (832)]

moteur de la croissance
engine of growth, growth engine

MOTIF
reason, cause, ground; basis; inducement; rationale

licenciement abusif du fait de l'invocation tardive des motifs
waiver of breach of contract

licenciement pour motif économique
dismissal for economic reasons, redundancy

motif illicite de discrimination
prohibited ground of discrimination

motif légitime (sans)
without just cause

motif de licenciement
ground / reason for dismissal

motif raisonnable / valable
just / good cause, reasonable ground, good reason

motif valable (sans)
without just cause

MOTIVATION
manque de motivation
lack of incentive / of motivation

motivation non financière
(occ.) intrinsic reward

motivation professionnelle
motivation to work, job motivation

motivation de réussite
achievement motivation

motivation au travail
work motivation, motivation to work

MOTIVÉ
absence motivée
explained / excusable absence

dûment motivé
properly substantiated

motivé (non)
without just cause

refus motivé
justifiable / justified refusal

MOTRICITÉ
troubles de la motricité
motor disability

MOULEUR
mouleurs de fonderie, soudeurs, tôliers-chaudronniers, monteurs de charpentes métalliques et assimilés [CITP-1988 (721)]
metal moulders, welders, sheet-metal workers, structural-metal preparers, and related trades workers [ISCO-1988 (721)]

MOURANT
malade mourant
terminally ill

MOUVEMENT
movement, shift, trend

abattement pour mouvements de personnel
adjustment for turnover of staff, turnover deduction

mouvement des années-personnes
person-year shift

mouvement ascendant
upward trend

mouvement des effectifs
turnover of labour, labour turnover; staff movement

mouvement de grève
strike movement

mouvement de la main-d'oeuvre
turnover of labour, labour turnover; staff movement

mouvements sur le marché du travail
labour market flow

mouvement migratoire
migration / migratory movement

mouvement du personnel
turnover of labour, labour turnover; staff movement; personnel action; (pl.) turnover; staff changes

mouvement de protestation
protest movement

mouvement revendicatif
job / industrial action

mouvement saisonnier
seasonal movement

mouvement social
industrial action

mouvement syndical
trade union movement; organised labour

mouvement transfrontière
cross-border / foreign movement

mouvement de travailleurs
flow of workers

MOYEN (adj.)
average, mean

âge moyen de cessation d'activité
mean age at separation from the labour force

âge moyen d'entrée en activité
mean age at accession to the labour force

augmentation moyenne
average increase

cadre moyen
middle manager; (pl.) middle (grade) management, middle management staff, middle-level manpower / personnel, executive staff

classes moyennes (Belg.)
small enterprises and traders

cotisation moyenne
average contribution

déficient (mental) moyen
trainable mentally retarded

durée moyenne des cas (de maladie)
average duration per case

durée moyenne du chômage
average duration of unemployment

durée moyenne de la vie active / professionnele
mean duration of working life

gain moyen
average earnings

montant moyen
average amount

nombre moyen
average number

nombre moyen de journées de maladie
mean number of days of illness

ouvrier moyen
average production worker

petites et moyennes entreprises (PME)
small and medium-sized enterprises
(SME)

profession de spécialisation moyenne
semi-skilled / medium-skilled occupation

rémunération moyenne
average earnings

revenu moyen
average income

salaire annuel moyen de base
basic average annual wage

salaire brut moyen
average gross / gross average wage

salaire hebdomadaire moyen
average weekly earnings / wage

salaire moyen
average wage; final average wage (for
calculation of a benefit); career average
salary (for calculation of pension)

MOYEN (n.)
resource; (pl.) resources, means; facilities

garantie des moyens d'existence
income security

garantir les moyens d'existence
to maintain income

manque de moyens
lack of means

**minimum de moyens d'existence
(MINIMEX) (Belg.)**
minimum income security, minimum
subsistence income

moyens d'action
policy instruments

moyens audio-visuels
audio-visual material

moyens d'étude et de formation
study and training facilities

moyens d'existence
means of support / subsistence, subsistence means, (means of) livelihood;
income; welfare

moyens de financement
financial facilities

moyens de formation
training facilities

moyens d'intervention
policy instruments

moyens légaux
legal means

moyens de preuve
evidence

moyens de production
means of production

moyens de protection individuelle
body / individual protection equipment

moyens de subsistance
(means of) livelihood, means of subsistence; maintenance

moyen de traitement ambulatoire
out-patient facility

obligation de moyens
best-endeavours obligation, duty to
exercise skill and care

perte de moyens d'existence
loss of income support

propres moyens (par ses)
on his/her own

répartition des moyens
allocation of resources, resource
allocation

socialisation des moyens de production
socialisation of the means of production

MOYENNE
average, mean

moyenne annuelle
annual / yearly average

moyenne arithmétique
arithmetic mean / average

moyenne mensuelle
monthly average

moyenne mobile
moving average

moyenne pondérée des indemnités de poste
weighted average of post adjustments

rémunération en-dessous de la moyenne
below-average salary

MULTICOMPÉTENT
multi-skilled

MULTIDISCIPLINAIRE
multidisciplinary

MULTIFAMILIAL
ménage multifamilial
multi-family / multiple(-)family household

MULTILATÉRAL
accord multilatéral
multilateral agreement

convention multilatérale
multilateral convention

convention multilatérale de sécurité sociale
multilateral social security convention

surveillance structurelle multilatérale
multilateral structural surveillance

MULTIPATRONAL
négociation multipatronale
multi-employer bargaining

MULTIPLE
allocation pour naissance multiple (Austr.)
multiple birth grant

famille à revenus multiples
multi-earner family

incapacités / infirmités multiples
multiple / several disabilities

ménage multiple
multi-person household

ménage à salaires multiples
multiple earner household

questionnaire à choix multiples
multiple choice / ipsative test / questionnaire

MULTIPLICATEUR
multiplier

création d'emplois par effet multiplicateur
employment spin-off

effet multiplicateur
multiplier (effect); spin-off

multiplicateur d'ajustement
post adjustment multiplier

multiplicateur corrigé par le facteur de correction de la rémunération
multiplier corrected by the remuneration correction factor

MULTIPLICATION
effet de multiplication
multiplier (effect); spin-off

MULTIRISQUE
assurance multirisques
comprehensive insurance

MUNICIPAL
conseil municipal
town council

conseiller municipal
town councillor

fonctionnaire municipal
local authority employee

prestation pour taxe municipale (UK)
council tax benefit

MUNICIPALITÉ
municipality

appartement loué à la municipalité
council flat

MUSCLE
maladie du système ostéo-articulaire et
des muscles
musculo-skeletal disease

MUSICIEN
musiciens, acteurs, danseurs et artistes
assimilés [CITP-1968 (1-7)]
composers and performing artists [ISCO-1968 (1-7)]

MUTATION
displacement; reassignment, transfer,
posting; change; move

avis de mutation
transfer notice

demande de mutation
request for transfer, transfer request

dossier de mutation
transfer record

mutation sans concours
transfer without competition

mutation disciplinaire
disciplinary transfer

mutation chez un même employeur
interplant transfer

mutation de fonctionnaire
transfer of staff member

mutation fonctionnelle
functional transfer

mutation interinstitutions
inter-agency transfer

mutation d'office
disciplinary posting / transfer

mutation de personnel
personnel move

**mutation du personnel déjà en
fonctions**
reassignment of existing staff

mutation par roulement
transfer on a rotating basis

MUTER
to transfer

muter un fonctionnaire
to transfer a staff member

travailleur muté
displaced worker

MUTILÉ
disabled

mutilé de guerre
disabled veteran / ex-serviceman, war
invalid / disabled / cripple

MUTUALISTE (adj.)
adhérent mutualiste
member of a mutual benefit society

adhésion mutualiste
membership of a mutual benefit society

association mutualiste
friendly society

assurance mutualiste
mutual insurance

ayant droit / bénéficiaire mutualiste
beneficiary of a mutual fund

caisse autonome mutualiste (Fr.)
autonomous mutual aid fund

carte mutualiste
mutual insurance card

convention locale mutualiste
local mutualistic convention / agreement

correspondant mutualiste (Fr.)
correspondent for a mutual benefit society

cotisation mutualiste
mutual insurance contribution

entraide mutualiste
mutualistic help

groupement / institution mutualiste
mutual benefit society

oeuvres mutualistes
institutions of mutual benefit societies

organisation mutualiste
mutual organisation

pharmacie mutualiste
mutual insurance dispensary

prestation mutualiste
mutual benefit

réassurance mutualiste
reinsurance of mutual benefit societies

société mutualiste
friendly / (mutual) benefit society

MUTUALISTE (n.)
member of a mutual benefit society

MUTUALITÉ
friendly society, mutual benefit movement; mutual benefit societies; mutual aid

Code de la mutualité
Code of mutual benefit societies

droit de la mutualité
law governing mutual benefit societies

mutualité sociale agricole (Fr.)
agricultural social insurance agency

MUTUEL
mutual

aide mutuelle
mutual aid

assurance basée sur une entente
d'exonération mutuelle
no fault insurance

assurance mutuelle
mutual insurance

**caisse d'assurance mutuelle agricole
(Fr.)**
agricultural mutual insurance fund

caisse mutuelle
mutual fund

cessation de service par accord mutuel
agreed termination

compagnie d'assurances mutuelles
mutual insurance company

licenciement par accord mutuel
agreed termination

secours mutuel
mutual aid

société de secours mutuel
mutual benefit / provident society

MUTUELLE
mutual insurance company; mutual aid
body; friendly / mutual benefit society;
benevolent fund; (occ.) (Belg.) social
security (fund)

tutelle sur les mutuelles
supervision of mutual benefit societies

NAISSANCE
birth

acte de naissance
birth certificate

allocation de naissance
birth / childbirth grant / allowance; (occ.)
maternity grant

**allocation pour naissance multiple
(Austr.)**
multiple birth grant

allocation spéciale de naissance
special childbirth allowance

congé de naissance
maternity / birth leave

déclaration de naissance
registration of birth

espérance de vie à la naissance
life expectancy at birth

indemnité de naissance
birth grant

invalide de naissance
congenitally disabled

prévention des naissances
birth control

prime de naissance
maternity / (child)birth grant / allowance /
premium

régulation des naissances
birth control

repos de naissance
maternity leave

statistiques de naissances
birth figures

NANTI
(pl.) the well-off, the better-off, the well-
to-do

nantis et les démunis (les)
haves and the have-nots (the)

NATALISTE
explosion nataliste
baby boom

NATION
comptes de la nation
national accounts / accounting

comptes sociaux de la nation
national social accounts

pupille de la nation
war orphan

NATIONAL (adj.)
national, domestic

agent de l'assurance nationale (UK)
(national) insurance officer

ascendance nationale
national extraction

assurance nationale (UK)
national insurance

autorités nationales
central government, national authorities

caisse d'assurance nationale (UK)
national insurance fund

**commissaire à l'assurance nationale
(UK)**
national insurance commissioner

comptabilité nationale
national accounts

convention nationale
national convention / agreement

cotisation à l'assurance nationale (UK)
national insurance contribution

marché national de l'emploi / du travail
domestic / national labour market

minorité nationale
national minority

numéro d'assurance nationale (UK)
national insurance number

organisation d'envergure nationale / à vocation nationale
nation-wide organisation

pension nationale
national pension, separate pension (UK), State pension (Denm.)

planification sanitaire nationale
national health planning

produit national brut
Gross National Product (GNP)

régime national de sécurité sociale
national social security scheme

retraite nationale par limite d'âge (UK)
national superannuation

revenu national
national income; social income

service national
military service; national service

service national de santé
national health service

système national de distribution de soins / de protection (médico-) sanitaire
national system of health care

travailleur national
national worker

NATIONAL (n.)
national

résidents qui sont des nationaux
national residents

résidents qui ne sont pas des nationaux
non-national residents

NATIONALITÉ
nationality, citizenship

NATURE
aide en nature
aid in kind

avantage en nature
benefit in kind; perk; fringe benefit

nature de l'accident / de la lésion
nature of injury

nature du travail
job content, type of activity / of job / of work

prestation en nature
benefit / payment in kind; non-cash benefit

prestation en nature de l'assurance maladie
health benefit in kind

prestation en nature de grande importance
major / substantial benefit in kind

prestation en nature de maladie ou de maternité
sickness or maternity benefit in kind

rétribution en nature
payment in kind

salaires et traitements en nature
wages and salaries in kind

secours en nature
relief / aid in kind, relief goods

versement en nature
payment in kind

NATUREL
calamité / catastrophe naturelle
natural disaster

départs naturels
natural wastage of labour

déperdition naturelle
natural wastage of labour

emplois résorbés par élimination naturelle
jobs eliminated by attrition

enfant naturel
illegitimate child, child born out of wedlock

jeu naturel des départs (par le)
by natural attrition

marché du travail naturel
natural labour market

médecine naturelle
naturopathy; natureopathy

taux de chômage naturel
full employment unemployment rate,
equilibrium rate of unemployment, natural
rate of unemployment, natural
unemployment rate

taux naturel de chômage
natural unemployment rate, natural rate of
unemployment

taux naturel d'emploi
natural employement rate, natural rate of
employment

usure naturelle des effectifs
natural wastage of labour

NAVAL
constructions navales
shipbuilding

NAVETTE
commuting

**navette entre son domicile et son lieu de
travail (faire la)**
to commute to and from work

navette quotidienne
day haul

NAVETTEUR
commuter

NAVIRE
ship

navire-usine
factory ship

propriétaire de / du navire
shipowner

N.C.
n.c. (non connu)
n.a. (not available)

N.C.A.
n.c.a. (non compris ailleurs)
n.i.e. (not included elsewhere)

N.D.A.
n.d.a. (non dénommé ailleurs)
n.e.s. (not elsewhere specified)

NÉCESSAIRE (adj.)
effectifs nécessaires
work / labour force requirements, labour /
manpower needs, labour requirements

formation nécessaire
required training

qualités nécessaires pour (avoir les)
to qualify for

**remplir les conditions nécessaires (pour
bénéficier / avoir droit)**
to qualify for; to fulfil requirements

NÉCESSAIRE (n.)
necessaries

strict nécessaire
bare necessities (of life)

NÉCESSITEUX
destitute, needy, deprived

**asile de vieillards, d'infirmes et de
nécessiteux**
home for the aged, infirm and needy

enfant nécessiteux
deprived child

NÉFASTE
detrimental

NÉGATIF
classe d'ajustement négatif
negative post adjustment class

impôt négatif
negative tax, tax credit system

NÉGLIGÉ
neglected

NÉGLIGENCE
lack of care / of diligence, negligence;
carelessness; malpractice

erreur et négligence administratives
administrative error and oversight

négligence (faire preuve de)
(occ.) to be remiss

NÉGLIGER
to disregard

NÉGOCE
trade, commerce, business

NÉGOCIATION
negotiation, bargain(ing), mediation talks

calendrier de négociation
bargaining schedule

cycle de négociations
bargaining round

cycle de négociations collectives
collective bargaining round

droit de / à la négociation collective
right to bargain collectively

négociation(s) collective(s)
collective bargaining / negotiations

négociation de compromis
concession bargaining

négociation de crise
crisis bargaining

négociation distributive
distributive / zero(-)sum bargaining

négociation au niveau de l'entreprise
plant bargaining

négociation intégrative
positive-sum bargaining

négociations interprofessionnelles
multi-trade bargaining

négociation monopatronale
single-employer bargaining

négociation multipatronale
multi-employer bargaining

négociations paritaires
joint talks

négociations salariales
pay round / negotiations, wage bargaining / negotiations / round

négociation volontaire
voluntary negotiation

phase de négociations collectives
collective bargaining round

**politique en matière de négociation
collective**
collective bargaining policy

pouvoir de négociation
bargaining power

prise de position dans une négociation
bargaining position

rupture des négociations
breakdown of (the) negotiations

série de négociations
bargaining round, round of negotiations

série de négociations collectives
collective bargaining round

NÉGOCIÉ
avantage négocié
negotiated benefit

NÉGOCIER
to negotiate, to bargain

permis de négocier (Irel.)
negotiation licence

NÉONATAL
neo-natal

soins infirmiers néonatals
neo-natal nursing

NERVEUX
tension nerveuse
strain

NET
actif net
net asset; equity

actif net successoral
net assets by inheritance

espérance nette de vie active
net expectation of working life

gain net
take-home pay, (pl.) net earnings

marge entre les rémunérations nettes
net remuneration margin

montant net
net amount

net d'impôts
tax-free

paie nette
take-home pay

profit net
net / retained profit

rémunération effective nette mensuelle
monthly take-home pay

rémunération nette
net salary / pay, take-home pay

revenu agricole net
net farm income

revenu net
net income

salaire net
net wage / pay / earnings; take-home pay;
disposable income

salaire net payable
net payable wage

traitement de base net
net base salary

NEUROPSYCHIATRIQUE
travailleur social neuropsychiatrique
psychiatric social worker

NEUTRE
méthode / système d'emploi neutre
neutral employment system

N.I.A.
n.i.a. (non inclus ailleurs)
n.i.e. (not included elsewhere)

NITRÉ
composés nitrés
nitro-compounds

NIVEAU
level, size; standard

augmentation en niveau des salaires
global percentage increase of salaries

compétence technique de haut niveau
high(er)-level technical skill

contrôle du niveau des ressources
means testing

cours de mise à niveau
remedial / refresher course

dérive des niveaux de salaire
earnings / wage drift

emploi de bas niveau
low-level job

fluctuations du niveau d'emploi
fluctuations in the level of employment

indicateur du niveau de vie
standard-of-living indicator

maintenir le niveau d'emploi
to maintain employment level

**maintenir les salaires au niveau du coût
de la vie**
to keep wages abreast of the cost of living

niveau absolu de l'emploi
employment in absolute terms

niveau acceptable d'exposition
acceptable level of exposure

niveau d'aptitude
skill level; functional level

niveau des attributions
level of work

niveau de capitalisation d'un régime
level of funding of a scheme

niveau de chômage
unemployment level

niveau de compétence
competence / skill level, level of skill

niveau des compétences actuelles
current skill level

niveau de compétence professionnelle
occupational proficiency level

niveau de / des cotisation(s)
contribution level, level of contributions

niveau de direction
executive level

niveau des effectifs
manning / staffing level

niveau élevé de compétence
high(er)-level skill

niveau d'emploi / de l'emploi
employment level, level of employment

niveau d'entrée
entry level

niveau d'entrée des diplômés
graduate entry (in a company)

niveau d'entrée en fonction
entrance level

niveau d'études
educational level, level of study / of
education / of schooling, academic /
educational achievement / attainment

niveau de financement
funding level

niveau de formation
education level

niveau des gains
earnings level

niveau général des gains
general level of earnings

niveau hiérarchique
layer of hierarchy

niveau d'hygiène
sanitation level

niveau d'imposition
level of taxation

niveau d'instruction
educational level, level of study / of
education / of schooling, academic /
educational achievement / attainment

niveau maximal de rendement
maximum performance level

niveau minimal / minimum
minimum level

niveau normal d'emploi
normal employment level

niveau de pleine capacité
full capacity level

niveau de poste
position level

niveau potentiel de salaire
earnings potential / power

niveau d'une / des prestation(s)
level of benefit, benefit level

niveau de qualification
competence / skill level, level of skill / of
qualification

niveau de qualification des emplois
skill content of jobs

niveau de rémunération
pay / salary / wage / compensation (USA)
level

niveau des ressources
resource level, level of resources

niveau de revenu
level of earnings

niveau de(s) salaire(s)
pay / salary / wage / earnings level; rate of
pay

niveau de salaire à l'embauche
accession rate of pay

niveau de satisfaction au travail
degree of job satisfaction

niveau de scolarité
academic attainment, level of study / of
education / of schooling, educational level

niveau de subsistance
subsistence level

niveau de technicité des emplois
skill content of jobs

niveau de traitement
pay / salary / wage level

niveau de / du travail
working level, level of work

niveau de vie
living standard, standard of living

niveau de vie minimum acceptable
minimum acceptable standard of living

postes de niveaux comparables
positions of the same level

stage de remise à niveau
updating course

**système de prestations lié au niveau des
ressources**
means-tested system of provision

test de niveau
aptitude / level / achievement test

NOCIF
harmful; injurious to (the) health

effet nocif
harmful effect

substance nocive
harmful / noxious subtance

NOCIVITÉ
harmful effect, health hazard

NOCTURNE
centre d'hébergement nocturne
night hostel

NODAL
entreprise nodale
network firm

NOIR
payé au noir (être)
to be paid off the books

travail au noir
black / hidden / moonlight / shadow /
submerged / twilight / underground / grey
economy; disguised / concealed /
unrecorded employment; moonlighting

travailler au noir
to moonlight; to work on the side (if
second occupation)

travailleur au noir
moonlighter

NOM
société en nom collectif
commercial partnership

NOMBRE
number
nombre de bénéficiaires
(occ.) coverage

nombre de chômeurs
number of unemployed; unemployment
(data / figures / statistics)

nombre d'élèves inscrits
(school) enrolment

nombre d'inscriptions
(occ.) enrolment

nombre de jours d'arrêt pour maladie
number of days lost to illness

nombre de lits
bed capacity

nombre moyen
average number

nombre moyen de journées de maladie
mean number of days of illness

nombre de personnes protégées
(occ.) (population) coverage

nombre de postes permanents
number of permanent jobs / posts; core staffing; establishment

nombre de travailleurs occupés
number of workers employed (in a company)

NOMBREUX
famille nombreuse
large family

famille peu nombreuse
small family

NOMENCLATURE
list, classification

acte hors nomenclature (Fr.)
medical treatment not covered by the social security scheme

nomenclature des actes médicaux
classification of items of care

nomenclature des activités
industrial classification

NOMINAL
rated, nominal

cotisation nominale
nominal contribution

coût des salaires nominaux
money-wage cost

revenu nominal
nominal / money income

salaire nominal
nominal / money wage

NOMINATIF
état nominatif des salaires
salary statement per person

liste nominative des cotisations
list / statement of contributions per person

tableau nominatif des emplois
nominative table of posts

NOMINATION
assignment, nomination, appointment

décret de nomination
instrument of appointment

nomination de carrière
career appointment

nomination conditionnelle
conditional appointment

nomination de caractère continu
continuing appointment

nomination définitive
permanent / career appointment

nomination de durée déterminée
fixed-term appointment

nomination pour une durée indéfinie / de durée indéterminée
appointment of indefinite duration / without limit of time

nomination intérimaire
acting appointment

nomination pour une période déterminée
specified period / term appointment

nomination pour une période indéterminée
indeterminate appointment

nomination à titre permanent
permanent appointment

nomination à titre régulier
regular appointment

nomination d'un type différent
conversion to another type of appointment

nouvelle nomination
re-appointment

révocation d'une nomination
revocation of an appointment

révoquer une nomination
to revoke an appointment

titulaire d'une nomination à titre permanent
holder of a permanent appointment

NOMMÉ
nommé sur proposition de
appointed on advice of

NOMMÉMENT
travailleur nommément désigné
specific named worker

NOMMER
to appoint

NON-ACTIF
(pl.) non-labour force, persons not in the labour force, non working population

NON-AFFILIATION
opter pour la non-affiliation au régime général de retraite complémentaire
to contract out

NON-APPLICATION
failure to comply

NON-ASSISTANCE
non-assistance à personne en danger
failure to render assistance to a person in danger

NON-ASSUJETTISSEMENT
opter pour le non-assujettissement au régime général de retraite complémentaire
to contract out

NON-CADRE
non-exempt employee

NON-CONCURRENCE
clause de non-concurrence
non-competition clause, (occ.) restrictive covenant

NON-CUMUL
non-cumul de prestations
prevention of overlapping of benefits

NON-DÉPENDANT
self-supporting person

NON-GRÉVISTE
non-striker, blackleg

NON-INVALIDANT
non-disabling

NON-PAIEMENT
non-paiement des cotisations
non-payment of contributions

NON-PRISE
non-prise en compte
disregard

NON-RECEVOIR
fin de non-recevoir
demurrer, objection; blunt refusal; dismissal

NON-RENOUVELLEMENT
non-renewal

NON-RÉSIDENT
non-resident

NON-RESPECT
failure to observe / to comply; violation, breach

non-respect de la procédure
procedural default / breach

NON-RÉTROACTIVITÉ
non-retroactivity

non-rétroactivité d'un avantage vieillesse
non-retroactivity of an old age benefit

NON-SALARIÉ
non-employee

non-salarié des professions agricoles
self-employed agricultural worker

non-salarié des professions artisanales
self-employed handicraft worker

NON-TITULAIRE
indemnité de non-titulaire
service benefit

NORMAL
normal; regular; standard

activité normale
normal activity

âge normal de fin de scolarité
normal / regular school-leaving age

âge normal de la retraite
normal retirement age

cotisation normale
regular contribution

durée normale du travail
standard working hours

durée normale du travail hebdomadaire
standard working week, standard weekly hours

école normale
college of education, teacher training college / school

effectif normal
normal workforce

emploi normal
regular employment

heures normales de travail
scheduled hours of work

horaire hebdomadaire normal
standard weekly hours

horaire de travail normal
normal working hours

journée de travail normale
normal working day

journée de travail normale à temps partiel
normal part-time working day

marché du travail normal
normal / open labour market

montant annuel normal
standard annual rate

niveau normal d'emploi
normal employment level

pension de retraite normale
standard retirement benefit

pension au taux normal
standard (rate) pension / retirement benefit

professeur d'école normale
teacher of a college of education; (occ.) teacher(-)educator

résidence normale
normal / permanent home

salaire hebdomadaire brut normal
normal gross weekly earnings / wage

salaire en horaire normal
straight-time pay; (occ.) regular wage

salaire normal
normal wage

semaine normale de travail
normal / standard work week, basic work week

taux normal
standard rate

travailler aux heures normales
to work regular hours

travailler en dehors des heures normales
to work unsocial hours

NORMALISÉ
standardised

avis normalisé de vacance de poste
standardised notice of vacancy

emploi / poste non normalisé
non-standard job

taux de chômage normalisé
standardised unemployment rate (SUR)

taux de production normalisé
standard rate of production

NORMALISER
to standardise

NORMATIF
standard-setting

NORME
standard

conforme aux normes établies / fixées (être)
to fulfil requirements

forme d'emploi hors normes
atypical form of employment

logement ne répondant pas aux normes d'habitabilité minimale
sub(-)standard housing

norme-cadre
master standard

norme de classement
standard of classification; grading standard

norme de comportement
standard of behaviour

normes de conduite
standard of conduct

norme d'emploi
employment standard

norme équitable en matière d'emploi
fair labour standard

norme établie
set standard

normes fondamentales du travail
basic / core labour standards

norme de mesure du travail
work measurement standard

norme minimale / minimum
minimum standard

normes minima de sécurité sociale
minimum standards for social security

norme non obligatoire
voluntary standard

norme pédagogique
academic standard

norme professionnelle
occupational standard / norm

norme de rendement
performance standard, standard of performance

norme salariale
wage standard

norme sanitaire / norme de santé
health standard

norme de sélection
qualification / selection standard

norme de service
standard of service

norme du travail
labour standard

norme du travail équitable
fair labour standard

travail hors normes
atypical work

travailleur hors normes
atypical worker

NOTATEUR
reporting officer; supervisor

deuxième notateur
second supervisor

NOTATION
grading; performance appraisal; reporting

échelle de notation du rendement
performance rating scale

notation par les étudiants (USA)
course student rate

notation au mérite
merit rating / rate

notation du rendement
performance rating

NOTE
note d'orientation
policy note

NOTICE
notice personnelle
personal history form

NOTIFICATION
notice, advice, notification; reporting
(illness)

**(formule de) notification administrative
de décharge**
personnel payroll clearance action (form)

notification administrative
(occ.) personnel action / form

**notification de la date du congé de
maternité**
notice of maternity absence

**notification obligatoire des emplois /
des postes vacants / des offres d'emploi
/ des vacances d'emploi**
compulsory notification of vacancies

notification d'une prestation
notification of benefit

système de notification
reporting system

NOTIFIÉ
poste notifié vacant
vacancy notified

vacance d'emploi notifiée
vacancy notified

NOTIFIER
to notify

notifier une lettre de promotion
to issue a letter of promotion

NOTION
concept, notion; (pl.) knowledge (ed.)

NOURRICE
enfant (placé) en nourrice
foster child

NOURRICIER
enfant sous la garde de parents nourriciers
foster child

famille nourricière
foster family

fonction nourricière
material need function

foyer nourricier
foster home

mère nourricière
house / foster mother

parents nourriciers
boarding / foster parents

placement nourricier
foster care

NOURRICIER (n.)
nourriciers (les)
boarding / foster parents

NOURRISSON
(new-born) baby / infant

aliment pour nourrissons
infant / baby food

consultation de nourrissons
baby / infant clinic, infant welfare centre

préparation pour nourrissons
infant formula

NOURRITURE
allocation de nourriture
food allowance

NOUVEAU
flux de nouveaux chômeurs
flow into unemployment

nouvel actif
labour force entrant, (new) entrant to the
workforce / labour force

nouvel arrivant
(new) entrant

nouvel assuré
newly insured

nouveaux besoins
additional needs / requirements / demand

nouveau calcul d'une prestation
recalculation of a benefit

nouveau diplômé
recent graduate

nouvel inscrit à un programme
entrant into a scheme

nouvelle nomination
re-appointment

nouveau participant à un programme
entrant into a scheme

nouvelle recrue
new hire

**nouveau secteur d'avenir / de
croissance**
new growth industry

nouveau venu
late entrant

nouveau venu sur le marché du travail
labour force entrant, (new) entrant on the
labour market

**programme d'initiation des nouveaux
employés**
orientation programme for new employees

NOUVEAU-NÉ
new-born infant / baby

NOYAU
hard core, nucleus

famille du type noyau conjugal
conjugal family

noyau familial
family nucleus

**noyau irréductible de chômage / de
chômeurs**
hard-core unemployment

NOYAUTAGE
infiltration

NUCLÉAIRE
effectifs nucléaires
core workforce / workers

famille nucléaire
nuclear family

main-d'oeuvre nucléaire
core workforce / workers

NUIRE
to prejudice

NUISIBLE
harmful, injurious, prejudicial

nuisible à la santé
injurious to (the) health

NUIT
asile de nuit
night shelter

équipe de nuit
night / twilight shift

garde de nuit
night nurse

hôpital de nuit
night hospital

indemnité de nuit
night shift allowance

infirmière de nuit
night nurse

postes permanents de nuit
regular night shift

prime de nuit
night shift premium

sursalaire de nuit
night differential

travail de nuit
night work

travail posté de nuit
nightshift

visite de nuit
night call

NUL
invalid; null

hypothèse nulle
null hypothesis

jeu à somme nulle
zero-sum game

NULLITÉ
invalidity

NUMÉRIQUE
importance numérique
strength

NUMÉRO
number

numéro d'affiliation
membership number

numéro d'assurance nationale (UK)
national insurance number

numéro d'assurance sociale
social insurance number

numéro d'immatriculation / matricule
identification / registration number;
insurance number

NUMERUS CLAUSUS
restricted intake

NUTRITION
hygiène de la nutrition
nutritional health

NUTRITIONNISTE
nutritionist

OBJECTIF (adj.)
licenciement pour raisons objectives (Sp.)
dismissal on objective grounds

pratique d'emploi objective
neutral / objective employment practice

OBJECTIF (n.)
aim, goal, objective; target; commitment

atelier d'objectif professionnel pour demandeurs d'emploi (Belg.)
vocational objectives workshop for jobseekers

objectif budgétaire
target budget

objectif de carrière
occupational goal; vocational development objective; career objective / goal

objectifs conflictuels
conflict of objectives / of goals, goal conflict

objectif de croissance
growth target

objectif éducatif / pédagogique
educational goal

objectif de plein emploi
full employment target / objective

objectif professionnel
occupational goal; vocational development objective; career objective / goal

objectif de rendement
performance target

prime d'objectif
objectives bonus

OBJECTION
objection; exception

OBLIGATION
duty; liability; commitment; requirement; rule

dégager des obligations professionnelles
to release from work

droits et obligations
rights and obligations

droit des obligations
law of obligations, contract law

inexécution des obligations de service
failure to discharge the duties attaching to a post

obligation alimentaire
(alimony) maintenance order / obligation / payment, obligation to maintain

obligation contractée
incurred obligation

obligation contractuelle
contractual obligation

obligation conventionnelle
treaty obligation

obligation de cotiser
liability for contribution

obligation de garder la chambre
confinement to bed

obligation inconditionnelle
absolute liability

obligations militaires
(compulsory) military service

obligation de moyens
best-endeavours obligation, duty to exercise skill and care

obligation de rémunération
duty to pay remuneration

obligation de rendre compte
obligation to report; accountability

obligation de réserve
obligation of discretion

obligation de rester chez soi
confinement to the house

obligation de résultat
obligation of result

obligation scolaire
compulsory education

obligation née d'un traité
treaty obligation

obligation de travailler
obligation to work

régime relatif aux obligations de l'employeur
scheme concerning the employer's liability

système d'obligations-logement (Icel.)
house-bond system

OBLIGATOIRE
compulsory, mandatory; binding; statutory

affichage obligatoire
compulsory posting

affiliation obligatoire
compulsory membership

âge de départ obligatoire à la retraite
automatic / compulsory / mandatory retirement age

âge de fin de scolarité (obligatoire)
school-leaving age

âge obligatoire de la retraite
automatic / compulsory / mandatory retirement age

âge de scolarité obligatoire
(compulsory) school age

arbitrage ayant force obligatoire (Malta)
binding arbitration

arrangement contractuel juridiquement obligatoire
legally binding contractual arrangement

assujetti à l'assurance obligatoire
subject to compulsory insurance, compulsorily covered

assujettissement à l'assurance obligatoire
liability to compulsory insurance

assujettissement obligatoire
compulsory coverage

assurance-chômage obligatoire
compulsory unemployment insurance

assurance obligatoire
compulsory insurance

assuré à titre obligatoire / au titre d'une assurance obligatoire
compulsorily insured

atelier pratiquant l'affiliation syndicale obligatoire
closed / union shop

communication obligatoire des emplois / offres d'emploi / postes vacants / vacances d'emploi
compulsory notification of vacancies

compétence obligatoire
compulsory jurisdiction

effectif(s) d'âge scolaire obligatoire
school age population

force obligatoire (ayant)
binding

instruction obligatoire
compulsory education

maladie à déclaration obligatoire
notifiable / reportable disease; scheduled disease

norme non obligatoire
voluntary standard

notification obligatoire des emplois / des postes vacants / des offres d'emploi / des

vacances d'emploi
compulsory notification of vacancies

obligatoire (non)
voluntary

obligatoire pour tous
generally binding

période d'assurance obligatoire
period of compulsory insurance

plage (obligatoire) de présence
core time / hours

prélèvement obligatoire
mandatory levy

prestation obligatoire
statutory benefit

rapport obligatoire
obligatory report

régime d'assurance obligatoire
compulsory insurance scheme

**régime d'assurance(-)vieillesse obliga-
toire**
compulsory pension insurance scheme

régime de retraite obligatoire
mandatory pension scheme / plan

retraite obligatoire
mandatory retirement

scolarité obligatoire
compulsory schooling

service militaire obligatoire
compulsory military service

service du travail obligatoire (Fr.
compulsory working

tribunal d'arbitrage obligatoire
compulsory arbitration tribunal

OBLITÉRÉ
timbre oblitéré
cancelled stamp

OBLITÉRER
oblitérer des timbres (national insurance)
(UK)
to cancel stamps

OBSÈQUES
funeral

allocation pour frais d'obsèques
funeral grant

congé pour obsèques
funeral leave

frais d'obsèques
cost of funeral, funeral expenses

OBSERVANCE
observance, compliance

OBSERVATION
centre d'observation
observation centre

observation du marché du travail
labour market monitoring

observation sur le terrain
field study

OBSERVER
to observe; to abide by, to comply

observer les règles (ne pas)
to fail to comply with rules

OBSTACLE
obstacle à l'emploi
barrier to employment, job barrier

obstacle lié à l'emploi
job-related barrier

obstacle matériel
physical barrier

obstacle à la mobilité
mobility barrier

obstacle physique
physical barrier

obstacle social
social barrier

OBSTÉTRICAL
soins obstétricaux
maternity / delivery care

OBSTÉTRIQUE (n.)
dispensaire d'obstétrique
midwifery clinic

OBTEMPÉRER
refus d'obtempérer
wilful disobedience

OBTURATION
filling

OCCASIONNEL
emploi occasionnel
casual / odd job / employment

emploi occasionnel vacant
casual vacancy

employé occasionnel
casual employee; short-term staff

main-d'oeuvre occasionnelle
casual labour

placement dans un emploi occasionnel
casual job placement

salaire occasionnel
casual wage

travail occasionnel
casual / irregular work; freelance work;
(pl.) casual employment

travaux occasionnels (pour des)
for casual labour

travailleur occasionnel
casual employee / worker / labourer,
occasional / contingent worker

vacance occasionnelle
casual vacancy

OCCUPANT (n.)
occupant sans titre
squatter

propriétaire occupant
owner-occupier

unité définie en fonction de l'occupant
unit based on occupancy

OCCUPATION
employment, activity, work; occupation;
sit-down protest, sit-in; occupancy

degré d'occupation d'un logement
degree of crowding of a dwelling

durée d'occupation d'un emploi
job tenure

grève avec occupation des locaux
sit-in / stay-in strike; worker occupation

mode d'occupation
tenancy, tenure

occupation accessoire
extra work

occupation dangereuse
hazardous occupation / work

occupation des lieux
occupation of premises

occupation d'un logement en (toute) propriété
owner-occupancy

occupation lucrative / rémunérée
remunerated employment

occupation sauvage
squatter take-over, squatting

occupation par les travailleurs
worker occupation

régime d'occupation
tenancy, tenure

roulement dans l'occupation des postes
rotation of staff

taux d'occupation
occupation rate

OCCUPÉ
actif occupé
employed; (pl.) population in employment, employed labour force / population

effectifs occupés
employed population

emploi effectivement occupé
current / actual job / occupation

emploi occupé
job / occupation held

formation des actifs occupés (Fr.)
training for employed people

logement insuffisamment occupé
under-occupied accommodation

nombre de travailleurs occupés
number of workers employed (in a company)

population active occupée
employed labour force / population

travailleur occupé
employed worker

OCCUPER
to employ

occuper un emploi
to hold a job

occuper un emploi de longue durée
to work on a long-term basis

occuper une fonction
to hold a position

occuper un poste
to encumber a post, to be the incumbent of a post, to hold a position

OCTROI
allocation, grant(ing), award; provision

condition d'octroi
qualifying condition; (pl.) eligibility, conditions of entitlement

conditions d'octroi des prestations
conditions governing eligibility for benefits

durée d'octroi des prestations
period for which benefit is allowed

octroi exceptionnel
exceptional / extra-statutory award

octroi d'une indemnité
award of compensation

octroi de licence
licensing

octroi d'une pension
provision / granting / award of pension

octroi de permis
licensing

octroi d'une prestation
provision / granting / award of a benefit

octroi des soins médicaux
provision of medical care

octroi de subventions salariales
subsidisation of wages

période d'octroi des prestations
period for which benefit(s) is/are allowed

OCTROYER
to grant, to award

octroyer une pension
to grant a pension

octroyer une prestation
to allow / to grant a benefit

octroyer un prêt
to grant a loan

OCULISTE
eye doctor / specialist, oculist

ODONTOLOGIQUE
(service de) consultations odontologiques
dental clinic

ODONTOLOGISTE
odontologist

OEUVRE
assistance fund; work; (pl.) social welfare work

conseil des oeuvres sociales
(occ.) community council

oeuvre d'adoption
adoption society

oeuvre de bienfaisance
relief / charitable association, assistance fund, charitable agency / institution, charity

oeuvre de caisse (Fr.)
fund institution

oeuvre caritative / charitable
charity, charitable association / agency

oeuvres mutualistes
institutions of mutual benefit societies

oeuvre privée
voluntary agency; private charity

oeuvre sociale
welfare agency / institution; (pl.) company
welfare facilities, staff amenities

oeuvre sociale privée
private / voluntary welfare agency

oeuvre reconnue d'utilité publique
corporation recognised to be of public
interest, charitable corporation; charity

OFFICE (D')
droit maintenu d'office
automatically maintained right, right
automatically maintained

hospitalisation d'office
involuntary hospitalisation

mise à la retraite d'office
compulsory retirement

mutation d'office
disciplinary posting / transfer

placement d'office
compulsory care

retraite d'office
compulsory retirement

retraite d'office (être mis à la)
to be compulsorily retired

OFFICE
bureau, office, board

office central du logement
central authority for housing

office de l'emploi
(labour) employment office, employment
agency / bureau (USA)

office de reclassement social
social re-adaptation service

office régional
regional office

office du travail
(labour) employment office, employment
agency / bureau (USA)

OFFICIEL (adj.)
official; statutory, legal

exercice de fonctions officielles
performance of official duties

fonction officielle
official function / duty; (pl.) public office

**imputable à l'exercice de fonctions
officielles**
attributable to the performance of official
duties

lieu d'affectation officiel
official duty station

marché du travail officiel
official / organised / formal labour market

organe officiel
official / statutory body

service officiel de réadaptation
public rehabilitation service

OFFICIEL (n.)
official

OFFICIELLEMENT
aviser officiellement
to give formal notice

OFFICIER
officier public
public officer

officiers publics et ministériels
public and ministerial officers

OFFICINE
dispensary

OFFRE
supply; provision; offer

acceptation d'une offre d'emploi
approval of a job offer

adéquation de l'offre et de la demande
matching supply and demand

adéquation de l'offre et de la demande d'emploi
job-worker / worker-job matching, matching of jobseekers and vacancies, job matching

annonce d'offre d'emploi
job advertisement

appariement informatique des offres et des demandes d'emploi
computerised matching of jobs and job seekers

approbation d'une offre d'emploi
approval of a job offer

courbe d'offre de main-d'oeuvre
supply curve of labour, labour supply schedule

diffuser des offres d'emploi
to circulate job vacancies

élasticité de l'offre de main-d'oeuvre
elasticity of labour supply

élasticité de l'offre de travail par rapport aux salaires
wage elasticity of labour supply

évolution de l'offre sur le marché du travail
changes in labour supply

inadéquation entre offres et demandes d'emploi
job mismatch

inadéquation de l'offre et de la demande de travail
(occ.) labour market mismatch

mise en correspondance des offres et des demandes d'emploi
job matching

notification obligatoire des offres d'emploi
compulsory notification of vacancies

offre et la demande (l')
supply and demand

offre d'éducation
education provision

offre d'emploi
job offer / advertisement / order; job opening / opportunity; job / appointment / situation vacant; (job) vacancy; (pl.) employment opportunities; availability of jobs

offre d'emploi authentique
bona fide job offer

offre d'emploi difficile à satisfaire
hard-to-fill vacancy

offre d'emploi discriminatoire
discriminatory job offer

offre d'emploi satisfaite
vacancy filled, filled vacancy

offre d'emploi non satisfaite
outstanding job / unfilled vacancy, unfilled demand for worker

offre d'engagement
offer of appointment

offre excédentaire de main-d'oeuvre
excess supply / oversupply of labour

offre ferme
firm offer

offre de formation
training provision / proposal, proposal for training

offre globale
aggregate / total supply

offre de main-d'oeuvre
manpower / labour supply, supply of labour; worker availability

offre de main-d'oeuvre excédentaire
excess supply / oversupply of labour

offre potentielle de main-d'oeuvre
potential manpower supply

offre de soins
available health services

offre de travail / de travailleurs
labour / manpower supply

prix d'offre de la main-d'oeuvre
supply price of labour

refuser une offre d'emploi
to refuse a job offer

registre des offres d'emploi
register of vacancies

système informatisé de traitement des offres d'emploi
automated job order system

tableau d'affichage des offres d'emploi
(occ.) job board

OKUN
courbe d'Okun
Okun curve

OLIGOPHRÈNE
mentally retarded / deficient, developmentally handicapped

OLIGOPHRÉNIE
mental retardation

OMNIPRATICIEN
general practitioner

OMNIPRÉSENT
technologie omniprésente
pervasive technology

OPÉRATEUR
operator; professional

opérateur sur machine
machine operator

opérateurs sur machines à traiter l'information [CITP-1968 (3-4)]
computing machine operators [ISCO-1968 (3-4)]

opérateurs de stations d'émissions de radio et de télévision, opérateurs d'appareils de sonorisation et projectionnistes de cinéma [CITP-1968 (8-6)]
broadcasting station and sound equipment operators and cinema projectionists [ISCO-1968 (8-6)]

opérateurs des téléphones et télégraphes [CITP-1968 (3-8)]
telephone and telegraph operators [ISCO-1968 (3-8)]

OPÉRATION
balance des opérations courantes
current account

cadres de direction, production et opérations [CITP-1988 (122)]
production and operations department managers [ISCO-1988 (122)]

compte des opérations courantes
current account

opération commerciale
(occ.) business venture

opération conjointe
joint venture

opération de planification
planning exercise

opération des promotions
promotion exercise

opération de sauvetage
rescue work

solde des opérations courantes
current account

OPÉRATIONNEL
cadre opérationnel
line manager

personnel opérationnel
operational staff / personnel, field staff

poste opérationnel
(occ.) field position

rapport opérationnel
operational report

recherche sociale opérationnelle
operational social research

structure opérationnelle
operational framework

OPHTALMOLOGISTE / OPH-TALMOLOGUE
ophthalmologist, eye doctor / specialist, oculist

OPINION
sondage d'opinion
opinion survey

OPPORTUN
suitable

OPPORTUNITÉ
coût d'opportunité
opportunity cost

OPPOSABLE
binding

référence médicale opposable (Fr.)
valid medical norm

tarif opposable
binding fee

OPPOSITION
mettre opposition sur un traitement
to attach salary

OPTER
opter pour la non-affiliation / le non-assujettissement au régime général de retraite complémentaire
to contract out

OPTICIEN
optician

OPTIMAL
quantification optimale
(occ.) target approach

OPTIMISATION
optimisation fiscale
(occ.) tax avoidance

OPTIMUM
budget optimum
target budget

optimum social
social optimum

programme optimum
target programme

OPTION
ajournement de l'option entre les prestations
deferment of choice of benefit

droit d'option
right of option

matière en option
optional / elective subject

option professionnelle
occupational alternative

OPTIONNEL
clause optionnelle d'adhésion
opting-in clause

clause optionnelle de désengagement / de sortie
opting-out clause

matière optionnelle
optional / elective subject

OPTIQUE (adj.)
soins optiques
eye care / treatment, vision care (USA)

ORAL
oral, verbal

avertissement oral
oral warning

ORDINAIRE
allocation ordinaire
regular allowance

allocation prévue par le régime ordinaire d'indemnisation
(occ.) standard benefit

budget ordinaire
regular budget

complément ordinaire de salaire (It.)
ordinary wage supplement

contrat d'apprentissage «ordinaire» (Belg.)
"ordinary" apprenticeship contract

coûts non salariaux ordinaires
recurring non-salary costs

dépenses ordinaires
recurrent expenditure

emploi en milieu ordinaire
open employment

enseignement ordinaire
formal education, mainstream education / schooling

manoeuvre ordinaire
ordinary labourer

manoeuvre ordinaire adulte masculin
ordinary adult male labourer

ménage ordinaire
family / private household

ouvrier ordinaire
common worker / labourer

vacance ordinaire
regular vacancy

ORDINATEUR
enseignement assisté par ordinateur (EAO)
computer-assisted learning (CAL)

(service de) placement assisté par ordinateur
computer-assisted placement (service)

ORDONNANCE
ordinance; statutory instrument; prescription (med.)

médicament délivré / vendu sur ordonnance
prescription drug

ordonnance provisoire
interim / interlocutory injunction

ordonnance médicale
medical prescription

ordonnance provisoire
interim / interlocutory injunction

ordonnance du service de santé (UK)
health prescription

participation au coût de l'ordonnance
prescription fee / charge

ORDONNANCEMENT
automatic workload regulation, work scheduling techniques, workload regulation; certification; order to pay

ORDONNER
to order, to prescribe

ORDRE
order; injunction; association

classer les traitements par ordre
to rank salary rates

compte d'ordre
suspense account

forces de l'ordre
police

membres des forces de l'ordre (Malta)
members of a disciplined force

ordre de (être de l')
to amount about

ordre d'exécution
mandatory injunction

ordre d'expulsion
deportation / expulsion order

ordre de grandeur
order of magnitude, range; estimate

ordre de grandeur de salaire
salary estimation / estimate

ordre d'interruption d'une activité (dangereuse)
prohibition notice

Ordre des Médecins (Fr.)
medical association

ordre mensuel de paiement
monthly payment order

ordre des pharmaciens
pharmaceutical society

ordre professionnel
professional association / body

ordre public
law and order

ordre de réintégration
reinstatement order

ordre de saisie-arrêt
attachment of earnings order

ordre de travail
work order

ORFÈVRE
joailliers et orfèvres [CITP-1968 (8-8)]
jewellery and precious metal workers
[ISCO-1968 (8-8)]

ORGANE
body; establishment

organe autonome
autonomous / self-governing / self-government body

organe consultatif
consultative / advisory body

organe de contrôle
enforcement body

organe de décision / décisionnel
decision-making body

organe directeur
governing body; steering group; policy-making body

organe d'une institution de sécurité sociale
organ of a social security institution

organe officiel
opfficial / statutory body

organe de surveillance / de tutelle
supervisory body

ORGANIGRAMME
divisional pattern, establishment / organisational / flow chart

organigramme en râteau
flat organisation chart

ORGANIQUE
organic; substantive

cadre organique
line manager

fonctions organiques
bodily processes

loi organique
organic law

personnel des services organiques
substantive staff

poste dans les services organiques
substantive post

service non organique
servicing unit

ORGANISATION
organisation, agency; management

comité d'organisation
organising / (occ.) steering committee

droit d'organisation
freedom of organisation, right to organise

ingénieur-conseil en organisation
management consultant

organisation bénévole
voluntary / volunteer agency, voluntary organisation

organisation des carrières
(occ.) career development

organisation civique
civic organisation

organisation communautaire
community organisation

organisation d'employeurs
organisation of employers

organisation d'envergure nationale
nation-wide organisation

**organisation non gouvernementale
semi-autonome**
quasi-autonomous non-governmental
organisation (quango)

organisation d'intérêt local
community(-based) organisation

organisation de jeunes
youth organisation

organisation matérielle
physical organisation

organisation mutualiste
mutual organisation

organisations ouvrières
organised labour

organisation patronale
employer's association / organisation,
association / organisation of employers,
trade association

organisation de la production
production engineering

organisation professionnelle
professional / industrial organisation;
workers' and employers' organisation

organisation de la protection sociale
(social) welfare provision

organisation en réseau
network organisation

**organisation sanitaire / de santé
publique**
(public) health practice

organisation scientifique du travail
(occ.) job engineering

organisation syndicale
labour organisation, labour / trade union

organisation du travail
work organisation

organisation à vocation nationale
nation-wide organisation

recherche en organisation sanitaire
health practice research

structure de l'organisation
organisational structure

ORGANISATIONNEL
structure organisationnelle
organisational structure

ORGANISÉ
marché du travail organisé
official / organised / formal labour market

secteur non organisé (de l'économie)
informal economy sector

travailleurs organisés
organised labour

ORGANISME
body; agency; establishment

organisme de l'administration locale
local government agency

organisme d'aide sociale
(social) welfare agency

organisme d'assistance
assistance body; charity

organisme d'assistance sociale
social assistance agency / body

organisme d'assurance
insurance institute

**organisme d'assurance contre les
accidents**
accident insurance institution

organisme assureur
insurance carrier, insuring body

organisme bénévole
voluntary / volunteer agency / organisation

organisme de bienfaisance
charitable agency / institution, charity

organisme-cadre
umbrella organisation

organisme caritatif
charity, charitable organisation

organisme client
client body

organisme communautaire
community organisation

organisme consultatif
consultative / advisory body

organisme de coordination
coordinating agency

organisme créancier
creditor body

organisme débiteur
debtor / paying body, paying office

organisme employeur
employing agency

organisme d'Etat
government(al) body / agency

organisme extérieur / externe
external / outside agency

organisme financier
financial institution

organisme de formation
training agency

organisme d'insertion socio-professionnelle (OISP) (Belg.)
social and vocational integration organisation / agency

organisme d'intérêt collectif / d'intérêt local
community(-based) organisation / agency

organisme de liaison
liaison body

organisme de paiement
paying body / office

organisme paraétatique / parapublic
semi-public body

organisme payeur
paying body / office

organisme doté de la personnalité morale
corporate body

organisme privé
voluntary body

organisme professionnel
professional body

organisme de protection sociale
(social) welfare agency

organisme public
governmental body, Government(al) agency; (pl.) public authorities

organisme public de bienfaisance / de secours
public charity

organisme de recherche
research establishment / institute

organisme de réglementation professionnelle
professional licensing authority

organisme sanitaire
health organisation

organisme de sécurité sociale
social security fund / agency

organisme social
welfare institution, social agency

organisme social privé
private / voluntary welfare agency

ORIENTATION
orientation; guidance, counselling; referral (of patients); policy; trend; (pl.) guidelines

agent d'orientation / responsable de l'orientation
guidance officer

agent d'orientation professionnelle
career guidance officer

centre d'information et d'orientation (Fr.)
information and guidance centre

centre d'orientation
referral centre

changement d'orientation
change of track

comité d'orientation
steering committee

conseil d'orientation conjugale / matrimoniale
marriage guidance council

conseiller d'orientation
career(s) adviser / officer, guidance counsellor; school counsellor

conseiller en / d'orientation professionnelle
vocational (guidance) counsellor, career officer

consultation d'orientation professionnelle
vocational counselling

contrat d'orientation (Fr.)
guidance / employment orientation contract

document d'orientation
policy paper

examen d'orientation professionnelle
vocational testing

grandes orientations
policy formulations, guidelines

instrument d'orientation professionnelle
vocational counselling tool

note d'orientation
policy note

orientation antérieure au placement
pre-employment counselling

orientation consécutive au placement
post-employment / post-placement counselling

orientation familiale
family guidance

orientation générale
(general) policy

orientation individuelle
individual counselling

orientation postérieure au placement
post-employment / post-placement counselling

orientation préalable / préparatoire à la retraite
pre-retirement counselling

orientation professionnelle
career / careers guidance / education, career(s) advice / counselling, job counselling / orientation, occupational counselling / guidance, vocational guidance / counselling

orientation professionnelle des adultes
adult vocational counselling

orientation professionnelle informatisée
computerised vocational guidance

orientation professionnelle personnalisée
personal career counselling

orientation psychologique
psychological guidance

orientations salariales
pay / wage guidelines

orientation scolaire
education(al) guidance

permanence d'accueil, d'information et d'orientation (PAIO) (Fr.)
reception, information and guidance office

professeur d'orientation (Malta)
guidance teacher

rapport d'orientation
policy report

responsable de l'orientation
guidance officer

service de consultation et d'orientation
counselling and guidance service

service d'orientation
guidance / counselling service

service d'orientation sur les carrières (UK)
career service

service d'orientation professionnelle
career counselling service, employment advisory service

service d'orientation professionnelle spécialisée
specialised vocational guidance service

spécialiste de l'orientation
guidance expert

stage d'orientation
orientation course / training

système d'orientation professionnelle informatisé
computer-based career orientation system

ORIENTEUR
vocational / career officer, guidance counsellor

orienteur professionnel
(vocational) guidance counsellor

ORIGINE
domicile d'origine
domicile of origin

famille d'origine
natural family

origine (d')
original

origine sociale
social background / origin

pays d'origine
home country

ORPHELIN
orphan (child)

allocation pour / d'orphelin
orphan's allowance, allowance for orphans; guardians's allowance (UK)

orphelin complet / double
full orphan, orphan whose parents are dead, orphan having lost both parents

orphelin de guerre
war orphan

orphelin de mère
orphan whose mother is dead

orphelin pauvre (Fr.)
orphan without subsistence means

orphelin de père
orphan whose father is dead

orphelin de père et de mère
full orphan, orphan whose parents are dead, orphan having lost both parents

orphelin de père ou de mère
orphan having lost one parent

pension d'orphelin
orphan's pension

pension d'orphelin complet (Austr.)
double orphan pension

pension de réversion d'orphelin
orphan's pension

prestation des / pour orphelin(s)
orphan's benefit

rente d'orphelin
orphan's pension

ORTHÈSE
orthesis

ORTHODONTIE
orthodontic treatment

ORTHOPÉDIQUE
appareil orthopédique
orthopaedic appliance

ORTHOPÉDISTE
orthopaedic specialist, orthopaedist

ORTHOPHONISTE
speech therapist

OSTÉO-ARTICULAIRE
maladie du système ostéo-articulaire et
des muscles
musculo-skeletal disease

OUÏE
perte de l'ouïe
hearing loss

OUTIL
outil de travail
work tool

OUTRE-MER
overseas

OUTREPASSER
outrepasser ses pouvoirs
to exceed one's powers / authority

OUVERT
accord ouvert
open-ended agreement

adhésion ouverte (sickness ins.)
open enrolment

assistance éducative en milieu ouvert
open educational support

atelier ouvert
open workshop

bureau ouvert (Fr.)
mother and child care centre

clinique ouverte
open clinic

crédits ouverts
appropriations

foyer ouvert
open-door house

hôpital ouvert
open-door hospital
marché ouvert
open market

ouvert à la signature
open to signature

syndicat ouvert
open union

OUVERTURE
âge d'ouverture des droits
age of eligibility

âge d'ouverture des droits à / ouvrant droit à pension
age of pension entitlement, pensionable age

condition minimale d'ouverture des droits
minimum qualifying condition

condition d'ouverture des droits
qualifying condition; condition of entitlement; eligibility

heures d'ouverture
trading / opening hours

ouverture des droits
entitlement

ouverture d'un droit à (des) prestations
acquisition of a right to benefits

période d'assurance requise pour l'ouverture du droit aux prestations
qualifying insurance / qualification period

remplir les conditions d'ouverture des droits aux prestations
to be eligible for / to qualify for benefit, to satisfy the conditions for acquisition

OUVRABLE
jour ouvrable
business / working / work day, week-day

- 560 -

jour non ouvrable
non-working day

OUVRAGE
travailleur à l'ouvrage
contract worker

OUVRÉ
heure effectivement ouvrée
hour actually worked

heure ouvrée
worked hour; (pl.) hours worked

heures ouvrées dans la journée
daily working hours

jour ouvré
business / working / work day, week-day

jour non ouvré
non-working day

salaire au prorata des heures ouvrées
wage in proportion to time worked

OUVRIER (adj.)
association ouvrière
workman's / workmen's association

assurance ouvrière
workers' insurance

classe ouvrière
working class

conscience ouvrière
working class consciousness

conseil ouvrier (Pol.)
workers' council

coopérative ouvrière
workers' cooperative

cotisation ouvrière
worker's contribution

éducation ouvrière
workers' education

enfant issu de famille ouvrière
child of working-class family

formation ouvrière
workers' education

logement ouvrier
tenement

milieu ouvrier
working(-)class environment

organisations ouvrières
organised labour

part ouvrière
employee's contribution

rente des retraites ouvrières et paysannes
annuity in addition to industrial and agricultural workers' pensions

rétention des cotisations ouvrières
retention of workers' contributions

retraites ouvrières et paysannes
industrial and agricultural workers' pensions

stage ouvrier
industrial placement

syndicat ouvrier
blue-collar union, employees' association

OUVRIER (n.)
wage earner; working man; (factory) hand; labourer; worker, workman; blue-collar (worker); manual worker; (pl.) industrial staff; (occ.) shop floor (the)

assurance des ouvriers
workers' insurance

assurance(-)vieillesse des ouvriers
manual workers' pension insurance, pension insurance of manual workers

emploi d'ouvrier spécialisé
semi-skilled occupation

ouvrier agricole
agricultural / farm labourer / worker, land worker

ouvriers de l'alimentation et des boissons [CITP-1968 (7-7)]
food and beverage processers [ISCO-1968 (7-7)]

ouvriers de l'assemblage [CITP-1988 (828)]
assemblers [ISCO-1988 (828)]

ouvrier du bâtiment
building worker

ouvriers du bâtiment (finitions) et assimilés [CITP-1988 (713)]
building finishers and related trades workers [ISCO-1988 (713)]

ouvriers du bâtiment (gros oeuvre) et assimilés [CITP-1988 (712)]
building frame and related trades workers [ISCO-1988 (712)]

ouvrier sur chantier
building site labourer

ouvrier compétent
qualified worker

ouvrier sans emploi
jobless worker

ouvriers et employés
industrial and non-industrial staff, manual workers and salaried employees, wage and salary workers

ouvriers et employés des mines
mineworkers and mine employees

ouvriers et employés non qualifiés [CITP-1988 (9)]
elementary occupations [ISCO-1988 (9)]

ouvrier de fabrication
production worker

ouvriers de la fabrication d'articles en caoutchouc et en matières plastiques [CITP-1968 (9-0)]
rubber and plastics product makers [ISCO-1968 (9-0)]

ouvrier à façon
jobbing workman

ouvriers du façonnage et de l'usinage des métaux [CITP-1968 (8-3)]
blacksmiths, toolmakers and machine-tool operators [ISCO-1968 (8-3)]

ouvrier du fond
underground worker

ouvrier hautement qualifié
highly skilled worker

ouvrier à la journée
day labourer

ouvriers et manoeuvres
production and related workers

ouvriers et manoeuvres non agricoles et conducteurs d'engins de transport [CITP-1968 (7/8/9)]
production and related workers, transport equipment operators and labourers [ISCO-1968 (7/8/9)]

ouvrier masculin qualifié
skilled manual male employee

ouvrier de métier
craftsman

ouvriers des métiers d'artisanat sur bois, sur textile, sur cuir et sur des matériaux similaires [CITP-1988 (733)]
handicraft workers in wood, textile, leather and related material [ISCO-1988 (733)]

ouvrier des mines
mineworker

ouvrier moyen
average production worker

ouvrier ordinaire
common worker / labourer

ouvrier le moins bien payé
worst-paid worker

ouvriers peintres, ravaleurs de façades et assimilés [CITP-1988 (714)]
painters, building structure cleaners and related trades workers [ISCO-1988 (714)]

ouvrier aux pièces
job worker, pieceworker

ouvrier à plein temps
full-time worker

ouvriers à la production et assimilés non classés ailleurs [CITP-1968 (9-4)]
production and related workers not elsewhere classified [ISCO-1968 (9-4)]

ouvriers de la production et du traitement des métaux [CITP-1968 (7-2)]
metal processers [ISCO-1968 (7-2)]

ouvrier professionnel
skilled / craft worker

ouvrier qualifié
skilled / qualified worker; (skilled) journeyman / craftsman, craft worker

ouvrier non qualifié
unskilled worker; (pl.) unskilled work-force

ouvrier qualifié type
person deemed typical of skilled labour

ouvrier spécialisé (OS)
semi-skilled / unskilled worker, specialised worker; operative

ouvriers des tabacs [CITP-1968 (7-8)]
tobacco preparers and tobacco product makers [ISCO-1968 (7-8)]

ouvrier à la tâche
jobbing workman, job worker, piece-worker

ouvrier temporaire
short-term worker

ouvriers du textile [CITP-1968 (7-5)]
spinners, weavers, knitters, dyers and related workers [ISCO-1968 (7-5)]

ouvrier (travaillant) à temps partiel
short-term worker

ouvrier d'usine
factory worker

poste d'ouvrier spécialisé
semi-skilled occupation

proportion ouvriers - employés
(occ.) labour mix

régime applicable aux ouvriers
scheme applicable to manual workers

rendement par ouvrier
labour productivity

OUVRIÈRE
woman / female worker, working woman

OUVRIR
ouvrir un droit
to entitle; to grant / to confer a right

ouvrir des emplois à
to provide employment for labour force

PACTE
covenant; pact; treaty

pacte pour l'emploi (Fr.)
employment scheme

pacte social
social agreement / convention; articles of / deed of partnership

PAIE
pay, wage, salary

bulletin de paie
pay statement / slip, payroll

bulletin de paie détaillé
detailed / itemised pay statement

bureau de paie
pay office

cycle de paie
pay cycle

enveloppe de paie
pay / wage packet

états de paie
payroll

feuille de paie
paylist, paysheet, payroll, earnings record, pay statement / slip

feuille / fiche de paie détaillée
detailed / itemised pay statement

fiche de paie
paylist, paysheet, payroll, earnings record, pay statement / slip

inscrit sur les états de paie
in pay status

jour de paie
pay(-)day

liste de paie
paylist, paysheet, earnings record

livre de paie
paybook, wage book, payroll ledger

paie nette
take-home pay

période de paie
pay period / cycle

registre de paie
payroll ledger

service de paie
payroll service

service de la paie (assurer le)
to meet the payroll

système de paie
pay / payment / payroll system

système de paie par paliers
stepped pay system

PAIEMENT
payment; settlement

balance des paiements
balance of payments

balance des paiements courants
current account

bordereau de paiement
payment form

bureau de paiement des indemnités de chômage
unemployment benefit (paying) office

centre de paiement
paying centre

compte des paiements courants
current account

conditions de paiement
terms of payment

délai de paiement
term of payment

exonération du paiement des primes
waiver of premiums

instruction relative au mode de paiement
payment instruction

modalités de paiement
method of payment

ordre mensuel de paiement
monthly payment order

organisme de paiement
paying body / office

paiement à l'acte
fee-for-service (system)

paiement par anticipation / anticipé
advance payment

paiement des arrérages / des arriérés
payment of arrears

paiement à la capitation
capitation payment

paiements de compensation
equalisation payments

paiement des cotisations
payment of contributions, contribution
payment

paiement des cotisations syndicales
payment of union fees

paiement en différé
deferred payment

paiement à l'étranger
payment abroad

paiement exceptionnel
(occ.) one-off payment

paiement excessif
overpayment

paiement forfaitaire
lump sum / one-off payment

paiement à titre gracieux / ex gratia
ex gratia payment

paiement hebdomadaire
weekly payment

paiement des heures supplémentaires
overtime compensation / pay

paiement par honoraires
fee-for-service system

paiement intégral
full payment

paiement intérimaire
interim payment

paiement libératoire
payment in full discharge

paiement mensuel
monthly payment

paiement de la pension
payment of the pension

paiement périodique
periodical payment; annuity

paiement des prestations
payment of benefits

paiement des prestations à un titulaire à l'étranger
payment of benefits abroad

paiement au prorata du travail effectué
(occ.) apportionment of wages

paiement en fonction des résultats
payment for results

paiement rétroactif
retroactive payment

paiement supplémentaire
additional payment

paiement en totalité
payment in full

paiement de transfert
transfer payment

paiement trimestriel
quarterly payment

paiement unique
non-recurrent payment, lump sum

procédure de paiement des prestations
procedure for the payment of benefits

récupération des frais afférents au paiement des prestations
recovery of expenses incurred in the
payment of benefits

relevé des paiements
record of payments

solde des paiements courants
current account

surseoir au paiement
to defer a payment

sursis de paiement
stay of collection

suspendre un paiement
to suspend a payment

système de paiement à l'acte
fee-for-service system

système de paiement des allocations
allowance payment system

système de paiement par honoraires
fee-for-service system

système de paiement des indemnités
allowance payment system

PAIX
clause de paix sociale
no-strike / peace clause

paix sociale
freedom from industrial disputes,
industrial harmony / peace, labour peace

PALIER
level

palier (atteindre un)
to level out / off

système de paie par paliers
stepped pay system

PALLIATIF
action palliative
affirmative / positive action, affirmative
action programme

soins palliatifs
palliative care

PANEL
panel; sample group

enquête par panel
panel survey

étude par panel
panel design / study

PANIER
indemnité de panier
meal(s) allowance

panier de la ménagère
basket of goods, shopping basket

prime de panier
meal(s) allowance

PANOPLIE
range

PAPETERIE
conducteurs de machines d'imprimerie, de
machines à relier et de machines de
papeterie [CITP-1988 (825)]
printing-, binding-and paper-products
machine operators [ISCO-1988 (825)]

PAPIER
conducteurs d'installations pour le travail
du bois et de la fabrication du papier
[CITP-1988 (814)]
wood-processing-and papermaking-plant
operators [ISCO-1988 (814)]

**ouvriers de la première préparation des
bois et de la fabrication du papier
[CITP-1968 (7-3)]**
wood preparation workers and paper
makers [ISCO-1968 (7-3)]

PARADIS
paradis fiscal
tax haven

PARAÉTATIQUE
parastatal

organisme paraétatique
semi-public body

PARAFISCAL
taxe parafiscale
additional levy

PARAGRAPHE
section

PARALLÈLE (adj.)
école parallèle
alternative school

économie parallèle
parallel / black / hidden / informal /
moonlight / shadow / submerged / twilight
/ underground / grey / invisible economy

emplois parallèles
dual jobholding

enseignement parallèle
informal education

formation parallèle
concurrent training

secteur parallèle de l'économie
informal economy sector

PARALYSÉ
crippled

PARAMÉDICAL
paramedical

personnel paramédical
paramedical staff / personnel / workers

profession paramédicale
paramedical profession

PARAPHARMACIE
parapharmaceuticals

PARAPROFESSIONNEL
activité paraprofessionnelle
non-professional activity

personnel paraprofessionnel
paraprofessional personnel

PARAPUBLIC
parapublic, quasi-public, semi-public,
parastatal

emploi dans le secteur parapublic
semi-public / (occ.) non-government
employment

employé du secteur parapublic
semi-public employee

organisme parapublic
semi-public body

PARASCOLAIRE
extracurricular

garderie parascolaire
(occ.) school-based care

PARC
park; supply; stock

parc immobilier
housing stock

parc scientifique
science park

PARCOURS
parcours de carrière
career path

PARENT
parent; relative; kin

allocation de / pour parent isolé
one-parent benefit (UK), single-parent /
lone parent's (Fr.) allowance

droit de garde des parents
parental custody

**enfant sous la garde de parents
nourriciers**
foster child

famille à parent unique
lone-parent / one-parent / single-parent
family

parents adoptifs / d'adoption
adoptive parents

parent non célibataire
non-single parent

**parent reconnu (légalement comme
parent) à charge**
dependent relative; (occ.) prescribed
relative

parent isolé
one(-)parent, lone(-)parent, single parent,
sole(-)parent

parents nourriciers
boarding / foster parents

pension de parent isolé (Austr.)
sole parent pension

prestation de parents (Icel.)
parents benefit

proche parent
close relative

PARENTAL
allocations parentales (Finl.)
parents' allowance

allocation parentale d'éducation
parental child care allowance

autorité parentale
parental authority; parental custody

congé parental
parental leave

congé parental d'éducation (Fr.)
parental childcare leave

congé parental rémunéré
paid parental leave

crèche parentale (Fr.)
family child care

déchéance de l'autorité parentale
loss of parental authority

fonction parentale
parenthood

PARENTÉ
kinship; relationship; parenthood

degré de parenté
degree of relationship

liens de parenté
kinship

parenté responsable
responsible parenthood

PARITAIRE
equal; joint

bureau paritaire de l'emploi
joint employment office

comité médical paritaire
joint medical committee

comité paritaire
joint committee

comité technique paritaire
joint technical committee

commission paritaire
joint commission / committee

commission salariale paritaire
wages council

consultation paritaire
joint consultation

négociations paritaires
joint talks

représentation paritaire
equal representation

système paritaire d'arbitrage
joint arbitration machinery

PARITÉ
parité des salaires
equal pay, wage parity

PART
part employé
employee's contribution

part (de l') employeur
employer's contribution

part fiscale
tax unit

part ouvrière
employee's contribution

part patronale
employer's contribution

part salariale
employee's contribution

pêcheur rémunéré à la part
share fisherman

PARTAGÉ (adj.)
accord de travail partagé
work sharing agreement

emploi sur poste partagé
shared job

prestation pour travail partagé
work sharing benefit

programme à frais partagés
shared-cost programme

salaire partagé
split pay

temps partagé
time sharing

travail partagé
work sharing

PARTAGE
distribution; sharing

partage d'emploi
job splitting / twinning / sharing

partage des frais
cost-sharing

partage de poste
job splitting / twinning / sharing

partage des responsabilités
division of responsibilities

partage du travail
distribution of the available volume of
work; job / work sharing

système de partage des frais
cost-sharing system

PARTENAIRE
conciliation entre partenaires sociaux
collective conciliation

partenaires sociaux
social partners; management and labour;
two / both sides of industry; unions and
management

relations entre partenaires sociaux
labour / employee / industrial relations;
social fabric

PARTENARIAT
partnership

partenariat social
social partnership

PARTI (n.)
prendre parti contre qqn
to have bias against somebody

prendre parti en faveur de / pour qqn
to have bias towards somebody

PARTI PRIS
bias, prejudice

parti pris favorable
favourably discriminatory treatment

PARTIALITÉ
bias, partiality

PARTICIPANT
nouveau participant à un programme
entrant into a scheme

PARTICIPATIF
participatory; participative

gestion participative
participative management, worker
participation

PARTICIPATION
participation; shareholding; attachment;
take-up; (occ.) membership

accord de participation
profit-sharing agreement

entreprise à participation mixte
joint venture

participation aux bénéfices
profit-sharing

participation au capital
equity stake

participation de la collectivité
community involvement

participation au coût
cost-sharing

participation au coût de l'ordonnance
prescription fee / charge

participation de l'Etat
State's contribution / share

participation aux frais
contribution towards / participation in cost
/ expenses

participation aux frais médicaux
contribution towards medical expenses

**participation aux investissements
sanitaires**
contribution in health investments

participation du malade aux frais
cost-sharing, patient's contribution

participation majoritaire
majority shareholding

participation au marché du travail
labour market / labour force attachment,
attachment to the labour force

participation minoritaire
minority shareholding

**participation pour prise en charge
exceptionnelle**
contribution for exceptional expenses

participation à la prise de décisions
co-determination

participation des salariés aux résultats
employee profit-sharing

participation des travailleurs
workers' participation

**participation des travailleurs à la
gestion des entreprises**
workers' participation in management

participation des usagers
customers' participation

pratiques de participation
participative practices

prise de participation
equity stake

**régime de retraite à participation
différée aux bénéfices**
deferred profit-sharing pension plan

reprise de la participation
re-entry into participation

**système de participation du malade aux
frais**
cost-sharing system

taux de participation
participation / take-up rate

PARTICULIER (adj.)
particular, specific; private

affectation particulière
specific job assignment

chambre particulière
private room

compétence particulière
specialised skill

cours particuliers
private tuition

régime particulier
special scheme

PARTICULIER (n.)
private individual

revenu disponible des particuliers
disposable personal income

services aux particuliers
personal services

PARTIE
partie à un contrat
party to a contract

partie prenante
party; income recipient

partie saisissable d'une pension
attachable part of a pension

tierce partie
third party

PARTIEL
activité à temps partiel
part-time / subsidiary activity, part-time
job

allocation de chômage partiel
short-time working allowance

allocation d'invalidité partielle (Neth.)
partial disability allowance

année partielle (en)
part(-)year

atteint d'incapacité partielle
partially incapacitated

atteint d'invalidité partielle
partially disabled

chômage partiel
short(-)time work(ing); partial
unemployment; under-employment

chômage partiel (en)
under-employed

chômage partiel (être en)
to be under-employed, to work short-time,
to be on short time

chômeur partiel
under-employed, partially unemployed
(worker), worker on short time, short-term
worker

congé spécial à traitement partiel
special leave with partial pay

congé (d'études) à temps partiel
part-time day release

contrat de travail à temps partiel
part-time employment contract

conversion partielle des pensions
partial commutation of retirement benefits

emploi permanent à temps partiel
permanent part-time employment

emploi à temps partiel
part-time employment / job

employé permanent à temps partiel
permanent part-time employee

employé à temps partiel
part-time employee

enseignement à temps partiel
part-time instruction / education

examen partiel
intermediate examination

formation à temps partiel
part-time training

incapacité (de travail) partielle
partial disablement / incapacity

**incapacité (de travail) partielle
permanente**
permanent partial incapacity / disablement

indemnisation pour chômage partiel
short-time working compensation

indemnité de chômage partiel
short-time working allowance

indemnité partielle
partial compensation

invalidité partielle
partial disability

**journée de travail normale à temps
partiel**
normal part-time working day

ouvrier (travaillant) à temps partiel
short-term worker

pension contributive partielle (Irel.)
partial contributory pension

pension de retraite partielle
partial pension

pension à temps partiel (Finl.)
part-time pension
personnel (employé) à temps

partiel
part-time staff

prestation pour chômage partiel
short-time working benefit

**régime de retraite par capitalisation
partielle**
partially funded-pension plan

**remboursement partiel des frais
salariaux**
partial wage reimbursement

remise totale ou partielle des retenues
full or partial waiver of deductions

retraite partielle
partial retirement

salaire partiel
part wage, partial pay

salarié permanent à temps partiel
permanent part-time employee

somme en capital résultant de / versée au titre de la conversion partielle de la pension
partial lump-sum withdrawal benefit, partial lump-sum commutation of pension benefit

stage à temps partiel
part-time course

temps partiel (à)
part-time

traitement partiel
part wage, partial pay

travail en année partielle
part-year work

travail à temps partiel
part-time employment / job / work

travailleur en année partielle
part-year worker

travailleur permanent à temps partiel
permanent part-time worker

travailleur à temps partiel
part-time worker

versement partiel
(occ.) instalment

PARTIR
partir en pré-retraite
to retire early

partir à la retraite
to retire (from work)

PASSAGE
transition

étranger de passage
alien visitor, non-resident / visiting alien

personne de passage
transient

passage à l'âge adulte
transition to adult life

passage à la vie active
transition to working life

passage de la vie active à la retraite
transition from work to retirement

taux de passage vers
transfer rate

PASSAGER (adj.)
temporary

PASSEPORT
passeport-formation
skills passport

PASSER
passer outre
to disregard

passer contrat avec
to contract with

passer une convention
to contract with, to make a convention

passer un entretien pour un poste
to interview for a job

passer un examen
to take an examination

PASSIBLE
subject, liable (to)

passible de droits
(occ.) taxable

passible de l'impôt
liable to tax

passible de poursuites judiciaires
subject to legal proceedings

PASSIF (adj.)
passive; inactive

mesure passive
passive measure

protection sociale passive
passive social protection

PASSIF (n.)
liabilities

élément de passif
liability

PATENT
faute patente
patent misconduct

PATENTE
occupation tax

PATERNITÉ
paternity; parenthood

allocation de paternité (Finl.)
paternity allowance

congé de paternité
paternity leave

PATHOLOGIE
pathology; disease pattern

pathologie professionnelle
occupational pathology / medicine

PATHOLOGIQUE
grossesse pathologique
pathological pregnancy

PATIENT (n.)
patient; case

patient inscrit
registered patient

PATRIMOINE
assets; endowment; wealth

patrimoine-retraite
pension wealth

revenu(s) du patrimoine
income from assets, revenue from estate

PATRON
manager; employer; (pl.) management

rapports patrons-salariés
labour-management / industrial relations

PATRONAL
accréditation patronale
certification of employer

association patronale
employer's association / organisation,

**association / organisation of employers,
trade association**

charges patronales
employer's contributions

comité (mixte) patronal - syndical
(joint) union - management committee

cotisation patronale
employer's contribution

cotisation patronale de sécurité sociale
employers' social security contribution

délégué patronal
management / employer's representative,
representative of employer

fédération patronale
employers' federation, industrial
federation (USA)

groupement patronal
employer's association / federation /
organisation

organisation patronale
employer's association / organisation,
association / organisation of employers,
trade association

part patronale
employer's contribution

représentant patronal
management / employer's representative,
representative of employer

- 574 -

responsabilité patronale
employer's liability

syndicat patronal
employer's association / federation / organisation

PATRONAT
management; employers; employer's organisations; (occ.) industry

patronat et salariés
employers and employed

syndicats et patronat
labour and management

PAUSE
break; time off

pause d'allaitement
nursing break

pause-déjeuner
meal interval

pause réglementaire
statutory / official break

pause salariale
wage standstill

période de pause
cooling-off period

PAUVRE
poor

orphelin pauvre (Fr.)
orphan without subsistence means

PAUVRETÉ
poverty

engrenage de la pauvreté
poverty trap

grande pauvreté
(occ.) destitution

piège de la pauvreté
poverty trap

poche de pauvreté
area of deprivation

seuil de pauvreté
poverty line / threshold / level, poverty datum line (PDL)

taux de pauvreté
poverty rate

PAVILLON
ward; flag

PAYABLE
due, payable

allocation hebdomadaire maximale payable
maximum weekly allowance payable

prestation payable
benefit due

salaire net payable
net payable wage

PAYANT
fee-paying, fee-charging

bureau de placement payant
fee-charging employment agency

service payant
user-fee service

stagiaire payant
fee-payer trainee

tiers(-)payant
cost of medical expenses, part paid by third fund; third-party payer / payment; direct payment system

PAYÉ
accorder un congé payé
to grant paid leave; to release an employee with pay

bien payé
well-paid, high-paid, highly paid

congé annuel payé, congé payé annuel
annual paid leave; paid vacation

congé-éducation payé
paid education(al) leave

congé payé
paid leave, leave / time off with pay; (pl.)
holiday with pay, paid holiday, vacation
pay (USA)

congé non payé
absence / leave without pay

cotisation payée
paid contribution

cotisation payée à l'étranger
contribution paid abroad

emploi mal payé
low-wage job

épuiser ses jours de congés payés
to use up one's holiday entitlement

**indemnité compensatrice de congés
payés**
compensation in lieu of paid holidays,
holidays paid in lieu

indemnité de congés payés
compensation for holiday leave

jour férié payé
paid public holiday

ouvrier le moins bien payé
worst-paid worker

payé à l'heure (être)
to be paid on an hourly basis / by the hour;
to be assigned to hourly rates

payé au noir (être)
to be paid off the books

payé à la pièce (être)
to be paid piecework

payé à la tâche (être)
to be paid by the job

payé à la vacation (être)
to be paid on a sessional basis

**pension payée en raison d'un accident
civil**
pension paid as a result of civil accident

pension payée par poste
pension paid through the post

pension payée à termes
pension paid out on a regular basis

**pension payée (à un titulaire) à
l'étranger**
pension paid abroad

préavis payé
pay under notice

prestation payée en une seule fois
benefit to be paid in a single amount

provisions pour congés payés
reserve for holiday leave

salaire payé à la semaine
wage paid by the week, weekly wage

salaire réellement payé
wage actually paid

semaine non payée
not paid week

travailleur payé à la journée
daily wage worker

PAYER
to pay (out), to remunerate

capacité de payer
ability to pay

payer les cotisations
to pay contributions

salaire restant à payer
outstanding pay

PAYEUR
organisme payeur
paying body / office

trésorier payeur général
accountant-general, paymaster-general

PAYS
pays d'accueil
receiving / host country

pays à bas salaires
low-wage country

pays bénéficiaire
receiving country

pays contractant
contracting / (occ.) agreement country

pays destinataire
receiving country

pays d'émigration
country of emigration, emigration /
sending country

pays d'immigration
immigration country

pays d'origine
home country

pays de recrutement
recruitment country

pays recruteur de main-d'oeuvre
labour(-)recruiting country

pièces justificatives requises attestant le pays de résidence
required proof of the country of residence

PAYSAN (adj.)
rente des retraites ouvrières et paysannes
annuity in addition to industrial and
agricultural workers' pensions

retraites ouvrières et paysannes
industrial and agricultural workers'
pensions

PÊCHE
agriculteurs et ouvriers qualifiés de
l'agriculture et de la pêche [CITP-1988
(6)]
skilled agricultural and fishery workers
[ISCO-1988 (6)]

PÊCHEUR
fisherman

marin pêcheur
fisherman, seafisherman

pêcheurs, chasseurs et trappeurs [CITP-1988 (615)]
fishery workers, hunters and trappers
[ISCO-1988 (615)]

pêcheurs, chasseurs et travailleurs assimilés [CITP-1968 (6-4)]
fishermen, hunters and related workers
[ISCO-1968 (6-4)]

pêcheur rémunéré à la part
share fisherman

PÉCULE
allowance; earnings in retrospect

pécule de vacances (Belg.)
holiday allowance; lump-sum holiday pay

PÉCUNIAIRE
assistance autre que pécuniaire
non-cash assistance

indemnité pécuniaire
cash benefit

perte pécuniaire
pecuniary loss

prestation autre que pécuniaire
non-cash benefit

sanction pécuniaire
financial penalty

PÉDAGOGIE
education

étudiant en pédagogie
teacher trainee

pédagogie de la transition
education for transition

PÉDAGOGIQUE
contrat pédagogique
educational agreement

ensemble pédagogique
training package (multimedia)

formation pédagogique
teacher training

institut (de formation) pédagogique
teacher training college / school

matériel pédagogique
teacher equipment

norme pédagogique
academic standard

objectif pédagogique
educational goal

réforme pédagogique
school / educational reform

PÉDIATRE
paediatrician

PÉDIATRIE
paediatrics

soins infirmiers de pédiatrie
paediatric nursing

PÉDIATRIQUE
soins infirmiers pédiatriques
paediatric nursing

soins pédiatriques
paediatric / child care

PÉDICURE
chiropodist

PÉDOPORNOGRAPHIE
child pornography

PEINTRE
peintres [CITP-1968 (9-3)]
painters [ISCO-1968 (9-3)]

PELLETERIE
tanneurs, peaussiers, mégissiers et ouvriers
de la pelleterie [CITP-1968 (7-6)]
tanners, fellmongers and pelt dressers
[ISCO-1968 (7-6)]

PÉNALITÉ
additional charge, surcharge

clause de pénalité
penalty clause

pénalité de retard
late payment charge

PENDULAIRE
migration pendulaire
journey to work; (pl.) commuting

PÉNIBILITÉ
prime de pénibilité
hardship allowance; heavy work bonus

PÉNIBLE
allocation pour situation pénible
hardship allowance

métier / profession pénible
arduous occupation

PÉNITENTIAIRE
administration pénitentiaire
prison service / administration

assistance pénitentiaire
prison welfare

**travailleur social en établissement
pénitentiaire**
prison welfare officer

PENSION
pension (benefit); annuity; (promised)
benefit; (pl.) (occ.) pension entitlements

accorder une pension
to grant a pension

âge d'admission à (la) pension
pensionable / retirement / pension age

**âge du droit à pension / d'ouverture des
droits à / ouvrant droit à pension / de
pension**
age of pension entitlement, pensionable
age

âge de pension (ayant atteint l')
of pensionable age

**ajustement des pensions aux variations
du coût de la vie**
cost-of-living pension adjustment

allouer une pension
to grant a pension

**annualisation du système d'ajustement
des pensions**
annualisation of the pension adjustment
system

anticipation de la pension
anticipation of the pension

arrérages de pension échus
pension arrears due

arrérages des pensions de retraite (Fr.)
old age pension arrears

assurance-pension
pension insurance

avance sur pension alimentaire
advance on alimony

barème des rémunérations considérées aux fins de la pension
scale of pensionable remuneration

bénéfice d'une pension (au)
in receipt of a pension

bénéficiaire d'une pension
beneficiary of a pension

bénéficiaire d'une pension d'invalidité
invalidity pensioner

bénéficiaire d'une pension de vieillesse
old age pensioner
bénéficier d'une pension
to receive / to draw a pension

Caisse (fédérale) de garantie des pensions
Pension Benefit Guaranty Corporation (USA)

caisse de pensions
pension fund

caisse de pension d'entreprise
enterprise pension fund

caisse de pensions financée suivant le principe de la capitalisation
funded pension fund

calcul de la pension
calculation of the pension

calcul de la pension vieillesse
calculation of old age pension

calculer une pension
to calculate a pension

cessation de la pension
cessation of the pension

coefficient de calcul des pensions vieillesse
factor applied to the calculation of old age pensions

Comité de supervision des pensions complémentaires (UK)
Reserve Pension Board

complément de pension
pension supplement, topping-up pension

complément de pension générale (Swed.)
general pension supplement

Conseil des pensions professionnelles (UK)
Occupational Pensions Board

conservation des droits à pension
preservation of rights to pension

conversion partielle des pensions
partial commutation of retirement benefits

cumul de pensions
multiple receipt of pensions

déchéance des droits à pension
loss of pension rights

demande de pension
application / claim for (a) pension, pension claim

demandeur d'une pension
pension claimant

droit à pension
pension right, right to pension; (pl.) pension entitlement

droit à pension (faire valoir un)
to claim a pension

droit(s) à pension transférable(s)
portable pension right(s)

élément soumis à retenue pour pension
pensionable element

emploi ouvrant droit à pension
(recognised) pensionable employment

emploi n'ouvrant pas droit à pension
employment not recognised pensionable employment

fonds détenus par les caisses de pensions
pension fund accumulations

fonds de pension
pension fund / foundation

fonds de pension d'entreprise
corporate / enterprise pension fund

formule de calcul de la pension
calculation of the pension

incessibilité de pension de vieillesse
non-transferability of old age pension

indice d'ajustement des pensions
pension adjustment index

indice révisé d'ajustement des pensions
revised pension adjustment index

liquidation d'une pension
award of pension; calculation /
determination of a pension

majoration de pension pour enfants
increase in pensions / pension increase /
pension supplement in respect of children

**majoration de la pension de retraite
pour conjoint à charge**
pension supplement / increase in respect of
a dependent spouse

méthode de calcul de la pension
calculation of the pension; pension
formula

minimum des pensions vieillesse
old age pension minimum

mise en pension
boarding out

mode de calcul de la pension
calculation of the pension

montant acquis de la pension
accrued pension income

montant ouvrant droit à pension
pensionable amount

montant de la pension
amount of the pension

**montant de la rémunération considérée
aux fins de la pension**
amount / level of pensionable
remuneration

octroi d'une pension
provision / granting / award of pension

octroyer une pension
to grant a pension

paiement de la pension
payment of the pension

partie saisissable d'une pension
attachable part of a pension

pension à 100%
full pension, full retirement benefit

pension d'adaptation (Swed.)
readjustment pension

pension additionnelle (UK)
additional pension

pension des agriculteurs (Finl.)
farmers' pension

pension de l'aide sociale (UK)
supplementary pension

pension alimentaire
maintenance; maintenance / subsistence
allowance / payment; separation
allowance; alimony (and support); child
support

pension d'ancienneté
company long-service pension, service
pension, seniority pension (It.)

pension anticipée
early / anticipated pension

**pension versée sur la base de
l'assurance du mari**
pension by virtue of husband's
contributions

**pension versée sur la base de son
assurance propre**
pension by virtue of one's own
contributions

pension relevant des assurances sociales
social insurance pension

pension d'aveugle (Irel.)
blind pension

pension d'ayant droit
dependant's pension

pension de base
basic pension / benefit; basic retirement
pension (UK)

pension de base de veuve (UK)
widow's basic pension

pension calculée sur la base de...
pension calculated on the basis of...

pension en cas de carrière mixte
mixed career pension

pension de cécité (Malta)
blindness pension
pension compensatrice
compensatory pension

pension complémentaire (UK)
supplementary pension

pension complémentaire du régime général (UK)
reserve pension

pension complète
full pension, full retirement benefit

pension contributive partielle (Irel.)
partial contributory pension

pension non contributive de veuvage (Irel.)
widows non-contributory pension

pension constituée par cotisations
contributory pension

pension définitive
life / permanent pension

pension liée à l'emploi (Finl.)
employment pension

pension d'enfant
child's benefit

pension pour enfant (Icel.)
child pension

pension entière
full pension, full retirement benefit

pension estimée
(occ.) hypothetical pension

pension de l'Etat liée aux revenus (UK)
State earnings-related pension

pension à titre familial
family pension

pension à fiscalité bonifiée
tax qualified pension

pension forfaitaire
standard pension

pension liée aux gains (antérieurs)
earnings-related pension

pension de guerre
war pension

pension indexée
indexed / (occ.) dynamised / pegged pension

pension individuelle anticipée (Finl.)
individual early pension

pension d'invalidité
disability / invalidity pension

pension d'invalidité suite à un accident du travail (Hung.)
accident disability pension

pension d'invalidité des anciens combattants
veterans' disability pension

pension d'invalidité non contributive
non-contributory invalidity pension

pension d'invalidité de veuve
invalid widow's pension (Fr.)

pension à jouissance différée
deferred pension

pension militaire d'invalidité
military disablement pension

pension minimale / minimum
minimum pension

pension nationale
national pension, separate pension (UK), State pension (Denm.)

pension d'orphelin
orphan's pension

pension d'orphelin complet (Austr.)
double orphan pension

pension de parent isolé (Austr.)
sole parent pension

pension payée en raison d'un accident civil
pension paid as a result of civil accident

pension payée par poste
pension paid through the post

pension payée à termes
pension paid out on a regular basis

pension payée (à un titulaire) à l'étranger
pension paid abroad

pension pour personnes âgées (Malta)
age pension

pension pour les personnes âgées de plus 80 ans (UK)
over-eighties pension

pension de personnes indirectement à charge
secondary dependants' benefit

pension pour personne seule (Liech.)
single pension

pension de préretraite-chômage (Finl.)
unemployment pension

pension professionnelle
company / occupational pension

pension proportionnelle
graduated / proportional pension

pension proportionnelle (assurance mixte) (Irel.)
pro-rata (mixed insurance) pension

pension proportionnelle de vieillesse (UK)
graduated retirement benefit

pension propre
pension on own insurance

pension provisoire
provisional pension

pension réduite de retraite différée
reduced deferred pension

pension au titre de son propre régime d'assurance
pension on own insurance

pension au titre d'un régime privé
private pension

pension au titre d'un régime public
public pension

pension de retraite
old(-)age pension, retirement / superannuation benefit, superannuation, retiring / retirement pension; service pension (Malta)

pension de retraite anticipée
early retirement allowance / benefit

pension de retraite complète
standard retirement benefit, full pension

pension de retraite indexée
index-linked pension

pension de retraite minimum (Belg.)
minimum retirement pension

pension de retraite normale
standard retirement benefit

pension de retraite partielle
partial pension

pension de réversion
reversionary annuity, reversion / dependant's / survivor's pension; widower's / widow's / survivor's benefit

pension de réversion à la suite d'un accident du travail
industrial death benefit

pension de réversion d'orphelin
orphan's pension

pension de sécurité sociale (It.)
social security pension

pension servie
pension in payment

pension simple (Liech.)
single pension

pension sociale
social pension

pension sociale d'invalidité (Port.)
social invalidity pension

pension pour soins (Austr.)
carer's pension

pension de substitution (Fr.)
old age pension replacing invalidity pension

pension de survie
survivor's pension

pension de survie minimum (Belg.)
minimum survivors' pension

pension de survivant
survivor's / survivors' (Irel.) pension

pension à taux minoré
reduced (rate) pension / retirement benefit

pension au taux normal
standard (rate) pension / retirement benefit

pension à taux plein
full pension, full retirement benefit

pension à taux réduit
reduced (rate) pension / retirement benefit

pension à temps partiel (Finl.)
part-time pension

pension théorique
theoretical pension

pension du titulaire
personal pension

pension transférable (between pension funds)
portable pension

pension des travailleurs indépendants (Finl.)
self-employed persons' pension

pension uniforme
flat-rate pension

pension uniforme de base
basic flat-rate pension

pension de veuf
widower's pension / benefit

pension de veuve
widow's pension / benefit (UK)

pension de veuve de guerre
war widow's pension

pension de victime de guerre (UK)
war pensioner's death benefit

pension à vie
life / permanent pension

pension de vieillesse
old(-)age pension, old persons' pension (UK), age pension (Malta)

pension de vieillesse constituée par cotisations
contributory old age pension

pension de vieillesse de veuf (Fr.)
old age widower's pension

pension de vieillesse de veuve (Fr.)
old age widow's pension

perte de droits à pension
loss of pension entitlements

plafond de pension vieillesse
old age pension ceiling

prestation exclue de la rémunération considérée aux fins de la pension
non-pensionable benefit

prestation considérée aux fins de la pension
pensionable benefit

prestation de pension ajustée
adjusted pension benefit

production imputée de services de caisses de pension
imputed service charge for pension funds

promesse de pension
pension promise

réexamen de la pension
pension review

régime contributif de pensions complémentaires du régime général (UK)
contributory reserve pension scheme

régime des / de pensions
pension scheme / system / plan

régime de pension d'entreprise
occupational pension scheme

régime de pensions privé
private pension plan

régime de pensions des salariés (Denm.)
employment pension scheme

**rémunération aux fins de la pension /
ouvrant droit à pension**
pensionable remuneration

revalorisation des pensions
revaluation / revalorisation / upgrading /
review of pensions

**revenu ouvrant droit à pension / pris en
compte pour la pension**
pensionable income

réversion d'une pension
transfer of pension rights to the surviving
beneficiary

salaire ouvrant droit à pension
pensionable wage

salaire soumis à retenue pour pension
pensionable wage

service ouvrant droit à pension
pensionable service

**somme en capital résultant de / versée
au titre de la conversion partielle de la
pension**
partial lump-sum withdrawal benefit,
partial lump-sum commutation of pension
benefit

supplément de pension
supplement to the pension

supplément de pension pour enfants
pension supplement / supplement to
pensions in respect of children

suppression d'une pension
withdrawal of a pension

suspension d'une pension
suspension of a pension

système d'ajustement des pensions
pension adjustment system

**système révisé d'ajustement des
pensions**
revised pension adjustment system

taux d'acquisition du droit à pension
(pension) accrual rate

taux de pension
rate of pension

**taux de pension de l'assurance
(-)vieillesse**
rate of the old age pension

titre de pension
certificate / document showing entitleme
to a pension; evidence of entitlement

titulaire d'une pension
beneficiary of a pension, pensioner, pers
entitled to a pension

titulaire de pension de vieillesse
old age pensioner

toucher une pension
to receive / to draw a pension

traitement ouvrant droit à pension
pensionable salary

**traitement soumis à retenue pour
pension**
pensionable salary

transférabilité des pensions
pension portability, portability of pensior

**validation aux fins de pension d'une
période de service**
validation for pension purposes of a peric
of service

valoir ses droits à pension (faire)
to claim pension rights; to qualify for a
pension

PENSIONNAIRE
inmate

PENSIONNÉ
retiree, retired person; pensioner; payee

**allocation de soins pour pensionnés
(Finl.)**
pensioner's care allowance

PÉNURIE
lack, shortage; short supply; scarcity

**indicateur-repère de pénurie de main-
d'oeuvre**
benchmark (labour / manpower) shortage
indicator

pénurie chronique
persistent shortage

pénurie d'emplois
job scarcity / shortage, lack / scarcity /
shortage of jobs / of work

pénurie de main-d'oeuvre
labour deficit / shortage / scarcity, shortage
of labour / manpower, man-power /
occupational / worker shortage, under-
supply of workers; labour / manpower
bottle-neck

pénurie de main-d'oeuvre agricole
farm labour shortage

pénurie de main-d'oeuvre qualifiée
skilled labour / skill shortage, shortage /
lack of skilled labour

pénurie persistante
persistent / long-term shortage

pénurie persistante de main-d'oeuvre
long-term / persistent manpower shortage

pénurie de personnel
staff shortage

pénurie de qualifications
skill bottleneck / shortage

pénurie de travail
work shortage

pénurie de travailleurs
manpower / occupational / worker
shortage, under-supply of workers

profession en pénurie de main-d'oeuvre
shortage occupation, occupation in short
supply

PÉPINIÈRE
pépinière d'entreprises
business / enterprise incubator

PERCEPTEUR
tax collector

PERCEPTION
collection; charge

perception des cotisations
collection of contributions, contribution
collection

perception fiscale
revenue receipt

perception des impôts
tax(-)collection

PERCEVOIR
to receive; to levy (taxes); to collect

cotisations à percevoir
contributions still due

percevoir une allocation
to be in receipt of a benefit

percevoir des allocations de chômage
to collect unemployment compensation, to
live on / to draw unemployment benefit

percevoir des cotisations
to collect contributions

percevoir des indemnités de chômage
to collect unemployment compensation, to
draw unemployment benefit, to live on
unemployment benefit

percevoir des prestations
to draw benefits

PERÇU
rembourser toutes les sommes perçues
to reimburse all amounts received

rémunération effectivement perçue
(occ.) take-home pay

PERDRE
perdre le droit à une / aux prestation(s)
to be disqualified for benefit, to disqualify
from receiving benefit

**perdre sa situation / son emploi / son
travail**
to lose one's job

PERDU
salaire perdu
lost wage

PÈRE
orphelin de père
orphan whose father is dead

orphelin de père et de mère
full orphan, orphan whose parents are
dead, orphan having lost both parents

orphelin de père ou de mère
orphan having lost one parent

père célibataire
unmarried father

PÉREMPTION
date de péremption
expiry date

PÉRENNITÉ
sustainability

PÉRÉQUATION
equalisation

fonds de péréquation
equalisation fund

péréquation des charges familiales
equalisation of family burdens

péréquation financière
financial adjustment / equilisation

péréquation fiscale
tax equalisation

péréquation salariale
wage equalisation

PERFECTIONNEMENT
upgrading; development; reskilling,
updating of skills

centre de perfectionnement
(occ.) training school

classe de perfectionnement
advanced / refresher / proficiency course

congé de perfectionnement
career / skill development leave, leave for
development purposes

cours de perfectionnement
advanced / refresher / proficiency course

perfectionnement des cadres
management development
perfectionnement des

compétences
skill improvement

perfectionnement de la main-d'oeuvre
development of manpower, manpower
development

perfectionnement du personnel
skill / staff / manpower development

perfectionnement professionnel
career / job development; in-service
(educational) training; on-site / on-the-job
training / learning, further vocational
training, occupational / skill up-grading,
vocational development

plan de perfectionnement professionnel
vocational development plan

programme de perfectionnement
developmental programme, retraining
scheme

**programme de perfectionnement des
cadres**
(occ.) executive programme

stade de perfectionnement
continuation stage

stage de perfectionnement
advanced / proficiency / retraining course;
in-service (educational) training, on-site /
on-the-job training / learning

PERFORMANCE
performance

indicateur de performance
performance indicator

mesure de la performance
performance measure

performances sur le plan de l'emploi
labour market performance

système de mesure de la performance
performance measure system

PÉRIODE
period, term

accomplir les périodes
to complete the periods

accomplissement d'une période d'assurance
completion of a period of insurance

addition des périodes
totalling of periods

attestation des périodes d'assurance
certification of periods of insurance, certified statement specifying the periods of insurance

durée de la période de stage
period of probationary service

engagement pour une période de stage
probationary appointment

interruption de la période de chômage
break in the period of unemployment

nomination pour une période déterminée
specified period / term appointment

nomination pour une période indéterminée
indeterminate appointment

période d'absence du travail
time absent from work

période active (en)
of working age

période d'activité
working life / age; term of office; period of employment

période d'activité non salariée
period of self-employment

période d'affiliation
period of / number of years of insurance; insurance period; period of membership; contributory service / period, period / length of contributory service

période d'affiliation conventionnelle
notional period of contributory service

période d'apprentissage
apprenticeship / learning period, period of apprenticeship

période assimilée
period treated as such

période d'assurance
insurance period

période d'assurance obligatoire
period of compulsory insurance

période d'assurance requise pour l'ouverture du droit aux prestations
qualifying insurance / qualification period

période d'astreinte
on-call time (USA)

période en atelier
workshop period

période d'attente
waiting period

période d'attribution
period of payment

période de chômage
period / spell of unemployment

période de chômage complète
completed spell of unemployment

période de chômage en cours
spell of unemployment in progress

périodes de chômage répétées
multiple spells of unemployment

période complète de chômage
completed spell of unemployment

période de congé
holiday period

période considérée
period under review / under consideration / under observation, report period

période de cotisation
contribution period, period of contribution

période cotisée
period for which contributions have been paid

période en cours
current period, spell in progress

période de croissance
period of growth

période de détachement
period / term of posting

période ouvrant droit
period of eligibility

période séparant deux échéances
period separating two dates for payment

période écoulée
completed period

période d'emploi
employment period, period of employment

période d'emploi courante
current period of employment

période d'emploi interrompue
split employment period

période d'emploi prévue
expected period of employment, period of expected employment

période d'emploi proposée
proposed period of employment

période couverte par l'enquête
inquiry / survey period

période équivalente
equivalent period

période d'essai
period of probation, probation (period), conditional employment / trial / probationary period

période couverte par l'étude
inquiry / survey period

période de formation
period of training, training period

période d'immatriculation (Lux.)
period of membership

période d'inadmissibilité
period of disqualification

période d'indemnisation du chômage
period for which a claimant receives unemployment benefits

période d'intégration
induction period

période d'interruption de travail
period of interruption of employment

période isolée
single spell

période isolée de chômage
single spell of unemployment

période de maladie
period of sickness

période maximale / maximum requise
maximum period required

période minimum d'affiliation
(occ.) qualifying period

période d'octroi des prestations
period for which benefit(s) is/are allowed

période de paie
pay period / cycle

période de pause
cooling-off period

période de pointe
peak work load period

période de post(-)cure
follow-up phase / period

période de préavis
notice period

période de prise en charge
period of coverage / of compensation, duration of benefit(s)

période probatoire
qualifying period; probation (period), trial / probationary period

période de prolongation
period of extension

période couverte par le rapport
report period

période de référence
recall / reckonable / reference / base reporting period

période de repos
rest period

période de résidence
period of residence

période de rodage
running-in period

période scolaire
(school) term

période de service ouvrant droit à ...
period of qualifying service

période de service des prestations
period for which benefit(s) is/are allowed

période de stage
qualifying / probationary period

période transitoire
transitional period

période de travail
(work) shift; period of work; period of
work experience

période de validité
period of validity

**personnel engagé pour une période de
courte durée**
short-term staff

récapitulation des périodes d'assurance
summary of the periods of insurance

relevé des périodes de résidence
statement of periods of residence

**restitution d'une période d'affiliation
antérieure**
restoration of prior contributory service

superposition de périodes d'assurance
overlapping of periods of insurance

totalisation des périodes
totalling of periods, adding together the
periods

totalisation des périodes d'assurance
adding (together) of periods of insurance,
aggregation of / totalling of insurance
periods

**validation aux fins de pension d'une
période de service**
validation for pension purposes of a period
of service

**validation d'une période de service
antérieure**
validation of previous service

PÉRIODIQUE
augmentation périodique de traitement
salary increment, within-grade (salary)
increment

formation périodique
recurrent training

indemnités périodiques
regular benefits

paiement périodique
periodical payment; annuity

prestation périodique
periodic / regular benefit

prestation périodique ajustée
periodically adjusted benefit

prestation périodique en espèces
periodical cash benefit

**retenue d'une augmentation périodique
de salaire**
withholding of salary increment

révision périodique
periodic review

**système d'établissement des rapports
périodiques**
periodic reporting system

PÉRIODIQUEMENT
periodically

PÉRIPHÉRIQUE
commission médicale périphérique
(occ.) district medical board

effectifs périphériques
peripheral workers

emploi périphérique
peripheral job

main-d'oeuvre périphérique
peripheral workers

zone périphérique
peripheral / suburban area

PÉRISCOLAIRE
activité périscolaire
extra-curricular activity; (pl.) extension /
extramural studies / work

PÉRI-UNIVERSITAIRE
activités péri-universitaires
university extension, extension / extramural studies / work

PERLÉ (adj.)
grève perlée
slow-down strike, go-slow (strike);
slowing down of work, work slow-down;
work-to-rule (strike)

PERMANENCE
permanence d'accueil, d'information et
d'orientation (PAIO) (Fr.)
reception, information and guidance office

permanence d'entraide sociale (UK)
Citizens' Advice Bureau

permanence téléphonique
hot line telephone

PERMANENT (adj.)
permanent; settled

admission permanente
permanent admission

aide / assistance permanente (Denm.)
continuing maintenance assistance

assurance-invalidité permanente
long-term disability insurance

chômage permanent
persistent unemployment

consigne permanente
standing order

consultation permanente
ongoing consultation

contrat permanent
permanent contract

droit permanent à dépassement (Fr.)
permanent right to overbilling

éducation permanente
continuing / lifelong / adult / further
education, lifelong training / learning

effectif(s) permanent(s)
regular establishment, core workforce /
workers, permanent workers / work-force /
staff; established posts

emploi permanent
permanent / regular job / employment /
post; (pl.) establishment

emploi permanent à temps partiel
permanent part-time employment

employé permanent
permanent employee

employé permanent à temps partiel
permanent part-time employee

employé permanent à temps plein
permanent full-time employee

engagement à titre permanent
permanent appointment

établissement d'éducation permanente
college of further education

fonctionnaire permanent
permanent civil servant

formation permanente
continuing / continued / continuous /
ongoing / further education, lifelong
training / learning

foyer permanent d'habitation
normal / permanent home

**incapacité (de travail) partielle
permanente**
permanent partial incapacity / disablement

incapacité (de travail) permanente
permanent incapacity /disablement

**indemnité pour incapacité permanente /
invalidité permanente**
permanent disability payment, permanency
award (USA)

infirmité / invalidité permanente
permanent disablement / disability /
invalidity, long-term disability

nombre de postes permanents
number of permanent jobs / posts; core
staffing; establishment

nomination à titre permanent
permanent appointment

personnel permanent
permanent workforce / staff, core
personnel, regular staff

poste permanent
permanent job / employment / post, career
/ core / established post; (pl.)
establishment

postes permanents de nuit
regular night shift

prestation d'invalidité permanente
industrial disablement benefit

programme permanent
permanent / ongoing programme

rente d'incapacité permanente
permanent disability pension

résidence permanente
permanent residence

résident permanent
permanent resident

salarié agricole permanent
full-time agricultural labourer

salarié permanent
permanent employee

salarié permanent (être)
to work on a regular basis

salarié permanent à temps partiel
permanent part-time employee

salarié permanent à temps plein
permanent full-time employee

subvention salariale permanente
permanent wage subsidy

**titulaire d'une nomination à titre
permanent**
holder of a permanent appointment

travailleur indépendant permanent
permanent self-employed

travailleur permanent
permanent worker

travailleur permanent à temps partiel
permanent part-time worker

PERMANENT (n.)
permanent employee; (pl.) establishment,
permanent workforce / staff / workers

permanent syndical
union employee

PERMIS
leave; permit; license

octroi de permis
licensing

permis de négocier (Irel.)
negotiation licence

permis de séjour
residence permit; registration certificate

permis de travail
work / labour / employment permit

PERMISSION
leave

permission (être en)
to be on furlough

PERMUTATION
exchange, interchange

permutation des employés
staff interchange

permutation des postes
exchange of jobs

PERSÉVÉRANCE
taux de persévérance scolaire
student retention rate

PERSISTANT
pénurie persistante
persistent / long-term shortage

pénurie persistante de main-d'oeuvre
long-term / persistent manpower shortage

PERSONNALISÉ
aide personnalisée au logement (APL)
housing subsidy

horaire de travail personnalisé
personalised hours of work, personalised
working hours

**orientation professionnelle
personnalisée**
personal career counselling

service personnalisé
personalised service

PERSONNALITÉ
personality; official

facteur de personnalité
personality factor

haute personnalité
(high-ranking) official

**organisme doté de la personnalité
morale**
corporate body

personnalité juridique
legal status

personnalité morale
legal personnality

principe de la personnalité
rule that a person is governed by his
personal law

test de personnalité
personality test

PERSONNE
année-personne
man-year, person-year, staff-year, work(-
)year

année-personne d'emploi / de travail
work-year of employment

heure-personne
man-hour

**impôt sur les revenus des personnes
physiques (Fr.)**
personal income tax

indemnité pour personne à charge
dependent allowance

jour-personne
person-day

majoration pour personne à charge
increase of benefits for a dependant,
supplement for dependant; family
supplement

majoration pour tierce personne
attendance allowance for third person,
constant attendance allowance (UK)

ménage d'une personne
one-person / single person household

personne (par)
per head, per capita

personne sans abri
homeless person

personne active
(pl.) economically active persons

personne ayant une activité lucrative
(pl.) economically active / gainfully
occupied / working population, labour
force

**personne n'exerçant pas d'activité
rémunérée**
non-employed person

personne qui exerce plusieurs activités
multiple jobholder

personne âgée
senior citizen; (pl.) old(er) people; the
aged, the elderly

personne âgée non autonome
elderly dependent person

personnes âgées à charge
aged dependants

personnes âgées dépendantes
dependent / (occ.) frail elderly

personnes âgées et les vieillards (les)
the aged and the elderly

personne à charge
dependant

**personne ayant des charges familiales /
chargée de famille**
person with family responsibilities,
breadwinner

personne compétente
relevant person

personne défavorisée
disadvantaged person

personne détachée
secondee

personne directement à charge
primary dependent

personne non directement à charge
secondary dependent

personne divorcée
divorced (person)

personne sans domicile
person of / with no fixed abode, vagrant

personne qui exerce une double activité
double jobholder / jobber

personne ayant droit aux prestations
person eligible for benefits

personne économiquement faible
person in need of financial assistance

**personne occupant un / exerçant un /
pourvue d'un emploi (rémunéré)**
employed, employee; (pl.) economically
active / gainfully occupied / working
population, labour force

personne employée (par)
per employee

personne exposée
person at risk

personne en fin de droits
exhaustee

personne gravement handicapée
seriously disabled person

personne habilitée
approved person

personne handicapée
handicapped person

personne handicapée apte au travail
employable person with disability / ies

personne hautement spécialisée
(occ.) professional

personne hospitalisée
(hospital) in-patient

personne imposable
taxpayer

**personne souffrant d'une incapacité
grave**
seriously disabled person

personne indirectement à charge
secondary dependent / dependant

personne intellectuellement diminuée
mentally disabled

personne invalide
disabled / handicapped person

personne isolée
single person / householder

personnes encore jeunes
non aged, non elderly

personne sans logement
homeless person

personne mariée
married person

personne maternante
mothering person

personne mise à disposition
secondee

personne à mobilité réduite
people with mobility handicap(s)

personne morale
legal entity / person, corporate body

personne de passage
transient

personne physique
natural person

personnes en quête de leur premier emploi [CITP-1968 (X-1)]
new workers seeking employment [ISCO-1968 (X-1)]

personne protégée
person protected, protected person

personne qualifiée
competent person

personnes du quatrième âge
old / frail elderly

personne à la recherche d'un emploi / en quête d'emploi
job hunter / seeker / searcher

personne recueillie de fait
de facto dependant

personne rémunérée
earner

personne sans résidence fixe
person of / with no fixed abode, vagrant

personne-ressource
resource person

personne aux revenus modestes
person on low income / with small means

personne de service
attendant

personne seule
single (person)

personne seule et sans abri
single homeless

personne suremployée
over-employed

personne travaillant à son compte
worker on own account; freelance (worker)

personnes du troisième âge
old people; (occ.) young elderly

personne valide
able-bodied (person)

personne veuve
widowed person

personne vivant sous le toit du travailleur salarié
person living under the same roof as the employed person

prestation pour personne(s) à charge
benefit for dependents, dependent's benefit

prestation pour personne indirectement à charge
secondary dependent's benefit

société de personnes
partnership; (occ.) private company

PERSONNEL (adj.)
personal, private

abattement personnel
personal allowance

absence pour convenance personnelle
compassionate leave

allocation d'assistance personnelle (It.)
personal assistance allowance

aptitude personnelle
personal ability

assurance personnelle
personal insurance

champ d'application personnel (ratione personae)
personal scope

congé pour convenance(s) personnelle(s) / pour raisons personnelles
leave of absence for personal reasons; (occ.) compassionate leave

convenance personnelle (pour raison de)
for personal reasons

dégrèvement personnel
personal (tax) relief

disposition prise à titre personnel
private arrangement

dossier personnel
personal record / file

entreprise personnelle
(sole) proprietorship

épanouissement personnel
self-fulfilment

grade attribué à titre personnel
personal grade

horaire de travail personnel
personalised working hours
indemnité personnelle provisoire
personal transitional allowance

informations personnelles
personal information / data

notice personnelle
personal history form

personnel (à titre)
in one's own right

plan personnel de recherche d'emploi
personal job-search plan

point personnel de rétribution (Ger.)
personal income point

projet fondé sur l'initiative personnelle
self-help project / scheme

régime d'assurance contre les accidents personnels
personal injuries scheme

régime de retraite personnel par capitalisation
personal pension scheme / plan

renseignements personnels
personal information / data

revenu personnel disponible
private disposable income, disposable personal income

services personnels
personal services

services sociaux et services personnels
social and personal services

soins personnels
(occ.) self-care

PERSONNEL (n.)
personnel, staff; employees; manpower; human resources

abattement pour mouvements de personnel
adjustment for turnover of staff, turnover deduction

accroissement de / du personnel
staff increase, expansion of staff

administration du personnel
staff / human resource(s) mnagement; personnel policy

affectation du personnel
staff allocation

affecter suffisamment de personnel (ne pas)
to understaff, to underman

agence de missions de personnel
personnel dispatching agency

assistant social du personnel
personnel social worker

association du personnel
staff association

attentes du personnel
staff aspirations

autre personnel des services directs aux particuliers [ISCO-1988 (514)]
other personal service workers [CITP-1988 (514)]

barème des contributions du personnel
(occ.) staff assessment plan

besoin global en personnel
overall staffing requirement

besoin(s) en personnel
manpower / labour / staff resource requirement(s), personnel needs

besoins en personnel qualifié
skill needs / requirements

bureau de conseils en personnel
personnel consultancy

bureau du personnel
personnel office

compression de personnel
staff / manpower / work force reduction, reduction in personnel / of staff, displacement; labour shake-out / shedding; employment cut-back

conseil du personnel
staff council

contribution du personnel
(occ.) staff assessment

court de personnel (être à)
to be understaffed / undermanned / short-handed / short-staffed / short of staff

défaire du personnel (se)
to shed staff

délégué du personnel
staff representative; chief steward

demande de dotation en personnel
staffing action request

département du personnel
personnel department

déploiement du personnel
deployment of staff

détachement de personnel
secondment of staff, staff secondment

directeur du personnel
labour / work director, personnel manager

division du personnel
personnel department

dossier du personnel
personnel file / record

dotation en personnel
staffing, provision of staff, manning

économies de personnel
staff savings

effectifs du personnel
staffing

embaucher du personnel
to hire staff

enquête de satisfaction du personnel
staff satisfaction survey

excédent de personnel
redundancy

exode de personnel
outflow of personnel

formation du personnel
staff training, training of personnel

formation du personnel enseignant
teacher training

formation de personnel qualifié
(occ.) skill training

former le personnel
to train staff

gel de la dotation en personnel
staff freeze

gestion du personnel
human resources / personnel management; manpower / personnel practices

gestion prévisionnelle du personnel
staff planning

indice de stabilité du personnel
labour stability index

maintien du personnel
employee retention

manque de personnel
shortage of staff, staff shortage, understaffing, undermanning

manque de personnel qualifié
shortage of skilled workers

manquer de personnel
to be understaffed / undermanned / short-handed / short-staffed, to be short of staff

mouvement du personnel
turnover of labour, labour turnover; staff movement; personnel action; (pl.) turnover; staff changes

mutation de personnel
personnel move

mutation du personnel déjà en fonctions
reassignment of existing staff

pénurie de personnel
staff shortage

perfectionnement du personnel
skill / staff / manpower development

personnel d'action sociale
social work personnel / staff

personnel en activité
serving staff

personnel administratif
clerical staff / employees; support staff

personnel administratif et travailleurs assimilés non classés ailleurs [CITP-1968 (3-9)]
clerical related workers not elsewhere classified [ISCO-1968 (3-9)]

personnel administratif et travailleurs assimilés [CITP-1968 (3)]
clerical and related workers [ISCO-1968 (3)]

personnel d'appoint
contingent workers

personnel d'appui
support staff

personnel auxiliaire
auxiliary / general duty personnel, servicing / ancillary staff; non-production workers

personnel de bureau
office staff, clerical personnel / staff / employees, white-collar workers, white-collars

personnel de carrière
career staff

personnel hors classes
ungraded staff

personnel clé
key staff / personnel

personnel commercial et vendeurs [CITP-1968 (4)]
sales workers [ISCO-1968 (4)]

personnel commercial et vendeurs non classés ailleurs [CITP-1968 (4-9)]
sales workers not elsewhere classified [ISCO-1968 (4-9)]

personnel à court terme
short-term staff

personnel détaché
seconded staff

personnel de direction
management; senior (directing / supervisory) staff, managerial staff

personnel engagé pour une durée déterminée
fixed-term staff

personnel d'encadrement
senior directing / supervisory staff, grade / managerial staff

personnel d'encadrement et de direction
supervisory and management staff

personnel enseignant
teaching staff / personnel

personnel enseignant [CITP-1968 (1-3)]
teachers [ISCO-1968 (1-3)]

personnel enseignant du service social
social work educators

personnel de l'enseignement
educational personnel

personnel d'établissement
residential staff

personnel d'état-major
staff personnel (mil.)

personnel étudiant
student staff

personnel excédentaire
labour redundancy, displaced / redundant labour, workers made redundant

personnel d'exécution
basic staff, operative workers, unskilled staff for executory work

personnel extérieur à l'entreprise
out-house staff

personnel de fonction
professional staff

personnel fonctionnel
(field) support staff

personnel formé
trained workers

personnel horaire
hourly paid personnel

personnel hospitalier
hospital staff / personnel / employees /
workers

personnel indispensable
key personnel

personnel infirmier
nursing staff / personnel

personnel infirmier auxiliaire
auxiliary nursing personnel

**personnel infirmier et sages-femmes
(niveau intermédiaire) [CITP-1988
(323)]**
nursing and midwifery associate
professionals [ISCO-1988 (323)]

personnel inscrit
employees on the payroll

personnel d'institution
residential staff

personnel intermédiaire
middle-level personnel

personnel de maison
domestic servants

personnel médical
medical personnel

personnel non médical
non-medical personnel

personnel médico-sanitaire
health personnel / staff / officers

personnel minimal
minimum / (occ.) skeleton staff

personnel de mission
dispatched workers

personnel mobile
mobile staff

personnel opérationnel
operational staff / personnel, field staff

personnel paramédical
paramedical staff / personnel / workers

personnel paraprofessionnel
paraprofessional personnel

**personnel engagé pour une période de
courte durée**
short-term staff

personnel permanent
permanent workforce / staff, core
personnel, regular staff

personnel en place
existing staff

**personnel des professions scientifiques,
techniques, libérales et assimilées
[CITP-1968 (0/1)]**
professional, technical and related workers
[ISCO-1968 (0/1)]

**personnel des professions scientifiques,
techniques, libérales et assimilées non
classé ailleurs [CITP-1968 (1-9)]**
professional, technical and related workers
not elsewhere classified [IS-CO-1968 (1-
9)]

personnel professionnel
professional personnel, trained workers

personnel qualifié
qualified employees, skilled / specialised
staff / personnel, trained personnel /
workers

**personnel recruté sur le plan
international**
internationally recruited staff

personnel recruté localement
locally recruited staff

personnel réduit
reduced / (occ.) skeleton staff

personnel salarié
salaried staff

personnel sanitaire / de santé
health personnel / staff / workers /
manpower / officers, health care workers

personnel de secrétariat
clerical staff / employees

personnel de service
service staff

personnel des services auxiliaires
ancillary workers

personnel des services directs aux particuliers et des services de protection et de sécurité [CITP-1988 (51)]
personal and protective services workers [ISCO-1988 (51)]

personnel du service d'immeuble, laveurs de vitres et assimilés [CITP-1988 (914)]
building caretakers, window and related cleaners [ISCO-1988 (914)]

personnel des services linguistiques
language staff

personnel des services organiques
substantive staff

personnel des services de protection et de sécurité (5-8)]
protective service workers [ISCO-1968 (5-8)]

personnel des services de protection et de sécurité [CITP-1988 (516)]
protective services workers [ISCO-1988 (516)]

personnel des services de santé
health personnel / staff / officers

personnel de service social
social work / welfare personnel / staff

personnel des services et vendeurs de magasin et de marché [CITP-1988 (5)]
service workers and shop and market sales workers [ISCO-1988 (5)]

personnel hors siège
field staff

personnel social
social work / welfare personnel / staff

personnel soignant
care staff

personnel soignant et assimilé [CITP-1988 (513)]
personal care and related workers [ISCO-1988 (513)]

personnel de soutien
support staff

personnel spécialisé
professional / skilled / trained / specialised personnel / staff

personnel statutaire
statutory staff

personnel subalterne
junior staff

personnel (de niveau) supérieur
managerial / grade / professional / senior personnel / supervisory staff

personnel de supervision
supervisory staff

personnel en sureffectif
overmanning

personnel en surnombre
labour redundancy, displaced / redundant labour, workers made redundant, surplus staff; overmanning

personnel syndical
trade union personnel

personnel technique
technical / professional staff
personnel temporaire
temporary staff / assistance

personnel (employé) à temps complet
full-time staff

personnel (employé) à temps partiel
part-time staff

personnel travaillant à son compte
freelance personnel

personnel visé par un accord
staff covered by an agreement

plan d'actionnariat du personnel
employee share ownership plan

planification du personnel
personnel / human resources planning

planification du personnel dans l'entreprise
company manpower planning, personnel planning at establishment level

politique du personnel
personnel policy; manpower / personnel practices

pourvoir en personnel
to staff

processus de sélection du personnel
staff selection process

protection des représentants du personnel
protection of staff representatives

recruter suffisamment de personnel (ne pas)
to understaff, to underman

réduction de personnel
staff / manpower / work force reduction, reduction in personnel / of staff, staff cut; employment cut-back

réduire le personnel
to reduce / to downsize / to shed staff

régime spécial des fonctionnaires ou du personnel assimilé
special scheme for civil servants and persons treated as such

registre du personnel
personnel register

règlement du personnel
staff rules

relations avec le personnel
staff / work relations, working relationship

renouvellement du personnel
labour / staff turnover

répartition géographique du personnel
geographical distribution of staff

représentant du personnel
staff representative

représentation du personnel
staff representation

ressources en personnel
labour / manpower resources / supply, staffing

rotation / roulement du personnel
turnover (of personnel), (personnel) turnover

service de missions de personnel
personnel dispatching service

service du personnel
personnel department

service social du personnel
personnel social work

statut du personnel
staff status

taux d'accroissement du personnel
accession rate

taux de conservation du personnel
retention rate, rate of retention

taux d'embauche du personnel
accession rate

taux de renouvellement / de roulement du personnel
personnel turnover rate

travailleur licencié pour compression de personnel
redundant worker

PERSPECTIVE
prospect, outlook

perspective d'avancement
promotion / advancement prospect, chance for promotion

perspective de carrière
career opportunity, career / occupational outlook / prospect / development; promotional ladder

perspectives conjoncturelles
business outlook / prospect

perspective de croissance
growth perspective / prospect

perspective démographique
population forecast

perspectives économiques
economic outlook / prospects

perspective d'emploi
job / employment opening, opportunity for employment, work opportunity, job prospect / outlook, placing / placement prospect; (pl.) employment outlook

Perspectives de l'emploi (OCDE)
Employment Outlook (OECD)

perspective d'évolution de carrière
career development prospect

perspective de gains
earnings prospect

perspective de placement
placing / placement prospect

perspective de promotion
promotion prospect, chance for promotion

perspectives sectorielles
sectoral outlook

perspective de travail
placing / placement prospect

PERTE
loss, deprivation

assurance-santé et perte de gains
health and loss of earnings insurance

compensation de / pour la perte de revenu(s)
compensation for loss of income, income replacement / compensation

fondé à réclamer une indemnisation pour perte de salaire (être)
to be entitled to claim restitution of lost salary / wage / earnings

indemnisation de / pour la perte de gain
compensation for loss of earnings, earnings replacement / compensation

indemnité de / pour perte d'emploi
indemnity for loss of job; redundancy payment, severance pay(ment)

indemnité pour perte de salaire
compensation for loss of wage(s)

perte de la capacité de gain / de travail
loss of earning capacity

perte d'un droit
loss of (a) right

perte de droits à pension
loss of pension entitlements

perte du droit aux prestations
loss of entitlement

perte d'échelle
diseconomy of scale

perte d'(un) emploi
loss of job, job loss

perte fonctionnelle
functional loss

perte de gain
loss of earnings

perte du gain
cessation of earnings

perte de moyens d'existence
loss of income support

perte de l'ouïe
hearing loss

perte pécuniaire
pecuniary loss

perte de revenus
loss of income

perte de salaire
loss of earnings / of wage

perte de soutien et dédommagement
death dependency and indemnity compensation

perte de traitement
loss of salary

taux de compensation de la perte de revenu
income replacement ratio

PERTINENCE
relevance; significance; pertinence; suitability

PERTINENT
relevant, concerned; suitable

PERTURBATEUR
comportement perturbateur
disruptive behaviour

PERTURBATION
perturbation du marché du travail
labour market / manpower dislocation, dislocation of the labour market

perturbation au / dans le travail
disruption at work

PERTURBÉ
enfant perturbé
emotionally disturbed child

PETIT
assurance petits risques
minor medical insurance

centre de la petite enfance
early childhood reception centre

petit appareillage
minor aids / appliances

petit boulot
odd job; (pl.) relief works

petit cultivateur
smallholder

petite enfance
early childhood, very young age

petite entreprise
small business

petit exploitant
smallholder

petite exploitation
smallholding

petite industrie
small-scale industries

petits métiers de la rue
light street industries

petites et moyennes entreprises (PME)
small and medium-sized enterprises (SME)

petits risques (Fr.)
minor medical expenses

petits salaires / salariés (les)
low-paid (the)

petite série
short production run

service d'aide à la petite enfance
infant care service

PEUPLEMENT
settlement

PHARE
école phare
magnet school

PHARMACEUTIQUE
indemnité pharmaceutique (Austr.)
pharmaceutical allowance

préparation pharmaceutique
drug, dosage form

produit pharmaceutique
pharmaceutical product, medicament, drug

spécialité pharmaceutique
patent medicine, proprietary drug

tarif pharmaceutique
maximum fixed price for medicines

PHARMACIE
chemist's shop, dispensary
pharmacie mutualiste
mutual insurance dispensary

préparateur en pharmacie
pharmacist's / chemist's assistant

PHARMACIEN
chemist, pharmacist

ordre des pharmaciens
pharmaceutical society

pharmacien assistant
assistant pharmacist

pharmacien-conseil
pharmaceutical adviser

pharmacien d'hôpital
hospital pharmacist

PHARMACODÉPENDANCE
drug dependence

PHARMACODÉPENDANT
drug-dependent

PHARMACOPÉE
pharmacopoeia

PHARMACOVIGILANCE
drug safety, monitoring of adverse
reactions to drugs

PHASE
malade en phase terminale
terminal patient

maladie dans sa / en phase terminale
terminal illness

phase ascendante
upturn, upswing

phase de contraction
downswing, downturn

phase de croissance
period of growth

phase descendante
downswing, downturn

phase de négociations collectives
collective bargaining round

phase pilote
pilot stage

phase de repli
downswing, downturn

PHILLIPS
courbe de Phillips
Phillips curve

courbe de Phillips élargie
augmented Phillips curve

PHYSICIEN
physiciens, chimistes et assimilés [CITP-
1988 (211)]
physicists, chemists and related
professionals [ISCO-1988 (211)]

PHYSIOLOGIE
physiologie du travail
occupational physiology

PHYSIQUE
aptitude physique
physical fitness

centre de réadaptation physique
remedial exercise clinic

diminué physique
physically disabled / handicapped

diminution de l'intégrité physique
(occ.) loss of faculty

enfant inadapté physique
physically handicapped child

éventualité d'ordre physique
physical contingency

handicap physique
physical handicap; bodily disablement

handicapé physique
physically disabled / handicapped; (pl.)
people with physical disabilities

**impôt sur les revenus des personnes
physiques (Fr.)**
personal income tax

incapacité physique
physical disability / disablement /
incapacity

infirmité physique
physical handicap / disability / disablement
/ impairment / infirmity

mobilité physique
geographic / spatial mobility

obstacle physique
physical barrier

personne physique
natural person

préjudice physique
physical injury

santé physique
physicl health / (occ.) fitness
travail physique
physical work; manual labour

trouble physique
physical disorder; (pl.) (occ.) bodily illness

PHYSIQUEMENT
personne physiquement diminuée
physically disabled / handicapped

travailleur physiquement handicapé
physically disabled worker

PIÈCE
piece; document, paper; evidence

ouvrier aux pièces
job worker, pieceworker

payé à la pièce (être)
to be paid piecework

pièce(s) (à la / aux)
at piece rate

pièces attestant un changement de résidence
evidence of relocation

pièce justificative
supporting document, voucher; proof; (pl.) documentary evidence

pièces justificatives requises attestant le pays de résidence
required proof of the country of residence

rémunéré à la pièce
employed on piecework basis

salaire à la pièce / aux pièces
piecework / piece wage, piece rate

salarié rémunéré à la pièce
worker paid on piecework basis

taux de rémunération / de salaire aux pièces
piecework rate

travail à la / aux pièce(s)
job work, piecework

travail à la pièce obéissant au système du temps alloué
time piecework

travailleur aux pièces
pieceworker; job worker

PIÈGE
piège du chômage
unemployment trap

piège de la pauvreté
poverty trap

PIERRE
mineurs, carriers, boutefeux et tailleurs de pierre [CITP-1988 (711)]
miners, shotfirers, stone cutters and carvers [ISCO-1988 (711)]

tailleurs et graveurs de pierres [CITP-1968 (8-2)]
stone cutters and carvers [ISCO-1968 (8-2)]

PILLAGE
pillage par les profits
profit piracy

pillage par les salaires
wage piracy

PILOTAGE
emplois en double pilotage
job shadowing

PILOTE
centre pilote
pilot centre

centre pilote de réadaptation
pilot rehabilitation centre

phase pilote
pilot stage

pilotes, officiers de pont et officiers mécaniciens (marine et aviation) [CITP-1968 (0-4)]
aircraft and ships' officers [ISCO-1968 (0-4)]

programme pilote
pilot programme

projet pilote
pilot project

PIQUET
former un piquet de grève
to picket

piquet de grève
(strike) picket; (pl.) picketing

piquet de grève mobile
roving picket

piquet de grève volant
flying picket

PIVOT
focal point
indice pivot (Belg.)
reference index

PLACARD
placard doré
[to be kicked upstairs]

PLACÉ (adj.)
enfant placé dans une famille d'accueil /
en foyer
foster child

enfant placé en internat
child boarded out

enfant placé en nourrice
foster child

haut placé
highly placed

PLACE (n.)
place; position

attribution de places de formation
allocation of training places

formation sur place
local training

garderie sur place
on-site day care facility

personnel en place
existing staff

place (sur)
on-the-job

place en apprentissage
apprenticeship place

place commerciale
business place

place de / en formation
training place

place de formation vacante
training vacancy

service sur place
on-site service

surveillance sur place
on-site monitoring

visite sur place
on-site visit

PLACEMENT
(job) placing / placement; finding of
employment; job matching

agence de placement
employment / placement agency, (labour)
employment office, employment exchange
/ bureau, labour exchange (service)

agence de placement privée
private employment agency

agence de placement publique
public employment agency

agent chargé du placement
(job) placement / placing officer

bureau de placement
employment / placement agency, (labour)
employment office, employment exchange
/ bureau, labour exchange (service)

bureau de placement payant
fee-charging employment agency

bureau privé de placement
private employment agency

centre de placement familial
family placement centre

convention de placement (Fr.)
placement agreement

**droit exclusif de placement des
travailleurs**
exclusive right to place workers in jobs,
placing monopoly

foyer de placement (familial)
foster house / home

intermédiaire de placement
boarding-out intermediary

monopole de placement des travailleurs
exclusive right to place workers in jobs, placing monopoly

orientation consécutive / postérieure au placement
post-employment / post-placement counselling

orientation préalable au placement
pre-employment counselling

perspective de placement
placing / placement prospect

placement assisté
assisted placement

placement assisté par ordinateur / automatisé
computer-assisted placement

placement conjoint
associate placement

placement direct
direct placement

placement dans un emploi agricole
agricultural job placement

placement dans un emploi occasionnel
casual job placement

placement dans un emploi régulier
regular job placement

placement des enfants
fostering / placement of children

placement des enfants en établissement
institutional care of children

placement en établissement
institutional care

placement d'étudiants
student placement

placement extérieur (familial)
boarding out

placement familial
family placement; foster (home) care

placement familial de vacances
holiday family placement

placement dans une famille
family placement; foster (home) care

placement en institution
placement in institution; institutional care

placement en internat
boarding out

placement libre d'enfant
voluntary placement of a child

placement de longue durée dans une institution
long-term institutional care

placement nourricier
foster care

placement d'office
compulsory care

placement par profession
placement by occupation

placement par secteur d'activité
placement by industry

placement sélectif
selective placement

placement des stagiaires
trainee placement

placement temporaire
(occ.) respite care

placement des travailleurs
placement of workers in jobs

politique de placement
placement policy

service de placement
placement agency; matching / placing / placement service; (labour) employment service / office; labour exchange (service)

service de placement automatisé / assisté par ordinateur
computer-assisted placement service

service de placement public
public employment agency

service privé de placement
private employment service

service de soutien après placement
post-employment support service

service spécialisé de placement
specialised job placement service

taux de placement
placement rate

PLACER
to place

chômeur difficile à placer
hard-to-place unemployed

placer dans un établissement
to institutionalise (in a social or medical
structure)

PLAFOND
ceiling; (maximum / upper) limit

plafond d'affiliation
membership ceiling

plafond d'assujettissement
liability ceiling

plafond assurable
insurability ceiling

plafond de cotisation
contribution ceiling

plafond d'exonération fiscale
tax exemption limit

plafond des gains
earnings limit / ceiling

plafond d'imposition
(tax) assessment ceiling

plafond du montant en espèces
cash limit

plafond de pension vieillesse
old age pension ceiling

plafond des prestations
maximum amount / rate of benefits;
benefit level

plafond de rémunération
remuneration ceiling / limit

plafond de ressources
maximum income limit

plafond de revenu
maximum income limit

plafond de salaire / salarial
upper earnings limit / level, wage ceiling

plafond de sécurité sociale
social security ceiling

relèvement du plafond des prestations
increase in benefit level

tarif plafond (Fr.)
maximum fee

PLAFONNÉ
subject to a ceiling

PLAFONNEMENT
cap; ceiling

plafonnement (sans)
without a ceiling

plafonnement des cotisations
upper limit on contributions

PLAFONNER
to level out / off

PLAGE
plage fixe
hard core, core hours / time

plage horaire
time frame / bracket

plage horaire fixe
fixed time bracket

plage horaire flexible / mobile / variable
flexible time bracket

plage mobile
flexible hours / band

plage (obligatoire) de présence
core time / hours

PLAINTE
claim, grievance, complaint

PLAN
plan; scheme; schedule; pattern

plan d'accompagnement
individual support scheme

plan d'accompagnement des chômeurs (Belg.)
support plan for the unemployed

plan d'accompagnement pour les sortants de l'école et des études (SAVE) (Belg.)
support plan for school and college leavers

plan d'action
action plan, plan of action

plan d'actionnariat du personnel
employee share ownership plan

plan d'aide aux salariés pour la prise en charge de leurs parents âgés
elder care scheme

plan d'austérité
austerity programme

plan autofinancé
self-funding scheme

plan de carrière
professional advancement, career development / advancement / planning, career (development) plan

plan à cotisations définies
defined contribution plan

plan des effectifs
staffing plan

plan d'épargne
savings scheme / plan

plan d'épargne d'entreprise (Fr.)
company / employee savings scheme

plan d'épargne logement
home (loan) saving plan (Fr.), private home ownership plan (USA)

plan d'épargne par prélèvement automatique
save-as-you-earn scheme

plan d'épargne retraite (Fr.)
savings-related retirement scheme

plan d'équipement social
social development plan

plan d'études
curriculum

plan famille (Fr.)
family scheme

plan de formation
training plan

plan de formation en apprentissage
apprenticeship training plan

plan de formation-insertion (Belg.)
employment-plus-training scheme

plan général
outline

plan d'intéressement
profit-sharing scheme

plan de licenciement
redundancy plan

plan de perfectionnement professionnel
vocational development plan

plan personnel de recherche d'emploi
personal job-search plan

plan à prestations définies
defined benefit plan

plan de prévention
prevention scheme

plan de programme
programme plan

plan de retraite à cotisations fixes
fixed contribution retirement plan

plan de retraite à prestations fixes
fixed benefit retirement plan

plan de sauvetage
rescue plan

plan social (Fr.)
collective redundancy programme

plan de succession
succession planning

plan de travail
work plan

plan d'urgence
contingency plan

PLANCHER
minimum level, lower limit; floor

plancher de revenu
minimum income limit

plancher de salaire / salarial
lower earnings limit / level, wage floor

rapport plancher
floor ratio

PLANIFICATION
planning

agent de planification de la famille / familiale
family-planning worker

opération de planification
planning exercise

planification de carrière
career planning

planification concertée
joint planning

planification en matière d'éducation
educational planning

planification des effectifs
manpower / work force planning

planification familiale
family planning, planned parenthood; birth control

planification de la main-d'oeuvre
manpower / work force planning

planification de la main-d'oeuvre des entreprises
company / corporate manpower planning

planification du personnel
personnel / human resources planning

planification du personnel dans l'entreprise
company manpower planning, personnel planning at establishment level

planification des ressources humaines
personnel / human resources planning

planification des ressources humaines dans l'entreprise
company manpower planning, personnel planning at establishment level

planification de la retraite
retirement planning

planification sanitaire
planning for health, health planning

planification sanitaire nationale
national health planning

planification pour la santé
planning for health, health planning

planification sociale
social planning

PLANNING
planning familial
family planning, planned parenthood; birth control

PLASTIQUE (adj.)
conducteurs de machines pour la fabrication de produits en caoutchouc et en matières plastiques [CITP-1988 (823)]
rubber- and plastic-products machine operators [ISCO-1988 (823)]

ouvriers de la fabrication d'articles en caoutchouc et en matières plastiques [CITP-1968 (9-0)]
rubber and plastics product makers [ISCO-1968 (9-0)]

PLEIN
année pleine (en)
full(-)year

budget de plein emploi
full(-)employment budget

capacité à pleine charge
full capacity

éducation à plein temps
full-time education

emploi à temps plein
full-time job / employment

employé permanent à temps plein
permanent full-time employee

employé à plein temps
full-time employee

équivalent de main-d'oeuvre à temps plein
full-time man equivalent

équivalent plein temps
full-time equivalent (FTE)

études à plein temps
full-time education

excédent budgétaire de plein emploi
full-employment budget surplus

formation à temps plein
full-time training

instruction à temps plein
full-time instruction

jour plein
full day

niveau de pleine capacité
full capacity level

objectif de plein emploi
full employment target / objective

ouvrier à plein temps
full-time worker

pension à taux plein
full pension, full retirement benefit

pleine capacité
full capacity

plein droit (de)
as of right

plein emploi
full employment

plein temps (à)
full time

politique de plein emploi
full employment policy, policy of full employment

population active à temps plein
full-time labour force

retraite à taux plein
full pension, full retirement benefit

salarié permanent à temps plein
permanent full-time employee

scolarisé à temps plein (être)
to be in full(-)time education

solde budgétaire en situation de plein emploi
full / high employment (budget) balance

stagiaire à temps plein
full-time trainee

statut de travailleur à temps plein
full-time status

taux de chômage en situation de plein emploi (des capacités)
full employment unemployment rate, equilibrium / natural rate of unemployment

taux plein
full rate

taux plein applicable à New York (au)
at the full New York rate

temps plein (à)
full-time

travail en année pleine
full-year work

travail à temps plein
full-time work / employment / job

travailler à pleine capacité
to work at full capacity

travailleur en année pleine
full-year worker

travailleur à temps plein
full-time worker; regular employee (USA)

PLOMBAGE
filling

PLOMBIER
plombiers soudeurs, tôliers-chaudronniers,
monteurs de charpentes et de structures
métalliques [CITP-1968 (8-7)]
plumbers, welders, sheet metal and
structural metal preparers and erectors
[ISCO-1968 (8-7)]

PLURALISME
pluralisme syndical
trade union pluralism

PLURALITÉ
régime applicable en cas de pluralité de
régimes
scheme applicable where there are a
number of schemes

PLURIACTIVITÉ
multiple jobholding

PLUS-VALUE
surplus; increase value; (occ.) unearned
increment

PME
agence pour la promotion des PME
SME / small business promotion agency

POCHE
poche de pauvreté
area of deprivation

PODOLOGUE
chiropodist

POIDS
weight; burden

poids de la fiscalité
fiscal / tax burden

poids des inactifs
dependency ratio

POINT
barème de conversion des points en classes
grade-point conversion scale

**évaluation des emplois selon une échelle
de points**
point-factor method of job evaluation

**fourchette de points pour les différentes
classes**
point range for classes

matrice de cotation par points
point-factor matrix

méthode des points
point method

point d'autonomie (Belg.)
autonomy point

point de comparaison
(occ.) comparator

point de contact
contact person

point de désaccord
area of contention

point d'indice
index point

point personnel de rétribution (Ger.)
personal income point

point de référence
benchmark

point de retraite
pension point (Fr.); (pl.) retirement
entitlement

rachat des points de retraite
purchase of retirement entitlement

**système de classement des emplois par
points**
point-factor system of job classification

POINTAGE
clocking (in / out); sign on (unempl.)

carte / carton de pointage
attendance / time (clock) card

feuille de pointage
punctuality record

fiche de pointage
time card

pointage à l'entrée
clocking-on

pointage à la sortie
clocking-off, clocking-out

POINTE
activité de pointe
leading industry

industrie de pointe
high(-)technology industry

période de pointe
peak work load period

pointe de travail
work peak

POINTER
to clock in / on, to clock out / off; to sign
on (unempl.)

POINTEUSE
time clock

PÔLE
focal point

pôle de croissance de l'emploi
employment growth area

POLÉMIQUE
dispute

POLICE
police; policy (ins.)

police d'assurance
insurance policy

police d'assurance-accidents
accident policy

police d'assurance générale
(occ.) blanket (insurance) policy
police d'assurance-vie à capital

récupérable
pure endowment policy

police tous risques
blanket (insurance) policy

police d'assurance-vie à capital différé
endowment policy

POLITIQUE
policy

politique anti-inflationniste
anti-inflationary policy

politique d'austérité
policy of restraint / of retrenchment

politique budgétaire
fiscal policy

politique-cadre
overall policy

politique de compression des dépenses
policy of retrenchment

politique conjoncturelle
business cycle policy

politique à court terme
short-term policy

politique de croissance
growth policy

politique dynamique de l'emploi
active employment policy

politique d'économies
policy of savings / of retrenchment

politique économique
economic policy

politique en matière d'éducation
educational policy

politique de l'emploi
employment / manpower / labour market
policy

politique d'emploi et de main-d'oeuvre
employment and manpower policy

politique fiscale
fiscal / tax policy

politique de formation
educational / training policy

politique globale
overall policy

politique d'intervention (directe) sur le marché du travail
active labour market policy

politique de non-intervention
laissez-faire policy

politique du marché du travail
labour market policy

politique en matière de négociation collective
collective bargaining policy

politique du personnel
personnel policy; manpower / personnel practices

politique de placement
placement policy

politique de plein emploi
full employment policy, policy of full employment

politique des prix
pricing policy

politique de rémunération
wage / compensation policy

politique de rétention de main-d'oeuvre
labour hoarding policy

politique des revenus
income policy

politique des salaires / salariale
wage / compensation policy

politique sanitaire / de (la) santé
health policy

politique sociale
social policy

politique sociale intégrée
integrated social policy

politique de stimulation de l'emploi
employment development policy

politique structurelle
structural policy

POLYCLINIQUE
private general hospital; nursing home

POLYHANDICAPÉ
multiply handicapped

POLYVALENCE
multi-skilling; versatility

polyvalence professionnelle des travailleurs
occupational flexibility of the workers

POLYVALENT
multi-skilled, broadly skilled, multidisciplinary, multipurpose

agent polyvalent
multipurpose / front-line worker

agent de santé polyvalent
multipurpose health worker

compétences polyvalentes
(occ.) transferable skills

école polyvalente
comprehensive school

formation polyvalente
broadly-based skill training, multi-skilling

PONCTUALITÉ
punctuality; timekeeping

manque de ponctualité
unpunctuality

PONCTUEL
punctual; selective, non-recurrent

grève ponctuelle
selective strike

soignant ponctuel
informal carer

PONDÉRATION
weight(ing)

coefficient de pondération
weight

coefficient de pondération constant
fixed weight

formule de pondération des prestations
weighted benefit formula

système de pondération
weighting system

PONDÉRÉ
moyenne pondérée des indemnités de
poste
weighted average of post adjustments

PONDÉRER
to weight

PONT
bridge; long weekend

POPULATION
population; community

accroissement de la population
population growth / increase

**accroissement / augmentation de la
population active**
labour force growth / increase

**base de données projectives sur la
population active**
labour force projections data base

caractéristiques de la population active
labour force characteristics

catégorie de population
segment / group of population

**charge supportée par la population
active**
dependency ratio

comportement de la population active
labour force behaviour

couverture sanitaire de la population
health care coverage

effectif de la population active
size of economically active population

**enquête (par sondage) sur la population
active**
labour force (sample) survey

ensemble de la population
general population

état de santé d'une population
health profile of a population

groupe de population
segment of population

intégration à la population active
labour force absorption

population active
economically active / gainfully occupied /
gainfully employed / working / active
population, labour / work force, gainful
workers; (occ.) manpower

population non active
non-active / unoccupied / economically
inactive population

population active agricole
agricultural workers

population active non agricole
non-agricultural workers

population active civile
civilian labour force / working population

population active ayant un emploi
gainfully occupied population

population active féminine
female labour (force)

population active industrielle
industrial population

population active intérieure
domestic labour force

population active masculine
male labour force

population active occupée
employed labour force / population

population active potentielle
potential labour force

population active primaire
primary labour force

population active de réserve
reserve labour force

population active secondaire
secondary labour force

population active à temps complet / à temps plein
full-time labour force

population ayant une activité lucrative
economically active / gainfully occupied / working population, labour force

population d'âge actif / en âge d'activité
population of working age, working (-)age labour force

population d'âge scolaire (obligatoire)
school age population

population en âge de travailler
working(-)age labour force

population agricole / vivant de l'agriculture
agricultural / farm population, population dependent on agriculture

population non agricole
non-farm population

population bénéficiaire / cible
target population

population domiciliée
resident population

population économiquement active
economically active / gainfully occupied / working population

population économiquement inactive
non working / unoccupied population, persons not in the labour force, non-labour force, economically inactive population

population occupant des emplois rémunérés
economically active / gainfully occupied / working population, labour force

population enfantine
child population

population estudiantine
number of students, student numbers

population habituellement active
usually active population

population inactive
non working / unoccupied population, persons not in the labour force, non-labour force, economically inactive population

population juvéno-infantile
child population

population des ménages collectifs (stat.)
institutional population

population résidante / de résidence habituelle
resident population

population à risque
population at risk

population rurale
rural population

population scolaire
school population

population type
standard population

population visée
target population

productivité de la population active
productivity of the labour force

projection de population
population projection

projection de la population active
labour force projection

rapport chômage/population
unemployment/population ratio

rapport emploi/population
employment/population ratio

recensement de la population
population census

régime intéressant la totalité de la population
universal scheme

réintégrer la population active
to re-enter the labour force

relogement de populations à bas revenus
rehousing of low-income groups

répartition de la population active
labour force distribution

retrait de la population active
departure from the labour force

statistiques de la population
population statistics

statistiques de la population active
labour force statistics

taux d'activité de la population active
labour force participation rate

taux d'utilisation des prestations par la population totale
beneficiary rate

taux d'utilisation des prestations par la population couverte
take-up rate

PORNOGRAPHIE
pornographie impliquant des enfants / infantile
child pornography

PORNOGRAPHIQUE
exploitation pornographique des enfants
child pornography

PORTAGE
portage d'entreprise
(occ.) piggy-backing

PORTANT
bien portant
healthy

PORTÉE
coverage; range; scope

clause de portée générale
(occ.) omnibus clause

longue portée (à)
long-run, long-range

PORTER
porter atteinte à
to affect, to prejudice

porter atteinte aux droits acquis
to jeopardise acquired rights

porter atteinte au libre exercice de l'industrie et du travail
to impair / to restrict the freedom of industry and labour

porter au crédit de
to credit

porter à l'effectif
to take on strength

porter malade (se faire)
to report sick

porter préjudice à
to prejudice

PORTEUR
porteur d'emploi
job creating

secteur porteur
leading edge industry

PORTUAIRE
manutentions / travail portuaire(s)
dock work

POSER
poser sa candidature à un emploi
to try / to apply for a job

POSITIF
positive

action positive
affirmative / positive action

discrimination positive
positive discrimination

prestation positive
positive performance

POSITION
position; situation; status; policy

fiche de position (Fr.)
benefit statement

position financière précaire
financial insecurity

position professionnelle
job status

position sociale
social situation / status

prise de position
policy statement

prise de position dans une négociation
bargaining position

POSSÉDANT (adj.)
classe possédante
proprietary class

POSSIBILITÉ
possibility, opportunity; scope; (pl.)
facilities

possibilité d'accès à l'emploi
accessibility to employment

possibilité d'avancement
opportunity / chance for promotion / for
advancement, potential for advancement,
promotability, promotional / career
opportunity, promotion / advancement
potential

possibilité de carrière
opportunity for advancement, career
opportunity

possibilités de création d'emplois
employment-generating potential

possibilité d'emploi
job / employment opening, opportunity for
employment, work / job opportunity, job
prospect / outlook, placing / placement
prospect; (pl.) employment opportunities;
availability of jobs

possibilité d'évasion fiscale
tax loophole

possibilité de formation
training opportunity

possibilité de promotion
opportunity for / chance for promotion /
for advancement, potential for
advancement, promotability, promotional
opportunity, promotion / advancement
potential

possibilités de rendement
potential for effectiveness

possibilité de transférer des droits
portability of rights

possibilité de travail
placing / placement prospect

POST(-)CURE
post-operative care; after care; follow-up

centre de post(-)cure
convalescent home, rest centre; after care
centre

foyer de post(-)cure (et de réadaptation)
(occ.) half-way house

période de post(-)cure
follow-up phase / period

service de post(-)cure
after care service

soins de post(-)cure
follow-up care

traitement de post(-)cure
follow-up treatment

POSTÉ (adj.)
sursalaire pour travail posté
shift differential

travail posté
shift work(ing)

travail posté de nuit
nightshift

POSTE (n.)
post, assignment, position, office, place;
employment, occupation; shift, manshift;
entry

abandon de poste
abandonment of post / of position;
desertion of one's post

abandonner son poste
to abandon one's post

accéder à un nouveau poste
to take on a new job

accéder à un poste important
to rise to an important position

affecté à un poste (être)
(to be) assigned to a position

aménagement du poste de travail
job adaptation / redesign

avis normalisé de vacance de poste
standardised notice of vacancy

barème des ajustements / des indemnités de poste
schedule of post adjustments

briguer un poste
to compete for a post, to canvass for / to covet a job

caractéristiques d'un / du poste (de travail)
particulars of a position, job specification / content

classement des postes
job classification; codification of posts

classement des postes par attributions
duty classification of posts

classement des postes fondé sur le rang
rank classification of posts

classer un poste
to classify a position

classification des postes
job classification

communication obligatoire des postes vacants
compulsory notification of vacancies

compression des postes
job squeeze
confirmer dans un poste / une fonction
to confirm in a job

confrontation des hommes et des postes
man-job matching

conversion des postes
job conversion

création de postes
job creation

déclarer une vacance de poste
to declare a post vacant

déclassement d'un poste
downgrading of post

dédoublement de poste
job splitting

définition de poste
job description ·

définition du / descriptif de poste
job specification

description de poste
job / position description

description sommaire de poste
summary job description

dotation d'un poste
staffing of a position

dotation des postes par voie de recrutement externe
external staffing

embauche sur poste(s) existant(s)
job replacement

embauche sur poste(s) existant(s) (par)
by replacement

emploi sur poste partagé
shared job

étude de(s) poste(s) de travail
job analysis

évaluation d'un poste
audit of a job / post

évaluation des postes de travail
job evaluation

exigence du poste
job requirement

fiche de poste à pourvoir
requisition form

fonctionnaire en poste à l'étranger
expatriate civil servant

formation hors poste
off-the-job training

garder un droit sur son poste
to retain a lien on one's post

gestion des vacances de poste
vacancy management

indemnité de poste
assignment allowance; post adjustment
(allowance)

intitulé de poste
job title

libérer un poste
to vacate a position

mission principale d'un poste
main job duty

moyenne pondérée des indemnités de poste
weighted average of post adjustments

niveau de poste
position level

nombre de postes permanents
number of permanent jobs / posts; core
staffing; establishment

notification obligatoire des postes vacants
compulsory notification of vacancies

occuper un poste
to encumber a post, to be the incumbent of
a post, to hold a position

partage de poste
job splitting / twinning / sharing

passer un entretien pour un poste
to interview for a job

pension payée par poste
pension paid through the post

permutation des postes
exchange of jobs

poste (en)
serving

poste à (être en)
to serve in

poste d'administrateur / administratif
administrative job, (occ.) professional post

poste de l'administration
civil service position

poste d'agent auxiliaire
ancillary post

poste d'agent local
local level post

poste alternant
rotating shift

poste antérieur
previous position

poste auxiliaire
servicing post

poste au bas de l'échelle
entry-level job

poste du budget / budgétaire
budget item / line

poste de chef de service
supervisor(y) post / position

poste hors classe
unclassified post

poste clé
key post / job / position

poste de commis
clerical post

poste de contrôle du travail
supervisory work station

poste de dépenses
item of expenditure

poste difficile
hardship post

poste difficile à pouvoir
hard-to-fill vacancy

poste de direction
executive position / job, managerial post

poste disponible
available post

poste de durée déterminée
position on a fixed-term basis

poste électif
elective office

poste élevé
high-ranking position

poste d'encadrement et de direction
supervisory and management position

poste d'exécutant
working level post

poste fonctionnel
functional / staff position

poste de formation
training / trainee position

poste fractionné
split shift

poste de haute direction
upper level management position

poste de jour
day shift

poste libéré
vacated position

poste médical
health station / post

postes de niveaux comparables
positions of the same level

poste non normalisé
non-standard job

poste notifié vacant
vacancy notified

poste opérationnel
(occ.) field position

poste d'ouvrier spécialisé
semi-skilled occupation

poste permanent
permanent job / employment / post, career
/ core / established post; (pl.)
establishment

postes permanents de nuit
regular night shift

poste à pourvoir
vacant position / post, (job) vacancy

poste pourvu
vacancy / job filled

poste non pourvu
unfilled vacancy

poste de premiers secours
first aid post / station

poste de recettes
item of receipts

poste de référence
benchmark position

poste de responsabilité
position of responsibility, senior post

poste sanitaire
health station / post

poste de secours
first aid post / station

poste de secrétaire
secretarial post

poste dans les services organiques
substantive post

poste de service social
social work appointment

poste au siège
headquarters assignment

poste hors siège
field post

poste signalé vacant
vacancy notified

poste stable
continuing post

poste de stagiaire
training / trainee position

poste subalterne
junior position

postes successifs
successive shifts

poste de surveillant
supervisory post / position

poste temporaire intermittent
recurrent temporary post

poste de travail
work station / place / shift; job

poste de travail (hors)
off-the-job

poste tremplin
ladder / bridging position

poste vacant
vacant position / post, situation vacant,
(job) vacancy

poste vacant inscrit
vacancy recorded

poste vacant signalé
registered vacancy

pourcentage de postes vacants
vacancy rate

**pourvoir un poste / à une vacance de
poste**
to fill a post / a job / a vacancy, to staff a
position

présenter sa candidature à un poste
to submit one's candidacy for a post

prime de poste
shift premium / differential

profil de poste
job profile; personnel specification

profil du poste
job / occupational characteristic

qualifié pour occuper un poste (être)
to be capable of filling a post

**qualités requises pour le poste (avoir
les)**
to have the qualifications for the job

quitter un poste
to vacate a position

rallier son poste
to report for / to duty

reclassement de poste
upgrading of post; (pl.) reclassification of
posts

reclasser un poste
to upgrade a post

réintégration dans un poste
reverting to a post

relèvement de l'indemnité de poste
increase of post adjustment

requalifier un poste
to upgrade a post

rotation des postes
job rotation

roulement dans l'occupation des postes
rotation of staff

salaire afférent à un poste
salary attached to a position

suppression de poste
abolition of post; (pl.) job dislocation /
displacement, labour displacement,
redundancy

supprimer un poste
to abolish a post

système de codage des postes
post coding system

système des indemnités de poste
post adjustment system

titulaire d'un poste
job holder, holder of a post, incumbent

titulaire d'un poste (être)
to encumber a post, to have tenure

transférer un poste
to transfer a post

transfert de postes
transfer of posts

travail à trois postes
three-shift work

vacance de poste
vacancy

POST-EMBAUCHE
post-entry

POSTÉRIEUR (adj.)
orientation postérieure au placement
post-employment / post-placement
counselling

POST-HOSPITALIER
centre post-hospitalier général de
réadaptation médicale
(occ.) medical rehabilitation centre

soins post-hospitaliers
follow-up care

POST-OPÉRATOIRE
soins post-opératoires
post-operative care

POSTNATAL
congé postnatal
post(-)natal leave

(service de) consultations postnatales
post-natal clinic

POST-NÉONATAL
post-neonatal

POST-OBLIGATOIRE
enseignement post-obligatoire
post-compulsory education

POST-PARTUM
soins post-partum
post-partum care

POST-SCOLAIRE
établissement d'éducation post-scolaire
college of further education

POST-SECONDAIRE
diplômé de niveau post-secondaire
post-secondary graduate

école post-secondaire
post-secondary school

enseignement post-secondaire
post-secondary / further education

**établissement (d'enseignement) post-
secondaire**
post-secondary educational institution

**établissement d'enseignement post-
secondaire communautaire (USA)**
community college

formation post-secondaire
post-secondary training

système d'enseignement post-secondaire
post-secondary system

POSTULANT
applicant

POSTULER
postuler un emploi
to apply for a job

POST-UNIVERSITAIRE
enseignement post-universitaire
postgraduate training

POTENTIEL (adj.)
allocataire / bénéficiaire potentiel
potential beneficiary

chômage potentiel
threat of unemployment

employeur potentiel
potential employer

main-d'oeuvre potentielle
manpower potential

niveau potentiel de salaire
earnings potential / power

offre potentielle de main-d'oeuvre
potential manpower supply

population active potentielle
potential labour force

revenu potentiel
potential income; (pl.) (occ.) earnings
prospect

sous-emploi potentiel
potential under-employment

POTENTIEL (n.)
potentiel de croissance / d'expansion
growth potential

potentiel de main-d'oeuvre
labour force / manpower potential

potentiel de production
productive capacity

POTIER
potiers, souffleurs de verre et assimilés
[CITP-1988 (732)]
potters, glass-makers and related trades
workers [ISCO-1988 (732)]

POUPONNIÈRE
day care centre, day(-care) nursery,
resident nursery, infant / infants' home

POURCENTAGE
pourcentage de l'accumulation
rate of accumulation

pourcentage d'actifs
employment rate

pourcentage de capitalisation
funded ratio

pourcentage des départs (naturels)
wastage rate

pourcentage global de capitalisation
aggregate funded ratio

pourcentage d'invalidité
degree of disability

pourcentage de postes vacants
vacancy rate

POURSUITE
continuation; follow-up

passible de poursuites judiciaires
subject to legal proceedings

poursuite des / d'études
continuation of studies

POURSUIVRE
poursuivre l'étude de
to keep under review

POURVOIR
emploi à pourvoir
(unfilled) (job) vacancy

fiche de poste à pourvoir
requisition form

poste difficile à pourvoir
hard-to-fill vacancy

poste à pourvoir
vacant position / post, (job) vacancy

pourvoir un emploi
to fill a post / a job / a vacancy, to staff a
position

pourvoir à l'entretien d'un enfant
to provide for a child

pourvoir en personnel
to staff

**pourvoir un poste / à une vacance de
poste**
to fill a post / a job / a vacancy, to staff a
position

POURVU
emploi / poste pourvu
vacancy / job filled

poste non pourvu
unfilled vacancy

pourvu (non)
unfilled

pourvu d'un emploi
in employment

POUSSÉ (adj.)
formation poussée
intensive training

POUSSÉE (n.)
poussée des salaires
wage inflation / push

POUVOIR (n.)
power, authority; ability

abus de pouvoir
abuse of position / of authority

baisse du pouvoir d'achat
loss of purchasing power

délégation de pouvoirs
delegation of authority

donner pouvoir de
to authorise

excéder ses pouvoirs
to act beyond one's authority

hausse du pouvoir d'achat
increase in purchasing power

logements financés / subventionnés par les pouvoirs publics
public housing

maintien du pouvoir d'achat
maintenance of purchasing power

outrepasser ses pouvoirs
to exceed one's powers / authority

pouvoir d'achat
buying / purchasing power

pouvoir d'achat des salaires
(occ.) real wage / earnings

pouvoir central
central government

pouvoir de décision
decision-making power

pouvoir discrétionnaire
discretionary power

pouvoirs locaux
local authorities

pouvoir de négociation
bargaining power
pouvoirs publics
(public) authorities

pouvoir de réglementation
regulatory power

pouvoir de substitution
power to appoint an agent

recours pour excès de pouvoir
application to set aside a decision on grounds of exceeding or misusing one's authority

relever du pouvoir discrétionnaire de
to be within the discretion of

renforcement du pouvoir des femmes
empowerment of women

PRATICIEN
practitioner; professional; (occ;) worker

association de praticiens libéraux
individual practices association (IPA)

médecin praticien
medical practitioner

praticien de l'action sociale
social (welfare) worker

praticien-conseil
health adviser

praticiens de la médecine traditionnelle et guérisseurs [CITP-1988]
traditional medicine practitioners and faith healers [ISCO-1988 (324)]

praticien de la santé
health practitioner

PRATIQUE (adj.)
bonnes connaissances pratiques
good working knowledge

connaissance pratique d'une langue
working knowledge of a language

connaissances théoriques et pratiques
knowledge and skills

cours de formation pratique
practical training course

enseignement pratique
(occ.) field teaching

enseignement universitaire pratique
graduate training

formation pratique
on-the-job training

formation pratique par simulation
simulated on-the-job training

manque d'expérience pratique
lack of practical experience / of work experience

stage pratique
field work practice

travaux pratiques
(occ.) field work

PRATIQUE (n.)
practice

actes de pratique médicale courante
standard medical service

apprentissage par la pratique
learning by doing

pratiques commerciales
business practices

pratiques commerciales courantes
customary business practices

pratique courante
standard / usual practice

pratique discriminatoire
discriminatory practice

pratiques (suivies en matière) d'embauche
hiring practices

pratique d'emploi impartiale / objective
neutral / objective employment practice

pratique d'emploi progressive
progressive employment practice

pratique infirmière
nursing practice

pratique loyale en matière d'emploi
fair employment practice

pratique médicale de groupe
group (medical) practice

pratiques de participation
participative practices

pratique d'une profession
professional practice

pratiques professionnelles
work practices

pratique de recrutement
recruitment practice

pratique restrictive en matière d'emploi
restrictive labour practice

pratique de sécurité syndicale (Fr.)
closed shop practice

pratiques de travail
work practices

PRATIQUÉ
taux pratiqué
prevailing / going rate

PRÉALABLE
accord préalable
prior agreement

approbation / autorisation préalable
prior approval

condition préalable
pre-condition

consultation préalable
prior consultation

déclaration préalable à l'embauche (Fr.)
prior registration of employee

demande préalable à l'emploi
pre-employment inquiry

entente préalable
prior agreement, pre-agreement

entretien préalable à la formation
pre-training interview

entretien préalable au licenciement
preliminary discussion before dismissal

formation préalable
pre-training

formation préalable à l'emploi
pre-service / pre-employment training

orientation préalable au placement
pre-employment counselling

orientation préalable à la retraite
pre-retirement counselling

programme de formation préalable à l'apprentissage
pre-apprenticeship training programme

sélection préalable
(pre-)screening (process)

PRÉ-APPRENTISSAGE
pre-apprenticeship

programme de pré-apprentissage
pre-apprentice scheme

PRÉAVIS
advanced notification / notice, prior notice
of termination, preliminary advice, proper
notice

délai minimum légal de préavis
statutory notice

délai de préavis
period of notice, notice period

démission sans préavis
resignation without prior notice

déposer un préavis de grève
to give notice of strike action

dispense de préavis
release from working out one's notice

donner un préavis
to give notice

durée de préavis
length of notice

effectuer / exécuter son préavis
to work out one's notice

grève sans préavis
wild(-)cat strike

indemnité compensatrice de préavis
compensation in lieu of notice, pay /
payment in lieu of notice

indemnité de préavis
compensation in lieu of notice

licenciement avec préavis
dismissal with notice

licenciement sans préavis
dismissal without notice

moyennant un préavis de six mois
upon six month's notice

période de préavis
notice period

préavis (sans)
without prior notice

préavis de cessation d'emploi
end-of-employment notice

préavis de démission écrit
written notice of resignation

préavis de grève
strike notice

préavis de licenciement
dismissal / termination notice, notice of
dismissal / of termination

préavis payé
pay under notice

préavis raisonnable
reasonable notice

recevoir un préavis de licenciement
to be served with a notice of termination

renvoi sans préavis
summary dismissal

renvoyer sans préavis
to dismiss summarily

terme d'un délai de préavis
end of a notice period

PRÉCAIRE
insecure; provisional

contrat de travail précaire
insecure employment contract

emploi précaire
insecure / unstable job

position / situation financière précaire
financial insecurity

situation précaire
hardship, predicament

PRÉCARISATION
reduction to casual status

PRÉCARITÉ
existence / practice of / reliance on casual /
irregular work; living on the bread-line

précarité de l'emploi
job insecurity, lack of job security

précarité financière
financial insecurity

PRECIO DOLORIS
pain and inconvenience

PRÉCIS (adj.)
contrat à durée déterminée à terme précis
(Fr.)
specified fixed-term contract

exigence précise
specific requirement

PRÉCISION
ajusteurs-monteurs, installateurs de
machines et mécaniciens de précision
(électriciens exceptés) [CITP-1968 (8-4)]
machinery fitters, machine assemblers and
precision instrument makers (except
electrical) [ISCO-1968 (8-4)]

PRÉCOCE
centre d'action médico-sociale précoce
early medical social work centre

PRÉCOMPTE
précompte immobilier (Belg.)
property tax deduction

précompte sur présomption
presumed deduction at source

précompte sur le salaire
deduction at source P.A.Y.E.

**système de précompte des cotisations
(UK)**
direct debit system

PRÉ-CONTRÔLE
pré-contrôle d'embauche (USA)
employment verification

PRÉDISPOSER
to prejudice

PRÉDISPOSITION
prédisposition aux accidents
accident proneness

PRÉDOMINANCE
profession à prédominance masculine
male-dominated occupation

PRÉDOMINANT
procédé à facteur travail prédominant
labour-intensive technology

PRÉ-EMBAUCHE
pre-entry

PRÉEMPTION
droit de préemption des travailleurs
workers' right of pre-emption

PRÉÉTABLI
stage à inscription préétablie
scheduled intake course

PRÉ-ÉVALUATION
consultation de pré-évaluation
pre-assessment consultation

PRÉEXISTANT
affection préexistante
previous illness

PRÉFECTORAL
arrêté préfectoral (Fr.)
prefectural order

PRÉFÉRENCE
préférence à l'embauche / au recrutement
preferential hiring

PRÉFÉRENTIEL
augmentation préférentielle des salaires
premium wage increase

avantage préférentiel
preferential benefit

clause d'embauche préférentielle
closed-shop clause

embauche préférentielle
preferential hiring

tarif préférentiel
preferential fee / rate, target payment (UK)

traitement préférentiel
preferential treatment; positive
discrimination (minorities)

PRÉFINANCÉ
régime de retraite préfinancé
funded pension plan

PRÉ-FORMATION
pré-formation professionnelle
occupational pre-training

PRÉHOSPITALIER
médecine préhospitalière d'urgence
prehospital medicine

PRÉJUDICE
prejudice, wrong; loss; hardship

porter préjudice à
to prejudice

préjudice corporel
personal injury

préjudice physique
physical injury

PRÉJUDICIABLE
harmful, detrimental, prejudicial, injurious

conséquence préjudiciable
harmful effect

préjudiciable à la santé
injurious to (the) health

PRÉJUDICIEL
prejudicial

PRÉJUGÉ (n.)
prejudice, bias

préjugé défavorable contre qqn
bias against somebody

préjugé favorable pour qqn
bias towards somebody

préjugé racial
racial prejudice

PRÉLÈVEMENT
deduction; levy; recovery charge; swab

assiette des prélèvements
contribution base

**plan d'épargne par prélèvement
automatique**
save-as-you-earn scheme

prélèvement compensatoire
compensatory levy

prélèvement fiscal
tax levy

prélèvement fiscal exceptionnel
exceptional tax levy

**prélèvement destiné à financer la
formation**
training levy

prélèvement obligatoire
mandatory levy

prélèvement sur salaire
deduction from wages / earnings

prélèvements fondés sur les salaires
payroll tax

prélèvement à la source
deduction at source P.A.Y.E.; withholding
tax; payroll deduction

système de subventions par prélèvement
levy-grant system

PRÉLEVER
to levy, to deduct from

prélever sur le salaire
to deduct from pay / wages

PRÉLIMINAIRE
allocation de subsistance pour visite
préliminaire
preliminary examination living allowance

allocation de visite préliminaire
preliminary examination allowance

sélection préliminaire
(pre-)screening (process), preselection

sélection préliminaire des travailleurs
preselection of workers

PRÉMATURÉ (adj.)
décès prématuré
early death

PRÉMATURÉ (n.)
soins aux prématurés
premature care

PREMIER
administration des premiers soins
provision of first aid

aide au premier emploi
first job allowance

aide au premier emploi des jeunes (Fr.)
allowance for young new workers

allocation de premier accueil (It.)
arrival grant

centre de premier accueil
emergency home shelter

centre de premier secours
emergency centre

demandeur d'un premier emploi
first(-time) job seeker, new entrant on the
labour market

emploi de premier échelon
entry-level job

enfant du premier âge
baby, infant

enseignement du premier degré
primary education

**enseignement secondaire du premier
cycle**
high school education

étudiant du premier cycle
undergraduate student

formation de première insertion (Fr.)
initial integration training

frais de premier établissement
initial outlay

médecin de premier contact
physician of first contact

poste de premiers secours
first aid post / station

premier commis
senior clerk

**premier cycle de l'enseignement
secondaire**
lower secondary

premier décile
first decile

première enfance
infancy

première entrée en activité
first accession to the labour force; entrance
/ entry into the labour force

première équipe
prime shift

premiers secours / soins
first aid

première tranche d'imposition
basic rate tax

prestataire de premier recours
first level provider

soins de premier recours
primary (health / medical) care

PRÉNATAL
prenatal

aide prénatale
aid to expectant mothers

allocation prénatale
pre(-)natal allowance, allowance for
pregnant women

congé prénatal
pre(-)natal leave

**(dispensaire de) consultations
prénatales, dispensaire prénatal**
ante-natal / pre(-)natal clinic

indemnité prénatale
allowance for pregnant women

repos prénatal
pre(-)natal leave

repos prénatal facultatif
optional pre(-)natal leave

secours prénatal
aid to expectant mothers

service de consultations prénatales
pre(-)natal clinic

soins prénatals
ante-natal / pre(-)natal care

PRENDRE
jour restant à prendre
remaining day

prendre acte de
to act; to register

prendre à sa charge
to assume responsibility for; to provide; to
bear; to absorb

prendre à sa charge les frais de
to bear the cost of

prendre en charge
to cover, to compensate, to defray

prendre sous contrat
to sign up

prendre effet
to take effect

prendre un emploi
to take / to accept a job, to enter into / to
take employment

prendre à l'essai
to take on probation

prendre fin
to expire

prendre ses fonctions
to take office, to report for / to duty

prendre parti contre qqn
to have bias against somebody

prendre parti en faveur de / pour qqn
to have bias towards somebody

prendre sa retraite
to retire (from work), to quit

prendre une retraite anticipée
to retire early

PRÉNUPTIAL
certificat prénuptial
prenuptial certificate

consultations prénuptiales
pre(-)marital counselling

PRÉPAIEMENT
système de prépaiement
prepaid group practice (PGP)

PRÉPARATEUR
préparateur en pharmacie
pharmacist's / chemist's assistant

PRÉPARATION
preparation, training

préparation à l'emploi
job preparation

préparation pour nourrissons
infant formula

préparation pharmaceutique
drug, dosage form

préparation professionnelle
(pre-)vocational training

préparation de la retraite
retirement planning

préparation à la vie de famille / familiale
family life education

préparation à la vie professionnelle
(pre-)vocational preparation

programme de préparation à l'emploi
(occ.) bridging programme

programme de préparation de la retraite
pre-retirement planning programme

stage de préparation à la vie professionnelle
vocational preparation course

PRÉPARATOIRE
école préparatoire
preparatory school

formation préparatoire
preparatory / vestibule training

orientation préparatoire à la retraite
pre-retirement counselling

stage préparatoire aux techniques industrielles
basic industrial skill course

PRÉPAYÉ
exercice de groupe prépayé, groupement médical prépayé (PGP)
prepaid group practice (PGP)

PRÉ(-)PENSION
pre-pension (Hung.), early pension (Belg.)

PRÉPOSÉ
attendant, servant; (pl.) (occ.) employees

préposé au reclassement (professionnel) des invalides (UK)
disablement resettlement officer

PRÉPOSER
préposer à une fonction
to appoint to an office

PRÉPRIMAIRE
enseignement préprimaire
pre-school / pre-primary education

instituteurs de l'enseignement primaire et préprimaire [CITP-1988 (233)]
primary and pre-primary education teaching professionals [ISCO-1988 (233)]

professions intermédiaires de l'enseignement préprimaire [CITP-1988)]
pre-primary education teaching associate professionals [ISCO-1988 (332)]

PRÉPROFESSIONNEL
pre(-)vocational

enseignement préprofessionnel
pre(-)vocational education

formation préprofessionnelle
pre(-)vocational training

PRÉQUALIFIANT
action préqualifiante
pre-skills training course

PRÉRETRAITE
pre-retirement; early retirement (pension); early retirement on a bridging pension; job release (UK)

départ volontaire à la préretraite
early retirement on a voluntary basis

mise en préretraite
compulsory early retirement

partir en préretraite
to retire early

pension de préretraite-chômage (Finl.)
unemployment pension

prestation de préretraite
pre-retirement benefit

régime de préretraite
early retirement plan

système de préretraite
early retirement scheme; job release (UK)

PRÉSCOLAIRE
âge préscolaire (d')
under school age

éducation préscolaire
early(-)childhood / pre(-)primary / pre-school education

enfant d'âge préscolaire
pre-school child

enseignement préscolaire
early(-)childhood / pre(-)primary / pre-school education

PRESCRIPTION
prescription; provision; limitation, statute
of limitations, statutory (time) limitations,
time limitations; specification;
requirement; regulations

délai de prescription
period / term of limitation

liberté de prescription
freedom of prescription

prescription abusive
overprescription

prescription d'un droit
limitation of a right

PRESCRIRE
to prescribe; to lapse

PRESCRIT
statute-barred; due; statutory, prescribed

délai prescrit
required / prescribed time(-limit)

délais prescrits (dans les)
in the required / prescribed time

emploi prescrit
prescribed employment

proroger le délai prescrit
to extend the time-limit

temps prescrit
prescribed time

PRÉSÉLECTION
preselection, (pre-)screening, screening
process

entrevue de présélection
screening interview

jury de présélection
screening board

présélection des candidats
shortlisting of candidates; screening of job
applicants

présélection des travailleurs
preselection of workers

PRÉSÉLECTIONNÉ
liste de candidats présélectionnés
shortlist of candidates

travailleur présélectionné
pre-selected worker

PRÉSÉLECTIONNER
to screen

PRÉSENCE
attendance

carte de présence
attendance card

état de présence
attendance record

feuille journalière de présence
daily attendance sheet

feuille des / fiche de présence(s)
attendance sheet / list, record of attendance

heures de présence
hours spent at work

jetons de présence des administrateurs
directors' fees

plage (obligatoire) de présence
core time / hours

présence aux cours
class attendance

présence au travail
work attendance

registre des présences
attendance sheet / list, record of attendance

**temps de présence ininterrompue au
travail**
(occ.) continuous employment

PRÉSENT
current

effectifs présents
staff at work

PRÉSENTATION
presentation; introduction; referral

entretien de présentation
referral interview

PRÉSENTÉISME
prime de présentéisme
well pay

PRÉSENTER
to present; to submit; to refer

présenter sa candidature à un poste
to submit one's candidacy for a post

présenter les conditions voulues (pour bénéficier / avoir droit)
to qualify for; to fulfil requirements; to be eligible

présenter à un concours (se)
to sit for a (competitive) examination

présenter une demande
to apply, to submit a claim

présenter une demande d'emploi
to apply for a job

présenter à un entretien (se)
to report for an interview

présenter un examen
to take an examination

présenter une réclamation
to submit a complaint

présenter régulièrement (se)
to report regularly

présenter au travail (se)
to report for / to duty / for work

PRÉSERVER
to protect

préserver des emplois
to safeguard / to preserve / to maintain (existing) jobs

PRÉSOMPTION
précompte sur présomption
presumed deduction at source

présomption d'imputabilité
presumption of responsibility / of liability

PRESSEUR
blanchisseurs, dégraisseurs et presseurs
[CITP-1968 (5-6)]
launderers, dry-cleaners and pressers
[ISCO-1968 (5-6)]

PRESSION
groupe de pression
pressure group, lobby

pression (faire)
to put under pressure; to lobby

pression fiscale
tax burden / load

pression(s) exercée(s) sur le marché du travail
labour market pressure

pression migratoire
migratory pressure

pression des salaires
wage pressure

PRESTATAIRE
provider; beneficiary; claimant; payee

main-d'oeuvre prestataire
statute labour

prestataire de premier recours
first level provider

prestataire de services
service provider

prestataire de soins médicaux
medical care provider

PRESTATION
allowance, benefit; supply; delivery; provision; performance; (item of) service; subsidy

abus de prestations
(social security) benefit fraud

accorder une prestation
to grant a benefit

acquisition d'un droit à (des) prestations
acquisition of a right to benefits

- 633 -

ajournement de l'option entre les prestations
deferment of choice of benefit

ajustement des prestations
benefit adjustment

allocataire d'une prestation
benefit recipient

allouer une prestation
to allow a benefit

année de prestations
benefit year

attestation de droit aux prestations
certificate of eligibility / of entitlement

attraction du droit à prestations
(occ.) eligibility effect

attribuer une prestation
to allow / to grant a benefit

attribution d'une prestation
provision / granting of a benefit

augmenter une prestation
to increase a benefit

avance sur prestations
advance on benefits, advance payment of benefits

barème des prestations
schedule of benefits

bénéficiaire d'une prestation
benefit recipient; (pl.) persons in receipt of benefits, recipients of benefits

bénéficier d'une prestation
to receive a benefit

calcul d'une prestation
calculation of a benefit

calculer une prestation
to calculate a benefit

catégorie de prestations
category of benefits

cessation d'un droit à (des) prestations
cessation of entitlement to / of a right to benefits, exhaustion of entitlement to benefits

cessation des prestations
exhaustion of benefits

clauses de réduction, de suspension ou de suppression de prestations
provisions for reduction, suspension or withdrawal of benefits

Commission des prestations complémentaires (UK)
Supplementary Benefits Commission

conditions d'attribution des prestations
conditions governing eligibility for benefits

conditions d'octroi des prestations
conditions governing eligibility for benefits

condition de / requise pour le versement des prestations
qualifying condition for benefits

conservation des prestations
preservation of benefits

convertir une prestation en une somme en capital
to commute a benefit in a lump sum

cumul de droits à (des) prestations
overlapping entitlement to benefits

cumul de / des prestations
overlapping (of) / plurality of / simultaneous payment of benefits, concurrent / duplicate benefits

cumul d'une prestation avec d'autres prestations de sécurité sociale
overlapping of one benefit with other social security benefits

date d'échéance des prestations
date on which the benefits fall due

débiteur de prestations
liable for benefits

déchéance du droit aux prestations
disqualification for benefit

déchu du droit à prestation
disentitled

demande de prestation
benefit claim, claim / application for benefit

demander une / des prestation(s)
to claim benefit(s)

dépenses au titre des prestations
benefit expenditure

déterminer le montant des prestations
to assess benefits

dispenser des prestations
to provide services

distribution des prestations
delivery of services

droit à prestation (faire valoir un)
to claim benefit

droit à (des) prestations
right to / eligibility for / entitlement to
benefit(s), benefit entitlement / claim

droit aux prestations (avoir)
to be eligible for / to qualify for benefit

**durée d'assurance ouvrant droit à
prestations**
qualifying insurance / qualification period

durée du droit à prestations
duration of benefit entitlement

durée d'octroi des prestations
period for which benefit is allowed

durée de la prestation
duration of benefit, benefit duration

durée de service des prestations
period for which benefit is allowed

éléments de prestations
benefit components

élusion des prestations sociales
evasion of social costs

enfant ouvrant droit aux prestations
eligible child

épuiser le droit aux prestations
to exhaust right / entitlement to benefit(s)

extension des prestations
increasing provision of benefits

fin des droits à (des) prestations
cessation / exhaustion of entitlement to / of
a right to benefits

formule de pondération des prestations
weighted benefit formula

indemnités et prestations
allowances and benefits

institution débitrice de prestations
institution responsible for payment / for
provision of benefits

**instruction d'une demande de
prestations**
investigation of a claim for benefits

**introduction d'une demande de
prestations**
submission of a claim for benefits

introduire une demande de prestations
to apply for / to lodge a claim for / to make
an application for benefits

**liquidation d'une demande de
prestation**
settlement of benefit claim, establishment
of entitlement to benefit

liquidation d'une prestation
award of a benefit

liquider des droits à prestations
to pay benefits

**litige concernant des / relatif aux
prestations**
benefit dispute

maintien d'un droit à (des) prestations
retention of a right to benefits

maintien du service des prestations
continued payment of benefits

majoration des prestations
benefit increase, increase of benefits

majorer une prestation
to increase a benefit

méthode de calcul des prestations
calculation of the benefits; benefit formula

**montant annuel de la prestation de
retraite**
annual pension benefit (amount)

montant effectif d'une prestation
actual amount of a benefit

montant de la prestation
amount of the / rate of benefit; (pl.) benefit level

niveau d'une / des prestation(s)
level of benefit, benefit level

non-cumul de prestations
prevention of overlapping of benefits

notification d'une prestation
notification of benefit

nouveau calcul d'une prestation
recalculation of a benefit

octroi d'une prestation
provision / granting / award of a benefit

octroyer une prestation
to allow / to grant a benefit

ouverture d'un droit à (des) prestations
acquisition of a right to benefits

paiement des prestations
payment of benefits

paiement des prestations à un titulaire à l'étranger
payment of benefits abroad

percevoir des prestations
to draw benefits

perdre le droit à une / aux prestation(s)
to be disqualified for benefit, to disqualify from receiving benefit

période d'assurance requise pour l'ouverture du droit aux prestations
qualifying insurance / qualification period

période d'octroi / de service des prestations
period for which benefit(s) is/are allowed

personne ayant droit aux prestations
person eligible for benefits

perte du droit aux prestations
loss of entitlement

plafond des prestations
maximum amount / rate of benefits; benefit level

plan à prestations définies
defined benefit plan

plan de retraite à prestations fixes
fixed benefit retirement plan

pouvoir prétendre à une prestation
to become entitled to a benefit

prestation accessoire
collateral benefit

prestation (en cas) d'accident du travail (et de maladies professionnelles)
accident benefit, benefit in respect of accidents at work, employment / industrial injury benefit, injury benefit (UK, Malta, Irel.)

prestation d'accouchement
confinement benefit

prestations d'adaptation pour les travailleurs
labour adjustment benefits

prestation d'aide sociale
welfare payment; supplementary benefit (UK); (pl.) welfare benefits, social fund (UK)

prestations alimentaires
(alimony) maintenance payments

prestation d'allaitement
nursing benefit

prestation d'ancienneté
long-service benefit

prestation anticipée de vieillesse
anticipatory old-age benefit

prestations d'assurance-accident à recevoir
casualty insurance claim receivable

prestation de l'assurance chômage
unemployment (insurance) benefit

prestation de l'assurance maladie
sick(ness) benefit

prestation de base
basic benefit

prestation en capital
lump-sum benefit / settlement

prestation de cessation de service
termination pay

prestation à la charge directe de l'employeur
employer-based benefit

prestation (en cas) de chômage
unemployment (insurance) benefit

prestation pour chômage partiel
short-time working benefit

prestation complémentaire
supplementary benefit

prestation complémentaire pour charges locatives (Irel.)
rent supplement

prestation complémentaire pour intérêts hypothécaires (Irel.)
mortgage interest supplement

prestation ouverte sans condition
unconditional / (occ.) vested benefit

prestation liée à / soumise à / subordonnée à une / versée sous condition de ressources
means-tested / income-tested benefit

prestation contributive
contributory benefit

prestation non contributive
non-contributory benefit

prestation de courte durée / à court terme
short-term benefit

prestation liée à / soumise à / subordonnée à un critère de ressources
means-tested / income-tested benefit

prestation (en cas) de décès
death benefit

prestation de décès à la suite / résultant d'un accident du travail, prestation pour décès professionnel
industrial death benefit

prestation due
benefit due

prestation hors emploi
non-work benefit

prestation pour enfant (UK)
child benefit

prestation en espèces
cash benefit, benefit / payment in cash

prestations autres qu'en espèces
non-cash benefits

prestation étendue
extended benefit

prestation exceptionnelle
exceptional / special benefit

prestation exclue de la rémunération considérée aux fins de la pension
non-pensionable benefit

prestation liée à l'exercice d'un emploi
in-work benefit

prestation liée à l'expatriation
expatriate benefit

prestation non liée à l'expatriation
non-expatriate benefit

prestation extra-légale
non-statutory benefit

prestation facultative
optional benefit

prestation familiale / aux familles
family benefit

prestation de femme abandonnée (Irel.)
deserted wife's benefit

prestation forfaitaire
flat-rate benefit, lump-sum grant

prestation de formation
training benefit

prestation pour frais funéraires
funeral benefit

prestation liée / dont le taux est lié aux gains (antérieurs)
(previous) pay-related / earnings-related (insurance) benefit

prestations générales d'aide sociale
general welfare assistance

prestation de grossesse
pregnancy benefit

prestation d'incapacité (UK)
disablement benefit

prestation individuelle
personal benefit / allowance

prestations infirmières
(occ.) nursing

prestation d'invalidité
disablement / disability / invalidity benefit

prestation d'invalidité causée par un accident du travail (ou une maladie professionnelle)
industrial disablement benefit

prestation d'invalidité permanente
industrial disablement benefit

prestation journalière
daily benefit

prestation légale
statutory benefit

prestation pour lésion ou maladie (professionnelle)
injury benefit (UK, Irel., Malta), industrial injury / employment injury benefit

prestation sans limitation de durée
open-ended benefit

prestation prévue par la loi
statutory benefit

prestation non prévue par la loi
non-statutory benefit

prestation de longue durée / à long terme
long-term benefit

prestation (en cas) (de) maladie
sick(ness) / medical benefit

prestation de maladie-maternité
sickness-maternity benefit

prestation de maladie professionnelle
benefit in respect of occupational disease(s)

prestation marginale
marginal / fringe benefit

prestation marginale d'assistance en espèces (Denm.)
marginal cash assistance benefit

prestation (en cas) de maternité
maternity benefit

prestation de maternité en espèces
maternity cash benefit

prestation maximale / maximum supérieure
overall highest maximum benefit

prestation médicale
medical benefit; (pl.) medicare (Austr.)

prestation médicale en cas de maternité
maternity medical benefit

prestation minimale
minimum benefit

prestation mutualiste
mutual benefit

prestation en nature
benefit / payment in kind; non-cash benefit

prestation en nature de l'assurance maladie
health benefit in kind

prestation en nature de grande importance
major / substantial benefit in kind

prestation en nature de maladie ou de maternité
sickness or maternity benefit in kind

prestation obligatoire
statutory benefit

prestation des / pour orphelin(s)
orphan's benefit

prestation de parents (Icel.)
parents benefit

prestation payable
benefit due

prestation payée en une seule fois
benefit to be paid in a single amount

prestation autre que pécuniaire
non-cash benefit

prestation considérée aux fins de la pension
pensionable benefit

prestation de pension ajustée
adjusted pension benefit

prestation périodique
periodic / regular benefit

prestation périodique ajustée
periodically adjusted benefit

prestation périodique en espèces
periodical cash benefit

prestation pour personne(s) à charge
benefit for dependents, dependent's benefit

prestation pour personne indirectement à charge
secondary dependent's benefit

prestation positive
positive performance

prestation de préretraite
pre-retirement benefit

prestation principale
main benefit

prestation proportionnelle au salaire
earnings-related benefit

prestation non proportionnelle au salaire
benefit not related to earnings

prestation à titre provisionnel
benefit payable on a provisional basis

prestation du régime général
basic scheme benefit

prestation réglementaire de maladie (UK)
statutory sick pay

prestation réglementaire de maternité (UK)
statutory maternity pay

prestation de retraite
pension benefit

prestation calculée en fonction des revenus
income-related benefit

prestation non liée aux revenus
benefit not related to earnings

prestation liée aux revenus antérieurs
(previous) earnings-related (insurance) benefit

prestation liée à des risques
contingency benefit

prestations sanitaires
health care (services / delivery)

prestation de sécurité sociale
social security benefit / payment

prestation servie
benefit provided, paid out benefit

prestation servie de droit
benefit paid as of right

prestation servie par l'Etat
State benefit

prestation de services
provision of services; contribution in service; (pl.) service trades / delivery

prestation sociale
welfare payment; social (security / insurance) benefit; (pl.) welfare benefits

prestation sociale des comités d'entreprise
social benefit paid by works committees

prestation sociale directe de l'employeur
unfunded employment welfare benefit

prestation pour soins constants (Norw.)
attendance benefit

prestation de soins infirmiers
provision of nursing care

prestation de sortie
withdrawal benefit

prestation spéciale assistante maternelle (Fr.)
special benefit for day-care attendant

prestation supplémentaire
supplementary / additional benefit

prestation supplémentaire en espèces en cas d'invalidité
supplementary disability income benefit

prestation supplémentaire pour la famille
family supplement

prestation de survivant
survivor's / survivors' (Irel.) benefit

prestation à taux uniforme
flat-rate benefit

prestation pour taxe communale (UK)
community charge benefit

prestation pour taxe municipale (UK)
council tax benefit

prestation théorique
notional benefit

prestation de transition (Denm.)
transition benefit

prestation pour travail partagé
work sharing benefit

prestation de veuve
widow's benefit

prestation (de) vieillesse
old age benefit

prétendre au bénéfice d'une / de prestation(s)
to claim benefit

procédure de paiement des prestations
procedure for the payment of benefits

recalcul d'une prestation
recalculation of a benefit

recevoir des prestations
to draw benefits

recouvrement d'un droit à (des) prestations
recovery of a right to benefits

recouvrer le droit à (des) prestations
to requalify for / to recover the right to benefits

récupération des frais afférents au paiement des prestations
recovery of expenses incurred in the payment of benefits

récupération de prestations indues
recovery of benefits which were not due

réduire une prestation
to reduce a benefit

refuser une demande de prestation
to reject a claim for benefit; (occ.) to disallow benefit

refuser une prestation
to refuse a benefit

régime de / des prestations
benefit scheme; benefits provisions

régime à prestations définies
defined benefit scheme

régime de prestations pour enfants (UK)
child benefit scheme

relèvement du plafond des prestations
increase in benefit level

remplir les conditions d'ouverture des droits aux prestations
to be eligible for / to qualify for benefit, to satisfy the conditions for acquisition of the rights to benefits

reprise du service des prestations après suspension ou suppression
resumption of provision of benefits after suspension or withdrawal

rétablir une prestation
to resume a benefit

rétablissement du versement des prestations
reinstatement of benefits

retrait du droit aux prestations
disqualification for benefit

revalorisation des prestations
benefit adjustment, adjustment / revalorisation / uprating / upgrading of benefits

risques couverts et prestations attribuées
contingencies covered and benefits granted

service d'une prestation
provision / granting of a benefit; payment of a benefit

service des prestations à un titulaire à l'étranger
payment of benefits abroad

servir une prestation
to provide / to pay a benefit

structure des prestations
benefit structure

supplément de prestation
benefit supplement

suppression des prestations
withdrawal of benefits

supprimer une prestation
to discontinue a benefit

suspendre une prestation
to suspend a benefit

suspension d'une prestation
suspension of benefit

système d'ajustement des prestations
benefit adjustment system

système indirect de prestations médicales
indirect system / pattern of providing medical care

système de prestations lié au niveau des ressources
means-tested system of provision

système de prestations sanitaires
health delivery system

système de prestation de services de main-d'oeuvre
manpower delivery system

système de prestation des soins
health care (delivery) system

taux d'une prestation
level / rate of benefit

taux de prestations d'aide sociale
rate of welfare benefits, (occ.) welfare rate

taux de prestations familiales
rate of family benefits

taux de réduction des prestations
benefit withdrawal rate

taux d'utilisation des prestations par la population totale
beneficiary rate

taux d'utilisation des prestations par la population couverte
take-up rate

titulaire d'une prestation
benefit recipient

transformation de prestations
commutation / conversion of benefits

tutelle aux prestations familiales (Fr.)
control on family benefits

tutelle aux prestations sociales (Fr.)
control on social benefits

versement d'une prestation
payment of a benefit

verser une prestation
to pay a benefit

PRESTER
to work (Belg.)

PRÉSUMÉ
date présumée de l'accouchement
expected date of confinement

semaine présumée d'accouchement
expected week of confinement

PRÊT (n.)
loan

consentir / octroyer un prêt
to grant a loan

prêt d'aide au budget (UK)
budgeting loan

prêt à l'amélioration de l'habitat / du logement
loan for housing improvement

prêt bonifié
bonified loan

prêt conventionné
low-interest / subsidised loan

prêt en cours
outstanding loan

prêt étudiant
student loan

prêt à faible taux d'intérêt
low-interest loan

prêt d'honneur
loan on trust

prêt impayé
outstanding loan

prêt sans intérêt
interest-free loan

prêt aux jeunes ménages
loan for young couples

prêt au logement
home loan

prêt de main-d'oeuvre
labour detachment

prêt non remboursé
outstanding loan

prêt social
social loan

prêt subventionné
subsidised loan

prêt d'urgence (UK)
crisis loan

PRÉTENDRE
droit de prétendre à (être en)
to be eligible

pouvoir prétendre à une prestation
to become entitled to a benefit

prétendre à (pouvant)
eligible

prétendre à (pouvoir)
to be entitled

prétendre au bénéfice d'une / de prestation(s)
to claim benefit

prétendre à une retraite
to claim a pension

PRÉTENTION
claim

prétention salariale
salary / wage expectation; wage demand

PRÊTER
prêter son assistance
to assist

PRETIUM DOLORIS
(damages for) pain and suffering

PREUVE
evidence

charge de la preuve
burden of proof, onus of the proof

éléments / moyens de preuve
evidence

preuves écrites
documentary evidence

PRÉVALENCE
prévalence des maladies
prevalence of diseases

PRÉVALENT
maladie prévalente
prevalent disease

PRÉVALOIR
prévaloir (pouvoir se) de
to be entitled

prévaloir de droits acquis (se)
to claim benefit of acquired rights

PRÉVARICATION
breach of duty

PRÉVENTIF
médecine préventive
preventive medicine

mesure préventive
preventive measure

mesure préventive d'emploi
preventive employment measure

service préventif individuel
personal preventive service

soins préventifs
preventive care

PRÉVENTION
prevention; safety; prejudice

plan de prévention
prevention scheme

prévention des accidents
accident prevention

prévention des accidents du travail
(occ.) industrial safety

**prévention des accidents du travail et
des maladies professionnelles**
industrial / occupational health and safety

prévention des maladies
prevention of diseases

prévention des naissances
birth control

prévention primaire
primary prevention

service de prévention
preventive (health) service

PREVENTORIUM
tuberculosis sanatorium; preventive health
centre (Belg.)

PRÉVISION
forecast; projection; outlook

prévision des besoins
anticipation of needs

prévision démographique
population forecast

prévision en matière d'emploi
manpower forecast

prévisions des entreprises
business expectations

statistiques et prévisions d'emploi
employment statistics and estimates

PRÉVISIONNEL
predictive, proactive

approche prévisionnelle de l'emploi
manpower forecast approach

**données prévisionnelles sur les
professions**
occupational outlook information

engagement prévisionnel (de dépenses)
commitment

**étude prévisionnelle des besoins de
main-d'oeuvre dans l'entreprise**
company manpower planning, personnel
planning at establishment level

**évolution prévisionnelle de la main-
d'oeuvre**
occupational forecast

gestion prévisionnelle de l'emploi (GPE)
(enterprise) manpower planning

**gestion prévisionnelle de l'emploi dans
l'entreprise**
company manpower planning, personnel
planning at establishment level

gestion prévisionnelle du personnel
staff planning

schéma prévisionnel de l'apprentissage
appenticeship plan for the future

PRÉVOIR
to provide; to foresee

prévoir au contrat
to set forth in a contract

PRÉVOYANCE
caisse / fonds de prévoyance (sociale)
provident / contingency / welfare fund,
company life and disability insurance,
social insurance fund

institution de prévoyance
welfare institute

prévoyance et aide sociale
social relief and welfare

prévoyance sociale
(social) welfare

régime de prévoyance
provident / welfare scheme, welfare system

société de prévoyance
friendly society

PRÉVU
activité prévue
planned activity

conditions prévues (dans les)
on the conditions provided for

période d'emploi prévue
expected period of employment, period of expected employment

PRIMAIRE
actif primaire
primary worker; (pl.) primary labour force

activité primaire
primary activity

agent sanitaire primaire / de santé primaire
primary health worker

caisse primaire d'assurance maladie (CPAM) (Fr.)
local health fund

centre de soins primaires
primary care centre

école primaire
elementary / grade school; grammar school

effectif(s) de l'enseignement primaire
primary-school enrolment

emploi sur le marché primaire
mainstream job

enseignement primaire
primary education

incapacité de travail primaire (Belg.)
primary incapacity for work

industrie primaire
primary industry

marché primaire de l'emploi / du travail
mainstream / primary labour market

population active primaire
primary labour force

prévention primaire
primary prevention

professions intermédiaires de l'enseignement primaire [CITP-1988 (331)]
primary education teaching associate professionals [ISCO-1988 (331)]

secteur primaire
primary industry / sector

service de soins primaires
primary care service

service de soins de santé primaire
primary health care service

soins médicaux primaires
primary medical care

soins primaires
primary care

soins de santé primaire
primary health care

travailleurs du marché primaire de l'emploi
primary labour force, mainstream workers

travailleur primaire
primary-level worker

travailleur sanitaire primaire
primary health worker

PRIME
premium (pay / payment); extra pay; bonus, grant, allowance; indemnity; gratuity; incentive; rate (ins.)

assurance à prime
premium insurance

barème des primes
schedule of premiums

droit à une prime (avoir)
to be eligible for a grant

droit à une prime de rapatriement
entitlement to repatriation grant

exonération du paiement des primes
waiver of premiums

prime d'accouchement
confinement grant; (occ.) maternity benefit

prime d'accouchement à domicile (UK)
home confinement grant

prime d'adoption (Belg.)
adoption grant

prime d'allaitement
nursing allowance

prime d'ancienneté
longevity / seniority pay / bonus

prime d'assiduité
attendance bonus

prime d'assistance
assistance grant

prime d'assurance
insurance premium

prime d'astreinte
on-call / stand-by pay

prime de connaissances linguistiques
language allowance / bonus

prime de déménagement
moving / removal / relocation allowance

prime de départ
severance pay / payment; (occ.) golden
handshake

prime de départ volontaire
voluntary leaving premium

prime de difficulté de vie
hardship allowance

prime d'éloignement
isolated post allowance

prime d'encouragement
incentive award / bonus

prime d'entrée dans les classes (Fr.)
allowance on entering the classes

prime d'équipement (Fr.)
equipment allowance

prime exceptionnelle
exceptional / special bonus

prime d'expatriation
expatriation allowance / bonus, over-seas
premium / allowance

prime familiale (Malta)
family bonus

prime de fin d'année
Christmas / end-of-year bonus

prime de grossesse (Icel.)
pregnancy subsidy

prime d'habillement
clothing allowance; (occ.) allowance for
wear and tear (of clothing)

prime d'heures supplémentaires
premium for extra duty, overtime pay

prime d'incitation
incentive bonus

prime d'insalubrité
allowance for unhealthy working
conditions

prime d'installation
installation / settling-in grant

prime d'intempéries
bad weather allowance / payment

prime d'intéressement
profit-sharing bonus; wage dividend

prime d'isolement
isolation pay

prime de langue
language allowance / bonus

prime de licenciement
severance pay / payment

prime linguistique
language allowance / bonus

prime de mariage
marriage grant / gratuity

prime de maternité (UK)
maternity grant / payment

prime de mobilité (UK)
mobility grant / allowance

prime de naissance
maternity / (child)birth grant / allowance / premium

prime de nuit
night shift premium

prime d'objectif
objectives bonus

prime de panier
meal(s) allowance

prime de pénibilité
hardship allowance; heavy work bonus

prime de poste
shift premium / differential

prime de présentéisme
well pay

prime à la qualification (Fr.)
skills allowance

prime de rapatriement
repatriation grant

prime de réinstallation
relocation grant

prime de rendement
efficiency / output / productivity / production / incentive bonus; incentive pay / award

prime de repas
meal(s) allowance

prime de répétitivité
bonus for repetitive work

prime liée aux résultats
performance-related bonus

prime de risque
hazard pay; danger money

prime de salissure
dirty allowance, dirty work pay

prime de secrétariat
secretarial allowance

prime semestrielle
half-yearly bonus

prime de stimulation
incentive award / bonus

prime de sujétion
hardship allowance

prime de transport
transport allowance

prime de vacances
holiday / vacation bonus, holiday allowance, vacation pay (USA)

prime de vie chère
cost-of-living allowance

prime de zone dangereuse
danger zone bonus

régime de primes de rendement
incentive bonus scheme

système de primes
bonus scheme

système de primes échelonnées
scaled premium system

système de primes d'encouragement
bonus incentive scheme

PRIMO-DEMANDEUR
primo-demandeur d'emploi
first(-time) job seeker, new entrant on the labour market

PRIMO-ENTRANT
new entrant on the labour market

PRINCIPAL
allocation principale
principal allowance

agent principal
senior officer

commis principal
principal / senior clerk

conseiller principal
senior adviser

entrepreneur principal
principal contractor

exploitant principal
main farmer

médecin principal
senior medical officer

mission principale d'un poste
main job duty

prestation principale
main benefit

principal apporteur de revenus
main / principal (wage) earner, primary earner

principal lieu d'affectation
main duty station

principal soutien économique
primary / principal (wage) earner

professeur principal
principal teacher

profession principale
primary occupation

source principale de revenu
primary / principal (wage) earner

superviseur principal
senior supervisor

PRINCIPE
principle

accord de principe
agreement in principle

approbation de principe
approval in principle

décision de principe
policy decision

déclaration de principe
policy statement

principe d'accélération
acceleration principle

principes actuariels équitables (selon des)
on an actuarial fair basis

principe d'assurance
insurance principle

principe de base
basic principle

principe directeur
basic principle; (pl.) policy considerations / guidelines, guidelines, policy

principe de l'égalité de traitement
principle of equal treatment

principe du mérite
merit principle

principe de la personnalité
rule that a person is governed by his personal law

principe de proportion
principle of proportionality

principe de recouvrement
recovery policy

principe de la répartition
(occ.) assessment

principe de la territorialité
rule of territoriality

principe à travail égal, salaire égal
equal pay for equal work principle

PRIORITAIRE
emploi prioritaire
preferential employment

groupe prioritaire
priority / target group

programme d'action prioritaire (Fr.)
priority action programme

zone d'éducation prioritaire (ZEP)
zone of educational priority (ZEP)

PRIORITÉ
carte de priorité
priority card

priorité d'emploi / de l'emploi
preferential access to employment, prior right of employment

priorité de réembauche
re(-)hiring priority, recall rights

PRISE
début de la prise en charge
commencement of benefit(s)

délai de prise en charge
period of liability for compensation

durée de la prise en charge
duration of benefit, benefit duration

heure de prise de service
starting time

participation pour prise en charge exceptionnelle
contribution for exceptional expenses

participation à la prise de décisions
co-determination

période de prise en charge
period of coverage / of compensation,
duration of benefit(s)

prise en charge
compensation; acceptance of
responsibility; reimbursement; defrayal,
defrayment; liability; benefit(s)

prise en charge intégrale / totale
full payment; total subsidisation

prise d'effet
entry into effect

prise d'emploi / de fonctions
appointment, assumption of duty / of
office

prise de participation
equity stake

prise de position
policy statement

prise de position dans une négociation
bargaining position

PRISON
service social des prisons
social work in penal institutions

PRISONNIER
prisonnier de guerre
war prisoner

PRIVATION
deprivation; loss; hardship

indemnité pour privation de jouissance
compensation for loss of property

PRIVATISER
to privatise

PRIVÉ (adj.)
personal, private; voluntary

agence de placement privée
private employment agency

assurance privée
commercial insurance

assurance-vie privée
(occ.) non-occupational coverage

bureau privé de placement
private employment agency

chambre privée (hosp.)
amenity bed

chambre privée ou semi-privée (hosp.) (Can.)
preferred accommodation

clientèle privée (des médecins)
private practice

clinique privée
private clinic

collège privé (UK)
public school

Conseil privé du Roi (Norw.)
King in Council

disposition prise à titre privé
private arrangement

école privée
private school

emploi dans le / du secteur privé
private (sector) employment

employeur du secteur privé
private sector employer

enseignement privé
private education

entreprise privée
private enterprise

établissement de bienfaisance privé
private charitable agency / charity

établissement privé
private institution

hôpital privé
voluntary / private hospital

initiative privée
voluntary effort

institution sociale privée
private / voluntary welfare agency

ménage privé
private household

oeuvre privée
voluntary agency; private charity

oeuvre sociale privée
private / voluntary welfare agency

organisme privé
voluntary body

organisme social privé
private / voluntary welfare agency

pension au titre d'un régime privé
private pension

propriété privée
private ownership

régime de pensions privé, régime privé
de retraite
private pension plan

régime de retraite complémentaire privé
private / contracted-out occupational
pension scheme

régime de retraite complémentaire privé
en gestion directe
self-administered pension scheme

secteur privé
business / private sector

service privé de placement
private employment service

soins en établissement privé
private care

supplément pour chambre privée
extra charge for private room

travailleur du secteur privé
private worker

PRIVER
to deprive

enfant privé d'affection
emotionally deprived child

priver du droit de faire qqch
to estop from doing something

PRIVILÉGIÉ
emploi privilégié
preferred employment

producteurs de soins privilégiés
preferred providers organisation (PPO)

salaire privilégié
premium wage

PRIX
price; charge, rate

ajusté / corrigé selon l'évolution des prix
adjusted for price changes

éventail de prix
price range

exprimé en prix constants
deflated
fourchette / gamme de prix
price range

indice des prix
price index

indice des prix à la consommation
consumer / retail price index

main-d'oeuvre à bas prix
cheap labour

mécanisme de formation des prix
price mechanism

modulé selon l'évolution des prix
adjusted for price changes

politique des prix
pricing policy

prix à la consommation
consumer price

prix coûtant
cost price

prix de détail
retail price

prix forfaitaire
overhead price

prix de journée (Fr.)
charge by the day, daily rate

prix de la main-d'oeuvre
labour price

prix d'offre de la main-d'oeuvre
supply price of labour

prix de revient
cost price

spirale des prix
price spiral

spirale des salaires et des prix
wage/price spiral

PROBABILITÉ
probabilité de cessation d'activité
probability of separation from the labour
force

probabilité d'entrée en activité
probability of accession to the labour force

probabilité de mortalité
probability of dying

probabilité de survie
probability of surviving

PROBABILISTE
sondage probabiliste
random sampling

PROBATOIRE
période probatoire
qualifying period; probation (period), trial
/ probationary period

PROBLÈME
problème d'intégration au marché du
travail
labour market entry difficulty

PROCÉDÉ
industries appliquant des procédés de
fabrication en continu
flow process industries

procédé à facteur travail prédominant
labour-intensive technology

**procédés et méthodes de production
(PMP)**
process and production methods (PPM)

PROCÉDURE
procedure; (pl.) (occ.) machinery

intenter une procédure disciplinaire
to institute disciplinary proceedings

non-respect de la procédure
procedural default / breach

procédure d'admission
admission / entitlement procedure

procédure d'admission à l'aide sociale
social assistance entitlement procedure

procédure d'agrément de l'entreprise
accreditation procedure for firms

procédure d'alerte
warning procedure

procédure de conciliation
conciliation arrangement / procedure

procédure de conciliation et d'arbitrage
conciliation and arbitration procedure

procédure contentieuse
litigation procedure

procédure de contrainte
coercive measures / action

procédure disciplinaire
disciplinary procedure / proceedings

procédure d'entrée
admission procedure

procédure gracieuse
non-contentious proceedings / procedure

procédure de licenciement
dismissal procedure

procédure de litige
litigation procedure

procédure de mise à pied
lay-off procedure

procédure de paiement des prestations
procedure for the payment of benefits

procédure paritaire de conciliation
joint conciliation procedure

procédure de promotion
promotion procedure

procédure prud'homale (Fr.)
procedure before an industrial tribunal

procédure de recours
complaints / grievance procedure

procédure de recrutement
selection / recruitment procedure

procédure en référé prud'homal
emergency interim proceedings for labour disputes

procédure de règlement d'un conflit social
(industrial) dispute procedure
procédure régulière conforme à la loi
due process of law

procédure de remboursement des dépenses
expense claim procedure

procédure de sélection
selection procedure

PROCÈS-VERBAL
procès-verbal de conciliation
minutes of conciliation

procès-verbal de désaccord
minutes of failure to agree

PROCESSUS
processus d'apprentissage
learning process

processus de (la) réadaptation
rehabilitation process

processus de recrutement
recruitment process

processus de sélection du personnel
staff selection process

PROCHE
famille proche
close relatives / relations

proche parent
close relative

PRO-CONJONCTUREL
pro-cyclical

PROCRÉER
femme en âge de procréer
woman of child-bearing age

PRO-CYCLIQUE
pro-cyclical

PRODUCTEUR (adj.)
activité productrice de recettes
income-producing / revenue-producing / income-generating / revenue-generating activity

industrie productrice de biens d'équipement
capital goods industry

PRODUCTEUR (n.)
producer

producteurs de soins privilégiés
preferred providers organisation (PPO)

PRODUCTIF
carrière productive
productive career

emploi / tâche / travail productif(ive)
productive employment, production job

travailleur productif
productive worker

PRODUCTION
production; output

agents de production
productive labour

biens de production
producer goods

cadence de production
production rate

capacité de production
productive capacity

capacité de production excédentaire
excess (plant) capacity

capacité de production inutilisée
idle capacity

chaîne de production
production / assembly line

coût de production
production cost

facteur de production
production factor; input

fonction de production
production function

formation sans production
out-of-production training

main-d'oeuvre à la production
productive labour

moyens de production
means of production

organisation de la production
production engineering

ouvrier à la production
production worker

potentiel de production
productive capacity

procédés et méthodes de production (PMP)
process and production methods (PPM)

production à la chaîne
line production

production en discontinu
batch production

production en flux tendus
just-in-time production

production imputée de services d'assurance-dommages
imputed service charge for casualty insurance

production imputée de services d'assurance-vie
imputed service charge for life insurance

production imputée de services de caisses de pension
imputed service charge for pension funds

production au plus juste
lean production

production juste à temps
just-in-time production

production de masse / en (grande) série
large-scale / mass production

ralentissement de la production
slowing down of work, work slow-down

rythme de production
production rate

salaire de la production réelle
real product wage

secteur de production
line of production

secteur de la production des services
service-producing sector

socialisation des moyens de production
socialisation of the means of production

taux de production normalisé
standard rate of production

taux d'utilisation des capacités de production
rate of capacity utilisation

travailleur extérieur à la production
non-production worker

travailleur à la / de la production
production employee / worker

PRODUCTIVITÉ
productivity

accords de productivité
productivity bargaining / deal

accroissement de la productivité
productivity increase

écart des salaires par rapport à la productivité
real wage gap

gain de productivité
productivity gain

hausse de la productivité
productivity increase

productivité horaire de la main-d'oeuvre
hourly productivity of labour

productivité de la main-d'oeuvre
productivity of labour, labour productivity

productivité de la population active
productivity of the labour force

productivité du travail
labour productivity

rémunération liée à la productivité
productivity payment

PRODUIRE
manque à produire
foregone output

PRODUIT (n.)
product; commodity; output; returns, proceeds

produit sous cachet (Fr.)
pharmaceutical product to be made up by the chemist

produit de l'impôt
tax proceeds / receipt

produit intérieur brut (PIB)
Gross Domestic Product (GDP)

produit marginal du travail
marginal product of labour

produit national brut (PNB)
Gross National Product (GNP)

produit pharmaceutique
pharmaceutical product, medicament, drug

produit de la rente
returns on the pension

PROFESSEUR
teacher

professeur certifié
certified teacher

professeur d'école normale
teacher of a college of education; (occ.) teacher(-)educator

professeur d'orientation (Malta)
guidance teacher

professeur principal
principal teacher

professeur de service social
social work teacher

professeurs de l'enseignement secondaire [CITP-1968 (232)]
secondary education teaching professionals [ISCO-1988 (232)]

professeurs d'université et d'établissements d'enseignement supérieur [CITP-1988 (231)]
college, university and higher education teaching professionals [ISCO-1988 (231)

PROFESSION
job, employment; occupation; profession; branch of economic activity; industry

analyse des professions
occupational analysis; (occ.) occupational distribution / composition / pattern

analyse des professions et métiers
occupational and trade analysis

autre profession
alternative / alternate employment, replacement job

autres professions intermédiaires de l'enseignement [CITP-1988 (334)]
other teaching associate professionals [CITP-1988 (334)]

autres professions intermédiaires [CITP-1988 (34)]
other associate professionals [ISCO-1988 (34)]

catégorie de professions
type of occupations

catégorie des professions libérales
professional category

changement de profession
change of occupation

choix de profession
career decision / options, occupational /
career / vocational choice

déséquilibre dans les professions
occupational imbalance

**données prévisionnelles sur les
professions**
occupational outlook information

épouse sans profession
housewife

exercice de la profession infirmière
nursing practice

grande profession
core occupation

groupe de professions
job family

inégalité d'accès aux professions
occupational segregation

information sur les professions
occupational / vocational information

initiation à la profession
pre-vocational training; vocational
preparation

membre d'une profession libérale
professional (worker)

mortalité par profession
occupational mortality

non-salarié des professions agricoles
self-employed agricultural worker

non-salarié des professions artisanales
self-employed handicraft worker

placement par profession
placement by occupation

pratique d'une profession
professional practice

profession (de)
professional

profession agricole
agricultural profession

profession ambulante
itinerant trade

profession artisanale
manual trade

profession de cadre supérieur
senior management occupation

profession civile
civilian occupation

profession commerciale
commercial profession

profession désignée
designated occupation

profession désuète
obsolete occupation

**professions et emplois d'accès
réglementé**
restricted occupations

profession envisagée
intended occupation

**profession en excédent de main-
d'oeuvre**
surplus occupation

**professions du forestage et assimilées
[CITP-1988 (614)]**
forestry and related workers [ISCO-1988
(614)]

profession à forte demande
high demand occupation

profession habituelle
usual occupation

**profession habituellement exercée par
des hommes**
(occ.) male-dominated occupation

**profession de haute qualification /
spécialisation / hautement spécialisée**
highly skilled / higher-skill / qualified
occupation

professions indépendantes (les)
professions (the)

professions industrielles et commerciales
industry and trade

profession infirmière
nursing profession

professions intellectuelles et scientifiques [CITP-1988 (2)]
professionals [ISCO-1988 (2)]

professions intermédiaires [CITP-1988 (3)]
technical and associate professionals [ISCO-1988 (3)]

professions intermédiaires de l'administration publique des douanes et des impôts, et assimilés [CITP-1988 (3-44)]
customs, tax and related government associate professionals [CITP-1988 (344)]

professions intermédiaires de la création artistique, du spectacle et du sport [CITP-1988 (347)]
artistic, entertainment and sports associate professions [ISCO-1988 (347)]

professions intermédiaires de l'éducation des handicapés [CITP-1988 (3-33)]
special education teaching associate professionals [ISCO-1988 (333)]

professions intermédiaires de l'enseignement [CITP-1988 (33)]
teaching associate professionals [ISCO-1988 (33)]

professions intermédiaires de l'enseignement préprimaire [CITP-1988)]
pre-primary education teaching associate professionals [ISCO-1988 (332)]

professions intermédiaires de l'enseignement primaire [CITP-1988 (331)]
primary education teaching associate professionals [ISCO-1988 (331)]

professions intermédiaires des finances et de la vente [CITP-1988 (341)]
finance and sales associate professionals [ISCO-1988 (341)]

professions intermédiaires de la gestion administrative [CITP-1988 (344)]
administrative associate professionals [ISCO-1988 (343)]

professions intermédiaires de la médecine moderne (à l'exception du personnel infirmier) [ISCO-1988 (322)]
modern health associate professionals (except nursing) [ISCO-1988 (322)]

professions intermédiaires des sciences physiques et techniques [CITP-1988 (31)]
physical and engineering science associate professionals [ISCO-1988 (31)]

professions intermédiaires des sciences de la vie et de la santé [CITP-1988 (32)]
life science and health associate professionals [ISCO-1988 (32)]

professions intermédiaires du travail social [CITP-1988 (346)]
social work associate professionals [ISCO-1988 (346)]

profession libérale
independent / learned / liberal profession, professional occupation / job; (pl.) professions

profession de manoeuvre
labouring occupation

profession de médecin / médicale
medical profession

profession ou métier
profession or trade

profession paramédicale
paramedical profession

profession pénible
arduous occupation

profession en pénurie de main-d'oeuvre
shortage occupation, occupation in short supply

profession à prédominance masculine
male-dominated occupation

profession principale
primary occupation

profession de rechange
alternative / alternate employment

profession recherchée
demand occupation

profession reclassée
transferred occupation

profession reconnue
recognised occupation

profession réglementée
regulated occupation

profession salariée
gainful occupation

profession de santé
health (care) profession

professions scientifiques, techniques, libérales et assimilées
(occ.) professionals

profession du secteur tertiaire
service occupation; (pl.) service trades

profession des / dans le domaine / dans le secteur des services
service occupation; (pl.) service trades

profession de spécialisation moyenne
semi-skilled / medium-skilled occupation

profession de spécialisation réduite
low-skilled occupation

profession spécialisée
skilled / trained occupation

profession non spécialisée
unskilled occupation

profession peu spécialisée
low-skilled occupation

profession non traditionnelle
non-traditional job

profession de niveau universitaire
graduate occupation / profession

profil des professions
occupational profile

répartition par branche d'activité et par profession
industrial and occupational composition

revalorisation des professions
upgrading of occupations

situation dans la profession
employment / industrial / occupational / work status, position in industry, work situation, status in employment

structure des professions / professionnelle
occupational structure / distribution / composition / pattern

système de classification des professions
occupational classification system

taux de croissance des professions
occupational growth rate

travailleurs ne pouvant être classés selon la profession [CITP-1968 (X)]
workers not classifiable by occupation [ISCO-1968 (X)]

travailleurs n'ayant déclaré aucune profession [CITP-1968 (X-3)]
workers not reporting any occupation [ISCO-1968 (X-3)]

travailleurs ayant fait au sujet de leur profession une déclaration imprécise ou insuffisante [CITP-1968 (X-2)]
workers reporting occupations unidentifiable or inadequately described [ISCO-1968 (X-2)]

travailleur employé dans les professions de santé
health worker

usages de la profession
professional practices

PROFESSIONNALISATION
occupational relevance; vocationalisation

PROFESSIONNALISME
workmanship

PROFESSIONNEL (adj.)
occupational, vocational; professional; industrial

abandon de l'activité professionnelle
cessation of the employment

accident non professionnel
non-occupational / non-industrial accident

accord professionnel
labour agreement

acte professionnel (Fr.)
medical treatment

action pour la défense des intérêts professionnels
(occ.) industrial action

activité professionnelle
occupation, gainful activity / occupation, occupational / professional / vocational work, employment

activité professionnelle du conjoint
working status of the spouse

activité professionnelle véritablement rémunératrice
substantially gainful occupation

âge minimal d'activité professionnelle
minimum active working age

agent d'orientation professionnelle
career guidance officer

aide à la mobilité professionnelle
occupational mobility incentive

allocation d'assistance à la formation professionnelle (RFA)
vocational assistance allowance (Ger.)

allocation pour déclassement professionnel
allowance for lowered standard of occupation

antécédents professionnels
employment / track record, occupational / employment / job / career / work history, past experience, (previous) work experience; work background

aptitude professionnelle
job / work / vocational skill, occupational aptitude

artiste professionnel
entertainer

aspiration professionnelle
career aspiration / expectation

assimilation d'un acte professionnel (Fr.)
assimilation of medical treatment

association professionnelle
industrial board / association, professional / trade association, trade guild, professional organisation / body

assurance (contre les) accidents du travail et les maladies professionnelles
industrial injury / injuries insurance, insurance against accident at work; employers' liability insurance; compensation scheme; accident insurance

assurance-déplacement professionnel
travel accident insurance

assurance (contre les) maladies professionnelles
insurance against occupational disease

atelier d'objectif professionnel pour demandeurs d'emploi (Belg.)
vocational objectives workshop for jobseekers

attente professionnelle
occupational expectation

avancement professionnel
career progress / path / advancement, professional advancement

bilan professionnel
vocational assessment

bourse de formation professionnelle
vocational training grant

branche professionnelle
occupation(al) sector, sector of industry

brevet d'enseignement professionnel (BEP) (Fr.)
certificate of vocational education

brevet d'études professionnelles agricoles (BEPA) (Fr.)
certificate of agricultural vocational education

but professionnel
occupational goal; vocational development objective; career objective / goal

caisse de compensation pour les accidents du travail et les maladies professionnelles
(occ.) workmen's compensation board

calcul de l'expérience professionnelle
reckoning of professional experience

capacité professionnelle
work skill, professional ability

capacité professionnelle réduite
reduced occupational capacity

catégorie professionnelle
occupation(al) group / category, job class;
class of worker

centre de formation professionnelle
vocational (training) centre

certificat d'aptitude professionnelle
certificate of competence, qualification /
occupational / trade proficiency / craft
certificate

certificat d'aptitude professionnelle
agricole (CAPA) (Fr.)
certificate of agricultural competence

certificat médical d'aptitude
professionnelle
occupational medical certificate

certificat professionnel
certificate of competence, qualification /
occupational certificate

cesser toute activité professionnelle
to drop out of / to leave the labour force; to
leave work

chambres professionnelle
business chamber

choix de l'activité professionnelle
choice of job, job choice

choix professionnels
career decision / options, occupational /
career / vocational choice

classification professionnelle
occupational classification

code d'éthique professionnelle
code of ethics / of behaviour

comité régional de formation
professionnelle (Fr.)
regional vocational training committee

compétence professionnelle
vocational / occupational skill,
employment / occupational / professional
qualification

comportement professionnel
employment behaviour; performance on
the job, job performance

composition professionnelle
occupational distribution / composition /
pattern

compte économique de la formation
professionnelle (Fr.)
vocational training economic account

conflit professionnel
labour / industrial / trade dispute

Conseil des pensions professionnelles
(UK)
Occupational Pensions Board

conseiller en / d'orientation
professionnelle
vocational (guidance) counsellor, career
officer

conseiller professionnel
careers adviser

consultation d'orientation
professionnelle
vocational counselling

contrat d'adaptation professionnelle
(Belg.)
vocational adaptation contract

contrat d'adaptation professionnelle
pour personnes handicapées (Belg.)
vocational adaptation contract for the
disabled

contrat de formation professionnelle
vocational training contract

convention de formation professionnelle
vocational training agreement

cours d'initiation / d'intégration
professionnelle
induction training / course, beginners'
course

décès dû à un accident du travail ou à
une maladie professionnelle
death from employment (injury)

déchéance professionnelle
professional disability

défendre les intérêts professionnels
to protect occupational interests

déformation professionnelle
job conditioning

dégager des obligations professionnelles
to release from work

dénomination / désignation professionnelle
professional description

deuxième activité professionnelle
second job

développement professionnel
staff development

devoir professionnel
official duty

discrimination professionnelle
occupational segregation

durée moyenne de la vie professionnelle
mean duration of working life

durée de la vie professionnelle
(duration of) working life

école professionnelle
training / trade / vocational school

éducation professionnelle
vocational education

égalité professionnelle (femmes-hommes)
equal opportunities for women and men at work

enseignement professionnel
vocational education

enseignement technique et formation professionnelle
vocational and technical education and training (VOTEC)

éthique professionnelle
professional code of ethics

étude de l'historique professionnel
career follow-up / career pattern study

évaluation professionnelle
vocational assessment

évolution professionnelle
occupational development

examen d'orientation professionnelle
vocational testing

examen professionnel
trade examination

exercer une activité professionnelle
to engage in an occupation, to hold a job

exigence professionnelle
skill requirement; (pl.) occupational requirements

exode de l'élite professionnelle
migration of highly trained personnel

expérience professionnelle
professional / job / work experience; work history

expérience professionnelle antérieure
past / previous (work) experience; work background; employment history

faute professionnelle
professional misconduct, malpractice

filière professionnelle
occupational career path

formation professionnelle
vocational education; occupational / vocational / job / skill training; professional education / training; skills development

formation professionnelle accélérée
accelerated / intensive vocational training

formation professionnelle des adultes
adult occupational training

formation professionnelle de base
basic job training

formation professionnelle continue
ongoing vocational training

formation professionnelle auprès d'une entreprise
vocational training with a company

formation professionnelle générale
generic skill training, general vocational training / education

formation professionnelle initiale
initial vocational training

formation professionnelle initiale agricole (Fr.)
initial agricultural vocational training

formation professionnelle spécialisée
occupational skills training, specialised vocational training

frais professionnels
professional expenses

gêne professionnelle
vocational disablement

grade professionnel
service grade

grand groupe professionnel
broad occupational group

groupe professionnel
occupational group / class; (occ.) industry, branch of economic activity

hygiène professionnelle
occupational health

incapacité professionnelle
incapacity for work in one's profession; occupational invalidity / disablement, vocational disablement

incompatibilité professionnelle
professional disqualification

indemnité de frais professionnels
professional expenditure allowance

infirmité professionnelle
occupational / vocational disablement

information professionnelle
vocational orientation

initiation aux techniques professionnelles
work-skill training

initiation à la vie professionnelle
introductory training to working life

insatisfaction professionnelle
job dissatisfaction

insertion professionnelle
vocational integration; integration into employment; job entry

instrument d'orientation professionnelle
vocational counselling tool

intégration professionnelle
vocational integration

intégrité professionnelle
professional integrity

intérêt professionnel
occupational interest

intoxication d'origine professionnelle
vocational poisoning

invalidité professionnelle
occupational disability

lésion professionnelle
employment injury

liste de maladies professionnelles
list of professional diseases

locaux professionnels
work / business premises

lycée professionnel
vocational upper secondary school

maladies et lésions d'origine professionnelle
work-related / occupational diseases and injuries

maladie professionnelle
occupational illness, industrial / occupational / professional disease

maladie non professionnelle
non-occupational disease

maladie professionnelle indemnisée
occupational disease for which the benefit has been awarded

maladie professionnelle reconnue
prescribed industrial disease

manque de compétences professionnelles
lack of occupational skills

mesure d'incitation à l'exercice d'une activité professionnelle
(occ.) in-work benefit

milieu professionnel
occupational environment

mobilité professionnelle
job / occupational / professional / inter-occupation mobility; occupational change

morale professionnelle
professional ethics

mortalité professionnelle
occupational mortality

motivation professionnelle
motivation to work, job motivation

niveau de compétence professionnelle
occupational proficiency level

norme professionnelle
occupational standard / norm

objectif professionnel
occupational goal; vocational development objective; career objective / goal

option professionnelle
occupational alternative

ordre professionnel
professional association / body

organisation professionnelle
professional / industrial organisation; workers' and employers' organisation

organisme professionnel
professional body

organisme de réglementation professionnelle
professional licensing authority

orientation professionnelle
career / careers guidance / education, career(s) advice / counselling, job counselling / orientation, occupational counselling / guidance, vocational guidance / counselling

orientation professionnelle des adultes
adult vocational counselling

orientation professionnelle informatisée
computerised vocational guidance

orientation professionnelle personnalisée
personal career counselling

orienteur professionnel
(vocational) guidance counsellor

ouvrier professionnel
skilled / craft worker

pathologie professionnelle
occupational pathology / medicine

pension professionnelle
company / occupational pension

perfectionnement professionnel
career / job development; in-service (educational) training; on-site / on-the-job training / learning, further vocational training, occupational / skill up-grading, vocational development

personnel professionnel
professional personnel, trained workers

plan de perfectionnement professionnel
vocational development plan

polyvalence professionnelle des travailleurs
occupational flexibility of the workers

position professionnelle
job status

pratiques professionnelles
work practices

pré-formation professionnelle
occupational pre-training

préparation (à la vie) professionnelle
(pre-)vocational training

prestation pour décès professionnel
industrial death benefit

prestation pour lésion ou maladie professionnelle
injury benefit (UK, Irel., Malta), industrial injury / employment injury benefit

prestation de maladie professionnelle
benefit in respect of occupational disease(s)

profil d'aptitudes professionnelles
occupational aptitude pattern

profil professionnel déterminé
specific vocational profile

progression professionnelle
career progress / path

projet professionnel
career objective

promotion professionnelle
job upgrading, vocational advancement

qualification professionnelle
occupational skill, employment /
occupational / vocational qualification

qualification professionnelle reconnue
recognised vocational qualification

rang professionnel
professional / work status

réadaptation professionnelle
vocational / job / occupational / industrial /
employment rehabilitation

**réadaptation professionnelle des
travailleurs invalides**
vocational rehabilitation of the disabled

reclassement professionnel
occupational reintegration

recyclage professionnel
(professional / occupational / vocational)
retraining, vocational upgrading; booster
training; reskilling, updating of skills

rééducation professionnelle
occupational therapy, vocational /
employment rehabilitation, occupational /
professional / vocational retraining

**régime légal complémentaire
professionnel**
occupation statutory complementary
scheme

régime professionnel
corporate / industrial scheme, occupational
plan / scheme

régime professionnel de retraite
occupational pension / company pension
plan / scheme

**régime de retraite professionnelle
(complémentaire) (UK)**
occupational pension scheme

**réinsertion / réintégration
professionnelle**
vocational / occupational reintegration, re-
entry (into the labour force)

relations professionnelles
labour / job / industrial relations; labour-
management relations

**relations professionnelles adversatives /
antagoniques**
adversarial industrial relations

rente de maladie professionnelle
pension for / in respect of an occupational
disease

réorientation professionnelle
career shift

**réparation des accidents du travail et
des maladies professionnelles**
workmen's compensation (for industrial
injuries and professional diseases)

répartition par catégorie professionnelle
industrial and occupational composition

retour à la vie professionnelle
reintegration into / return to / re-entry into
working life

**retraite professionnelle
(complémentaire)**
company / occupational pension

réussite professionnelle
career achievement, job success

revenus professionnels
occupational income / earnings, earned
income

risque professionnel
occupational hazard / risk

santé professionnelle
occupational health

satisfaction professionnelle
job / work satisfaction

secret professionnel
professional secrecy / privilege

secteur professionnel
occupational field / area / sector

sécurité professionnelle
occupational safety

ségrégation professionnelle
occupational segregation

ségrégation professionnelle fondée sur le sexe
sex-based occupational segregation

service d'orientation professionnelle
career counselling service, employment advisory service

service d'orientation professionnelle spécialisée
specialised vocational guidance service

service professionnel
professional service

service de réadaptation professionnelle
vocational rehabilitation service

situation professionnelle
employment / industrial / occupational / work status, position in industry, work situation, status in employment

situation professionnelle actuelle
current employment status

stage de formation professionnelle
occupational / skill / vocational course

stage d'initiation à la vie professionnelle (SIVP)
work experience programme

stage d'insertion à la vie professionnelle
integration to working life course
stage d'intégration professionnelle
induction course

stage de préparation à la vie professionnelle
vocational preparation course

stage de réadaptation professionnelle
occupational rehabilitation course

statut professionnel
industrial / professional / employment / occupational / work status, position in industry, status in employment, work situation

structure professionnelle
occupational structure / distribution / composition / pattern

syndicat professionnel
professional organisation / association; industrial association; occupational union; craft / horizontal union

système d'orientation professionnelle informatisé
computer-based career orientation system

(système de) rapport d'appréciation du comportement professionnel
performance evaluation report (system)

tableau des maladies professionnelles
table of occupational diseases

taux de maladies professionnelles
occupational illness rate

taux de mortalité par suite de maladie professionnelle
occupational fatality rate

taxe professionnelle
occupation tax

titre professionnel
occupational certification

travail professionnel
workmanship

travail social professionnel
professional social work

travailleur professionnel
(occ.) trained worker

travailleur professionnel qualifié
skilled / trained / qualified worker; skilled craftsman; professional

travailleur social professionnel
professional social worker

valorisation professionnelle
staff development; upgrading

victime d'une maladie professionnelle
person who contracts an occupational disease

vie professionnelle
working / professional life

PROFESSIONNEL (n.)
skilled / professional worker

professionnel hautement qualifié
highly skilled professional employee

professionnel qualifié
(occ.) low-level technician

professionnel de la santé
health worker / practitioner / professional
(worker), health care worker

PROFESSORAL
corps professoral
teaching profession

PROFIL
profile, pattern; cross section

**candidat correspondant au profil
recherché / requis**
suitable candidate

**candidat n'ayant pas le profil recherché
/ requis**
unsuitable candidate

établissement d'un profil professionnel
vocational assessment

profil d'aptitudes professionnelles
occupational aptitude pattern

profil de carrière
career pattern / profile

profil des compétences
skill profile

profil d'emploi
employment profile

profil de l'emploi / des emplois
job / occupational characteristic

profil de poste
job profile; personnel specification

profil du poste
job / occupational characteristic

profil des professions
occupational profile

profil professionnel déterminé
specific vocational profile

profil de qualifications
skill profile

profil sanitaire
health profile (of a country)

PROFIT
profit; (pl.) returns

centre de profit
profit centre

pillage par les profits
profit piracy

profit net
net / retained profit

PROFOND
arriéré profond
profoundly / severely mentally retarded

cause profonde
underlying cause

débile / déficient (mental) profond
profoundly / severely mentally retarded

invalide profond
severely disabled

PROGRAMMATION
programming

programmation commune
joint programming

programmation sociale
social programming

PROGRAMME
programme, scheme; schedule
accès à un programme
access to / entry into a scheme

activité hors programme (ed.)
extra-curricular activity

administrer un programme
to manage / to run a programme

agent de programme
programme officer

budget de programme
programme budgeting

chargé / directeur de programme
programme manager

durée d'un programme
term of a programme

exécuter un programme
to administer a programme

exécution d'un programme
programme delivery

gérer un programme
to manage / to run / to administer a
programme

inscription à un programme
entry into a scheme

**nouvel inscrit / nouveau participant à
un programme**
entrant into a scheme

plan de programme
programme plan

programme accéléré
accelerated / crash programme

programme d'accès à l'égalité
affirmative action programme

programme d'action prioritaire (Fr.)
priority action programme

programme d'action sociale
social action programme

programme d'actionnariat des salariés
employee stock ownership plan

**programme d'aide à la collectivité /
d'aide communautaire**
community assistance programme

programme d'aide sociale
social support programme

programme d'alternance travail-études
work-study programme

programme d'appoint
(occ.) add-on programme

programme d'apprentissage
apprenticeship programme

programme d'apprentissage accéléré
accelerated programme of apprenticeship

programme d'austérité
austerity programme

programme d'auto-assistance
self-help project / scheme

programme ciblé
target programme

**programme de construction
d'habitations / de logements**
housing programme

**programme de construction
d'habitations / de logements à bon
marché / de logements sociaux**
low-cost housing programme

programme en cours d'emploi
on-the-job programme

**programme de création d'emplois /
favorisant la création d'emplois**
job-creation / work-creation / employment-
creation programme / scheme, scheme
aimed at creating employment / jobs

programme de crédit-formation
training grants scheme

programme de départs volontaires
voluntary severance / redundancy scheme

programme pour / en faveur de l'emploi
employment scheme

**programme d'emploi des collectivités
locales**
community employment programme

programme d'emploi et de formation
employment and training scheme

programme d'emploi d'intérêt local
community employment programme

programme d'encouragement
incentive programme

programme d'enseignement
curriculum

programme d'équipement
capital programme

programme d'évaluation analytique des tâches / du travail
analytical job evaluation scheme

programme expérimental
pilot programme

programme en faveur de la famille
family scheme

programme destiné aux / en faveur des / intéressant les femmes
women's programme

programme de formation
training programme / scheme

programme de formation en établissement scolaire
in-school training programme

programme de formation individuelle
individual training programme

programme de formation pour jeunes diplômés
graduate training scheme

programme de formation préalable à l'apprentissage
pre-apprenticeship training programme

programme de formation universitaire
university-based training programme

programme à frais partagés
shared-cost programme

programme d'incitation
incentive programme

programme d'initiation
induction programme

programme d'initiation à l'arithmétique
numeracy programme

programme d'initiation des nouveaux employés
orientation programme for new employees

programme intensif
crash programme

programme axé sur / orienté vers les jeunes
youth-specific programme

programme de logements
housing programme

programme en faveur de la main-d'oeuvre
manpower programme

programme du / intéressant le marché du travail
labour market programme / scheme

programme optimum
target programme

programme de perfectionnement
developmental programme, retraining scheme

programme de perfectionnement des cadres
(occ.) executive programme

programme permanent
permanent / ongoing programme

programme pilote
pilot programme

programme de pré-apprentissage
pre-apprentice scheme

programme de préparation à l'emploi
(occ.) bridging programme

programme de préparation de la retraite
pre-retirement planning programme

programme pour la promotion interne (Sp.)
internal development programme

programme de protection sociale
(social) welfare programme

programme de rattrapage
bridging programme

programme de recherche
research programme

programme de reconversion
retraining scheme

programme de recrutement dans les universités
university recruitment programme

programme de recyclage
retraining programme / scheme

programme de rééducation
rehabilitation / remedial programme

programme de réorientation
(occ.) transition programme

programme scolaire
syllabus; curriculum

programme sélectif
target programme

programme socio-récréatif
social programme

programme de subventions
incentive programme

programme subventionné (de construction) d'habitations / de logements
social housing scheme, subsidised housing programme

programme témoin
pilot programme

programme de transferts (de revenus)
income transfer programme

responsable de programme
programme official

PROGRÈS
progress, development, advancement

contrat de progrès (Fr.)
contract for progress

impôt de progrès social
social development tax

progrès social
social development

PROGRESSIF
progressive; incremental; graduated

allocation familiale progressive
progressive family allowance

contribution progressive
progressive contribution

impôt progressif
graded / graduated tax

impôt progressif sur le revenu, impôt sur le revenu progressif
graduated / progressive income tax

pratique d'emploi progressive
progressive employment practice

retour progressif au travail
drift back to work

retrait progressif
(occ.) phasing-out

retraite progressive
progressive / phased retirement

taux progressif
progressive rate

PROGRESSION
progression; increase

progression automatique des salaires
automatic wage progression

progression dans la carrière
career progression / path

progression de l'emploi
increase in / expansion of employment

progression professionnelle
career progress / path

progression des traitements à l'intérieur d'une même classe
intra-grade salary progression

PROGRESSIVITÉ
impôt sur le revenu fondé sur la progressivité
graduated / progressive income tax

progressivité de l'impôt sur le revenu
graduated / progressive income tax

PROJECTIF
base de données projectives sur la population active
labour force projections data base

PROJECTION
projection

projection des besoins en main-d'oeuvre
projected manpower requirement

projection démographique / de population
population projection

projection de la population active
labour force projection

PROJET
project; scheme

agent de projet
project officer

calendrier des activités d'un projet
project management schedule

chef / directeur de projet
project manager

projet d'auto-assistance
self-help project / scheme

projet des / entrepris par les collectivités locales
community project

projet conjoint
joint project

projet d'entraide
self-help project / scheme

projet d'entreprise
business plan; mission statement

projet expérimental
pilot project

projet fondé sur l'initiative personnelle
self-help project / scheme

projet d'intérêt collectif
community project

projet de formation
training project / initiative

projet de logements sociaux
low-income housing project

projet mixte
joint project

projet pilote
pilot project

projet professionnel
career objective

projet de recherche
research project

projet de relèvement rural
rural rehabilitation project

projet témoin
pilot project

prolongation d'un projet
extension of a project, project renewal

PROLONGATION
période de prolongation
period of extension

prolongation de contrat
extension of contract

prolongation d'emploi
extension of employment

prolongation d'un engagement
extension of appointment

prolongation d'un projet
extension of a project, project renewal

PROLONGÉ
affection prolongée et coûteuse
prolonged and expensive illness

congé prolongé
extended leave

incapacité prolongée
prolonged / long-term disability

maladie prolongée
prolonged illness

prolongé (être)
to be extended

service temporaire prolongé
extended temporary duty

soins prolongés
continuing care

PROLONGEMENT
continuation; extension; (occ.) follow-up

PROLONGER
prolonger un contrat
to extend a contract

prolonger un engagement
to extend an appointment

PROMESSE
promesse d'embauche
promise of employment

promesse de pension
pension promise

PROMOTION
promotion; career development /
progression; career / professional /
occupational advancement; upward
mobility

agence pour la promotion des PME
SME / small business promotion agency

ajourner une promotion
to suspend (implementation of) a
promotion

droit à une promotion
right to promotion

fondé à escompter une promotion (être)
to have a justified expectation to be
promoted

lettre de promotion
letter of promotion

logements de promotion publique (Sp.)
public promotion housing

notifier une lettre de promotion
to issue a letter of promotion

opération des promotions
promotion exercise

perspective de promotion
promotion prospect, chance for promotion

possibilité de promotion
opportunity for / chance for promotion /
for advancement, potential for
advancement, promotability, promotional
opportunity, promotion / advancement
potential

procédure de promotion
promotion procedure

**programme pour la promotion interne
(Sp.)**
internal development programme

promotion accélérée
accelerated promotion

promotion à l'ancienneté
advancement / promotion by seniority

promotion de l'emploi
employment promotion, promotion of
employment / of job creation

promotion de la / des femme(s)
advancement of women

promotion interne
internal advancement, promotion from
within; inbreeding

promotion au mérite
promotion according to merit

promotion professionnelle
job upgrading, vocational advancement

promotion sanitaire / de la santé
health promotion

promotion sociale
social advancement / betterment /
development; (social) welfare; upgrading

recommander en vue d'une promotion
to recommend for promotion

système de promotion
promotion scheme

PROMOUVOIR
to promote; to upgrade

PROMU
conditions requises pour être promu
(remplir les / satisfaire aux)
to be eligible for promotion, to satisfy the
standards required for promotion

PROMULGUER
to issue; to introduce, to pass, to
promulgate

PRONOSTIC
prognosis

PROPENSION
propension à travailler
propensity to work

PRO-PHARMACIEN
doctor authorised to provide drugs

PROPHYLAXIE
prevention of diseases

mesure de prophylaxie
preventive health measure

service de prophylaxie
preventive (health) service

PROPORTION
proportion; ratio, rate

principe de proportion
principle of proportionality

proportion d'actifs
labour (force) participation; activity rate /
ratio

proportion ouvriers - employés
(occ.) labour mix

PROPORTIONNEL
proportional; graduated

cotisation proportionnelle au salaire
earnings-related contribution

impôt proportionnel
proportional tax

**méthode d'ajustement proportionnel
sur un an**
annualised method of prorated adjustment

pension proportionnelle
graduated / proportional pension

**pension proportionnelle (assurance
mixte) (Irel.)**
pro-rata (mixed insurance) pension

**pension proportionnelle de vieillesse
(UK)**
graduated retirement benefit

prestation proportionnelle au salaire
earnings-related benefit

**prestation non proportionnelle au
salaire**
benefit not related to earnings

**proportionnel au salaire / aux gains /
aux revenus**
earnings-related

**régime d'assurance(-)vieillesse
proportionnelle au salaire**
(occ.) graduated pension scheme

retraite proportionnelle
proportional pension

**revenu salarial proportionnel à ses
compétences**
salary commensurate with one's abilities

PROPORTIONNELLEMENT
proportionally

PROPOSÉ
période d'emploi proposée
proposed period of employment

PROPOSITION
proposition d'emploi
offer of employment

proposition de formation
proposal for training, training proposal

proposition salariale
pay offer

PROPRE
assurance propre
own insurance

fonds propres
equity base

pension propre
pension on own insurance

propres moyens (par ses)
on his/her own

propre régime d'assurance (au titre de son)
on his own insurance

PROPRIÉTAIRE
logement occupé par son propriétaire
owner-occupied dwelling

propriétaire exploitant
self-employed farmer; farm-owner; owner-operator, owner-manager; working proprietor

propriétaires-gérants de commerces de gros et de détail [CITP-1968 (4-1)]
working proprietors (wholesale and retail trade) [ISCO-1968 (4-1)]

propriétaires-gérants d'hôtel, de cafés ou de restaurants [CITP-1968 (5-1)]
working proprietors (catering and lodging services) [ISCO-1968 (5-1)]

propriétaire de son logement (Austr.)
homeowner

propriétaire de / du navire
shipowner

propriétaire occupant
owner-occupier

propriétaire unique, seul propriétaire
sole proprietor / owner

PROPRIÉTÉ
ownership

accession à la propriété
home ownership

occupation d'un logement en (toute) propriété
owner-occupancy

propriété collective
collective ownership

propriété de l'Etat
State ownership

propriété immobilière
real estate / property

propriété privée
private ownership

PRO QUOTA
pro quota

PRORATA
pro rata

application d'un prorata
pro-rating

fraction au prorata du temps / prorata temporis
pro-rata fraction

prorata (au)
on a pro-rata basis, proportionally, pro rata

prorata temporis du travail effectué (au)
in proportion to time worked

prorata du temps (au)
pro-rata temporis

règle du prorata temporis
pro-rata temporis rule

salaire au prorata des heures ouvrées
wage in proportion to time worked

PRORATISÉ
unité bénéficiaire proratisée (Fr.)
pro-rata beneficiary unit

PROROGATION
extension

prorogation de délai
extension of deadline

prorogation d'un mandat
renewal of tenure

PROROGER
proroger le délai prescrit
to extend the time-limit

PROSPECTION
exploration

aide au déplacement et à la prospection
relocation and exploratory assistance

aide à la prospection
exploratory assistance

prospection des carrières
career exploration

prospection du marché du travail
(occ.) job exploration

PROSPÉRITÉ
wealth; well-being; welfare

PROSTITUTION
prostitution d'enfants / enfantine
child prostitution

PROTECTEUR
Etat protecteur
welfare State

PROTECTION
protection; care; welfare

agent de protection de l'enfance
child welfare officer

agent de protection sociale
(social) welfare officer / worker, social
worker, social service officer

bureau de protection de l'enfance
child welfare authority

**centre de protection maternelle et
infantile**
maternity child welfare centre

clause de protection syndicale
closed-shop / union security clause

compte satellite de la protection sociale
satellite account for social welfare

consultation de protection infantile
consulting centre for child health

**établissement de protection sanitaire et
sociale de l'enfance**
health and social care institution for
children

filet de protection sociale
social security net

mineur sous protection conjointe (Fr.)
legally and socially protected minor

moyens de protection individuelle
body / individual protection equipment

organisation de la protection sociale
(social) welfare provision

organisme de protection sociale
(social) welfare agency

programme de protection sociale
(social) welfare programme

protection de la collectivité
community welfare

protection de l'emploi
job / employment protection

protection de l'enfance
child care / welfare

protection de la famille
family welfare

protection de la famille et de l'enfance
family and child welfare

protection infantile
child care / welfare

**protection contre le(s) licenciement(s)
(abusif(s))**
(unfair) dismissal protection, protection
against (unfair) dismissal

protection maternelle
maternal welfare; maternity care

protection maternelle et infantile
maternal and child welfare

protection de la maternité
maternity protection / care

protection médico-sanitaire
health care

protection médico-sociale de l'enfance
medical and social child welfare

protection des représentants du personnel
protection of staff representatives

protection des revenus
income protection

protection du salaire
wage protection

protection sanitaire
health care / protection

protection de sécurité sociale
social security coverage

protection sociale
social welfare / defence / protection / care, social welfare work

protection sociale et juridique de l'enfance
social and legal child welfare

protection sociale passive
passive social protection

protection syndicale
union security

protection-travail
workfare, welfare employment (USA)

rente-protection
annuity-welfare

service de protection de la famille et de l'enfance
family and child welfare service

service de protection infantile
child / infant welfare service

service de protection maternelle
maternity service

service de protection maternelle et infantile
maternal and child health service

service de protection sociale
(social) welfare service

système national de protection (médico-) sanitaire
national system of health care

système de protection (médico-) sanitaire / de protection de santé
health care (delivery) system

système de protection sociale
social protection / welfare (scheme)

PROTÉGÉ
atelier protégé
sheltered workshop

catégories de personnes protégées
population coverage

emploi en milieu non protégé
open employment

emploi protégé
protected job; sheltered employment

enfant protégé
protected child

habitat / logement protégé
sheltered housing

milieu protégé
sheltered (working) environment

nombre de personnes protégées
(occ.) (population) coverage

personne protégée
person protected, protected person

résidence protégée
protected residence

salarié protégé
protected employee; protected staff representative (Fr.)

travail protégé
sheltered employment

PROTÉGER
to protect, to guarantee

PROTESTATION
grève de protestation
protest strike

grève de protestation contre des / les licenciements
redundancy strike

mouvement de protestation
protest movement

PROTHÈSE
prosthesis, prosthetic appliance

allocation pour prothèse dentaire (Ger.)
dental replacement allowance

appareil de prothèse
prosthetic appliance

prothèse auditive
hearing aid

prothèse capillaire
hair replacement

PROTHÉSISTE
prosthetic technician

prothésiste dentaire
dental technician

PROTOCOLE
protocole d'accord / d'entente
memorandum of understanding, statement
of agreement

protocole d'expertise
(occ.) memorandum of appraisal

PROVENANCE
provenance des fonds
source of funds

PROVIDENCE
Etat providence
welfare State

PROVISION
supply; allowance; allocation

provision alimentaire
maintenance

provision budgétaire
budgetary provision

provisions pour congés payés
reserve for holiday leave

provision sur honoraires
retainer fee

provision pour risques
risk allowance

PROVISIONNÉ
régime de retraite provisionné
funded pension plan

régime de retraite entièrement provisionné
fully funded pension plan

PROVISIONNEL
provisional

indemnité provisionnelle
provisional compensation

prestation à titre provisionnel
benefit payable on a provisional basis

versement provisionnel
provisional payment

PROVISOIRE
provisional; temporary; interim; tentative

accord provisoire
interim / tentative agreement

affectation provisoire
secondment

allocation provisoire
provisional benefit

douzième provisoire
credit vote

emploi provisoire
interim job / employment

indemnité personnelle provisoire
personal transitional allowance

injonction provisoire
interim / interlocutory injunction

inscription provisoire
provisional registration

ordonnance provisoire
interlocutory injunction

pension provisoire
provisional pension

PROXIMITÉ
centre de proximité
community centre

emploi de proximité
neighbourhood job

service de proximité
community / neighbourhood service

soins de proximité
community(-based) care

PRUD'HOMAL
procédure prud'homale (Fr.)
procedure before an industrial tribunal

procédure en référé prud'homal
emergency interim proceedings for labour
disputes

PRUD'HOMMES
conseil des prud'hommes (Fr.)
industrial court / tribunal (UK), labour
court

conseiller / juge prud'hommes
labour court member

PSYCHIATRE
psychiatrist
psychiatre consultant
consultant psychiatrist

PSYCHIATRIE
psychiatry

psychiatrie du travail
occupational psychiatry

PSYCHIATRIQUE
expertise psychiatrique
expert psychiatric report

hôpital psychiatrique
mental home / hospital, psychiatric
hospital

infirmière du secteur psychiatrique
psychiatric nurse

soins psychiatriques
psychiatric nursing / treatment

trouble psychiatrique
mental disorder

PSYCHIQUE
trouble psychique
(pl.) mental illness

PSYCHOLOGIE
psychology

psychologie du travail
occupational / work / industrial
psychology

PSYCHOLOGIQUE
orientation psychologique
psychological guidance

PSYCHOLOGUE
psychologist

PSYCHO-MEDICO-PEDAGOGIQUE
(centre /service) (de consultations) psycho-
médico-pédagogique(s)
child guidance clinic / centre

PSYCHOMETRICIEN
psychometric test administrator

PSYCHOMOTEUR
aptitude psychomotrice
(occ.) manipulative skill

PSYCHO-PÉDAGOGIQUE
consultations psycho-pédagogiques
child guidance clinic / centre

PUBLIC (adj.)
action de santé publique
(public) health work

administrateur de (la) santé publique
(public) health officer / administrator

administration des finances publiques
fiscal administration

administration publique
government department

administration de (la) santé publique
(public) health administration

agence de placement publique
public employment agency

agent de la fonction publique
public / civil servant, public official

agent public
public servant

agent de santé publique
public health worker

aide sur fonds publics / publique / du secteur public
public / Government aid

allocation d'aide publique (Fr.)
State help allowance

assistance publique
national assistance, public care / assistance, State care (institution), poor relief

association reconnue d'utilité publique
association recognised to be of public interest, charitable association; charity

assurance accidents corporels du secteur public (Ger.)
public accident insurance

bâtiment et travaux publics
building and civil industry

centre public d'aide sociale (CPAS) (Belg.)
public centre for social welfare, public welfare centre

centre sanitaire public / de santé publique
Government / public health centre

charge publique
official duty

clientèle de malades pris en charge par le service public
(occ.) public practice

Code de la santé publique
Public Health Code

collectivité publique
public corporation

comptabilité publique
fiscal / public accounting

concours public
open competition

congé pour exercice de fonctions publiques
time off (work) for public duties

contrat public
public contract

deniers publics
public money / monies / funds

dépenses publiques
Government / public spending / expenditure

Directeur de la santé publique (UK)
State health officer

école publique
government / public school

emploi dans la fonction publique
public service employment

emploi public
public job / employment; (occ.) public office

emploi public temporaire
temporary public job

emploi dans le secteur public
public (sector) employment

employé du secteur public
public employee

employé d'un service public
public servant

entreprise publique / du secteur public
public undertaking / utility / corporation

entreprise de service public
public utility

établissement public
Government-owned establishment /
corporation, public institution,
governmental corporation; statutory body

établissement public (financièrement) autonome
governmental / Government-owned
corporation

établissement d'utilité publique
charitable corporation; charity

finances publiques
public finance

fonction publique
public administration / service; civil
service (corps); official duty

fonctionnaire de la santé publique
(public) health officer

fonds publics
public funds / money, Government funds

fonds public d'assurance
State insurance fund

formation en santé publique
public health training

hôpital public
public hospital

hygiène publique
public health

infirmière de santé publique
public health nurse

logements financés / subventionnés par les pouvoirs publics
public housing

logements de promotion publique (Sp.)
public promotion housing

manoeuvres des mines, du bâtiment et des travaux publics [CITP-1988 (-931)]
mining and construction labourers [ISCO-1988 (931)]

médecin de (la) santé publique / des services de santé publique
medical officer of health, public health
physician / medical officer

membres des corps législatifs et cadres supérieurs de l'administration publique [CITP-1968 (2-0)]
legislative officials and governments
administrators [ISCO-1968 (2-0)]

membres de l'exécutif et des corps législatifs, et cadres supérieurs de l'administration publique [CITP-1988 (11)]
legislators and senior officials [ISCO-1988 (11)]

membre de la fonction publique
civil servant

oeuvre reconnue d'utilité publique
corporation recognised to be of public
interest, charitable corporation; charity

officier public
public officer

officiers publics et ministériels
public and ministerial officers

ordre public
law and order

organisation de santé publique
(public) health practice

organisme public
governmental body, Government(al)
agency; (pl.) public authorities

organisme public de bienfaisance / de secours
public charity

pension au titre d'un régime public
public pension

pouvoirs publics
(public) authorities

recettes publiques
public revenue

régime d'assistance publique (Can.)
assistance plan

règlement d'administration publique
administrative regulation

salarié du secteur public
public sector employee

salubrité publique
public health

salut public
public welfare

santé publique
public / (occ.) community health

secours public
public relief

secteur public
public sector; public / State enterprise

service infirmier de santé publique
public health nursing service

service de placement public
public employment agency

service public
public authorities / service; public utility;
(pl.) public / Government services

service public de l'emploi
public employment service

service public hospitalier
hospital public service

service public de soins infirmiers
public health nursing service, district
nursing service (UK)

société de droit public
public corporation

société de service public
public utility

travaux d'intérêt public
public works

Trésor public
fiscal administration

PUÉRICULTRICE
child care worker; paediatric nurse

PUÉRICULTURE
child / infant care; mothercraft

puériculture et économie domestique
home and mother craft

PUPILLAIRE
deniers pupillaires
ward property

PUPILLE
foster child; ward

pupille de l'Etat
child in care

pupille de la nation
war orphan

PUPITREUR
pupitreurs et autres opérateurs de matériels
informatiques [CITP-1988 (312)]
computer associate professionals [ISCO-
1988 (312)]

PYRAMIDE
pyramide des âges
age / population pyramid, age distribution /
pattern / structure

pyramide des besoins
needs hierarchy

QUALIFIANT
stage de formation qualifiante
skill training course

QUALIFICATION
qualification; competence, competency;
skill

amélioration des qualifications
skill development, up-skilling

année de qualification
qualifying year

certificat de qualification
certificate of competence, qualification /
occupational / trade proficiency / craft
certificate

contrat de qualification
qualification / skills contract

déficit de qualifications
skill gap

degré de qualification
skill level

dépréciation des qualifications
deskilling

éventail de qualifications
range of skills, skill mix

haute qualification (de)
(occ.) professional

inadéquation des qualifications
skill mismatch

intensité de qualification
skill intensity

manque de qualification
lack of skill

niveau de qualification
competence / skill level, level of skill / of
qualification

niveau de qualification des emplois
skill content of jobs

pénurie de qualifications
skill bottleneck / shortage

prime à la qualification (Fr.)
skills allowance

profession de haute qualification
highly skilled / higher-skill / qualified
occupation

profil de qualifications
skill profile

qualification de base
basic / generic / entry skill; (pl.) key / core
skills

qualification intermédiaire
intermediate skill

qualification professionnelle
occupational skill, employment / occupational / vocational qualification

qualification professionnelle reconnue
recognised vocational qualification

qualification recherchée
skill in demand

qualification requise
job requirement

qualification spéciale (sans)
(occ.) untrained

qualification du travail
job evaluation / qualification

qualifications d'un travailleur
worker's qualifications

reconnaissance des qualifications
recognition of (educational) qualifications

relèvement des qualifications requises
upgrading of educational requirements

structure des qualifications
skill profile / structure

validation des qualifications
skill certification / recognition, recognition of skills

QUALIFIÉ
qualified; skilled; trained; eligible

agent qualifié
skilled employee, trained worker

candidat qualifié
suitable candidate

chômeur non qualifié
unemployed unskilled worker

déficit de main-d'oeuvre qualifiée
(occ.) skill gap

emploi qualifié
qualified / skilled job

employé non qualifié
unskilled employee

formation de personnel qualifié
(occ.) skill training

hautement qualifié
highly qualified / skilled; professional

homme de métier qualifié
qualified journeyman

infirmière qualifiée
trained nurse

main-d'oeuvre qualifiée
qualified / skilled manpower, skilled labour

main-d'oeuvre non qualifiée
common / unskilled labour

main-d'oeuvre hautement qualifiée
highly qualified / skilled manpower

manque de main-d'oeuvre / de personnel qualifié(e)
lack / shortage of skilled workers / labour / manpower

métier qualifié
skilled trade

ouvriers et employés non qualifiés [CITP-1988 (9)]
elementary occupations [ISCO-1988 (9)]

ouvrier hautement qualifié
highly skilled worker

ouvrier masculin qualifié
skilled manual male employee

ouvrier qualifié
skilled / qualified worker; (skilled) journeyman / craftsman, craft worker

ouvrier non qualifié
unskilled worker; (pl.) unskilled workforce

ouvrier qualifié type
person deemed typical of skilled labour

pénurie de main-d'oeuvre hautement qualifiée
high-skill shortage, shortage / lack of highly skilled manpower

pénurie de main-d'oeuvre qualifiée
skilled labour / skill shortage, shortage / lack of skilled labour

personne qualifiée
competent person

personnel qualifié
qualified employees, skilled / specialised staff / personnel, trained personnel / workers

professionnel hautement qualifié
highly skilled professional employee

professionnel qualifié
(occ.) low-level technician

qualifié (non)
unskilled; untrained; unqualified

qualifié pour occuper un poste (être)
to be capable of filling a post

travail qualifié
skilled work

travailleur hautement qualifié
highly skilled worker

travailleur (professionnel) qualifié
skilled / trained / qualified worker; skilled craftsman; professional

travailleur non qualifié
unskilled worker / labourer

QUALIFIER
to entitle; to qualify

QUALITATIF
couverture qualitative
qualitative coverage

QUALITÉ
cercle de qualité
quality circle, quality improvement group

cercle de recherche active d'emploi (Fr.)
job club

inspecteurs d'immeubles, de sécurité, d'hygiène et de qualité [CITP-1988 (315)]
safety and quality inspectors [ISCO-1988 (315)]

logement de mauvaise qualité / de qualité médiocre
sub(-)standard housing

maîtrise totale de la qualité (MTQ)
total quality control (TQC)

manuel d'assurance-qualité (MQ)
quality assurance manual

qualité (en)
in the capacity

qualité pour (avoir)
to be entitled

qualité pour (ayant)
entitled, eligible

qualité de chef d'entreprise
entrepreneur skill

qualité comportementale
behavioural skill

qualités nécessaires pour (avoir les)
to qualify for

qualités relationnelles
interactive / interpersonal skills

qualité requise
qualification; requirement

qualités requises (qui n'a pas les)
unqualified

qualités requises pour le poste (avoir les)
to have the qualifications for the job

qualité de la vie
quality of life

qualité de la vie au travail
quality of working life

système de gestion de la qualité
quality management system

système qualité
quality system

QUANTIFIABLE
quantifiable; measurable

emploi quantifiable
quantifiable employment

QUANTIFICATION
quantification optimale
(occ.) target approach

QUANTITATIF
couverture quantitative
quantitative coverage

flexibilité quantitative
numerical flexibility

mesure quantitative du travail
work count

QUANTUM DOLORIS
assessment of pain and sufferings

QUART
chef de quart
shift supervisor

QUARTIER
neighbourhood; district

centre social de quartier
neighbourhood (welfare / social) centre

comité de quartier
neighbourhood committee

équipements de quartier
neighbourhood facilities

maison de quartier
neighbourhood centre

QUARTILE
quartile

QUATRIÈME
(personnes du) quatrième âge
old / frail elderly

quatrième état
working class

troisième et le quatrième âge (le)
the aged and the elderly

QUESTIONNAIRE
questionnaire

questionnaire d'auto-évaluation
self-appraisal questionnaire

questionnaire à choix multiples
multiple choice / ipsative test /
questionnaire

questionnaire d'embauche
employment questionnaire

questionnaire d'état de santé / médical
medical questionnaire

QUÊTE
quête d'emploi (en)
looking for / seeking work

quête d'emploi (être en)
to seek employment / work

QUINZAINE
quinzaine (par)
per fortnight

QUITTANCE
receipt

quittance de loyer
rent receipt

QUITTER
to quit, to leave

quitter un emploi volontairement
to voluntarily leave employment

quitter un poste
to vacate a position

quitter le travail
to leave work

quitter la vie active
to withdraw from / to leave the labour
force

QUOTA
quota

QUOTE-PART
établissement / fixation de la quote-part
assessment of contributions

fixer la quote-part
to assess contributions

QUOTIDIEN (adj.)
daily

acte de la vie quotidienne
daily task

allocation de trajets quotidiens
commuting allowance

gestes essentiels de la vie quotidienne
basic activities of daily life

geste de la vie quotidienne
daily task

migrant quotidien
commuter

migration quotidienne
(pl.) commuting

navette quotidienne
day haul

réduction de la durée quotidienne du travail
reduction of daily hours

taux quotidien
daily rate; per diem rate

trajet quotidien
day haul; (pl.) commuting

QUOTIENT
quotient familial
dependants' allowance set against tax, tax
relief with respect to dependants

quotient de mortalité
probability of dying

quotient de survie
probability of surviving

système du quotient familial
system of (income) tax relief with respect
to dependants

QUOTITÉ
quotité saisissable
attachable portion (of wages)

RABAIS
médecine au rabais
cheap medicine

RACHAT
rachat en capital (d'une rente)
capital compensatory settlement

rachat de cotisations
purchase of contributions

rachat (d'une entreprise)
buy-out

rachat d'une entreprise par ses cadres avec effet de levier (RECEL)
leveraged management buy-out (LMBO)

rachat d'une entreprise par ses salariés (RES)
leveraged management buy-out (LMBO)

rachat des points de retraite
purchase of retirement entitlement

rachat de rente
compensatory settlement; redemption of annuity

valeur de rachat
amount of the (capital) compensatory settlement; surrender value (ins.)

RACE
harcèlement en raison de la race
racial harassment

RACIAL
déséquilibre racial
racial imbalance

discrimination raciale
racial discrimination

équilibre racial
racial balance

préjugé racial
racial prejudice

RACISME
racialism; racial prejudice

RADIATION
removal

RADIÉ
radié du chômage (être)
to be struck off the unemployment register

radié des garanties (être)
to be excluded form insurance coverage

RADIER
radier du chômage
to strike off the unemployment register

RADIOGRAPHIQUE
examen radiographique
x-ray examination

RADIOLOGIE
radiology

RADIOSCOPIE
x-ray examination

RADIOTHÉRAPIE
X-ray therapy

RAISON
absence pour raison(s) familiale(s) / de famille
compassionate leave

congé pour raisons personnelles
leave of absence for personal reasons; (occ.) compassionate leave

congé pour raisons spéciales
leave of absence for special reasons; (occ.) compassionate leave

licencié pour raisons économiques (être)
to be made redundant

licenciement pour raisons objectives (Sp.)
dismissal on objective grounds

raison d'être
rationale

raisons humanitaires
humanitarian reasons; compassionate circumstances

raisons de santé (pour)
for reasons of health, for health reasons

raison de service
exigency of the service

raison valable
just / good cause, good reason

raison valable (sans)
without just cause

RAISONNABLE
diligence raisonnable
due diligence

motif raisonnable
just / good cause, reasonable ground, good reason

préavis raisonnable
reasonable notice

RAISONNABLEMENT
dépenses raisonnablement et légitime-ment engagées
just and reasonable expenses

RAJEUNIR
rajeunir les effectifs
to recruit younger employees

RAJUSTEMENT
re-adjustment

rajustement de la rémunération
salary / remuneration adjustment

RALENTISSEMENT
ralentissement de l'activité économique
economic slack / downswing / down-turn

ralentissement des affaires
business recession

ralentissement du marché du travail
labour market slack

ralentissement de la production / du travail
slowing down of work, work slow-down

RALLIER
rallier son poste
to report for / to duty

RAMPANT
inflation rampante
creeping inflation

RANG
rank; status; seniority

administrateurs et fonctionnaires de rang supérieur
(occ.) professional and higher categories

classement (des postes) fondé sur le rang
rank classification (of posts)

fonctionnaire de rang élevé
senior officer

fonctionnaires de rang supérieur
staff in the higher categories

haut rang (de)
high-ranking

rang professionnel
professional / work status

responsable de haut rang
senior-ranked official

RAPATRIÉ
repatriate

allocation viagère aux rapatriés (Fr.)
annuity for repatriates

RAPATRIEMENT
droit à une prime de rapatriement
entitlement to repatriation grant

indemnité de rapatriement
repatriation allowance

prime de rapatriement
repatriation grant

rapatriement de salaires
(cash) remittances

rapatriement sanitaire
repatriation for health reasons, sanitary
repatriation

voyage de rapatriement
repatriation travel

RAPIDE
équipe de rotation rapide
rapid rotation shift work

RAPPEL
retrospective pay / payment, back salary /
pay / payment, retroactive payment; recall

rappel d'ancienneté
grant of additional seniority / of (additional) years of service

rappel d'impôt(s)
back tax(es)

rappel de traitement
(payment of) arrears of salary

RAPPELER
rappeler un travailleur
to recall a worker

RAPPORT
report; ratio; returns

période couverte par le rapport
report period

rapport à (qui a)
relevant

rapport d'activité
activity / progress report, report on the
activities

rapport annuel
annual report

rapport d'appréciation d'un travailleur
evaluation report of an employee

rapport chômage/population
unemployment/population ratio

rapport de continuité
continuation rate

rapport coût-rendement
cost-efficiency

rapport de dépendance économique
rate of dependency, dependency ratio

**rapport de dépendance économique des
personnes âgées**
old age dependency ratio

rapport emploi/population
employment/population ratio

rapport d'enquête sociale
social (inquiry) report

rapport d'évaluation d'un travailleur
evaluation report of an employee

rapport de forces
power relationship; bargaining power

rapport inactifs/actifs
dependency / support ratio, rate of
dependency

rapport intérimaire
progress report

rapport médical
medical record

rapport obligatoire
obligatory report

rapport opérationnel
operational report

rapport d'orientation
policy report

rapports patrons-salariés
labour-management / industrial relations

rapport plancher
floor ratio

rapport de situation
progress report

rapport sur la situation des employés
status report on employees

rapport social
social reporting / accounts, personnel report

rapport de soutien économique
support ratio

rapport de soutien économique des personnes âgées
old age support ratio

rapport spécial relatif au licenciement
special report relating to termination
rapport de stage
probation report

système d'établissement des rapports périodiques
periodic reporting system

(système de) rapport d'appréciation du comportement professionnel
performance evaluation report (system)

RARETÉ
scarcity

RASSEMBLEMENT
collation; collection

rassemblement de données
data collection

RASSEMBLER
rassembler des informations / des données
to collect information / data

RATEAU
organigramme en râteau
flat organisation chart

RATIFICATION
instrument de ratification
instrument of ratification

RATIO
ratio

RATIONALISATION
rationalisation

RATIONALISER
to rationalise, to streamline

RATIONNAIRE
liste de rationnaires
relief roll

RATTRAPAGE
cours de rattrapage
remedial classes / course / training / teaching / education

programme de rattrapage
bridging programme

rattrapage de salaire
make-up pay, back salary / pay

rattrapage scolaire
educational / academic upgrading

RATTRAPER
to make up

RAVITAILLEMENT
bon de ravitaillement
food stamp / voucher

RAYÉ
rayé de l'effectif
struck off strength

RAYON
rayon d'action
scope

rayon de migration journalière
commuting distance

RÉADAPTATION
retraining; (re-)adjustment, readaptation, rehabilitation; rehabilitation education, re-education; reintegration

centre de convalescence, de cure ou de réadaptation (Fr.)
nursing, care or rehabilitation centre

centre pilote de réadaptation
pilot rehabilitation centre

centre post-hospitalier général de réadaptation médicale
(occ.) medical rehabilitation centre

centre de réadaptation
rehabilitation centre

centre de réadaptation physique
remedial exercise clinic

congé de réadaptation
rehabilitation leave

conseil en matière de réadaptation
(pl.) rehabilitation counselling

conseiller en réadaptation
rehabilitation counsellor

consultation pour la réadaptation
rehabilitation counselling

contrat d'emploi de réadaptation (Irel.)
remedial work

coordonnateur de réadaptation
rehabilitation co-ordinator

équipe de réadaptation
rehabilitation team

formation pour la réadaptation
rehabilitation education

foyer de (post-)cure et de réadaptation
(occ.) half-way house

indemnité de réadaptation
retraining (Hung.) / rehabilitation (Pol.) allowance

processus de (la) réadaptation
rehabilitation process

réadaptation des aveugles
rehabilitation of the blind

réadaptation fonctionnelle
functional rehabilitation

réadaptation des invalides
disablement rehabilitation, rehabilitation of the disabled

réadaptation médicale
medical rehabilitation

réadaptation professionnelle
vocational / job / occupational / industrial / employment rehabilitation

réadaptation professionnelle des travailleurs invalides
vocational rehabilitation of the disabled

réadaptation sociale
social rehabilitation

service officiel de réadaptation
public rehabilitation service

service de réadaptation
rehabilitation department, rehabilitative service

service de réadaptation professionnelle
vocational rehabilitation service

soins de réadaptation
rehabilitative care

stage de réadaptation professionnelle
occupational rehabilitation course

RÉADAPTÉ
rehabilitated

RÉAFFECTATION
reassignment; redeployment

fonctionnaire en instance de réaffectation
civil servant awaiting reappointment (redundant)

réaffectation de crédits
re-allocation of funds

réaffectation de la main-d'oeuvre
redeployment of labour

réaffectation d'un service à un autre
internal reassignment

RÉAFFECTER
to reassign, to redeploy

RÉAJUSTEMENT
réajustement automatique des salaires
automatic wage adjustment

réajustement du marché du travail
adjustment of the labour market

RÉAJUSTER
to (re)adjust

RÉALISATION
délai de réalisation
lead time

moment de la réalisation du risque
time when risk / the contingency arises

réalisation du risque
occurrence of the event

RÉAMÉNAGEMENT
adjustment; rehabilitation

réaménagement des effectifs
labour force / manpower / work force
adjustment

réaménagement du marché du travail
adjustment of the labour market

RÉANIMATION
service mobile d'urgence et de
réanimation (SMUR)
mobile emergency and intensive care
service

RÉASSURANCE
réassurance mutualiste
reinsurance of mutual benefit societies

REBOURS
discrimination à rebours
reverse discrimination

RECALCUL
recalcul d'une prestation
recalculation of a benefit

RÉCAPITULATIF
bordereau récapitulatif de cotisations
summary statement of contributions

document récapitulatif
summary / round-up document

état récapitulatif
summary / consolidated statement

tableau récapitulatif
summary table

RÉCAPITULATION
summary

récapitulation des périodes d'assurance
summary of the periods of insurance

RECENSÉ (adj.)
chômage recensé
registered unemployment

chômage non recensé
unregistered / unrecorded unemployment

RECENSÉ (n.)
respondent

RECENSEMENT
census; survey

**données (statistiques) provenant d'un
recensement**
census material

**recensement effectué auprès des entre-
prises**
establishment census

recensement industriel
industrial census

recensement de la population
population census

RÉCENT
chômeur récent
short-term / short-duration unemployed

RECENTRAGE
mainstreaming

RÉCÉPISSÉ
receipt

RÉCEPTION
receipt

accusé de réception
receipt

date limite de réception des candidatures
application deadline

réception d'une demande
receipt of an application

RÉCESSION
recession; slump, economic slack / down-swing / downturn

récession économique
economic crisis

RECETTE
receipt; (pl.) earnings, revenue, returns, income

poste de recettes
item of receipts

recettes accessoires
miscellaneous income

recettes affectées
earmarked receipts

recettes brutes
gross earnings

recettes budgétaires
fiscal revenue

recettes comptabilisées d'avance
deferred income

recettes tirées / provenant des cotisations
contribution revenue

recettes extraordinaires
below-the-line income

recettes financières
fiscal revenue

recettes fiscales
financial / tax / fiscal revenue

recettes générales
general revenue

recettes publiques
public revenue

RECEVABILITÉ
eligibility, admissibility

conditions de recevabilité
(occ.) eligibility

RECEVABLE
eligible, admissible

RECEVEUR
chefs de train et receveurs [CITP-1968 (3-6)]
transport conductors [ISCO-1968 (3-6)]

RECEVOIR
to receive

prestations d'assurance-accident à recevoir
casualty insurance claim receivable

recevoir (à)
receivable

recevoir des allocations d'aide / une aide sociale
to be on welfare

recevoir congé
to receive notice to quit

recevoir un préavis de licenciement
to be served with a notice of termination

recevoir des prestations
to draw benefits

RECHANGE
profession de rechange
alternative / alternate employment

RECHERCHÉ
compétences recherchées
skill in demand

profession recherchée
demand occupation

qualification recherchée
skill in demand

RECHERCHE
research

atelier d'entraînement à la recherche d'emplois (Belg.)
job-finding workshop

cercle (Fr.) / club (Belg.) de recherche active d'emploi
job club

critère de recherche effective d'emploi
(occ.) work test

méthode de recherche d'emploi
job-finding / job-search skills / technique, job-hunting method

organisme de recherche
research establishment / institute

plan personnel de recherche d'emploi
personal job-search plan

programme de recherche
research programme

projet de recherche
research project

recherche orientée vers l'action
action research

recherche économique appliquée
applied economic research

recherche d'emploi
job seeking / search / hunting

recherche d'un emploi (à la)
looking for / seeking work

recherche d'un emploi (être à la)
to seek employment / work

recherche d'emploi autonome
independent job search

recherche d'emploi individuelle
private job search

recherche fondamentale
basic research

recherche de logement
house hunting

recherche en organisation sanitaire
health practice research

recherche sociale
social research

recherche sociale opérationnelle
operational social research

technique(s) de recherche d'emploi
job(-)search / job-finding skill(s) / technique; job-hunting method

RÉCIPROCITÉ
accord de réciprocité
reciprocal agreement

RÉCIPROQUE
mutual

accord réciproque
mutual agreement

RÉCLAMATION
claim , complaint, grievance

présenter une réclamation
to submit a complaint

RÉCLAMER
to claim

fondé à réclamer une indemnisation pour perte de salaire (être)
to be entitled to claim restitution of lost salary

RECLASSÉ
profession reclassée
transferred occupation

RECLASSEMENT
social integration; re-adjustment, (vocational) rehabilitation; job transfer; transfer of workers to other jobs; redeployment; re(-)employment; relocation; resettlement; upgrading

allocation de formation reclassement (Fr.)
resettlement / re-deployment (Fr.) training allowance

allocation de reclassement
re-adjustment benefit

antenne / cellule de reclassement
redeployment unit

demande de reclassement
request for reclassification

itinéraire de reclassement
outplacement schedule

office de reclassement social
social re-adaptation service

préposé au reclassement (professionnel) des invalides (UK)
disablement resettlement officer

reclassement externe
out(-)placement

reclassement interne
in-placement

reclassement de poste
upgrading of post; (pl.) reclassification of posts

reclassement professionnel
occupational reintegration

reclassement social
social resettlement

RECLASSER
to upgrade; to regrade; to redeploy

chômeur difficile à reclasser
(occ.) hard-core unemployed

reclasser un poste
to upgrade a post

RECOMMANDATION
recommandation; reference

lettre de recommandation
letter of reference / of recommendation

recommandation à un employeur
introduction to employer

RECOMMANDER
to recommend; to refer

recommander l'avancement
to recommend for promotion

recommander en vue d'une promotion
to recommend for promotion

RÉCOMPENSE (n.)
récompense en espèces
money / cash award

RECOMPOSÉ
famille recomposée
reconstituted family; step family

RECONDUCTION
reconduction d'un contrat
renewal of a contract

reconduction tacite
renewal by tacit agreement, tacit renewal

RECONDUIRE
to renew

RECONDUIT
reconduit dans ses fonctions
re-designated

RECONDUITE
reconduite de force
forcible return

reconduite à la frontière
deportation

RECONFIGURATION
re(-)engineering (business management)

RECONNAISSANCE
certificat de reconnaissance
recognition certificate

indemnité sans reconnaissance de responsabilité
without prejudice payment

reconnaissance des qualifications
recognition of (educational) qualifications

reconnaissance de responsables syndicaux
accreditation of union officials

reconnaissance syndicale / d'un syndicat
(trade) union recognition

reconnaissance des titres
recognition of (educational) qualifications

RECONNAÎTRE
to recognise; to approve

reconnaître un syndicat
to recognise a union

RECONNU
certified; registered; recognised; approved

besoin reconnu
recognised / felt need

diplôme reconnu
recognised diploma

maladie professionnelle reconnue
prescribed industrial disease

maladie reconnue
prescribed / scheduled disease

profession reconnue
recognised occupation

qualification professionnelle reconnue
recognised vocational qualification

reconnu apte au travail (être)
to be certified fit to work

stage de formation reconnu
approved training course

syndicat reconnu
registered (trade) union

RECONSTITUÉ
famille reconstituée
reconstituted family, stepfamily

RECONSTITUER
reconstituer la carrière d'assurance
to draw up someone's insurance history / record

RECONVENTIONNEL
demande reconventionnelle
counter-claim

RECONVERSION
(vocational) retraining; shift; redeployment

aide à la reconversion (des structures)
adjustment assistance

formation de reconversion
retraining, conversion training

programme de reconversion
retraining scheme

reconversion industrielle
industrial redeployment

stage de reconversion
retraining course

RECONVERTIR
to re(-)train

RECORD
chômage record
peak unemployment

RECOURIR
recourir contre une décision
to appeal against a decision

RECOURS
appeal; claim

commission de recours
appeals board

délai de recours
time-limit for an appeal

droit de recours
right of / to appeal

former un recours
to enter / to lodge an appeal, to appeal

instance de recours
appeal body

prestataire de premier recours
first level provider

procédure de recours
complaints / grievance procedure

recours administratif
appeal to a higher administrative authority

recours en matière d'aide sociale
legal action against a decision relating to
social welfare

recours pour excès de pouvoir
application to set aside a decision on
grounds of exceeding or misusing one's
authority

recours gracieux
application to reconsider a decision;
submission for an out-of-court settlement

recours hiérarchique
application for disciplinary proceedings,
disciplinary complaint; appeal to superior
administrative authority

recours juridique
legal action

recours à des ressources extérieures
out(-)sourcing

recours sur succession (Fr.)
action to recover from succession arrears
of complementary allowance

**recours sur succession en matière
d'aide sociale (Fr.)**
action to recover social benefits from
succession

recours de tiers
third party claim

recours contre des tiers
recourse / remedy against third parties

soins de premier recours
primary (health / medical) care

susceptible de recours contentieux
challengeable

voies et délais de recours
legal remedies and periods allowed for
appeals

voie de recours
remedy; complaints / grievance procedure

RECOUVRÉ
fonds / montants recouvrés
recovery funds

RECOUVREMENT
recovery; offset; enforcement; collection

contrainte de recouvrement
enforced payment

principe de recouvrement
recovery policy

recouvrement de(s) cotisations
recovery / collection of contributions,
contribution collection

recouvrement des coûts
cost recovery

recouvrement des droits
recovery of rights

**recouvrement d'un droit à (des) pres-
tations**
recovery of a right to benefits

recouvrement forcé
enforced payment

recouvrement des impôts
tax collection

**recouvrement des trop-payés / des
versements excédentaires**
over-payment recovery

système de recouvrement des frais
cost recovery system

RECOUVRER
to collect, to levy, to recover

recouvrer des cotisations
to collect contributions

recouvrer le droit à (des) prestations
to requalify for / to recover the right to
benefits

RÉCREATIF
activité récréative
leisure activity

équipements récréatifs
recreational facilities

foyer récréatif et culturel
(occ.) community centre

groupe récréatif
play group

matériel récréatif
play equipment / material

RECRUE
nouvelle recrue
new hire

RECRUTÉ
agent recruté localement
locally recruited staff member

**personnel recruté sur le plan
international**
internationally recruited staff

personnel recruté localement
locally recruited staff

RECRUTEMENT
recruitment; engagement, hiring; manning

accord de recrutement
recruitment agreement

agence de recrutement
recruitment / staff agency

bureau de recrutement
recruitment office

cabinet de recrutement
(occ.) recruitment consultancy

campagne de recrutement
recruitment drive

chargé de recrutement
recruitment officer

coefficient de recrutement différé
delayed recruitment factor

convention de recrutement
recruitment agreement

coût de recrutement
hiring cost

**dotation des postes par voie de recru-
tement externe**
external staffing

frais de recrutement
recruitment costs

gel du recrutement
freeze in recruitment

interdiction de recrutement
ban on recruitment, recruitment ban

lieu de recrutement
place of recruitment

mode de recrutement
recruitment process

pays de recrutement
recruitment country

pratique de recrutement
recruitment practice

préférence au recrutement
preferential hiring

procédure de recrutement
selection / recruitment procedure

processus de recrutement
recruitment process

**programme de recrutement dans les
universités**
university recruitment programme

recrutement et affectations
(occ.) staffing

recrutement par approche directe
executive search

recrutement de diplômés universitaires
graduate recruitment

recrutement à l'étranger
foreign recruiting, foreign worker
recruitment; off-shore recruitment

recrutement extérieur
external recruitment

recrutement à l'extérieur
outside recruitment

recrutement externe
external recruitment

recrutement sur le plan local
local recruitment

recrutement de la main-d'oeuvre
manpower recruitment

recrutement dans les services locaux
local authority appointment

recrutement de travailleurs
worker recruitment

recrutement de travailleurs étrangers
foreign recruiting, foreign worker
recruitment; off-shore recruitment

service de recrutement
recruitment service

spécialiste en recrutement
recruiting specialist

stratégie de recrutement
recruitment strategy

système de recrutement
recruitment system

système de recrutement de bouche à oreille
word-of-mouth recruitment system

taux de recrutement
hiring / recruitment rate / ratio

zone de recrutement de main-d'oeuvre
labour recruiting area

RECRUTER
to engage, to take on, to hire, to recruit

recruter suffisamment de personnel (ne pas)
to understaff, to underman

recruter en surnombre
to overstaff

RECRUTEUR
pays recruteur de main-d'oeuvre
labour(-)recruiting country

RECTIFIER
to adjust

REÇU (adj.)
candidat non reçu
unsuccessful candidate

REÇU (n.)
receipt

reçu pour solde de tout compte (Fr.)
receipt of final pay

RECUEIL
compendium

recueil des accords d'entreprise
compendium of company agreements

recueil annuel
annual series

recueil des lois
statute book

RECUEILLI
enfant recueilli
foster child

enfant temporairement recueilli
temporarily fostered child

personne recueillie de fait
de facto dependant

RECUEILLIR
to collect; to raise

recueillir des fonds
to raise funds

recueillir des renseignements
to collect information

RECUL
decrease

recul sur (en)
behind

RÉCUPÉRABLE
reclaimable, recoverable

assurance-vie à capital récupérable
pure endowment insurance

avance récupérable
recoverable advance

**police d'assurance-vie à capital
récupérable**
pure endowment policy

RÉCUPÉRATION
recovery; time off in lieu

heures de récupération
hours off in lieu, hours (not worked) to be
made up later

jour de récupération
day off in lieu, day (not worked) to be
made up later

récupération des capacités
recovery of capacities

**récupération des frais afférents au
paiement des prestations**
recovery of expenses incurred in the
payment of benefits

récupération de prestations indues
recovery of benefits which were not due

système de récupération du temps
time recovery scheme

RÉCURRENT
recurrent

chômage récurrent
recurrent unemployment, multiple spells
of unemployment

éducation récurrente
recurrent education

récurrent (non)
non-recurrent

RECYCLAGE
retraining, re-skilling, updating / refresher
training, upgrading

cours de recyclage
refresher course

programme de recyclage
retraining programme / scheme

recyclage de la main-d'oeuvre
retraining of manpower

recyclage professionnel
(professional / occupational / vocational)
retraining, vocational upgrading; booster
trai-ning; reskilling, updating of skills

stage de recyclage
retraining / upgrading course

RECYCLÉ
retrained

RECYCLER
to re(-)train, to upgrade

REDÉFINI
emploi redéfini
redesigned job

REDÉFINIR
redéfinir un emploi
to redesign a job

REDÉFINITION
redifinition; requalification

redéfinition des tâches
job redefinition / restructuring

REDÉMARRAGE
indemnité de redémarrage (Austr.)
new start allowance

REDÉPLOIEMENT
redeployment; reassignment

redéploiement des effectifs
redeployment of labour, labour adjustment

redéploiement industriel
industrial redeployment

redéploiement de la main-d'oeuvre
redeployment of labour

REDEVANCE
fee; charge; rental; royalty

REDIMENSIONNEMENT
right-sizing; downsizing

REDISTRIBUTIF
effet redistributif
distributive effect

REDISTRIBUTION
reassignment; redeployment; shift

redistribution des fonctions
reassignment of duties

redistribution des revenus
redistribution of income

redistribution du volume de travail
redistribution of the volume of work

REDRESSEMENT
upturn, upswing, recovery; relief; adjustment

loi de redressement
economic recovery act

mesure de redressement
remedial action / measure

redressement fiscal
tax adjustment

RÉDUCTION
reduction; decrease; allowance; rebate

bon de réduction sur les denrées alimentaires (UK)
food rebate coupon

clauses de réduction, de suspension ou de suppression de prestations
provisions for reduction, suspension or withdrawal of benefits

convention d'aménagement et de réduction du temps de travail (ARTT) (Fr.)
agreement to reform and reduce working hours

coefficient de réduction
reduction factor

exonérations et réductions des cotisations
exemptions from and reductions of contributions

réduction selon des calculs actuariels
actuarial reduction

réduction de la durée du travail
reduction of / cut in working hours

réduction de la durée hebdomadaire du travail
reduction of the working week

réduction de la durée quotidienne du travail
reduction of daily hours

réduction des / d'effectifs
staff / manpower / work force reduction, reduction in personnel / of staff, staff cut; employment cut-back; post reduction, reduction in staffing levels; downsizing

réduction d'emplois
employment cut-back

réduction fiscale
tax reduction / cut

réduction d'impôts
tax abatement / concession / cut / reduction

réduction du loyer
rent rebate

réduction de personnel
staff / manpower / work force reduction,
reduction in personnel / of staff, staff cut;
employment cut-back

réduction de salaire
wage cut

réduction des taxes locales (UK)
rate rebate

réduction du temps de travail
reduction in / of working hours, shortening of working hours; shortened
working week

taux de réduction des prestations
benefit withdrawal rate

RÉDUIRE
to reduce; to downsize

réduire le chômage
to reduce unemployment

réduire les effectifs
to reduce / to downsize / to shed staff

réduire la masse salariale
to cut the payroll

réduire le personnel
to reduce / to downsize / to shed staff

réduire une prestation
to reduce a benefit

RÉDUIT (adj.)
allocation de revenus réduits (UK)
reduced earnings allowance

annuité réduite
reduced annual (periodic) benefit

capacité professionnelle réduite
reduced occupational capacity

capacité de travail réduite
reduced working capacity

durée de travail réduite
short time

effectif réduit
(occ.) skeleton staff

enseignement à horaire réduit
part-time education

horaire réduit (à)
part-time; short(-)time

pension réduite de retraite différée
reduced deferred pension

pension à taux réduit
reduced (rate) pension / retirement benefit

personne à mobilité réduite
people with mobility handicap(s)

personnel réduit
reduced / (occ.) skeleton staff

profession de spécialisation réduite
low-skilled occupation

semaine de travail réduite
compressed work(ing) week, reduced /
short work week

tarif réduit
reduced fee, concessional fare

tarif réduit (à)
at reduced fee

taux réduit
reduced rate

temps réduit
compressed / reduced time

**temps réduit indemnisé longue durée
(Fr.)**
short-time work on benefit for a long
period

travail à horaires réduits
short-time work / working; partial
unemployment

**travailler en horaires réduits / à temps
réduit**
to be on / to work short time

verser à un taux réduit
to pay at a reduced rate

RÉÉCHELONNER
rééchelonner une dette
to reschedule a debt

RÉÉDUCATIF
médecine rééducative
rehabilitation medicine

RÉÉDUCATION
re-education; readaptation, rehabilitation;
rehabilitation education; retraining

allocation de rééducation
(re)training allowance

centre de rééducation
rehabilitation centre

centre de rééducation pour aveugles
rehabilitation centre for the blind; training
centre for the blind

conseiller en rééducation
rehabilitation counsellor

programme de rééducation
rehabilitation / remedial programme

rééducation fonctionnelle
functional rehabilitation

rééducation des invalides
disablement rehabilitation, rehabilitation
of the disabled

rééducation médicale
medical rehabilitation

rééducation professionnelle
occupational therapy, vocational /
employment rehabilitation, occupational /
professional / vocational retraining

RÉÉDUQUÉ
rehabilitated; rehabilitatee; retrained

RÉEL
avance des salaires réels
real wage gap

besoin réel
real / felt need

cause réelle et sérieuse
just cause; genuine and proper ground

cause réelle et sérieuse de licenciement
genuine and proper ground for dismissal

date réelle de l'accouchement
effective date of confinement

frais réels
real cost, actual expenses, total expenses
incurred

gains réels
actual earnings

impôt réel
property tax

**licenciement abusif sans cause réelle et
sérieuse**
dismissal without just cause

rémunération horaire effective / réelle
actual hourly earnings

retard des salaires réels
real wage gap

revenu réel
real income; (pl.) actual earnings

salaire de la consommation réelle
real consumption wage

salaire de la production réelle
real product wage

salaire réel
actual / real wage / earnings

termes réels (en)
in real terms

RÉELLEMENT
salaire réellement payé
wage actually paid

RÉEMBAUCHE
rehiring

priorité de réembauche
re(-)hiring priority, recall rights

RÉEMBAUCHER
to rehire, to re-engage, to re-employ; to
recall

RÉEMPLOI
re(-)employment; resettlement

RÉEMPLOYER
to re(-)employ

RÉÉVALUATION
re-assessment

RÉEXAMEN
re-assessment; review

droit de réexamen
right of review

réexamen de la pension
pension review

RÉEXAMINER
to review

RÉFÉRANT
médecin référant (Fr.)
refering doctor

RÉFÉRÉ
procédure en référé prud'homal
emergency interim proceedings for labour
disputes

RÉFÉRENCE
reference; letter of reference / of recommendation; referee (person); (pl.)
credentials

année de référence
base / reckonable / relevant year

**bonnes références pour un poste (avoir
de)**
to have good credentials for a job

cadre de référence
terms of reference

centre de référence
referral centre

date de référence
reference date

estimation de référence
benchmark estimate

groupe de référence
comparison / control group

indice de référence
benchmark / reference index

jour de référence
reference day / date

lettre de référence
letter of reference / of recommendation

mois de référence
base month

période de référence
recall / reckonable / reference / base
reporting period

point de référence
benchmark

poste de référence
benchmark position

référence médicale opposable (Fr.)
valid medical norm

référence morale
character reference

revenu de référence
reckonable earnings; income standard

salaire de référence
official / reference wage

semaine de référence
reference week

taux de référence
benchmark rate

REFONTE
redrafting; review; amendment

RÉFORME
commission de réforme
discharge board

réforme de l'enseignement
educational reform

réforme fiscale / de la fiscalité
fiscal reform

réforme pédagogique
school / educational reform

réforme sociale
social reform

REFUGE
maison de refuge
assistance home

RÉFUGIÉ
refugee

aide aux réfugiés
aid for refugees

réfugié économique
economic refugee

REFUS
refusal

refus d'emploi
denial of employment

refus d'entretien
failure to maintain; non-support

refus justifié
(occ.) non-disqualifying refusal

refus motivé
justifiable / justified refusal

refus d'obtempérer
wilful disobedience

refus de soins
refusal of health care

refus de travailler
refusal to work

REFUSER
refuser une demande d'allocation / de
prestation
to reject a claim for benefit, (occ.) to
disallow benefit

refuser une offre d'emploi
to refuse a job offer

refuser une prestation
to refuse a benefit

refuser un service
to withhold a service

REGARD
droit de regard
right to examine

RÉGI
régi par
governed by, subject to

RÉGIME
scheme, plan; provisions; regulations;
system; rule; tenure

**affiliation à un régime de sécurité
sociale**
insurance under a social security scheme

**allocation prévue par le régime
ordinaire d'indemnisation**
(occ.) standard benefit

**allocation prévue par les régimes
spéciaux d'indemnisation**
(occ.) special benefit

**cotisations sociales du régime général
de sécurité sociale**
insurance contributions for the general
social security scheme

niveau de capitalisation d'un régime
level of funding of a scheme

**opter pour la non-affiliation / le non-
assujettissement au régime général de
retraite complémentaire**
to contract out

**pension complémentaire du régime
général (UK)**
reserve pension

**pension au titre de son propre régime
d'assurance**
pension on own insurance

pension au titre d'un régime privé
private pension

pension au titre d'un régime public
public pension

prestation du régime général
basic scheme benefit

propre régime d'assurance (au titre de son)
on his own insurance

régime agricole
agricultural scheme

régime d'aide sociale
welfare plan

régime d'allocations familiales
family allowances scheme

régime d'allocations (de) logement
rental subsidy scheme

régime d'allocations (de) logement révisé
revised rental subsidy scheme

régime d'allocations et de retenues au titre du loyer
rental subsidy/deduction scheme

régime ambulatoire (en)
on an out-patient basis

régime d'assistance
assistance scheme

régime d'assistance publique (Can.)
assistance plan

régime d'assurance
insurance scheme

régime d'assurance contre les accidents personnels
personal injuries scheme

régime d'assurance-chômage
unemployment insurance (scheme)

régime d'assurance-maladie
health insurance scheme

régime d'assurance maladie ou maternité
sickness or maternity insurance scheme, scheme for sickness or maternity insurance

régime d'assurance obligatoire
compulsory insurance scheme

régime d'assurance salaire
wage loss insurance plan, wage loss replacement plan

régime d'assurance-traitement collectif
group salary insurance scheme

régime d'assurance(-)vieillesse
pension (insurance) scheme

régime d'assurance(-)vieillesse obligatoire
compulsory pension insurance scheme

régime d'assurance(-)vieillesse proportionnelle au salaire
(occ.) graduated pension scheme

régime d'assurance volontaire
voluntary insurance scheme

régime autonome
independent scheme

régime de base
basic scheme

régime par / reposant sur la capitalisation
funded scheme

régime ne reposant pas sur la capitalisation
unfunded scheme

régime par / reposant sur la capitalisation intégrale
fully funded scheme

régime commun
common system

régime commun des traitements
common salary scheme

régime complémentaire
complementary scheme

régime complémentaire de retraite
company / occupational pension plan / scheme

régime complémentaire des travailleurs des charbonnages / des houillères
colliery workers supplementary scheme

régime contributif
contributory scheme

régime non contributif
non-contributory scheme

régime contributif de pensions complémentaires du régime général (UK)
contributory reserve pension scheme

régime à cotisations définies
defined contribution scheme

régime dérogatoire (Fr.)
exceptional arrangement

régime différentiel
different treatment

régime discriminatoire
discriminatory / different treatment

régime applicable aux employés
scheme applicable to clerical workers

régime d'entreprise
enterprise-based / employer-based /
occupational scheme

régime fin de carrière
final average earnings plan

régime fiscal
(system of) taxation

régime non garanti (Can.)
uninsured plan

régime général
general / basic scheme

régime général de (la) sécurité sociale
general social security scheme, standard
social security health and retirement
insurance (for private industry)

régime des hôpitaux
hospital regulations

régime hospitalier
hospital system

régime d'indemnisation
compensation scheme; benefit plan

régime d'indemnisation en cas d'accident ou de maladie
compensation scheme for industrial
injuries

régime d'indemnisation du chômage
unemployment compensation scheme

régime légal
statutory scheme

régime légal complémentaire professionnel
occupation statutory complementary
scheme

régime légal de retraite
statutory pension scheme

régime légal de sécurité sociale
statutory social security scheme

régime national de sécurité sociale
national social security scheme

régime relatif aux obligations de l'employeur
scheme concerning the employer's
liability

régime d'occupation
tenancy, tenure

régime applicable aux ouvriers
scheme applicable to manual workers

régime particulier
special scheme

régime des / de pensions
pension scheme / system / plan

régime de pension d'entreprise
occupational pension scheme

régime de pensions privé
private pension plan

régime de pensions des salariés (Denm.)
employment pension scheme

régime applicable en cas de pluralité de régimes
scheme applicable where there are a
number of schemes

régime de préretraite
early retirement plan

régime de / des prestations
benefit scheme; benefits provisions

régime à prestations définies
defined benefit scheme

**régime de prestations pour enfants
(UK)**
child benefit scheme

régime de prévoyance
provident / welfare scheme, welfare
system

régime de primes de rendement
incentive bonus scheme

régime privé de retraite
private pension plan

régime professionnel
corporate / industrial scheme, occupational plan / scheme

régime professionnel de retraite
occupational pension / company pension
plan / scheme

régime de rémunération
wage / pay / compensation plan / system

régime de rémunération au mérite
merit pay system

régime par répartition
pay-as-you-go scheme, PAYG scheme,
unfunded / assessment scheme

**régime fondé sur la responsabilité de
l'employeur**
employer's liability scheme

régime de retraite
retirement plan; pension / superannuation
scheme / plan

régime de retraite agréé
registered pension plan

régime de retraite en assurance
insured pension plan

régime de retraite des cadres
managers' pension scheme

régime de retraite par capitalisation
funded pension plan / system

régime de retraite sans capitalisation
unfunded pension plan

**régime de retraite par capitalisation
intégrale**
fully funded pension plan

**régime de retraite par capitalisation
partielle**
partially-funded pension plan

régime de retraite complémentaire
complementary pension scheme

**régime de retraite complémentaire géré
par l'Etat**
State earnings-related pension scheme

**régime de retraite complémentaire
privé**
private / contracted-out occupational
pension scheme

**régime de retraite complémentaire
privé en gestion directe**
self-administered pension scheme

régime de retraite non contributif
non-contributory pension plan / scheme

régime de retraite contributif (mixte)
contributory pension scheme / plan

**régime de retraite proposé / mis en
place par l'employeur**
employer-sponsored pension plan

régime de retraite facultatif
optional pension plan

régime de retraite en fiducie
trusteed pension plan

régime de retraite des fonctionnaires
public service pension scheme

régime de retraite obligatoire
mandatory pension scheme / plan

**régime de retraite à participation
différée aux bénéfices**
deferred profit-sharing pension plan

**régime de retraite personnel par capi-
talisation**
personal pension scheme / plan

régime de retraite préfinancé
funded pension plan

régime de retraite professionnelle (complémentaire) (UK)
occupational pension scheme

régime de retraite provisionné
funded pension plan

régime de retraite entièrement provisionné
fully funded pension plan

régime de retraite par répartition
pay-as-you-go pension plan / system, pay-as-you-go (PAYG)

régime de retraite-vieillesse
old age pension scheme

régime des salaires
salary system

régime salaire de carrière
career earnings pension plan

régime salaire meilleures années
average best earnings plan

régime de sécurité sociale
social security scheme

régime de solidarité (Fr.)
solidarity scheme

régime spécial
special scheme

régime spécial des fonctionnaires ou du personnel assimilé
special scheme for civil servants and persons treated as such

régime spécial de sécurité sociale
specific / special social security scheme

régime spécial de travailleurs non salariés
special scheme for self-employed persons

régime statutaire
statutory scheme

régime à taux fixe / uniforme
flat-rate scheme

régime intéressant la totalité de la population
universal scheme

régime des traitements
salary scheme / system

régime de travail sous contrat
contract labour system

régime applicable aux travailleurs manuels
scheme applicable to manual workers

régime universel
universal scheme

régime volontaire
voluntary scheme

rythme de croisière d'un régime
mature status of scheme / plan

soins en régime hospitalier ou ambulatoire
in-patient or out-patient care

RÉGION
region; area

autorité sanitaire de région
regional health authority

région assistée (UK)
assisted area

région d'emploi
region for work

région à excédent de main-d'oeuvre
labour surplus area

région sanitaire
health area

RÉGIONAL
bureau régional
branch / regional office

caisse régionale
regional fund

caisse régionale d'assurance maladie (CRAM) (Fr.)
regional health fund

centre hospitalier régional (CHR)
regional hospital

comité régional de formation professionnelle (Fr.)
regional vocational training committee

conseil régional
county / district council

conseil régional des hôpitaux (UK)
hospital regional board

hôpital régional
regional hospital

institut régional d'assurance
regional insurance office

mobilité régionale
regional mobility

office régional
regional office

service sanitaire régional
regional health administration

RÉGISSEUR
bailiff

REGISTRE
register; record; range

médecin inscrit au registre
registered practitioner

registre des accidents du travail
accident book

registre des congés
leave record

registre des offres d'emploi
register of vacancies

registre de paie
payroll ledger

registredu personnel
personnel register

registre des présences
attendance sheet / list, record of attendance

registre de suivi médical
health register

registre des vacances d'emploi
register of vacancies

tenue de registres
record keeping

RÉGLÉ (adj.)
settled

conflit non réglé
unresolved dispute

RÈGLE (n.)
rule; standard; requirement

observer les règles (ne pas)
to fail to comply with rules

règle (en)
valid

règles régissant l'accès / l'admission / l'affiliation
entrance / admission rules

règle d'attribution
qualifying requirement

règle de droit
law

règle empirique
rule-of-thumb

règles régissant l'entrée
entrance rules

règle de fond
substantive rule

règles d'hygiène
health practices

règle impérative
mandatory rule

règle du prorata temporis
pro-rata temporis rule

règle des quatre mois
four-month rule

règle de sécurité
safety regulation

règle du service fait
service performed rule

règle statutaire
statutory rule; (pl.) (occ.) legislation

RÈGLEMENT
regulation(s), rules and regulations; arrangement; settlement

conditions de règlement
terms of settlement

édicter des règlements
to issue / to make regulations

grève du règlement
work-to-rule (strike)

lois et règlements
laws and regulations

modalités de règlement
method of payment

procédure de règlement d'un conflit social
(industrial) dispute procedure

règlement d'administration publique
administrative regulation

règlement (à l') amiable
out-of-court / friendly settlement

règlement d'application
implementing regulation

règlement d'atelier
works regulations / rule-book

règlement en capital
lump-sum payment / settlement

règlement d'un conflit / d'un différend
dispute settlement / resolution, settlement of a dispute

règlement d'entreprise
works / staff regulations, works rule-book

règlement intérieur
works regulations / rule-book; rules of procedure; standing orders

règlement interne
rules of association

règlement d'un litige
dispute settlement / resolution, settlement of a dispute

règlement du personnel
staff rules

règlement sanitaire
health regulation(s)

règlement de sécurité
safety regulation(s)

règlement du travail
work rules

service de règlement
(occ.) award section

RÉGLEMENTAIRE
statutory; due

augmentation réglementaire
statutory increase

avantage réglementaire
statutory benefit

condition réglementaire
statutory condition

délai réglementaire
prescribed time

dispositions législatives et réglementaires
laws and regulations

disposition réglementaire
regulatory rule; (pl.) regulation(s)

pause réglementaire
statutory / official break

prestation réglementaire de maladie (UK)
statutory sick pay

prestation réglementaire de maternité (UK)
statutory maternity pay

textes législatifs et/ou réglementaires
statutory instruments / regulations

texte réglementaire
(pl.) regulation(s)

RÉGLEMENTATION
regulations; provisions

**organisme de réglementation profes-
sionnelle**
professional licensing authority

pouvoir de réglementation
regulatory power

**réglementation régissant l'admission /
l'entrée / l'inscription**
entrance / admission rules

RÉGLEMENTÉ
professions et emplois d'accès réglementé
restricted occupations

profession réglementée
regulated occupation

réglementé (non)
uncontrolled

RÉGLER
to provide for; to settle

**régler un conflit / un différend / un
litige**
to settle a dispute

RÉGRESSION
régression de l'emploi
decline in employment

régression sociale
(occ.) downward mobility

REGROUPEMENT
regroupement familial
family reunion

**regroupement familial des travailleurs
migrants**
reuniting of migrant workers' families

RÉGULARISATION
regularisation; correction

régularisation annuelle des cotisations
annual regularisation of contributions

régularisation en fin d'année
year-end regularisation

RÉGULATION
régulation des naissances
birth control

RÉGULÉ
concurrence régulée
managed competition

RÉGULIER
allocation régulière
regular allowance

emploi régulier
regular employment

emploi régulier vacant
regular vacancy

engagement à titre régulier
regular appointment

enseignement régulier
formal education

formation régulière
formal training

intervalles réguliers (à)
periodically

nomination à titre régulier
regular appointment

placement dans un emploi régulier
regular job placement

procédure régulière conforme à la loi
due process of law

salaire régulier
regular wage

subvention régulière
recurrent grant

travailleur sans emploi régulier
casual labourer / worker, occasional
worker

RÉGULIÈREMENT
présenter régulièrement (se)
to report regularly

séjournant régulièrement
lawfully present

RÉHABILITATION
rehabilitation

RÉIMPLANTATION
relocation

RÉINSERTION
reintegration; reinstatement; rehabilitation; resettlement; reemployment

contrat de réinsertion
return to work contract

formation de réinsertion
(occ.) remedial training

réinsertion sur le marché de l'emploi / du travail
reintegration into the labour market

réinsertion professionnelle
vocational / occupational reintegration, reentry (into the labour force)

réinsertion sociale
social integration / resettlement

RÉINSTALLATION
relocation; resettlement

allocation / indemnité de réinstallation
reestablishment / resettlement allowance

prime de réinstallation
relocation grant

RÉINTÉGRATION
reintegration; rehabilitation; reinstatement; rehire, re-employment

ordre de réintégration
reinstatement order

réintégration dans un poste
reverting to a post

réintégration professionnelle
vocational / occupational reintegration, reentry (into the labour force)

RÉINTÉGRER
to reinstate; to rehire

réintégrer le marché du travail / la population active
to re-enter the labour force

travailleur mis à pied non réintégré
non-return lay-off

REJETER
to reject; to dismiss; to disallow

RELAIS
allocation-relais
bridging allowance

RELANCE
recovery

mesures de relance
reflationary measures / policy

relance économique
economic upswing / recovery

RELATIF
intensité relative de main-d'oeuvre / de travail
labour intensity

RELATION
relation; relationship

cessation de la relation de travail
cessation / termination of employment

relations collatérales
(occ.) staff relations

relations employeur-employé
staff relations

relations employeurs-travailleurs
labour-management / industrial relations

relations familiales
family / (occ.) domestic relations

relations fonctionnelles
functional relations

relation hiérarchique
managerial relationship

relations horizontales
lateral relations

relations humaines / interpersonnelles
interpersonal relations

relations entre partenaires sociaux
labour / employee / industrial relations;
social fabric

relations avec le personnel
staff / work relations, working relationship

relations professionnelles
labour / job / industrial relations; labour-
management relations

**relations professionnelles adversatives /
antagoniques**
adversarial industrial relations

relations sociales
labour / employee / industrial relations;
social fabric

relation de travail
employment relationship; (pl.) staff / work
/ industrial / labour relations, working
relationship; job attachment

relations verticales
line relationships

RELATIONNEL
qualités relationnelles
interactive / interpersonal skills

soins relationnels
supportive care

RELEVÉ (n.)
statement; record; returns

relevé concernant l'absentéisme
record of absenteeism

relevé de congé annuel
annual leave record

relevé des cotisations (versées)
contribution record

relevé des gains
statement of income

relevé hospitalier
hospital record

relevé des paiements
record of payments

relevé des périodes de résidence
statement of periods of residence

relevé statistique d'activité
statistical activity report

relevé des tâches
task inventory

RELÈVEMENT
upward adjustment; increase, rise; upswing, recovery, upturn, upgrading;
rehabilitation

projet de relèvement rural
rural rehabilitation project

relèvement des cotisations
raising of contributions

relèvement de fonctions
removal from office

relèvement de l'indemnité de poste
increase of post adjustment

relèvement du niveau d'instruction
educational upgrading

relèvement du plafond des prestations
increase in benefit level

relèvement des qualifications requises
upgrading of educational requirements

relèvement des traitements
upward adjustment of salaries

RELEVER
to raise, to increase; to come under

relever de ses fonctions
to dismiss, to relieve of one's duties, to
discharge

relever du pouvoir discrétionnaire de
to be within the discretion of

RELIGIEUX
appartenance religieuse
religious affiliation

fête religieuse
religious holiday

RELIQUAT
unexpended / unencumbered balance

reliquat non affecté
unallotted balance

reliquat de congés
residual leave

RELOCALISATION
relocation

RELOCALISÉ
industrie relocalisée
migrant industry

RELOGEMENT
aide au logement et au relogement
housing and rehousing help

relogement de populations à bas revenus
rehousing of low-income groups

REMANIEMENT
redrafting; shake-up

REMARIAGE
remarriage

REMARIÉ
remarried

REMBOURSABLE
reclaimable, recoverable

remboursable (non)
non-recoverable

REMBOURSÉ
prêt non remboursé
outstanding loan

traitement non remboursé
(occ.) private treatment

REMBOURSEMENT
refund, repayment, reimbursement, defrayal, defrayment

demande de remboursement
refund request / claim

dispense de remboursement
waiver of reimbursement

formulaire / formule de demande de remboursement
request for settlement form

modalités de remboursement
repayment terms

mode de remboursement
method of reimbursement

procédure de remboursement des dépenses
expense claim procedure

remboursement de cotisations
contribution refund, reimbursement of contributions

remboursement en espèces
cash refund

remboursement excédentaire
over-reimbursement

remboursement sur la base de forfaits
refund on the basis of lump-sum payments

remboursement forfaitaire
lump-sum reimbursement / refund, refund in a lump sum

remboursement entre institutions
reimbursement between institutions

remboursement maximal au titre des salaires
maximum wage reimbursement

remboursement partiel des frais salariaux
partial wage reimbursement

remboursement au titre du salaire
wage reimbursement

remboursement en totalité
repayment in full

tarif / taux de remboursement
refund rate, rate of reimbursement

REMBOURSER
to reimburse, to pay off, to refund, to defray

rembourser toutes les sommes perçues
to reimburse all amounts received

REMÈDE
remedy; cure

REMERCIER
to dismiss; to discharge

REMISE
remission; rebate; remittance

remise de cotisation(s)
reduction / cancellation of (a) contribution(s)

remise en état
rehabilitation

remise gracieuse de cotisations
discretionary reduction of contributions

remise totale ou partielle des retenues
full or partial waiver of deductions

remise au travail
re-employment

remise en vigueur
re-enactment; reinstatement

stage de remise à niveau
updating course

REMONTRANCE
admonition

REMPLACEMENT
replacement

allocation de remplacement (Fr.)
replacement allowance

allocation de remplacement de revenus (Belg.)
income replacement allowance

coefficient de remplacement du revenu
income replacement ratio

coût de remplacement
replacement cost

emploi de remplacement
alternative / alternate employment, replacement job

équipe de remplacement
relief shift

remplacement des générations
generation replacement

revenu de remplacement
replacement income

taux de remplacement
replacement rate

taux de remplacement des gains
earnings replacement ratio / rate

taux de remplacement du revenu
income replacement ratio / rate

taux de remplacement des travailleurs
workers' replacement rate

REMPLIR
remplir une condition
to satisfy a condition; (pl.) to comply with / to fulfil the conditions

remplir les conditions (ne pas)
(occ.) to be ineligible

remplir les conditions d'admission
to qualify for membership

remplir les conditions d'ouverture des droits aux prestations
to be eligible for / to qualify for benefit, to satisfy the conditions for acquisition of the rights to benefits

**remplir les conditions nécessaires /
requises / voulues (pour bénéficier /
avoir droit)**
to qualify for; to fulfil requirements: to be
eligible

**remplir à nouveau les conditions
requises pour**
to requalify for

remplir les fonctions de
to serve as

RÉMUNÉRATEUR
profitable; gainful; remunerative

**activité professionnelle véritablement
rémunératrice**
substantially gainful occupation

activité rémunératrice
income-producing / revenue-producing /
income-generating / revenue-generating
activity

emploi peu rémunérateur
low-wage job

travail rémunérateur
remunerative work

RÉMUNÉRATION
remuneration; earnings; wage, salary;
wages and salaries; pay, payment;
consideration; fee

arrêt de rémunération
interruption of earnings

augmentation de la rémunération
salary increase

barème courant de rémunération
ordinary scale of remuneration

**barème des rémunérations considérées
aux fins de la pension**
scale of pensionable remuneration

cadre unique de rémunération
single salary schedule

**comparaison portant sur la
rémunération totale**
total compensation comparison

complément de rémunération
earnings supplement

différence / écart de rémunération
salary gap / disparity / differential, pay
differential

échelle de rémunération
salary / pay / wage scale / range, range /
scale of wages

échelon de rémunération
pay grade; salary section

égalité de / des rémunération(s)
equal pay, pay equity

élément non salarial de rémunération
non-wage award

excédent de rémunération
salary surplus

feuille de rémunération
paylist, paysheet, payroll, earnings record,
pay statement / slip

gestion des rémunérations
salary administration

marge entre les rémunérations nettes
net remuneration margin

**méthode de la double courbe des
rémunérations**
dual pay-line approach

**méthode de rémunération à l'acte / par
honoraires**
fee-for-service / item of service method of
remuneration

montant des rémunérations
amounts earned

**montant de la rémunération considérée
aux fins de la pension**
amount / level of pensionable remuneration

**multiplicateur corrigé par le facteur de
correction de la rémunération**
multiplier corrected by the remuneration
correction factor

niveau de rémunération
pay / salary / wage / compensation (USA)
level

obligation de rémunération
duty to pay remuneration

plafond de rémunération
remuneration ceiling / limit

politique de rémunération
wage / compensation policy

**prestation exclue de la rémunération
considérée aux fins de la pension**
non-pensionable benefit

rajustement de la rémunération
salary / remuneration adjustment

régime de rémunération
wage / pay / compensation plan / system

régime de rémunération au mérite
merit pay system

rémunération à l'acte
fee-for-service

rémunération annuelle
annual remuneration

rémunération de base
basic remuneration

rémunération liée aux bénéfices
profit-related pay

rémunération brute
gross pay / earnings / salary

**rémunération brute à prendre en
compte / en considération**
gross reckonable earnings

rémunération à convenir
negotiable salary

rémunération courante
going salary

rémunération en début d'activité
beginning / starting salary

rémunération de départ
beginning / starting salary

rémunération à déterminer
negotiable salary

rémunération effective
actual earnings

rémunération effective nette mensuelle
monthly take-home pay

rémunération effectivement perçue
(occ.) take-home pay

rémunération en espèces
salary paid in cash

rémunération fictive
notional earnings

rémunération fixe
basic / fixed salary

rémunération des fonctions
remuneration for duties

rémunération forfaitaire par personne
(occ.) capitation

rémunération globale
comprehensive package; pay / remuneration package, compensation package
(USA); emoluments

rémunération hebdomadaire assurable
weekly insurable earnings

**rémunération des heures
supplémentaires**
overtime compensation / pay

rémunération horaire
hourly earnings

rémunération horaire effective / réelle
actual hourly earnings

rémunération après impôts
after-tax pay

**rémunération inchangée en cas
d'absence**
pay not affected by absence

rémunération indexée
index-tied wage, indexed pay

rémunération initiale
starting salary

rémunération par malade inscrit
capitation(-fee) system

rémunération mensuelle
monthly salary
rémunération au mérite
merit pay

rémunération moyenne
average earnings

rémunération en-dessous de la moyenne
below-average salary

rémunération moyenne finale
final average remuneration

rémunération nette
net salary / pay, take-home pay

rémunération ouvrant droit à pension / aux fins de la pension
pensionable remuneration

rémunération liée à la productivité
productivity payment

rémunération au rendement
pay / payment by results, performance (-related) pay

rémunération rétroactive
retroactive remuneration

rémunération salariale
wage earnings

rémunération des salariés
compensation of employees

rémunération à la tâche
piecework remuneration

rémunération théorique
notional earnings

rémunération du travail
earned income

responsable de la rémunération et des avantages sociaux (USA)
compensation and benefits manager

supplément de rémunération
remuneration supplement; top-up

système de rémunération
wage / pay / compensation plan / system

système de la rémunération par malade inscrit
capitation-fee system

système de la rémunération d'après le nombre de clients (med.)
capitation-fee system

système de rémunération aux résultats
incentive scheme

système de rémunération à la tâche
task payment system

système de la rémunération par tête
capitation-fee system

taux de rémunération
salary / pay / wage rate, rate of pay

taux de rémunération courant
prevailing rate of pay

taux de rémunération hebdomadaire
weekly wage / pay rate

taux de rémunération des heures supplémentaires
overtime rate of pay

taux de rémunération local
local wage / pay rate

taux de rémunération maximal
maximum rate of pay

taux de rémunération aux pièces
piecework rate

taux de rémunération en vigueur
going (pay) rate

RÉMUNÉRÉ
remunerated, paid

activité rémunérée
gainful activity / occupation / employment; economic activity; (occ.) market work

activité non rémunérée
unpaid occupation / work / employment; (occ.) non-market work

aide / auxiliaire familial(e) non rémunéré(e)
unpaid family worker

bien rémunéré
well-paid, high-paid, highly paid

capacité de travail rémunéré
wage-earning capacity

congé parental rémunéré
paid parental leave

congé rémunéré
leave / time off with pay; (pl.) paid holiday

emploi mal rémunéré
low-wage job

emploi rémunéré
paid /gainful employment

exercer une activité rémunérée
to be gainfully occupied / employed

exercer un emploi rémunéré
to be gainfully occupied / employed

occupation rémunérée
remunerated employment

pêcheur rémunéré à la part
share fisherman

personne n'exerçant pas d'activité rémunérée
non-employed person

personne occupant un emploi rémunéré
employed, employee; (pl.) economically active / gainfully occupied / working population, labour force

personne rémunérée
earner

population occupant des emplois rémunérés
economically active / gainfully occupied / working population, labour force

rémunéré (non)
unpaid

rémunéré à la commission
employed on a commission basis

rémunéré à la pièce
employed on piecework basis

salarié rémunéré
paid employee

salarié rémunéré à la pièce
worker paid on piecework basis

travail rémunéré
paid / gainful work

travailleur familial non rémunéré
unpaid family worker

travailleur rémunéré
gainfully occupied worker / person, gainfully employed person, paid / gainful worker

travailleur rémunéré à l'heure
hourly paid worker

RÉMUNÉRER
to remunerate, to pay; to retain

RENCENSEMENT
rencensement de la main-d'oeuvre manpower inventory

RENDEMENT
performance; output; efficiency; returns

analyse de rendement / coûts-rendement
benefit-cost analysis

appréciation du rendement
performance appraisal

échelle de notation du rendement
performance rating scale

évaluation du rendement
performance appraisal / rating

mesure du rendement
performance measure

méthode d'évaluation du rendement
performance evaluation system

niveau maximal de rendement
maximum performance level

norme de rendement
performance standard, standard of
performance

notation du rendement
performance rating

objectif de rendement
performance target

possibilités de rendement
potential for effectiveness

prime de rendement
efficiency / output / productivity /
production / incentive bonus; incentive
pay / award

rapport coût-rendement
cost-efficiency

régime de primes de rendement
incentive bonus scheme

rémunération au rendement
pay / payment by results, performance
(-related) pay

rendement de la formation
pay-offs to training

rendement général
overall performance

rendement du marché du travail
labour market performance

rendement par ouvrier
labour productivity

rendement au travail
job performance

rendement du travailleur
worker performance

salaire au rendement
incentive wage, wage incentive

système d'évaluation du rendement
performance evaluation system

système de mesure du rendement
performance measure system

taux de rendement
rate of return

test de rendement
achievement / performance test

travail au rendement
job work

RENÉGOCIATION
clause de renégociation
reopening clause

RENFORCEMENT
renforcement de l'effectif
staff increase

renforcement du pouvoir des femmes
empowerment of women

RENFORT
travailleur en renfort
relief worker

RENGAGEMENT
re-appointment, re-employment

RENGAGER
to re-engage, to re-employ

RENONCER
to waive; to forfeit

renoncer à des droits
to waive / to relinquish rights

RENONCIATION
waiver

RENOUVELABLE
renewable

caisse renouvelable
revolving fund

dépenses renouvelables
recurrent expenditure

dépenses non renouvelables
non-recurrent / non-recurring / one-time
expenditure

fonds renouvelable
revolving fund

renouvelable (non)
non-recurrent

subvention renouvelable
recurrent grant

RENOUVELLEMENT
replacement; renewal; turnover

expectative juridique du renouvellement d'un engagement
legal expectation of renewal of contract

renouvellement d'un contrat
renewal of a contract

renouvellement des effectifs
labour turnover

renouvellement des générations
generation replacement

renouvellement de la main-d'oeuvre
labour / staff turnover

renouvellement de mandat
re(-)appointment (on the expiry of the term of office)

renouvellement du personnel
labour / staff turnover

taux de renouvellement
replacement / turnover rate

taux de renouvellement du personnel
personnel turnover rate

RÉNOVATION
rehabilitation

RENSEIGNEMENT
information; particulars; input; data

bureau de renseignements
inquiry office

fiche de renseignements
fact sheet

recueillir des renseignements
to collect information

renseignements personnels
personal information / data

service de renseignements
inquiry office

RENTABILITÉ
profitability, economic viability; profit-earning capacity, cost-effectiveness

rentabilité des entreprises
business profitability

seuil de rentabilité
profitability break-even point, cut-off rate (of return)

seuil de rentabilité (atteindre le)
to break even

taux de rentabilité
rate of return

RENTABLE
profitable; cost-effective, cost-efficient

rentable (non)
non profitable, uneconomic(al)

RENTE
periodic payment; annuity; pension; allowance; private income

assurance-rente
pension insurance

comité des rentes
pensions committee

constituer une rente
to purchase an annuity

conversion d'une rente
commutation of annuity

demandeur d'une rente
pension claimant

produit de la rente
returns on the pension

rachat de rente
compensatory settlement; redemption of annuity

- 720 -

rente d'accident du travail
industrial injury pension, pension for accident at work

rente d'ayant droit
survivor's annuity

rente complémentaire pour épouse (Switz.)
wife's supplementary pension

rente de conjoint
spouse life pension

rente pour couple (Switz.)
married couple's pension

rente après décès
survivor's pension

rente différée
deferred annuity / pension

rente hypothécaire
reverse mortgage

rente d'incapacité
disablement / disability pension

rente d'incapacité permanente
permanent disability pension

rente d'invalidité
disability / invalidity / disablement pension

rente de maladie professionnelle
pension for / in respect of an occupational disease

rente d'orphelin
orphan's pension

rente-protection
annuity-welfare

rente des retraites ouvrières et paysannes
annuity in addition to industrial and agricultural workers' pensions

rente de réversion
survivor's annuity

rente simple (Switz.)
single pension

rente de survie
survivor's pension

rente de veuve
widow's pension

rente viagère
life annuity

rente (viagère) de réversion / avec réversion / réversible
survivor's / survivorship annuity

rente (de) vieillesse
old-age pension / annuity

réversion d'une pension / d'une rente
transfer of pension rights to the surviving beneficiary

révision d'une rente
review of a pension

suppression d'une rente
withdrawal of a pension

suspension d'une rente
suspension of a pension

titre de rente
certificate / document showing entitlement to a pension; evidence of entitlement

titulaire d'une rente
beneficiary of a pension, pensioner, person entitled to a pension

RENTIER
person of independent means, rentier

rentier viager
annuitant

RENTRÉE
receipt; (pl.) earnings; revenue; returns; back-to-school

allocation de rentrée scolaire
back-to-school allowance, back-to-school clothing and footwear allowance (Irel.)

rentrées de cotisations
contribution revenue

rentrée fiscale
tax receipt

rentrée sur le marché du travail
re-entry into the labour force

RENTRER
femme rentrante (Belg.)
woman re-entering the labour market

rentrer sur le marché du travail
to re-enter the labour force

RENVERSEMENT
upturn, upswing

renversement de tendance
reversal of trend, trend reversal

RENVOI
discharge; dismissal; removal (from office); referral

indemnité de renvoi
dismissal compensation

menace de renvoi
threat of dismissal

renvoi immédiat / sans préavis
dismissal without notice, immediate / summary dismissal

RENVOYER
to dismiss

renvoyer pour faute
to dismiss for misconduct

renvoyer sans préavis
to dismiss summarily

renvoyer des salariés
to pay off workers

RÉORGANISATION
reorganisation; shake-up; redeployment; reassignment

RÉORIENTATION
programme de réorientation
(occ.) transition programme

réorientation professionnelle
career shift

subvention au titre de la réorientation
reestablishment grant

RÉPANDU
maladie la plus répandue
prevalent disease

RÉPARATEUR
médecine réparatrice
restorative services

RÉPARATION
compensation; relief

droit à réparation
(enforceable) right to (receive) compensation

indemnité de réparation
rehabilitation allowance

réparation pour un / des accident(s)
accident compensation

réparation d'un accident du travail
compensation for an accident at work

réparation des accidents du travail et des maladies professionnelles
workmen's compensation (for industrial injuries and professional diseases)

réparation des dommages de guerre
war damage compensation

réparation forfaitaire
lump-sum / standard compensation

réparation intégrale
full / global compensation

RÉPARER
to compensate

RÉPARTIR
to allocate; to apportion, to spread; to deal out provisions

RÉPARTITION
allocation; composition; spread(ing), apportionment, distribution, break-down; (occ.) assessment

financement par répartition
current(-)income / pay-as-you-go financing

modèle de répartition
allocative model

principe de la répartition
(occ.) assessment

régime par répartition
pay-as-you-go scheme, PAYG scheme, unfunded / assessment scheme

régime de retraite par répartition
pay-as-you-go pension plan / system, pay-as-you-go (PAYG)

répartition (par)
pay-as-you-go (PAYG)

répartition par âge(s)
age distribution / pattern / structure

répartition par branche d'activité et par profession / par catégorie professionnelle
industrial and occupational composition

répartition de la charge de travail
distribution of the workload

répartition des dépenses
(occ.) cost-sharing

répartition des effectifs par âge
breakdown of headcount by age

répartition des emplois
distribution of jobs

répartition géographique équitable
equitable geographical distribution

répartition géographique du personnel
geographical distribution of staff

répartition de la main-d'oeuvre
allocation of labour

répartition des moyens
allocation of resources, resource allocation

répartition de la population active
labour force distribution

répartition des ressources
allocation of resources, resource allocation

répartition des revenus
distribution of income, income distribution

répartition du risque
spreading the risk

répartition par sexes
sex structure / distribution

répartition des tâches / du travail
division / segregation of duties; division of work / labour, work allocation / distribution, workload breakdown

système de répartition
pay-as-you-go scheme, PAYG scheme

REPAS
chèque-repas
luncheon voucher

frais de repas
meal expenses

indemnité / prime de repas
meal(s) allowance

repas à domicile
home meals

service de repas à domicile
(occ.) meals on wheels

ticket-repas
luncheon voucher, meal ticket (USA)

REPÈRE
benchmark

emploi repère
benchmark job

indicateur-repère d'excédent de main-d'oeuvre
benchmark (labour / manpower) surplus indicator

indicateur-repère de pénurie de main-d'oeuvre
benchmark (labour / manpower) shortage indicator

RÉPERTOIRE
répertoire des métiers
trades register

RÉPERTORIER
to list

RÉPÉTÉ
périodes de chômage répétées
multiple spells of unemployment

RÉPÉTITIF
travail répétitif
monotonous / repetitive work

RÉPÉTITIVITÉ
prime de répétitivité
bonus for repetitive work

REPLI
phase de repli
downswing, downturn

RÉPONDANT
respondent

tiers répondant
third surety

RÉPONSE
taux de réponse
response rate

REPORT
posting; deferment, deferral; transfer

effet de report
carry-over effect

report de jours de congé accumulés
transfer of accrued leave

REPORTÉ
charge reportée
deferred charge

REPORTER
to defer

reporter des congés d'une année à l'autre
to carry over outstanding holidays from one year to the next

REPOS
rest

indemnité journalière de repos
daily rest allowance

jour de repos
rest day, day off, non-working day

jour de repos hebdomadaire
weekly rest day

maison de repos
convalescent / rest / nursing home

période de repos
rest period

repos compensateur
time off in lieu

repos dominical
Sunday rest

repos des femmes en couches (Fr.)
leave for women after childbirth

repos hebdomadaire
weekly rest

repos de maternité / de naissance
maternity leave

repos prénatal
pre(-)natal leave

repos prénatal facultatif
optional prenatal leave

REPRENDRE
apte à reprendre le travail
(physically) fit to resume work

aptitude à reprendre le travail
(physical) fitness to return to / resume work

reprendre un emploi
to resume work, to re-enter employment, to return to employment / to work

reprendre (le) service
to resume service

reprendre le travail
to resume work, to re-enter employment, to return to employment / to work

REPRÉSAILLE
mesure de représailles
retaliatory measure

REPRÉSENTANT
representative

protection des représentants du personnel
protection of staff representatives

représentant (de commerce)
commercial traveller

représentant désigné
official representative, (occ.) prescribed person

représentant de la direction / de l'employeur
management / employer's representative, representative of employer

représentant auprès des employeurs
employment representative

représentant patronal
management / employer's representative, representative of employer

représentant du personnel
staff representative

représentant syndical
(trade) union / labour representative, union steward; business agent (USA)

représentant des travailleurs
labour / union / worker representative, union steward, representative of workers

REPRÉSENTATIF
typical

échantillon représentatif
representative / adequate sample

effectif non représentatif
non-representative workforce

REPRÉSENTATION
congé de représentation (Fr.)
representation leave (in order to carry out elected duties)

droit de représentation syndicale
representational right

frais de représentation
entertainment expenses / allowance, expense account, office allowance

indemnité de représentation
entertainment / hospitality allowance

représentation paritaire
equal representation

représentation du personnel
staff representation

REPRESENTATIVITÉ
representativeness

représentativité syndicale
representativeness of a union

taux de représentativité
participation rate

taux de représentativité des femmes
women's participation rate

RÉPRIMANDE
admonition

REPRISE
reprise d'activité
re-entry into the labour force / into working life, return to working life

reprise d'ancienneté
credit for previous service, restoration of earlier / of prior service

reprise économique
economic upswing / recovery

reprise de la participation
re-entry into participation

reprise du service des prestations après suspension ou suppression
resumption of provision of benefits after suspension or withdrawal

reprise du travail
resumption of work

sorties du chômage pour reprise d'emploi
outflow to jobs from unemployment

visite médicale de reprise
medical examination before returning to work

REQUALIFICATION
reskilling

REQUALIFIER
to upgrade

requalifier un poste
to upgrade a post

REQUÉRANT
applicant, claimant

REQUÊTE
application, claim

REQUIS
requested; due

compétence requise
skill requirement; (pl.) necessary skills

condition requise
requirement, required / relevant condition; qualification; (pl.) (occ.) eligibility

conditions requises (qui ne remplit pas les)
unqualified

conditions requises (remplissant les / réunissant les / répondant aux)
eligible; qualified; suitable

conditions requises pour être promu (remplir les)
to be eligible for promotion

période maximale / maximum requise
maximum period required

qualification requise
job requirement

qualité requise
qualification; requirement

qualités requises (qui n'a pas les)
unqualified

qualités requises pour le poste (avoir les)
to have the qualifications for the job

remplir les conditions requises (pour bénéficier / avoir droit)
to qualify for; to fulfil requirements: to be eligible

scolarité requise
educational requirements

RÉQUISITION
réquisition de travailleurs
requisitioning of workers

RÉSEAU
économie de réseau
network economy

entreprise-réseau
network firm

organisation en réseau
network organisation

réseau hospitalier
hospital network / system

réseau local de soutien
neighbourhood support network / system

réseau médico-hospitalier
health care (delivery) system

réseau de soins coordonnés
health maintenance organisation (HMO)

RÉSERVE
reserve; supply; pool; exception, limitation, proviso; qualification

emploi réservé
(pre-)arranged employment; (pl.) job reservation

Etat auteur d'une réserve
reserving State (treaty)

fonctionnaire de réserve
relieving officer

fonds de réserve
reserve fund

obligation de réserve
obligation of discretion

population active de réserve
reserve labour force

réserve (avec)
qualified

réserve (sans)
unqualified

réserve que (sous)
provided that

réserve de (sous)
subject to

réserve de cessation de l'emploi (-sous)
subject to a retirement condition

réserve des dispositions de (sous)
except as provided in, subject to the provisions of

réserve distribuable
revenue reserve

réserve de main-d'oeuvre
labour / manpower reserve

réserve de main-d'oeuvre disponible
(occ.) stand-by workforce

réserve mathématique
mathematical reserve

réserve de sécurité
contingency reserve

soumis à des réserves
subject to limitations

RÉSERVER
to reserve, to save; to earmark

RÉSERVOIR
pool

réservoir de main-d'oeuvre
labour pool, pool of workers / of labour

RÉSIDANT
population résidante
resident population

RÉSIDENCE
(place of) residence; home

changement de résidence
change of residence; removal, relocation

clause de résidence
residence clause

compter trois années de résidence
to have complete three years' residence

condition de résidence
residence requirement

durée de résidence
period of residence

fixer sa résidence
to make one's abode

indemnité de résidence
residence allowance

institution du lieu de résidence
institution of the place of residence

lieu de résidence
place of residence

période de résidence
period of residence

personne sans résidence fixe
person of / with no fixed abode, vagrant

pièces attestant un changement de résidence
evidence of relocation

pièces justificatives requises attestant le pays de résidence
required proof of the country of residence

population de résidence habituelle
resident population

relevé des périodes de résidence
statement of periods of residence

résidence à l'étranger
residence abroad

résidence de famille
family / matrimonial home

résidence habituelle
normal / ordinary / regular residence

résidence médicalisée
(occ.) serviced flat

résidence normale
normal / permanent home

résidence permanente
permanent residence

résidence protégée
protected residence

résidence secondaire
vacation / second home

résidence temporaire
temporary residence

transfert de résidence
transfer of residence

RÉSIDENT
resident

carte de résident
residence permit

étranger résident
resident alien

résident étranger
alien resident

résident habituel
normal resident

résidents qui sont des nationaux
national residents

résidents qui ne sont pas des nationaux
non-national residents

résident permanent
permanent resident

résident de retour
returning resident

statut de résident
resident status

RÉSIDENTIEL
complexe résidentiel
housing project / estate

mobilité résidentielle
residential mobility

RÉSIDUEL
capacité résiduelle
residual capacity

capacité résiduelle de gain
residual capacity to earn

cas résiduels
(occ.) hard core

chômage résiduel
residual / hard-core / frictional / transitional unemployment

incapacité résiduelle
residual disability

versement résiduel
residual settlement / payment

RÉSILIATION
annulment; termination

avis de résiliation
notice of termination

clause de résiliation
termination clause

résiliation d'un accord
termination of an agreement

résiliation d'un contrat
termination of a contract

RÉSILIER
to terminate; to rescind; to annul

résilier une clause
to annul a clause

résilier un contrat
to terminate a contract

RÉSISTANCE
marge de résistance au travail
work(ing) tolerance

RESOCIALISATION
resocialisation

RÉSOLUTION
resolution; termination

RÉSORBÉ
emplois résorbés par élimination naturelle
jobs eliminated by attrition

RÉSORBER
to absorb

RÉSORPTION
résorption du chômage
reduction of unemployment

RESPECT
respect, observance, compliance

respect des droits acquis
respect for acquired rights

RESPECTER
to abide by, to comply

RESPONSABILITÉ
responsibility; accountability; liability;
charge; (pl.) (occ.) assignement of duties

acquitter de ses responsabilités (s')
to fulfill one's duties / responsibilities

assurance en responsabilité civile
third party insurance, liability insurance

**assurance-responsabilité de
l'employeur**
employer's liability insurance

**indemnité sans reconnaissance de
responsabilité**
without prejudice payment

indemnité de responsabilité
liability allowance

partage des responsabilités
division of responsibilities

poste de responsabilité
position of responsibility, senior post

**régime fondé sur la responsabilité de
l'employeur**
employer's liability scheme

responsabilité du fait d'autrui
vicarious liability

responsabilité à raison de dommages
responsibility for injuries

**responsabilité de l'employeur /
patronale**
employer's liability

sphère de responsabilité
competency area

tarif de responsabilité
liability fee

RESPONSABLE (adj.)
responsible for; liable

agent responsable
officer-in-charge

parenté responsable
responsible parenthood

tiers responsable
person vicariously liable

RESPONSABLE (n.)
manager; policy-maker; official; officer;
officer-in-charge; (pl.) authorities

habilitation de responsables syndicaux
accreditation of union officials

haut responsable
senior executive

reconnaissance de responsables syndi-
caux
accreditation of union officials

responsable d'entreprise
(occ.) workers' representative, shop
steward

responsable de la formation
training officer

responsable de groupe
group leader

responsable de haut rang
senior-ranked official

responsable de l'homologation des
syndicats (UK)
certification officer

responsable de l'hygiène et de la
sécurité
(health and) safety officer

responsable de l'orientation
guidance officer

responsable de programme
programme official

responsable de la rémunération et des
avantages sociaux (USA)
compensation and benefits manager

responsable de secteur
area manager

responsable syndical
(trade / labour) union official, labour
leader

RESSENTI
besoin ressenti
felt need

RESSERREMENT
resserrement du marché du travail / de
l'emploi
tightening of the job market

RESSORT
competence, competency

dernier ressort (en)
without appeal; in the last instance

RESSORTISSANT (n.)
citizen, national

ressortissant d'un Etat membre
national of a Member State

RESSOURCE
resource; (pl.) means, means of support,
subsistence means; income; wealth (occ.)
endowment

affectation / allocation des ressources
resource allocation, allocation of resources

assujetti à une condition de ressources
subject to means test

bilan ressources-emploi
employment(-)resources balance sheet

condition de ressources
means test

condition de ressources (sans)
without means test

condition de ressources (sous)
on a means-test basis; means-tested

contrôle (du niveau) des ressources
means testing

critère de ressources
means test

département des ressources humaines
personnel department

développement des ressources humaines
human resources / manpower development

directeur des ressources humaines
labour / work director, personnel manager

division des ressources humaines
personnel department

fiscalisation des ressources
funding by taxation of revenue

garantie de ressources
income guarantee / maintenance, guaranteed minimum income, minimum income security; income support (allowance)

garantie des ressources après la retraite
income maintenance after retirement

gestion des ressources humaines
human resources / personnel management

mise en valeur des ressources
resource development

mise en valeur des ressources humaines
labour / human resources / manpower / staff development

mobilisation des ressources
(occ.) resource securing

niveau des ressources
resource level, level of resources

personne-ressource
resource person

plafond de ressources
maximum income limit

planification des ressources humaines
personnel / human resources planning

planification des ressources humaines dans l'entreprise
company manpower planning, personnel planning at establishment level

prestation liée à / soumise à / subordonnée à une / versée sous condition de ressources
means-tested / income-tested benefit

recours à des ressources extérieures
out(-)sourcing

répartition des ressources
allocation of resources, resource allocation

ressources (être sans)
to be without means of support / destitute

ressources affectées
income specially earmarked

ressources financières
financial resources

ressources humaines
manpower, human capital / resources

ressources humaines disponibles
human resources supply

ressources de / en main-d'oeuvre
labour / manpower resources / supply, staffing

ressources de main-d'oeuvre inutilisées
employment / labour market slack

ressource matérielle
physical resource

ressources en personnel
labour / manpower resources / supply, staffing

service des ressources humaines
personnel department

soumis à (une) / subordonné à une condition de res-sources, subordonné au critère des ressources
subject to a means test, means-tested

système de prestations lié au niveau des ressources
means-tested system of provision

valorisation des ressources humaines
human resources / manpower / staff development

versé sous conditions de ressources
means-tested

RESTANT
jour restant à prendre
remaining day

salaire restant à payer
outstanding pay

RESTAURANT
chèque-restaurant
luncheon voucher

directeurs d'hôtels, de cafés ou de restaurants [CITP-1968 (5-0)]
managers (catering and lodging services) [ISCO-1968 (5-0)]

foyer-restaurant (Fr.)
home meals

propriétaires-gérants d'hôtel, de cafés ou de restaurants [CITP-1968 (5-1)]
working proprietors (catering and lodging services) [ISCO-1968 (5-1)]

ticket-restaurant
luncheon voucher, meal ticket (USA)

RESTAURATION
rehabilitation; catering

hôtellerie-restauration
catering

intendants et personnel des services de restauration [CITP-1988 (512)]
housekeeping and restaurant services workers [ISCO-1988 (512)]

RESTE
reste (de)
surplus

RESTER
obligation de rester chez soi
confinement to the house

rester en activité
to continue to work, to remain / to stay in employment; to stay in the job

RESTITUTION
restoration

restitution d'une période d'affiliation antérieure
restoration of prior contributory service

RESTREINDRE
to restrict, to limit; to qualify

restreindre l'accès à
to restrict / to limit access

RESTREINT
enquête auprès d'un / sur échantillon restreint
sample survey

marché du travail restreint
tight labour market

RESTRICTIF
clause restrictive
restrictive clause, proviso

pratique restrictive en matière d'emploi
restrictive labour practice

RESTRICTION
limit, limitation, restriction; proviso; qualification

mesure de restriction
restraint measure

restrictions (sous certaines)
subject to certain limitations

restriction d'accès / d'admission / à l'admission / d'affiliation
restriction on access / on entry, entrance / entry limitation / restriction, limitation on entrance / entry, restricted entrance / entry, admission restriction

restriction budgétaire
budgetary constraint

restriction des dépenses
expenditure restraint

restriction à l'entrée
admission restriction, restriction / limitation on entry, entry limitation, restricted entry

restriction de service
service limitation

RESTRUCTURATION
re(-)organisation, restructuring; shake-up

restructuration de l'emploi
employment adjustment

restructuration des emplois
job redefinition / restructuring

RÉSULTAT
result; finding; (pl.) (occ.) returns

élève ayant des résultats scolaires médiocres
under-achiever, low performer / achiever

indicateur de résultat
performance indicator

mauvais résultats scolaires
(occ.) under-achievement

obligation de résultat
obligation of result

paiement en fonction des résultats
payment for results

participation des salariés aux résultats
employee profit-sharing

prime liée aux résultats
performance-related bonus

résultats sur le plan de l'emploi
labour market / employment performance

résultats obtenus à l'examen / aux examens
examination performance

résultats scolaires
educational achievement / attainment, performance at / in school, school achievement / performance

résultats (atteints) au travail
job performance, performance on the job

résultats trimestriels
quarterly figures

système de rémunération aux résultats
incentive scheme

test de résultat
achievement / performance test

RÉTABLIR
to restore, to re-establish; to reinstate; to resume; to recuperate

rétablir une prestation
to resume a benefit

RÉTABLISSEMENT
reinstatement; recovery; restoration

rétablissement de la garde
restoration of custody

rétablissement du versement des prestations
reinstatement of benefits

RETARD
delay; deferment; retardation

pénalité de retard
late payment charge

retard (en)
in arrears

retard injustifiable
unjustifiable delay

retard des salaires
wage gap

retard des salaires réels
real wage gap

retard technologique
technological gap

RETARDÉ (adj.)
départ à la retraite retardé
deferred retirement

enfant retardé
(mentally) retarded child

RETARDÉ (n.)
retardé mental
mentally retarded, developmentally handicapped

RETARDER
to delay; to defer

retarder le départ à la retraite
to defer retirement

RETENIR
to retain; to deduct; (occ.) to shortlist

retenir la cotisation sur le salaire
to deduct contributions from pay / wages

retenir sur le salaire
to deduct from pay / wages

retenir à la source
to tax at source

RÉTENTION
politique de rétention de main-d'oeuvre
labour hoarding policy

rétention des cotisations ouvrières
retention of workers' contributions

rétention d'effectifs / de main-d'oeuvre
labour hoarding

taux de rétention (des effectifs)
retention rate

taux de rétention des salariés à mi-carrière
(occ.) half-life survival rate

RETENU
candidat retenu
successful candidate

candidature non retenue
unsuccessful job application

retenu à la source
deducted at source

RETENUE
deduction

carte des retenues (UK)
deduction card

élément soumis à retenue pour pension
pensionable element

régime d'allocations et de retenues au titre du loyer
rental subsidy/deduction scheme

remise totale ou partielle des retenues
full or partial waiver of deductions

retenue d'une augmentation périodique de salaire
withholding of salary increment

retenue de la cotisation
deduction of contribution

retenue (opérée) au titre du loyer
rental deduction

retenue sur salaire
deduction from wages / earnings, wage assignment

retenue salariale
payroll deduction

retenue à la source
withholding tax, pay-as-you-earn (PAYE), deduction at source P.A.Y.E., payroll deduction

retenue de traitement
withholding of salary

retenue sur le traitement
deduction from earnings / salary, wage assignment

salaire soumis à retenue pour pension
pensionable wage

système de retenue de la cotisation sur le salaire (UK)
direct debit system

traitement soumis à retenue (pour pension)
pensionable salary

RETIRER
retirer du marché du travail (se)
to withdraw from the labour force

retirer de la vie active (se)
to withdraw from working life, to retire
(from work)

RÉTORSION
mesure de rétorsion
retaliatory measure

RETOUR
contrat de retour à l'emploi (Fr.)
back-to-work contract

information en retour
feedback

migrant de retour
returning migrant

migration de retour
return migration

résident de retour
returning resident

retour sur le marché du travail
re-entry (into the labour force)

retour progressif au travail
drift back to work

retour tardif de congés
late return from holidays

retour au travail
back to work, return to employment / to
work

retour à la vie active / professionnelle
reintegration into / return to / re-entry into
working life

RETOURNEMENT
retournement de la conjoncture
cyclical upturn

RETOURNER
retourner au travail
to resume work, to re-enter employment,
to return to employment / to work

RETRAIT
withdrawal

droit d'alerte et de retrait (Fr.)
right of worker to notify a potential risk to
his safety and to stop work

droit de retrait (Fr.)
right to stop work

retrait d'accréditation syndicale
withdrawal of union certification, (occ.)
decertification

retrait d'agrément
revocation / withdrawal of registration,
withdrawal of accreditation; deregistration

retrait de candidature
withdrawal of candidacy

retrait du droit aux prestations
disqualification for benefit

retrait d'emploi
removal from office

retrait de la population active
departure from the labour force

retrait progressif
(occ.) phasing-out

retrait de la vie active
withdrawal from work / from working life
/ from employment

RETRAITE
retirement; (retiring / retirement) pension;
retirement pay / income; superannuation

abaissement de l'âge de la retraite
lowering of the retirement age

administrateur d'une caisse de retraite
trustee of a pension fund

âge de départ obligatoire à la retraite
automatic / compulsory / mandatory
retirement age

âge de départ à la retraite
retirement age

âge légal de départ à la / en retraite
statutory retirement age

âge légal de la retraite
(legal) retirement age, prescribed
pensionable age

âge de la mise à la retraite
pensionable age

âge modulable de la prise de / du
départ à la retraite
flexible pensionable / retirement age

âge normal de la retraite
normal retirement age

âge obligatoire de la retraite
automatic / compulsory / mandatory
retirement age

âge fixé pour la prise de / pour le
départ à la retraite anticipée
age for early retirement

âge de la retraite
age at retirement / at withdrawal; pensionable / retiring age

âge de la retraite anticipée
age for early retirement

âge de retraite facultative
optional retirement age

âge statutaire de la retraite
statutory age of retirement

ajournement de la prise de retraite
deferred retirement

ajourner la prise de / le départ à la
retraite
to defer retirement

anticipation de la prise de retraite
early retirement

anticiper le départ à la retraite
to retire early

arrérages des pensions de retraite (Fr.)
old age pension arrears

caisse de retraite
retirement fund / system, superannuation /
pension fund

caisse de retraite complémentaire
complementary pension fund

cessation de fonctions par mise à la
retraite
termination of appointment by retirement

contrat collectif de retraite
group annuity policy

contrat individuel de retraite
individual annuity policy

date d'effet de la retraite
effective date of retirement

départ forcé à la retraite
involuntary retirement

départ à la / en retraite
retirement (from labour force); (pl.) (occ.)
staff attrition

départ à la retraite ajourné
deferred retirement

départ à la retraite anticipé
early retirement

départ à la retraite retardé
deferred retirement

départ volontaire à la retraite
voluntary retirement

droit à la retraite (ayant)
eligible for retirement

droits à la retraite (faire valoir ses)
to claim retirement benefit

engagement au titre des retraites
pension liability

garantie des ressources / des revenus
après la retraite
income maintenance after retirement

indice courant des retraites (Ger.)
current pension value

institution de retraite
pension institute

liquidation de retraite
pension calculation

livret de retraite
pension book

maison de retraite
old people home, nursing home (USA);
custodial care

**majoration de la pension de retraite
pour conjoint à charge**
pension supplement / increase in respect
of a dependent spouse

mettre à la retraite
to pension off

mise à la retraite
retirement; superannuation

mise à la retraite anticipée
advanced retirement

mise à la retraite d'office
compulsory retirement

**montant annuel de la prestation de
retraite**
annual pension benefit (amount)

**opter pour la non-affiliation / le non-
assujettissement au régime général de
retraite complémentaire**
to contract out

**orientation préalable / préparatoire à la
retraite**
pre-retirement counselling

partir à la retraite
to retire (from work)

passage de la vie active à la retraite
transition from work to retirement

patrimoine-retraite
pension wealth

pension réduite de retraite différée
reduced deferred pension

pension de retraite
old(-)age pension, retirement / superannuation benefit, superannuation,
retiring / retirement pension; service
pension (Malta)

pension de retraite anticipée
early retirement allowance / benefit

pension de retraite complète
standard retirement benefit, full pension

pension de retraite indexée
index-linked pension

pension de retraite minimum (Belg.)
minimum retirement pension

pension de retraite normale
standard retirement benefit

pension de retraite partielle
partial pension

plan d'épargne retraite (Fr.)
savings-related retirement scheme

plan de retraite à cotisations fixes
fixed contribution retirement plan

plan de retraite à prestations fixes
fixed benefit retirement plan

planification de la retraite
retirement planning

point de retraite
pension point (Fr.); (pl.) retirement
entitlement

prendre sa retraite
to retire (from work), to quit

prendre une retraite anticipée
to retire early

préparation de la retraite
retirement planning

prestation de retraite
pension benefit

prétendre à une retraite
to claim a pension

**programme de préparation de la
retraite**
preretirement planning programme

rachat des points de retraite
purchase of retirement entitlement

régime complémentaire de retraite
company / occupational pension plan /
scheme

régime légal de retraite
statutory pension scheme

régime privé de retraite
private pension plan

régime professionnel de retraite
occupational pension / company pension
plan / scheme

régime de retraite
retirement plan; pension / superannuation
scheme / plan

régime de retraite agréé
registered pension plan

régime de retraite en assurance
insured pension plan

régime de retraite des cadres
managers' pension scheme

régime de retraite par capitalisation
funded pension plan / system

régime de retraite sans capitalisation
unfunded pension plan

**régime de retraite par capitalisation
intégrale**
fully funded pension plan

**régime de retraite par capitalisation
partielle**
partially funded-pension plan

régime de retraite complémentaire
complementary pension scheme

**régime de retraite complémentaire géré
par l'Etat**
State earnings-related pension scheme

**régime de retraite complémentaire
privé**
private / contracted-out occupational
pension scheme

**régime de retraite complémentaire
privé en gestion directe**
self-administered pension scheme

régime de retraite non contributif
non-contributory pension plan / scheme

régime de retraite contributif (mixte)
contributory pension scheme / plan

**régime de retraite proposé / mis en
place par l'employeur**
employer-sponsored pension plan

régime de retraite facultatif
optional pension plan

régime de retraite en fiducie
trusteed pension plan

régime de retraite des fonctionnaires
public service pension scheme

régime de retraite obligatoire
mandatory pension scheme / plan

**régime de retraite à participation
différée aux bénéfices**
deferred profit sharing pension plan

**régime de retraite personnel par capi-
talisation**
personal pension scheme / plan

régime de retraite préfinancé
funded pension plan

**régime de retraite professionnelle
(complémentaire) (UK)**
occupational pension scheme

régime de retraite provisionné
funded pension plan

**régime de retraite entièrement provi-
sionné**
fully funded pension plan

régime de retraite par répartition
pay-as-you-go pension plan / system, pay-
as-you-go (PAYG)

régime de retraite-vieillesse
old age pension scheme

**rente des retraites ouvrières et
paysannes**
annuity in addition to industrial and
agricultural workers' pensions

retarder le départ à la retraite
to defer retirement

retraite (à la / en)
retired; superannuated

retraite à 100 %
full pension, full retirement benefit

retraite anticipée
early retirement, pre-retirement

retraite de base
basic pension

retraite par capitalisation
pre-funded pension plan / scheme

retraite à la carte
flexible retirement

retraite complémentaire
company / occupational pension;
complementary pension

retraite complète
full pension, full retirement benefit

retraite différée
deferred pension / retirement benefit

retraite entière
full pension, full retirement benefit

retraite par étapes
phased retirement

retraite versée par l'Etat
State pension

retraite facultative
optional retirement

retraite forfaitaire
flat-rate pension

retraite par limite d'âge
retirement on account of age

retraite modulée
flexible retirement

retraite nationale par limite d'âge (UK)
national superannuation

retraite obligatoire
mandatory retirement

retraite d'office
compulsory retirement

retraite d'office (être mis à la)
to be compulsorily retired

retraites ouvrières et paysannes
industrial and agricultural workers'
pensions

retraite partielle
partial retirement

retraite professionnelle (complémentaire)
company / occupational pension

retraite progressive
progressive / phased retirement

retraite proportionnelle
proportional pension

retraite de réversion
survivor's pension

retraite à taux minoré
reduced (rate) pension / retirement benefit

retraite à taux plein
full pension, full retirement benefit

revenu sous forme de retraite
retirement income

salaire de base pour le calcul de la retraite
pensionable earnings

système de retraite
retirement / pension scheme / system

système de retraite par capitalisation
funded pension system

RETRAITÉ (adj.)
fonctionnaire retraité
retired staff member

RETRAITÉ (n.)
pensioner, retiree, retired (person); old age
/ retirment pensioner; superannuated

carte de retraité
pension card

RÉTRÉCISSEMENT
rétrécissement du marché du travail / de
l'emploi
tightening of the job market

RÉTRIBUÉ
salaried

emploi rétribué
paid / gainful employment

exercer un emploi rétribué
to be gainfully occupied / employed

rétribué (non)
unpaid; honorary

RÉTRIBUTION
payment; compensation; consideration;
fee

point personnel de rétribution (Ger.)
personal income point

rétribution garantie-traitement (Belg.)
guaranteed remuneration

rétribution en nature
payment in kind

RÉTROACTIF
retroactive, retrospective; ex post facto

augmentation salariale rétroactive
retroactive increase in wages

effet rétroactif (avec)
retroactively; backdated

loi rétroactive
retroactive statute

mesure à effet rétroactif
retroactive measure

paiement rétroactif
retroactive payment

rémunération rétroactive
retroactive remuneration

RÉTROACTIVITÉ
retroactivity

RÉTROCESSION
reassignment

RÉTROGRADATION
downgrading; demotion

RÉTROGRADER
to downgrade; to demote

RÉTROSPECTIF
retrospective

données rétrospectives
retrospective / back data

RÉTROSPECTION
erreur de rétrospection
recall error

RÉUNION
droit de réunion
right of assembly

liberté de réunion
freedom of assembly

RÉUNIR
réunir les conditions
to fulfil the conditions

réunir les conditions (ne pas)
(occ.) to be ineligible

réunir des données
to collect data

réunir des fonds
to raise funds

réunir des informations
to collect information

RÉUSSIR
réussir un examen
to pass an examination

RÉUSSITE
motivation de réussite
achievement motivation

réussite professionnelle
career achievement, job success

taux de réussite
success / completion rate

REVALORISATION
(upward) adjustment; uprating, upgrading; rehabilitation; revaluation;
revalorisation

coefficient de revalorisation
revalorisation coefficient

majoration de revalorisation
revalorisation increase

revalorisation des pensions
revaluation / revalorisation / upgrading /
review of pensions

revalorisation des prestations
benefit adjustment, adjustment / revalorisation / uprating / upgrading of
benefits

revalorisation des professions
upgrading of occupations

revalorisation des salaires
upward adjustment of wages

revalorisation du travail manuel
upgrading of manual work

REVALORISER
to upgrade

REVENDICATIF
action / mouvement revendicatif (ive)
job / industrial action

REVENDICATION
claim, grievance; demand

cahier des revendications syndicales
list of union demands

journée de revendication
day of action

revendication catégorielle
group claim; (pl.) sectional claims

revendication de salaire / salariale
wage claim / demand; (pl.) pressure of
wages

revendication sociale
social demand

revendication syndicale
union demand

REVENDIQUER
to claim

REVENIR
revenir à
to amount to

revenir sur
to revoke

revenir sur le marché du travail
to re-enter the labour force

REVENU
income; earnings; returns

**abattement fiscal sur le revenu profes-
sionnel de l'épouse**
wife's earned income allowance

**abattement fiscal sur le revenu du
travail**
earned income allowance

**allocation de remplacement de revenus
(Belg.)**
income replacement allowance

allocation de revenus réduits (UK)
reduced earnings allowance

année de revenu
earning year

apporteur de revenu
earner, breadwinner

assujetti à l'impôt sur le revenu
subject to income tax(ation)

calculer l'impôt sur le revenu
to assess income tax

catégorie de personnes à faibles revenus
low-income (population) group

catégorie de revenus
class of income

coefficient de remplacement du revenu
income replacement ratio

**compensation de / pour la perte de
revenu(s)**
compensation for loss of income, income
replacement / compensation

complément au / de revenu familial
family supplement, family income
supplement (UK); family credit (UK)

complément de revenu
income supplement, supplementary
income, income support allowance

**crédit d'impôt au titre des revenus du
travail**
earned income tax credit (USA)

critère de revenu
income test

déclaration de l'impôt sur le revenu
income tax return / form

déclaration de revenus
statement of income

déclaration de revenus modifiée
modified statement of income, amended
tax return

déductible du revenu imposable
tax(-)deductible

**déterminer le montant de l'impôt sur le
revenu**
to assess income tax

deuxième apporteur de revenu
second (family) earner / breadwinner,
secondary family worker, secondary
(wage) earner

différence(s) / disparité de revenus
income differential; earnings gap

distribution du revenu
income distribution

écart entre les revenus
income differential; earnings gap

effet de revenu
income effect (of a wage increase)

égaliser les revenus
to level out earnings

**élasticité de la demande par rapport au
revenu**
income elasticity of demand

famille à deux revenus
two-income / two-earner family

**famille à plusieurs revenus / à revenus
multiples**
multi-earner family

famille à revenu unique
one-earner family

garantie de revenu
income maintenance / support

garantie de revenu minimal
minimum / basic income support

garantie des revenus après la retraite
income maintenance after retirement

groupe à faibles revenus
low-income (population) group

haut de la hiérarchie des revenus
upper income bracket

hiérarchie des revenus
salary scale; wage bracket; scale of
income / salaries

impôt progressif sur le revenu
graduated / progressive income tax

impôt sur le revenu
income tax

**impôt sur les revenus des personnes
physiques (Fr.)**
personal income tax

**impôt sur le revenu progressif / fondé
sur la progressivité**
graduated / progressive income tax

incidence sur les revenus
income effect

**logements pour les groupes sociaux à
faibles revenus**
low-income housing

ménage à faible revenu
low-income household

ménage à revenu unique
one-earner household

mise en commun des revenus
income pooling

niveau de revenu
level of earnings

pension de l'Etat liée aux revenus (UK)
State earnings-related pension

personne aux revenus modestes
person on low income / with small means

perte de revenus
loss of income

plafond de revenu
maximum income limit

plancher de revenu
minimum income limit

politique des revenus
income policy

prestation calculée en fonction des revenus
income-related benefit

prestation non liée aux revenus
benefit not related to earnings

prestation liée aux revenus antérieurs
(previous) earnings-related (insurance) benefit

principal apporteur de revenus
main / principal (wage) earner, primary earner

programme de transferts de revenus
income transfer programme

progressivité de l'impôt sur le revenu
graduated / progressive income tax

proportionnel aux revenus
earnings-related

protection des revenus
income protection

redistribution des revenus
redistribution of income

relogement de populations à bas revenus
rehousing of low-income groups

répartition des revenus
distribution of income, income distribution

revenu accessoire
incidental / additional income; (pl.) subsidiary income

revenu accumulé / acquis
accrued income

revenu d'activité
income from work

revenu additionnel
secondary income

revenu agricole
farm income

revenu agricole net
net farm income

revenu annuel
yearly / annual income

revenu d'appoint
secondary / complementary income

revenu d'appoint temporaire
temporary income support

revenu d'aubaine
windfall income

revenu brut
gross income

revenu complémentaire
secondary / complementary income

revenu à prendre en compte / en considération
reckonable earnings

revenu différé
deferred income

revenu discrétionnaire
discretionary income

revenu disponible
spendable / disposable income

revenu disponible des particuliers
disposable personal income

revenu ouvrant droit à pension
pensionable income

revenus effectifs
actual earnings

revenus provenant / tirés d'un emploi
employment earnings / income, earnings
from employment

revenus exonérés d'impôts
tax-free income

revenus externes
outside earnings

revenu familial
family / household income

revenu fixe
fixed / regular income

revenu foncier
landed income

revenu gagné
accrued income; (pl.) earned income

revenu non gagné
investment / unearned income

revenu par habitant
per capita income

revenu hebdomadaire
weekly earnings

revenu imposable
assessed / assessable / taxable income

revenu non imposable
tax-free income

revenu de l'impôt
tax yield

revenus industriels et commerciaux
income from business

revenu intermédiaire
middle income

revenu marginal du travail
marginal revenue of labour

revenu du ménage
household income

revenu minimum
minimum income, income support (UK)

revenu minimum familial
family minimum income

revenu minimum garanti
guaranteed minimum income

revenu minimum d'insertion (RMI)
minimum social income, guaranteed
minimum income

revenu minimum légal
statutory minimum income

revenu moyen
average income

revenu national
national income; social income

revenu net
net income

revenu nominal
nominal / money income

revenu(s) du patrimoine
income from assets, revenue from estate

revenu pris en compte pour la pension
pensionable income

revenu personnel disponible
private disposable income, disposable
personal income

revenu potentiel
potiential income; (pl.) (occ.) earnings
prospect

revenus professionnels
occupational income / earnings, earned
income

revenu réel
real income; (pl.) actual earnings

revenu de référence
reckonable earnings; income standard

revenu de remplacement
replacement income

revenu sous forme de retraite
retirement income

revenu salarial
earned / wage / labour income

revenu non salarial
non-wage income; (pl.) investment /
unearned income

revenu salarial proportionnel à ses compétences
salary commensurate with one's abilities

revenu par semaine
weekly earnings

revenu social brut
gross social (insurance) income

revenus de sociétés
company / corporate earnings

revenu statutaire
statutory income

revenu de subsistance
subsistence income

revenu de substitution
income replacement

revenu supplémentaire
additional income; secondary income

revenu par tête
per capita income

revenu (provenant) de transferts
transfer income

revenu du travail
income from work, earned income; (pl.) labour income

revenus autres que ceux du travail / ne provenant pas d'un travail
investment / unearned income

seuil d'exonération fiscale des revenus
lower earnings limit of tax exemption

seuil de faible revenu
low-income cut-off / threshold / limit

source principale de revenu
primary / principal (wage) earner

source de revenu
earner

source secondaire de revenus
second breadwinner, secondary (wage) earner, second family earner

soutien du revenu familial
family income support

soutien du revenu hebdomadaire
weekly income support

supplément de revenu familial (UK)
family income supplement

supplément de revenu garanti
guaranteed income supplement, supplemental security income (Can.)

taux de compensation de la perte de revenu
income replacement ratio

taux effectif d'imposition sur le revenu
real income tax rate

taux de remplacement du revenu
income replacement ratio / rate

tranche de revenus
class of income, wage / income bracket

transfert de revenus
income transfer

travailleur à faibles revenus
worker with low income

versé sous condition de revenu
income-tested

REVERSÉ
reversé (être)
to revert

RÉVERSIBLE
transferable; passing on the survivor

rente viagère réversible
survivor's / survivorship annuity

RÉVERSION
clause de réversion
survivorship provision

pension de réversion
reversionary annuity, reversion / dependant's / survivor's pension; widower's / widow's / survivor's benefit

pension de réversion à la suite d'un accident du travail
industrial death benefit

pension de réversion d'orphelin
orphan's pension

rente (viagère) de / avec réversion
survivor's / survivorship annuity

retraite de réversion
survivor's pension

réversion d'une pension / d'une rente
transfer of pension rights to the surviving
beneficiary

REVIENT
prix de revient
cost price

RÉVISÉ
indice révisé d'ajustement des pensions
revised pension adjustment index

**régime d'allocations (de) logement
révisé**
revised rental subsidy scheme

**système révisé d'ajustement des
pensions**
revised pension adjustment system

RÉVISER
to review

réviser à la baisse
to review downwards

réviser à la hausse
to review upwards

réviser les salaires
to review salaries / wages

RÉVISION
review; re-assessment

comité de révision
review board

révision annuelle
annual review

révision générale
general review

révision générale des traitements
major salary review

révision en hausse
upward adjustment

révision à la hausse des traitements
upward adjustment of salaries

révision périodique
periodic review

révision d'une rente
review of a pension

révision des salaires
pay / salary / wage review

RÉVOCATION
removal (from office); dismissal

révocation d'accréditation syndicale
withdrawal of union certification, (occ.)
decertification

révocation d'une nomination
revocation of an appointment

REVOIR
to review

RÉVOLU
année révolue
complete year

RÉVOQUER
to revoke; to dismiss

révoquer une nomination
to revoke an appointment

RHUMATOLOGIE
rheumatology

**RHUMATOLOGISTE / RHUMATO-
LOGUE**
rheumatologist

RICHESSE
wealth, affluence

signe extérieur de richesse
external indication of wealth

RIGIDITÉ
rigidité du marché du travail
labour market rigidity

rigidité des salaires
wage rigidity

RIGUEUR
délai de rigueur
strict time-limit

rigueur salariale
wage restraint

RISQUE
risk, contingency; event; hazard; venture;
claim

amélioration de la couverture des risques
improvement in coverage

assurance générale risques graves (Neth.)
general insurance against serious risks

assurance gros risques
major medical insurance

assurance petits risques
minor medical insurance

assurance tous risques
comprehensive insurance

barème des risques
scale of risks

clause de risque de grève
strikes clause

couverture des risques de maladie
health insurance cover

couverture du risque vieillesse
old age coverage

délai d'exposition au risque
risk exposure time

étalement du risque
spreading the risk

fonction de risque
hazard function

groupe à haut(s) risque(s)
high-risk group

moment de la réalisation du risque
time when risk / the contingency arises

petits risques (Fr.)
minor medical expenses

police tous risques
blanket (insurance) policy

population à risque
population at risk

prestation liée à des risques
contingency benefit

prime de risque
hazard pay; danger money

provision pour risques
risk allowance

réalisation du risque
occurrence of the event

répartition du risque
spreading the risk

risque (à)
at risk; disadvantaged

risques (sans)
safe

risque d'accident du travail
occupational hazard / risk

risque avéré
proven risk

risques couverts et prestations attribuées
contingencies covered and benefits granted

risque d'invalidité
probability / risk of disability

risque moral
moral hazard

risque professionnel
occupational hazard / risk

risque pour la santé
health hazard

risque de sécurité
safety hazard

risque social
social contingency / risk

risque subjectif
moral hazard (insurance)

salarié à risques
accident-prone worker

survenance du risque
occurrence of the event

taux de risque
hazard rate

type de risques couverts
type of coverage

RISTOURNE
rebate

RÔDAGE
période de rodage
running-in period

RÔLE
role; function

établissement des rôles d'imposition
tax assessment

rôle (à tour de)
by / in rotation

rôle consultatif
advisory capacity

rôle d'imposition
tax roll

rôle social
social responsibility / role

ROMPRE
rompre un contrat
to terminate a contract

ROTATION
rotation, turnover

affectation par rotation
rotational assignment

équipe de rotation rapide
rapid rotation shift work

rotation des effectifs
turnover (of staff), (staff) turnover

rotation des / d'emplois / d'un emploi à l'autre
job rotation

rotation de la main-d'oeuvre
turnover (of labour), (labour) turnover

rotation du personnel
turnover (of personnel), (personnel) turnover

rotation des postes
job rotation

taux de rotation
turnover rate

taux de rotation des effectifs
staff turnover rate

taux de rotation des emplois
job turnover rate

taux de rotation de la main-d'oeuvre
labour turnover rate

ROUAGE
(pl.) machinery

rouages du marché de l'emploi / du travail
functioning / operation of the labour market

ROULANT
fauteuil roulant
wheel-chair

matériel roulant
rolling stock (railways)

ROULEMENT
rotation

liste de roulement
rota

mutation par roulement
transfer on a rotating basis

roulement (par)
by / in rotation

roulement des effectifs
turnover (of staff), (staff) turnover

roulement de la main-d'oeuvre
turnover (of labour), (labour) turnover

roulement dans l'occupation des postes
rotation of staff

roulement du personnel
turnover (of personnel), (personnel)
turnover

système par roulement
rota system

taux de roulement
turnover rate

taux de roulement du personnel
personnel turnover rate

travail par roulement
shift work(ing)

travailler par roulement
to work shifts

ROUTE
délai de route
travel(ling) time

accident de la route
traffic accident

ROUTINE
examen médical de routine
routine medical test

ROUTINIER
travail routinier
monotonous / repetitive work

ROYAL
arrêté royal (Belg.)
Royal decree

RUBAN
sténographes dactylographes et opérateurs sur machines perforatrices de cartes
et de rubans [CITP-1968 (3-2)]
stenographers, typists and card- and tape-
punching machine operators [ISCO-1968
(3-2)]

RUBRIQUE
heading

RUE
cireurs de chaussures et autres travailleurs des petits métiers des rues [CITP-
1988 (912)]
shoe cleaning and other street services
elementary occupations [ISCO-1988
(912)]

éducateur de rue
(community) supervision officer, street
educator

enfant des rues
street child

petits métiers de la rue
light street industries

RUPTURE
termination; severance; breakdown

clause de rupture
termination clause

**date effective de la rupture du contrat
de travail**
effective date of termination

rupture abusive du contrat de travail
wrongful / unfair dismissal, wrongful
discharge (USA)

rupture anticipée
anticipatory breach

rupture dans la continuité du service
break in service

rupture de contrat
breach of contract

rupture du contrat de travail
breach of contract of employment

rupture d'un contrat de travail
termination of a contract of employment

rupture des négociations
breakdown of (the) negotiations

rupture d'union
broken / dissolved marriage, termination
of marriage

RURAL (adj.)
rural

artisan rural (Fr.)
rural self-employed

Code rural (Fr.)
rural Code

développement rural
rural development

exode rural
rural depopulation

groupe sanitaire rural
rural health unit

modernisation rurale
rural modernisation

population rurale
rural population

projet de relèvement rural
rural rehabilitation project

service de santé rural
rural health service

service social rural
rural social work

RURAL (n.)
rural dweller

RYTHME
pace; rate

rythme de croisière d'un régime
mature status of scheme / plan

rythme de production
production rate

rythme de sorties
rate of outflow (register)

SABBATIQUE
sabbatical

année sabbatique
sabbatical year / (occ.) leave

congé sabbatique
sabbatical leave

SAGE-FEMME
midwife

cadres infirmiers et sages-femmes [CITP-1988 (223)]
nursing and midwifery professionals [ISCO-1988 (223)]

personnel infirmier et sages-femmes (niveau intermédiaire) [CITP-1988 (323)]
nursing and midwifery associate professionals [ISCO-1988 (323)]

sage-femme visiteuse
domiciliary midwife

SAIN
healthy; sound

sain et sauf
uninjured

SAISI
tiers saisi
garnishee

SAISIE
attachment; seizure; sequestration

saisie du / sur salaire
attachment of wages / earnings, income execution, wage garnishment

saisie sur le salaire (faire)
to attach salary

SAISIE-ARRÊT
ordre de saisie-arrêt
attachment of earnings order

saisie-arrêt
attachment, garnishee order, garnishment

saisie-arrêt du / sur salaire
attachment of wages / earnings, income execution, wage garnishment

SAISISSABLE
partie saisissable d'une pension
attachable part of a pension

quotité saisissable
attachable portion (of wages)

SAISONNIER (adj.)
seasonal

activité saisonnière
seasonal operation / business

ajustement saisonnier
seasonal adjustment

chômage saisonnier
seasonal unemployment

contrat de travail saisonnier
seasonal employment / work contract

correction des variations saisonnières
seasonal adjustment

corrigé des variations saisonnières
seasonally adjusted

demande saisonnière
seasonal demand

emploi agricole saisonnier
seasonal agriculture work

emploi saisonnier
employment of a seasonal nature, seasonal job / employment / work

emploi saisonnier pour étudiants
(occ.) vacation job / work

employé saisonnier
seasonal employee

facteur saisonnier
seasonal factor

fluctuation saisonnière
seasonal fluctuation / variation

fluctuations saisonnières de l'emploi
seasonal employment variations

main-d'oeuvre saisonnière
seasonal manpower / labour force

mouvement saisonnier
seasonal movement

travail agricole saisonnier
seasonal agriculture work

travail (à caractère) saisonnier
work of (a) seasonal nature, seasonal job /
employment / work

travailleur saisonnier
seasonal worker / employee

variation saisonnière
seasonal fluctuation / variation

SAISONNIER (n.)
seasonal employee /worker

saisonnier agricole
seasonal agricultural labourer

SALAIRE
wage; pay; earnings; remuneration; salary; (pl.) (occ.) salary scale

accessoires de salaire
fringe benefits

accord collectif sur les salaires
collective pay agreement

acompte sur salaire
advance on salary

alignement des salaires
(occ.) pay comparability

allocation de salaire unique
single wage allowance

arriéré de salaire
arrear of wages, back wage / salary / pay,
wage arrear

assurance-maintien du salaire
salary continuation insurance

assurance(-)salaire
wage loss insurance

augmentation en niveau des salaires
global percentage increase of salaries

augmentation préférentielle des salaires
premium wage increase

augmentation de / du / des salaire(s)
salary increase / award, salary / wage /
pay rise / increase

avance sur salaire
salary advance

avance des salaires
wage gap

avance des salaires réels
real wage gap

avantage de salaire
wage premium

baisse de salaire
wage cut

barème local des salaires
local salary / wage scale

barème des salaires
salary / wage scale

blocage des salaires
wage freeze

bloquer les salaires
to withhold wages

bulletin de salaire
payroll

cession de salaire
wage transfer

chèque de salaire
pay cheque

classe de salaire
wage class

**complément extraordinaire de salaire
(It.)**
extraordinary wage supplement

complément ordinaire de salaire (It.)
ordinary wage supplement

complément de salaire
pay / wage supplement

complément de salaire lié à la situation du marché de l'emploi (Swed.)
market pay supplement

compléter le salaire
to make up wage(s)

compression des salaires
wage compression

compte salaire
payroll account

congé sans salaire
leave without pay

conseil des salaires (UK)
wage council

cotisation perçue sur le salaire (USA)
wages tax

cotisation proportionnelle au salaire
earnings-related contribution

courbe d'augmentation des salaires
salary progression curve

courbe des salaires
wage curve / trend

course entre les salaires
wage-wage spiral

coût des salaires nominaux
money-wage cost

déduire la cotisation du salaire
to deduct contributions from wages

demi-salaire
half-pay, half-wage

dérapage / dérive des salaires
earnings / wage drift

dernier salaire
final salary

différence de salaires
wage / earnings gap / differential,
difference in wages

disparité de salaires
wage disparity

double salaire sans enfants
double income no kids (DINK)

écart de salaires
wage / earnings gap / differential,
difference in wages

écart des salaires par rapport à la productivité
real wage gap

échelle mobile des salaires
sliding wage scale, incremental scale

échelle mobile des salaires établie sur le coût de la vie
cost-of-living sliding scale

échelle de(s) salaires
wage / pay / salary scale / range, range /
scale of wages, wage bracket

économie de salaires
wage economy

égalité des salaires
equal pay, wage parity

élasticité de l'offre de travail par rapport aux salaires
wage elasticity of labour supply

élément fixe des salaires
fixed wage element

encadrement des salaires
wage control

enquête sur les salaires
salary survey

enveloppe de salaire
pay / wage packet

état nominatif des salaires
salary statement per person

éventail des salaires
range of wages; (occ.) wage differential

famille à salaire unique
one-earner family

feuille de salaire
paylist, paysheet, payroll, earnings record,
pay statement / slip

fixation des salaires
salary determination

fixer les salaires
to set wages

**fondé à réclamer une indemnisation
pour perte de salaire (être)**
to be entitled to claim restitution of lost
salary / wage / earnings

formation des salaires
wage formation

fourchette de salaires
wage range / band / bracket

garantie de créances de salaires
wage claim guarantee

gel des salaires
wage / pay freeze

glissement de salaires
incidental wage increase, wage drift / shift

grille des salaires
salary scale

harmonisation interne des salaires
internal alignment of wages

hausse contractuelle de salaires
pay / wage settlement

hausse inflationniste de salaires
wage inflation

hausse du / des salaire(s)
wage / salary rise / increase, pay increase

hiérarchie des salaires
salary scale; wage bracket; scale of
income / salaries

impôt sur la masse des / sur les salaires
payroll tax

indemnité pour perte de salaire
compensation for loss of wage(s)

indemnité de salaire
wage replacement / compensation

indemnité se substituant au salaire
compensation in lieu of salary

indexation des salaires
wage indexation

indexation des salaires sur l'inflation
indexing of wages to inflation

indicateur de dispersion des salaires
(occ.) comparatio

indice des salaires
wage index

inégalité de salaires
wage disparity

inflation par les / des salaires
wage(-push) inflation

juste salaire
fair wage

limitation des salaires
wage restraint

**maintenir les salaires au niveau du coût
de la vie**
to keep wages abreast of the cost of living

maintien du salaire
continued payment of wage, wage
continuation

majoration du / des salaire(s)
salary / wage / pay rise / increase

masse des salaires industriels
industrial payroll

ménage à salaire unique
one-earner family

ménage à salaires multiples
multiple earner household

niveau potentiel de salaire
earnings potential / power

niveau de(s) salaire(s)
pay / salary / wage / earnings level; rate of
pay

niveau de salaire à l'embauche
accession rate of pay

ordre de grandeur de salaire
salary estimation / estimate

parité des salaires
equal pay, wage parity

pays à bas salaires
low-wage country

perte de salaire
loss of earnings / of wage

petits salaires (les)
low-paid (the)

pillage par les salaires
wage piracy

plafond de salaire
upper earnings limit / level, wage ceiling

plancher de salaire
lower earnings limit / level, wage floor

politique des salaires
wage / compensation policy

poussée des salaires
wage inflation / push

pouvoir d'achat des salaires
(occ.) real wage / earnings

précompte sur le salaire
deduction at source P.A.Y.E.

prélèvement sur salaire
deduction from wages / earnings

prélèvements fondés sur les salaires
payroll tax

prélever sur le salaire
to deduct from pay / wages

pression des salaires
wage pressure

prestation proportionnelle au salaire
earnings-related benefit

prestation non proportionnelle au salaire
benefit not related to earnings

principe à travail égal, salaire égal
equal pay for equal work principle

progression automatique des salaires
automatic wage progression

proportionnel au salaire
earnings-related

protection du salaire
wage protection

rapatriement de salaires
(cash) remittances

rattrapage de salaire
make-up pay, back salary / pay

réajustement automatique des salaires
automatic wage adjustment

réduction de salaire
wage cut

régime d'assurance salaire
wage loss insurance plan, wage loss replacement plan

régime d'assurance(-)vieillesse proportionnelle au salaire
(occ.) graduated pension scheme

régime des salaires
salary system

régime salaire de carrière
career earnings pension plan

régime salaire meilleures années
average best earnings plan

remboursement maximal au titre des salaires
maximum wage reimbursement

remboursement au titre du salaire
wage reimbursement

retard des salaires
wage gap

retard des salaires réels
real wage gap

retenir la cotisation sur le salaire
to deduct contributions from pay / wages

retenir sur le salaire
to deduct from pay / wages

retenue d'une augmentation périodique de salaire
withholding of salary increment

retenue sur salaire
deduction from wages / earnings, wage assignment

revalorisation des salaires
upward adjustment of wages

revendication de salaire
wage claim / demand; (pl.) pressure of
wages

réviser les salaires
to review salaries / wages

révision des salaires
pay / salary / wage review

rigidité des salaires
wage rigidity

saisie du / sur salaire
attachment of wages / earnings, income
execution, wage garnishment

saisie sur le salaire (faire)
to attach salary

saisie-arrêt du / sur salaire
attachment of wages / earnings, income
execution, wage garnishment

salaire annuel moyen de base
basic average annual wage

salaire d'appoint
complementary / secondary income

salaire de base
base wage / pay / rate; (occ.) tariff wage

**salaire de base pour le calcul de la
retraite**
pensionable earnings

salaire de base maximal imposable
maximum taxable wage rate

salaire brut
gross pay / wage / earnings

salaire brut moyen
average gross / gross average wage

salaire concurrentiel
competitive wage

salaire dû pendant les congés
holiday pay

salaire de la consommation réelle
real consumption wage

salaire contractuel
contractual / negotiated wage

salaire convenu
agreed / standard wage

**salaire donnant lieu / soumis à
cotisation**
earnings subject to contribution, contributory wage

salaire-coût
labour cost

salaire en début d'activité / de départ
starting wage

salaire différé
deferred wage

salaires différenciés
differential wages

salaire ouvrant droit à pension
pensionable wage

salaire dû
outstanding pay

salaire effectif
active / actual wage / earnings

salaire d'efficience
efficiency wage

salaire égal
equal pay

salaire élevé (à)
high-paid, highly paid

salaire d'embauche
starting wage; recruitment ratio / rate,
hiring rate

salaire équivalent
equivalent earnings

salaire en espèces
(occ.) money wage

salaire exigé
wage required

salaire en fin de carrière
final salary

salaire fixe
basic / fixed wage

salaire de formation
training wage

salaire garanti
warranted wage

salaire gonflé
inflated salary

salaire de gréviste
strike pay

salaire hebdomadaire
weekly wage / pay, earnings / wage per week

salaire hebdomadaire brut
gross weekly pay, weekly earnings before deductions

salaire hebdomadaire brut normal
normal gross weekly earnings / wage

salaire hebdomadaire maximal admissible
maximum allowable weekly earnings / wage

salaire hebdomadaire moyen
average weekly earnings / wage

salaire horaire
hourly / time wage

salaire en horaire normal
straight-time pay; (occ.) regular wage

salaire après impôt
take-home / after-tax pay

salaire indexé
index-tied wage, indexed pay

salaires indexés sur l'inflation
wages geared to inflation

salaire indirect
indirect wage / compensation

salaires dans l'industrie
industrial wages

salaire initial
starting wage

salaire intégral
full wage

salaire journalier
daily wage

salaire légal de maternité (UK)
statutory maternity pay

salaire du marché
market salary

salaire médian
median wage

salaire mensuel
monthly wage

salaire minimal / minimum
minimum wage

salaire minimum accepté
acceptance / reserve / reservation wage

salaire minimum garanti
guaranteed minimum wage, minimum wage rate; (occ.) fall-back pay (when linked to performance)

salaire minimum d'insertion (Sp.)
minimum integration wage

salaire minimum interprofessionnel (Sp.)
minimum interprofessional wage

salaire minimum interprofessionnel de croissance (SMIC) (Fr.)
guaranteed / statutory minimum wage

salaire minimum interprofessionnel garanti
intertrade minimum wage

salaire minimum légal
statutory minimum wage

salaire minimum vital
minimum living wage

salaire de misère
subsistence wage

salaire moyen
average wage; final average wage (for calculation of a benefit); career average salary (for calculation of pension)

salaire net
net wage / pay / earnings; take-home pay;
disposable income

salaire net payable
net payable wage

salaire nominal
nominal / money wage

salaire normal
normal wage

salaire occasionnel
casual wage

salaire partagé
split pay

salaire partiel
part wage, partial pay

salaire payé à la semaine
wage paid by the week, weekly wage

salaire perdu
lost wage

salaire à la pièce / aux pièces
piecework / piece wage, piece rate

salaire afférent à un poste
salary attached to a position

salaire privilégié
premium wage

salaire de la production réelle
real product wage

salaire au prorata des heures ouvrées
wage in proportion to time worked

salaire de référence
official / reference wage

salaire réel
actual / real wage / earnings

salaire réellement payé
wage actually paid

salaire régulier
regular wage

salaire au rendement
incentive wage, wage incentive

salaire restant à payer
outstanding pay

salaire soumis à retenue pour pension
pensionable wage

**salaire pratiqué dans les secteurs
syndiqués**
union wage

salaire social
social wage

salaire social minimal (Lux.)
minimum social salary

salaire pour solde de tout compte
terminated employee's final pay

**salaire de subsistance / tout juste
suffisant pour vivre**
subsistence wage

salaire à la tâche
piecework / piece wage, piece rate

salaires et traitements
wages and salaries

salaires et traitements en nature
wages and salaries in kind

salaire unique
single wage

salaire dû pendant les vacances
holiday pay

salaire variable
variable wage

salaire versé
wage paid

salaire vital
living wage

spirale des salaires
wage spiral

spirale des salaires et des prix
wage/price spiral

structure des salaires
wage / salary / pay structure

substitut de salaire
cash benefit(s) in lieu of wage

supplément de salaire
extra pay

supplément lié / proportionnel au salaire
earnings-related supplement

système (de détermination) du salaire minimum
minimum wage system

système d'indexation des salaires
pay indexation system

système de retenue de la cotisation sur le salaire (UK)
direct debit system

taux de chômage non accélérateur des salaires
non accelerating wage rate of unemployment (NAWRU)

taux horaire de salaire
hourly wage rate

taux de / du salaire
salary / pay / wage rate

taux de salaire fixé par arbitrage
award (wage) rate

taux de salaire courant
prevailing rate of pay

taux de salaire horaire
hourly wage rate

taux de salaire maximal
maximum rate of pay

taux de salaire mensuel
monthly wage rate

taux de salaire minimum
minimum wage rate

taux de salaire aux pièces
piecework rate

taxe sur la masse des salaires / sur les salaires
payroll tax

toucher son salaire
to draw one's pay, to receive one's wage

traitements et salaires
salaries

tranche inférieure des salaires (la)
lower paid (the)

tranche de salaire
wage / pay / salary bracket

travailleur à bas salaire
low-wage earner

versement des salaires
payment of wages

viscosité des salaires
wage stickiness

zone de salaires
wage zone

SALARIAL
accord salarial
wage / pay settlement

aspirations salariales
wage aspirations / expectations

augmentation salariale
salary increase / award, salary / wage / pay rise / increase

augmentation salariale rétroactive
retroactive increase in wages

avantage salarial
wage premium

bien salarial
wage good

calcul du coût salarial
calculation of wage / salary cost(s), salary costing

catégorie salariale
earnings category

charge salariale
labour cost; (pl.) employee's contributions; hired labour charges

charges salariales fixes
overhead labour costs

commission salariale (paritaire)
wages council

complément salarial
remuneration supplement, top-up

conditions salariales
wage conditions; details of salaries

conflit salarial
pay / wage dispute

convention salariale
wage settlement

cotisation salariale
worker's / employee's contribution

cotisation salariale de sécurité sociale
employees' social security contribution

coût de main-d'oeuvre non salarial
non-wage labour cost

coût salarial
wage / labour cost; (pl.) payroll / salary
costs, wage bill

coût non salarial
non-salary / non-wage cost

coûts salariaux directs
direct labour costs

coûts salariaux indirects
indirect labour costs

coûts non salariaux ordinaires
recurring non-salary costs

créance salariale
pay claim

différence / écart salarial(e)
wage / earnings gap / differential,
difference in wages

échelle salariale
wage / pay / salary scale / range, range /
scale of wages, wage bracket

élément non salarial de rémunération
non-wage award

établissement du coût salarial
calculation of wage / salary cost(s), salary
costing

flexibilité salariale
wage flexibility

gains salariaux
wage earnings

hausse salariale
wage / salary rise / increase, pay increase

hausse salariale compensatoire
compensatory wage increase

impôt sur la masse salariale
payroll tax

indexation salariale
wage indexation

majoration salariale
salary / wage / pay rise / increase

masse salariale
wage / pay bill, total payroll / wage (bill);
payroll; total earnings

masse salariale brute
total gross earnings

masse salariale investie (dans...)
invested pay, investment wage

modération salariale
pay restraint, wage moderation

négociations salariales
pay round / negotiations, wage bargaining / negotiations / round

norme salariale
wage standard

octroi de subventions salariales
subsidisation of wages

orientations salariales
pay / wage guidelines

part salariale
employee's contribution

pause salariale
wage standstill

péréquation salariale
wage equalisation

plafond salarial
upper earnings limit / level, wage ceiling

plancher salarial
lower earnings limit / level, wage floor

politique salariale
wage / compensation policy

prétention salariale
salary / wage expectation; wage demand

proposition salariale
pay offer

réduire la masse salariale
to cut the payroll

remboursement partiel des frais salariaux
partial wage reimbursement

rémunération salariale
wage earnings

retenue salariale
payroll deduction

revendication salariale
wage claim / demand; (pl.) pressure of wages

revenu salarial
earned / wage / labour income

revenu non salarial
non-wage income; (pl.) investment / unearned income

revenu salarial proportionnel à ses compétences
salary commensurate with one's abilities

rigueur salariale
wage restraint

structure salariale
wage / salary / pay structure

subvention salariale
wage (cost) subsidy

subvention salariale directe
direct wage subsidy

subvention salariale permanente
permanent wage subsidy

subvention salariale transférable
portable wage subsidy

surenchère salariale
wage-wage spiral

taux salarial
wage rate

taux salarial convenu
agreed wage rate

taxe sur la masse salariale
payroll tax

SALARIÉ (adj.)
employed, salaried

abandon de l'activité salariée
cessation of the employment / of the gainful activity

activité salariée
gainful activity / occupation, activity as an employed person; economic activity; employment

activité non salariée
self-employment; activity as a self-employed person

allocation aux vieux travailleurs salariés
allowance for old employees

co-investissement du salarié
employee's co-participation

début d'une activité non salariée
entry into self-employment

détachement d'un travailleur salarié
posting of an employed person

effectifs salariés
salaried / payroll employees

emploi salarié
wage / dependent employment, employment as an employee, payroll job / employment

emploi non salarié
non-wage employment, self-employment

emploi salarié déguisé
disguised wage employment

employé salarié
wage earner

étudiant salarié
student employee, working student

main-d'oeuvre salariée
dependent labour force / working
population, hired labour

membres salariés de la famille
earning members of the family

période d'activité non salariée
period of self-employment

**personne vivant sous le toit du
travailleur salarié**
person living under the same roof as the
employed person

personnel salarié
salaried staff

profession salariée
gainful occupation

**régime spécial de travailleurs non
salariés**
special scheme for self-employed persons

salarié (non)
self-employed

salarié (être)
(occ.) to be on the payroll

salarié (ne pas être)
(occ.) to be off the payroll

travail salarié
paid / gainful occupation

travailleur salarié
wage earner, employed earner / worker /
person, employee; dependent / hired
worker

travailleur non salarié
non-wage / self-employed (earner /
worker / person)

travailleurs salariés de l'industrie
employed persons in industry

**travailleur salarié des transports inter-
nationaux**
person employed in international transport

SALARIÉ (n.)
wage / salary earner, employed earner /
person, employee; worker; staffer (USA);
(pl.) wage and salary earners / workers,
wage earners and salaried employees;
employees; salaried staff; hired labour

association de salariés
workers' organisation

carte d'immatriculation du salarié
employee registration card

**congé individuel de formation pour les
salariés (Fr.)**
individual training leave for employees

dossier individuel d'un salarié
employee file

droit d'expression des salariés
employees' right of expression

droits des salariés
employee / employees' rights

participation des salariés aux résultats
employee profit-sharing

patronat et salariés
employers and employed

petits salariés (les)
low-paid (the)

**plan d'aide aux salariés pour la prise en
charge de leurs parents âgés**
elder care scheme

programme d'actionnariat des salariés
employee stock ownership plan

**rachat d'une entreprise par ses salariés
(RES)**
leveraged management buy-out (LMBO)

rapports patrons-salariés
labour-management / industrial relations

régime de pensions des salariés (Denm.)
employment pension scheme

rémunération des salariés
compensation of employees

renvoyer des salariés
to pay off workers

salarié (par)
per employee

salarié agricole
agricultural / farm labourer / worker

salarié agricole permanent
full-time agricultural labourer

salarié ayant une longue / beaucoup d'ancienneté
long-serving employee, senior employee (USA)

salarié de l'Etat
Government employee

salarié éventuel
prospective employee

salarié permanent
permanent employee

salarié permanent (être)
to work on a regular basis

salarié permanent à temps partiel
permanent part-time employee

salarié permanent à temps plein
permanent full-time employee

salarié protégé
protected employee; protected staff representative (Fr.)

salarié rémunéré
paid employee

salarié rémunéré à la pièce
worker paid on piecework basis

salarié à risques
accident-prone worker

salarié secondaire
secondary wage earner

salarié du secteur public
public sector employee

sur-utilisation des salariés
overutilisation of employees

taux de rétention des salariés à mi-carrière
(occ.) half-life survival rate

SALISSURE
prime de salissure
dirty allowance, dirty work pay

SALLE
instruction en salle
bench / vestibule training

salle d'allaitement
nursing room

salle d'hôpital
ward

SALUBRE
healthy, healthful; safe

SALUBRITÉ
sanitation; healthiness; safety

inspecteur de salubrité
sanitary inspector

mesure de salubrité
health measure; (pl.) sanitation

salubrité de l'environnement / du milieu
environmental health

salubrité publique
public health

SALUT
salut public
public welfare

SALUTAIRE
healthful

SANATORIUM
sanatorium

SANCTION
sanction; penalty

sanction disciplinaire
disciplinary sanction

sanction pécuniaire
financial penalty

SANGUIN
transfusion sanguine
blood transfusion

SANITAIRE
action sanitaire
health measures / activities / promotion

action sanitaire et sociale
health and welfare activities, health and
social promotion

administrateur sanitaire
health officer / administrator

administration sanitaire
health administration / authorities

administration sanitaire intermédiaire
intermediate health administration

agent sanitaire
health (care) worker; (pl.) health personnel / staff

agent sanitaire primaire
primary health worker

agent sanitaire visiteur
(pl.) domiciliary health staff

assistant sanitaire
health assistant

autorité sanitaire
(pl.) health authorities

autorité sanitaire de circonscription
area health authority (UK)

autorité sanitaire de région
regional health authority

auxiliaire sanitaire
health assistant

besoin sanitaire
health need

carte sanitaire
(occ.) list of health services

centre sanitaire public
government / public health centre

circonscription sanitaire
health area

Commission de l'équipement sanitaire
Health Facilities Commission

contrôle sanitaire
health control / checks, sanitary inspection

couverture sanitaire (de la population)
health care coverage

éducateur sanitaire
health educator

éducation sanitaire
health education

enquête sanitaire
health survey

équipe sanitaire
health team

équipement sanitaire
health equipment / (pl.) facilities

équipement sanitaire et médical
health and medical equipment / facilities

**établissement de protection sanitaire et
sociale de l'enfance**
health and social care institution for
children

établissement sanitaire
health facility

état sanitaire
health / physical condition, state of health,
health status

formation sanitaire
hospital / health unit; health training

génie sanitaire
public health engineering

groupe sanitaire
health unit
groupe sanitaire rural
rural health unit

infrastructure sanitaire
health infrastructure, health care (delivery) system

infrastructure sanitaire et sociale
health and welfare infrastructure

inspecteur des affaires sanitaires et sociales
health and sanitary inspector

inspecteur sanitaire
sanitary inspector

inspection sanitaire
sanitary inspection

institution sanitaire
health agency

investissement sanitaire et social
health and social investment

norme sanitaire
health standard

organisation sanitaire
(public) health practice

organisme sanitaire
health organisation

participation aux investissements sanitaires
contribution in health investments

personnel sanitaire
health personnel / staff / workers / manpower / officers, health care workers

planification sanitaire
planning for health, health planning

planification sanitaire nationale
national health planning

politique sanitaire
health policy

poste sanitaire
health station / post

prestations sanitaires
health care (services / delivery)

profil sanitaire
health profile (d'un pays)

promotion sanitaire
health promotion

protection sanitaire
health care / protection

rapatriement sanitaire
repatriation for health reasons, sanitary repatriation

recherche en organisation sanitaire
health practice research

région sanitaire
health area

règlement sanitaire
health regulation(s)

sectorisation sanitaire et sociale
division into health and social sectors

service sanitaire
health service / administration; (pl.) health facilities

service sanitaire destiné à la collectivité
community health service

service sanitaire régional
regional health administration

spécialiste en éducation sanitaire
health educator

statistiques sanitaires
health statistics

système d'information sanitaire
health information system

système national de protection sanitaire
national system of health care

système de prestations sanitaires
health delivery system

système de protection sanitaire
health care (delivery) system

transport sanitaire
sanitary transportation

travailleur sanitaire
health (care) worker

travailleur sanitaire primaire
primary health worker

travailleurs sanitaires et sociaux
health and social workers

unité sanitaire locale (It.)
local health unit

visite sanitaire
sanitary inspection

visiteuse sanitaire
health visitor

SANS-ABRI
homeless person

SANS-EMPLOI
unemployed (worker)

SANS-LOGIS
homeless person

SANTÉ
health (care)

action de santé publique
(public) health work

administrateur de (la) santé publique
(public) health officer / administrator

administration de (la) santé publique
(public) health administration

agent de la santé
health (care) worker

agent de (la) santé mentale
mental health worker

agent de santé polyvalent
multipurpose health worker

agent de santé primaire
primary health worker

agent de santé publique
public health worker

assurance-santé et perte de gains
health and loss of earnings insurance

assurance-soins de santé
health care insurance

autorité locale de la santé (UK)
local health authority

bonne santé (en)
healthy

bien de santé
(pl.) health goods

bilan de santé
medical checkup, health check

carnet de santé
health booklet / passport / record

centre d'examens de santé
medical examination centre

centre de santé
health centre / unit

centre de santé intégré
integrated health centre

centre de santé publique
Government / public health centre

certificat de santé
health certificate; (occ.) medical clearance

Code de la santé publique
Public Health Code

consommateur de soins de santé
medical consumer

consommation de soins de santé
consumption of medical care

couverture santé
health coverage

dépenses de santé
health expenditure

Directeur de la santé publique (UK)
State health officer

distribution des soins de santé
health care delivery

éducation pour / à la santé
health education

enquête sur la / de santé
health survey

espérance de vie en bonne santé
health expectation, healthy life expectancy

établissement de santé auxiliaire
peripheral health establishment

état de santé
health / physical condition, state of health, health status

état de santé d'une population
health profile of a population

examen de santé
health examination

fiche de santé infantile
child health card

fonctionnaire de la santé publique
(public) health officer

formation en santé publique
public health training

hygiène et santé individuelles
personal health

indicateur de l'état de santé
health status indicator

infirmière de santé publique
public health nurse

inspecteur de la santé et de l'assainissement
health and sanitary inspector

inspection de la santé
health inspectorate

maison de santé
nursing home

maison de santé mentale
mental home

maîtrise des dépenses de santé
health expenditure control

médecin de (la) santé publique
medical officer of health, public health physician / medical officer

médecin (de santé) scolaire
school health / medical doctor

médecin des services de santé publique
medical officer of health, public health physician / medical officer

norme de santé
health standard

nuisible à la santé
injurious to (the) health

ordonnance du service de santé (UK)
health prescription

organisation de santé publique
(public) health practice

personnel de santé / des services de santé
health workers / manpower / personnel / officers / staff, health care workers

planification pour la santé
planning for health, health planning

politique de (la) santé
health policy

praticien de la santé
health practitioner

préjudiciable à la santé
injurious to (the) health

professions intermédiaires des sciences de la vie et de la santé [CITP-1988 (32)]
life science and health associate professionals [ISCO-1988 (32)]

profession de santé
health (care) profession

professionnel de la santé
health worker / practitioner / professional (worker), health care worker

promotion de la santé
health promotion

questionnaire d'état de santé
medical questionnaire

raisons de santé (pour)
for reasons of health, for health reasons

risque pour la santé
health hazard

santé de la / des collectivité(s)
community health

santé de l'enfant
child health

santé de la famille / familiale
family health

santé génésique
reproductive health

santé infantile de base
basic child health

santé maternelle
maternal health

santé maternelle et infantile
maternal and child health

santé mentale
mental / (occ.) emotional health

santé physique
physical health / (occ.) fitness

santé professionnelle
occupational health

santé publique
public / (occ.) community health

santé scolaire
school health

santé au travail
occupational health

santé des travailleurs
workers' health

sécurité et santé au travail
occupational safety and health

sécurité et santé des travailleurs
safety and health of workers

service infirmier de santé publique
public health nursing service

service local de la santé
local health unit

service national de santé
national health service

service de santé
health service; medical department; (pl.)
health care / medical services

service de santé de base
basic health service

service de santé des collectivités
community health service

service de santé dentaire
dental health service

service de santé de la famille / familiale
family health service

service de santé général
general health service

service de santé individuel
personal health service

service de santé intermédiaire
intermediate health service

service de santé local
local health service

service de santé rural
rural health service

service de santé scolaire
school health service

service de santé urbain
urban health service

service de soins de santé primaire
primary health care service

soins de santé
health care

soins de santé de base
basic health care

soins de santé primaire
primary health care

spécialistes des sciences de la vie et de la
santé [CITP-1988 (22)]
life science and health professionals
[ISCO-1988 (22)]

statistiques des services de santé
health service statistics

système national de santé
national system of health care

système de protection de santé
health care (delivery) system

système de santé
health system

technicien de la santé
health (care) worker

techniciens et travailleurs assimilés des sciences de la vie et de la santé [CITP-1988 (321)]
life science technicians and related associate professionals [ISCO-1988 (321)]

travailleur employé dans les professions de santé
health worker

troubles de santé
health disorder

SATELLITE
compte satellite de la protection sociale
satellite account for social welfare

SATISFACTION
degré de satisfaction au travail
degree of job satisfaction

enquête de satisfaction du personnel
staff satisfaction survey

indice de satisfaction générale
general satisfaction rating

niveau de satisfaction au travail
degree of job satisfaction

satisfaction professionnelle / au / dans le travail
job / work satisfaction

SATISFAIRE
to satisfy, to fulfil

offre d'emploi difficile à satisfaire
hard-to-fill vacancy

satisfaire à une condition
to satisfy a condition

satisfaire aux conditions requises pour être promu
to satisfy the standards required for promotion

SATISFAIT
besoin social non satisfait
unmet social need

offre d'emploi satisfaite
vacancy filled, filled vacancy

offre d'emploi non satisfaite
outstanding job / unfilled vacancy, unfilled demand for worker

SATURNIN
intoxication saturnine
lead poisoning

SATURNISME
lead poisoning

SAUF (adj.)
sain et sauf
uninjured

SAUT
saut d'indexation
not applied index-adjustment

SAUVAGE
grève sauvage
outlaw / unofficial / wild(-)cat strike

occupation sauvage
squatter take-over, squatting

SAUVEGARDE
clause de sauvegarde
safety / escape / saving / hardship clause

SAUVER
sauver des emplois
to save / to safeguard / to preserve / to maintain (existing) jobs

SAUVETAGE
opération de sauvetage
rescue work

plan de sauvetage
rescue plan

SAVOIR (n.)
knowledge

économie du savoir
knowledge(-based) economy

SAVOIR-FAIRE
expertise, skill, know-how

SCHÉMA
scheme; outline; pattern

schéma de carrière
career plan; (pl.) (occ.) career structures

schéma directeur
master plan

schéma prévisionnel de l'apprentissage
appenticeship plan for the future

SCIENCE
sciences humaines
humanistic studies, humanities

sciences de l'ingénieur
engineering sciences

sciences ménagères
home economics

sciences sociales
social sciences

SCIENTIFIQUE
complexe scientifique
science park

organisation scientifique du travail
(occ.) job engineering

parc scientifique
science park

**professions intellectuelles et
scientifiques [CITP-1988 (2)]**
professionals [ISCO-1988 (2)]

**professions scientifiques, techniques,
libérales et assimilées**
(occ.) professionals

SCOLAIRE
[school]; academic

abandon scolaire
drop-out, dropping out

âge scolaire
(compulsory) school age

allocation de rentrée scolaire
back-to-school allowance, back-to-school
clothing and footwear allowance (Irel.)

année scolaire
school / academic year

assistante d'hygiène scolaire
school nurse

bagage scolaire
schooling

**centre médical scolaire / de médecine
scolaire**
school health clinic / centre

circonscription scolaire
school district

commission scolaire
school board

congés scolaires
school holidays / vacation

conseil scolaire
school board

décrochage scolaire
drop-out

déperdition scolaire
educational wastage

dossier scolaire
school record

échec scolaire
school failure; under-achievement

effectif(s) d'âge scolaire (obligatoire)
school age population

effectifs scolaires
school population / enrolment

**élève en difficulté scolaire / ayant des
résultats scolaires médiocres**
under-achiever, low performer / achiever

enfant d'âge scolaire
school(-)child

enseignement scolaire
formal education

enseignement non scolaire
non-formal education

établissement scolaire
educational institution

formation en milieu scolaire
in-school / (occ.) classroom training

fréquentation scolaire
school enrolment, school attendance (rate)

hygiène scolaire
school health; health education

infirmier scolaire
school nurse

jeune sorti du système scolaire
school-leaver

mauvais résultats scolaires
(occ.) under-achievement

médecin (de santé) scolaire
school health doctor / medical officer

médecine scolaire
school health

obligation scolaire
compulsory education

orientation scolaire
education(al) guidance

période scolaire
(school) term

population d'âge scolaire (obligatoire)
school age population

population scolaire
school population

programme de formation en établisse-ment scolaire
in-school training programme

programme scolaire
syllabus; curriculum

rattrapage scolaire
educational / academic upgrading

résultats scolaires
educational achievement / attainment,
performance at / in school, school
achievement / performance

santé scolaire
school health

service de santé scolaire
school health service

service social scolaire
school social work

taux d'abandon scolaire
drop-out rate

taux de fréquentation scolaire
school attendance (rate), attendance ratio

taux de persévérance scolaire
student retention rate

travail social scolaire
school social work

vacances scolaires
school holidays / vacation

SCOLARISATION
school enrolment / attendance (rate)

taux de scolarisation
educational enrolment, (school) enrolment
ratio

SCOLARISÉ
effectifs scolarisés
school enrolment

enfant scolarisé
school child

enfant non scolarisé
out-of-school child

jeunes non scolarisés
out-of-school young people / youth

scolarisé (être)
to attend school

scolarisé (non)
out-of-school

scolarisé à temps plein (être)
to be in full(-)time education

SCOLARITÉ
schooling; school attendance (rate); tuition; education

abandon de la scolarité
(early) school-leaving

âge de fin de scolarité (obligatoire)
school-leaving age

âge légal de fin de scolarité
statutory school-leaving age

âge normal de fin de scolarité
normal / regular school-leaving age

âge de scolarité obligatoire
(compulsory) school age

certificat de fin de scolarité
school-leaving certificate

certificat de scolarité
certificate of (school) attendance

degré de scolarité
educational level

droits / frais de scolarité
tuition / school fees

jeune ayant achevé sa scolarité / en fin de scolarité
school-leaver

niveau de scolarité
academic attainment, level of study / of education / of schooling, educational level

scolarité obligatoire
compulsory schooling

scolarité requise
educational requirements

SCRUTIN
scrutin décidant de la tenue d'une grève
strike vote / ballot

SCULPTEUR
sculpteurs, peintres, photographes et artistes créateurs assimilés [CITP-1968 (1-6)]
sculptors, painters, photographers and related creative artists [ISCO-1968 (1-6)]

SÉANCE
séance de formation
training session

séance de travail
working session; workshop

SECOND
second; secondary; junior

enseignement du second degré
secondary education

examen d'entrée dans le second cycle universitaire (USA)
graduate record examination

second employeur
secondary employer

SECONDAIRE
secondary; ancillary

actif secondaire
secondary worker

activité secondaire
secondary / ancillary activity

certificat d'enseignement secondaire inférieur (CESI)
lower secondary education certificate

certificat de fin d'études secondaires
high-school leaving certificate

deuxième cycle de l'enseignement secondaire
upper secondary (education)

école secondaire
secondary school

enseignement secondaire
secondary education

enseignement secondaire du premier cycle
high school education

établissement d'enseignement secondaire
secondary school, high school (USA)

établissement secondaire technique
technical college

marché secondaire de l'emploi / du travail
secondary labour market

métier secondaire
alternative / alternate / secondary employment

population active secondaire
secondary labour force

premier cycle de l'enseignement secondaire
lower secondary

professeurs de l'enseignement secondaire [CITP-1968 (232)]
secondary education teaching professionals [ISCO-1988 (232)]

résidence secondaire
vacation / second home

salarié secondaire
secondary wage earner

secteur secondaire
secondary industry / secondary sector

soins médicaux secondaires
secondary medical care

soins secondaires
secondary care

source secondaire de revenus
second breadwinner, secondary (wage) earner, second family earner

travailleurs du marché secondaire
secondary labour force

SECONDER
to assist, to help, to support

SECOURISTE
first-aid worker

SECOURS
help, assistance, aid, relief; compassionate benefits

caisse de secours
relief / contingency fund

centre de premier secours
emergency centre

devoir de secours
duty of assistance

domicile de secours (Fr.)
place of residence for welfare purposes

fonds de secours
relief / contingency fund

organisme public de secours
public charity

poste de (premiers) secours
first aid post / station

premiers secours
first aid

secours chômage
unemployment relief

secours à l'enfance
aid to children

secours en espèces
relief in cash

secours exceptionnel
exceptional relief

secours mutuel
mutual aid

secours en nature
relief / aid in kind, relief goods

secours prénatal
aid to expectant mothers

secours public
public relief

secours d'urgence
emergency relief / aid

secours viager
life allowance for the surviving spouse of an elderly worker

société de secours
provident society; relief association

société de secours mutuel
mutual benefit / provident society

travailleur de secours
relief worker

SECOURU
on relief

chômeur secouru
unemployed on relief

enfant secouru
child on relief

SECRET (adj.)
vote à bulletin secret
secret ballot

SECRET (n.)
secret de fonctions
official secret

secret médical
medical secrecy

secret professionnel
professional secrecy / privilege

SECRÉTAIRE
poste de secrétaire
secretarial post

secrétaire de direction
executive secretary, personal assistant

secrétaires et opérateurs sur claviers (411)]
secretaries and keyboard-operating clerks [ISCO-1988 (411)]

SECRÉTARIAT
secretariat; (occ.) office, staff

école de secrétariat
secretarial college

emploi de secrétariat
clerical occupation / job, office occupation

personnel de secrétariat
clerical staff / employees

prime de secrétariat
secretarial allowance

secrétariat social (It.)
social welfare secretariat

travail de secrétariat
secretarial work

SECTEUR
sector; district; area

aide du secteur public
public / Government aid

assurance accidents corporels du secteur public (Ger.)
public accident insurance

bureau de secteur
zone office

échelle d'un secteur (à l')
industry-wide

emploi dans le secteur parapublic
semi-public / (occ.) non-government employment

emploi dans le / du secteur privé
private (sector) employment

emploi dans le secteur public
public (sector) employment

emploi dans le secteur des / dans les services
service / tertiary employment

emploi dans le tiers secteur
third sector employment

employé du secteur parapublic
semi-public employee

employé du secteur public
public employee

employé du secteur des services
service worker

employé du secteur de la vente
sales worker

employeur du secteur privé
private sector employer

entreprise du secteur public
public undertaking / utility / corporation

infirmière du secteur psychiatrique
psychiatric nurse

nouveau secteur d'avenir / de croissance
new growth industry

placement par secteur d'activité
placement by industry

profession du secteur tertiaire
service occupation; (pl.) service trades

responsable de secteur
area manager

salaire pratiqué dans les secteurs syndiqués
union wage

salarié du secteur public
public sector employee

secteur d'activité
branch of the economy; (sector of) industry; line of business

secteur des affaires
business community

secteur agricole
agricultural sector

secteur en amont
(occ.) supplying sector

secteur associatif
voluntary / third sector; community organisations

secteur d'avenir
growth sector

secteur du bâtiment
building / construction industry

secteur clé
key sector

secteur du commerce
trade industry

secteur de la construction
building / construction industry

secteur de croissance
growth sector

secteur en déclin
declining industry

secteur de l'économie
economic sector, branch of the economy

secteur de l'économie sociale
(occ.) third sector

secteur économique
economic sector, branch of the economy

secteur des entreprises
corporate sector

secteur en expansion
growth industry

secteur formel de l'économie
formal economy sector

secteur à honoraires libres (Fr.)
free-fee sector

secteur hospitalier
hospital system

secteur de l'industrie / industriel
sector of industry; industrial sector

secteur industriel à forte croissance
high-growth industrial sector

secteur informel de l'économie
informal economy sector

secteur du marché de l'emploi / du travail
labour market sector, segment of labour market

secteur non organisé / parallèle (de l'économie)
informal economy sector

secteur porteur
leading edge industry

secteur primaire
primary industry / sector

secteur privé
business / private sector

secteur de production
line of production

secteur de la production des services
service-producing sector

secteur professionnel
occupational field / area / sector

secteur public
public sector; public / State enterprise

secteur secondaire
secondary industry / secondary sector

secteur des services
tertiary / service sector / industries;
service / social trades

secteur socialisé
socialist sector

secteur structuré de l'économie
formal economy sector

secteur non structuré de l'économie
informal economy sector

secteur syndiqué
unionised sector

secteur tertiaire
service industry; (pl.) service / tertiary
industries, service / social trades

tiers secteur
third sector

travailleur du secteur privé
private worker

travailleur du secteur tertiaire
service worker

SECTION
section; branch; unit

section locale d'un / des syndicat(s)
(trade) union local / branch

section syndicale
(in-company) union branch / section

section transversale
cross section

SECTORIEL
sectoral

accord sectoriel
sectoral agreement

analyse sectorielle
sector analysis

chômage sectoriel
sectoral unemployment

conseiller sectoriel
industrial consultant

convention (collective) sectorielle
industry-wide (collective) agreement

expert-conseil sectoriel
industrial consultant

grève sectorielle
industry-wide strike

mobilité sectorielle
inter-industry / sectoral mobility

perspectives sectorielles
sectoral outlook

SECTORISATION
sectorisation sanitaire et sociale
division into health and social sectors

SÉCURITÉ
safety, security

acte de sécurité sociale (Fr.)
social security action

**affiliation à un régime de sécurité
sociale**
insurance under a social security scheme

affiliation à la sécurité sociale
social security membership

agent contrôle de la sécurité sociale
social security inspector

amélioration de la sécurité et de l'hygiène du travail
improvement in safety and health conditions at work

branche de (la) sécurité sociale
branch of social security

caisse de sécurité sociale
social security fund

circonscription de caisse de sécurité sociale
social security fund district

clause de sécurité syndicale
closed-shop / union security clause

Code de la sécurité sociale
Social Security Code

Comité d'hygiène, de sécurité et des conditions de travail (Fr.)
Health and Safety at Work Committee

comité d'hygiène et de sécurité
health and safety / safety and health committee

consigne de sécurité
safety regulation; (pl.) safety instructions / code

contentieux de la sécurité sociale
social security claims

contribution au titre de la sécurité sociale
social security charge

contrôleur de sécurité
safety inspector

convention multilatérale de sécurité sociale
multilateral social security convention

convention de sécurité sociale
convention on social security, social security convention

cotisation patronale de sécurité sociale
employers' social security contribution

cotisation salariale de sécurité sociale
employees' social security contribution

cotisation de / à la / au titre de la sécurité sociale
social security contribution / charge / tax (USA)

cotisations sociales du régime général de sécurité sociale
insurance contributions for the general social security scheme

couverture de sécurité sociale
social security coverage

déficit de la sécurité sociale
deficit in social security

délégué à la sécurité
safety representative

dépenses de sécurité sociale
social security expenditure

droit à la sécurité sociale
right to social security

équipement de sécurité
safety equipment

escroquerie à la sécurité sociale
(social security) benefit fraud

exclu de la sécurité sociale
not protected by social security

expert en matière de sécurité (Gr.)
safety technician

fichier de sécurité sociale
social security record

filet de sécurité
safety net

filet de sécurité sociale
social security net

financement de la sécurité sociale
financing of social security

formation à la sécurité
safety training

hygiène et sécurité
health and safety

hygiène et sécurité du travail
industrial / occupational health and safety

hygiène et sécurité sur le lieu de travail / au travail
health and safety at work

impôt de sécurité sociale des travailleurs indépendants
self-employment social security tax

ingénieur de sécurité (Ger.)
safety engineer

institution de sécurité sociale
social security agency / institution

marché de la sécurité sociale
social security contract

mesure de sécurité
safety measure / precaution

normes minima de sécurité sociale
minimum standards for social security

organe d'une institution de sécurité sociale
organ of a social security institution

organisme de sécurité sociale
social security fund / agency / institution

pension de sécurité sociale (It.)
social security pension

personnel des services directs aux particuliers et des services de protection et de sécurité [CITP-1988 (51)]
personal and protective services workers [ISCO-1988 (51)]

personnel des services de protection et de sécurité (5-8)]
protective service workers [ISCO-1968 (5-8)]

personnel des services de protection et de sécurité [CITP-1988 (516)]
protective services workers [ISCO-1988 (516)]

plafond de sécurité sociale
social security ceiling

pratique de sécurité syndicale (Fr.)
closed shop practice

prestation de sécurité sociale
social security benefit / payment

protection de sécurité sociale
social security coverage

régime général de (la) sécurité sociale
general social security scheme, standard social security health and retirement insurance (for private industry)

régime légal de sécurité sociale
statutory social security scheme

régime national de sécurité sociale
national social security scheme

régime de sécurité sociale
social security scheme

régime spécial de sécurité sociale
specific / special social security scheme

règle / règlement de sécurité
safety regulation(s)

réserve de sécurité
contingency reserve

responsable de l'hygiène et de la sécurité
(health and) safety officer

risque de sécurité
safety hazard

sécurité (en)
safe

sécurité de l'emploi / d'emploi
employment / job security, security of employment, employment protection; job guarantee

sécurité et hygiène (du travail)
safety and health (at work)

sécurité dans l'industrie
industrial safety engineering
sécurité de jouissance
security of tenure

sécurité professionnelle
occupational safety

sécurité et santé au travail
occupational safety and health

sécurité et santé des travailleurs
safety and health of workers

sécurité sociale
social security; welfare programme

sécurité syndicale
union security

sécurité au travail / sur le lieu de travail
job / occupational safety, safety at work
sécurité de la vieillesse (Can.)
old-age security

Système international de conservation des droits en matière de sécurité sociale
International System for the Maintenance of Rights in Social Security

système de sécurité sociale
social insurance / social security system

trou de la sécurité sociale
deficit in social security

SÉDENTAIRE
sedentary; settled

travail sédentaire
sedentary work

SÉDENTARISATION
settlement

SEGMENTATION
segmentation du marché du travail
labour market segmentation

SÉGRÉGATION
ségrégation professionnelle
occupational segregation

ségrégation professionnelle fondée sur le sexe
sex-based occupational segregation

SÉJOUR
stay; residence

allocation de séjour hors du foyer
living-away from home allowance

autorisation / carte de séjour
residence permit

carte de séjour et de travail
work and residence permit, green card (USA)

centre de long séjour
nursing home

Commission de séjour (Fr.)
Residence Committee

durée de séjour
duration / length of stay

établissement de séjour
residential facility

frais de séjour
subsistence expenses

frais de voyage et de séjour
travel and accommodation / travel and subsistence expenses

hôpital de court séjour
(occ.) somatic hospital

hôpital de long séjour / pour séjours de longue durée
long-term hospital

indemnité de séjour
subsistence / living allowance

institution du lieu de séjour
institution of the place of stay

lieu de séjour
place of stay

permis de séjour
residence permit; registration certificate

séjour à l'étranger
stay abroad

séjour temporaire
temporary stay / residence

transfert de séjour
transfer of stay

SÉJOURNANT
séjournant régulièrement
lawfully present

SÉLECTIF
selective; differentiated; discriminatory

application sélective
differentiated application

grève sélective
whipsaw strike

mesure sélective
selective measure

mesure sélective d'emploi
selective employment measure

placement sélectif
selective placement

programme sélectif
target programme

sélectif (non)
non-discriminatory

SÉLECTION
critère de sélection
criterion for selection, selection criterion

jury de sélection
selection board

méthode de sélection
selection procedure

méthode de sélection de candidats en groupe
group selection method

norme de sélection
qualification / selection standard

procédure de sélection
selection procedure

processus de sélection du personnel
staff selection process

sélection aléatoire
random assignment

sélection sur / par / par voie de concours
competitive method of selection

sélection préalable / préliminaire
(pre-)screening (process), preselection

sélection préliminaire des travailleurs
preselection of workers

système de sélection
screening device

test de sélection
selection test

test de sélection en temps limité
in-tray exercice, in-basket test

SÉLECTIONNER
to select; to screen; to shortlist

SEMAINE
revenu par semaine
weekly earnings

salaire payé à la semaine
wage paid by the week, weekly wage

semaine d'accouchement
week of confinement

semaine de cotisation
contribution week

semaine fiscale
income tax week

semaine normale de travail
normal / standard work week, basic work week

semaine non payée
not paid week

semaine présumée d'accouchement
expected week of confinement

semaine de référence
reference week

semaine de travail
work(ing) week

semaine de travail réduite
compressed work(ing) week, reduced / short work week

semaine de travail variable
variable work week

semaine travaillée
work-week worked

SEMESTRE
half-year

SEMESTRIEL
semi-annual, six-monthly

prime semestrielle
half-yearly bonus

SEMI-AUTONOME
organisation non gouvernementale semi-autonome
quasi-autonomous non-governmental organisation (quango)

SEMI-BRUT
traitement semi-brut
half-gross salary

SEMI-CONTINU
travail en semi-continu
split shift

SEMI-ÉDUCABLE
déficient semi-éducable
trainable mentally retarded

SEMI-LIBERTÉ
foyer de semi-liberté
semi-custodial home

SEMI-PRIVÉ
chambre privée ou semi-privée (-hosp.) (Can.)
preferred accommodation

SEMI-PROFESSIONNEL (n.)
semi-professional

SEMI-PROTÉGÉ
emploi semi-protégé
semi-sheltered employment

SEMI-QUALIFIÉ
main-d'oeuvre semi-qualifiée
semi-skilled labour

travailleur semi-qualifié
semi-skilled worker

SEMI-RETRAITE
semi-retirement

SEMI-RETRAITÉ
semi-retired person

SEMONCE
admonition

SENSIBILISATION
awareness- / consciousness-raising; outreach

matériel de sensibilisation
sensitivity material

SENSIBLE
sensible aux variations de la conjoncture
(occ.) cyclically sensitive

SENSORIEL
centre d'éducation sensorielle
education centre for people with sensory disability

incapacité sensorielle
sensory disability

SENTENCE
sentence arbitrale
arbitration award

SÉPARATION
separation; leaving; severance

indemnité de séparation
separation allowance

séparation à l'amiable
negotiated termination

SÉPARÉMENT
vivant ensemble séparément
living apart together

SÉPARER
séparer de (se)
to part with

SÉQUELLE
after-effect

SÉRAIL
homme du sérail
insider

SÉRIE
grande série
long production run

petite série
short production run

production en (grande) série
large-scale / mass production

série de négociations
bargaining round, round of negotiations

série de négociations collectives
collective bargaining round

SÉRIEUX
cause réelle et sérieuse
just cause; genuine and proper ground

cause réelle et sérieuse de licenciement
genuine and proper ground for dismissal

licenciement abusif sans cause réelle et sérieuse
dismissal without just cause

SERMENT
serment de fonctionnaire
official oath

serment d'Hippocrate
Hippocratic oath

SERRÉ (adj.)
marché du travail serré
tight labour market

SERVI
pension servie
benefit in payment, pension in payment

prestation servie
paid out benefit

prestation servie de droit
benefit paid as of right

prestation servie par l'Etat
State benefit

SERVICE
service; branch, section, department, unit;
authority; office, bureau; facility; payment
(of benefits); (pl.) service (and
distribution) industries, tertiary industries

accident lié au service
service-incurred injury

achat de services
purchase of services

administrateur de service(s) socia(l)-(ux)
social (welfare) administrator

administration du / des service(s) socia(l)(ux)
social (welfare) administration

agents de service
servicing staff

agent de service social / des services sociaux
(social) welfare officer / worker, social
worker, social service officer

allocation de fin de service
severance allowance

allocation des services ménagers (Fr.)
home help allowance

années de service
seniority

attribuable au service
attributable to service

branche de services
service industry

cadre de service social
social work supervisor

capital des services humanitaires
human overhead capital

capital des services sociaux
social overhead capital

centre de services
service centre

certificat de service(s)
certificate of service

cessation de service
separation from service, termination,
leaving

cessation des services
termination of services

cessation de service par accord mutuel
agreed termination

chef de service (hosp.)
medical officer

chef des services médicaux
chief medical officer

circonscription de service social
social service district

**clientèle de malades pris en charge par
le service public**
(occ.) public practice

commis aux services aux usagers
help-desk clerk

condition de durée de service
service requirement / eligibility

conseiller de service social
social welfare adviser

continuité du service
continuity of service

contrat d'engagement de service
employment contract

contrat de louage de services
(institutional) service contract; (occ.)
employment contract

**contrat de louage de services
individuels**
individual service contract

contrat de service
contract of service, service contract

contrat spécial de service
special service agreement

demande de services
service request

déplacement de service
official travel / journey

document de cessation de service
separation document

durée minimale de service (benefits)
minimum period of payment

durée de service
duration / length of service / of employment; period of payment (benefits)

durée de service des prestations
period for which benefit is allowed

école de service social
social work school

éducateur spécialiste du service social
social work educator

**emploi dans le secteur des / dans les
services**
service / tertiary employment

emploi de service
service job

employé du secteur des services
service worker

employé de service
employee on duty

employé d'un service public
public servant

entreprise de service
service enterprise

entreprise de service public
public utility

entrer au service de ... en qualité de
to be recruited by ... as

équipement de service social
social welfare (material) facility

esprit de / du service social
social work approach

état de service
service record, record / length of service

étudiant de service social
social work student

exempt de service
excused from duty

externalisation des services
facilities management

faute de service
administrative / official error

formation des enseignants en cours de service
INSET (in-service training)

formation en cours de service
in-service (educational) training

formation au service social
social work education

heure de prise de service
starting time

heures de service
hours of duty; working time

imputable au service
service-incurred

imputable au service (non)
non-service connected

inapte au service
unfit for service

indemnité de cessation de service / lors de la cessation de service / versée à la cessation de service
separation / terminal / severance pay / payment / benefit, allowance for separation; (occ.) completion bonus

indemnité de frais de service
official expenditure allowance

industrie de services
service / tertiary industry

inexécution des obligations de service
failure to discharge the duties attaching to a post

interruption des services
break in service

libre service
self-service

maintien du service des prestations
continued payment of benefits

médecin des services de santé publique
medical officer of health, public health physician / medical officer

membre des services sociaux
social (welfare) worker

méthode de / du service social
social work method / process

moniteur de service social
social work educator

norme de service
standard of service

ordonnance du service de santé (UK)
health prescription

période de service ouvrant droit à ...
period of qualifying service

période de service des prestations
period for which benefit(s) is/are allowed

personne de service
attendant

personnel enseignant du service social
social work educators

personnel de service
service staff

personnel des services auxiliaires
ancillary workers

personnel des services linguistiques
language staff

personnel des services organiques
substantive staff

personnel des services de santé
health workers / manpower / personnel /
officers / staff, health care workers

personnel de service social
social work / welfare personnel / staff

poste de chef de service
supervisor(y) post / position

poste dans les services organiques
substantive post

poste de service social
social work appointment

prestataire de services
service provider

prestation de cessation de service
termination pay

prestation de services
provision of services; contribution in
service; (pl.) service trades / delivery

**production imputée de services d'assu-
rance-dommages**
imputed service charge for casualty
insurance

**production imputée de services d'assu-
rance-vie**
imputed service charge for life insurance

**production imputée de services de
caisses de pension**
imputed service charge for pension funds

professeur de service social
social work teacher

**profession des / dans le domaine / dans
le secteur des services**
service occupation; (pl.) service trades

raison de service
exigency of the service

réaffectation d'un service à un autre
internal reassignment

recrutement dans les services locaux
local authority appointment

refuser un service
to withhold a service

règle du service fait
service performed rule

reprendre (le) service
to resume service

**reprise du service des prestations après
suspension ou suppression**
resumption of provision of benefits after
suspension or withdrawal

restriction de service
service limitation

rupture dans la continuité du service
break in service

secteur de la production des services
service-producing sector

secteur des services
tertiary / service sector / industries;
service / social trades

service (de)
on duty; in active employment

service (en)
active, in service

service d'adaptation à l'emploi
employment adjustment service

service d'aide familiale / à la famille
home service; (pl.) family counselling;
home-maker services

service d'aide maternelle / aux mères
mother care service; child care service;
(pl.) home-maker services; child care
facilities

**service d'aide médicale d'urgence
(SAMU)**
emergency medical relief service

service d'aide à la petite enfance
infant care service

service d'aide sociale
(social) welfare service; (occ.) public
charity

service d'aiguillage
referral centre

service antérieur
prior service

service d'approche
outreach service

service d'assistance
assistance board / department / service

service auxiliaire
ancillary service

services de base
basic services

service bénévole
voluntary agency

services de bureau
clerical assistance

service de carrière
career system / service

service collectif
community service; (pl.) community
facilities

**service auprès de / fourni à la
collectivité**
community service / work; (pl.) (occ.)
community, social and personal services

**service axé sur la collectivité et la
famille**
community and family-based service

service de conseils
counselling service

service de conseils en matière d'emploi
employment advisory service

services de conseils familiaux
counselling for families, family counselling

service consultatif
consultative service; (pl.) provision of
advice

service de consultation
counselling service

**Service de consultation, de conciliation
et d'arbitrage (UK)**
Advisory, Conciliation and Arbitration
Service (ACAS)

service de consultations conjugales
marriage counselling / guidance

service de consultation dentaire
dental clinic

service de consultations pour enfants
child care / children's clinic

service de consultations externes
out-patient services / clinic / department;
(pl.) out-patient facilities

service de consultations infantiles
child care / children's clinic

service de consultations matrimoniales
marriage counselling / guidance

service de consultations odontologiques
dental clinic

service de consultations postnatales
post-natal clinic

service de consultations prénatales
pre(-)natal clinic

**service de consultations psycho-médico-
pédagogiques**
child guidance clinic / centre

service du contentieux
claims / legal department

service contractuel
external contract

services de crèche et de garderie
child care facilities

service curatif
remedial service

Service des demandes (UK)
Claims Section

service diplomatique
foreign service

service domestique
domestic service

service ouvrant droit à pension
pensionable service

service d'éducation surveillée
correctional service

service de l'emploi
labour / manpower administration /
service, employment agency / service;
placing / placement service; job service

services aux employeurs
employer services, services to employers

services aux entreprises
business services

services essentiels
basic facilities

**service en faveur des / s'adressant aux
femmes**
women's service

service de formation
training service

service de garderie (d'enfants)
day nursery; (pl.) day-care facilities for
children

service gouvernemental
Government department

service hospitalier
in-patient unit / service; (pl.) hospital
services

service d'hospitalisation
in-patient department; (occ.) ward

service d'hygiène et d'aide sociale
health and social welfare service

service infirmier
nursing service

service infirmier des collectivités
community health nursing service

service infirmier de santé publique
public health nursing service

services d'infrastructure
(occ.) basic services

services intégrés en faveur de l'enfance
integrated services for children

service d'intérêt collectif
community service

service d'inventaires
(occ.) referral centre

service juridique
legal department

service local de la santé
local health unit

**services recevant des malades hospita-
lisés**
in-patient facilities / units

service de la main-d'oeuvre
employment service; (pl.) labour services

service de maternité
maternity unit; (occ.) lying-in clinic

service de médecine du travail
occupational health service

services médicaux
medical care services

service médico-pédagogique
child guidance clinic / centre

service médico-social
medical and social service / (occ.) work

service militaire
military service

service militaire obligatoire
compulsory military service

service minimum
minimum (level of) service

service de missions de personnel
personnel dispatching service

**service mobile d'urgence et de
réanimation (SMUR)**
mobile emergency and intensive care
service

service national
military service; national service

service national de santé
national health service

service officiel de réadaptation
public rehabilitation service

service non organique
servicing unit

service d'orientation
guidance / counselling service

service d'orientation sur les carrières (UK)
career service

service d'orientation professionnelle
career counselling service, employment advisory service

service d'orientation professionnelle spécialisée
specialised vocational guidance service

service de paie
payroll service

service de la paie (assurer le)
to meet the payroll

services aux particuliers
personal services

service payant
user-fee service

service personnalisé
personalised service

services personnels
personal services

service du personnel
personnel department

service sur place
on-site service

service de placement
placement agency; matching / placing / placement service; (labour) employment service / office; labour exchange (service)

service de placement automatisé / assisté par ordinateur
computer-assisted placement service

service de placement public
public employment agency

service de postcure
after care service

service d'une prestation
provision / granting of a benefit; payment of a benefit

service des prestations à un titulaire à l'étranger
payment of benefits abroad

service préventif individuel
personal preventive service

service de prévention
preventive (health) service

service privé de placement
private employment service

service professionnel
professional service

service de prophylaxie
preventive (health) service

service de protection de la famille et de l'enfance
family and child welfare service

service de protection infantile
child / infant welfare service

service de protection maternelle
maternity service

service de protection maternelle et infantile
maternal and child health service

service de protection sociale
(social) welfare service

service de proximité
community / neighbourhood service

service psycho-médico-pédagogique
child guidance clinic / centre

service public
public authorities / service; public utility; (pl.) public / Government services

service public de l'emploi
public employment service

service public hospitalier
hospital public service

service public de soins infirmiers
public health nursing service, district nursing service (UK)

service de réadaptation
rehabilitation department, rehabilitative
service

service de réadaptation professionnelle
vocational rehabilitation service

service de recrutement
recruitment service

service de règlement
(occ.) award section

service de renseignements
inquiry office

service de repas à domicile
(occ.) meals on wheels

service des ressources humaines
personnel department

service sanitaire
health service / administration; (pl.) health
facilities

service sanitaire destiné à la collectivité
community health service

service sanitaire régional
regional health administration

service de santé
health service; medical department; (pl.)
health care / medical services

service de santé de base
basic health service

service de santé des collectivités
community health service

service de santé dentaire
dental health service

service de santé de la famille / familiale
family health service

service de santé général
general health service

service de santé individuel
personal health service

service de santé intermédiaire
intermediate health service

service de santé local
local health service

service de santé rural
rural health service

service de santé scolaire
school health service

service de santé urbain
urban health service

service signalétique
referral centre

service social
social agency; social welfare; (social)
welfare service / work / provision; social
work (activity / practice); (pl.) social
administration / services / provision /
welfare; welfare (facilities)

services sociaux de la collectivité
community welfare services

**services sociaux et services connexes
fournis à la collectivité**
social and related community services

service social de communauté
community social work, social work with
communities

service social d'entreprise
industrial social work

service social de groupe
social group work

service social à l'hôpital
hospital social work

service social dans l'industrie
industrial welfare service

services sociaux et services personnels
social and personal services

service social du personnel
personnel social work

service social des prisons
social work in penal institutions

service social rural
rural social work

service social scolaire
school social work

service social du travail
industrial welfare, industrial social work

service de soins ambulatoires
ambulatory service

service de soins à domicile
home care service

service de soins infirmiers à domicile pour personnes âgées
home care nursing for the elderly

service de soins primaires
primary care service

service de soins de santé primaire
primary health care service

service de soutien
backstop / supportive / support service

service de soutien après placement
post-employment support service

service spécialisé
specialised / (occ.) professional service

service spécialisé de placement
specialised job placement service

service temporaire prolongé
extended temporary duty

service de traitement de jour
day-care patient facility

service du travail
job service

service du travail obligatoire (Fr.)
compulsory working

service aux travailleurs
service to workers

service de travailleuses familiales
home help services

service des urgences
emergency / casualty department / ward

service à valeur ajoutée
value added / enhanced service

service validable
reckonable / pensionable service

service de visiteuses d'hygiène
health visiting service

société de service public
public utility

somme due à la cessation de service
terminal entitlement

spécialiste de l'enseignement du service social
social work educator

spécialiste des questions de service social
(social) welfare officer

statistiques des services de santé
health service statistics

système de prestation de services de main-d'oeuvre
manpower delivery system

tableau de service
duty roster, rota

travailleurs spécialisés dans les services [CITP-1968 (5)]
service workers [ISCO-1968 (5)]

travailleurs spécialisés dans les services non classés ailleurs [CITP-1968 (5-9)]
service workers not elsewhere classified [ISCO-1968 (5-9)]

validation aux fins de pension d'une période de service
validation for pension purposes of a period of service

validation d'une période de service antérieure
validation of previous service

valider les services antérieurs
to have previous services credited

versement à la cessation de service
separation pay / payment

versement de fin de service
end-of-service payment

voiture de service
company car

SERVIR
servir à (faire)
to make available for

servir une prestation
to provide / to pay a benefit

SERVITUDE
servitude; limitation, constraint

servitude des enfants
child bondage / slavery

SEUIL
limit, level, threshold (level); (occ.) low
cut-off point

indice de seuil
threshold index

seuil d'accélération de l'emploi
employment threshold

seuil critique
trigger level

seuil de décence
decency threshold

seuil de déclenchement
trigger level

seuil d'effectifs
staff level

seuil d'exonération fiscale des revenus
lower earnings limit of tax exemption

seuil de faible revenu
low-income cut-off / threshold / limit

seuil d'imposition
tax threshold

seuil d'indifférence
range of indifference

seuil de l'indigence
poverty line / threshold / level

seuil d'intervention
trigger level

seuil de pauvreté
poverty line / threshold / level, poverty
datum line (PDL)

seuil de rentabilité
profitability break-even point, cut-off rate
(of return)

seuil de rentabilité (atteindre le)
to break even

valeur seuil
threshold limit value

SEUL
femme seule chef de famille
single woman family head

pension pour personne seule (Liech.)
single pension

personne seule
single (person)

personne seule et sans abri
single homeless

seul propriétaire
sole proprietor / owner

SÉVICE
(pl.) ill treatment, maltreatment; bodily
harm

sévices à enfant
child abuse

SEXE
répartition par sexes
sex structure / distribution

**ségrégation professionnelle fondée sur
le sexe**
sex-based occupational segregation

SEXISME
sexism

SEXISTE
sexist

SEXUEL
discrimination sexuelle
sexual discrimination

harcèlement sexuel
sexual harassment

SIÈGE
head office; (registered) office

affectation hors siège
field service / assignment

lieu d'affectation hors siège
field duty station, non-headquarters duty
station

personnel hors siège
field staff

poste au siège
headquarters assignment

poste hors siège
field post

siège central
head office

siège social
head office

ville siège
headquarters location / duty station

SIGNALÉ
gains non signalés
unreported earnings

**poste signalé vacant, poste vacant
signalé**
registered vacancy

vacance signalée
registered vacancy

SIGNALEMENT
reporting; signalling

théorie du signalement
signalling theory

SIGNALER
to notify

SIGNALÉTIQUE
fiche signalétique
identification sheet

service signalétique
referral centre

SIGNATAIRE
signataire d'un contrat
party to a contract

SIGNATURE
ouvert à la signature
open to signature

SIGNE
signe extérieur de richesse
external indication of wealth

SIMILAIRE
mécaniciens de précision sur métaux et
matériaux similaires [CITP-1988 (731)]
precision workers in metal and related
materials [ISCO-1988 (731)]

**ouvriers des métiers d'artisanat sur
bois, sur textile, sur cuir et sur des
matériaux similaires [CITP-1988 (733)]**
handicraft workers in wood, textile,
leather and related material [ISCO-1988
(733)]

SIMPLE
pension simple (Liech.)
single pension

rente simple (Switz.)
single pension

SIMPLIFICATION
simplification des tâches
work simplification

SIMULATEUR
simulateur cardiaque
pacemaker

SIMULATION
formation pratique par simulation
simulated on-the-job training

SIMULTANÉ
emplois simultanés
dual jobholding

SINISTRE
accident; casualty; loss

SINISTRÉ
victim; disaster-stricken; claimant

SITE
site

délégué de site (Fr.)
workplace staff representative

site industriel
industrial site

SITUATION
situation; condition; status; employment,
post, position

allocation pour situation difficile
hardship allowance

**allocation pour situation
particulièrement difficile (UK)**
special hardship allowance

allocation pour situation pénible
hardship allowance

contrôle de la situation de fortune
means testing

**déclaration de situation de famille et
demande d'indemnités pour charges de
famille**
family status report and request for
payment of dependency allowances

égalité de situation
equality of condition

étranger en situation irrégulière
illegal alien

formation par mise en situation
vestibule training

main-d'oeuvre en situation irrégulière
unauthorised / undocumented labour

perdre sa situation
to lose one's job

rapport de situation
progress report

rapport sur la situation des employés
status report on employees

situation d'activité (en)
in active service

situation au regard de l'activité
activity status

situation difficile
hardship, predicament

situation économique
economic / business situation

situation de l'emploi
employment / manpower / job situation

**situation relative à / au regard de
l'emploi**
employment / work situation / status

situation au regard des études
school attendance status

situation familiale / de famille
marital / conjugal / dependency / family /
parental status

situation financière
fiscal position

situation financière précaire
financial insecurity

situation devant l'impôt
tax status

**situation du marché de l'emploi / du
travail**
manpower / job situation, labour market
situation / conditions

situation matrimoniale
marital / civil / conjugal status, marital
condition

situation précaire
hardship, predicament

**situation dans la profession /
professionnelle**
employment / industrial / occupational /
work status, position in industry, work
situation, status in employment

situation professionnelle actuelle
current employment status

situation socio-professionnelle
social status

situation stable
(occ.) steady job

travailleur en situation irrégulière
illegal / undeclared / unauthorised /
undocumented worker

S.O.
s.o. (sans objet)
n.a. (not applicable)

SOCIAL
social

accompagnement social
social support

acquis social
social standard; (pl.) social rights

action sanitaire et sociale
health and welfare activities, health and
social promotion

action sociale
social measures / work, social welfare /
development / action

action sociale curative
remedial social action

activité sociale et culturelle
social event

**administrateur social / de service(s)
socia(l)-(ux)**
social (welfare) administrator

**administration du / des service(s)
socia(l)(ux)**
social (welfare) administration

admission à l'aide sociale
social assistance / welfare entitlement,
eligibility for / admission to social
assistance / welfare

**affiliation à un régime de sécurité
sociale**
insurance under a social security scheme

affiliation à la sécurité sociale
social security membership

agent d'aide sociale
(social) welfare officer

agent contrôle de la sécurité sociale
social security inspector

**agent de protection sociale / de service
social / des services sociaux**
(social) welfare officer / worker, social
worker, social service officer

aide sociale
social assistance / welfare, public /
welfare assistance; supplementary benefit
(UK)

aide sociale à l'enfance
child welfare (authorities); child care

aide sociale à la famille
social assistance for the family
(members), family welfare

aide sociale aux handicapés
social assistance for disabled people

aide sociale aux personnes âgées
social assistance for old people, (occ.)
provision for old age

allocation d'aide sociale
(occ.) supplementary allowance

allocation logement social (Fr.)
social housing allowance

allocation sociale
social allowance

**allocation sociale complémentaire
(Irel.)**
supplementary welfare allowance

ascension sociale
upward mobility

assiette des cotisations sociales
basis of social insurance contribution

assistance sociale
social assistance / welfare, welfare
assistance

assistance sociale et médicale
social and medical assistance

assistant social
welfare assistant / worker, social worker

assistante sociale de garderie
child-minder

assistant social d'hôpital / des hôpitaux
(occ.) almoner

assistant social du personnel
personnel social worker

assisté social
welfare recipient; [on welfare]

assurance sociale
social insurance

assuré social
insured person; insured; (pl.) members of
the National Insurance Scheme (UK)

audit social
social / personnel audit

auxiliaire social
social aid; unqualified social worker

avantage social
fringe / marginal / social benefits; (pl.)
(occ.) staff amenities

avantage social contributif
contributory social benefit

avantage social non contributif
non-contributory social benefit

avantage social indirect
indirect (social) benefit

bénéficiaire d'aide sociale
welfare / social assistance recipient; [on
welfare]

besoin social
social (welfare) need

besoin social non satisfait
unmet social need

bien-être social
social welfare

bilan social
social audit / reporting

branche de (la) sécurité sociale
branch of social security

budget social
social budget

bureau d'aide / d'assistance sociale
social assistance / (social) welfare office

cadre de service social
social work supervisor

caisse d'assurances sociales
social insurance fund

caisse de sécurité sociale
social security fund

capillarité sociale
inter-generational social mobility

capital des services sociaux
social overhead capital

**carte d'assurance sociale / d'assuré
social**
(social) insurance card

cas social
person with social problems, needy /
hardship case, social misfit

catégorie sociale
social status / socio-economic group

centre communal d'action sociale
social work municipal centre

**centre d'information et de coordination
de l'action sociale**
social work information and co-ordination centre

**centre public d'aide sociale (CPAS)
(Belg.)**
public centre for social welfare, public
welfare centre

centre social
welfare / social centre

centre social de quartier
neighbourhood (welfare / social) centre

charges sociales
social burden / charges; payroll tax; social security contributions; welfare costs

circonscription de caisse de sécurité sociale
social security fund district

circonscription de service social
social service district

classe sociale
social class

clause de paix sociale
no-strike / peace clause

Code de la famille et de l'aide sociale
Family and Social Welfare Code

Code de la sécurité sociale
Social Security Code

cohésion sociale
social cohesion

Commission d'admission à l'aide sociale (Fr.)
Commission deciding on the eligibility for social welfare

Commission centrale d'aide sociale
Social Welfare Central Commission

complément social
(occ.) marginal benefit

comptabilité sociale
social accounts / accounting

compte satellite de la protection sociale
satellite account for social welfare

comptes sociaux de la nation
national social accounts

conciliation sociale / entre partenaires sociaux
collective conciliation

conditions d'admission à l'aide sociale
qualifying conditions to welfare benefits

condition sociale
social status; position

conflit social
labour / industrial dispute; (pl.) labour / industrial unrest

conseil des oeuvres sociales
(occ.) community council

conseiller pour les / aux affaires sociales
social adviser

conseiller de service social
social welfare adviser

conseiller social
employment / staff / work counsellor; social adviser

contentieux de l'aide sociale
social welfare claims

contentieux de la sécurité sociale
social security claims

contrainte sociale
inescapable social fact

contrat social
social contract

contribution au titre de la sécurité sociale
social security charge

contribution sociale généralisée (CSG) (Fr.)
general social contribution

convention multilatérale de sécurité sociale
multilateral social security convention

convention de sécurité sociale
convention on social security, social security convention

corps social
social entity

cotisation patronale de sécurité sociale
employers' social security contribution

cotisation salariale de sécurité sociale
employees' social security contribution

cotisation de / à la / au titre de la sécurité sociale
social security contribution / charge / tax (USA)

cotisation sociale
welfare / social / insurance contribution

cotisation sociale complémentaire
supplementary welfare contribution

cotisations sociales du régime général de sécurité sociale
insurance contributions for the general social security scheme

cotisation sociale des travailleurs indépendants
self-employment insurance contribution

coût social du travail
social (opportunity) cost of labour

couverture de sécurité sociale
social security coverage

couverture sociale
social coverage; insurance coverage (USA)

déclaration annuelle de données sociales (Fr.)
annual declaration of salaries

défense sociale
social defence

déficit de la sécurité sociale
deficit in social security

demande d'admission à l'aide sociale
welfare benefits request

demande sociale d'éducation
social demand for education

demander une aide sociale
to apply for welfare benefits / for relief

démographie sociale
social demography

dépense d'infrastructure sociale
social overhead cost

dépenses de sécurité sociale
social security expenditure

dépenses sociales
social expenditure

désinsertion sociale
(occ.) dropping out

développement social
social development

diagnostic social
social diagnosis

dialogue social
concertation, social dialogue

dimension sociale
social dimension

diminué social
socially handicapped

dispensaire de médecine sociale
social medicine centre

droit à la sécurité sociale
right to social security

droit social
social / welfare law / legislation; (pl.) social rights

droit social dérivé
subordinate social right

dumping social
social dumping

école de service social
social work school

économie de marché sociale
social market economy

éducateur spécialiste du service social
social work educator

élusion des prestations sociales
evasion of social costs

enquête sociale
social inquiry

équipement de service social
social welfare (material) facility

équipement social
social resources / development / facilities / services, community / welfare facilities

escroquerie à la sécurité sociale
(social security) benefit fraud

esprit de / du service social
social work approach

établissement de protection sanitaire et sociale de l'enfance
health and social care institution for children

étudiant de service social
social work student

exclu de la sécurité sociale
not protected by social security

fichier de sécurité sociale
social security record

filet de protection / de sécurité sociale
social security net

financement de l'aide sociale
social welfare funding

financement de la sécurité sociale
financing of social security

fonds de prévoyance sociale
welfare fund

fonds social
social fund

formation au service social
social work education

foyer social
(occ.) settlement (house)

garantie sociale
social guarantee

groupe social
social (status) group, socio-economic group

handicapé social
socially handicapped; social misfit

hygiène sociale
preventive medicine and social welfare

immatriculation à l'assurance sociale
social insurance registration

impôt de progrès social
social development tax

impôt de sécurité sociale des travailleurs indépendants
self-employment social security tax

inadapté social
social misfit; socially maladjusted / inadequate

indicateur social
social indicator; (pl.) (occ.) key personnel statistical data

infrastructure économique et sociale
economic and social infrastructure / facilities / overhead

infrastructure sanitaire et sociale
health and welfare infrastructure

infrastructure sociale
social overhead / facilities / infrastructure

ingénierie sociale
social engineering

injustice sociale
social inequality

insertion sociale
social integration

inspecteur des affaires sanitaires et sociales
health and sanitary inspector

inspection générale des affaires sociales
social affairs general inspectorate

institution de sécurité sociale
social security agency / institution

institution sociale
social / welfare agency / institution; (pl.) social services

institution sociale privée
private / voluntary welfare agency

interlocuteurs sociaux
social partners

investissement sanitaire et social
health and social investment

juge social
(occ.) social assessor

justice sociale
social fairness

législation sociale
welfare / social legislation

logements pour les groupes sociaux à faibles revenus
low-income housing

logement social
social housing, low-cost dwelling / housing unit; (pl.) low-cost / council / subsidised / public housing

loi sociale
(pl.) social legislation

malaise social
industrial / labour unrest

marché de la sécurité sociale
social security contract

mécontentement social
social discontent

médecine sociale
social medicine

membre des services sociaux
social (welfare) worker

mesure d'action sociale
socially supportive measure

méthode de / du service social
social work method / process

migration sociale
social mobility

milieu social
social environment / background

mineur confié à l'aide sociale (Fr.)
minor in custody of a social welfare institution

mise en oeuvre des droits économiques et sociaux
realisation of economic and social rights

mobilité sociale
social mobility

moniteur de service social
social work educator

mouvement social
industrial action

mutualité sociale agricole (Fr.)
agricultural social insurance agency

normes minima de sécurité sociale
minimum standards for social security

numéro d'assurance sociale
social insurance number

obstacle social
social barrier

oeuvre sociale
welfare agency / institution; (pl.) company welfare facilities, staff amenities

oeuvre sociale privée
private / voluntary welfare agency

office de reclassement social
social re-adaptation service

optimum social
social optimum

organe d'une institution de sécurité sociale
organ of a social security institution

organisation de la protection sociale
(social) welfare provision

organisme d'aide sociale
(social) welfare agency

organisme d'assistance sociale
social assistance agency / body

organisme de protection sociale
(social) welfare agency

organisme de sécurité sociale
social security fund / agency / institution

organisme social
welfare / social agency / institution

organisme social privé
private / voluntary welfare agency

origine sociale
social background / origin

pacte social
social agreement / convention; articles of / deed of partnership

paix sociale
freedom from industrial disputes, industrial harmony / peace, labour peace

partenaires sociaux
social partners; management and labour; two / both sides of industry; unions and management

partenariat social
social partnership

pension de l'aide sociale (UK)
supplementary pension

pension relevant des assurances sociales
social insurance pension

pension de sécurité sociale (It.)
social security pension

pension sociale
social pension

pension sociale d'invalidité (Port.)
social invalidity pension

permanence d'entraide sociale (UK)
Citizens' Advice Bureau

personnel d'action sociale
social work personnel / staff

personnel enseignant du service social
social work educators

personnel (de service) social
social work / welfare personnel / staff

plafond de sécurité sociale
social security ceiling

plan d'équipement social
social development plan

plan social (Fr.)
collective redundancy programme

planification sociale
social planning

politique sociale
social policy

politique sociale intégrée
integrated social policy

position sociale
social situation / status

poste de service social
social work appointment

praticien de l'action sociale
social (welfare) worker

prestation d'aide sociale
welfare payment; supplementary benefit (UK); (pl.) welfare benefits, social fund (UK)

prestations générales d'aide sociale
general welfare assistance

prestation de sécurité sociale
social security benefit / payment

prestation sociale
welfare payment; social (security / insurance) benefit; (pl.) welfare benefits

prestation sociale des comités d'entre-prise
social benefit paid by works committees

prestation sociale directe de l'employeur
unfunded employment welfare benefit

prêt social
social loan

prévoyance et aide sociale
social relief and welfare

prévoyance sociale
(social) welfare

procédure d'admission à l'aide sociale
social assistance entitlement procedure

procédure de règlement d'un conflit social
(industrial) dispute procedure

professeur de service social
social work teacher

professions intermédiaires du travail social [CITP-1988 (346)]
social work associate professionals [ISCO-1988 (346)]

programmation sociale
social programming

programme d'action sociale
social action programme

programme d'aide sociale
social support programme

programme de construction de logements sociaux
low-cost housing programme

programme de protection sociale
(social) welfare programme

progrès social
social development

projet de logements sociaux
low-income housing project

promotion sociale
social advancement / betterment / development; (social) welfare; upgrading

protection de sécurité sociale
social security coverage

protection sociale
social welfare / defence / protection / care, social welfare work

protection sociale et juridique de l'enfance
social and legal child welfare

protection sociale passive
passive social protection

rapport d'enquête sociale
social (inquiry) report

rapport social
social reporting / accounts, personnel report

réadaptation sociale
social rehabilitation

recevoir des allocations d'aide / une aide sociale
to be on welfare

recherche sociale
social research

recherche sociale opérationnelle
operational social research

reclassement social
social resettlement

recours en matière d'aide sociale
legal action against a decision relating to social welfare

recours sur succession en matière d'aide sociale (Fr.)
action to recover social benefits from succession

réforme sociale
social reform

régime d'aide sociale
welfare plan

régime général de (la) sécurité sociale
general social security scheme, standard social security health and retirement insurance (for private industry)

régime légal de sécurité sociale
statutory social security scheme

régime national de sécurité sociale
national social security scheme

régime de sécurité sociale
social security scheme

régime spécial de sécurité sociale
specific / special social security scheme

régression sociale
(occ.) downward mobility

réinsertion sociale
social integration / resettlement

relations sociales / entre partenaires sociaux
labour / employee / industrial relations; social fabric

responsable de la rémunération et des avantages sociaux
compensation and benefits manager (USA)

revendication sociale
social demand

revenu social brut
gross social (insurance) income

risque social
social contingency / risk

rôle social
social responsibility / role

salaire social
social wage

salaire social minimal (Lux.)
minimum social salary

sciences sociales
social sciences

secrétariat social (It.)
social welfare secretariat

secteur de l'économie sociale
(occ.) third sector

sectorisation sanitaire et sociale
division into health and social sectors

sécurité sociale
social security; welfare programme

service d'aide sociale
(social) welfare service; (occ.) public
charity

service d'hygiène et d'aide sociale
health and social welfare service

service de protection sociale
(social) welfare service

service social
social agency; social welfare; (social)
welfare service / work / provision; social
work (activity / practice); (pl.) social
administration / services / provision / welfare; welfare (facilities)

services sociaux de la collectivité
community welfare services

**services sociaux et services connexes
fournis à la collectivité**
social and related community services

service social de communauté
community social work, social work with
communities

service social d'entreprise
industrial social work

service social de groupe
social group work

service social à l'hôpital
hospital social work

service social dans l'industrie
industrial welfare service

services sociaux et services personnels
social and personal services

service social du personnel
personnel social work

service social des prisons
social work in penal institutions

service social rural
rural social work

service social scolaire
school social work

service social du travail
industrial welfare, industrial social work

siège social
head office

**spécialiste de l'enseignement du service
social**
social work educator

**spécialiste des questions de service
social**
(social) welfare officer

station sociale (Ger.)
social station

statut d'assisté social
(occ.) welfare status

stratification sociale
social stratification

structure sociale
social fabric

**Système international de conservation
des droits en matière de sécurité sociale**
International System for the Maintenance
of Rights in Social Security

système de protection sociale
social protection / welfare (scheme)

système de sécurité sociale
social insurance / social security system

taux de prestations d'aide sociale
rate of welfare benefits, (occ.) welfare rate

tissu social
social fabric

traitement social individuel
individual social treatment

transfert social
social transfer; (pl.) social transfer
payments, social benefits

travail social
social work (activity / practice); (social)
welfare work

travail social d'entreprise
industrial social work

travail social professionnel
professional social work

travail social scolaire
school social work

travail d'utilité sociale
community service / work; community
work schemes, workfare

travailleurs sanitaires et sociaux
health and social workers

travailleur social
social / welfare worker, (social) welfare
officer / worker

travailleur social d'entreprise
industrial social / welfare worker

**travailleur social en établissement
pénitentiaire**
prison welfare officer

travailleur social de groupe
group (social) worker

travailleur social neuropsychiatrique
psychiatric social worker

travailleur social professionnel
professional social worker

trou de la sécurité sociale
deficit in social security

trouble social
(pl.) industrial / labour unrest

tutelle aux prestations sociales (Fr.)
control on social benefits

unité sociale
social unit

valeur sociale
social value / effectiveness

visiteuse sociale
home visitor

SOCIALEMENT
famille socialement défavorisée
socially deprived family

socialement défavorisé
socially deprived

travail socialement utile (Ger.)
socially useful work

SOCIALISATION
socialisation des moyens de production
socialisation of the means of production

SOCIALISÉ
secteur socialisé
socialist sector

SOCIALISER
to socialise

SOCIÉTAL
societal

SOCIÉTÉ
society; community; corporation, corporate body, company

acte de société
articles of / deed of partnership

aptitude à vivre en société
social skill(s)

contrat de société
articles of / deed of partnership

directeurs de société [CITP-1988 (12)]
corporate managers [ISCO-1988 (12)]

entreprise constituée en société
corporate business / enterprise, incorporated business / enterprise

impôt sur les bénéfices des sociétés
tax on corporate profits

impôt sur les sociétés
corporate tax

revenus de sociétés
company / corporate earnings

société d'abondance
affluent society

société active
active society

société d'aide à l'enfance
child helping society

société attentive aux besoins
caring society

société de bien-être
welfare society

société de consommation
consumer society

société de développement de l'emploi local
(occ.) community employment corporation

société de droit public
public corporation

société duale
dual society

société d'épargne et de financement immobilier
(occ.) building society

société mixte
joint venture

société mutualiste
friendly / (mutual) benefit society

société en nom collectif
commercial partnership

société de personnes
partnership; (occ.) private company

société de prévoyance
friendly society

société de secours
provident society; relief association

société de secours mutuel
mutual benefit / provident society

société de service public
public utility

société à deux vitesses
two-tier / dual society

voiture de société
company car

SOCIO-CULTUREL
animateur socio-culturel
community worker

centre socio-culturel
social / socio-cultural centre

SOCIO-ÉCONOMIQUE
indicateur socio-économique
socio-economic indicator

indice des disparités socio-économiques
socio-economic disparity index

SOCIO-ÉDUCATIF
équipement socio-éducatif
socio-educational facility

SOCIO-PÉDAGOGIE
educational sociology

SOCIO-PÉDAGOGIQUE
animateur socio-pédagogique
social welfare organiser

moniteur socio-pédagogique
social welfare instructor

SOCIO-PROFESSIONNEL
catégorie socio-professionnelle
social and economic category, social
status / socio-economic group; social
status

**organisme d'insertion socio-
professionnelle (OISP) (Belg.)**
social and vocational integration
organisation / agency

situation / statut socio-professionnel(le)
social status

SOCIO-RÉCRÉATIF
programme socio-récréatif
social programme

SOCIOTHÉRAPIE
social therapy

SOIGNANT (adj.)
équipe soignante
health team

personnel soignant
care staff

SOIGNANT (n.)
(health) care provider, care giver, care
taker, carer

allocation pour soignant (Irel.)
carer's allowance

soignant ponctuel
informal carer

SOIGNÉ
travail soigné
high quality work

SOIN
(pl.) care; treatment; attendance

administration des premiers soins
provision of first aid

administration des soins infirmiers
provision of nursing care

aide et soins à domicile
home help and care

allocation de / pour soins
nursing / care allowance

allocation pour soins constants
(constant) attendance allowance, attendance benefit (Norw.)

allocation de soins à domicile (Irel.)
domiciliary care allowance

allocation pour soins aux enfants (Finl.)
child care allowance

allocation pour soins hospitaliers (UK)
hospital treatment allowance

**allocation pour soins en institution
(UK)**
residential allowance

allocation pour soins à (un) invalide
invalid care allowance

allocation de soins majorée (Finl.)
increased care allowance

allocation pour soins médicaux
(medical) treatment allowance

**allocation de soins pour pensionnés
(Finl.)**
pensioner's care allowance

allocation de soins spéciale (Finl.)
special care allowance

allocation de soins aux tuberculeux
tuberculosis allowance

assurance-soins dentaires
dental insurance, dental health scheme

assurance-soins de santé
health care insurance

carnet de soins
health care booklet / record

centre collectif de soins
community health centre

centre de soins
(health / nursing) care centre

centre de soins primaires
primary care centre

Comité des allocations pour soins constants (UK)
Attendance Allowance Board

congé pour soins aux enfants (Swed.)
child care leave

consommateur de soins de santé / de soins médicaux
medical consumer

consommation de soins de santé / de soins médicaux
consumption of medical care

dispensateur de soins
care giver / provider

dispensateur de soins médicaux
medical care provider

distribution des soins médicaux / des soins de santé
health care delivery

établissement de soins
health facility

état nécessitant des soins médicaux
condition requiring medical care

feuille de soins (Fr.)
medical (expenses refund) claim form

forfait journalier de soins et d'hébergement
patient's daily charge for care and accommodation

gratuité des soins
free medical care

hôpital de soins aigus
acute care / active treatment / somatic hospital

indemnité de soins aux tuberculeux
tuberculosis allowance

octroi des soins médicaux
provision of medical care

offre de soins
available health services

pension pour soins (Austr.)
carer's pension

premiers soins
first aid

prestataire de soins médicaux
medical care provider

prestation pour soins constants (Norw.)
attendance benefit

prestation de soins infirmiers
provision of nursing care

producteurs de soins privilégiés
preferred providers organisation (PPO)

refus de soins
refusal of health care

réseau de soins coordonnés
health maintenance organisation (HMO)

service public de soins infirmiers
public health nursing service, district nursing service (UK)

service de soins ambulatoires
ambulatory service

service de soins à domicile
home care service

service de soins infirmiers à domicile pour personnes âgées
home care nursing for the elderly

service de soins primaires
primary care service

service de soins de santé primaire
primary health care service

soins ambulatoires
ambulatory / out-patient care

soins auto-administrés
self-care

soins cliniques
clinical care

soins communautaires
community (health) care

soins complets
comprehensive care

soins conservateurs
conservative treatment

soins constants
constant attendance

soins continuels
regular care

soins courants
routine care

soins curatifs
curative care

soins dentaires
dental treatment / care

soins dentaires d'entretien
conservative dental care

soins directs
direct care

soins à domicile
domiciliary / in-house care, home nursing, home (medical) care

soins aux enfants
child care

soins d'entretien et de continuité de la vie
daily care to compensate dependence

soins en établissement
institutional / residential care

soins dans des établissements de jour
day care

soins en établissement privé
private care

soins à l'étranger
health care abroad

soins dispensés par la famille
family care / support

soins génésiques
reproductive health

soins gradués
progressive patient care

soins hospitaliers
hospital care / treatment; institutional care

soins non hospitaliers
(occ.) out-patient care

soins d'hygiène et de confort
basic nursing care

soins indirects
indirect care

soins individuels
personal health care

soins aux individus
individual patient care

soins infirmiers
nursing (care)

soins infirmiers à domicile
home nursing, visiting nurse services

soins infirmiers intensifs
intensive nursing care

soins infirmiers aux malades mentaux
mental health nursing

soins infirmiers néonatals
neo-natal nursing

soins infirmiers de pédiatrie / pédiatriques
paediatric nursing

soins en institution
institutional / residential care

soins intensifs
intensive care

soins intermédiaires (Can.)
intermediate care

soins de longue durée
long-term care

soins aux malades
patient care

soins aux malades hospitalisés
(occ.) residential care

soins aux malades non hospitalisés
(occ.) non-residential care

soins aux malades en traitement de jour
day patient care

soins de maternité
maternity care

soins médicaux
medical care / treatment / (occ.) attention,
course of treatment

soins médicaux en consultation externe
out-patient treatment

soins médicaux à domicile
home medical care, medical home relief
(USA)

soins médicaux primaires
primary medical care

soins médicaux secondaires
secondary medical care

soins médicaux tertiaires
tertiary medical care

soins de médecine générale
general medical care, general practitioner
care

soins du ménage
household care

soins aux mères et aux enfants
mother and child care

soins en milieu hospitalier
hospital care / treatment; (occ.)
institutional care

soins minimaux
minimum care

soins obstétricaux
maternity / delivery care

soins optiques
eye care / treatment, vision care (USA)

soins palliatifs
palliative care

soins pédiatriques
paediatric / child care

soins aux personnes âgées
care of old people

soins personnels
(occ.) self-care

soins de post-cure
follow-up care

soins post-hospitaliers
follow-up care

soins post-opératoires
post-operative care

soins post-partum
post-partum care

soins aux prématurés
premature care

soins de premier recours
primary (health / medical) care

soins prénatals
ante-natal / pre(-)natal care

soins préventifs
preventive care

soins primaires
primary care

soins prolongés
continuing care

soins de proximité
community(-based) care

soins psychiatriques
psychiatric nursing / treatment

soins de réadaptation
rehabilitative care

**soins en régime hospitalier ou ambula-
toire**
in-patient or out-patient care

soins relationnels
supportive care

soins de santé
health care

soins de santé de base
basic health care

soins de santé primaire
primary health care

soins secondaires
secondary care

soins de spécialistes
specialist care

soins tertiaires
tertiary care

soins ultérieurs
(occ.) after-treatment

soins d'urgence
first aid, emergency health care

supplément de soins (Pol.)
medical care supplement

système d'administration des soins
health care (delivery) system

système national de distribution de soins
national system of health care

système de prestation des soins
health care (delivery) system

unité de soins
nursing unit, patient care / health care unit

unité de soins intensifs
intensive care unit

SOIR
cours du soir
evening school / classes, night course / school / classes

école (dispensant des cours) du soir
evening / night school

équipe du soir
backs / evening shift

établissement dispensant des cours du soir
evening / night school

SOLDE
balance; pay

congé sans solde
unpaid leave, leave without pay; absence without pay

délégation de solde
order to pay somebody's salary to dependants

indemnité de congé de maternité sans solde (Austr.)
unpaid maternity leave allowance

reçu pour solde de tout compte (Fr.)
receipt of final pay

salaire pour solde de tout compte
terminated employee's final pay

solde non affecté
unallotted balance

solde budgétaire en situation de plein emploi
full / high employment (budget) balance

solde disponible
unexpended / unencumbered balance

solde des droits
balance of entitlements

solde non engagé
unobligated balance

solde de jours de congé annuel accumulés
accrued annual leave balance

solde migratoire
balance of migration, migration balance

solde des opérations courantes / des paiements courants
current account

solde non utilisé
unexpended / unencumbered balance

SOLIDAIRE
interdependent; interrelated; integrated; sympathetic; [in solidarity with]

SOLIDARITÉ
mutual help, solidarity, interrelationship

allocation conventionnelle de solidarité (Fr.)
contractual solidarity allowance

allocation de solidarité
solidarity allowance

allocation de solidarité de chômage total (Fr.)
total unemployment solidarity allowance

allocation de solidarité spécifique (Fr.)
specific solidarity allowance

allocation spéciale de solidarité (Fr.)
special solidarity allowance

contrat emploi-solidarité (CES) (Fr.)
solidarity employment contract, employment contract to facilitate reintegration of disadvantaged persons

contrat de solidarité
solidarity contract

contribution de solidarité
solidarity contribution

fonds de solidarité
solidarity fund

fonds de solidarité vieillesse (Fr.)
old age solidarity fund

grève de solidarité
secondary / sympathetic / sympathy strike, secondary industrial action

groupe de solidarité
(mutual) self-help group

impôt de solidarité
solidarity tax

régime de solidarité (Fr.)
solidarity scheme

SOLLICITER
solliciter un emploi
to apply for a job

SOLVABILITÉ
ability to pay

SOMATIQUE
somatic; physical

SOMMAIRE (adj.)
description sommaire de poste
summary job description

SOMMATIF
évaluation sommative
summative assessment

SOMMATION
notice; summons; subpoena

SOMME
sum, total; amount

débiteur de sommes
liable to pay sums

jeu à somme nulle
zero-sum game

rembourser toutes les sommes perçues
to reimburse all amounts received

somme assignée
allocation

somme en capital
capital sum; lump(-sum) payment

somme en capital résultant de / versée au titre de la conversion partielle de la pension
partial lump sum withdrawal benefit, partial lump sum commutation of pension benefit

somme due à la cessation de service
terminal entitlement

somme fixe
fixed sum

somme forfaitaire / globale
lump(-sum) / single payment, lump sum

somme de travail accrue
increased workload

somme unique
lump(-sum) / single payment, lump sum

SOMMET
sommet d'une carrière
peak of a career

SONDAGE
enquête par sondage
sample survey

enquête par sondage sur la population active
labour force sample survey

sondage aléatoire
random sampling

sondage d'opinion
opinion survey

sondage probabiliste
random sampling

SONDÉ (n.)
respondent

SORTANT
plan d'accompagnement pour les sortants de l'école et des études (SAVE) (Belg.) support plan for school and college leavers

SORTIE
exit; discharge; withdrawal; release

âge de sortie de l'école
school-leaving age

clause (optionnelle) de sortie
opting-out clause

date de sortie
date of discharge; date of leaving (hosp.)

date de sortie d'un employé
departure date of an employee

pointage à la sortie
clocking-off, clocking-out

prestation de sortie
withdrawal benefit

rythme de sorties
rate of outflow (register)

sortie du chômage
outflow from / flow out of unemployment

sorties du chômage pour reprise d'emploi
outflow to jobs from unemployment

sortie de l'hôpital
release from hospital

sortie du marché de l'emploi / du travail
withdrawal from employment / from the labour force

visa de sortie
exit permit

SOUFFRANCE
pain

travail en souffrance
work in abeyance

SOULAGER
to relieve (the plight)

SOULEVER
to raise

SOUMIS
soumis à (une) condition de ressources subject to a means test, means-tested

soumis à cotisation
liable for / subject to contribution

soumis à l'impôt
taxable

soumis à des réserves
subject to limitations

SOUPLE
aménagement souple du temps de travail variable / flexible working time

formes d'emploi souples
flexible employment

forme de travail souple
flexible work

horaire souple
flexible working hours / time, flexible time / hours; flexitime

horaire de travail souple
flexible work schedule, flexible hours

SOUPLESSE
flexibility; elasticity

souplesse des horaires de travail
flexibility of working hours

SOURCE
imposé à la source
taxed at source

imposer à la source
to tax at source

impôt prélevé / retenu à la source
tax deducted at source, pay-as-you-earn
(PAYE) tax, withholding tax

prélèvement à la source
deduction at source P.A.Y.E.; withholding tax; payroll deduction

retenir à la source
to tax at source

retenu à la source
deducted at source

retenue à la source
withholding tax, pay-as-you-earn
(PAYE), deduction at source P.A.Y.E.,
payroll deduction

source de financement
funding source

source de main-d'oeuvre
manpower / supply source

source principale de revenu
primary / principal (wage) earner

source de revenu
earner

source secondaire de revenus
second breadwinner, secondary (wage)
earner, second family earner

source de subsistance
source of subsistence / of livelihood

source de travail
source of employment

source de travailleurs
manpower / supply source

système de retenue à la source
pay-as-you-earn (PAYE)

SOUS-ASSURANCE
underinsurance

SOUSCRIPTEUR
company underwriter (ins.)

SOUS-DIRECTEUR
deputy manager

SOUS-EFFECTIF
understaffing, undermanning

sous-effectif (être en)
to be understaffed / undermanned

SOUS-EMPLOI
under-employment; employment slack;
growth gap unemployment; short-time
work / working

sous-emploi des capacités
under-utilisation of capacity

sous-emploi dissimulé
concealed under-employment

sous-emploi invisible
invisible under-employment

sous-emploi de la main-d'oeuvre
under-utilisation of labour

sous-emploi potentiel
potential under-employment

sous-emploi visible
visible under-employment

SOUS-EMPLOYÉ
underworked; marginally employed; under-employed

SOUS-ENCADRÉ
inadequately trained

SOUS-GROUPE
sub-group; minor group

SOUS-JACENT
underlying

SOUS-OFFICIER
non-commissioned officer (NCO)

SOUS-ORDRE
travailler en sous-ordre
to work under close control

SOUS-PAYÉ
underpaid

SOUS-PEUPLÉ
logement sous-peuplé
insufficiently occupied dwelling

SOUS-QUALIFIÉ
underqualified, underskilled

SOUS-REPRÉSENTATION
under-representation

SOUS-REPRÉSENTER
to underrepresent

SOUS-SALAIRE
dumping wage

SOUS-SYSTÈME
sub-system

SOUS-TRAITANCE
subcontracting; contracting out; out
(-)sourcing; offshore work

contrat de sous-traitance
subcontracting; (occ.) contract for
services

sous-traitance de main-d'oeuvre
labour subcontracting

SOUS-TRAITANT
subcontractor

SOUS-TRAITER
to subcontract; to contract out; to farm out
work

SOUS-UTILISATION
underspending, underexpenditure; under-
run, under-utilisation

sous-utilisation de la main-d'oeuvre
under-utilisation of labour

**sous-utilisation de la main-d'oeuvre et
des installations**
under-utilisation of labour and capacity

SOUTENIR
to help, to second, to support; to claim

soutenir l'emploi
to sustain employment

SOUTENU
croissance économique soutenue
sustained economic growth

SOUTERRAIN
économie souterraine
black / hidden / informal / moonlight /
shadow / submerged / twilight /
underground / grey / invisible economy

SOUTIEN
support; earner

**allocation de soutien de famille /
familial**
family support allowance

enseignement de soutien
remedial teaching / education

mesure de soutien
support measure

personnel de soutien
support staff

perte de soutien et dédommagement
death dependency and indemnity
compensation

principal soutien économique
primary / principal (wage) earner

rapport de soutien économique
support ratio

rapport de soutien économique des personnes âgées
old age support ratio

réseau local de soutien
neighbourhood support network / system

service de soutien
backstop / supportive / support service

service de soutien après placement
post-employment support service

soutien de famille
primary / principal (wage) earner;
(family) breadwinner; family support

soutien du revenu familial
family income support

soutien du revenu hebdomadaire
weekly income support

SOUTIER
baggage handler

SPÉCIAL
activité spéciale
special occupation

affectation spéciale
special assignment, reserved occupation

allocation d'éducation spéciale
special education allowance, allowance
for severely disabled children (Fr.)

allocation prévue par les régimes spéciaux d'indemnisation
(occ.) special benefit

allocation de soins spéciale (Finl.)
special care allowance

allocation spéciale
special allowance

allocation spéciale de chômage (Fr.)
special unemployment allowance

allocation spéciale pour les enfants de femmes divorcées (UK)
child's special allowance

allocation spéciale de naissance
special childbirth allowance

allocation spéciale de solidarité (Fr.)
special solidarity allowance

allocation spéciale vieillesse (Fr.)
old age special allowance

Commission spéciale (UK)
Select Committee

compte d'affectation spéciale
earmarked account

congé pour raisons spéciales
leave of absence for special reasons;
(occ.) compassionate leave

congé spécial
special leave

congé spécial d'ancienneté
special long-service leave

congé spécial à demi-traitement
special leave with half pay

congé spécial à plein traitement
special leave with full pay

congé spécial sans traitement
special leave without pay

congé spécial à traitement partiel
special leave with partial pay

contrat d'apprentissage spécial (Belg.)
special apprenticeship contract

contrat spécial d'engagement / de service
special service agreement

disposition spéciale
special provision

éducation spéciale
special education

établissement d'éducation spéciale / d'enseignement spécial
special school

fonds d'affectation spéciale
trust fund, funds-in-trust

impôt spécial
special tax

indemnité journalière de subsistance au taux spécial
special rate of daily subsistence allowance

indemnité spéciale de déplacement
special travel allowance

mission spéciale
special assignment

prestation spéciale assistante maternelle (Fr.)
special benefit for day-care attendant

qualification spéciale (sans)
(occ.) untrained

rapport spécial relatif au licenciement
special report relating to termination

régime spécial
special scheme

régime spécial des fonctionnaires ou du personnel assimilé
special scheme for civil servants and persons treated as such

régime spécial de sécurité sociale
specific / special social security scheme

régime spécial de travailleurs non salariés
special scheme for self-employed persons

tâche spéciale
special assignment

SPÉCIALISATION
specialisation / specialist training; specialised skill

métier de haute spécialisation
highly skilled / higher-skill trade

profession de haute spécialisation
highly skilled / higher-skill / qualified occupation

profession de spécialisation moyenne
semi-skilled / medium-skilled occupation

profession de spécialisation réduite
low-skilled occupation

spécialisation flexible
flexible specialisation

SPÉCIALISÉ
specialised; professional, skilled

conseiller spécialisé
specialist counsellor

dirigeants et cadres supérieurs d'organisations spécialisées [CITP-1988 (114)]
senior officials of special-interest organisations [ISCO-1988 (114)]

éducateur spécialisé
teacher of children with learning difficulties

emploi d'ouvrier spécialisé
semi-skilled occupation

enseignement dispensé par des établissements spécialisés
(occ.) institutionalised education

établissement spécialisé
specialised institution

formation aux / dans les métiers spécialisés
skilled trades training

formation professionnelle spécialisée
occupational skills training, specialised vocational training

formation spécialisée
specialised / specialisation / specialist training

formation hautement spécialisée
high-skill training

formation peu spécialisée
lower-level skill training

formation spécialisée en établissement
institutional skill training

fournisseur spécialisé
specialised supplier

hautement spécialisé
highly qualified / skilled; professional

hôpital spécialisé
specialised hospital

instituteur spécialisé (Fr.)
special school teacher

main-d'oeuvre spécialisée
semi-skilled labour

médicament spécialisé
patent medicine

métier hautement spécialisé
highly skilled / higher-skill trade

ouvrier spécialisé (OS)
semi-skilled / unskilled worker, specialised worker; operative

personne hautement spécialisée
(occ.) professional

personnel spécialisé
professional / skilled / trained / specialised personnel / staff

poste d'ouvrier spécialisé
semi-skilled occupation

profession hautement spécialisée
highly skilled / higher-skill / qualified
occupation

profession spécialisée
skilled / trained occupation

profession non spécialisée
unskilled occupation

profession peu spécialisée
low-skilled occupation

**service d'orientation professionnelle
spécialisée**
specialised vocational guidance service

service spécialisé
specialised / (occ.) professional service

service spécialisé de placement
specialised job placement service

spécialisé (non)
unskilled

travail hautement spécialisé
highly skilled work

travail technique hautement spécialisé
high-skill technical work

travailleur manuel spécialisé
semi-skilled manual worker

SPÉCIALISTE
specialist; consultant; officer; resource
person; substantive officer; professional;
consultant doctor

**autres spécialistes de l'enseignement
[CITP-1988 (235)]**
other teaching professionals [ISCO-1988
(235)]

**autres spécialistes des professions
intellectuelles et scientifiques [CITP-
1988 (24)]**
other professionals [ISCO-1988 (24)]

soins de spécialistes
specialist care

spécialiste en éducation sanitaire
health educator

spécialiste en emploi
employment specialist

**spécialistes de l'enseignement [CITP-
1988 (23)]**
teaching professionals [ISCO-1988 (23)]

**spécialiste de l'enseignement du service
social**
social work educator

**spécialistes des fonctions
administratives et commerciales des
entreprises [CITP-1988 (241)]**
business professionals [ISCO-1988 (241)]

**spécialistes de l'informatique [CITP-
1988 (213)]**
computing professionals [ISCO-1988
(213)]

spécialiste de l'orientation
guidance expert

spécialiste en recrutement
recruiting specialist

spécialiste des questions de service social
(social) welfare officer

spécialistes des sciences physico-chimiques et techniciens assimilés [CITP-1968 (0-1)]
physical scientists and related technicians [ISCO-1968 (0-1)]

spécialistes des sciences physiques, mathématiques et techniques [CITP-1988 (21)]
physical, mathematical and engineering science professionals [ISCO-1988 (21)]

spécialistes des sciences sociales et humaines [CITP-1988 (244)]
social science and related professionals [ISCO-1988 (244)]

spécialistes des sciences de la vie [CITP-1988 (221)]
life science professionals [ISCO-188 (221)]

spécialistes des sciences de la vie et de la santé [CITP-1988 (22)]
life science and health professionals [ISCO-1988 (22)]

spécialiste du domaine du travail
labour expert

SPÉCIALITÉ
spécialité pharmaceutique
patent medicine, proprietary drug

SPÉCIFICATION
specification; standard

SPÉCIFIÉ
specified

contrat à durée déterminée à terme non spécifié (Fr.)
unspecified (but fixed) term contract

SPÉCIFIQUE
specific

allocation de solidarité spécifique (Fr.)
specific solidarity allowance

étude spécifique
case study

formation spécifique à un emploi
job-related training

SPECTACLE
performance; entertainment

artiste du spectacle
entertainer

domaine / industrie / monde du spectacle
entertainment industry; show business

SPÉCULATIF
candidature spéculative
speculative application

SPHÈRE
sphère de responsabilité
competency area

SPIRALE
spirale inflationniste
inflationary spiral

spirale des prix
price spiral

spirale des salaires
wage spiral

spirale des salaires et des prix
wage/price spiral

SPONTANÉ
voluntary

candidature spontanée
unsolicited candidacy / job application

habitat spontané
squatter settlement

SPORADIQUE
chômage sporadique
casual unemployment

SPORT
professions intermédiaires de la création artistique, du spectacle et du sport [CITP-1988 (347)]
artistic, entertainment and sports associate professions [ISCO-1988 (347)]

sport d'entreprise
sports activities for workers

SPORTIF
centre de médecine sportive
sports medicine centre

SQUATTAGE
squatting

SQUATTER (n.)
squatter

colonie de squatters
squatter settlement

STABILISATION
stabilisation du marché du travail
labour market stabilisation

STABILISÉ
incapacité stabilisée
arrested incapacity

STABILITÉ
stability; sustainability

indice de stabilité du personnel
labour stability index

stabilité d'emploi
job stability, security of tenure; job tenure

STABLE
emploi stable
steady job, stable / secure employment

établissement stable
permanent establishment

logement stable (Icel.)
secure dwelling

main-d'oeuvre stable
stable workforce

poste stable
continuing post

situation stable
(occ.) steady job

STADE
stade de perfectionnement
continuation stage

STAGE
course; field experience; training; traineeship; probation (period), trial / training / probationary period; qualifying / waiting period

abandonner un stage
to withdraw from a training course

condition de stage
qualifying period

condition de stage (sans)
without qualifying period

convention de stage (Fr.)
training agreement

durée de la période de stage
period of probationary service

écourter un stage
to reduce a probationary period

effectuer un stage
to complete a training period

engagement pour une période de stage
probationary appointment

envoyer en stage de formation
to refer for training

imposer aucune condition de stage (n')
to impose no qualifying period

inscription conditionnelle à un stage
-conditional referral to a course

inscrire à un stage de formation
to refer for training

période de stage
qualifying / probationary period

rapport de stage
probation report

stage d'affirmation de soi
assertiveness training

stage conventionné
agreement-regulated training course

stage de cotisation
qualifying period of contribution

stage pour débutants
beginners' course

stage diplômant
qualifying training period / working
experience

stage d'emploi
qualifying period of employment

stage en entreprise
(occ.) internship

stage d'été
summer course

**stage de fin de formation en entreprise
(Belg.)**
enterprise-based end of training course

stage de formation
training course

stage de formation accélérée
rapid training course

stage de formation en alternance (Fr.)
sandwich integration course

stage de formation de base
basic / low-level training course

stage de formation intensive
intensive / rapid training course

stage de formation professionnelle
occupational / skill / vocational course

stage de formation qualifiante
skill training course

stage de formation reconnu
approved training course

stage d'initiation
beginners' / introductory / induction
course

stage d'initiation au travail
pre-employment course

**stage d'initiation à la vie
professionnelle (SIVP)**
work experience programme

stage à inscription préétablie
scheduled intake course
stage d'insertion
work-experience job

**stage d'insertion et de formation à
l'emploi (Fr.)**
employment integration and training
course

stage d'insertion à la vie professionnelle
integration to working life course

stage d'intégration professionnelle
induction course

stage intensif
intensive / crash course

stage d'orientation
orientation course / training

stage ouvrier
industrial placement

stage de perfectionnement
advanced / proficiency / retraining course;
in-service (educational) training, on-site /
on-the-job training / learning

stage pratique
field work practice

**stage de préparation à la vie profes-
sionnelle**
vocational preparation course

**stage préparatoire aux techniques
industrielles**
basic industrial skill course

stage de réadaptation professionnelle
occupational rehabilitation course

stage de reconversion
retraining course

stage de recyclage
retraining / upgrading course

stage de remise à niveau
updating course

stage à temps partiel
part-time course

stage de terminologie technique
technical language training course

stage de travail et d'étude
(occ.) work study

subordonné à une condition de stage
subject to a qualifying period

STAGIAIRE
trainee; probationer, probationary employee; student; junior

allocation de stagiaire
trainee allowance

apprenti stagiaire
trainee apprentice

fonctionnaire stagiaire
civil servant on probation

formation des stagiaires
training of trainees

placement des stagiaires
trainee placement

poste de stagiaire
training / trainee position

stagiaire non apprenti
non-apprentice trainee

stagiaire chômeur
unemployed trainee

stagiaire en formation
active trainee

stagiaire payant
fee-payer trainee

stagiaire à temps complet / à temps plein
full-time trainee

subvention de voyage de stagiaire
trainee travel grant

STANDARD (adj.)
calcul des coûts standard
standard costing

coût standard
standard cost

STANDARDISÉ
taux de chômage standardisé (TCS)
standardised unemployment rate (SUR)

STATION
station climatique / de cure
health resort

station sociale (Ger.)
social station

station thermale
health resort

STATISTICIEN
statisticiens, mathématiciens, analystes de systèmes et techniciens assimilés [CITP-1968 (0-8)]
statisticians, mathematicians, systems analysts and related technicians [IS-CO-1968 (0-8)]

statisticien du travail
labour statistician

STATISTIQUE (adj.)
données statistiques provenant d'un recensement
census material

relevé statistique d'activité
statistical activity report

tableau statistique d'activité
statistical table of activity

STATISTIQUE (n.)
(pl.) statistics; record; returns

statistiques du chômage
unemployment data / figures / statistics

statistiques démographiques
population statistics

statistiques de l'emploi
labour market / manpower statistics;
employment figures

statistiques de l'état civil
vital statistics

statistiques de flux
flow statistics

statistiques relatives au marché du travail
labour market statistics

statistiques de naissances
birth figures

statistiques de la population
population statistics

statistiques de la population active
labour force statistics

statistiques et prévisions d'emploi
employment statistics and estimates

statistiques sanitaires
health statistics

statistiques des services de santé
health service statistics

statistiques syndicales
trade union statistics

statistiques du travail
labour / manpower statistics

STATU QUO
status quo; standstill

STATURE
size

STATUT
status; statute; position; regulations; articles; memorandum of association

aménagement de statut
status adjustment

statut des agents
staff status; staff regulations

statut d'assisté social
(occ.) welfare status

statut-cadre
managerial status

statut contractuel
contractual status

statut légal
legal status

statut du personnel
staff status

statut professionnel
industrial / professional / employment / occupational / work status, position in industry, status in employment, work situation

statut de résident
resident status

statut socio-professionnel
social status

statut de travailleur à temps complet / à temps plein
full-time status

STATUTAIRE
statutory; provided by the articles

âge statutaire de la retraite
statutory age of retirement

condition d'emploi statutaire
statutory condition of service

disposition statutaire
statutory provision, provision in the articles

personnel statutaire
statutory staff

régime statutaire
statutory scheme

règle statutaire
statutory rule; (pl.) (occ.) legislation

revenu statutaire
statutory income

STATUTAIREMENT
under the articles

STÉNOGRAPHE
sténographes dactylographes et opérateurs sur machines perforatrices de cartes
et de rubans [CITP-1968 (3-2)]
stenographers, typists and card- and tape-
punching machine operators [ISCO-1968
(3-2)]

STIMULANT
inducement; incentive

STIMULATION
mesure de stimulation de l'emploi
employment incentive, employment
development measure

politique de stimulation de l'emploi
employment development policy

prime de stimulation
incentive award / bonus

stimulation de l'emploi
job stimulation; employment development

STIMULER
stimuler l'emploi
to stimulate employment

STIPULATION
provision; specification

STIPULER
to provide

STOCK
stock; supply

données de stocks
stock data

STRATÉGIE
stratégie des besoins essentiels
basic needs strategy

stratégie d'emploi
employment strategy

**stratégie industrielle orientée vers la
satisfaction des besoins essentiels**
basic needs-oriented industrial strategy

stratégie de recrutement
recruitment strategy

STRATIFICATION
stratification sociale
social stratification

STRICT
strict nécessaire
bare necessities (of life)

STRUCTURÉ (adj.)
enseignement structuré
organised education

entretien structuré
directed interview

formation structurée
formal training

formation non structurée
informal training

secteur structuré de l'économie
formal economy sector

secteur non structuré de l'économie
informal economy sector

STRUCTURE (n.)
structure; composition; pattern; (pl.) facilities

aménagement de structure
structural adjustment

structure d'accueil pour (les) enfants
child care facility

structure par âge(s)
age distribution / pattern / structure

structure par classe
grade-level structure

structure des classes
grading structure

structure à n classes
n-grade level structure, n-level grading
structure

structure de l'emploi
employment structure / pattern, patterns of
employment

structure d'évaluation
evaluation framework

structures familiales
(occ.) family patterns

structure du marché du travail
labour market structure

structure opérationnelle
operational framework

**structure de l'organisation / organisa-
tionnelle**
organisational structure

structure des prestations
benefit structure

**structure des professions / profession-
nelle**
occupational structure / distribution /
composition / pattern

structure des qualifications
skill profile / structure

structure des salaires / salariale
wage / salary / pay structure

structure sociale
social fabric

structure des traitements
salary / pay structure

STRUCTUREL
structural; organisational

ajustement structurel
structural adjustment

chômage structurel
structural unemployment

discrimination structurelle
structural / systemic / systematic
discrimination

faiblesse structurelle d'un système
inbuilt weakness of a system

politique structurelle
structural policy

surveillance structurelle multilatérale
multilateral structural surveillance

tendance structurelle
trend over time

SUBALTERNE (adj.)
subordinate; junior

cadre subalterne
junior official / executive; (pl.) executive
staff

employés / personnel subalterne(s)
junior staff

poste subalterne
junior position

tâche subalterne
menial task

SUBALTERNE (n.)
(pl.) junior staff

SUBDIVISION
subsection; unit

SUBJECTIF
risque subjectif
moral hazard (insurance)

SUBORDONNÉ (adj.)
subordinate; inferior; subject (to)

subordonné à
subject to

subordonné à une condition de ressources
subject to a means test, means-tested

subordonné à une condition de stage
subject to a qualifying period

subordonné au critère des ressources
subject to a means test, means-tested

SUBROGÉ
assureur subrogé
insurer substituting for ... / entering into the rights of ... / involved

subrogé tuteur
surrogate guardian

SUBSIDE
grant

subside pour la formation
training grant / subsidy

SUBSIDIAIRE
subsidiary

SUBSISTANCE
subsistence, maintenance; continued coverage

assurer la subsistance
to maintain, to support

agriculteurs et ouvriers de l'agriculture et de la pêche de subsistance [CITP-1988 (62)]
subsistence agricultural and fishery workers [ISCO-1988 (62)]

agriculteurs et ouvriers de l'agriculture et de la pêche de subsistance [CITP-1988 (621)]
subsistence agricultural and fishery workers [ISCO-1988 (621)]

allocation de subsistance
subsistence / living allowance

allocation de subsistance pour invalides (UK)
disability living allowance

allocation de subsistance pour visite préliminaire
preliminary examination living allowance

caisse de subsistance (Fr.)
subsistence fund

frais de subsistance
living costs / expenses

indemnité journalière de subsistance
daily subsistence / living allowance; per diem

indemnité journalière de subsistance au taux spécial
special rate of daily subsistence allowance

indemnité de subsistance
subsistence allowance / payment, maintenance allowance; stipend

moyens de subsistance
(means of) livelihood, means of subsistence; maintenance

niveau de subsistance
subsistence level

revenu de subsistance
subsistence income

salaire de subsistance
subsistence wage

source de subsistance
source of subsistence / of livelihood

SUBSISTANT (n.)
beneficiary covered by a fund other than his own

SUBSTANCE
substance chimique dangereuse
hazardous chemical

substance engendrant une dépendance
dependence-producing drug

substance médicale
medicine, drug

substance nocive
harmful / noxious subtance

SUBSTITUT
substitut du lait maternel
infant formula

substitut de salaire
cash benefit(s) in lieu of wage

SUBSTITUTION
substitution

coût de substitution
replacement / opportunity cost

effet de substitution
displacement / substitution effect

emploi de substitution
alternative / alternate employment,
replacement job

pension de substitution (Fr.)
old age pension replacing invalidity
pension

pouvoir de substitution
power to appoint an agent

revenu de substitution
income replacement

substitution d'assurance
substitution of insurance

substitution de condition
substitution of condition

SUBVENIR
incapable de subvenir à ses (propres)
besoins
incapable of self-support

subvenir aux besoins
to maintain, to support, to provide for

SUBVENTION
subsidy; grant, grant-in-aid

octroi de subventions salariales
subsidisation of wages

programme de subventions
incentive programme

subvention en capital
capital grant

subvention directe à l'emploi
direct employment subsidy

subvention à l'embauche
recruitment subsidy

subvention en espèces
cash grant

subvention de l'Etat
State / Government subsidy

subvention de fonctionnement
operating subsidy

subvention forfaitaire
lump-sum grant

subvention globale
block grant

subvention à l'industrie
industrial incentive

subvention à l'investissement
(incremental) investment subsidy

**subvention pour le maintien à domicile
(UK)**
community care grant

subvention à la mobilité
mobility grant

**subvention de mobilité des étudiants /
destinée aux étudiants**
student mobility grant
subvention régulière / renouvelable
recurrent grant

subvention au titre de la réorientation
reestablishment grant

subvention salariale
wage (cost) subsidy

subvention salariale directe
direct wage subsidy

subvention salariale permanente
permanent wage subsidy

subvention salariale transférable
portable wage subsidy

**subvention supplémentaire de
transition**
supplementary transition grant

subvention transférable
portable subsidy

subvention de voyage
travel grant

subvention de voyage de stagiaire
trainee travel grant

système de subventions par prélèvement
levy-grant system

SUBVENTIONNÉ
construction subventionnée
social housing

contrat (de travail) subventionné (-Sp.)
grant-assisted (employment) contract

emploi subventionné
subsidised employment

logement subventionné
social housing

prêt subventionné
subsidised loan

programme subventionné (de construction) d'habitations / de logements
social housing scheme, subsidised
housing programme

travailleur subventionné
subsidised worker

SUBVENTIONNER
to subsidise

subventionner un emploi
to subsidise a job

SUCCÈS
taux de succès
success / completion rate

SUCCESSIF
équipes / postes successifs(ves)
successive shifts

SUCCESSION
droits de succession
death / estate duties

plan de succession
succession planning

recours sur succession (Fr.)
action to recover from succession arrears
of complementary allowance

recours sur succession en matière d'aide sociale (Fr.)
action to recover social benefits from
succession

SUCCESSORAL
actif net successoral
net assets by inheritance

SUCCINCT
exposé succinct
summary statement

SUCCURSALE
branch (office); subsidiary

SUFFISANT
sufficient; adequate

expérience suffisante (avoir / posséder une)
(occ.) to qualify for

salaire tout juste suffisant pour vivre
subsistence wage

titres suffisants (avoir / posséder des)
to qualify for

SUITE
donner suite
to follow up; to implement

suite à donner
follow-up

SUIVI (adj.)
grève largement suivie
widespread strike

SUIVI (n.)
follow-up, monitoring

assurer le suivi
to follow up

enquête de suivi
follow-up survey

registre de suivi médical
health register

suivi du marché du travail
labour market monitoring

suivi téléphonique
telephone follow-up

SUIVRE
marche à suivre
procedure

suivre des études
to attend school

suivre l'évolution de
to keep under review

SUJET (adj.)
subject; liable

SUJET (n.)
subject; case

SUJÉTION
prime de sujétion
hardship allowance

SUPERFICIE
surface; acreage (agr.)

SUPÉRIEUR (adj.)
superior; upper

brevet de technicien supérieur agricole (BTSA) (Fr.)
agricultural senior technician's certificate

cadre supérieur
top / senior (level) / upper level / executive manager, senior / top / higher professional executive, executive; technologist; (pl.) (upper / senior / top) management, senior directing staff, managerial / senior / executive (supervisory) staff

décile supérieur
upper decile

diplômé de l'enseignement supérieur
college graduate, tertiary-education graduate

directeurs et cadres administratifs supérieurs [CITP-1968 (2)]
administrative and managerial workers [ISCO-1968 (2)]

échelon supérieur
top grade

école supérieure de commerce / de gestion
business school

encadrement supérieur
top / executive management

enseignement supérieur
college / higher education

établissement d'enseignement supérieur
establishment / institution of higher education, (higher education) college

études universitaires supérieures
postgraduate studies

étudiant de l'enseignement supérieur
student in higher education; (occ.) scholar

étudiant des quatre premières années de l'enseignement supérieur
undergraduate

fonctionnaires de rang supérieur
staff in the higher categories

formation supérieure
advanced / postbasic education

formation supérieure (de)
(occ.) professional

intérêt supérieur de la collectivité
ultimate interest of the community

limite d'âge supérieure
upper age limit

limite supérieure
maximum / upper limit; ceiling; high cut-off point

limite supérieure pour l'assiette des cotisations de la catégorie n
upper earnings limit of class n contributions

limite supérieure des gains
upper earnings limit / level

personnel (de niveau) supérieur
managerial / grade / professional / senior personnel / supervisory staff

prestation maximale / maximum supérieure
overall highest maximum benefit

professeurs d'université et d'établissements d'enseignement supérieur [CITP-1988 (231)]
college, university and higher education teaching professionals [ISCO-1988 (231)

profession de cadre supérieur
senior management occupation

régime de retraite complémentaire pour cadres supérieurs
top hat pension plan

supérieur à
in excess of

technicien supérieur
advanced technician

tranche d'imposition supérieure
upper income bracket

tranche supérieure d'imposition
higher tax bracket

SUPÉRIEUR (n.)
supervisor

supérieur hiérarchique
(official / hierarchical) superior

supérieur hiérarchique direct
immediate superior / supervisor

SUPERPOSITION
superposition de périodes d'assurance
overlapping of periods of insurance

SUPERVISER
to supervise

SUPERVISEUR
supervisor

superviseur principal
senior supervisor

SUPERVISION
supervision

agent de supervision
supervisor

Comité de supervision des pensions complémentaires (UK)
Reserve Pension Board

personnel de supervision
supervisory staff

SUPPLÉANT
acting

travailleur suppléant
replacement worker

SUPPLÉER
to make up, to supply; to compensate; to replace

SUPPLÉMENT
supplement; addition; extra payment

supplément pour chambre privée
extra charge for private room

supplément à la cotisation
supplement to contribution

supplément pour enfant
child's supplement

supplément pour épouse (Swed.)
wife's supplement

supplément pour impossibilité de se procurer un emploi (UK)
unemployability supplement

supplément d'indemnisation
additional compensation

supplément de pension
supplement to the pension

supplément de pension pour enfants
pension supplement / supplement to pensions in respect of children

supplément de prestation
benefit supplement

supplément de rémunération
remuneration supplement; top-up

supplément de revenu familial (UK)
family income supplement

supplément de revenu garanti
guaranteed income supplement, supplemental security income (Can.)

supplément de salaire
extra pay

supplément lié / proportionnel aux gains / au salaire
earnings-related supplement

supplément de soins (Pol.)
medical care supplement

SUPPLÉMENTAIRE
supplementary; incremental

allocation supplémentaire
supplementary / additional allowance, added benefit

allocation supplémentaire d'attente (Fr.)
interim supplementary allowance

allocation supplémentaire famille (Fr.)
supplementary family allowance

allocation supplémentaire vieillesse (Fr.)
supplementary old age allowance

appel à de la main-d'oeuvre supplémentaire (faire)
(occ.) to take on extra hands

avantage supplémentaire
added benefit

besoins supplémentaires
additional needs / requirements / demand

corrigé des variations du nombre d'heures supplémentaires
adjusted for overtime

cotisation supplémentaire pour la catégorie n
secondary class n contribution

frais supplémentaires
additional expenses; extras

heures supplémentaires
overtime (work / working)

heures supplémentaires (faire des)
to work overtime, to work after / extra hours

hypothèse travailleur supplémentaire
additional worker hypothesis

indemnité de fonctions supplémentaires
extra-duty pay

interdiction d'heures supplémentaires
overtime ban

jour supplémentaire
additional day

paiement des heures supplémentaires
overtime compensation / pay

paiement supplémentaire
additional payment

prestation supplémentaire
supplementary / additional benefit

prestation supplémentaire en espèces en cas d'invalidité
supplementary disability income benefit

prestation supplémentaire pour la famille
family supplement

prime d'heures supplémentaires
premium for extra duty, overtime pay

rémunération des heures supplémentaires
overtime compensation / pay

revenu supplémentaire
additional income; secondary income

subvention supplémentaire de transition
supplementary transition grant

taux d'heures supplémentaires
overtime rate

taux de rémunération des heures supplémentaires
overtime rate of pay

travailleur supplémentaire
relief worker

SUPPLÉTIF
caisse supplétive (Switz.)
supplementary insurance fund

indicateur supplétif
proxy measure

SUPPORT
support

SUPPORTER
to support; to absorb; to cover

SUPPRESSION
withdrawal; removal

clauses de réduction, de suspension ou de suppression de prestations
provisions for reduction, suspension or withdrawal of benefits

mesure d'accompagnement des suppressions d'emplois
redundancy mitigation measure

reprise du service des prestations après suspension ou suppression
resumption of provision of benefits after suspension or withdrawal

suppression d'emploi
job cut / loss; (pl.) job dislocation / displacement, labour displacement, redundancy

suppression d'une fonction
discontinuance of a function

suppression d'une pension
withdrawal of a pension

suppression de poste
abolition of post; (pl.) job dislocation / displacement, labour displacement, redundancy

suppression des prestations
withdrawal of benefits

suppression d'une rente
withdrawal of a pension

travailleur victime de suppressions d'emploi(s)
redundant / displaced worker

SUPPRIMÉ
suppressed; discontinued

travailleur dont l'emploi a été supprimé
displaced / redundant worker

SUPPRIMER
to suppress; to abolish; to discontinue

supprimer des emplois
to displace workers / labour

supprimer un poste
to abolish a post

supprimer une prestation
to discontinue a benefit

SÛR (adj.)
safe

lieu sûr
safe place

SURCAPACITÉ
overcapacity; excess (plant) capacity

SURCHARGE
surcharge de travail
overwork

SURCHARGER
surcharger en effectif
to overstaff

SURCONSOMMATION
surconsommation médicale
excessive medical demand

SURCROÎT
surcroît de travail
increased workload; extra work; pressure
of work

SURDÉPLOIEMENT
featherbedding (of labour)

SURDIPLÔMÉ
overqualified

SUREFFECTIF
surplus; (pl.) overmanning, overstaffing;
redundant labour, workers made redundant; labour hoarding; featherbedding

personnel en sureffectif
overmanning

sureffectif (être en)
to be overmanned / overstaffed

SUREMPLOI
excess employment, over
(-)employment; over(-)full employment

SUREMPLOYÉ
over-employed

SURENCHÈRE
leap-frogging

surenchère salariale
wage-wage spiral

SUR-INDEMNISATION
over-compensation

SUR-LE-CHAMP
licenciement sur-le-champ
summary / immediate dismissal

SURMENAGE
strain; overwork

SURMENÉ
overworked

SURNOMBRE
effectifs / main-d'oeuvre / personnel en
surnombre
labour redundancy, displaced / redundant
labour, workers made redundant, surplus
staff; overmanning

recruter en surnombre
to overstaff

travailleur en surnombre
redundant worker, surplus employee

SURNUMÉRAIRE (adj.)
supernumerary

travailleur surnuméraire
redundant worker, surplus employee

SURNUMÉRAIRE (n.)
occasional help / hand; (pl.) casual labour

SURPAIEMENT
over-payment

SURPAYER
to overpay

SURPEUPLÉ
logement surpeuplé
overcrowded dwelling

SURPEUPLEMENT
overcrowding

SURPLUS
surplus

surplus actuariel
actuarial / experience surplus

surplus de travailleurs
over-supply of workers, worker surplus

SURPRISE
contrôle surprise
random inspection

grève surprise
lightning / guerilla strike

visite surprise
random inspection

SURQUALIFICATION
overqualification, overskilling

SURQUALIFIÉ
overqualified

SURREPRÉSENTATION
over-concentration

SURSALAIRE
bonus, extra pay; salary differential

sursalaire de nuit
night differential

sursalaire pour travail posté
shift differential

SURSEOIR
to defer

surseoir au paiement
to defer a payment

SURSIS
stay

sursis à exécution
stay of execution

sursis de paiement
stay of collection

SURTAXE
tax surcharge

SUR-UTILISATION
sur-utilisation des salariés
overutilisation of employees

SURVEILLANCE
supervision; monitoring; after care

comité de surveillance
inspection / monitoring / supervising
committee

conseil de surveillance
supervisory board

fonction de surveillance
supervisory duty / function

organe de surveillance
supervisory body

surveillance constante
constant attendance

surveillance médicale (ultérieure)
medical supervision / follow-up

surveillance médicale (sous)
under medical supervision

surveillance sur place
on-site monitoring

surveillance structurelle multilatérale
multilateral structural surveillance

SURVEILLANT
supervisor

poste de surveillant
supervisory post / position

SURVEILLÉ
centre d'éducation surveillée
correctional school; (occ.) training school

enfant surveillé
supervised child

service d'éducation surveillée
correctional service

SURVEILLER
to supervise, to monitor

SURVENANCE
beginning; occurrence

survenance du risque
occurrence of the event

SURVIE
survival

gain de survie
advantage accruing to the survivor

pension de survie
survivor's pension

pension de survie minimum (Belg.)
minimum survivors' pension

probabilité de survie
probability of surviving

quotient de survie
probability of surviving

rente de survie
survivor's pension

SURVIVANT
survivor

assurance de survivant
survivor's assurance / insurance

assurance(-)vieillesse et survivants
old age and survivors' insurance

conjoint survivant
surviving spouse

pension de survivant
survivor's / survivors' (Irel.) pension

prestation de survivant
survivor's / survivors' (Irel.) benefit

survivant en état de célibat
single survivor

survivant en état de non-célibat
ever-married survivor

survivant ayant droit
eligible survivor

taux survivant (Fr.)
survivor rate

SUS
sus de (en)
over and above

SUSPENDRE
to suspend

suspendre un paiement
to suspend a payment

suspendre une prestation
to suspend a benefit

SUSPENDU
suspendu de ses fonctions (être)
to be suspended from one's position

SUSPENSION
suspension; stay

clauses de réduction, de suspension ou de suppression de prestations
provisions for reduction, suspension or withdrawal of benefits

reprise du service des prestations après suspension ou suppression
resumption of provision of benefits after suspension or withdrawal

suspension d'un contrat de travail
suspension of an employment contract

suspension pendant enquête
suspension pending investigation

suspension de fonctions
suspension from office

suspension du gain
suspension of earnings

suspension de mesures administratives
suspension of administrative action

suspension d'une pension
suspension of a pension

suspension d'une prestation
suspension of benefit

suspension d'une rente
suspension of a pension

suspension avec traitement
suspension with pay

suspension sans traitement
suspension without pay

SYMBOLIQUE
nominal

grève symbolique
token (protest) strike

SYMPTÔME
symptom, sign, manifestation

SYNDICAL
accréditation syndicale
union certification

affiliation / appartenance syndicale
(trade) union membership

atelier syndical / pratiquant l'affiliation syndicale obligatoire
closed / union shop

base syndicale (la)
shop floor (the), shop-floor workers

cadre syndical
union officer

cahier des revendications syndicales
list of union demands

carte syndicale
union card

centrale syndicale
central trade union organisation

chambre syndicale
employers' federation

clause de protection / de sécurité syndicale
closed-shop / union security clause

comité (mixte) patronal - syndical
(joint) union - management committee

conseil syndical local
local labour council

convention d'exclusivité syndicale
closed shop agreement

cotisation syndicale
union fee / subscription; (pl.) (trade) union dues

délégué syndical
(labour / trade) union representative / delegate; (shop / union) steward

dirigeant syndical
(trade) union official / leader

droit de représentation syndicale
(occ.) representational right

droit syndical
right of association / of union organisation / to organise; trade union law; (pl.) trade union rights

effectifs syndicaux
union membership

fonds syndical
union fund

habilitation de responsables syndicaux
accreditation of union officials

implantation syndicale
union density

législation interdisant le monopole syndical d'embauche (USA)
right-to-work laws

liberté syndicale
right of association / of union organisation / to organise; freedom of association

local syndical
union room

militant syndical
trade union worker, militant unionist

militantisme syndical
union militancy

monopole syndical d'embauche / d'emploi
closed-union shop / system

mouvement syndical
trade union movement; organised labour

organisation syndicale
labour organisation, labour / trade union

paiement des cotisations syndicales
payment of union fees

permanent syndical
union employee

personnel syndical
trade union personnel

pluralisme syndical
trade union pluralism

pratique de sécurité syndicale (Fr.)
closed shop practice

protection syndicale
union security

reconnaissance de responsables syndicaux
accreditation of union officials

reconnaissance syndicale
(trade) union recognition

représentant syndical
(trade) union / labour representative, union steward; business agent (USA)

représentativité syndicale
representativeness of a union

responsable syndical
(trade / labour) union official, labour leader

retrait d'accréditation syndicale
withdrawal of union certification, (occ.) decertification

revendication syndicale
union demand

révocation d'accréditation syndicale
withdrawal of union certification, (occ.) decertification

section syndicale
(in-company) union branch / section

sécurité syndicale
union security

statistiques syndicales
trade union statistics

tarif syndical
union wage

SYNDICALISATION
unionisation; union membership

taux de syndicalisation
union rate / density

SYNDICALISME
(trade) unionism; organised labour

SYNDICALISTE
(militant) (trade) unionist

SYNDICAT
(trade) union; labour organisation / union; trade association

adhérent d'un syndicat
(trade) union member

adhérer / s'affilier à un syndicat
to join a / to gain to a union

antenne locale d'un syndicat
(occ.) local union

appartenance à un syndicat
membership of a trade union

cotiser à un syndicat
to contribute to a union

exclure d'un syndicat
to expel from a union

exclusion d'un syndicat
expulsion from a union

fonder des syndicats
to form trade unions

membre d'un syndicat
(trade) union member; unionist

mise à l'écart des syndicats
labour exclusion

reconnaissance syndicale / d'un syndicat
(trade) union recognition

reconnaître un syndicat
to recognise a union

responsable de l'homologation des syndicats (UK)
certification officer

section locale d'un / des syndicat(s)
(trade) union local / branch

syndicat non affilié
non-affiliated union

syndicat agréé
recognised union

syndicat autonome
independent / non-affiliated (trade) union

syndicat de branche
industrial union

syndicat de classe (Sp.)
non-corporatist union

syndicat corporatiste
corporatist union

syndicat de corps de métier
occupational / craft / (occ.) horizontal union

syndicat d'employeurs
employer's association / federation / organisation

syndicat d'entreprise
works / in-house union

syndicat général
general (workers') union

syndicat indépendant
independent / non-affiliated (trade) union

syndicat interbranches
multi-industry union

syndicat inter-hospitalier
interhospital group

syndicat interprofessionnel
general union, interprofessional union (Cyp.)

syndicat maison
house / in-house / company union

syndicat de métier
professional organisation / association; industrial association; occupational / craft / horizontal union

syndicat ouvert
open union

syndicat ouvrier
blue-collar union, employees' association

syndicat patronal
employer's association / federation / organisation

syndicats et patronat
labour and management

syndicat professionnel
professional organisation / association; industrial association; occupational / craft / horizontal union

syndicat reconnu
registered (trade) union

syndicat unifié
amalgamated union

union de syndicats
federation of trade unions

SYNDIQUÉ (adj.)
unionised

atelier n'admettant pas d'ouvriers non syndiqués
closed / union shop

atelier non syndiqué
non-union / open shop

établissement non syndiqué
non-union establishment

main-d'oeuvre syndiquée
unionised labour

salaire pratiqué dans les secteurs syndiqués
union wage

secteur syndiqué
unionised sector

syndiqué (non)
non-unionised; unorganised

travailleur syndiqué
trade unionist; unionised worker; (pl.) organised labour; (occ.) union membership

travailleur non syndiqué
non-union(ised) worker

SYNDIQUÉ (n.)
(trade) union member; unionist

liste des syndiqués
union roll

SYNDIQUER
to organise

droit de se syndiquer
right to organise

SYNTHÈSE
review; survey; consolidation

loi de synthèse
consolidation act

synthèse bibliographique / documentaire
literature review / survey

SYNTHÉTIQUE
indicateur synthétique
summary indicator / measure

SYSTÉMATIQUE
discrimination systématique
structural / systemic / systematic discrimination

SYSTÈME
system; scheme

annualisation du système d'ajustement des pensions
annualisation of the pension adjustment system

faiblesse structurelle d'un système
inbuilt weakness of a system

jeune sorti du système scolaire
school-leaver

maladie du système ostéo-articulaire et des muscles
musculo-skeletal disease

système d'accréditation
certification / qualification system

système d'acquisition de compétences
skill acquisition system

système d'administration des soins
health care (delivery) system

système d'aide
support system

système d'aiguillage
referral system

système d'ajustement des pensions
pension adjustment system

système d'ajustement des prestations
benefit adjustment system

système par capitalisation
advance-funded plan

système capitalisé
funded plan

système des classes alternées
double-shift system; dual sessions

système de classement
system of classification, classification system; (occ.) grading system

système de classement des emplois par points
point-factor system of job classification

système de classification des professions
occupational classification system

système de codage des postes
post coding system

système combiné
dual / combined system

système commun
common system

système continu (3 x 8)
continuous work system

système du conventionnement
licensing regulations (health care institutions)

système de cotation des emplois
point-factor method of job evaluation

système (de détermination) du salaire minimum
minimum wage system

système de la double filière (pensions)
two-track pension adjustment system

système dual (ed.)
dual system

système éducatif
education(al) system

système d'emploi neutre / non discriminatoire
neutral employment system

système d'enseignement post-secondaire
post-secondary system

système d'établissement des rapports périodiques
periodic reporting system

système d'évaluation
evaluation system

système d'évaluation analytique des tâches / du travail
analytical job evaluation scheme

système d'évaluation du rendement
performance evaluation system

système de fabrication flexible
flexible manufacturing system

système foncier
land-tenure system

système de formation
training system

système de gestion de la qualité
quality management system

système d'incitation
incentive scheme

système des indemnités de poste
post adjustment system

système d'indexation des salaires
pay indexation system

système indirect de prestations médicales
indirect system / pattern of providing medical care

système d'information sanitaire
health information system

système informatisé de traitement des offres d'emploi
automated job order system

système intégré
integrated model / system / scheme

Système international de conservation des droits en matière de sécurité sociale
International System for the Maintenance of Rights in Social Security

système du marché du travail
labour market system

système de mesure de la performance / du rendement
performance measure system

système de modulation des loyers (Irel.)
differential rent scheme

système national de santé / de distribution de soins / de protection (médico-) sanitaire
national system of health care

système de notification
reporting system

système d'obligations-logement (Icel.)
house-bond system

système d'orientation professionnelle informatisé
computer-based career orientation system

système de paie
pay / payment / payroll system

système de paie par paliers
stepped pay system

système de paiement à l'acte
fee-for-service system

système de paiement des allocations
allowance payment system

système de paiement par honoraires
fee-for-service system

système de paiement des indemnités
allowance payment system

système paritaire d'arbitrage
joint arbitration machinery

système de partage des frais / de participation du malade aux frais
cost-sharing system

système de pondération
weighting system

système de précompte des cotisations (UK)
direct debit system

système de prépaiement
prepaid group practice (PGP)

système de préretraite
early retirement scheme; job release (UK)

système de prestations lié au niveau des ressources
means-tested system of provision

système de prestations sanitaires
health delivery system

système de prestation de services de main-d'oeuvre
manpower delivery system

système de prestation des soins
health care (delivery) system

système de primes
bonus scheme

système de primes échelonnées
scaled premium system

système de primes d'encouragement
bonus incentive scheme

système de promotion
promotion scheme

système de protection (médico-) sanitaire / de protection de santé
health care (delivery) system

système de protection sociale
social protection / welfare (scheme)

système qualité
quality system

système du quotient familial
system of (income) tax relief with respect to dependants

système de rapport d'appréciation du comportement professionnel
performance evaluation report system

système de recouvrement des frais
cost recovery system

système de recrutement
recruitment system

système de recrutement de bouche à oreille
word-of-mouth recruitment system

système de récupération du temps
time recovery scheme

système de rémunération
wage / pay / compensation plan / system

système de la rémunération par malade inscrit / d'après le nombre de clients (med.)
capitation-fee system

système de rémunération aux résultats
incentive scheme

système de rémunération à la tâche
task payment system

système de la rémunération par tête
capitation-fee system

système de répartition
pay-as-you-go scheme, PAYG scheme

système de retenue de la cotisation sur le salaire (UK)
direct debit system

système de retenue à la source
pay-as-you-earn (PAYE)

système de retraite
retirement / pension scheme / system

système de retraite par capitalisation
funded pension system

système révisé d'ajustement des pensions
revised pension adjustment system

système par roulement
rota system

système de santé
health system

système de sécurité sociale
social insurance / social security system

système de sélection
screening device

système de subventions par prélèvement
levy-grant system

système du temps alloué
time-allowed system (piece work)

système du tiers garant (Switz.)
third party guarantee system

système du tiers(-)payant
third party payment system, direct payment system

système du travail sous contrat
contract labour system

système de travail par équipes alternant jour et nuit
alternating shift system

système de travail par équipes chevauchantes
coupled shift system

systèmes unifiés
compatible systems

système de versement des allocations / des indemnités
allowance payment system

système à deux vitesses
two-tier system

travail à la pièce obéissant au système du temps alloué
time piecework

TABAC
ouvriers des tabacs [CITP-1968 (7-8)]
tobacco preparers and tobacco product
makers [ISCO-1968 (7-8)]

TABLE
table d'activité
table of working life

table de conversion
conversion table

table d'(entrée en) invalidité
disability table

TABLEAU
table; schedule

inscrit au tableau d'avancement (être)
to be included in the promotion register

tableau d'affichage des offres d'emploi
(occ.) job board

tableau d'avancement
promotion roster / register, promotional
ladder

tableau comparatif
comparative table

tableau d' / des effectifs
staffing / manning table

tableau des emplois
table of posts, establishment table

tableau d'horaires
duty roster

tableau des maladies professionnelles
table of occupational diseases

tableau de morbidité
disease pattern

tableau nominatif des emplois
nominative table of posts

tableau récapitulatif
summary table

tableau de service
duty roster, rota

tableau statistique d'activité
statistical table of activity

TABLEUR
spreadsheet, worksheet

TÂCHE
task; job; function; work; responsibility;
commitment

accomplir des tâches
to perform duties

analyse des tâches
task / job analysis, work study

attribution des tâches
work assignment

classification des tâches
classification of tasks; job grading

contrôle des tâches
job control

définition des tâches
job design / description, task definition;
work structuring

déqualification des tâches
deskilling

description des tâches
job / position description

distribution des tâches
work allocation / distribution, workload
breakdown

diversification des tâches
(occ.) job enlargement

enrichissement des tâches
job enrichment

étude des tâches
work study

évaluation analytique des tâches
analytical job evaluation

évaluation des tâches
job evaluation

ouvrier à la tâche
jobbing workman, job worker, piece-worker

payé à la tâche (être)
to be paid by the job

programme d'évaluation analytique des tâches
analytical job evaluation scheme

redéfinition des tâches
job redefinition / restructuring

relevé des tâches
task inventory

rémunération à la tâche
piecework remuneration

répartition des tâches
division / segregation of duties; division of work / labour, work allocation / distribution, workload breakdown

salaire à la tâche
piecework / piece wage, piece rate

simplification des tâches
work simplification

système d'évaluation analytique des tâches
analytical job evaluation scheme

système de rémunération à la tâche
task payment system

tâche (à la)
at piece, by the job

tâche assignée
assignment

tâche dangereuse
hazardous occupation / work

tâche habituelle
routine task

tâche horaire
hour task

tâche ingrate
invidious task

tâche productive
productive employment, production job

tâche spéciale
special assignment

tâche subalterne
menial task

travail à la tâche
job work, piecework

travailleur à la tâche
pieceworker; job worker

TACITE
tacit

reconduction tacite / tacite reconduction
renewal by tacit agreement, tacit renewal

TACITEMENT
by tacit agreement

TAILLE
size

taille de l'échantillon
sample size

taille de la famille
(average) family size

taille du ménage
household size

TAILLEUR
tailleurs, couturiers, couseurs, tapissiers et ouvriers assimilés [CITP-1968 (7-9)]
tailors, dressmakers, sewers, upholsterers and related workers [ISCO-1968 (7-9)]

tailleurs et graveurs de pierres [CITP-1968 (8-2)]
stone cutters and carvers [ISCO-1968 (8-2)]

TALENT
talent; ability; skill

talent d'entrepreneur
entrepreneurial skill

TANNEUR
tanneurs, peaussiers, mégissiers et
ouvriers de la pelleterie [CITP-1968 (7-
6)]
tanners, fellmongers and pelt dressers
[ISCO-1968 (7-6)]

TARDIF
adhésion tardive à l'assurance
late entrance into insurance

demande tardive
late claim

retour tardif de congés
late return from holidays

TARIF
fee; charge; schedule; rate; scale

dépassement de tarif
overbilling, extra-billing

dépasser le tarif conventionnel agréé
to charge more than the standard agreed
fee

tarif d'autorité (Fr.)
recommended medical fee, set rate

tarif de base
basic rate

tarif de convention / conventionnel
standard (agreed) fee

tarif forfaitaire
flat rate

tarif imposé
set rate

tarif d'indemnisation
rate of compensation

tarif journalier
day / daily rate

tarif médical conventionnel
standard medical fee

tarif opposable
binding fee

tarif pharmaceutique
maximum fixed price for medicines

tarif plafond (Fr.)
maximum fee

tarif préférentiel
preferential fee / rate, target payment
(UK)

tarif réduit
reduced fare, concessional fare

tarif réduit (à)
at reduced fee

tarif de remboursement
refund rate, rate of reimbursement

tarif de responsabilité
liability fee

tarif syndical
union wage

tarif uniforme
flat rate

TARIFAIRE
contrat tarifaire
wage contract

convention tarifaire
agreement on fees

loi tarifaire
collective (wage) agreements act

TARIFICATION
pricing; rates

tarification collective
collective rates

TARIFÉ
honoraire tarifé
scheduled fee

TAS
formation sur le tas
on-site / on-the job / in-service training /
learning

grève sur le tas
sit-down / sit-in / stay-in strike; worker
occupation

tas (sur le)
in-house; on-the-job

TASSEMENT
slack (econ.)

TASSER
tasser (se)
to level out / off

TAUX
rate; level; degree; charge; amount

allocation à taux uniforme
flat-rate allowance / benefit

Commission des taux (UK)
Rating Board

cotisation à taux forfaitaire / à taux uniforme
flat-rate contribution

détermination du taux d'invalidité
determination of impairment / of invalidity

échelle des taux
schedule of rates

indemnité journalière de subsistance au taux spécial
special rate of daily subsistence allowance

majoration du taux de base
increase of the basic amount

pension à taux minoré
reduced (rate) pension / retirement benefit

pension au taux normal
standard (rate) pension / retirement benefit

pension à taux plein
full pension, full retirement benefit

pension à taux réduit
reduced (rate) pension / retirement benefit

prestation à taux uniforme
flat-rate benefit

prêt à faible taux d'intérêt
low-interest loan

régime à taux fixe / uniforme
flat-rate scheme

retraite à taux minoré
reduced (rate) pension / retirement benefit

retraite à taux plein
full pension, full retirement benefit

taux d'abandon (scolaire)
drop-out rate

taux d'absentéisme
absenteeism rate, rate of absenteeism

taux d'absorption des nouveaux venus sur le marché du travail
rate of absorption of labour market entrants

taux des accidents
accident frequency rate

taux d'accroissement du personnel
accession rate

taux d'acquisition du droit à pension
(pension) accrual rate

taux d'activité
participation rate

taux d'activité des femmes / féminine
female (labour force) / women's participation rate

taux d'activité global
aggregate / total participation rate

taux d'activité de la main-d'oeuvre
labour force participation rate

taux d'activité masculine
male participation rate

taux d'activité de la population active
labour force participation rate

taux d'actualisation
updating rate

taux d'admissibilité
eligibility rate

taux d'admission
admission rate; (occ.) transfer rate

taux des allocations
allowance rate / level, rate / level of allowances

taux des allocations de formation
rate / level of training allowances

taux annuel
annual rate, annualised percentage rate

taux d'appel (Fr.)
coefficient used to calculate the effective rate of contributions

taux applicable
appropriate rate

taux de base
basic rate / amount; basic wage; (occ.) straight-time rate

taux de bonification
bonus rate

taux de cessation d'activité
rate of separation from the labour force

taux de change
exchange rate, rate of exchange

taux de chômage
level of unemployment; unemployment / jobless rate

taux de chômage non accélérateur de l'inflation
non accelerating inflation rate of unemployment (NAIRU)

taux de chômage non accélérateur des salaires
non accelerating wage rate of unemployment (NAWRU)

taux de chômage familial
family unemployment rate

taux de chômage global
aggregate unemployment rate

taux de chômage naturel
full employment unemployment rate, equilibrium rate of unemployment, natural rate of unemployment, natural unemployment rate

taux de chômage normalisé / standardisé (TCS)
standardised unemployment rate (SUR)

taux de chômage en situation d'équilibre / de plein emploi (des capacités)
full employment unemployment rate, equilibrium / natural rate of unemployment

taux de compensation
replacement ratio / rate

taux de compensation de la perte de revenu
income replacement ratio

taux de conservation des effectifs / des travailleurs / du personnel
retention rate, rate of retention

taux de (la) cotisation
contribution rate, amount / rate of contribution; (pl.) level of contributions

taux de couverture
coverage (ratio)

taux de croissance
growth rate

taux de croissance de l'emploi
employment growth rate

taux de croissance des professions
occupational growth rate

taux courant
standard / going / prevailing rate

taux des départs
separation rate

taux de dépendance (économique)
dependency ratio

taux de dépendance des personnes âgées
old age dependency ratio

taux de déperdition d'effectifs (ed.)
drop-out rate

taux différentiel (de traitement)
salary differential

taux de diminution des effectifs
attrition rate

taux de disparition (des entreprises)
mortality rate (of companies)

taux d'échec
failure rate

taux effectif d'imposition sur le revenu
real income tax rate

taux élevé
high rate

taux d'embauche du personnel
accession rate

taux d'emploi
employment rate

taux de non-emploi
non-employment rate

taux d'encadrement (ed.)
teacher/pupil ratio

taux d'entrée en activité
rate of accession to the labour force

taux fixe
flat / set rate

taux fixe (à)
at flat rate

taux forfaitaire
flat / standard / fixed rate

taux forfaitaire (à)
at flat rate

taux de fréquence des accidents
accident frequency rate

taux de fréquentation
participation rate

taux de fréquentation scolaire
school attendance (rate), attendance ratio

taux garanti
guaranteed rate

taux de gravité
severity rate

taux de gravité des accidents
accident severity rate

taux hebdomadaire
weekly rate

taux hebdomadaire applicable
appropriate weekly rate

taux d'heures supplémentaires
overtime rate

taux horaire
hourly / time rate

taux horaire minimal
minimum hourly rate

taux horaire de salaire
hourly wage rate

taux d'imposition marginal
marginal rate of tax, marginal tax rate

taux d'inactivité
inactivity rate

taux d'incapacité
degree of incapacity / of disablement

taux d'incidence
incidence rate

taux des indemnités
allowance rate, rate of allowances

taux d'inemploi
non-employment rate

taux d'inscription
enrolment rate

taux d'invalidité
degree of invalidity / of disability,
disability / invalidity rate

taux journalier
day / daily rate

taux légal
prescribed rate

taux de la main-d'oeuvre excédentaire des jeunes
youth labour surplus rate

taux de maintien en fonction
retention rate, rate of retention

taux majoré
increased / enhanced rate

taux majoré de moitié
(occ.) time and a half rate

taux de maladies professionnelles
occupational illness rate

taux du marché
market rate

taux marginaux d'imposition effectifs
marginal effective tax rates (METR)

taux mobile
loose rate

taux de mortalité
mortality / death / fatality rate

taux de mortalité par suite de maladie professionnelle
occupational fatality rate

taux naturel de chômage
natural unemployment rate, natural rate of unemployment

taux naturel d'emploi
natural employment rate, natural rate of employment

taux normal
standard rate

taux d'occupation
occupation rate

taux de participation
participation / take-up rate

taux de passage vers
transfer rate

taux de pauvreté
poverty rate

taux de pension
rate of pension

taux de pension de l'assurance
(-)vieillesse
rate of the old age pension

taux de persévérance scolaire
student retention rate

taux de placement
placement rate

taux plein
full rate

taux plein applicable à New York (au)
at the full New York rate

taux pratiqué
prevailing / going rate

taux d'une prestation
level / rate of benefit

taux de prestations d'aide sociale
rate of welfare benefits, (occ.) welfare rate

taux de prestations familiales
rate of family benefits

taux de production normalisé
standard rate of production

taux progressif
progressive rate

taux quotidien
daily rate; per diem rate

taux de recrutement
hiring / recruitment rate / ratio

taux de réduction des prestations
benefit withdrawal rate

taux réduit
reduced rate

taux de référence
benchmark rate

taux de remboursement
refund rate, rate of reimbursement

taux de remplacement
replacement rate

taux de remplacement des gains
earnings replacement ratio / rate

taux de remplacement du revenu
income replacement ratio / rate

taux de remplacement des travailleurs
workers' replacement rate

taux de rémunération
salary / pay / wage rate, rate of pay

taux de rémunération courant
prevailing rate of pay

taux de rémunération hebdomadaire
weekly wage / pay rate

**taux de rémunération des heures sup-
plémentaires**
overtime rate of pay

taux de rémunération local
local wage / pay rate

taux de rémunération maximal
maximum rate of pay

taux de rémunération aux pièces
piecework rate

taux de rémunération en vigueur
going (pay) rate

taux de rendement
rate of return

taux de renouvellement
replacement / turnover rate

taux de renouvellement du personnel
personnel turnover rate

taux de rentabilité
rate of return

taux de réponse
response rate

taux de représentativité
participation rate

taux de représentativité des femmes
women's participation rate

taux de rétention des effectifs
retention rate

**taux de rétention des salariés à mi-
carrière**
(occ.) half-life survival rate

taux de réussite
success / completion rate

taux de risque
hazard rate

taux de rotation
turnover rate

taux de rotation (des effectifs)
labour turnover rate

taux de rotation des emplois
job turnover rate

taux de rotation de la main-d'oeuvre
labour turnover rate

taux de roulement
turnover rate

taux de roulement du personnel
personnel turnover rate

taux de / du salaire
salary / pay / wage rate

taux de salaire fixé par arbitrage
award (wage) rate

taux de salaire courant
prevailing rate of pay

taux de salaire horaire
hourly wage rate

taux de salaire maximal
maximum rate of pay

taux de salaire mensuel
monthly wage rate

taux de salaire minimum
minimum wage rate

taux de salaire aux pièces
piecework rate

taux salarial
wage rate

taux salarial convenu
agreed wage rate

taux de scolarisation
educational enrolment, (school) enrolment
ratio

taux de succès
success / completion rate

taux survivant (Fr.)
survivor rate

taux de syndicalisation
union rate / density

taux théorique
theoretical amount

taux de traitement
salary / pay / wage rate

taux uniforme
flat rate

taux uniforme (à)
at flat rate

taux d'utilisation
utilisation rate

taux d'utilisation des capacités (de production)
rate of capacity utilisation

taux d'utilisation des prestations par la population totale
beneficiary rate

taux d'utilisation des prestations par la population couverte
take-up rate

taux de vacances comblées
vacancy fill rate

taux de vacances d'emploi
vacancy rate

taux variable
variable / loose rate

taux en vigueur
prevailing / going rate

verser à un taux réduit
to pay at a reduced rate

TAXATION
taxation; imposition; assessment; levy

double taxation
double imposition

TAXE
tax; levy; charge; fee

droits / impôts et taxes
dues and taxes

exonération de la taxe d'apprentissage (Fr.)
exemption from apprenticeship tax

prestation pour taxe communale (UK)
community charge benefit

prestation pour taxe municipale (UK)
council tax benefit

réduction des taxes locales (UK)
rate rebate

taxes (hors)
tax-free

taxe d'apprentissage
apprenticeship tax; training levy (Fr.)

taxe de compensation
compensatory charge; equalisation levy (Neth.)

taxe fédérale de chômage (USA)
employer's excise tax

taxe foncière
property tax

taxe d'habitation (Fr.)
community charge

taxe locale (UK)
rate

taxe sur la masse des salaires / sur la masse salariale
payroll tax

taxe parafiscale
additional levy

taxe professionnelle
occupation tax

taxe sur les salaires
payroll tax

TAXER
to put / to impose a tax, to tax; to assess for tax

TAYLORIEN
taylorist

TAYLORISME
taylorism

TECHNICIEN
technician, technical worker; professional
brevet de technicien agricole (BTA) (Fr.)
agricutural technician's certificate

brevet de technicien supérieur agricole (BTSA) (Fr.)
agricultural senior technician's certificate

techniciens d'appareils optiques et électroniques [CITP-1988 (313)]
optical and electronic equipment operators [ISCO-1988 (313)]

technicien breveté
professional technician

technicien de laboratoire
laboratory technician

techniciens des moyens de transport maritime et aérien [CITP-1988 (314)]
ship and aircraft controllers and technicians [ISCO-1988 (314)]

technicien de la santé
health (care) worker

techniciens des sciences physiques et techniques [CITP-1988 (311)]
physical and engineering science technicians [ISCO-1988 (311)]

technicien supérieur
advanced technician

techniciens et travailleurs assimilés des sciences de la vie et de la santé [CITP-1988 (321)]
life science technicians and related associate professionals [ISCO-1988 (321)]

TECHNICITÉ
technical nature; craftsmanship; skill / knowledge intensity

niveau de technicité des emplois
skill content of jobs

TECHNIQUE (adj.)
technical

agent technique
middle-level / sub-professional technician, technician worker; maintenance worker; clerk of works

aide technique
technical assistance / aid

chômage technique
(intermittent / temporary) lay(-)off

chômage technique (en)
(temporarily) laid-off, temporarily stopped, on furlough

comité technique paritaire
joint technical committee

compétence technique de haut niveau
high(er)-level technical skill

connaissances techniques
(occ.) expertise, know-how

conseiller technique
technical advisor

contentieux technique
technical claims

efficience technique
technical efficiency

enseignement technique
technical education

enseignement technique et formation professionnelle
vocational and technical education and training (VOTEC)

établissement secondaire technique
technical college

formation technique
technical training

inefficience technique
technical inefficiency

mettre en chômage technique
to lay off (temporarily)

personnel technique
technical / professional staff

professions intermédiaires des sciences physiques et techniques [CITP-1988 (31)]
physical and engineering science associate professionals [ISCO-1988 (31)]

professions scientifiques, techniques, libérales et assimilées
(occ.) professionals

spécialistes des sciences physiques, mathématiques et techniques [CITP-1988 (21)]
physical, mathematical and engineering science professionals [ISCO-1988 (21)]

stage de terminologie technique
technical language training course

techniciens des sciences physiques et techniques [CITP-1988 (311)]
physical and engineering science technicians [ISCO-1988 (311)]

travail technique hautement spécialisé
high-skill technical work

travailleur en chômage technique
laid-off worker, (occ.) lay(-)off

TECHNIQUE (n.)
technique; engineering; practice; skill; (pl.) technology

évolution des techniques
technological change

formation aux techniques de base / élémentaires
basic skills training

initiation aux techniques professionnelles
work-skill training

stage préparatoire aux techniques industrielles
basic industrial skill course

techniques de base
basic skill(s)

technique d'entretien
interviewing skill

technique de formation
training technique

technique de gestion
management technique

techniques interactives
interacting skills

technique d'une profession
professional practice

technique(s) de recherche d'emploi
job(-)search / job-finding skill(s) / technique; job-hunting method

technique thérapeutique / de traitement
remedial skill

TECHNOLOGIE
technology

industrie de haute technologie
high(-)technology industry

institut de technologie
institute of technology

technologie de base / fondamentale
basic / core technology

technologie habilitante
enabling technology

technologie omniprésente
pervasive technology

transfert de technologies
technology transfer, transfer of technology

TECHNOLOGIQUE
chômage d'adaptation technologique
frictional / transitional unemployment

chômage technologique
technological unemployment

écart technologique
technological gap

évolution des techniques / technologique
technological change

retard technologique
technological gap

TÉLÉ-APPRENTISSAGE
distance learning

TÉLÉ-ENSEIGNEMENT
distance learning / education / teaching

TÉLÉGESTION
facilities management

TÉLÉGRAPHE
opérateurs des téléphones et télégraphes
[CITP-1968 (3-8)]
telephone and telegraph operators [ISCO-1968 (3-8)]

TÉLÉGUIDAGE
long-distance counselling

TÉLÉPHONIQUE
permanence téléphonique
hot line telephone

suivi téléphonique
telephone follow-up

TÉLÉTRAVAIL
long-distance / remote control work;
telecommuting, telework(ing)

TÉLÉTRAVAILLEUR
telecommuter

télétravailleur électronique
computer-linked home worker

TÉMOIN
centre témoin
pilot centre

groupe témoin
comparison / control group

programme témoin
pilot programme

projet témoin
pilot project

TEMPORAIRE (adj.)
temporary; interim; short-term

affectation temporaire
temporary assignment

agence de travail temporaire
temporary work (agency), temp agency,
temporary employment agency,
temporary help contractor / service (USA)

allocation temporaire
transitional allowance

assistance temporaire
temporary assistance

contrat de travail temporaire
temporary work contract

déplacement temporaire
temporary relocation

disposition temporaire
transitional provision

emploi public temporaire
temporary public job

emploi temporaire
interim / temporary job / employment

employé temporaire
temporary employee

engagement à titre temporaire
temporary appointment

incapacité (de travail) temporaire
short-term / temporary disablement /
incapacity

invalidité temporaire
short-term / temporary disability / invalidity

main-d'oeuvre temporaire
interim / temporary / casual labour

mise à pied temporaire
intermittent / temporary lay-off

ouvrier temporaire
short-term worker

personnel temporaire
temporary staff / assistance

placement temporaire
(occ.) respite care

poste temporaire intermittent
recurrent temporary post

résidence temporaire
temporary residence

revenu d'appoint temporaire
temporary income support

séjour temporaire
temporary stay / residence

service temporaire prolongé
extended temporary duty

travail temporaire
temporary work / employment / job;
temping

travailleur immigré temporaire
temporary immigrant / migrant worker;
(occ.) guest worker

travailleur temporaire
temporary (help) employee / worker; temp

TEMPORAIRE (n.)
temporary (help) employee / worker

TEMPORAIREMENT
enfant temporairement recueilli
temporarily fostered child

licencier temporairement
to lay off (temporarily)

temporairement mis à pied
(temporarily) laid-off

TEMPOREL
comparaison temporelle / dans le temps
time-to-time comparison

indice temporel
time-to-time index

TEMPS
activité à temps partiel
part-time / subsidiary activity, part-time
job

ajustement dans le temps
time-to-time adjustment

aménagement du temps de travail
new patterns / redistribution of working
time; flexible working hours / time

budget-temps
time budget

capital temps-formation
right to a number of hours' training

comparaison dans le temps
time-to-time comparison

congé (d'études) à temps partiel
part-time day release

contrat de travail à temps partiel
part-time employment contract

**convention d'aménagement et de
réduction du temps de travail (ARTT)
(Fr.)**
agreement to reform and reduce working
hours

**école dispensant un enseignement à
temps complet**
full-time school

éducation à plein temps
full-time education

emploi permanent à temps partiel
permanent part-time employment

emploi à temps complet
full-time job / employment

emploi à temps partiel
part-time job / employment

emploi à temps plein
full-time job / employment

employé permanent à temps partiel
permanent part-time employee

employé permanent à temps plein
permanent full-time employee

**employé à plein temps / à temps
complet**
full-time employee

employé à temps partiel
part-time employee

enseignement à temps partiel
part-time instruction / education

équivalent de main-d'oeuvre à temps plein
full-time man equivalent

équivalent plein temps
full-time equivalent (FTE)

études à plein temps
full-time education

flexibilité dans l'aménagement du temps de travail
flexibility of working time arrangements

formation à temps complet
full-time training

formation à temps partiel
part-time training

formation à temps plein
full-time training

fraction au prorata du temps / prorata temporis
pro-rata fraction

instruction à temps plein
full-time instruction

journée de travail normale à temps partiel
normal part-time working day

modulation du temps de travail
flexible working hours / scheduling

ouvrier à plein temps
full-time worker

ouvrier (travaillant) à temps partiel
short-term worker

pension à temps partiel (Finl.)
part-time pension

personnel (employé) à temps complet
full-time staff

personnel (employé) à temps partiel
part-time staff

population active à temps complet / à temps plein
full-time labour force

production juste à temps
just-in-time production

prorata du temps (au)
pro-rata temporis

réduction du temps de travail
reduction in / of working hours, shortening of working hours; shortened working week

salarié permanent à temps partiel
permanent part-time employee

salarié permanent à temps plein
permanent full-time employee

scolarisé à temps plein (être)
to be in full(-)time education

stage à temps partiel
part-time course

stagiaire à temps complet / à temps plein
full-time trainee

statut de travailleur à temps complet / à temps plein
full-time status

système de récupération du temps
time recovery scheme

système du temps alloué
time-allowed system (piece work)

temps complet (à)
full-time

temps contraint
tied time

temps d'hospitalisation
stay in hospital

temps libre(s)
leisure / spare time

temps partagé
time sharing

temps partiel (à)
part-time

temps plein (à)
full-time

temps prescrit
prescribed time

temps de présence ininterrompue au travail
(occ.) continuous employment

temps réduit
compressed / reduced time

temps réduit indemnisé longue durée (Fr.)
short-time work on benefit for a long period

temps de trajet
journey / travelling time

temps de travail
hours of work, working time / hours; work period

temps voulu (en)
by the required date

travail à la pièce obéissant au système du temps alloué
time piecework

travail à temps complet
full-time work / employment / job

travail à temps partiel
part-time employment / job / work

travail à temps plein
full-time work / employment / job

travailler à temps réduit
to be on / to work short time

travailleur permanent à temps partiel
permanent part-time worker

travailleur à temps partiel
part-time worker

travailleur à temps plein
full-time worker; regular employee (USA)

TENDANCE
trend

renversement de tendance
reversal of trend, trend reversal

tendance ascendante
upward trend

tendance du chômage
unemployment pattern, pattern of unemployment

tendance conjoncturelle
business / cyclical trend

tendance économique
economic trend

tendance de l'emploi
labour market trend

tendance à la hausse
upward trend

tendance du marché de l'emploi / du travail
labour market trend

tendance structurelle
trend over time

TENDU
tight

marché du travail tendu
tight labour market

production en flux tendus
just-in-time production

TENSION
tension; stress

tension nerveuse
strain

TENTATIVE
tentative de conciliation
arbitration / conciliation attempt

TENUE
keeping; behaviour; performance

tenue de dossiers
record keeping

tenue de l'emploi
labour market / employment performance

tenue de registres
record keeping

TERME
term; expiry; (pl.) terms

arriver à terme
to expire

contrat à durée déterminée à terme imprécis (Fr.)
unspecified fixed-term contract

contrat à durée déterminée à terme précis (Fr.)
specified fixed-term contract

contrat à durée déterminée à terme non spécifié (Fr.)
unspecified (but fixed) term contract

contrat à long terme
long-term contract

court terme
short-term

court terme (à)
in the short-run

formation à court terme
short-term training

long terme
long-term, long-run, long-range

pension payée à termes
pension paid out on a regular basis

personnel à court terme
short-term staff

politique à court terme
short-term policy

prestation à court terme
short-term benefit

prestation à long terme
long-term benefit

terme (à)
in the long run

terme d'un contrat
expiry date / end of contract; (pl.) wording / terms and conditions of a contract

termes d'un contrat de travail
terms and conditions of employment

terme d'un délai de préavis
end of a notice period

termes de l'échange
terms of trade

termes réels (en)
in real terms

TERMINAISON
termination

TERMINAL (adj.)
malade en phase terminale
terminal patient

maladie dans sa / en phase terminale
terminal illness

TERMINER
terminer sa formation
to finish / to complete one's training

TERMINOLOGIE
stage de terminologie technique
technical language training course

TERRAIN
activité de / sur le terrain
field work

effectifs de terrain
field forces

enquête sur le terrain
field survey

expérience du terrain
field experience

matériel pour terrains de jeux
playground equipment

observation sur le terrain
field study

terrain de jeux
recreation ground, playground

travail de / sur le terrain
field work

TERRITORIAL
administration / autorité / collectivité
territoriale
local government

TERRITORIALITÉ
principe de la territorialité
rule of territoriality

TERTIAIRE (adj.)
activité tertiaire
service industry; (pl.) service / tertiary
industries, service / social trades

emploi tertiaire
service / tertiary employment

enseignement tertiaire
tertiary education

profession du secteur tertiaire
service occupation; (pl.) service trades

secteur tertiaire
service industry; (pl.) service / tertiary
industries, service / social trades

soins médicaux tertiaires
tertiary medical care

soins tertiaires
tertiary care

travailleur du secteur tertiaire
service worker

TERTIAIRE (n.)
service industry; service / tertiary industries, service / social trades

TERTIARISATION
labour market shift

TEST
test

test d'aptitude
aptitude test

test d'aptitude à l'emploi
employment aptitude test

test d'aptitude(s) générale(s)
general aptitude test

test de compétence
skill / proficiency test

test de connaissances
knowledge test, test of knowledge

test de niveau
aptitude / level / achievement test

test de personnalité
personality test

test de rendement / de résultat
achievement / performance test

test de sélection
selection test

test de sélection en temps limité
in-tray exercice, in-basket test

TESTER
to test

TÊTE
allocation par tête
per capita allocation

revenu par tête
per capita income

système de la rémunération par tête
capitation-fee system

tête (par)
per capita / head

TEXTE
text; (occ.) version

textes faisant également foi
texts equally authoritative

texte législatif
legal / statutory instrument; (pl.)
legislation

textes législatifs fondamentaux
basic legislation

textes législatifs et/ou réglementaires
statutory instruments / regulations

texte de loi
act, legal / statutory instrument; (pl.)
legislation

texte réglementaire
(pl.) regulation(s)

TEXTILE
ouvriers du textile [CITP-1968 (7-5)]
spinners, weavers, knitters, dyers and
related workers [ISCO-1968 (7-5)]

THALASSOTHÉRAPIE
thalassatherapy

THÉORIE
théorie de l'apprentissage
learning theory

théorie des attentes
expectancy theory

théorie conjoncturelle
business cycle theory

théorie économique
economic theory

théorie du signalement
signalling theory

THÉORIQUE
theoretical; academic; cognitive; notional;
off-the-job (training)

connaissances théoriques et pratiques
knowledge and skills

cours théoriques
classroom / theoretical training

formation théorique
theoretical / off-the-job training

gains théoriques
notional earnings

**montant maximal / maximum
théorique**
highest theoretical amount

montant théorique
theoretical amount

pension théorique
theoretical pension

prestation théorique
notional benefit

rémunération théorique
notional earnings

taux théorique
theoretical amount

THÉRAPEUTIQUE (adj.)
therapeutic; remedial

appartement thérapeutique
half-way house

atelier thérapeutique
therapeutic workshop

centre d'accueil thérapeutique
(occ.) drop-in centre

équipement thérapeutique
treatment facility

technique thérapeutique
remedial skill

THÉRAPEUTIQUE (n.)
therapy; therapeutics

thérapeutique d'entretien
maintenance therapy

thérapeutique par le travail
work / industrial therapy

THÉRAPIE
therapy

thérapie par le travail
work / industrial therapy

THERMAL
cure thermale
spa (course of) treatment, hydrotherapy

forfait thermal (Fr.)
fixed rate for spa course of treatment

hôpital thermal
hydropathic hospital

station thermale
health resort

THÉSAURISEUR
acquisitive

TICKET
exemption du ticket modérateur
exemption from patient's contribution

ticket modérateur
cost of medical expenses, part not
reimbursed to insured persons; patient's
contribution; co-payment (lump sum), co-
insurance (proportional)

ticket-repas, ticket-restaurant
luncheon voucher, meal ticket (USA)

TIERS (adj.)
aide / assistance constante d'une tierce
personne
constant attendance

assistance d'une tierce personne
(occ.) invalid care allowance (UK)

emploi dans le tiers secteur
third sector employment

majoration pour tierce personne
attendance allowance for third person,
constant attendance allowance (UK)

tierce partie
third party

tierce personne
third person; attendant

tiers secteur
third sector

TIERS (n.)
third party

aide / assistance constante d'un tiers
constant attendance

assurance aux tiers
third party insurance

recours de tiers
third party claim

recours contre des tiers
recourse / remedy against third parties

système du tiers garant (Switz.)
third party guarantee system

système du tiers(-)payant
third party payment system, direct
payment system

tiers financier / gestionnaire
funding agency

tiers(-)payant
cost of medical expenses, part paid by
third fund; third-party payer / payment;
direct payment system

tiers répondant
third surety

tiers responsable
person vicariously liable

tiers saisi
garnishee

TIMBRE
stamp

méthode des timbres
stamp method

**oblitérer des timbres (national
insurance) (UK)**
to cancel stamps

timbre d'assurance (UK)
insurance stamp

timbre de cotisation (UK)
contribution stamp

timbre oblitéré
cancelled stamp

TISSU
tissu social
social fabric

TITRE
title; heading; function; qualification;
charge; entitlement; permit; security

occupant sans titre
squatter

reconnaissance des titres
recognition of (educational) qualifications

titre (à)
as, in the capacity

titres et certificats
(occ.) credentials

titre fonctionnel
functional / post title

titre médecin (Fr.)
coupon for medical consultation in a third
party system

titre de pension
certificate / document showing entitlement to a pension; evidence of entitlement

titre professionnel
occupational certification

titre de rente
certificate / document showing entitlement to a pension; evidence of entitlement

titres suffisants (avoir / posséder des)
to qualify for

TITULAIRE
recipient; beneficiary; holder; tenured

agent non titulaire de l'Etat
non-established State employee

fonctionnaire titulaire
established civil servant

fonctionnaire non titulaire
temporary / non-established civil servant

**pension payée à un titulaire à
l'étranger**
pension paid abroad

pension du titulaire
personal pension

**service des prestations à un titulaire à
l'étranger**
payment of benefits abroad

titulaire d'une allocation
beneficiary of an allowance

titulaire d'un diplôme
diploma holder, holder of a diploma

titulaire d'un diplôme (être)
to hold a diploma

titulaire d'un diplôme universitaire
degree holder, holder of a degree

titulaire d'un droit
person entitled to a right

titulaire d'un emploi
job holder

titulaire de deux emplois
second job holder

**titulaire d'une nomination à titre per-
manent**
holder of a permanent appointment

titulaire d'une pension
beneficiary of a pension, pensioner,
person entitled to a pension

titulaire de pension de vieillesse
old age pensioner

titulaire d'un poste
job holder, holder of a post, incumbent

titulaire d'un poste (être)
to encumber a post, to have tenure

titulaire d'une prestation
benefit recipient

titulaire d'une rente
beneficiary of a pension, pensioner,
person entitled to a pension

TITULARISATION
conversion to established basis; tenure

TITULARISÉ
employé titularisé
employee with tenure

fonctionnaire titularisé
established civil servant

fonctionnaire non titularisé
temporary / non-established civil servant

titularisé (être)
to get tenure

TOIT
vivre sous le même toit
to live in the same house, to live together

TOMBER
to fall; to lapse

tomber malade
to be taken ill

TORT
prejudice, wrong
tort à (faire)
to prejudice

TOTAL (adj.)
complete, total

allocation de chômage total
total unemployment allowance

allocation de solidarité de chômage total (Fr.)
total unemployment solidarity allowance

chômage total
total unemployment

chômage total (au)
totally / wholly unemployed

comparaison portant sur la rémunération totale
total compensation comparison

incapacité (de travail) totale
total / absolute disablement, total incapacity

invalidité totale
absolute disablement, total disability

invalidité totale consécutive à un accident du travail
total disability due to work injury

maîtrise totale de la qualité (MTQ)
total quality control (TQC)

montant total
total amount
prise en charge totale
full payment; total subsidisation

remise totale ou partielle des retenues
full or partial waiver of deductions

totale indigence
absolute distress

TOTAL (n.)
total; (occ.) amount

total des congés annuels accumulés
accrued annual leave balance

TOTALISATION
totalling; aggregation

totalisation des périodes
totalling of periods, adding together the periods

totalisation des périodes d'assurance
adding (together) of periods of insurance, aggregation of / totalling of insurance periods

TOTALITÉ
paiement en totalité
payment in full

régime intéressant la totalité de la population
universal scheme

remboursement en totalité
repayment in full

TOUCHER
to affect; to receive

toucher des allocations / des indemnités de chômage
to live on / to draw unemployment benefit

toucher une pension
to receive / to draw a pension

toucher son salaire
to draw one's pay, to receive one's wage

TOURNANT (adj.)
équipe tournante
rotating / swing shift

formation tournante
carousel training

grève tournante
rotating / staggered / selective / guerilla strike

TOXICITÉ
valeur attribuée à la toxicité
toxicity rating

TOXICOMANE
drug addict

TOXICOMANIE
drug dependence / addiction

TRACE
record; evidence

TRACTATION
(pl.) bargaining

TRADITIONNEL
activité traditionnelle
traditional / mainstream activity

emploi non traditionnel
non-traditional job

enseignement non traditionnel
non-formal education

formation des femmes dans les métiers non traditionnels
non-traditional training for women

profession non traditionnelle
non-traditional job

TRAFIC
trafic d'enfants
child trafficking

trafic de main-d'oeuvre
labour traffic / trafficking

TRAIN
train de mesures
series of measures; (occ.) package deal

train de vie
life style, style of living; standard of living criteria; rate of expenditure

TRAITANT
médecin traitant
attending physician; family doctor; doctor in attendance

visites du médecin traitant à l'hôpital
in-hospital doctor's care

TRAITE
traite d'enfants
child trafficking

TRAITÉ (n.)
treaty

obligation née d'un traité
treaty obligation

TRAITEMENT
salary, pay; remuneration; treatment; (occ.) wage; (pl.) salary / pay scales

allocation pour traitement hospitalier (UK)
hospital treatment allowance

augmentation périodique de traitement
salary increment, within-grade (salary) increment

augmentation du traitement
salary increase

augmentation de traitement accélérée
accelerated salary increment

barème des traitements
salary / pay scales, salary rate, salaries
range

barème des traitements de base
base salary scale

**barème unique et uniforme de
traitements de base**
single uniform base salary scale
classer les traitements par ordre
to rank salary rates

conduite du traitement (med.)
(occ.) case management

congé spécial à demi-traitement
special leave with half pay

congé spécial à plein traitement
special leave with full pay

congé spécial sans traitement
special leave without pay

congé spécial à traitement partiel
special leave with partial pay

congé sans traitement
leave without pay

demande d'avance de traitement
request for salary advance

disparité de traitement
disparity of treatment

échelle de traitement / des traitements
wage / pay / salary scale / range, range /
scale of wages, wage bracket

égalité de traitement
equal treatment, equality of treatment

étude des traitements
review of salary scales

éventail des traitements
salaries range

fourchette des traitements
salary range / band / bracket

indemnité de traitement
wage / salary replacement

inégalité de traitement
unequal treatment, (occ.) discrimination

malade en traitement ambulatoire
(hospital) out-patient

malade en traitement de jour
day patient

mauvais traitements
ill treatment, abuse

mauvais traitements à enfant
child abuse

mettre opposition sur un traitement
to attach salary

moyen de traitement ambulatoire
out-patient facility

niveau de traitement
pay / salary / wage level

perte de traitement
loss of salary

principe de l'égalité de traitement
principle of equal treatment

**progression des traitements à
l'intérieur d'une même classe**
intra-grade salary progression

rappel de traitement
(payment of) arrears of salary

régime d'assurance-traitement collectif
group salary insurance scheme

régime commun des traitements
common salary scheme

régime des traitements
salary scheme / system

relèvement des traitements
upward adjustment of salaries

retenue de traitement
withholding of salary

retenue sur le traitement
deduction from earnings / salary, wage
assignment

rétribution garantie-traitement (Belg.)
guaranteed remuneration

révision générale des traitements
major salary review

révision à la hausse des traitements
upward adjustment of salaries

salaires et traitements
wages and salaries

salaires et traitements en nature
wages and salaries in kind

service de traitement de jour
day-care patient facility

soins aux malades en traitement de jour
day patient care

structure des traitements
salary / pay structure

suspension avec traitement
suspension with pay

suspension sans traitement
suspension without pay

système informatisé de traitement des offres d'emploi
automated job order system

taux différentiel de traitement
salary differential

taux de traitement
salary / pay / wage rate

technique de traitement
remedial skill

traitement ambulatoire
out-patient / ambulatory treatment

traitement annuel
annual salary

traitement annuel courant
current annual salary

traitement de base
basic salary

traitement de base net
net base salary

traitement brut
gross salary

traitement chimiothérapique
drug treatment

traitement ouvrant droit à pension
pensionable salary

traitement effectif
take-home salary

traitements et autres émoluments
salaries and emoluments

traitement en établissement
institutional / residential care

traitement d'exception
special treatment

traitement de faveur
preferential treatment

traitement fixe
basic / fixed salary

traitement (en milieu) hospitalier
hospital care / treatment; institutional care

traitement sans hospitalisation
out-patient treatment

traitements et indemnités
salaries and allowances

traitement inégal
unequal treatment

traitement inéquitable
unfair treatment

traitement en institution
institutional / residential care

traitement intensif
intensive care

traitement juste et équitable
fair and equitable treatment

traitement médical
medical treatment, course of treatment

traitement partiel
part wage, partial pay

traitement de post-cure
follow-up treatment

traitement préférentiel
preferential treatment; positive discrimination (minorities)

traitement non remboursé
(occ.) private treatment

traitement soumis à retenue (pour pension)
pensionable salary

traitements et salaires
salaries

traitement semi-brut
half-gross salary

traitement social individuel
individual social treatment

tranche de traitement
salary bracket

valeurs indiciaires des traitements
(salary) scale relativities

TRAJET
accident de / du trajet
injury / accident while travelling (to or from work), accident between home and work, commuting accident; accident in transit

allocation de trajets quotidiens
commuting allowance

temps de trajet
journey / travelling time

trajet domicile-travail
work journey

trajet journalier / quotidien
day haul; (pl.) commuting

TRANCHE
bracket; instalment

impôt par tranches
graduated tax (rate)

première tranche d'imposition
basic rate tax

tranche d'âge
age bracket

tranche de barème fiscal / d'imposition
tax bracket

tranche d'imposition inférieure
lower income bracket

tranche d'imposition supérieure
upper income bracket

tranche inférieure des salaires (la)
lower paid (the)

tranche de revenus
class of income, wage / income bracket

tranche de salaire
wage / pay / salary bracket

tranche supérieure d'imposition
higher tax bracket

tranche de traitement
salary bracket

TRANSACTION
transaction; negotiated financial compensation

coûts de transaction
transaction costs (job seeking and hiring of staff)

TRANSFÉRABILITÉ
transferability, portability

transférabilité des compétences
skill transferability

transférabilité des pensions
pension portability, portability of pensions

TRANSFÉRABLE
portable, transferable

droit(s) de pension transférable(s)
portable pension right(s)

pension transférable (between pension funds)
portable pension

subvention salariale transférable
portable wage subsidy

subvention transférable
portable subsidy

TRANSFÉRÉ
chômage transféré
shift of unemployment, transferred
unemployment

TRANSFÉRER
to transfer

possibilité de transférer des droits
portability of rights

transférer un poste
to transfer a post

TRANSFERT
transfer; assignment

allocation de transfert (Neth.)
transfer allowance

paiement de transfert
transfer payment

programme de transferts (de revenus)
income transfer programme

revenu (provenant) de transferts
transfer income

transfert des crédits
credits transfer

**transfert des droits acquis d'une caisse
à une autre (pension)**
transferability / portability of pension
rights

transfert des droits d'ancienneté
transfer of seniority rights

transfert de fonds (migr.)
remittance

transfert monétaire
cash transfer

transfert de postes
transfer of posts

transfert de résidence
transfer of residence

transfert de revenus
income transfer

transfert de séjour
transfer of stay

transfert social
social transfer; (pl.) social transfer
payments, social benefits

transfert de technologies
technology transfer, transfer of technology

transfert lié au travail
work(-)tested transfer

TRANSFORMATION
industrie de transformation
processing / manufacturing industry

transformation de prestations
commutation / conversion of benefits

TRANSFRONTALIER
cross-frontier, cross-border

TRANSFRONTIÈRE
cross-frontier, cross-border

mouvement transfrontière
cross-border / foreign movement

TRANSFUSION
transfusion sanguine
blood transfusion

TRANSITION
transition

**allocation de chômage de transition
(Belg.)**
transitional unemployment allowance

foyer de transition
transit home

pédagogie de la transition
education for transition

prestation de transition (Denm.)
transition benefit

subvention supplémentaire de transition
supplementary transition grant

TRANSITIONNEL
chômage transitionnel
transitional unemployment

TRANSITOIRE
transitional; temporary

période transitoire
transitional period

TRANSMISSIBLE
lutte contre les maladies transmissibles
communicable disease control

maladie transmissible
communicable disease

TRANSNATIONAL
entreprise transnationale
transnational company

TRANSPARENCE
transparence dans l'entreprise
accessibility of information within a
company

TRANSPLACEMENT
transplacement

TRANSPORT
conducteurs d'engins de transport [CITP-
1968 (9-8)]
transport equipment operators [ISCO-
1968 (9-8)]

**employés d'approvisionnement, d'or-
donnancement et des transports [CITP-
1988 (413)]**
material-recording and transport clerks
[ISCO-1988 (413)]

frais de transport
travelling / travel / transportation expenses

indemnité de transport
travel allowance

**manoeuvres des mines, du bâtiment et
des travaux publics, des industries
manufactu-rières et des transports
[CITP-1988 (93)]**
labourers in mining, construction,
manufacturing and transport [ISCO-1988
(93)]

**ouvriers et manoeuvres non agricoles et
conducteurs d'engins de transport
[CITP-1968 (7/8/9)]**
production and related workers, transport
equipment operators and labourers
[ISCO-1968 (7/8/9)]

prime de transport
transport allowance

transport maritime
shipping

transport sanitaire
sanitary transportation

**travailleur salarié des transports inter-
nationaux**
person employed in international transport

travailleur des transports
transport worker

TRANSPORTEUR
armateur transporteur
shipowner carrier

TRANSVERSAL
section transversale
cross section

TRAPPEUR
pêcheurs, chasseurs et trappeurs [CITP-
1988 (615)]
fishery workers, hunters and trappers
[ISCO-1988 (615)]

TRAUMATISME
injury

traumatisme léger
minor injury

TRAVAIL
work; employment; job; (pl.) work(s)

abandonner le travail
to leave work

abattement fiscal sur le revenu du travail
earned income allowance

accident de / du travail
accident at work, labour / work / industrial accident, occupational accident / injury, industrial / work / employment injury

accident survenu sur le chemin du travail
accident (or injury) while travelling (to or from work); accident (or injury) in transit

accidenté du travail
industrial injury / accident victim, person who sustains an accident at work

accord collectif de travail
collective agreement

accord de travail partagé
work sharing agreement

acte commis à l'occasion d'un conflit du travail
act done in furtherance of a trade dispute

acte commis en vue d'un conflit du travail
act done in contemplation of a trade dispute

action-travail
employee's share

adaptation au travail
work adjustment

administration du travail
labour administration

âge d'aptitude au travail
employable age

âge d'entrée au travail
age at accession to the labour force, age at entry into employment

agence de travail intérimaire / temporaire
temporary work (agency), temp agency, temporary employment agency, temporary help contractor / service (USA)

allocation pour incapacité de travail (UK)
disablement benefit

allocation d'incapacité par suite d'un accident du travail (UK)
industrial injury disability benefit

allocation de travail pour invalides (UK)
disability working allowance

allocation pour travaux insalubres et dangereux (Gr.)
unhealthy and dangerous work allowance

allonger la durée du travail
to increase hours of work

amélioration de la sécurité et de l'hygiène du travail
improvement in safety and health conditions at work

aménagement du poste de travail
job adaptation / redesign

aménagement souple du temps de travail
variable / flexible working time

aménagement du temps de travail
new patterns / redistribution of working time; flexible working hours / time

amplitude de la journée de travail
work day span

analyse du marché du travail
labour market analysis

analyse du travail
work study

année-personne de travail
work-year of employment

année de travail
work(-)year, person-year, staff-year

apte à reprendre le travail
(physically) fit to resume work

apte au travail
capable of work, able to work; able-bodied; employable

aptitude à reprendre le travail
(physical) fitness to return to / resume work

aptitude au travail
occupational fitness; working ability, ability to work; job readiness; employability

arrêt de / du travail
absence from work; stoppage / suspension / cessation of work, work stoppage, cessation from work, walkout; disruption of employment

arrêt de travail (en)
absent from work

arrêt de travail collectif
collective work stoppage
arrêt de travail pour maladie
sick leave, absence from work owing to illness

arrêt de travail pour maladie (en)
absent from work owing to illness

arrêt de travail pour raison médicale
(occ.) medical suspension

assurance (contre les) accidents du travail (et les maladies professionnelles)
industrial injury / injuries insurance, insurance against accident at work; employers' liability insurance; compensation scheme; accident insurance

atteinte à la liberté du travail
violation of the freedom of labour

autorisation de travail
work / labour permit

autorités (responsables) du marché du travail
labour market institutions / authorities

avis d'arrêt de travail
notice of cessation of work / of having ceased work; sick leave notice

bâtiment et travaux publics
building and civil industry

besoins du marché du travail
labour market needs

bourse du travail
job / labour exchange (service)

cadre de travail
work setting / surroundings, working environment

caisse de compensation pour les accidents du travail et les maladies professionnelles
(occ.) workmen's compensation board

calendrier de travail / des travaux
work schedule, scheduling of work

camarade de travail
fellow(-worker)

capacité d'absorption du marché du travail
labour market absorption capacity

capacité de travail
capacity to / for work, ability to work, working capacity

capacité de travail réduite
reduced working capacity

capacité de travail rémunéré
wage-earning capacity

carte de séjour et de travail
work and residence permit, green card (USA)

carte de travail
work permit

centre d'aide par le travail
work-based support centre

certificat d'arrêt de travail
sick leave certificate

certificat d'incapacité de travail
certificate of incapacity for work

certificat de travail
certification / certificate of service, employment / work certificate

cessation collective de travail
collective work stoppage

cessation d'un contrat de travail
termination of a contract of employment

cessation de la relation de travail
cessation / termination of employment

cesser le travail
to stop work, to walk off the job; to leave work

champ d'action et effet du travail
scope and effect of work

charge de travail
(volume of) work()load

chercher du travail
to look for employment / for a job, to seek employment / work

chômeur apte au travail
able-bodied unemployed

climat de travail
working atmosphere / environment, work climate

code du travail
Labour Code, labour laws

Comité d'hygiène, de sécurité et des conditions de travail (Fr.)
Health and Safety at Work Committee

comité de travailleurs pour l'amélioration des conditions de travail (USA)
employee action committee

compagnon de travail
fellow(-worker)

comportement du marché du travail
labour market performance

condition légale de travail
legal employment requirement

conditions de travail
work(ing) / employment conditions, conditions of work; work environment; work practices

conducteur de travaux
site foreman

conflit de / du travail
labour / industrial conflict / dispute, trade dispute

congé d'accident de travail
injury-on-duty leave

conjoncture du marché du travail
labour market conditions

conseil du travail (au niveau local)
local labour council

conseiller du travail
employment / work counsellor; industrial social / welfare worker; staff counsellor

contrat collectif de travail
collective agreement

contrat individuel de travail
(occ.) indenture contract

contrat de travail
contract of employment / of labour / of service, work contract / agreement, labour / employment / service contract

contrat de travail à / de durée déterminée
fixed-term / fixed-duration (employment / work) contract, fixed-term appointment

contrat de travail à durée indéterminée
indefinite / open-ended (employment / work) contract, indefinite appointment

contrat de travail intermittent
intermittent work contract

contrat de travail précaire
insecure employment / work contract

contrat de travail saisonnier
seasonal employment / work contract

contrat de travail temporaire
temporary work contract

contrat de travail à temps partiel
part-time employment contract

contrat de travail subventionné (Sp.)
grant-assisted (employment) contract

contrat-type de travail
standard work / employment / service contract

contre-incitation au travail
work disincentive

convention d'aménagement et de réduction du temps de travail (ARTT) (Fr.)
agreement to reform and reduce working hours

convention collective du travail
collective labour agreement

cotation du travail
job evaluation

cotisation accident de travail (Fr.)
industrial injury contribution

Cour du travail
Labour Court of Appeal

coût marginal du travail
marginal cost of labour

coût social du travail
social (opportunity) cost of labour

coût du travail
labour cost

crédit d'impôt au titre des revenus du travail (USA)
earned income tax credit

cycle de travail
job / work cycle

décalement des horaires de travail
staggered working hours

décès dû à un accident du travail ou à une maladie professionnelle
death from employment (injury)

déclaration d'accident du travail
declaration / notification of an accident at work

degré d'incapacité de travail
degree of incapacity / of disablement

degré de satisfaction au travail
degree of job satisfaction

demande d'indemnisation pour accident du travail
accident claim, workmen's compensation claim

demande sur le marché du travail
labour market demand

demande de travail
demand for labour, labour demand

déplacement domicile-travail / entre domicile et lieu de travail
travel / journey to work; commuting

déséquilibre du marché du travail
labour market imbalance, imbalance / disequilibrium on the labour market

désorganisation du marché du travail
labour market / manpower dislocation, dislocation of the labour market

dévalorisation du travail manuel
downgrading of manual labour

différend du travail
industrial dispute

diminution de la capacité de travail
reduction of working capacity

disponibilité pour le travail
availability for work

disposition au travail
willingness to work; attitude to work

distribution du travail
work allocation / distribution, workload breakdown

division internationale du travail
international division of work / of labour

division du travail
division of labour / of work

droit au travail
right of / to work

droit du travail
labour law / legislation

durée annuelle de travail
annual working time

durée annuelle effective du travail
annual hours worked

durée convenue du travail hebdomadaire
standard working week, standard weekly hours

durée hebdomadaire du travail
hours worked weekly, weekly hours of
work, work(ing) week

**durée hebdomadaire du travail prévue
par la loi**
statutory working week

durée légale du travail
statutory working hours

**durée légale maximale du travail, durée
maximale du travail prévue par la loi**
statutory maximum working hours

durée normale du travail
standard working hours

**durée normale du travail
hebdomadaire**
standard working week, standard weekly
hours

durée du travail
hours of work, working time / hours

durée de travail réduite
short time

dynamique du marché du travail
labour market dynamics

échelonnement des horaires de travail
scheduling of work

économie du travail
labour market theory, labour economics

effet du travail
impact of work

efficacité du marché du travail
labour market efficiency

éloignement du travail
distance from work

enquête sur les forces de travail
labour force survey

enrichissement du travail
job enrichment

entrave à la liberté du travail
interference with freedom of employment

entrave au travail
work hindrance

entrée au travail
entry into employment

**entreprise de travail adapté (ETA)
(Belg.)**
adapted work company

**entreprise de formation par le travail
(EFT) (Belg.)**
training-through-work venture

équilibre du marché du travail
labour market equilibrium, balance of /
equilibrium on the labour market

équipe de travail
work shift

état du marché du travail
labour market conditions

étude de(s) poste(s) de travail
job analysis

évaluation analytique du travail
analytical job evaluation

évaluation des postes de travail
job evaluation

évaluation du travail
work assessment

évolution du marché du travail
labour market development

**évolution de l'offre sur le marché du
travail**
changes in labour supply

expérience concrète du travail
practical (work) / hands-on / on-the job
experience

expérience de travail
job / work experience

expérience en milieu de travail
practical (work) / hands-on / on-the job
experience

fête du travail
Mayday, Labor Day (USA)

feuille d'accident du travail
work injury form

feuille / fiche de travail
worksheet

flexibilité dans l'aménagement du temps de travail
flexibility of working time arrangements

flexibilité du marché du travail
labour market flexibility

fonctionnement du marché du travail
functioning / operation of the labour market, labour market operation(s)

formation sur les lieux de travail / en milieu de travail
on-the-job training / learning

formes de travail
work patterns

forme de travail atypique
non-standard form of working

forme de travail souple
flexible work

gêne pour le travail
work hindrance

grève par le travail
work-in

groupe de travail
task force / group; (occ.) syndicate

habitude de travail
work habit, working pattern; attitude to work

heures normales de travail
scheduled hours of work

heures de travail
hours of work, working hours

heure de travail effectuée
worked hour; (pl.) hours (actually) worked

horaire de travail
working time / hours; work(ing) schedule

horaire de travail assoupli / flexible
flexible work schedule, flexible hours

horaire de travail individualisé
personalised hours of work, personalised working hours

horaire de travail normal
normal working hours

horaire de travail personnel / personnalisé
personalised working hours

horaire de travail souple / variable
flexible work schedule, flexible hours

hygiène et sécurité du travail
industrial / occupational health and safety

hygiène et sécurité sur le lieu de travail / au travail
health and safety at work

hygiène du travail
industrial / occupational health

inadéquation de l'offre et de la demande de travail
(occ.) labour market mismatch

inapte au travail
incapable for / of work; unfit for work; not able / unable to work

inaptitude au travail
inability to work, incapacity for / to work, unfitness for work

incapacité de travail
disablement / incapacitation / disability for work, industrial / occupational / vocational disablement, working disability, working / vocational incapacity, inability to work, incapacity for / to work, unfitness for work

incapacité de travail définitive
permanent incapacity / disablement

incapacité de travail partielle
partial disablement / incapacity

incapacité de travail partielle permanente
permanent partial incapacity / disablement

incapacité de travail permanente
permanent incapacity /disablement

incapacité de travail primaire (Belg.)
primary incapacity for work

incapacité de travail temporaire
short-term / temporary disablement /
incapacity

incapacité de travail totale
total / absolute disablement, total
incapacity

indemnisation des accidents du travail
worker's compensation (for industrial
injury)

indemnité d'accident / pour accident de travail
workmen's compensation (award /
benefit); employment / industrial injury
benefit; injury benefit (UK, Irel., Malta)

indemnité d'invalidité pour accident du travail (ou maladie professionnelle)
industrial disablement payment / gratuity

indemnités maladie / accident du travail pour travailleurs indépendants
occupational sick pay for self-employed
workers

industrie à forte intensité de travail
labour-intensive industry

initiation au monde du travail
introductory training; (occ.) career(s)
education

initiation au travail
pre-employment orientation, (job)
induction; job training

insatisfaction au travail
job dissatisfaction

inspecteur du travail
labour inspector

inspection du lieu de travail
inspection of work surroundings

inspection sur le lieu de travail
on-site inspection

inspection du travail
labour inspectorate, factory inspectorate /
inspection; Occupational Safety and
Health Administration (USA)

intégration au marché du travail
labour market integration / entry

intensité (relative) de travail
labour intensity

interruption de travail
interruption of employment / of work

interruption du travail
cessation of / from work

intervenant sur le marché du travail
labour market partner

invalidité totale consécutive à un accident du travail
total disability due to work injury

jour / journée de travail
work()day, working day

journée de travail normale
normal working day

journée de travail normale à temps partiel
normal part-time working day

législation du travail
labour law / legislation

libérer qqn de son travail
to release someone from work

liens avec le marché du travail
labour market attachment

lieu de travail
job site, place of work / of employment,
work site, work()place; (pl.) work
premises

lieu(x) de travail (sur le / les)
on-the-job

limitation de la durée du travail
restrictions on working hours

livret de travail (Gr.)
labour permit

loi sur les accidents du travail
workmen's compensation law

maladie du travail
industrial / occupational / professional
disease

manque de travail
lack / shortage of work, work shortage

manquement au contrat de travail
breach of contract of employment

marche du travail
work flow

marché national du travail
domestic / national labour market

marché primaire du travail
mainstream / primary labour market

marché secondaire du travail
secondary labour market

marché du travail
employment / job / labour market

marché du travail agricole
agricultural / farm labour market

marché du travail civil
civilian labour market

marché du travail externe
external labour market

marché du travail intérieur
domestic labour market

marché du travail interne
internal labour market

marché du travail local
local labour market

marché du travail naturel
natural labour market

marché du travail normal
normal / open labour market

marché du travail officiel / organisé
official / organised / formal labour market

marché du travail restreint / serré / tendu
tight labour market

marge de résistance au travail
work(ing) tolerance

mauvaises conditions de travail
poor working conditions

médaille du travail
long-service award, seniority / service / long-service medal

médecin-inspecteur du travail
occupational health inspector

médecin du travail
occupational health doctor; works (Gr.) / industrial medical officer, industrial doctor

médecine du travail
industrial / occupational medicine / health

mesure d'incitation au travail
(occ.) in-work benefit

mesure quantitative du travail
work count

mesure du travail
work measurement

méthode de travail
work process; (pl.) work practices

migration de travail
labour migration

milieu de travail
work(ing) environment

modalités de travail
work patterns

modulation du temps de travail
flexible working hours / scheduling

mois de travail
(occ.) staff-month

monde du travail
working life

motivation au travail
work motivation, motivation to work

mouvements sur le marché du travail
labour market flow

nature du travail
job content, type of activity / of job / of work

navette entre son domicile et son lieu de travail (faire la)
to commute to and from work

niveau de satisfaction au travail
degree of job satisfaction

niveau de / du travail
working level, level of work

normes fondamentales du travail
basic / core labour standards

norme de mesure du travail
work measurement standard

norme du travail
labour standard

norme du travail équitable
fair labour standard

nouveau venu sur le marché du travail
labour force entrant, (new) entrant on the labour market

observation du marché du travail
labour market monitoring

office du travail
(labour) employment office, employment agency / bureau (USA)

offre de travail
labour / manpower supply

ordre de travail
work order

organisation scientifique du travail
(occ.) job engineering

organisation du travail
work organisation

outil de travail
work tool

paiement au prorata du travail effectué
(occ.) apportionment of wages

partage du travail
distribution of the available volume of work; job / work sharing

participation au marché du travail
labour market / labour force attachment, attachment to the labour force

pension d'invalidité suite à un accident du travail (Hung.)
accident disability pension

pension de réversion à la suite d'un accident du travail
industrial death benefit

pénurie de travail
work shortage

perdre son travail
to lose one's job

période d'absence du travail
time absent from work

période d'interruption de travail
period of interruption of employment

période de travail
(work) shift; period of work; period of work experience

permis de travail
work / labour / employment permit

personne handicapée apte au travail
employable person with disability / ies

perspective de travail
placing / placement prospect

perte de la capacité de travail
loss of earning capacity

perturbation du marché du travail
labour market / manpower dislocation, dislocation of the labour market

perturbation au / dans le travail
disruption at work

physiologie du travail
occupational physiology

plan de travail
work plan

pointe de travail
work peak

politique d'intervention (directe) sur le marché du travail
active labour market policy

politique du marché du travail
labour market policy

porter atteinte au libre exercice de l'industrie et du travail
to impair / to restrict the freedom of industry and labour

possibilité de travail
placing / placement prospect

poste de contrôle du travail
supervisory work station

poste de travail
work station / place / shift; job

poste de travail (hors)
off-the-job

pratiques de travail
work practices

présence au travail
work attendance

présenter au travail (se)
to report for / to duty / for work

pression(s) exercée(s) sur le marché du travail
labour market pressure

prestation (en cas) d'accident du travail (et de maladies professionnelles)
accident benefit, benefit in respect of accidents at work, employment / industrial injury benefit, injury benefit (UK, Malta, Irel.)

prestation de décès à la suite / résultant d'un accident du travail
industrial death benefit

prestation d'invalidité causée par un accident du travail (ou une maladie professionnelle)
industrial disablement benefit

prestation pour travail partagé
work sharing benefit

prévention des accidents du travail
(occ.) industrial safety

prévention des accidents du travail et des maladies professionnelles
industrial / occupational health and safety

principe à travail égal, salaire égal
equal pay for equal work principle

problème d'intégration au marché du travail
labour market entry difficulty

procédé à facteur travail prédominant
labour-intensive technology

productivité du travail
labour productivity

produit marginal du travail
marginal product of labour

programme d'alternance travail-études
work-study programme

programme d'évaluation analytique des tâches / du travail
analytical job evaluation scheme

programme du / intéressant le marché du travail
labour market programme / scheme

prorata temporis du travail effectué (au)
in proportion to time worked

prospection du marché du travail
(occ.) job exploration

protection-travail
workfare, welfare employment (USA)

psychiatrie du travail
occupational psychiatry

psychologie du travail
occupational / work / industrial psychology

qualification du travail
job evaluation / qualification

qualité de la vie au travail
quality of working life

quitter le travail
to leave work

ralentissement du marché du travail
labour market slack

ralentissement du travail
slowing down of work, work slowdown

réajustement / réaménagement du marché du travail
adjustment of the labour market

reconnu apte au travail (être)
to be certified fit to work

redistribution du volume de travail
redistribution of the volume of work

réduction de la durée du travail
reduction of / cut in working hours

réduction de la durée hebdomadaire du travail
reduction of the working week

réduction de la durée quotidienne du travail
reduction of daily hours

réduction du temps de travail
reduction in / of working hours, shortening of working hours; shortened working week

régime de travail sous contrat
contract labour system

registre des accidents du travail
accident book

règlement du travail
work rules

réglementation du travail
labour regulations

réinsertion sur le marché du travail
reintegration into the labour market

réintégrer le marché du travail
to re-enter the labour force

relation de travail
employment relationship; (pl.) staff / work / industrial / labour relations, working relationship; job attachment

remise au travail
re-employment

rémunération du travail
earned income

rendement du marché du travail
labour market performance

rendement au travail
job performance

rente d'accident du travail
industrial injury pension, pension for accident at work

rentrée sur le marché du travail
re-entry into the labour force

rentrer sur le marché du travail
to re-enter the labour force

réparation d'un accident du travail
compensation for an accident at work

réparation des accidents du travail et des maladies professionnelles
workmen's compensation (for industrial injuries and professional diseases)

répartition de la charge de travail
distribution of the workload

répartition du travail
division / segregation of duties; work allocation / distribution, job / work sharing; workload breakdown

reprendre le travail
to resume work, to re-enter employment, to return to employment / to work

reprise du travail
resumption of work

resserrement du marché du travail
tightening of the job market

résultats (atteints) au travail
job performance, performance on the job

retirer du marché du travail (se)
to withdraw from the labour force

retour sur le marché du travail
re-entry (into the labour force)

retour progressif au travail
drift back to work

retour au travail
back to work, return to employment / to work

retourner au travail
to resume work, to re-enter employment, to return to employment / to work

rétrécissement du marché du travail / de l'emploi
tightening of the job market

revalorisation du travail manuel
upgrading of manual work

revenir sur le marché du travail
to re-enter the labour force

revenu marginal du travail
marginal revenue of labour

revenu du travail
income from work, earned income; (pl.) labour income

revenus autres que ceux du travail / ne provenant pas d'un travail
investment / unearned income

rigidité du marché du travail
labour market rigidity

risque d'accident du travail
occupational hazard / risk

rouages du marché du travail
functioning / operation of the labour market, labour market operations

rupture abusive du contrat de travail
wrongful / unfair dismissal, wrongful discharge (USA)

rupture du contrat de travail
breach of contract of employment

rupture d'un contrat de travail
termination of a contract of employment

santé au travail
occupational health

satisfaction au / dans le travail
job / work satisfaction

séance de travail
working session; workshop

secteur du marché du travail
labour market sector, segment of labour market

sécurité et hygiène du travail
safety and health at work

sécurité et santé au travail
occupational safety and health

sécurité au travail / sur le lieu de travail
job / occupational safety, safety at work

segmentation du marché du travail
labour market segmentation

semaine normale de travail
normal / standard work week, basic work week

semaine de travail
work(ing) week

semaine de travail réduite
compressed work(ing) week, reduced / short work week

semaine de travail variable
variable work week

service de médecine du travail
occupational health service

service social du travail
industrial welfare, industrial social work

service du travail
job service

service du travail obligatoire (Fr.)
compulsory working

situation du marché du travail
manpower / job situation, labour market situation / conditions

somme de travail accrue
increased workload

sortie du marché du travail
withdrawal from employment / from the labour force

souplesse des horaires de travail
flexibility of working hours

source de travail
source of employment

spécialiste du domaine du travail
labour expert

stabilisation du marché du travail
labour market stabilisation

stage d'initiation au travail
pre-employment course

stage de travail et d'étude
(occ.) work study

statisticien du travail
labour statistician

statistiques relatives au marché du travail
labour market statistics

statistiques du travail
labour / manpower statistics

structure du marché du travail
labour market structure

suivi du marché du travail
labour market monitoring

surcharge de travail
overwork

surcroît de travail
increased workload; extra work; pressure of work

sursalaire pour travail posté
shift differential

suspension d'un contrat de travail
suspension of an employment contract

système d'évaluation analytique du travail
analytical job evaluation scheme

système du marché du travail
labour market system

système du travail sous contrat
contract labour system

système de travail par équipes alternant jour et nuit
alternating shift system

système de travail par équipes chevauchantes
coupled shift system

système de travail par équipes avec périodes d'interruption entre les équipes
discontinuous shifts

taux d'absorption des nouveaux venus sur le marché du travail
rate of absorption of labour market entrants

temps de présence ininterrompue au travail
(occ.) continuous employment

temps de travail
hours of work, working time / hours; work period

tendance (du marché) du travail
labour market trend

termes d'un contrat de travail
terms and conditions of employment

thérapeutique / thérapie par le travail
work / industrial therapy

trajet domicile-travail
work journey

transfert lié au travail
work(-)tested transfer

travail (du)
[work]; (occ.) industrial

travail accompli
work performed

travail administratif
administrative / clerical work

travail agricole
agricultural work

travail agricole saisonnier
seasonal agriculture work

travail analogue
equivalent occupation

travail en année complète
full-year work

travail en année partielle
part-year work

travail en année pleine
full-year work

travail sur appel
work on call

travail d'appoint
subsidiary job

travail d'artisanat
handicraft

travail atypique
atypical work

travail bénévole
volunteer work

travail de bureau
clerical / office work; white-collar job /
occupation; office duty

travail caché
disguised employment

travail à la chaîne
assembly-line work, flow process work,
production line work; flow / line
production

travail clandestin
black / hidden / moonlight / shadow /
submerged / twilight / underground / grey
economy; clandestine work, moonlighting

travail à la commande
jobbing work; outwork

travail au profit de la communauté
community service / work

travail non conforme
below-standard work

travail consciencieux
competent work

travail continu
non-stop work

travail en continu
shift work(ing)

travail continu en équipe
continuous shiftwork

travail sous contrat
contract work; indentured labour

travail courant
normal workload; routine work

travail dangereux
hazardous occupation / work

travail non déclaré
undeclared / disguised / concealed /
unrecorded employment; unrecorded
work

travail déguisé
disguised employment

travail en deux-huit
double day shift, two-shift work

travail le dimanche
Sunday work

travail dissimulé
disguised employment / work, concealed /
unrecorded employment

travail à distance
remote control work; telecommuting,
telework(ing)

travail domestique
domestic / household work

travail à domicile
home business / work, (occ.) homebound
employment

travail dominical
Sunday work

travail égal
equal work

travail des enfants
child employment / labour

travail enrichissant
rewarding work

travail d'équipe
team()work

travail en / par équipe
shift work(ing)

travail par équipes fixes
fixed shift system

travail à façon
hire service contract; special order work;
jobbing work; outwork

travail familial
family work; (occ.) cottage industry

travail forcé
forced labour

travail à forfait
contract work

travail formateur
formative work

travail gratifiant
rewarding work

travail de / en groupe
group work

travail hautement spécialisé
highly skilled work

travail à l'heure
time work

travail à horaires réduits
short-time work / working; partial
unemployment

travail illicite
irregular employment, illegal work

travail indépendant
self-employment

travail dans l'industrie
industrial work

travaux infirmiers
nursing work

travail ingrat
unrewarding work

travail insalubre
unhealthy work

travail intellectuel
intellectual / professional work

travail d'intérêt général (TIG)
community service / work

travaux d'intérêt public
public works

travail intérimaire
temporary work; temping

travail en intermittence / intermittent
periodic work

travail invisible
disguised employment

travail irrégulier
irregular employment

travail latent
disguised employment

travaux légers
light work

travail manuel
manual work / labour

travail non manuel
non-manual / white-collar job / work /
occupation

travail marchand
market work

travail non marchand
non-market work

travail masqué
disguised employment

travail médico-social
medical and social work; almoning (UK)

travail à mi-temps
half-time employment / work

travail monotone
monotonous / repetitive work

travail au noir
black / hidden / moonlight / shadow /
submerged / twilight / underground / grey
economy; disguised / concealed /
unrecorded employment; moonlighting

travail hors normes
atypical work

travail de nuit
night work

travail occasionnel
casual / irregular work; freelance work;
(pl.) casual employment

travaux occasionnels (pour des)
for casual labour

travail partagé
work sharing

travail physique
physical work; manual labour

travail à la / aux pièce(s)
job work, piecework

**travail à la pièce obéissant au système
du temps alloué**
time piecework

travail portuaire
dock work

travail posté
shift work(ing)

travail posté de nuit
nightshift

travaux pratiques
(occ.) field work

travail productif
productive employment, production job

travail professionnel
workmanship

travail protégé
sheltered employment

travail qualifié
skilled work

travail rémunérateur
remunerative work

travail rémunéré
paid / gainful work

travail au rendement
job work

travail répétitif
monotonous / repetitive work

travail par roulement
shift work(ing)

travail routinier
monotonous / repetitive work

travail (à caractère) saisonnier
work of (a) seasonal nature, seasonal job /
employment / work

travail salarié
paid / gainful occupation

travail de secrétariat
secretarial work

travail sédentaire
sedentary work

travail en semi-continu
split shift

travail social
social work (activity / practice); (social)
welfare work

travail social d'entreprise
industrial social work

travail social professionnel
professional social work

travail social scolaire
school social work

travail socialement utile (Ger.)
socially useful work

travail soigné
high quality work

travail en souffrance
work in abeyance

travail à la tâche
job work, piecework

travail technique hautement spécialisé
high-skill technical work

travail temporaire
temporary work / employment / job;
temping

travail à temps complet
full-time work / employment / job

travail à temps partiel
part-time employment / job / work

travail à temps plein
full-time work / employment / job

travail de / sur le terrain
field work

travail à trois postes / en trois-huit
three-shift work

travail en usine
factory work

travail d'utilité collective (TUC) / sociale
community service / work; community work scheme, workfare

travailleur apte au travail
employable worker

tribunal du travail
industrial court / tribunal (UK), labour court

type de travail
kind of work

unité de travail
work unit, unit of work

unité travail-année
man-year unit, year work unit

valorisation du travail
job enrichment

variation de la charge de travail
workload shift

victime d'(un) accident du travail
industrial accident / injury victim, person who sustains an accident at work

volume de travail
(volume of) work(-)load, volume level of activities

zone de déplacement domicile-travail
journey(-)to(-)work / travel(-)to(-)work area

zone de travail
work area

TRAVAILLÉ
heure effectivement travaillée
hour actually worked

heure travaillée
worked hour; (pl.) hours / time worked

semaine travaillée
work-week worked

TRAVAILLER
to work; to hold a job

âge minimum légal pour travailler
minimum legal working age

âge de travailler (en)
of working age

capable de travailler (pas)
incapable of working, not able / unable to work; (occ.) unemployable

femme mariée qui travaille
working wife

incapable de travailler
incapable of working, not able / unable to work; (occ.) unemployable

incapacité de travailler (dans l')
unfit for work, not able / unable to work

légalement autorisé à travailler
legally entitled / eligible to work

obligation de travailler
obligation to work

personne travaillant à son compte
worker on own account; freelance (worker)

personnel travaillant à son compte
freelance personnel

population en âge de travailler
working(-)age labour force

propension à travailler
propensity to work

refus de travailler
refusal to work

travailler (en état de)
able to work

travailler (à même de)
available for work

travailler à la chaîne
to work on the production line

travailler comme collaborateur indépendant
to work freelance

travailler comme extra
to work as an extra

travailler aux heures normales
to work regular hours

travailler en dehors des heures normales
to work unsocial hours

travailler en horaires réduits
to be on / to work short-time

travailler comme indépendant
to work freelance

travailler à mi-temps
to work half-time

travailler au noir
to moonlight; to work on the side (if second occupation)

travailler à pleine capacité
to work at full capacity

travailler par roulement
to work shifts

travailler en sous-ordre
to work under close control

travailler à temps réduit
to be on / to work short time

TRAVAILLEUR
worker; labourer; employee; workman; (pl.) work force, labour, manpower; working / active population

allocation aux vieux travailleurs
allowance for elderly / old workers

allocation aux vieux travailleurs salariés
allowance for old employees

association de travailleurs
workers' organisation

autogestion par les travailleurs
workers' self-management

comité de travailleurs pour l'amélioration des conditions de travail
employee action committee (USA)

congé de formation jeunes travailleurs (Fr.)
young workers training leave

contrat passé avec un travailleur indépendant
freelance contract

cotisation sociale des travailleurs indépendants
self-employment insurance contribution

cotisation des travailleurs
workers' contribution

délégué des travailleurs
labour / union representative, union steward

demande de travailleurs
worker / manpower demand

déplacement des travailleurs
manpower movement, movement of / flow of workers

détachement d'un travailleur salarié
posting of an employed person

disponibilité de travailleurs
worker availability

droit exclusif de placement des travailleurs
exclusive right to place workers in jobs, placing monopoly

droit de préemption des travailleurs
workers' right of pre-emption

durée de disponibilité du travailleur
length of time worker available

effet travailleur ajouté
added worker effect

effet travailleur découragé
discouraged worker effect

envoi de fonds des travailleurs émigrés / immigrés
workers' remittance

excédent de travailleurs
over-supply of workers, worker surplus

fonds d'indemnisation des travailleurs licenciés (pour raisons économiques)
redundancy fund

former un travailleur
to train a worker

foyer de jeunes travailleurs
young workers hostel

hypothèse travailleur découragé
discouraged worker hypothesis

hypothèse travailleur supplémentaire
additional worker hypothesis

impôt de sécurité sociale des travailleurs indépendants
self-employment social security tax

impôt des travailleurs indépendants
self-employment tax

indemnités maladie / accident du travail pour travailleurs indépendants
occupational sick pay for self-employed workers

inscription du travailleur
worker registration

jeune travailleur
young worker

liberté de circulation des travailleurs
freedom of movement for workers

libre circulation des travailleurs
free movement of workers

manque de travailleurs
lack / shortage / under-supply of workers, labour / manpower / worker shortage

mobilité des travailleurs
labour / manpower / work force / worker mobility

monopole de placement des travailleurs
exclusive right to place workers in jobs, placing monopoly

mouvement de travailleurs
flow of workers

nombre de travailleurs occupés
number of workers employed (in a company)

occupation par les travailleurs
worker occupation

offre de travailleurs
labour / manpower supply

participation des travailleurs
workers' participation

participation des travailleurs à la gestion des entreprises
workers' participation in management

pension des travailleurs indépendants (Finl.)
self-employed persons' pension

pénurie de travailleurs
manpower / occupational / worker shortage, under-supply of workers

personne vivant sous le toit du travailleur salarié
person living under the same roof as the employed person

placement des travailleurs
placement of workers in jobs

polyvalence professionnelle des travailleurs
occupational flexibility of the workers

présélection des travailleurs
preselection of workers

prestations d'adaptation pour les travailleurs
labour adjustment benefits

qualifications d'un travailleur
worker's qualifications

rappeler un travailleur
to recall a worker

rapport d'appréciation / d'évaluation d'un travailleur
evaluation report of an employee

réadaptation professionnelle des travailleurs invalides
vocational rehabilitation of the disabled

recrutement de travailleurs
worker recruitment

recrutement de travailleurs étrangers
foreign recruiting, foreign worker recruitment; off-shore recruitment

régime complémentaire des travailleurs des charbonnages / des houillères
colliery workers supplementary scheme

régime spécial de travailleurs non salariés
special scheme for self-employed persons

régime applicable aux travailleurs manuels
scheme applicable to manual workers

regroupement familial des travailleurs migrants
reuniting of migrant workers' families

relations employeurs-travailleurs
labour-management / industrial relations

rendement du travailleur
worker performance

représentant des travailleurs
labour / union / worker representative, union steward, representative of workers

réquisition de travailleurs
requisitioning of workers

santé des travailleurs
workers' health

sécurité et santé des travailleurs
safety and health of workers

sélection préliminaire des travailleurs
preselection of workers

service aux travailleurs
service to workers

source de travailleurs
manpower / supply source

statut de travailleur à temps complet / à temps plein
full-time status

surplus de travailleurs
over-supply of workers, worker surplus

taux de conservation des travailleurs
retention rate, rate of retention

taux de remplacement des travailleurs
workers' replacement rate

travailleur actif
active / employed worker

travailleur âgé
old(er) / elderly worker

travailleur d'âge très actif
prime-age worker

travailleur d'un certain âge
older worker

travailleur agricole
farm / agricultural worker; (pl.) agricultural manpower / workers

travailleurs agricoles [CITP-1968 (6-2)]
agriculture and animal husbandry workers [ISCO-1968 (6-2)]

travailleur ajouté
added worker

travailleur alternant
rotating worker

travailleur ayant une longue / beaucoup d'ancienneté
long-serving worker, senior worker (USA)

travailleur en année complète
full-year worker

travailleur en année partielle
part-year worker

travailleur en année pleine
full-year worker

travailleur apparenté à l'employeur
employee / worker related to the employer

travailleur approprié
suitable worker

travailleur apte à occuper un emploi / apte au travail
employable worker

travailleur assidu
steady worker

travailleur assimilé
related worker

travailleur atypique
atypical worker

travailleur autochtone
native / national / indigenous / aboriginal / worker

travailleur autonome (Can.)
self-employed (person / worker)

travailleur non autorisé
illegal worker

travailleur auxiliaire
auxiliary worker

travailleur à bas salaire
low-wage earner

travailleurs de la base
rank and file workers

travailleur du bâtiment
construction worker

travailleur bénévole
voluntary / volunteer worker

travailleur célibataire
single worker

travailleur des charbonnages
colliery worker

travailleur ayant charge de famille
worker with dependants / with family
responsibilities

travailleur chevronné
experienced worker

travailleur en chômage technique
laid-off worker, (occ.) lay(-)off

travailleur clandestin
illegal / clandestine / undeclared /
unauthorised / undocumented worker

**travailleur appartenant aux classes
d'âge de forte activité**
prime-age worker

travailleur à compétence unique
single-skilled employee

travailleur compétent
skilled / suitable / qualified worker;
skilled craftsman

travailleur pour compte d'autrui
employee

travailleur confirmé
experienced worker

travailleur contractuel
contract labourer

travailleur sous contrat
contract employee / worker

travailleurs engagés sur contrat
contract labour

travailleur déclaré
regular employee

travailleur non déclaré
illegal / clandestine / undeclared /
unauthorised / undocumented worker

travailleur découragé
discouraged worker

travailleur défavorisé
disadvantaged worker

travailleur dépendant
dependent worker

travailleur déplacé
displaced worker

travailleur détaché
seconded worker

travailleur disponible
available worker; (pl.) manpower supply,
supply of labour

travailleur domestique
domestic / household worker

travailleur à domicile
cottage / home worker, outworker

travailleur-élève (Malta)
pupil worker

travailleur ayant un emploi
employed worker

travailleur sans emploi
unemployed (worker), jobless worker

travailleur occupant un emploi
employee in employment

travailleur occupant plus d'un emploi
multiple jobholder

travailleur sans emploi régulier
casual labourer / worker, occasional worker

travailleur dont l'emploi a été supprimé
displaced / redundant worker

travailleurs et employeurs
(occ.) labour and management

travailleur à l'essai
probationary employee / worker

travailleur établi à son compte
self-employed (person / worker)

travailleur étranger
foreign worker

travailleur excédentaire
redundant worker; surplus employee

travailleur exempté
excluded employee

travailleur expérimenté
experienced worker

travailleur extérieur
outside worker

travailleur extérieur à la production
non-production worker

travailleur externe
outside worker

travailleur à faibles revenus
worker with low income

travailleur familial non rémunéré
unpaid family worker

travailleur de force
heavy worker

travailleurs forestiers [CITP-1968 (6-3)]
forestry workers [ISCO-1968 (6-3)]

travailleur en formation
(occ.) trainee worker

travailleur formé
trained worker

travailleur frontalier
border / frontier worker; cross-border worker (Belg.)

travailleur handicapé
disabled / handicapped worker

travailleur handicapé reconnu par l'Etat
registered disabled person

travailleur hautement qualifié
highly skilled worker

travailleur horaire
hourly paid worker

travailleur des houillères
colliery worker

travailleur immigré
migrant / immigrant worker

travailleur immigré temporaire
temporary immigrant / migrant worker; (occ.) guest worker

travailleur atteint d'incapacité
disabled worker

travailleur indépendant
self-employed (earner / worker / person); freelance / independent / own-account worker, worker on own account

travailleur indépendant permanent
permanent self-employed

travailleur de l'industrie
industrial worker; (pl.) industrial staff

travailleurs des industries de base
(occ.) key workers

travailleur intellectuel
intellectual / professional worker; (occ.) salaried worker / employee

travailleur intérimaire
temporary / casual worker

travailleur intermittent
casual / occasional worker

travailleur invalide
disabled worker

travailleur itinérant
itinerant / transient worker

travailleur licencié pour compression de personnel / pour raisons économiques
redundant worker

travailleur soumis à un lock-out
locked-out worker

travailleur malentendant
hearing-impaired worker

travailleur manuel
blue-collar (worker); manual worker; (pl.) (occ.) industrial staff

travailleur non manuel
clerical / office / non-manual worker, white-collar (worker); (pl.) (occ.) clerical and office workers

travailleur manuel spécialisé
semi-skilled manual worker

travailleurs du marché primaire de l'emploi
primary labour force, mainstream workers

travailleurs du marché secondaire
secondary labour force

travailleur marginal
marginal worker

travailleur migrant
migrant labourer / worker; transient worker; (pl.) migrant labour

travailleur des mines et des établissements assimilés
worker in mines and similar undertakings

travailleur à mi-temps
half-time worker; half-timer

travailleur mis à pied non réintégré
non-return lay-off

travailleur muté
displaced worker

travailleur national
national worker

travailleur au noir
moonlighter

travailleur nommément désigné
specific named worker

travailleur hors normes
atypical worker

travailleur occasionnel
casual employee / worker / labourer, occasional / contingent worker

travailleur occupé
employed worker

travailleurs organisés
organised labour

travailleur à l'ouvrage
contract worker

travailleur payé à la journée
daily wage worker

travailleur permanent
permanent worker

travailleur permanent à temps partiel
permanent part-time worker

travailleur physiquement handicapé
physically disabled worker

travailleur aux pièces
pieceworker; job worker

travailleur présélectionné
pre-selected worker

travailleur primaire
primary-level worker

travailleur productif
productive worker

travailleur à la / de la production
production employee / worker

travailleurs ne pouvant être classés selon la profession [CITP-1968 (X)]
workers not classifiable by occupation [ISCO-1968 (X)]

travailleurs n'ayant déclaré aucune profession [CITP-1968 (X-3)]
workers not reporting any occupation [ISCO-1968 (X-3)]

travailleurs ayant fait au sujet de leur profession une déclaration imprécise ou insuffisante [CITP-1968 (X-2)]
workers reporting occupations unidentifiable or inadequately described [ISCO-1968 (X-2)]

travailleur employé dans les professions de santé
health worker

travailleur professionnel
(occ.) trained worker

travailleur (professionnel) qualifié
skilled / trained / qualified worker; skilled craftsman; professional

travailleur non qualifié
unskilled worker / labourer

travailleur rémunéré
gainfully occupied worker / person, gainfully employed person, paid / gainful worker

travailleur rémunéré à l'heure
hourly paid worker

travailleur en renfort
relief worker

travailleur saisonnier
seasonal worker / employee

travailleur salarié
wage earner, employed earner / worker / person, employee; dependent / hired worker

travailleur non salarié
non-wage / self-employed (earner / worker / person)

travailleurs salariés de l'industrie
employed persons in industry

travailleur salarié des transports internationaux
person employed in international transport

travailleur sanitaire
health (care) worker

travailleur sanitaire primaire
primary health worker

travailleurs sanitaires et sociaux
health and social workers

travailleur du secteur privé
private worker

travailleur du secteur tertiaire
service worker

travailleur de secours
relief worker

travailleur semi-qualifié
semi-skilled worker

travailleurs spécialisés dans les services [CITP-1968 (5)]
service workers [ISCO-1968 (5)]

travailleurs spécialisés dans les services non classés ailleurs [CITP-1968 (5-9)]
service workers not elsewhere classified [ISCO-1968 (5-9)]

travailleur en situation irrégulière
illegal / undeclared / unauthorised / undocumented worker

travailleur social
social / welfare worker, (social) welfare officer / worker

travailleur social d'entreprise
industrial social / welfare worker

travailleur social en établissement pénitentiaire
prison welfare officer

travailleur social de groupe
group (social) worker

travailleur social neuropsychiatrique
psychiatric social worker

travailleur social professionnel
professional social worker

travailleur subventionné
subsidised worker

travailleur suppléant
replacement worker

travailleur supplémentaire
relief worker

travailleur victime de suppressions d'emploi(s)
redundant / displaced worker

travailleur en surnombre / surnuméraire
redundant worker, surplus employee

travailleur syndiqué
trade unionist; unionised worker; (pl.) organised labour; (occ.) union membership

travailleur non syndiqué
non-union(ised) worker

travailleur à la tâche
pieceworker; job worker

travailleur temporaire
temporary (help) employee / worker; temp

travailleur à temps partiel
part-time worker

travailleur à temps plein
full-time worker; regular employee (USA)

travailleur des transports
transport worker

voyage d'étude de travailleurs
study tour for workers

TRAVAILLEUSE
female worker, working woman

service de travailleuses familiales
home help service

travailleuse familiale
home-maker, home / mother's help; family / home aid, family help / helper / worker; (pl.) home-maker services (Fr.)

TREIZIÈME
treizième mois
extra month's salary

TREMPLIN
poste tremplin
ladder / bridging position

TRÉSOR
public revenue

Trésor public
fiscal administration

TRÉSORERIE
treasury; cash

besoins de trésorerie
cash requirement / needs

TRÉSORIER
paymaster

trésorier payeur général
accountant-general, paymaster-general

TRÊVE
trêve fiscale
tax holiday

TRI
screening

TRIBUNAL
pouvoir être invoqué devant les tribunaux
to be enforceable in a court of law

tribunal d'arbitrage obligatoire
compulsory arbitration tribunal

tribunal du travail
industrial court / tribunal (UK), labour court

TRIBUTAIRE
dependent

TRIER
to screen

TRILATÉRAL
convention trilatérale
trilateral convention

TRIMESTRE
term

TRIMESTRIEL
chiffres trimestriels
quarterly figures

paiement trimestriel
quarterly payment

résultats trimestriels
quarterly figures

TRIPARTITE
tripartite

financement tripartite
tripartite / three-party financing

TROIS
travail à trois postes / en trois-huit
three-shift work

trois-huit (les)
three shift system

TROISIÈME
enseignement du troisième degré
tertiary education

études de troisième cycle universitaire
postgraduate studies

étudiant du troisième cycle
(post)graduate student

personnes du troisième âge
old people; (occ.) young elderly

troisième âge
old people / age, (occ.) young elderly; the aged, (occ.) the elderly

troisième et le quatrième âge (le)
the aged and the elderly

TRONC
tronc commun
common core, core courses

TROP-PAYÉ
over(-)payment

avis de trop-payé
notice of overpayment

recouvrement des trop-payés
over-payment recovery

TROP-PERÇU
overpayment; overcharge

TROU
trou de la sécurité sociale
deficit in social security

TROUBLE
difficulty; trouble, disorder; disability

enfant présentant des troubles affectifs
emotionally disturbed child

trouble fonctionnel
functional disturbance, disturbance of function

trouble mental
mental disorder; (pl.) mental disability

troubles moteurs / de la motricité
motor disability

trouble physique
physical disorder; (pl.) (occ.) bodily illness

trouble psychiatrique
mental disorder

trouble psychique
(pl.) mental illness

troubles de santé
health disorder

trouble social
(pl.) industrial / labour unrest

trouble(s) de la vue
sight impairment

TROUSSE
kit; pack

trousse de maternité
maternity pack

TROUVER
trouver un emploi
to find / to obtain / to secure employment

TRUST
trust

TUBERCULEUX
allocation de soins aux tuberculeux
tuberculosis allowance

établissement pour tuberculeux
tuberculosis clinic

indemnité de soins aux tuberculeux
tuberculosis allowance

TUBERCULOSE
assurance contre la tuberculose (It.)
tuberculosis insurance

TUTELLE
supervision; guardianship; ward; care;
guidance

allocation de tutelle
after care allowance; guardian's allowance (UK)

autorité de tutelle
supervisory board

compte de tutelle
guardianship account

conseil de tutelle
supervisory board

délégué à la tutelle
guardianship officer

organe de tutelle
supervisory board

tutelle sur les mutuelles
supervision of mutual benefit societies

tutelle aux prestations familiales (Fr.)
control on family benefits

tutelle aux prestations sociales (Fr.)
control on social benefits

TUTEUR
guardian

allocation de tuteur (Austr.)
guardian allowance

subrogé tuteur
surrogate guardian

TYPE (adj.)
standard; typical; model

accord(-)type
model agreement

bénéficiaire type
standard beneficiary

calcul-type
model calculation

clause-type
standard clause

contrat-type de travail
standard service contract

erreur-type
standard error

exploitation type (agr.)
standard farm

manoeuvre(-)type
typical unskilled male worker, person
deemed typical of unskilled labour

ouvrier qualifié type
person deemed typical of skilled labour

population type
standard population

TYPE (n.)
type; form; kind
nomination d'un type différent
conversion to another type of appointment

type d'activité
kind / type of activity, type of job / of
work

type d'emploi
kind of job

type de risques couverts
type of coverage

type de travail
kind of work

TYPIQUE
typical

TYPOLOGIE
typology; pattern

ULTÉRIEUR
soins ultérieurs
(occ.) after-treatment

surveillance médicale ultérieure
medical supervision / follow-up

UNIFAMILIAL
ménage unifamilial
one-family household

UNIFICATION
unifying; consolidation

UNIFIÉ
loi unifiée
consolidation act

syndicat unifié
amalgamated union

systèmes unifiés
compatible systems

UNIFORME (adj.)
flat; standard(ised)

allocation à taux uniforme
flat-rate allowance / benefit

augmentation uniforme
(occ.) across-the-board increase

**barème unique et uniforme de
traitements de base**
single uniform base salary scale

cotisation (à taux) uniforme
flat-rate contribution

pension uniforme
flat-rate pension

pension uniforme de base
basic flat-rate pension

prestation à taux uniforme
flat-rate benefit

régime à taux uniforme
flat-rate scheme

tarif / taux uniforme
flat rate

taux uniforme (à)
at flat rate

UNIFORMISER
to standardise

UNILATÉRAL
accord unilatéral
unilateral / one-sided agreement

UNILINGUE
emploi unilingue
monolingual job

UNION
union

rupture d'union
broken / dissolved marriage, termination
of marriage

union consensuelle
companionate marriage, consensual union

union illégitime
illegitimate union

union légitime
legitimate union, (occ.) marriage

union libre
free / non-marital union; cohabitation

union libre (en)
cohabiting

union de syndicats
federation of trade unions

vivre en union libre
to cohabit

UNIQUE
allocation de salaire unique
single wage allowance

**barème unique et uniforme de
traitements de base**
single uniform base salary scale

cadre unique de rémunération
single salary schedule

candidat unique
sole candidate

employeur unique
sole employer

famille à enfant unique
one-child family

famille à parent unique
lone-parent / one-parent / single-parent
family

famille à revenu / salaire unique
one-earner family

ménage à revenu / salaire unique
one-earner household

paiement unique
non-recurrent payment, lump sum

propriétaire unique
sole proprietor / owner

salaire unique
single wage

somme unique
lump(-sum) / single payment, lump sum

travailleur à compétence unique
single-skilled employee

versement forfaitaire unique
lump-sum / flat-rate payment

UNITAIRE
calcul des coûts unitaires
unit costing

**coût de main-d'oeuvre unitaire / coût
unitaire de main-d'oeuvre**
unit labour cost

coût unitaire
unit cost

heure unitaire de main-d'oeuvre
unit hour of operation

UNITÉ
unit; section

heure-unité
unit hour

unité allocataire
benefit unit

unité bénéficiaire proratisée (Fr.)
pro()rata beneficiary unit

unité d'habitation / de logement
dwelling (unit), housing unit

unité ménagère
household unit

unité en mer (Denm.)
offshore unit

unité définie en fonction de l'occupant
unit based on occupancy

unité sanitaire locale (It.)
local health unit

unité sociale
social unit

unité de soins
nursing unit, patient care / health care unit

unité de soins intensifs
intensive care unit

unité de travail
work unit, unit of work

unité travail-année
man-year unit, year work unit

unité de valeur
unit of competence; module

unité de voisinage
neighbourhood unit

UNIVALENT
agent univalent
single purpose / single(-)skill worker

UNIVERSEL
ayant droit à titre universel
residuary beneficiary

couverture maladie universelle (Fr.)
universal health coverage

régime universel
universal scheme

UNIVERSITAIRE (adj.)
[university]; academic

année universitaire
academic year

centre hospitalier universitaire (CHU)
university hospital

crédit universitaire
university credit

diplôme universitaire
university diploma / degree

diplômé universitaire
graduate, degree holder, university graduate

emploi de niveau universitaire
graduate-level job; (pl.) jobs for (university) graduates

enseignement universitaire pratique
graduate training

études de troisième cycle universitaire, études universitaires supérieures
postgraduate studies

examen d'entrée dans le second cycle universitaire (USA)
graduate record examination

hautes études universitaires
postgraduate studies

hôpital universitaire
teaching / training hospital, hospital school

profession de niveau universitaire
graduate occupation / profession

programme de formation universitaire
university-based training programme

recrutement de diplômés universitaires
graduate recruitment

titulaire d'un diplôme universitaire
degree holder, holder of a degree

UNIVERSITAIRE (n.)
chômage des universitaires
graduate unemployment, unemployment amongst graduates

UNIVERSITÉ
université d'été
summer school

URBAIN
urban

aménagement urbain
urban planning

logement urbain
urban housing

service de santé urbain
urban health service

URBANIFICATION
urban development

URBANISATION
urban development

URBANISÉ
zone urbanisée
urban area

URBANISER
zone à urbaniser
urban development area

URGENCE
aide médicale d'urgence
emergency medical aid

médecine préhospitalière d'urgence
prehospital medicine

médecine d'urgence
emergency medicine

mesure d'urgence
emergency measure

plan d'urgence
contingency plan

prêt d'urgence (UK)
crisis loan

secours d'urgence
emergency relief / aid

service d'aide médicale d'urgence (SAMU)
emergency medical relief service

service mobile d'urgence et de réanimation (SMUR)
mobile emergency and intensive care service

service des urgences
emergency / casualty department / ward

soins d'urgence
first aid, emergency health care

urgence médicale
emergency health care

USAGE
practice

code d'usages / de l'usage
code of practice

coût d'usage
user cost

usage consacré / établi
established practice

usages du métier / de la profession
professional practices

USAGER
user; client, customer (social services); (pl.) (occ.) clientele

commis aux services aux usagers
help-desk clerk

participation des usagers
customers' participation

USINE
factory; works; installation; shop

employé d'usine
factory employee

navire-usine
factory ship

ouvrier d'usine
factory worker

travail en usine
factory work

USURE
allocation pour usure (anormale) des vêtements
allowance for wear and tear (of clothing)

usure et détérioration
wear and tear

usure naturelle des effectifs
natural wastage of labour

UTILE
useful; relevant, effective; profitable

travail socialement utile (Ger.)
socially useful work

UTILISATEUR
user

UTILISATION
taux d'utilisation
utilisation rate

taux d'utilisation des capacités (de production)
rate of capacity utilisation

taux d'utilisation des prestations par la population totale
beneficiary rate

taux d'utilisation des prestations par la population couverte
take-up rate

utilisation de la main-d'oeuvre
utilisation of manpower

UTILISÉ
solde non utilisé
unexpended / unencumbered balance

UTILITÉ
usefulness; use; interest; efficacy

association reconnue d'utilité publique
association recognised to be of public interest, charitable association; charity

établissement d'utilité publique
charitable corporation; charity

fonction (d') utilité
utility function

oeuvre reconnue d'utilité publique
corporation recognised to be of public
interest, charitable corporation; charity

**travail d'utilité collective (TUC) /
sociale**
community service / work; community
work scheme, workfare

VACANCE
vacancy; (pl.) holiday, vacation

aide aux vacances
holiday subsidy

allocation de vacances (Neth.)
holiday allowance

avis normalisé de vacance de poste
standardised notice of vacancy

avis de vacance d'emploi
notice of a vacant post, notified vacancy,
vacancy announcement / notice

bon vacances
holiday voucher

camp de vacances
summer camp

chèque vacances
holiday voucher

colonie de vacances
summer / holiday camp

**communication obligatoire des
vacances d'emploi**
compulsory notification of vacancies

déclarer une vacance de poste
to declare a post vacant

durée de vacance (de poste / d'emploi)
duration of vacancy, vacancy duration

échelonner les vacances
to stagger holidays

étalement des vacances
staggered holidays

gestion des vacances de poste
vacancy management

grandes vacances
summer holidays

indemnité de vacances
vacation allowance

maison familiale de vacances
family holiday home

**notification obligatoire des vacances
d'emploi**
compulsory notification of vacancies

pécule de vacances (Belg.)
holiday allowance; lump sum holiday pay

placement familial de vacances
holiday family placement

pourvoir à une vacance de poste
to fill a post / a job / a vacancy, to staff a
position

prime de vacances
holiday / vacation bonus, holiday
allowance, vacation pay (USA)

registre des vacances d'emploi
register of vacancies

salaire dû pendant les vacances
holiday pay

taux de vacances comblées
vacancy fill rate

taux de vacances d'emploi
vacancy rate

vacance comblée
vacancy filled

vacance non comblée
unfilled vacancy

vacance à combler
outstanding vacancy

vacance d'emploi
(job) vacancy

vacance d'emploi notifiée
vacancy notified

vacances d'été
summer holidays

vacance occasionnelle
casual vacancy

vacance ordinaire
regular vacancy

vacance de poste
vacancy

vacances scolaires
school holidays / vacation

vacance signalée
registered vacancy

VACANT
vacant; unfilled

communication obligatoire des postes vacants
compulsory notification of vacancies

emploi occasionnel vacant
casual vacancy

emploi régulier vacant
regular vacancy

emploi vacant
vacant position / post; (job) vacancy

logement vacant
unoccupied dwelling

notification obligatoire des postes vacants
compulsory notification of vacancies

place de formation vacante
training vacancy

poste notifié / signalé vacant
vacancy notified

poste vacant
vacant position / post, situation vacant, (job) vacancy

poste vacant inscrit
vacancy recorded

poste vacant signalé
registered vacancy

pourcentage de postes vacants
vacancy rate

VACATAIRE (adj.)
médecin vacataire
part-time doctor

VACATAIRE (n.)
(pl.) part-time / sessional staff

VACATION
session, sitting

payé à la vacation (être)
to be paid on a sessional basis

VACCINATION
vaccination

VAGABOND
vagrant

enfant vagabond
vagrant child

VALABLE
valid; effective

motif / raison valable
just / good cause, reasonable ground, good reason

motif / raison valable (sans)
without just cause

valable (non)
invalid

VALEUR
équivalent en valeur actuarielle
equivalent actuarial value

mise en valeur des ressources
resource development

mise en valeur des ressources humaines
labour / human resources / manpower / staff development

service à valeur ajoutée
value added / enhanced service

unité de valeur
unit of competence; module

valeur actuarielle
actuarial value

valeur ajoutée
added value

valeur en capital
capital value

valeurs indiciaires des traitements
(salary) scale relativities

valeur locative
rental value

valeur mobilière
security

valeur de rachat
amount of the (capital) compensatory
settlement; surrender value (ins.)

valeur seuil
threshold limit value

valeur sociale
social value / effectiveness

valeur attribuée à la toxicité
toxicity rating

VALIDABLE
service validable
reckonable / pensionable service

VALIDATION
validation; approval; authentication; accreditation

validation des connaissances
skill recognition, recognition of skills

validation gratuite
free validation

**validation aux fins de pension d'une
période de service**
validation for pension purposes of a
period of service

**validation d'une période de service
antérieure**
validation of previous service

validation des qualifications
skill certification / recognition, recognition of skills

VALIDE
valid; fit; able-bodied

encore valide
(occ.) unexpired

personne valide
able-bodied (person)

VALIDER
to validate; to authenticate; (occ.) to
support

valider les services antérieurs
to have previous services credited

VALIDITÉ
validity; adequacy

durée / période de validité
period of validity

VALOIR
valoir (faire)
to claim

valoir ses droits à pension (faire)
to claim pension rights; toqualify for a
pension

VALORISATION
valorisation professionnelle
staff development; upgrading

valorisation des ressources humaines
human resources / manpower / staff
development

valorisation du travail
job enrichment

VARIABLE (adj.)
coût variable
variable cost

horaire (de travail) variable
flexible working hours / time, flexible
time / hours; flexible work schedule;
flexitime

plage horaire variable
flexible time bracket

salaire variable
variable wage

semaine de travail variable
variable work week

taux variable
variable / loose rate

VARIABLE (n.)
variable de comportement
behaviour variable

VARIANTE
alternative version

VARIATION
variation; fluctuation

ajustement des pensions aux variations du coût de la vie
cost-of-living pension adjustment

correction des variations saisonnières
seasonal adjustment

corrigé des variations du nombre d'heures supplémentaires
adjusted for overtime

corrigé des variations saisonnières
seasonally adjusted

sensible aux variations de la conjoncture
(occ.) cyclically sensitive

variation de la charge de travail
workload shift

variation saisonnière
seasonal fluctuation / variation

VARIÉTÉ
range

VENDEUR
personnel commercial et vendeurs [CITP-1968 (4)]
sales workers [ISCO-1968 (4)]

vendeurs ambulants et assimilés [CITP-1988 (911)]
street vendors and related workers [ISCO-1988 (911)]

vendeurs et démonstrateurs en magasin [CITP-1988 (522)]
shop salespersons and demonstrators [ISCO-1988 (522)]

vendeurs à l'étal et sur les marchés [CITP-1988 (523)]
stall and market salespersons [ISCO-1988 (523)]

VENDREDI
Vendredi Saint
Good Friday

VENTE
employés non qualifiés des services et de la vente [CITP-1988 (91)]
sales and services elementary occupations [ISCO-1988 (91)]

employé du secteur de la vente
sales worker

entreprise de vente par correspondance
mail-order business

médicament en vente libre
over-the-counter drug

professions intermédiaires des finances et de la vente [CITP-1988 (341)]
finance and sales associate professionals [ISCO-1988 (341)]

VENTILATION
composition, distribution, disaggregation, disaggregating, breakdown; allocation

VENTILER
to breakdow; to apportion

VENU
nouveau venu
late entrant

nouveau venu sur le marché du travail
labour force entrant, (new) entrant on the labour market

VENUE
venue à expiration du contrat
expiry of contract

venue à maturité
maturation

VERBAL
verbal

accord verbal
verbal agreement

avertissement verbal
verbal warning

VÉHICULE
véhicules et engins
vehicles and equipment

VÉRIFICATION
check(ing), monitoring; audit

VERRE
verres de contact
contact lenses

verres correcteurs
corrective lenses

VERRIER
verriers, potiers et travailleurs assimilés
[CITP-1968 (8-9)]
glass formers, potters and related workers
[ISCO-1968 (8-9)]

VERSÉ
capital versé en une seule fois
lump sum

cotisations versées
paid contributions, contribution record

salaire versé
wage paid

versé sous conditions de ressources
means-tested

versé sous condition de revenu
income-tested

versé en trois fractions
paid in three instalments

VERSEMENT
payment; charge; remittance

condition de / requise pour le versement des prestations
qualifying condition for benefits

modalités de versement
method of payment

recouvrement des versements excédentaires
over-payment recovery

rétablissement du versement des prestations
reinstatement of benefits

système de versement des allocations / des indemnités
allowance payment system

versement des allocations
payment of allowances

versement par anticipation / anticipé
advance payment

versement d'appoint
top-up / deficiency payment

versement en capital
payment in capital, (payment of a) lump sum; capital compensation

versement à la cessation de service
separation pay / payment

versement de départ au titre de la liquidation des droits
withdrawal settlement

versement direct
direct payment

versement échelonné
instalment

versement en espèces
payment in cash

versement excédentaire
over-payment

versement exceptionnel
(occ.) one-off payment

versement de fin de service
end-of-service payment

versement forfaitaire (unique)
lump-sum / flat-rate payment

versement à titre gracieux
ex gratia payment

versement d'indemnités
compensation payment, payment of
benefits / allowances

versement intérimaire
interim payment

versement libératoire
payment in full discharge

versement mensuel
monthly instalment / payment

versement en nature
payment in kind

versement partiel
(occ.) instalment

versement d'une prestation
payment of a benefit

versement provisionnel
provisional payment

versement résiduel
residual settlement / payment

versement des salaires
payment of wages

VERSER
to pay; to provide

verser les / des cotisations
to pay contributions, to contribute

verser une prestation
to pay a benefit

verser à un taux réduit
to pay at a reduced rate

VERTICAL
mobilité verticale
upward / vertical mobility

relations verticales
line relationships

VESTIMENTAIRE
indemnité vestimentaire
clothing allowance

VÊTEMENT
allocation pour usure (anormale) des
vêtements
allowance for wear and tear (of clothing)

VEUF (adj.)
allocation de mère veuve (UK)
widowed mother's allowance

personne veuve
widowed person

VEUF (n.)
widower

**allocation au conjoint pour veufs et
veuves (Can.)**
widowed spouse's allowance

pension de veuf
widower's pension / benefit

pension de vieillesse de veuf (Fr.)
old age widower's pension

veuf ou divorcé
ever-married

VEUVAGE
widowhood

allocation de veuvage
widow's / widowhood (UK) allowance,
widowed person's allowance (Australia)

assurance veuvage
widow's insurance

**pension non contributive de veuvage
(Irel.)**
widows non-contributory pension

VEUVE
widow

allocation complémentaire de veuve
widow's supplementary allowance

allocation au conjoint pour veufs et veuves (Can.)
widowed spouse's allowance

allocation de veuve
widow's allowance

indemnité (forfaitaire) pour veuve
widow's (lump sum) payment, widow's grant

pension de base de veuve (UK)
widow's basic pension

pension d'invalidité de veuve (Fr.)
invalid widow's pension

pension de veuve
widow's pension / benefit (UK)

pension de veuve de guerre
war widow's pension

pension de vieillesse de veuve (Fr.)
old age widow's pension

prestation de veuve
widow's benefit

rente de veuve
widow's pension

veuve blanche
grass widow

veuve de guerre
war widow

veuve de jour
grass widow

VIABILITÉ
sustainability

VIABLE
emploi viable
(occ.) self-sustaining employment

VIAGER (adj.)
(for) life

allocation viagère aux rapatriés (Fr.)
annuity for repatriates

avantage viager
annuity benefit

indemnisation viagère de départ
annuity for withdrawal from work

rente viagère
life annuity

rente viagère de réversion / avec réversion / réversible
survivor's / survivorship annuity

rentier viager
annuitant

secours viager
life allowance for the surviving spouse of an elderly worker

VIAGER (n.)
(life) annuity

VICTIME
victim; injured person, casualty

allocation / pension de victime de guerre (UK)
war pensioner's death benefit

victime d'accident de la circulation
road accident victim

victime d'(un) accident du travail
industrial accident / injury victim, person who sustains an accident at work

victime civile de la guerre
civilian war victim

victime de (la) guerre
war victim, victim of war; (occ.) war pensioner

victime d'une maladie professionnelle
person who contracts an occupational disease

VIE
life

accidenté de la vie
adventiously handicapped

acte de la vie quotidienne
daily task

âge d'entrée dans la vie active
age at entry into employment

âge limite de la vie active
maximum active working age

allocation de vie chère
cost-of-living allowance / compensation / adjustment

aptitudes nécessaires à la vie courante
living skills

assurance-groupe sur la vie
group life insurance

assurance-vie
life insurance, life assurance (UK)

assurance-vie à capital différé
endowment insurance

assurance-vie à capital récupérable
pure endowment insurance

assurance-vie privée
(occ.) non-occupational coverage

auxiliaire de vie
home help

cadre de vie
home / human environment; setting of life

certificat de vie
life certificate

communauté de vie
conjugal life

conditions de vie
conditions of living, living conditions; (occ.) welfare

coût de la vie
cost of living

débutant dans la vie active
labour force entrant

différentiel de coût de la vie
cost-of-living differential factor

durée moyenne de la vie active / professionnelle
mean duration of working life

durée de la vie active / de la vie professionnelle
(duration of) working life

échelle mobile (des salaires) établie sur le coût de la vie
cost-of-living sliding scale

emploi à vie
lifetime job / employment

emploi quasiment à vie
near lifetime job

entrée dans la vie active
access to the labour force, access to / entrance into / entry into working life

entrer dans la vie active
to enter the labour force / market, to enter employment / into economic life, to take up employment, to begin / to start work

espérance brute de vie active
gross expectation of working life

espérance nette de vie active
net expectation of working life

espérance de vie
life expectancy

espérance de vie active
expectation of working life

espérance de vie en bonne santé
health expectation, healthy life expectancy

espérance de vie corrigée en fonction du bien-être
quality-adjusted life-year (QUALY)

espérance de vie à la naissance
life expectancy at birth

gestes essentiels de la vie quotidienne
basic activities of daily life

geste de la vie quotidienne
daily task

indemnité de cherté de vie / de vie chère
cost-of-living allowance / compensation / adjustment

indexation sur le / au titre du coût de la vie
cost-of-living adjustment, adjustment to cost of living

indicateur du niveau de vie
standard-of-living indicator

indice du coût de la vie
cost-of-living index

initiation à la vie professionnelle
introductory training to working life

insertion dans la vie active
integration into working life

lieu de vie
(occ.) sheltered home

maintenir les salaires au niveau du coût de la vie
to keep wages abreast of the cost of living

milieu de vie
human environment

mode de vie
lifestyle, life pattern, living arrangement

niveau de vie
living standard, standard of living

niveau de vie minimum acceptable
minimum acceptable standard of living

passage à la vie active
transition to working life

passage de la vie active à la retraite
transition from work to retirement

pension à vie
life / permanent pension

police d'assurance-vie à capital différé
endowment policy

police d'assurance-vie à capital récupérable
pure endowment policy

préparation à la vie de famille / familiale
family life education

préparation à la vie professionnelle
vocational preparation

prime de difficulté de vie
hardship allowance

prime de vie chère
cost-of-living allowance

production imputée de services d'assurance-vie
imputed service charge for life insurance

qualité de la vie
quality of life

qualité de la vie au travail
quality of working life

quitter la vie active
to withdraw from / to leave the labour force

retirer de la vie active (se)
to withdraw from working life, to retire (from work)

retour à la vie active / professionnelle
reintegration into / return to / re-entry into working life

retrait de la vie active
withdrawal from work / from working life / from employment

soins d'entretien et de continuité de la vie
daily care to compensate dependence

spécialistes des sciences de la vie [CITP-1988 (221)]
life science professionals [ISCO-188 (221)]

stage d'initiation à la vie professionnelle (SIVP)
work experience programme

stage d'insertion à la vie professionnelle
integration to working life course

stage de préparation à la vie professionnelle
vocational preparation course

train de vie
life style, style of living; standard of living criteria; rate of expenditure

vie (à / de toute une)
lifelong; for life

vie active
working life

vie associative
associative / associational life; voluntary activities

vie conjugale
married life

vie maritale
cohabitation

vie professionnelle
working / professional life

VIEILLARD
asile de vieillards, d'infirmes et de nécessiteux
home for the aged, infirm and needy

personnes âgées et les vieillards (les)
the aged and the elderly

VIEILLESSE
old age

allocation de base vieillesse (Fr.)
old age basic allowance

allocation complémentaire / supplémentaire vieillesse (Fr.)
supplementary old age allowance

allocation spéciale vieillesse (Fr.)
old age special allowance

allocation (de) vieillesse
old age allowance; (occ.) age allowance

allocation de vieillesse agricole (Fr.)
agricultural old age allowance

assurance(-)vieillesse
old-age insurance, insurance in respect for old-age

assurance(-)vieillesse des employés
pensions insurance of salaried employees

assurance(-)vieillesse des ouvriers
manual workers' pension insurance, pension insurance of manual workers

assurance(-)vieillesse et survivants
old age and survivors' insurance

avantage complémentaire vieillesse (Fr.)
supplementary old age benefit

avantage (de) vieillesse
old age benefit / bonus

bénéficiaire d'une pension de vieillesse
old age pensioner

caisse d'assurance(-)vieillesse
old age pension fund

calcul de la pension vieillesse
calculation of old age pension

coefficient de calcul des pensions vieillesse
factor applied to the calculation of old age pensions

couverture (du risque) vieillesse
old age coverage

déduction (d'impôt) pour vieillesse (UK)
age relief

durée d'assurance(-)vieillesse
period of old age insurance

fonds d'assurance(-)vieillesse
old age security fund

fonds de solidarité vieillesse (Fr.)
old age solidarity fund

incessibilité de pension de vieillesse
non-transferability of old age pension

institution d'assurance(-)vieillesse
old-age insurance institution

maladie de la vieillesse
geriatric disorder

minimum des pensions vieillesse
old age pension minimum

minimum vieillesse
basic old-age pension, old age minimum
(Fr.)

**non-rétroactivité d'un avantage
vieillesse**
non-retroactivity of an old age benefit

**pension proportionnelle de vieillesse
(UK)**
graduated retirement benefit

pension de vieillesse
old(-)age pension, old persons' pension
(UK), age pension (Malta)

**pension de vieillesse constituée par
cotisations**
contributory old age pension

pension de vieillesse de veuf (Fr.)
old age widower's pension

pension de vieillesse de veuve (Fr.)
old age widow's pension

plafond de pension vieillesse
old age pension ceiling

prestation anticipée de vieillesse
anticipatory old-age benefit

prestation (de) vieillesse
old age benefit

régime d'assurance(-)vieillesse
pension (insurance) scheme

**régime d'assurance(-)vieillesse obliga-
toire**
compulsory pension insurance scheme

**régime d'assurance(-)vieillesse propor-
tionnelle au salaire**
graduated pension scheme

régime de retraite-vieillesse
old age pension scheme

rente (de) vieillesse
old-age pension / annuity

sécurité de la vieillesse (Can.)
old-age security

**taux de pension de l'assurance
(-)vieillesse**
rate of the old age pension

titulaire de pension de vieillesse
old age pensioner

VIEILLISSEMENT
ageing

VIEUX
old; aged

allocation aux vieux travailleurs
allowance for elderly / old workers

**allocation aux vieux travailleurs
salariés**
allowance for old employees

VIGNETTE
price label on medicines for reimbursement by social security; identification
label to affix on claim forms for reimbursement by mutual benefit societies

VIGUEUR
contrat en vigueur
current contract

date d'entrée en vigueur
commencement / effective date

entrée en vigueur
entry into effect

entrer en vigueur
to come into force

mettre en vigueur
to enforce, to bring into force

mise en vigueur
enforcement

remise en vigueur
re-enactment; reinstatement

taux de rémunération en vigueur
going (pay) rate

taux en vigueur
prevailing / going rate

vigueur (en)
current; in force; operative

VILLAGE
chefs traditionnels et chefs de village
[CITP-1988 (113)]
traditional chiefs and heads of villages
[ISCO-1988 (113)]

VILLE
médecin de ville
non-hospital doctor; doctor working in a
town

médecine de ville
general medicine as practised in towns

ville de base
base city

ville dortoir
dormitory town

ville siège
headquarters location / duty station

VIOLATION
violation; breach

violation des devoirs de fonction
breach of professional / official duty

violation des droits acquis
breach of acquired rights

VIREMENT
transfer

VISA
visa d'entrée
entry permit

visa global
blanket visa

visa de sortie
exit permit

VISCOSITÉ
viscosité de la main-d'oeuvre
manpower rigidity

viscosité des salaires
wage stickiness

VISÉ
concerned; specified (in)

personnel visé par un accord
staff covered by an agreement

population visée
target population

VISIBLE
chômage visible
measured / open / overt / visible unemployment

sous-emploi visible
visible under-employment

VISITE
visit; inspection; (pl.) attendance

**allocation de subsistance pour visite
préliminaire**
preliminary examination living allowance

allocation de visite préliminaire
preliminary examination allowance

visite de contrôle
monitoring / follow-up visit; medical
inspection at home

visite à domicile (med.)
doctor's home visit, domiciliary consultation / visiting, home call / visit

visite dominicale
Sunday call

visite impromptue
(occ.) cold call

visite d'inspection
monitoring visit

visite médicale
medical inspection / examination

visite médicale d'embauche
pre-employment medical examination

visite médicale de reprise
medical examination before returning to
work

visites du médecin traitant à l'hôpital
in-hospital doctor's care

visite de nuit
night call

visite sur place
on-site visit

visite sanitaire
sanitary inspection

visite surprise
random inspection

voyage de visite familiale
family visit travel

VISITEUR
agent sanitaire visiteur
(pl.) domiciliary health staff

conseillère-visiteuse
home visitor

infirmière visiteuse
domiciliary / home / district nurse, health
visitor

sage-femme visiteuse
domiciliary midwife

service de visiteuses d'hygiène
health visiting service

visiteuse d'hygiène
health visitor

visiteur médical
medical representative

visiteuse sanitaire
health visitor

visiteuse sociale
home visitor

VITAL
chirurgie non vitale
elective surgery

minimum vital
subsistence level / minimum; living /
subsistence wage; (occ.) demogrant;
poverty line

salaire minimum vital
minimum living wage

salaire vital
living wage

VITESSE
société à deux vitesses
two-tier / dual society

système à deux vitesses
two-tier system

VIVIER
pool

vivier de compétences
pool of talent

VIVRE
aptitude à vivre en société
social skill(s)

**personne vivant sous le toit du
travailleur salarié**
person living under the same roof as the
employed person

salaire tout juste suffisant pour vivre
subsistence wage

vivre (faire)
to support

vivre du chômage
to live on unemployment benefit

vivant ensemble séparément
living apart together

vivre au jour le jour
living on a hand-to-mouth basis

vivre maritalement
to cohabit

vivre sous le même toit
to live in the same house, to live together

vivre en union libre
to cohabit

VOCATION
commitment

VOIE
voie administrative
official channel(s)

voies et délais de recours
legal remedies and periods allowed for
appeals

voies d'exécution
means of enforcement

voie hiérarchique
official channel(s); (occ.) chain of
command

voie de recours
remedy; complaints / grievance procedure

VOIRIE
sanitation

VOISINAGE
comité de voisinage
neighbourhood committee

foyer de voisinage
neighbourhood house

groupe de voisinage
neighbourhood group

unité de voisinage
neighbourhood unit

VOITURE
voiture de fonction
company car

voiture pour handicapé
(occ.) invalid carriage; trike

voiture de service / de société
company car

VOLANT (adj.)
équipe volante
floating staff

piquet de grève volant
flying picket

VOLANT (n.)
volant de main-d'oeuvre
labour / manpower reserve

VOLONTAIRE (adj.)
voluntary

abandon volontaire d'un emploi
voluntary leaving of employment

admission à l'assurance volontaire
admission to voluntary insurance

assurance volontaire
voluntary / optional insurance

assuré (à titre) volontaire
voluntarily insured

chômage volontaire
voluntary unemployment

chômeur volontaire
voluntary unemployed

cotisation volontaire
voluntary contribution

départ volontaire
voluntary separation, quit(ting)

départ volontaire à la préretraite
early retirement on a voluntary basis

départ volontaire à la retraite
voluntary retirement

**interruption volontaire de grossesse
(IVG)**
voluntary termination of pregnancy

négociation volontaire
voluntary negotiation

prime de départ volontaire
voluntary leaving premium

programme de départs volontaires
voluntary severance / redundancy scheme

régime d'assurance volontaire
voluntary insurance scheme

régime volontaire
voluntary scheme

volontaire (se porter)
to volunteer

VOLONTAIRE (n.)
volunteer

VOLONTAIREMENT
quitter un emploi volontairement
to voluntarily leave employment

VOLONTARIAT
voluntary aid / work

licenciement par appel au volontariat
voluntary redundancy

VOLONTARISTE
voluntary

VOLUME
volume; size; level; turnover

redistribution du volume de travail
redistribution of the volume of work

volume des activités
(volume of) work(-)load, volume level of
activities

volume (global) de l'emploi
(overall) level of employment

volume de travail
(volume of) work(-)load, volume level of
activities

VOTE
vote à bulletin secret
secret ballot

vote décidant de la tenue d'une grève
strike vote / ballot

VOTER
voter une loi
to introduce / to pass legislation

VOULU
présenter / remplir les conditions voulues
(pour bénéficier / avoir droit)
to qualify for; to fulfil requirements; to be
eligible

**remplissant les conditions requises /
voulues**
qualified for; suitable; eligible

temps voulu (en)
by the required date

VOYAGE
travel

aide de voyage
travel assistance

allocation de voyage
travel allowance

conditions de voyage
travel conditions / arrangements

frais de voyage
transportation / travel expenses / costs

frais de voyage et de séjour
travel and accommodation / travel and
subsistence expenses

subvention de voyage
travel grant

subvention de voyage de stagiaire
trainee travel grant

voyage autorisé
official travel / journey

voyage d'étude de travailleurs
study tour for workers

voyage en mission
travel on official business

voyage de rapatriement
repatriation travel

voyage de visite familiale
family visit travel

VOYAGER
to travel

VOYAGEUR
commis voyageur, voyageur de commerce
commercial traveller

VUE
trouble(s) de la vue
sight impairment

VULGARISATEUR
extension worker

VULGARISATION
extension, outreach (ed.)

cours de vulgarisation
extension course, extramural studies

VULNÉRABILITÉ
vulnerability; helplessness

VULNÉRABLE
vulnerable; at risk; disadvantaged

ZÈLE
grève du zèle
work(ing)-to-rule (strike), go-slow (strike)

grève du zèle (faire la)
to work to rule

ZÉRO
croissance zéro
zero growth

zéro défaut
zero defect

ZONE
area

prime de zone dangereuse
danger zone bonus

zone d'activité
enterprise zone

zone artisanale
(occ.) development estate

zone d'attraction
catchment area

zone critique / défavorisée
depressed area

zone de déplacement domicile-travail
journey(-)to(-)work / travel(-)to(-)work
area

zone déshéritée
depressed area

zone d'éducation prioritaire (ZEP)
zone of educational priority (ZEP)

zone d'entreprises
enterprise zone

zone frontalière
frontier zone

zone industrielle
development / enterprise zone; industrial
estate

zone d'influence
catchment area

zone non intégrée
(occ.) marginal area

zone périphérique
peripheral / suburban area

zone de recrutement de main-d'-oeuvre
labour recruiting area

zone de salaires
wage zone

zone de travail
work area

zone urbanisée
urban area

zone à urbaniser
urban development area

Sales agents for publications of the Council of Europe
Agents de vente des publications du Conseil de l'Europe

AUSTRALIA/AUSTRALIE
Hunter Publications, 58A, Gipps Street
AUS-3066 COLLINGWOOD, Victoria
Fax: (61) 33 9 419 7154
E-mail: Robd@mentis.com.au

AUSTRIA/AUTRICHE
Gerold und Co., Graben 31
A-1011 WIEN 1
Fax: (43) 1512 47 31 29
E-mail: buch@gerold.telecom.at

BELGIUM/BELGIQUE
La Librairie européenne SA
50, avenue A. Jonnart
B-1200 BRUXELLES 20
Fax: (32) 27 35 08 60
E-mail: info@libeurop.be

Jean de Lannoy
202, avenue du Roi
B-1060 BRUXELLES
Fax: (32) 25 38 08 41
E-mail: jean.de.lannoy@euronet.be

CANADA
Renouf Publishing Company Limited
5369 Chemin Canotek Road
CDN-OTTAWA, Ontario, K1J 9J3
Fax: (1) 613 745 76 60

CZECH REPUBLIC/RÉPUBLIQUE TCHÈQUE
USIS, Publication Service
Havelkova 22
CZ-130 00 Praha 3
Fax: (420) 2 242 21 484

DENMARK/DANEMARK
Munksgaard
Østergade 26A – Postbox 173
DK-1005 KØBENHAVN K
Fax: (45) 77 33 33 77
E-mail: direct@munksgaarddirect.dk

FINLAND/FINLANDE
Akateeminen Kirjakauppa
Keskuskatu 1, PO Box 218
FIN-00381 HELSINKI
Fax: (358) 9 121 44 50
E-mail: akatilaus@stockmann.fi

FRANCE
C.I.D.
131 boulevard Saint-Michel
F-75005 Paris
Fax: (33) 01 43 54 80 73
E-mail: lecarrer@msh-paris.fr

GERMANY/ALLEMAGNE
UNO Verlag
Proppelsdorfer Allee 55
D-53115 BONN
Fax: (49) 228 21 74 92
E-mail: unoverlag@aol.com

GREECE/GRÈCE
Librairie Kauffmann
Mavrokordatou 9
GR-ATHINAI 106 78
Fax: (30) 13 23 03 20

HUNGARY/HONGRIE
Euro Info Service/Magyarország
Margitsziget (Európa Ház),
H-1138 BUDAPEST
Fax: (361) 302 50 35
E-mail: euroinfo@mail.matav.hu

IRELAND/IRLANDE
Government Stationery Office
4-5 Harcourt Road
IRL-DUBLIN 2
Fax: (353) 14 75 27 60

ISRAEL/ISRAËL
ROY International
41 Mishmar Hayarden Street
PO Box 13056
IL-69865 TEL AVIV
Fax: (972) 3 648 60 39
E-mail: royil@netvision.net.il

ITALY/ITALIE
Libreria Commissionaria Sansoni
Via Duca di Calabria 1/1, CP 552
I-50125 FIRENZE
Fax: (39) 0 55 64 12 57
E-mail: licosa@ftbcc.it

MALTA/MALTE
L. Sapienza & Sons Ltd
26 Republic Street, PO Box 36
VALLETTA CMR 01
Fax: (356) 233 621

NETHERLANDS/PAYS-BAS
De Lindeboom Internationale Publikaties
PO Box 202
NL-7480 AE HAAKSBERGEN
Fax: (31) 53 572 92 96
E-mail: lindeboo@worldonline.nl

NORWAY/NORVÈGE
Akademika, A/S Universitetsbokhandel
PO Box 84, Blindern
N-0314 OSLO
Fax: (47) 23 12 24 10

POLAND/POLOGNE
Głowna Księgarnia Naukowa im. B. Prusa
Krakowskie Przedmiescie 7
PL-00-068 WARSZAWA
Fax: (48) 22 26 64 49

PORTUGAL
Livraria Portugal
Rua do Carmo, 70
P-1200 LISBOA
Fax: (351) 13 47 02 64

SPAIN/ESPAGNE
Mundi-Prensa Libros SA
Castelló 37
E-28001 MADRID
Fax: (34) 915 75 39 98
E-mail: libreria@mundiprensa.es

SWITZERLAND/SUISSE
Buchhandlung Heinimann & Co.
Kirchgasse 17
CH-8001 ZÜRICH
Fax: (41) 12 51 14 81

BERSY
Route d'Uvrier 15
CH-1958 LIVRIER/SION
Fax: (41) 27 203 73 32

UNITED KINGDOM/ROYAUME-UNI
TSO (formerly HMSO)
51 Nine Elms Lane
GB-LONDON SW8 5DR
Fax: (44) 171 873 82 00
E-mail: denise.perkins@theso.co.uk

UNITED STATES and CANADA/
ÉTATS-UNIS et CANADA
Manhattan Publishing Company
468 Albany Post Road, PO Box 850
CROTON-ON-HUDSON, NY 10520, USA
Fax: (1) 914 271 58 56
E-mail: Info@manhattanpublishing.com

STRASBOURG
Librairie Kléber
Palais de l'Europe
F-67075 STRASBOURG Cedex
Fax: +33 (0)3 88 52 91 21

Council of Europe Publishing/Editions du Conseil de l'Europe
F-67075 Strasbourg Cedex
Tel. +33 (0)3 88 41 25 81 – Fax +33 (0)3 88 41 39 10
E-mail: publishing@coe.int – Website: http://book.coe.fr